The Magic Mirror

THE MAGIC MIRROR
Law in American History

KERMIT L. HALL

New York   Oxford
OXFORD UNIVERSITY PRESS
1989

Oxford University Press

Oxford   New York   Toronto
Delhi   Bombay   Calcutta   Madras   Karachi
Petaling Jaya   Singapore   Hong Kong   Tokyo
Nairobi   Dar es Salaam   Cape Town
Melbourne   Auckland
and associated companies in
Berlin   Ibadan

Published by Oxford University Press, Inc.,
198 Madison Avenue, New York, New York 10016-4314

Library of Congress Cataloging-in-Publication Data
Hall, Kermit L. The magic mirror.
Includes index.
1. Law—United States—History and criticism.
I. Title.   KF352.H35   1989   349.73   88-15138
ISBN 0-19-504459-2   347.3
ISBN 0-19-504460-6 (pbk.)

10 12 14 16 18 19 17 15 13 11
Printed in the United States of America
on acid-free paper

For Phyllis

Preface

This book is about the history of American legal culture and the law in action. It is not a technical history of substantive law, nor is it an intensive study of case law development in either private or public law. That important task remains to be done, and surely we would know a good deal more about American legal culture if we had a better understanding of the law's technical interstices. This book, however, has a different purpose: to elucidate the interaction of law and society as revealed over time through the main lines of development in American legal culture. Thus, much of what follows seeks to fit legal change with social, economic, and political developments from the first English settlement to the present.

This is a book of synthesis and interpretation. What follows expresses, I hope, our best current understanding about the evolution of American legal culture. One of the reasons it is possible to write such a book is that since World War II, and especially since the early 1960s, research and writing in legal history—of both private and public law, of legal and judicial institutions, and of attitudes and values toward the law—have exploded. Yet much remains to be done. There are huge gaps in our knowledge about the nation's legal past. We have no history of substantive criminal law, and only the beginnings of work in contract, tort, and procedure. We know far more about the functioning of the Supreme Court than we do about the day-to-day business in the thousands of lower state and local courts that mete out justice in matters such as medical malpractice, homicide, and speeding automobiles. Moreover, although legal historians have lavished attention on courts and judges, we still have no good history of the rise and impact of regulatory bodies and of administrative law. American historians have preferred, despite the repeated admonitions of James Willard Hurst, to treat legislatures—one of the greatest sources of lawmaking authority in the American system—as political rather than legal entities. We know the most about nineteenth-century legal culture; we know far less about the beginnings of American law in the seventeenth and eighteenth centuries, and its more recent manifestations in the twentieth century. A good deal more attention has been given in the past decade or so to the history of the civil law in Louisiana especially and the Southwest more generally, but we still have only a vague appreciation of the contributions of civil law to our common law traditions. Important new work has appeared dealing with legal developments in the South and West; however, much of the best research has focused on New England, the Middle Atlantic states, and one Middle Western state—Wisconsin. In short, attempting to write a synthesis of American legal culture is a huge presumption, not just because of the scope of the subject but because so much remains to be done before historians can reveal that past with authority.

If we are to make progress, we must have works that attempt to sum up our legal past. We must pause occasionally to try to synthesize and integrate into a larger body of knowledge that which we do know, and, in so doing, press future scholars to cast a revisionist eye on its assumptions. This book, of course, is not the first effort at such integration. Lawrence M. Friedman's *A History of American Law,* which first appeared in 1973 and was issued in a somewhat revised second edition in 1985, audaciously summarized what was then known about the history of American legal culture. Legal historians of all stripes owe Friedman an enormous debt; he played the vital role of constructing a broad-gauged sociolegal history of American law. This book, of course, is fashioned along the same lines; it, too, is about law and society. Moreover, whatever its limitations, this book is that much better because of Friedman's pioneering efforts. While similar in approach to Friedman's study, though, this book is fundamentally different in its organization, which is fitted much more closely to the main lines of the historiography of American history, and in its more systematic treatment of the twentieth century. On the whole, as the title suggests, this is a book about law in American history rather than strictly a history of American law. The book also combines themes of private and public law, of criminal justice and social control, of minority rights and majority control, and of political power and legal legitimacy far more explicitly than does Friedman.

I have no qualms about having written this book. But I do have considerably more humility than when I began it—humility based on admiration for Friedman's synthesizing efforts, for social historians who seek to extract generalizations from legal materials, and for legal historians who have accomplished so much in so short a time, but who have, it is now clear to me, so much left to do.

I tackled this project with a good number of friends. Over the several years that were required to complete it, many of them have surely grown weary of seeing me at their doors with a handful of manuscript. Nancy Lane of Oxford University Press, who originally proposed this project to me, probably wishes I had shown up at her door earlier. She has shown remarkable patience and great kindness, but she has been, when necessary, a demanding yet supportive editor. I have learned a great deal from several friends who doubtless concluded long ago that I was too early and too often at their doors with some or all of the manuscript. John W. Johnson, Paul L. Murphy, and James W. Ely, Jr., read the entire manuscript and provided valuable interpretive insights while spotting many egregious errors of fact. David Colburn, Augustus Burns III, and Jeffrey Adler read and commented on various parts of the manuscript, and Burns was especially helpful in breathing life into often-limp prose. Laura Kalman read and commented on all of the twentieth-century chapters, and she forced me to rethink and reorganize much of that material. Mel Leffler was supportive as always.

Without institutional support, this book would still be a glimmer in my mind's eye. Dean Jeffrey Lewis of the University of Florida College of Law provided a place and resources to get this project under way, and Rick Donnelly, Bob Munro, and Pam Williams of the University of Florida Legal Information Center were unstinting in locating materials. David Colburn, chair of the department of history at the University of Florida, has created the kind of atmosphere that respects scholarship in general and the study of legal history in particular. Most of the rewriting for this book was carried out during a year as a visiting scholar at the American Bar Foundation. I am indebted to Jack Heinz and Bill Felstiner for the opportunity to draw on their fine resources. While at the Bar Foundation, I benefited from the wonderful intellectual support of Ray Solomon (who unselfishly shared his considerable knowledge of twentieth-century legal history with me), Stephen Daniels, Lori Andrews, Bob Nelson, and David Rabban. John Flood was a relentless (and therefore therapeutic) squash partner during the year in Chicago.

To all of these persons and institutions I express my greatest appreciation and admiration. They are in the well-deserved position of deserving credit for whatever is of value in this book while bearing no responsibility for any errors of fact and interpretation that may follow.

Gainesville, Florida   K.L.H.
March 1988

Contents

The Magic Mirror

Introduction

What is Legal History? A Magic Mirror

"This abstraction called the Law," Justice Oliver Wendell Holmes, Jr., once observed, is "a magic mirror, [wherein] we see reflected, not only our own lives, but the lives of all men that have been!"[1] Holmes believed that this "magic mirror" offered historians an opportunity to explore the social choices and moral imperatives of previous generations. This book is about what that magic mirror reveals to us; it is about law, constitutions, legal institutions, and the idea of the rule of law as separate subjects and as part of our social history.

The contemporary definitions of law fully stress its connection to society. The dictionary is very direct, describing the law as "a rule established by authority, society, or custom . . . governing the affairs of man within a community or among states. . . ."[2] The legal scholar Donald Black offered an even shorter definition. He described law as "governmental social control."[3] In sum, law is a system of social choice, one in which government provides for the allocation of resources, the legitimate use of violence, and the structuring of social relationships.

These simple definitions have one element in common: they define the law in social context. Without society we need no law; without law we would have no society. The rules of behavior for both individuals and government take on historical meaning as they affect and are affected by the social order. When we look back into Holmes's magic mirror, we seek in it answers to questions about how previous generations went about using the law to affect values and moral principles they deemed important. We tend, of course, to think of the law as something complex, as something that only lawyers and judges deal with in often obscure ways. But the internal workings of the law offer a beginning not an ending to historical understanding.

As the legal historian Lawrence M. Friedman has observed, we can think of these matters in a somewhat simple way.[4] The law can be viewed as a black box that contains various rules. Examining the chronological development of the rules would yield a literal, internal history of American law; until the mid-1960s most writers on legal history have done just that. Such an approach had the undesirable effect of confirming the mystery and complexity of law, making the black box all the more foreboding.

But the law can be understood in another way. What is important is not only what is in that box but what consequences its contents have had for the society it is meant to serve. Though an interesting intellectual exercise, what good does it do to know what went on in the box, if we do not understand what significance it had for the larger external world it aimed to serve? In the past two decades this concern with the *external* history of the law has taken on greater urgency. The legal historian still has to know what went on in the box, but now he or she must also address a large set of causal relationships. We want to know the law by what it has done, or by what has been done to it, rather than simply by what it was.

There is yet another reason to pursue this external approach to legal history. Law is, after all, a human institution; its history is a tale of human choices. Its abstract rules deal with the most central of human issues: the preservation of life, the protection of property, the exercise of individual liberty, the fashioning of creative knowledge, and the allocating of scarce resources. All encounters in the law, therefore, have been personal, human encounters. Its history is that of individuals caught up in the efforts of the state to allocate blame, to deter criminal behavior, to punish wrongdoing, and to encourage socially valuable activity.

The law, as Justice Holmes understood, is indeed a cultural artifact, a moral deposit of society. Because its life stretches beyond that of a single individual, its meaning reaches to the values of society. Thus, we cannot know the law only through the individuals who have administered and lived under it. We trivialize the rule of law, and we miss the opportunity to sort out the clashing views about it, when we disregard its inner logic and rules, its institutions, and its processes. This book seeks to encourage you to think about both the internal and external history of American law.

Elements of the Legal System

This book is about more than rules and their place in American society. It concerns also the structures, institutions, and processes through which the law has operated historically. The component elements—the connective tissue, if you will—of this legal system have been its structure, substance, and culture.

Structure

The institutions *and* the means through which they have operated constitute the structure of American law. Most persons, if asked to name a "legal" institution, would doubtless respond with "court." The life of the law, to many of us, has been the adversarial process; the drama of lawyer confronting lawyer, of judge and jury. But this view is needlessly and misleadingly narrow. The formal product of the law has emanated not just from courts and lawyers, but from legislatures, administrative agencies and the executive branch. In the legal history of the United States, courts have usually been reactive institutions; the great limit on the judicial power has been the necessity of judges waiting for litigation to reach them so they might decide an issue. Legislators, executives, and administrators, on the other hand, have most often had the initiative in the lawmaking process, although the courts, through the process of judicial review, have gradually developed the power to decide what the law is.

The legal structure has also included informal and nongovernmental institutions, such as the family, private associations, and trade groups. In some instances, moreover, these nongovernmental and informal associations have developed their own procedures. Witness, for example, the development of Roberts Rules of Order in the late nineteenth century, and the effort it embodied to bring procedural order to the operation of private, nongovernmental groups.

This book, however, gives attention to the formal, governmental structure of the legal system. The purpose of legal history is not to explain all social choices and all aspects of social control. The distinctiveness of the American legal system has been its reliance on a formal structure, and it is with the understanding of the place of that formal structure in society that American legal history is concerned.

Substance

The operation of the formal legal structure produces substantive results. Substance is what Oliver Wendell Holmes, Jr. meant by the legal system's "moral deposit." It is the primary rules—against murder, the treatment of agreement between bargaining parties, the awarding of damages to injured parties, the establishment of fault and liability, for example—that the legal structure produces. The substance of the legal system has been more than the sum of judicial pronouncements; it has also included statutes, executive orders, and administrative regulations produced at the federal, state, and local levels. It offers a direct measure of the extent to which cultural and moral values have penetrated the legal system.

Both the structure and the substance of the law have been multiform. There has never been only one American legal system, but permutations and deviations. From the beginning of white settlement, the substance of the legal system evolved through many forums: federal, state, and local. Geography and topography encouraged diversity in the substantive results of the legal system, but so too did the U.S. Constitution through the concept of federalism. The framers in Philadelphia in 1787 indeed fashioned a national government, but they did not create a national law. Rather, the principle of federalism recognized that the states retained important elements of sovereign authority, and that they could, within the terms of that authority, enact laws for themselves. The states retained authority under the police powers to deal with questions of health, safety, morals, and welfare. The federal government, on the other hand, had broad responsibilities for national concerns, such as war and peace, foreign relations, commerce among the states and with foreign nations. This bifurcated scheme left the states through much of the nineteenth century to develop large areas of the legal system. The law was not a free-for-all, but it did manifest important differences from state to state.

Culture

The third element of the American legal system, legal culture, is genuinely elusive. Legal culture is the matrix of values, attitudes, and assumptions that have shaped both the operation and the perception of the law.

Legal culture has had two components. First, it is a manifestation of ideology. Persons often hold strong ideas about how the world should and does operate, and those beliefs have had an impact on the legal system. That is why what prominent figures in the legal system have said about it is of such importance. Ideology is both a statement of expectations and a rationalization of what has occurred.

Second, legal culture has evolved in response to individual and group interest. American historians have argued endlessly about whether ideas or interests have provided the mainsprings of historical action. Have people within the American legal system acted as a result of what they believed or who they were? Or were interest and ideology so intertwined that separating them only caused further confusion? There seems little doubt that what persons have been has shaped what they expected of and how they viewed the legal system. Property holding, social class position, wealth, and race, for example, provide individuals with tangible interests to be secured through the law. What has been good for some property holders has not necessarily been good for others.

Legal culture through ideology and interest provides the mainsprings of the legal system in the United States. Structure and substance provide the institutional manifestations of the system; legal culture embodies the motivating forces in response to which the other two develop. The plurality of interests and ideas in American history has bred controversy over the purposes of the legal system. Diversity has spawned disagreement, and one measure of the significance of the rule of law in our history has been the extent to which it has promoted consensus.

The nature, direction, and velocity of legal adaptation is one of the central issues of this book and it is also a measure of the effectiveness of the rule of law. The rule of law is one of our culture's most important concepts and one of the great forces in the history of western civilization. Its origins reach back to the Roman Empire, but beginning only in the seventeenth century, with the rise of humanistic rationalism, did it assume anything like its present identity. The rule of law meant that there existed a body of rules and procedures governing human and governmental behavior that have an autonomy and logic of their own. The rule of law—the rule of rules, if you will— proposed to make all persons equal before a neutral and impartial authority. Its legitimacy derived largely from the possibility of applying it on a reasoned basis free from the whim and caprice of both individuals and government. Social position, governmental office, family of birth, wealth, and race ideally had nothing to do with the dispensation of justice. By the eighteenth and nineteenth centuries the very notion of justice had become an abstraction. To do justice was to administer the law in a procedurally correct manner, because such attention to the process of law guaranteed a reasonable and hence just conclusion to any dispute. The rule of law made persons in authority— police, legislators, and judges—bound to it. It promised impartiality, fairness, and equality; all persons were to receive the same treatment.[5]

Legal historians have disagreed sharply about whether the rule of law has actually performed in such a manner. Some of them, notably scholars identified with the critical legal studies movement, insist that the rule of law is so much humbug. As John Henry Schlegel has observed: *"LAW IS POLITICS,* pure and simple."[6] These critics of our legal system complain that the law merely provided a formal device by which the most powerful elements of a capitalist society—the ruling class—perpetuated their control. The law furnished the elite with an amoral device that promoted their social hegemony. In such circumstances, these historians explain, minorities—blacks, Native Americans, women, and poor white working class—have suffered. Impartiality and fairness have not only been in short supply, but the rule of law has masked blatant class oppression.

A contrary interpretation reaches quite different conclusions. This so-called pluralist consensus view, most fully identified with this century's greatest historian of law in the United States, J. Willard Hurst, holds that given the enormous diversity of the population and the great geographic size of the United States, the abstract rule of law has fostered economic growth and the maintenance of free expression and dissent, and has limited the authority of government.[7] The law, in this interpretation, has functioned as an honest broker through which conflicting interests have sought to achieve their own ends. The results of the clash of pluralistic social interests appear in the historical rise of a large, prosperous middle class. The rule of law, in short, has opened fresh opportunities for large numbers of persons, certainly more so than was ever the case in Europe with its feudal past. This book suggests that neither interpretation quite captures the supple nature of the American historical experience nor the powerful contradictions that have beset it.

Private Law and Public Law

All law is a system of social choice backed by the power of the state. But the state has varying degrees of interest in those choices. Private law, though implemented through public courts, aims to resolve disputes in which the interests of individuals, rather than the state, are directly involved. The state, for example, has a direct interest in whether you speed in your car or murder your neighbor, but it has only an indirect interest in whether you keep a promised contractual agreement with that neighbor. Private law, therefore, encompasses the major categories of substantive legal rules, such as contracts, real property, and torts. Private law is private because of the character of the parties in dispute and the absence of a direct state interest.

Public law, on the other hand, involves social choices where the state has a direct interest. Public law embraces those rules that affect the organization of the state, the relations between the state and the people who compose it (including control over the means of legitimate violence and punishment of deviant social acts), the responsibilities of the officers of the state to each other and to the public, and the relations of states within the nation to one another. Public law, like private law, also has several categorical divisions. It consists of criminal, administrative, international, and constitutional law. The last of these, constitutional law, treats the establishment, construction, and interpretation of constitutions and the validity of legal enactments passed under them.

This book is about both private and public law, about private law rules and public law doctrines. Although historians have frequently treated these as subjects distinct from one another, this book seeks to show the relationships among them, as they have been shaped by legal institutions and as they have formed a part of the legal culture. We might think of them as complementary themes played in different modes.[8] Both contribute to the ordering of society and each contributes to the life of the other. Both have formed the magic mirror of our legal past.

1

Social and Institutional Foundations of Early American Law

Origins

When the first settlers in the early seventeenth century pushed ashore on the North American continent, two great systems of law dominated the Western world. One was the civil law of western Europe; the other was the common law of England. The American legal system owed something to both, though much more to the latter than to the former.

Civil Law

The Roman Empire contributed its system of civil law to the growth of Western civilization. The Romans formulated their law through written codes susceptible to easy replication throughout their vast empire. Emperor Justinian of Constantinople in the early sixth century A.D. captured the essence of the Roman legal system in the *Corpus Juris Civilis,* a four-volume restatement that ordered most of the earlier law of the Empire. Justinian was a reactionary concerned about the decadence of the Empire, and he believed that a thorough codification of the law would strengthen its moral fiber. On the publication of the *Corpus Juris Civilis,* the emperor forbade any further reference to the older law of Rome. The *Corpus* failed in its social purposes, but its preparation was nonetheless propitiously timed. The civil law system went into eclipse following the Germanic invasion of the Empire, but thanks to the *Corpus* Roman law survived, though in a less sophisticated version.

During the Middle Ages, clerics in the Roman Church ''rediscovered'' Justinian's *Corpus* and with it the great civil law tradition. The rulers of the new Holy Roman Empire embraced it, not only because the civil law legitimated their connection with the Caesars, but because it offered a ready-made device by which to extend their rule over western Europe. Thereafter waves of exploration from the sixteenth century on spread it to Latin America and elsewhere, including French-speaking Canada and the Mississippi River Valley and Spanish settlements in present-day Louisiana, Florida, the Southwest, and California. But only in Louisiana and Quebec did the civil law system win a lasting hold on the North American continent.

The civil law was a system of positive rules arranged in books called codes. Its commands, whether from a sovereign body or a royal ruler, spoke directly to the ruled. Its authority depended on neither broad notions of morality nor assumptions about human character rooted in nature, but on the powers inherent in the person or persons promulgating it. This comprehensive body of rules established what law or laws governed a particular situation. When a controversy reached a lawyer or judge, their immediate task involved finding the appropriate code provision and then applying it. The civil law system placed a premium on the judicial *administration* of the law rather than on the judicial *interpretation* of it, a feature that typified English common law. Civil law judges had limited discretion; they applied existing law rather than initiating it. The civil law system that emerged from medieval Europe was responsive to social change, but it trusted in legislative action and the scholarly endeavors of academic lawyers rather than judges to systematize, criticize, and develop it. Past cases were important, but judicial precedent lacked the influence it assumed in the common law system.

Civil law countries regularly updated their codes through major restatements. Perhaps the most influential in modern times was the French Civil Code, or Code Napoleon, of 1804. It had enormous influence throughout western Europe and beyond, serving as the major source of authority for the hybrid version of civil law practiced in Louisiana.

The civil law tradition contributed only modestly to the origins of American law. In the nineteenth and twentieth centuries American law reformers, however, repeatedly invoked the concept of codification—of a rational, written body of rules for all to see—as a way of imposing order on the unruly common law. Legal systems composed part of the cultural baggage of colonial expansion; the English settlers not only came in larger numbers, but they came to stay with concentrated settlement on the vital Atlantic beachhead. Therefore, although the Dutch briefly carved out a civil law system in New Amsterdam, the common law system flourished after control of the colony passed to the Duke of York in 1664.

English Common Law

English common law was more diffuse in its historical origins and in its application than was the civil law. Rome for three and a half centuries (A.D. 43–407) ruled England, but that occupation left few legal marks. More important was the later migration by, among others, the Angles and the Saxons from the European continent. They laid down a body of law based largely on custom, practice, and folkways, although it was partly codified. Unlike Roman civil law, which had the administration of an extended empire as a principal objective, the Anglo-Saxon laws reflected the diversity and diffusion of interests within England after the end of Roman occupation.

A two-tiered legal system grew from this early experience. The first level supported the powerful centralizing system of feudalism introduced in 1066 by William the Conqueror and his successors. The common law was "common" because it spread throughout England, not because it served the lower social orders. To the contrary, William intended the common law to apply only to the aristocratic tip of highly stratified English society. Over the course of several centuries, the common law system matured into a complex body of rules that only trained lawyers and judges fully comprehended, and then only after long, arduous study.

The common law also functioned on a second, local level. Its Anglo-Saxon inheritance gave it a customary quality; that is, it rested on long-established practices of the community. Legislation, which was so important to the civil law, played a relatively insignificant role in the development of the common law until the mid-nineteenth century. Even the high common law developed from customary practices accepted by the royal courts. Custom also held sway on the local level—in the counties, manors, and boroughs—where royal law did not regularly intervene in the day-to-day lives of the people until the beginning of the seventeenth century. Thus, the common law developed in the royal courts had a meaning larger than just the technical rules of pleading; it was also the customary practices associated with the conduct of local affairs.

At both the royal and the local level, the English evolved rules and procedures that laid the foundation for American law. Between 1066 and the abolition of feudalism in 1660, the English courts formulated the law of real property, of obligations and duties in society, and of criminal justice. After settlement of the American colonies in the early seventeenth century, English law remained the source of authority, and this transatlantic connection persisted even after the colonies achieved independence.

Through the organizational legacy of the feudal state Englishmen also gradually evolved the rudiments of constitutionalism. With constitutionalism government is limited in its powers and is based on the existence of certain overarching principles. The nobility was acutely aware of its rights and liberties, and it sought to protect them against the growing strength of the Crown. When civil war broke out against King John (1199–1216), the nobility attempted to limit the king's prerogatives through the famous Magna Carta, or Great Charter. This historic document, which was not a constitution in the way we would think of one today, was forced on the king by his rebellious vassals. In it he pledged to respect their traditional rights. It was neither a bill of rights nor a charter of liberty; it was simply a feudal contract. It had no application to the general public, and it was revised three times over the next twenty years. It only became a permanent part of the law in England in 1225. Still, Magna Carta was a turning point in the constitutional history of England and later a source of reference for English settlers in North America. Certain of its key provisions, notably those dealing with matters of criminal justice, were later included in the Bill of Rights to the American Constitution.

The Magna Carta was only one phase of the more than five-hundred-year struggle between the Crown and the nobility, or between the king and Parliament, over the basis of sovereign authority in the English government. Equally important were questions about the relationship of government to the people, the proper balance among the various branches of government, and the role of government in promoting both the public good and private interest. Unlike the Americans the English never developed a written constitution to deal with these questions. Instead, they relied on the customs and practices of the common law and on a handful of documents, including Magna Carta, to establish their unwritten constitution.

The origins of public and private law in the United States flowed from a multiform and dynamic common law tradition. The evolution of England from a feudal society with a subsistence-agricultural economy to a commercial or mercantile-oriented economy contributed mightily to the legal tradition that the English settlers brought with them. North America never experienced a feudal regime, but the origins of its legal structure, substance, and culture were inextricably linked, even in today's world, to the form and content of the common law as it evolved from the eleventh through the seventeenth centuries.

Receiving and Carrying

"No one can tell," wrote an anonymous "American" at the beginning of the eighteenth century, "what is law and what is not in the plantations. Some hold that the law of England is chiefly to be respected. . . . others are of the opinion that the laws of the Colonies are to take the first place."[1] The willingness of colonial Americans to register uncertainty about their law cautions us against generalizing about an early American law. No single legal institution dominated the colonies; no set of legal rules, or no particular ruling document, unified it. The ambiguity early Americans felt about their law stemmed from the disjunctions created by the affiliation of English legal traditions in the environment of the New World.

Historians frequently invoke the noun "reception" to describe the transplantation of English laws and institutions to American soil. The reception metaphor affirms our continuing fascination with the frontier's influence on American culture, a fascination that pervaded the writings of earlier lawyer-historians, who equated good law with technical complexity. They shuddered at its absence for much of the colonial era. For them, the wild American environment was little more than a land without law.

The frontier thesis and the reception metaphor deflect our attention from the colonists' shrewd legal sensibilities. Early Americans *carried* a body of legal ideas with them that they applied, as they would and could, in their new environment. The notion of "carrying" as opposed to "receiving" law properly emphasizes the active process by which informed persons made choices that were always important under often novel, and invariably difficult, circumstances. The frontier was less an impediment to the full reception of a preferred system of English law than a mold in which colonists in places as diverse as Massachusetts and Virginia went about making social choices.

The Setting of Early American Law

Growth of the population and of the land area occupied was the central fact of the colonial setting of American law. The white population in 1660 would barely have filled present-day Yankee Stadium. The native American population, decimated by disease and warfare, numbered only 25,000. While it steadily dwindled, the white population multiplied. By 1690 the white population had tripled, and by 1760 it had quadrupled again to more than one million persons. Benjamin Franklin, in 1751, predicted that within a century "the greatest number of Englishmen will be on this side of the water."[2] The black slave population, which barely existed in 1660, grew thereafter at a rate even faster than the white population. Aided by the slave trade and an escalating birthrate, the number of blacks in bondage in 1750 was almost 236,000, and their number nearly doubled again by 1770.

The colonies expanded in size as well as population. Initially, the early seventeenth-century settlements in Massachusetts, New York, and Virginia were little more than patches of coastal life clinging to a huge forested continent. By 1750, however, the colonies spread from the district of Maine to Georgia and inland from the Atlantic to the Appalachian Mountains. The spacious continent readily absorbed the expanding population, propelling economic activity and making labor a dear commodity.

Sources of Discontinuity

Variations in geography, in immigration patterns, and in religious experience produced important economic and social differences within and among the colonies. The resulting discontinuities at once shaped and were shaped by the colonists' carried legal tradition.

The rough soils, heavy forests, and few navigable waterways of New England encouraged the exploitation of natural resources—fish, timber, and furbearing animals—and an agricultural system that produced foodstuffs and grazing animals for export. New England became enmeshed in the sugar trade with the West Indies, and Boston emerged as a terminus for transatlantic commerce. This same geography, abetted by the congregational form of church organization and the predominately English village background of the New England settlers, encouraged small independent towns based on the common field system of agriculture and pasturage. New England imported few class distinctions, at least in comparison with the Old World. It was a middle-class haven, although the emergence of larger towns and commercial activity in the eighteenth century spurred social stratification. Attitudes of deference rather than caste influenced the focus of political action, with a small upper class leading the majority.

In the middle colonies, which the Hudson River separated from New England, there was a richer ethnic mix. German, Scotch-Irish, Dutch, and Swedes established communities in which they produced beef, pork, wheat and other livestock, and supplied farm implements and hardware to other colonies. Class patterns became more blurred than in New England, although the "middling sort" predominated as well.

Of these settlements, Quaker Pennsylvania was more socially democratic; New York, with its Hudson River patricians, was more aristocratic. With Philadelphia as the colonies' leading port city, urban settlement was more highly developed. By the mid-eighteenth century, plain folk crowded into Philadelphia and other port cities.

In the Chesapeake and southern colonies, geography dealt yet another hand. Fertile soils and broad rivers flowing to the Atlantic encouraged staple agricultural production; tobacco was the primary crop, and in the eighteenth century rice and indigo in South Carolina and Georgia. The pattern of settlement differed from New England. Although Virginia and Maryland were the most populous colonies before the Revolution, their populations were scattered among widely separated plantations and farms. Moreover, the leading immigrants to these colonies often came from the gentry class,

some of them former sugar planters experienced with slavery in the West Indies. Of all
of the colonies, class distinctions were sharpest in the Chesapeake region and further
south. Yet even there the middle class was pervasive. Most planters held few slaves,
and widespread property ownership permitted an extensive franchise. More than any-
where else, deference influenced the social context of legal authority.

Religion separated the colonies as well, both internally and from one another.
Religious and economic motives led to immigration. True enough, in Massachusetts
Bay the original settlers promised, according to their leader John Winthrop, to establish a "cittie upon a hill." But idiosyncratic biblicism and intolerance characterized
their religious experiment, and many hundreds of thousands who came to the New
World did so as much with an eye on economic opportunity as with strong religious
attachments. The Puritan and Separatist dissenters from the Anglican Church who
settled in early New England had trouble enough agreeing with one another, let alone
with the staunch Anglicans in Virginia. When Quakers attempted in the mid-seventeenth century to settle in the Massachusetts Bay colony, they encountered ear crop-
ping, even execution. The Quakers founded Pennsylvania, but next door in Maryland
the Roman Catholic Church was predominant under Lord Baltimore. The mid-eighteenth century Great Awakening set believers trembling, splintering American Protestantism into additional denominational fragments. Early America was not an un-
churched land; rather it was a mosaic of faiths confronting the growing forces of
secularism.

The legal division of British North America produced a patchwork of conflicting
authority. In theory the king ruled over all, but in practice, local autonomy prevailed.
Of the thirteen original colonies, only seven had been founded by 1660. Georgia, the
last officially established, did not come into existence until 1733. Some were royal
colonies (like Virginia) controlled directly by the Crown, while others were charter
colonies (like Massachusetts Bay) in which members of a chartered company had
extensive governing rights; still others were proprietary colonies (like Maryland and
Pennsylvania) in which a single owner exercised seemingly vast control. Following the
Glorious Revolution in 1688, English authorities labored for the next ninety years to
impose a scheme of imperial organization, but their efforts only stirred the colonists to
resistance while making more shadowy the precise basis for imperial authority.

Taken together, these discontinuities invited the colonists to apply eclectically
their imported legal traditions. The result was a richly textured pattern of legal institutions and activity.

Threads of Shared Experience

Shared experiences channeled the development of law in all of the colonies. Colonial
America was overwhelmingly agricultural and rural, and the rhythms of the land in
every colony dictated the priorities of the law. Questions of holding, alienating, and
inheriting land, the status of indentured servants and slaves who worked on it, the
contractual issues raised by the sale of goods from it, and the penalties to be suffered
when livestock or fire strayed over it crowded the private law agenda of every colony.

Despite its divisiveness, religion was also a unifying force in the colonial experience. Post-Reformation Protestant thought proclaimed the existence of fixed standards
of justice, based on Divine Reason that was superior to man-made law. In the seven-

teenth-century colonies, this higher law found expression in the idea of natural law. "The Law of Nature," explained the Reverend John Davenport in 1669, "is God's law, written as with a pen of iron and the point of a diamond."[3] By the eighteenth century under the influence of the Enlightenment, the notion of higher law became more secular and rational; still loaded with moral imperative, it found its way into emerging American constitutional law, first in the form of the Declaration of Independence and later in the Constitution.

In yet another way, religion shaped early American law. The Protestant practice of making covenants, in New England and elsewhere, encouraged the view that law should flow from a consensus based on written agreements. In the post-Reformation world, amidst the growth of commerce and international trade, the law increasingly became a tool rather than a set of rigid and unalterable prescriptions. The savagery, and perhaps the mystery, of the New World invited the colonists to believe that they rather than kings could mold their own social choices. Disaster, after all, always lurked close to the surface. The Pequot Indians in the 1630s, for example, ambushed five colonists, dispatching three immediately, roasting one alive, and "the other came down drowned to us . . . with an arrow shot into his eyes through his head."[4] Survival under these circumstances depended on enforced discipline, but the early colonists also recognized that mutual assent to rules offered the best hope for survival in the face of danger.

The famous Mayflower Compact of 1620 typified the way in which the first colonists blended religious authority and consent. The compact was a contractual agreement in which the Pilgrim Separatists bound themselves into a single government. The enormous distance from England and the looming challenge of the North American wilderness induced a sense of mutual commitment among like-minded believers.

Political covenants appealed to ordinary settlers as well as religious ideologues. Seventeenth-century New England towns adopted bylaws that specified the operations of government. In other instances, adventurers pledged their mutual commitment at the beginning of a new enterprise. For example, the eight original founders of Springfield, Massachusetts in 1636 drew up a compact. "Wee whose names are underwritten," it began, "beinge by God's p'vidence ingaged to make a Plantation . . . , do mutually agree to certayne articles and orders to be observed and kept by us and our successors."[5] Personal liberty and individual order depended on God's laws but also on understood compacts.

It may seem incongruous that a system of religious authority could stimulate the notion that law ought to be based on individual will. Yet that was the case. For too long we have fixed our eyes on the sources of early American law without appreciating fully the importance of the form in which it appeared. The colonial enthusiasm for codes offers a good example of the way in which a moral order based on religious authority expressed itself through the form of consensual, rational law.

No man in a position of leadership who came to North America could have been unaware of the agitation for law reform in England. One of its chief objectives was to produce a rational body of readily understood and readily obeyed law. In the Massachusetts Bay colony, for example, Puritan leaders urgently sought such a formulation as a way of distancing themselves from England. Differences over content slowed adoption. The Reverend John Cotton in 1636 offered a code of law known as "Moses, His Judicials," that wove together secular legal ideals and Hebraic law. The "Judicials'' were never adopted, but the quest for a set of uniform rules persisted. In 1641 Nathaniel Ward, another minister and one of the colony's first trained lawyers, formulated the "Body of Liberties," but it too failed to receive formal support.

These disagreements among the Puritans typified the colonists' unease with the English common law tradition. But they also bred political contention based on frustration about what the law was. Dr. Robert Child in 1646 issued his "Remonstrances" against John Winthrop and other magistrates on the Massachusetts General Court, the chief governing body of the Bay colony. Child complained that the colony had deviated from the "Fundamental and wholesome Lawes" of England. He insisted that the religious leaders of the Massachusetts Bay colony should broaden the base of church membership and, in so doing, secure for all colonists—Puritan and non-Puritan— "civil liberty and freedom."[6] Child's complaints fell on deaf ears (he was subsequently convicted of defaming the government and slandering the church), but two years later the Massachusetts Bay colony did adopt a written code that met some of Child's demands.

The *Book of the General Lawes and Libertyes* of the Massachusetts Bay colony in 1648 was the most successful of the Puritan efforts to formulate a rational, consensual rule of law. The Puritans were not democrats, but they were sensitive to the need to win obedience through shared commitment. The *Lawes and Libertyes* injected religious fervor into the English common law heritage. Each crime and punishment, for example, cited biblical authority: "If any man or woman be a *witch* . . . they shall be put to death. *Exod.* 22. 18 *Levit.* 20. 27. *Deut.* 18. 10. 11."[7]

The *Lawes and Libertyes* spread over fifty-nine pages and, despite its religious configuration, it influenced other colonies. Pragmatic legal borrowing was quite strong. Provisions of the code migrated widely to Connecticut, New York, New Jersey, Pennsylvania, and even Virginia. The code jettisoned much of the technical apparatus of the English common law. The profusion of biblical citations should not obscure the quite practical way in which the code dealt with matters of crime, business, and economics. Typical was the provision under the heading "Summons" that dispensed with the intricacies of process in England when issuing a summons or arrest warrant. The *Lawes and Libertyes* mandated a simple course of action: "No . . . Judgement or any kinde of proceedings . . . shall be reversed on any kinde of circumstantial errors or mistakes, if the person and the Cause be rightly understood and intended by the Court."[8]

Colonial leaders everywhere sought the certainty of written codes. The form of the law seemed as important as its content. Some codes were quite harsh, even draconian, as was Dale's Code of 1611 in Virginia. But even there, early settlers knew in writing what rules governed their actions. Named after Sir Thomas Dale, the colony's first governor, the Code treated violators roughly. For instance, it specified execution for persons found to have stolen from public stores or boats. Such provisions reflected the grim realities of the "starving time" in Virginia, but the Code enunciated "Laws Divine" and "Moral" as well as "Martial."[9] All who participated in the colony had first to know the rules, to accept the notion of Divine Reason behind them, and to conduct themselves with the best interests of the group as a whole in mind. As conditions improved in Virginia, Dale's Code faded. The House of Burgesses, America's first legislative assembly, appeared in 1619, and its elected members gradually crafted a more supple body of law.

In every other colony, similar legislative bodies appeared as colonial Americans busily marshaled their own resources to fashion societies out of the wilderness. The ready availability of property made the franchise extensive. In the eighteenth century, between 75 and 90 percent of the adult white male population was qualified to vote. Social deference proscribed sharply the limits of direct popular control over government, and the lawmaking process remained tightly held by the upper ranks of society. Still, popular will was a genuine source of consensual authority in every colony, and its growth during the eighteenth century contributed directly to the eventual acccptance of a popular will theory of law. That is, legitimate law had to be derived from the people.

All of the colonies developed law under the umbrella of imperial authority. The imperial system changed from the seventeenth to the eighteenth centuries in reaction to developments in English society. Regicide, Civil War, Restoration, and the ascendancy of Parliament all shook seventeenth-century England. The commercial and mercantile interests that gained power following the Restoration expected the American colonies to contribute directly to the welfare of the empire. Parliament in 1691 established the Board of Trade to oversee mercantilist policies aimed at bringing the colonies fully within the imperial economy. New and more comprehensive regulations—and squads of officals to administer them—appeared. These officials brought with them a determination to impose English common law, in all of its complexity, on the colonies. The common law became a tool of the empire, a means of bringing uniformity to the seemingly ragged and disjointed practice of law in the American plantations. Although forced to acknowledge the imperial demands, Americans actively shaped their institutions to fit more their needs than those of their English masters.

Beginnings of American Legal Institutions

The colonists held to a unitary view of legal institutions and their responsibilities. They did not subscribe to the modern notion of a functional separation of powers in government nor did they believe in sharply drawn lines in the administration of the law. Through two centuries, the colonists indeed developed more complex, formal, and hierarchical legal institutions, but even at the end of the era they were less differentiated than they became in the nineteenth and twentieth centuries. The quest for economic self-reliance, rooted in the practice of capitalism, and the tightening grip of imperial control, generated by the empire's greater costs, fueled the growing complexity of legal institutions.

The Courts

Seventeenth-century Americans viewed lawmaking and judging as synonymous activities. John Winthrop, for example, repeatedly referred to the "High Court of Parliament," a position echoed in England by Sir Thomas Smith in *De Republica Anglorum*.[10] There were, of course, courts lesser than Parliament. Lord Edward Coke, the greatest writer on the common law in the seventeenth century, counted more than one hundred courts, ranging from the powerful royal courts that administered the complex body of common law rules to local courts, leet and baron, that depended as much, if not more, on custom as law. The colonists' modest social origins (coupled with the absence of a trained bench and bar during the seventeenth century) meant that they were most familiar with the local courts. The colonists replicated what they knew, and what they knew best was local not royal judicial structure. Throughout they gave Old World institutions a New World character.

Every colony developed a simple layered system of courts. At the top were the colonial legislatures, whose members regarded themselves, sometimes in alliance with the governor, as the highest court in their jurisdiction. Unlike Parliament, the colonial legislatures occasionally took cases in original jurisdiction. The Virginia legislature in 1619 tried Captain Henry Spelman for illegal correspondence with the Indians and required him to serve a term of seven years as the governor's interpreter as punishment. The General Court of Massachusetts, which was that colony's lawmaking body, took an expansive view of its judicial power. For example, it tried Dr. Robert Child and his associates for heresy (adhering to unorthodox religious views) and sedition (defaming a political official). But the legislatures were most important as courts of appeal, especially in criminal proceedings. Even in Virginia and Maryland, where the king granted authority to the proprietors or governors, the legislators made themselves into the forums of last legal resort. The same bodies that made the law often decided the fate of persons accused of breaking it.

A layer of superior courts below the legislatures functioned as courts of assize and original jurisdiction in some colonies. The authority for these courts might be a charter, a voluntary association, or royal instructions. Their composition also varied. In the Chesapeake colonies, superior courts consisted of an appointed governor and council, and they were called the General or Quarter Court in Virginia and the Provincial Court in Maryland. In New England, the governor and the assistants made up the superior court, and they were elected either by freemen or the legislature. In Massachusetts these courts were styled Assistants Courts, in Rhode Island the Court of Tryals, in Connecticut the Particular Court, and in New Haven the Court of Magistrates.

Although generalizations are difficult, these superior courts shared two features. First, civil matters constituted most of their dockets, but they also exercised original jurisdiction over capital criminal cases and appellate jurisdiction from lower courts. Second, the politics that swirled through each colony buffeted these courts. In Maryland, for example, the Provincial Court was a battleground between the Calverts and their opponents, and charges of sedition and treason fill the court's records. In Massachusetts, a clique of the self-proclaimed elect dominated the Assistants Court through most of the seventeenth century, anxiously superintending the colony's moral condition.

The local courts made up the third and most important layer of judicial authority. In Massachusetts and New York in the mid-seventeenth century the quarter session courts (so called because they met in session every three months or so) began to appear. In the Chesapeake region similar institutions were known originally simply as county courts, although Maryland briefly experimented with a full-blown scheme of manorial courts. The individuals on these courts were variously termed commissioners, councilors, magistrates, or justices of the peace. They numbered from three (Massachusetts) to fifteen (Virginia), and in every colony the social elite controlled them. Their duties included legislative as well as judicial responsibilities. These courts, for example, decreed the level of taxation, oversaw its collection, stood in judgment of those persons who failed to pay, supervised road building, licensed taverns and inns, granted poor relief, and tried criminal offenders.

Local courts had social and symbolic as well as legal functions. Court day brought large numbers of persons to town. It was an opportunity to discuss politics, to conduct business, and to socialize. Court day fostered continuity in the lives of colonial Americans through its palpable demonstration of the existence of legal authority. By the eve of the Revolution, court days were often more important for the political rhetoric outside the courtroom than for the legal proceedings inside.

From the establishment of the colonies to the Revolution, the legal tenor of these courts gradually changed. Initially, lay judges administered an informal and often discretionary form of justice. These local courts were not duplications of a specific English model, but "crude imitation[s] of inaccurately remembered things."[11] The "things" inaccurately remembered were local laws and customs spiced, in some colonies, with religious fervor. There was little of the technical precision insisted on in the royal courts of the mother country, which prescribed rigid verbal formulas for different descriptions of wrongs and requests for remedies. Rather, in keeping with the law reform impulse of seventeenth-century England, local courts administered justice based more on the substance of the case than the way in which it was presented. Sentencing patterns suggest the discretionary role of these courts as agencies of social control and as safety valves for individuals in society. In New York, for example, a woman suspected of theft was ordered out of the county, while another thief was ordered to be given twenty-one lashes, and yet a third was "remitted to the correction of his father."[12]

By the end of the seventeenth century these courts became more formal. The Essex County, Massachusetts court typified this process. Until the 1680s, that court had taken an informal and creative approach to law. But two developments prompted change. First, as Essex filled up with settlers and as commerce expanded, land titles came under increasing scrutiny. Many were found wanting. The county court, once an institution most attuned to maintaining local consensus, now found itself cast as a neutral agent, an honest broker, expected to resolve social conflict through the formal legal processes. At the same time, the restored Stuart monarchy in England wished to knit the colonists more fully into the fabric of the empire, and they proposed to do so by making colonial law confrom to English practices. To this end, the Crown instituted in 1691 the short-lived Dominion of New England, which reorganized county government and brought new members to the Essex County bench. Although the Dominion subsequently collapsed, the reforms it brought persisted.

Both developments introduced a previously unheard of degree of formality. Thus, in the late 1680s there appeared for the first time the use of the fictitious parties of John Doe and Richard Roe in cases involving ejectment from lands. The Essex court also began to enforce technical requirements of procedure, leading to the dismissal of actions and undermining the traditional role of informal community norms on the actions of the judges. Litigation in the late 1690s declined sharply because people balked at having their cases argued according to unfamiliar common law procedures. By the early eighteenth century, however, a trained bar offered its services and litigation in Essex exploded beyond seventeenth-century levels. The same pattern developed in nearby Connecticut, where once-neighborly modes of dispute settlement yielded before an increasingly formal legal system that treated neighbors and strangers alike.[13] As colonies became provinces in the eighteenth century, and as economic activity extended in scope beyond local boundaries, the courts became both more active and more formal. Formal institutional roles first flowed from and then abetted economic and demographic growth.

Settlers in the Chesapeake and southern colonies experienced much the same with local courts as did their New England and middle colonies counterparts. Still, differences appeared. The somewhat sharper division of social status in these colonies gave the gentry, which had by experience greater exposure to the technical forms of the common law than did the middle class, a firm hold on the county courts. The law reform movement in seventeenth-century England had less influence in these colonies, and the courts had greater respect for technical pleading. But the differences existed on the margins; county court justice in seventeenth-century Virginia could be as arbitrary as that in Plymouth plantation. Thus, the Virginia House of Burgesses in 1658 passed a statute urging the courts to render judgment "according as the right of the cause and the matter in lawe shall appeare unto them, without any regard of any imperfection, default or want of forme in any writt, returne, plaint or proces."[14] By century's end, however, the same economic and demographic forces that promoted a more formal scheme of justice in Essex County appeared in Virginia and Maryland.

The dispersed landholdings of the Chesapeake and southern colonies militated against efficient justice. Judges presided over scattered populations. They were notorious for their reluctance to leave the safe confines of home. South Carolina, for example, for the first forty years of its existence had only one court that met in Charles Town, creating hardships for backcountry residents. It was not until the Regulator Movement of the 1760s, which was brought about in large part by the failure of local government outside of the low country, that judicial authority became truly provincewide.

Even when the judges did venture forth, they sometimes exercised insufficient authority in problematic ways. Tobacco prices provide a good example. Planters with vast stretches of land (often the county court officials expected to implement laws setting the price of tobacco) went their own way and cultivated excessive acreage. At the end of the seventeenth century, the planters' disdain of the rule of law brought about a serious crisis as small farmers, who wanted to improve their economic position by reducing the amount of tobacco in production, engaged in "plant cutting" riots. A worried local magistry, anxious for their own prerogatives, retreated to the certainty of formalized common law. In turn, the legal profession, itself made up of the sons of planters, rose to serve the law's increasing technicality.

Justices of the Peace

The justices of the peace constituted the lowest and most ubiquitous layer of colonial legal institutions. Long a bulwark of the English legal system, the justice of the peace served a similar function in the colonies. In a society in which social status and authority were closely linked, the office commanded influence. Although the tasks of the justice of the peace varied from colony to colony, considerable responsibility was attached to the office. In addition to trying serious criminal matters together in a sessions or county court, the justices acting alone exercised wide civil jurisdiction and extensive power to try minor criminal matters. In many colonies the justice of the peace fulfilled what amounted to a modern-day policing function, first investigating then trying purported crimes.

Although the justices of the peace "were the embodiment of the law to the ordinary man, they were themselves lay persons not formally trained in the law."[15] The early history of the justices of the peace gave a firm tradition of lay participation in the judicial process. They were also deeply implicated in colonial political affairs. In Virginia, for example, the governor ostensibly appointed justices, but local power brokers, on whose support the governor depended, effectively controlled the selection process. The result was that justices there served longer terms (often twenty to thirty years) than did their New England counterparts.

Appeals to England

In hindsight the English could have promoted a rational scheme of empire by imposing legal uniformity on the colonies through the royal courts. They did not. Great distance merely reinforced their disdain of the colonial legal order.

An appeal mechanism, however, was available to the colonists through a committee of the Privy Council. Its duties included hearing legal appeals as well as reviewing colonial legislation. It had little opportunity to exercise its review power over colonial courts; fewer than three cases a year between 1696 and 1775 were appealed. This council usually placed the necessities of imperial policy over the rationalization of colonial law. As a scholar studying the work of the Privy Council has observed, its "jurisdiction . . . was largely exercised in an *ad hoc* fashion, from appeal to appeal with little lasting effect."[16]

The same was true of the Privy Council's review of colonial legislation, to which it took a benign view. The council overturned slightly more than 5 percent of all colonial legislation. The council's weakly exercised review power not only encouraged Americans to fashion their carried legal traditions independently of the mother country, but in the eighteenth century it made hollow Crown demands for the colonies to heed the technical character of the common law.

Special Courts: Vice-Admiralty and Chancery

Vice-admiralty and chancery courts developed independently of the hierarchical layering of the indigenous colonial courts. The former provided imperial control and commercial coherence to ocean trading. In the seventeenth century governors had acted in the capacity of vice-admirals, handling disputes arising out of maritime matters such as prize, wrecks, insurance, and seaman's wages. Parliament in 1696 authorized separate vice-admiralty courts as part of its larger program to tighten the imperial grip. These new courts brought the highly technical law of admiralty to the colonies. The judges received fixed fees and percentage payments of the goods they condemned, a practice that denied colonial assemblies control over their salaries.

The colonists resented the courts even though they offered important commercial advantages. Vice-admiralty judges, who were often Americans, placed colonial merchants and customs racketeers on short legal leashes in commercial dealings with their

English masters. Moreover, the colonists, who coveted the benefits of local control through trial by jury, resented the prerogative nature of the vice-admiralty proceedings.

Chancery courts were also controversial because governors sought in their capacity as chancellors to seek political ends rather than justice. The English courts of chancery, which by the seventeenth century had become as complex as the common law courts, were not easily transferred to the colonies. Massachusetts and Pennsylvania rejected them outright; elsewhere, they developed only fitfully.

Equity, however, had emerged in the colonies as a matter of practice if not of form. Seventeenth century colonial lay judges exercised a kind of equity through the laxity with which they followed common law precedents. But as the English tightened control over the colonies in the eighteenth century, governors discovered that by assuming the status of chancellors they could extend the reach of their authority. In New York, for example, Governor William Burnet established himself as chancellor and proceeded to collect feudal dues owed in the form of quit rents in the Hudson River Valley. (Tenants paid a fee to quit, to be free of personal service or other obligations to a lord.) Burnet's successor went so far as to use his position as chancellor to question the validity of one of the colonies most extensive land patents.

The furor over equity practice subsided by the mid-eighteenth century, and the growing technicality of the common law system in the colonies revived interest in it. There was a "generally recognized need for equity as a part of the . . . American legal system," but it was accepted only after the colonies had either adopted viable chancery courts free of gubernatorial influence or granted this jurisdiction to the common law courts.[17]

The Bench and Bar

In the seventeenth century, there were few lawyers and their status was problematic. Of the sixty-five men who landed at Plymouth in 1620, not one was a lawyer. The colony's first trained lawyer, Thomas Lechford, did little to instill enthusiasm. He was disbarred for trying to influence a jury. Antilawyer sentiment was pervasive elsewhere as well, and the "ancient English prejudice against lawyers secured new strength in America."[18] The framers of the Fundamental Constitutions of the Carolinas in 1669 declared it a "base and vile thing to plead for money or reward."[19] Connecticut and Virginia during a portion of the seventeenth century prohibited lawyers from practicing. Early lawyers were often laymen helping friends or women serving the legal interests of absent husbands.

Too much, however, should not be made of antilawyer sentiment. Since the Middle Ages lawyers had played an ever-increasing role in joining human activity to established rules of government, and they carried on this function in colonial society, especially as capitalism bloomed in the late seventeenth century. The legal practitioners of eighteenth-century America were important as agents of both social stability and economic coherence. Initially, most trained colonial lawyers came from the Inns of Court, but by the mid-eighteenth century a rough apprenticeship system emerged in which would-be lawyers studied with a practicing attorney or judge. There were no law schools, and the entire educational process had a pragmatic and dronelike quality.

Nonetheless, the rudiments of what would become the American legal profession appeared, stimulated by more than just crude opportunities for training. By legislative enactment, executive decree, and court order every colony bestowed on some persons the professional status of officers of the court. Thereafter an emerging hierarchy of lawyers appeared. The stratification was relatively simple: lawyers residing in and operating from eighteenth-century colonial capitals believed they were superior to county court attorneys. Economic growth provided a further impetus. The scarcity of specie made credit relations vital to the success of the colonial economies. Lawyers busied themselves arbitrating these arrangements. Economic necessity stimulated a demand for skilled interpreters of the labyrinth of provincial and local economic regulatory legislation. It also enabled colonial lawyers to begin to Americanize the substantive portions of the English common law.

Imperial demands in the eighteenth century for fuller allegiance to the English common law system also abetted the institutionalization of the bar and eroded the informal character of early American law practice. People caught up in the legal system increasingly thought first to seek counsel, and their actions merely confirmed the need for more and better-trained lawyers. Moreover, the rise of social discord in eighteenth-century Massachusetts accompanied a decline in legal fees. As competent legal counsel became more important it also became more available. Lawyers also dressed to reflect their new status: by the 1760s in both New York and Massachusetts lawyers wore robes and wigs as they performed their courtroom duties. In those colonies and others, the formalization of the legal process meant that the legal system emerged as the standard for all forms of dispute settlement.

The colonial economy never generated sufficient legal business to bring about a division of the profession similar to that in England, where barristers (who practiced before the courts) and solicitors (who only provided legal advice) fielded highly technical legal disputes. American lawyers survived as generalists; they literally did not have the luxury of specialization. The absence in most colonies of explicit provisions for admission to the bar confirmed the tentative character of the legal profession.

The development of the colonial bench paralleled that of the bar. Early magistrates were often unschooled in the law. William Penn in 1681, for example, appointed Nicholas More, a London physician and husband of a wealthy Quaker, chief justice of Pennsylvania. The chief justice, however, brought to the bench ignorance of the law, personal arrogance, and avarice, a combination that prompted the Pennsylvania Assembly four years later to impeach him. The eighteenth-century colonial judiciary was more professional, a change induced by both English authorities and a bar anxious to practice before more competent judges. From the beginning of American legal history, the bar took a special interest in the judiciary, on whose behavior its livelihood depended.

The predominance of lay judges often meant that juries exercised important responsibilities in settling questions of law as well as fact. The celebrated trial of John Peter Zenger for seditious libel against the governor of New York in 1735 revealed, among other things, that a jury could disregard or interpret judicial instructions with some impunity. That jury found Zenger not guilty, although the judge's instructions left no doubt that it should have decided the opposite. Similarly, a Virginia statute in the seventeenth century provided that if jurors were not "clear" regarding a particular case, they might choose "in open Court to advise with any man they shall think fit to resolve or direct them, before they give in their verdict."[20] Governor William Shirley of Massachusetts, himself a trained lawyer and a proponent of the adoption of English legal forms in colonies, acknowledged that juries were often powerful engines of local interest. "A trial by jury," he complained, "is only trying one illicit trader by his fellows, or at least by his well-wishers."[21]

The precarious state of the colonial judiciary stemmed from more than its indifferent legal training. Judges also lacked independence. The doctrine that the king had exclusive authority to erect courts made colonial judges agents of the Crown. Distance created an insuperable burden. "If that prerogative power was too distant when exercised from London," a historian has observed, "it was far too immediate when institutionalized under the auspices of the royal governors representing the king."[22] The governors appointed most judges, but they did so for only limited terms. Parliament in 1701 provided good-behavior tenure for English judges, but that guarantee of independence, so essential to the functioning of the judiciary, never reached colonial America. The judiciary, as a result, was an item of political debate and compromise among contesting colonial factions. The Privy Council sealed the matter in 1761 when it decreed that no judicial commission was good unless it specifically stated that its holder served at "the pleasure of the crown."[23]

The independence of colonial judges was limited in another way. The lower houses of the assemblies in the eighteenth century grew increasingly restive with the exercise of judicial power, and they turned to impeachment to limit judicial influence. Unlike the earlier judicial impeachments—such as that against More in Pennsylvania, aimed at criminal wrongdoing in office—these new proceedings had important political overtones. Particularly significant were the impeachments and near-impeachments of Chester County Judge William Moore of Pennsylvania in 1758, Chief Justice Charles Shinner of South Carolina, and Chief Justice Peter Oliver of Massachusetts, both in 1774. In these cases impeachment became "a method of expressing the people's grievances (as enunciated in their assemblies) against imperial rules" rather than a means of chastising corruption in office.[24]

Legislative Authority of the Assembly and the Town

The colonists developed their carried legal tradition most fully in the lawmaking institutions of colonywide and local government. The lower houses of the assembly, the town, and the county decisively shaped the substantive content of colonial law. Lawmaking, as a result, became the effective center of colonial politics.

Under English law the lower houses were subordinate, corporate councils called into session under the king's instructions to his governors or under a specific charter provision. The governor exercised something less than a whip hand. He was invariably forced to make significant concessions to the assembly merely to make government work. The steady accretion of legislative power in the colonies mirrored events in seventeenth-century England. There the Glorious Revolution of 1688 secured the sovereignty of Parliament, and American colonists thereafter insisted on the primacy of their own assemblies and the subordination of the governor to them. Colonial impertinence grew bolder in the eighteenth century. So too did threats against it. A pamphleteer in New York, supporting the British position, advised the colonial assembly "to drop those parliamentary airs and style about liberty and property, and keep within their sphere."[25] When Massachusetts in 1733 appealed to the actions of the House of Commons as precedent for their own position, Parliament renounced it as a "high insult upon his Majesty's government."[26] No matter, the assemblies repeatedly demonstrated their command of events on this side of the Atlantic.

The assemblies became potent lawmaking institutions because somebody had to take responsibility for the mundane chores of day-to-day provincial life. Areas of legislative activity included the building of roads, ferries, and wharves; the formulation of land policy; the establishment of trade with the Indians; the regulation of immigration into the colony; settlement of boundary disputes; and the designation of fishing grounds. The assemblies necessarily gained control of the colonial purse strings through the exercise of taxing and spending powers. They also managed their internal affairs, including the freedom of their members to speak, to initiate legislation, and to fix qualifications of membership.

Strong colonial assemblies nourished a federal-like system of legal authority in which different levels of government exercised influence over particular matters. There was in reality a hierarchy of lawmaking authority. One of the chief responsibilities of the assemblies, for example, was that of establishing a loose but effective framework of legal constraints for the operation of towns.

Municipal corporations were the first colonial entities charged with promoting the public welfare. The Massachusetts Town Act of 1635 typified measures subsequently adopted in other colonies. It recognized the diversity of existing practices in the towns rather than attempting to dictate rights and privileges based on higher authority. Thus, the towns were to "dispose of their owne land, and woods," to "make such orders as may concerne the well ordering of their townes," to enforce these orders with bylaws establishing penalties not exceeding twenty shillings, and "to chuse their owne particulr officers, as constables, surveyors for highwayes, and the like."[27] Regarding individual lives, this and other municipal incorporation acts left basic decisions about the role of the community to the towns.

Until about the 1740s, the single most important function of the incorporated town was to provide "the commercial community . . . the service of trade and industry."[28] It established and regulated the marketplace. Like the English borough, colonial American towns actively intervened in the local economy. Among town-owned stalls strolled town officials employing town standards of weights and measures to gauge the produce sold by town-licensed butchers and town-admitted freemen.

The New England town meeting afforded a popular basis for the establishment of local law. Some historians claim that a ruling elite imposed rather than earned mutual accord; others argue that the spirit of consensus was real enough, and that influential town leaders simply settled troublesome issues through quiet agreement outside the meeting hall. Whatever its precise operation, the town meeting reinforced the consensual basis of early American law, not so much in a spirit of public policy formed through open government, as much as through a wish to avoid conflict. The New England settlers brought far more of their experience with them than has heretofore been recognized, and attitudes toward law and its implementation composed a significant part of their "English ways." Their inheritance included the notion, reinforced by the congregational scheme of church organization, that individuals ought to work in harmony. The bylaws of one Massachusetts town suggested as much. They expressed the wish that "no Intrested Disputes may make any breach of Union," so that the town could "advise and agree upon measures" and thereby obtain "Love and Unity [and] Peace."[29]

The town meeting invariably settled disputes involving groups rather than individuals. For example, the town of Rochester, Massachusetts in 1722 confronted the sticky issue of who would pay the taxes owed by Quakers who refused to support the local Congregational minister. The town decided that it would pay. Yet many of the decisions made in the meetings, while aimed at groups, required specific implementation, and that task fell to the selectmen elected by the freeholders of the town. The towns legislated, for example, to dispose of tramps and itinerants, to punish rowdy youths, to control loose hogs, and to establish the rights of fishermen in local waters. The selectmen, however, had the job of actually expelling strangers and securing roving swine.

On the eve of the American Revolution economic change, population growth, religious ferment, and imperial intervention placed these "peaceable kingdoms" under serious strain. As ripples of economic activity widened in the eighteenth century, social conflict spread to individuals and groups in different towns, even colonies. The conscious effort of the English authorities to enhance the common law system also pushed disputants in New England to seek judicially enforceable legal remedies. The town remained a source of local governmental authority through its rule-making power, but as an institution of formal and informal dispute resolution, it became less important. Beginning in the 1760s, growing numbers of disputes between persons from different towns crowded the county and session court dockets, indicating the mounting attention given to judicial resolution of social controversies. The courts laid claim to new authority at the expense of the towns.

With a few exceptions—Williamsburg, for example—towns in the Chesapeake and southern colonies were pale images of their counterparts in New England and the middle colonies. The county rather than the town fostered commercial activity and regulated the local marketplace. The pattern of scattered settlement over a large area made the county and its court the center of local legislative activity. And because the leadership from the tobacco and rice planting social elite was not interested in setting up villages with churches as the focus of life, society in Virginia, Maryland, and the Carolinas spread out into tobacco plantations of various sizes. The dispersion of legal institutions followed the dispersion of society.

The Church

The law of God and the Bible were important sources of colonial law. Early Americans identified wrongdoing with sin, and they looked to their churches as institutions of conflict resolution and social control. The clergy enjoyed a prominent role both as a source of social authority in its own right and as a voice in civil affairs. The congregation and town government overlapped in New England; the vestry and county government coincided in the Chesapeake. Positive secular law had always to be conscious of, if not consonant with, moral values supported by religious authority. Even the Quakers in Pennsylvania, with their loosely structured religious units, anticipated that the church would enhance—but not dictate—secular authority. Yet nowhere did the church run civil government, and the notion of separation of church and state itself became a major unifying tenet in the development of American public life.

Still, churches were significantly less important as legal institutions than in England. The Anglican Church never fully established itself (i.e., became an official state religion) in the New World and, as a result, ecclesiastical courts never appeared. These courts in England were powerful engines of moral authority, treating crimes such as drunkenness, fornication, buggery (sexual perversion), and adultery. The civil courts in America took responsibility for these matters. Individual churches indeed punished misconduct, but their authority ran only to the members of their congregations and parishes. The churches did not distinguish between civil and criminal acts, but instead attempted to foster a sense of Christian forgiveness and consensus. Even where the church was strong, economic growth imported divisions into local communities that resisted resolution by local nonlegal institutions. As formal legal institutions grew in authority, the significance of arbitration and church disciplinary procedures waned. Religious ideals supplied a moral tone to the operation of criminal law and business relationships, but the churches proved incapable of resolving disputes among nonmembers. Finally, religious pluralism precluded any one church from dominating the character of colonial legal culture. In order to enhance settlement on its western frontier, Virginia, for example, had to waive provisions of a law that required non-Anglicans to pay a tax to maintain the parish clergy.

The Institutional Legacy

By the time of the American Revolution, the colonists had forged a distinctive set of legal institutions to serve colonial conditions. Over the course of almost two centuries they became increasingly complex and formal, and they also became more powerful. Law became less communal, in part, because the community itself changed, with law becoming more general and the community more particular.[30] From these institutions in each colony emerged a body of rules that, while owing something to remembered English ways, also reflected the circumstances of the New World. The resulting ambiguity in law troubled colonists and English imperial authorities alike.

2

Law, Society, and Economy in Colonial America

Colonial Law and Social Control

The crude provinces that in time formed the United States were elements of a greater historical context. Protestant toleration, nationalism, and capitalism shaped the English society and economy. These same forces affected the colonies, but with them the situation was different: they had no feudal past. The colonists matured their legal tradition under this unique circumstance. The substantive body of law that poured forth from early American legal institutions promoted both a more open society and one in which individuals could experience greater economic opportunity than existed in the mother country. Yet among the early settlers were losers as well as winners, and decisions about how to treat the poor, punish the deviant, and enforce economic obligations touched some persons more than others. The ambiguity in early American law extended to its social and distributive consequences, not just to differing notions of law among the colonies and with the mother country.

Dependency

Colonial Americans accepted poverty as a natural, expected condition of frontier life. They did not, however, so willingly embrace its social consequences. The poor were an economic drain on the community, an unwanted example of sinfulness, and, in the eighteenth century, a potential criminal threat.

We shall never know exactly the extent of colonial poverty. What we do know is that, despite the strong middle-class character of early North America, the poor constituted an identifiable class. For example, James Glen, governor of South Carolina in the mid-eighteenth century, concluded that, while his province had "plenty of the good things of life," it also included—among a population of 30,000—about 5000 white persons who only had a "bare subsistence."[1] Subsistence and poverty, of course, are two different things. Josiah Quincy of Massachusetts offered a more biting assessment of class and poverty in South Carolina; he found that the colony divided into "opulent and lordly planters, poor and spiritless peasants and vile slaves."[2] Even strongly middle-class New England was conscious of its poor. Religious activists thought of Boston as a kind of Babylon, teeming with vice and poverty.

By the eighteenth century, in all the colonies a new kind of poor had emerged: the wandering or "strolling poor," consisting of the unskilled, the widowed, and the aged. Some of these people were not truly indigent, but instead were itinerant male laborers constantly searching for work, having been displaced from their hometowns. Establishing the residency of these individuals confounded leaders of different towns, each of whom sought to prove that responsibility for a transient belonged elsewhere. The courts of New England and the middle colonies became the forums in which these disputes were settled, and a decline in the traditional informal basis of social cohesion followed.

Sentiments of class and humanity influenced the legal response to the poor. Every colony enacted some sort of "poor law" based on the Elizabethan model. Colonial legislatures prescribed the terms of relief for the poor, but the responsibility for implementation fell on local communities. Because the towns and counties had to levy taxes to fill the relief coffers, their leaders decisively controlled the treatment of the poor. They expected families and neighbors to take care of their own and, when they did not, the overseers of the poor (a committee appointed by the county court or the town selectmen) sought court action. In 1752, for example, a sessions court in Massachusetts ordered the relatives of two "aged" women to care for them.[3] In seventeenth-century New England the family was held accountable for the well-being of its members and therefore rescued the deserving local poor from their fate.

Family and neighbors were also important in the Chesapeake and southern colonies, but demography and geography worked against their effectiveness. The scarcity of women in the seventeenth century, the low life expectancy of males, and the remoteness of scattered settlements over large areas prompted a more active role for judicial authority. The most significant development from these circumstances was the appearance of orphans' courts. These institutions attempted to prevent poverty before it began by binding children without families into apprenticeships.

The transient poor stirred great anxiety because they threatened the bonds of community. All of the colonies adopted the practice of "warning out," which was part of the carried legal tradition brought by the settlers from life in the English boroughs. Persons who could not prove their self-sufficiency, by either posting a bond or securing a community sponsor, were ordered by the selectmen or overseers of the poor to leave, usually within three days. In some instances communities attempted to deal with transients and idlers—the so-called undeserving poor—by shaming them. A Pennsylvania statute of 1718, for example, prescribed that the habitually poor were to wear a "large Roman 'P' " on their shoulder.[4] The stocks also became a favored punishment.

But by the end of the eighteenth century, the legal status of the poor was in transition from the earlier local and familial solutions toward a state-sponsored, institutional mode of action. The Massachusetts General Court in 1794, for example, enacted a new Poor Law that formally replaced the practice of warning out with routinized procedures for the removal of the poor and instructions to each town to provide care and immediate relief for up to three months without regard to an indigent's residence.

Early Americans generally rejected what was one of the most striking features of the Elizabethan Poor Laws: imprisonment for debt. The colonists rearranged their legal tradition to fit New World exigencies, and their actions caution us against drawing a fine line between colonial experience and the practices of the new nation. In a labor-scarce economy, the work force was an important commodity that could be tapped for the benefit of the community. By the middle of the eighteenth century the leaders of New England and the middle colonies, while still committed to treating the poor on the basis of family and neighborhood assistance, forged a modest institutional solution to the seemingly ever-increasing problem of the poor: the workhouse. Pennsylvania law makers, for example, began to specify periods of incarceration for those persons unable to pay their debts. Their reasons for doing so, however, were altogether different from those of the English. Under Quaker influence, the Pennsylvania Assembly concluded that putting the poor to work at hard labor would teach them the discipline necessary to become productive future citizens while providing the community with much-needed labor. The workhouse subsequently provided the model for the American penitentiary.

Deviancy

Colonial society bred little crime. Although crime increased in absolute numbers from the seventeenth through the eighteenth centuries, the population expanded more rapidly. Colonial Americans nonetheless had a fearsome interest in controlling social deviancy, and the repeated denunciations of licentiousness and vice in every colony confirm that they worried a good deal about crime, even though it was far less pervasive than today.

The low but growing incidence of crime was largely a social artifact. Total populations were small, and especially in the seventeenth century everyone had a place in which he or she was known to live. Homicide, for example, was often the product of frustration rather than premeditation; it was a violent explosion of built-up social pressures. The cramped quarters in which colonial families lived appear to have been fertile ground for the small numbers of violent crimes. Francis Brooke, for example, became convinced that his wife was pregnant by another man, and he abused her badly on several occasions. He finally attempted an abortion with a pair of tongs, and a badly bruised child was born dead. Brooke claimed that his wife had fallen from a peach tree; the doubtless terrified woman agreed. He received from the court only a warning of God's wrath.[5]

By the eighteenth century, with the appearance of the wandering poor, larger towns, and greater geographic mobility, the consensual nature of early American society ebbed. The greater ethnic heterogeneity further disrupted old social bonds. Homicides, assaults, and thievery occured more frequently, and those persons charged with capital crimes seem to have had a significantly greater history of mobility than did the average colonist. Geographic mobility freed the already alienated felon from the informal mechanisms of social control: family, neighborhood, and religious congregation. For example, John Smith, a prominent counterfeiter, traveled throughout the colonies before being caught and hanged at Albany, New York in 1773.

Crimes against property, which had seldom been prosecuted in the seventeenth century, appeared with greater frequency on court dockets. Only with the emergence of conspicuous wealth at the end of the colonial era do we find sufficiently compelling motives for individuals to become career criminals. Owen Sullivan, the most notorious criminal in colonial America (he had six aliases), was the acknowledged leader of a gang of counterfeiters (that included John Smith) operating throughout New England and New York; like Smith's, his life ended on the gallows.

Americans made social discipline the handmaiden of moral behavior. The Bible and religion were important sources of authority for criminal law, more so in New England than elsewhere. In four of the five colonies in which radical Protestantism prevailed, the Bible furnished transcendent precedents for criminal law. Even in the Chesapeake and southern colonies, which most fully embraced English criminal law sources, an offense against God was also an offense against society.

The close equation of crime with sin and of biblical phrases with statutory language should not obscure the most important source of early American criminal rules: English law. All of the original thirteen colonies derived most of their substantive criminal law from England, but the colonists seem to have been far more influenced by the criminal reform movement in England than were the English. Francis Bacon and Matthew Hale had urged major reforms in criminal law, and colonial legislators knew of and appreciated their efforts.

By our modern standards, colonial criminal law seems harsh, even ruthless. Quakers had their ears cropped, witches were hanged, riotous slaves were burned at the stake, and even some forms of torture were recognized. The *Body of Liberties* of 1641 in Massachusetts approved torture when "it is very apparent there be other conspirators, or confederates with him. Then he may be tortured, yet not with such Tortures as be Barbarous and Inhumane."[6] In the famous Salem witchcraft trials of 1692, Giles Corey, who refused to enter a plea, was subjected to the medieval torture of *peine forte et dure:* heavy weights were laid on his body until, still refusing to plea, he was pressed to death.

Yet, when measured against practices in England and Europe generally, colonial America's criminal law was less severe. In the late seventeenth century, for example, only eleven crimes in Pennsylvania were punishable by death, while in England the number was fifty, and that number expanded over the next century to more than two hundred. Moreover, of the eleven capital crimes, only murder and treason mandated capital punishment. The executioner played an important role as a guardian of the social order, in some places with greater prominence than others. South Carolina, at the beginning of the revolutionary era, had ten times as many capital crimes listed in its legal code as did Massachusetts.

Everywhere in the colonies, judges had great discretion when invoking the death penalty, as did juries. Both could, and did, find defendants guilty of lesser, noncapital crimes. Even when convicted, the condemned had a reasonable chance to escape the hangman, sometimes through the practice of benefit of clergy, other times through commuted sentences. For instance, in New York between 1691 and 1776, 51.7 percent of all persons condemned to death were pardoned.[7]

Americans favored what they believed to be the rational and just provisions of English law. Crimes against property offer a striking example. In England, theft was the most common crime, regularly punished by death. The early colonial settlements were not plagued by thieves, in part because there was little to steal. What was stolen was often consumable (food and clothing), and under the precarious circumstances of life such theft was often a serious matter. Dale's Code, for example, made such thievery during the "starving time" in Virginia a capital crime.

The death penalty was seldom invoked there or elsewhere for crimes against property. Only one person, Daniel Franke of Virginia, was executed for larceny in the colonies before 1660. He had stolen a calf, a chicken, and a napkin. In the eighteenth century, as the incidence of crimes against property increased, so too did harsher penalties. But the colonists refrained from the terror of English law, reserving capital punishment for crimes against property to repeat offenders. In Maryland, for example, where hogs were valued (as was true of all livestock in colonial America), the death penalty was only meted out to persons convicted for a third offense. First-time offenders were usually subjected to punishments meant to degrade and humiliate: branding, whipping, time in the stocks, and multiple restitution. When two Harvard students in the mid-seventeenth century burgled two homes, the college president whipped both in public and sentenced them to pay double restitution.

The colonies founded in the seventeenth century at first gave broad discretion to judges to define the criminal law. By the beginning of the eighteenth century, however, only about 24 percent of the criminal law was based on common law principles; the rest of it was written in codes.

In New England discretionary justice came under sharper attack than in the other colonies. There, by the end of the seventeenth century, more than 90 percent of all criminal actions were defined by statute. Discretionary justice generated political opposition, and as the colonies grew more heterogeneous there were increasing fears that a particular group would come to control the judiciary. Demographic shifts, the rise of a class of wandering poor, and the first stirrings of commercial activity made greater precision in the criminal law useful. The New England colonies moved first, with the *Lawes and Libertyes* of Massachusetts in 1641, and then the middle and Chesapeake colonies followed, the last with the least fervor.

In the Chesapeake and southern colonies, wealth was in the land, and it could be unlocked only with the compliance of a subservient work force. In Virginia and Maryland, for example, indentured servants comprised a large portion of the population, and black slaves south of the Chesapeake in the eighteenth century often outnumbered white masters. The tobacco colonies permitted judges significant discretion in sentencing masters found guilty of abusing their servants, apprentices, and slaves. The death penalty typically fell only on masters with long histories of mistreating their subordinates. In 1667 John Dandy of Maryland killed his servant, Henry Gouge, and removed the boy's clothes before throwing him into a creek to make it appear that he had drowned. Dandy had previously beaten Gouge, and on one occasion inflicted a severe head wound with an axe. Dandy was hanged.

At the same time, it made no economic sense to hang valuable workers in either the North or the South. Whipping, branding, mutilation, and other forms of corporal punishment seemed a sufficient means of striking fear into servants and slaves. The gallows, for both master and servant, was a mechanism of last resort to control persons with homicidal urges.

Nor was criminal misconduct confined to such matters as theft, battery, and murder. A concern with moral behavior infused the colonial criminal codes. Seventeenth-century men and women were adventurous and innovative sexual creatures, and cases of adultery, fornication, buggery, bestiality, homosexuality, rape, and incest enlivened the docket of every court, making court attendance a principal spectator sport. Rural life apparently invited extraordinary sexual activity. Consider, for example, Thomas Granger of Plymouth. In 1642 he was indicted for "buggery . . . with a mare, a cowe, two goats, five sheep, 2 calves, and a turkey."[8] Benjamin Goad in 1673 was sentenced to death in Massachusetts for having committed the "unnatural and horrid act of Bestialitie on a mare in a highway or field."[9] The 1660 case of George Spencer of New Haven shows why colonists regarded bestiality with such horror: they feared the birth of humanoid monsters. This same fascination also figured in their anxiety about witches. Spencer had a deformed eye, and part of the evidence brought against him included a grotesque piglet that "had butt one eye in the middle of the face like some blemished eye of a man."[10] Spencer was sentenced to death, and the sow with which he had had his way was killed with a sword within Spencer's sight before the execution.

Adultery and fornication consumed most of the attention of colonial lawmakers, judges, and juries. The upper classes in colonial society considered it a part of their moral responsibility to impose appropriate forms of morality on the lower orders. Such legislation also served as a handy instrument of social control. Pregnancy reduced the efficiency of servant women, and it created a class of bastards that burdened the already meager local resources. In the eighteenth century, the Chesapeake and southern colonies enacted fervently worded statutes against miscegenation based on the concern that a class of mulatto children would confound the social order. The practice of infanticide was the most shocking response to unwanted pregnancy. Mary Martin, a Boston servant, killed her newborn bastard daughter and hid the body in a trunk. She was hanged. As one student of crime in Virginia has concluded, "the more severe injunctions against immorality were directed in support of a stabilized class system."[11]

New England was no different from the Chesapeake colonies in dealing with sex offenders. The New Englanders relied more extensively on biblical authority as a source of stringent rules against sexual misconduct, but there and elsewhere prosecutions of adulterers and fornicators were both numerous and largely unsuccessful—at least in terms of stemming illicit practices and illegitimate children. Massachusetts, for example, initially made adultery a capital crime, and the colonies of Connecticut and New Haven followed suit. The punishment was too great for the crime, and the crimes were too numerous to be effectively curbed by the punishment. A sense of resignation set in. The authors of the Rhode Island Code, for example, made it clear that they despised the act "whereby men do turn aside from the natural use of their own wives and do burn in their lusts for strange flesh."[12] Like the English, they designated adultery as a minor crime, but with "this momento, that the Most High will judge them."[13]

By the mid-eighteenth century the initial quest for sexual purity had flagged. In New England individuals found guilty of fornication and bastardy were treated with considerable leniency, so much so that men were seldom charged and women were given a reprimand and small fine. By the end of the century the dockets of new state courts, which had earlier bulged with prosecutions against sexual crimes, were filled with an increasing number of cases dealing with the protection of property.

Attempts at social control appeared also in the substantive law of personal misconduct. Puritan New England was in no way unique. Drunkenness, cursing, idleness, and Sabbath violations were matters of great concern in the colonies, as they were in England. The somewhat more stratified social hierarchy of the Chesapeake and southern colonies gave such measures class overtones. For example, Virginia legislation in the eighteenth century prohibited ten specific games to persons of the lower classes. Such measures were aimed as well at encouraging a steady work force. There is little evidence, except in the most controlled circumstances between master and servant, that such measures had any impact. If anything, the Chesapeake and southern colonies were somewhat more lenient in their punishment of personal misconduct.

The colonists placed a premium on schemes of punishment that emphasized retribution, humiliation, and shame. Incarceration was a temporary rather than a punitive measure; it was intended to detain rather than rehabilitate. The colonial judiciary sentenced offenders to wear letters, suffer branding, be whipped, and be subjected to the stocks. Punishment was public and full of warning to potential offenders. In the Puritan colonies the practice developed of delivering a sermon either before the execution or at the gallows. The condemned offered a recital of their crime, and ministers wove together biographical details, scripture, and comment to show how small sins had progressed inevitably into enormous crimes. In some instances, convicted persons were made to suffer with the noose around their neck while the sermon was delivered, even though they were ultimately not to be executed. More than one execution seems to have been bungled. Mary Martin, who had killed her bastard daughter, after confessing on the gallows, "through the Unskilfulness of the Executioner, . . . was turned off the Ladder *twice,* before She Dyed."[14]

Punishment also reflected the weight of social class. The pillory, which held up the victim's head, was reserved for the well-to-do, while the stocks, which allowed the head to hang down, were used for the common folk. The challenge of colonial criminal law was not to save or change the offender, but to cow him or her into future cooperation and, at the same time, present society with an example of the consequences of wrongdoing.

The Quakers of Pennsylvania broke most fully with this standard. In 1682, they developed a criminal code that prefigured later developments in the late eighteenth and early nineteenth centuries. The code emphasized the use of prisons and fines, and it forbade capital punishment. The Pennsylvania scheme assumed that individuals incarcerated for long terms would have the opportunity to improve themselves. The introduction of increased English control over the colony in the eighteenth century undermined the plan (the death penalty was restored), but it nonetheless set a precedent for the subsequent introduction of the penitentiary. The Pennsylvania reforms demonstrated how colonial Americans could bend their carried legal tradition to achieve rational and humane ends.

The fairness and efficiency of colonial treatment of the socially deviant remains open to debate. Colonial jurisdictions seem to have extended and clarified concepts of fair procedure, a result influenced by English legal reformers. In practice, therefore, the almost two hundred years of experience with criminal justice in America molded the movement to establish bills of rights in state constitutions beginning in 1775 and later in the federal Constitution. The oppressive acts of the English in the years before the Revolution merely confirmed American belief in due process.

The criminal justice system was extremely limited in the resources it commanded and perhaps inconsistent and unjust in the use of the legal process. Social control based on appeals to moral authority were an everyday reality. The Salem witchcraft trials that began in 1692, disregarding the social context that explains them, were a brutal demonstration of the potential excesses that lurked in much of early American criminal law. Yet those trials gained such notoriety because they were exceptional. The criminal justice system of the American colonies were in some ways the most lenient in the Western world.

The system also depended on a good deal of informal bargaining to function. Colonial court records reveal many cases in which prosecutions suddenly stopped—perhaps in part because of restitution made on a private basis to victims. There was apparently great incentive to do so, because once put on trial, a person was likely to be found guilty. High rates of conviction and low rates of acquittal were typical of colonial criminal courts.

Colonial society was self-policing and the rule of law was often subverted by popular rather than legitimate institutional forms. The sheriff, the constable, and the nightwatchman were hardly police officers in the modern sense of the word. The inability of colonial officials to deliver effectively constituted authority to the distant western regions of the colonies often stirred popular justice, including vigilantism. When, for example, the governor of South Carolina in 1767 pardoned five of six criminals convicted for robbery and horse-stealing in that colony's western counties, its residents formed the Regulator movement. The Regulators tried, convicted, and punished offenders in total disregard of the established criminal justice system of South Carolina. Vigilantism became the darker side of an emerging public will theory of American law.

Women in the Colonial Legal System

Social necessity also gave shape to the legal position of colonial women. English society placed married women on a pedestal, but it imposed significant legal disabilities in return. The principal legal doctrine affecting women was coverture, the condition into which women passed when married. It merged two individuals into one, and the person who remained was always a man. The woman's legal existence essentially disappeared, with her property rights passing to her husband. She could not make contracts or sue in court. The social insistence on protecting women reached extraordinary conclusions. If a woman committed a crime, the law assumed that she had done so under her husband's coercion. As a result, husbands were tried for the crimes of their wives, even to the absurdity of whipping and fining husbands whose wives had committed adultery.

Single English women enjoyed fuller rights, but they were also vulnerable to the rigors of a male-dominated society. They could own property, engage in contracts, and conduct businesses, as well as sue and be sued. Even the position of single English women during the eighteenth century became increasingly tenuous, as the rise of capitalism brought with it legal disabilities that favored males over females in business and the professions.

Colonial Americans modified this carried legal tradition in ways that offered women somewhat greater freedom, although women clearly remained legally dependent. The simple agrarian conditions of the seventeenth century revived the function of the family as the unit of production, placing greater economic responsibility on married women and enlarging their legal personality. Early America had no leisure class, and society could not afford to restrict the activities of willing and able workers. Both married and single women also engaged in every business open to men from apothecary to undertaker.

Colonial law offered incentives for such cooperation. The practice of dower in England, for example, provided that the wife was to receive one-third of her husband's real property upon his death. The English erected a host of legal barriers that often frustrated the purpose of dower. In New England, however, the magistrates recognized the plight of widows in the middle and upper classes, and courts took it upon themselves to increase the wife's share where they deemed it appropriate. Widows also benefited indirectly in the Chesapeake and southern colonies by the provision that slaves could be counted as part of a dower, thus giving women extra flexibility in adjusting resources to meet their changing economic needs.

The theory of coverture created the same legal disabilities in colonial America as in England, but colonial courts and legislators modified it in ways that produced a less authoritarian model. The simplification of justice in early New England made it easier in practice for married women to assert some limited legal personality. Women, for example, not just in New England but in the other colonies, often served as attorneys in the absence of their husbands. While this practice had precedent stretching back into feudal times, it was apparently practiced much more regularly in the colonies. Maryland was the only colony to prohibit it, and Governor Fendall did so because of what he perceived as the abuses of women coming to court claiming that "shee had a Letter of Attorney from her husband to doe any business whatsoever."[15] The colonies also counted married women as separate individuals and gave them grants of land. Women sued in their own names and they acted on their own in contract and tort claims, both significant departures from the common law tradition.

Some American courts also embraced the practice of separate estates, through which married women owned and controlled property independently of their husbands. These separate estates were an attempt by women, despite coverture, to retain a legal claim to property that they either had before marriage or earned while married. The common law courts typically refused to uphold these agreements, because they were deemed to violate coverture; equity courts, however, did sustain them. Thus, in the colonies, "tremendous variation [was] evident in early American rules on married women's property rights. . . ."[16] In those colonies (New York, Maryland, Virginia, and South Carolina) with equity courts, married women attained more independence than in those jurisdictions with only common law courts or with courts that blended both forms of jurisdiction.

Women's active economic roles enabled them to have a modicum of political power. On the eve of the Revolution, only Pennsylvania, Delaware, and South Carolina had laws disfranchising women who otherwise met the property and residency requirements. Custom and cultural assumptions, not law, were the most significant limitation on the participation of women in politics. The notion of deference pervaded colonial America, and men, not women, were viewed as society's natural leaders. Richard Henry Lee paternalistically admonished his complaining sister that women had "as legal a right to vote as any other person," but that they too often lacked the initiative to do so.[17]

Although women did not hold office, they were involved extensively in extralegal political conduct. Women joined and led mobs, and their actions were often decisive—even deadly. In Marblehead, Massachusetts in 1677 during King Philip's War, a mob of women attacked and murdered two Indian captives, stoning their white male protectors while "seizing [the Indians] by the hair. . . . Then with stones, billets of wood, and what else they might, they made an end of these Indians."[18]

Colonial women appear to have benefited from a significant divergence from the application (if not the letter) of divorce law in England. English law treated marriage as a sacramental act, and this view was carried over into the southern colonies. In New England, however, marriage had a stronger secular contractual base, and it might be expected that acts of nonperformance such as desertion or cruelty would have been grounds to void it. Such was not the case, because colonial law made the sexual definition of marriage its essence and, in the absence of ecclesiastical courts, colonial civil courts considered sexual incapacity or illicit practices as the chief basis for its dissolution. But where divorce through parliamentary legislation had been available in England only to very rich men, in the colonies a few women from a wide social spectrum won divorce through court proceedings. A laborer, a poor woman, and a black servant, for example, all gained freedom from their husbands in Massachusetts during the eighteenth century.

Colonial women had "equality of function and dependency of status."[19] They typically suffered the brunt of punishment for fornication and adultery. Men were far more successful in obtaining divorces, and they enjoyed economic independence, political and religious leadership, greater literacy, and greater control over geographic moves. By the late eighteenth century, the forces of economic liberalism and a rising commercial economy diminished the functional equality of women and eroded their already problematic legal standing.

Labor, Race, and Slavery

Race gradually joined gender as a defining social category within the colonial law of personal status. The colonists had to secure sufficient labor in order to forge a viable economy capable of sustaining permanent settlement. They relied extensively on Elizabethan labor policy, but they produced a law of labor that varied significantly from English practices, especially in its recognition of slavery.

Because of a scarcity of workers, the colonies evolved two major schemes of labor. The first was indentured servitude (so-called because the servant signed a document called an indenture). This system organized labor, financed immigration, provided training (there were apprenticeship indentures, as in England) for the young, and offered a sort of welfare system for those too poor to care for themselves but capable of work. They became the personal property of their masters for a specified period of time, usually four to seven years. Their freedom during this period was sharply curtailed: they could not enter into a marriage contract, make business agreements, or engage in trade. Indentured servants did not give up all of their legal rights. Brutal masters were hauled into court for beating, starving, and sexually abusing their servants. Doubtless most such offenses, given the cowed state of servants, went unreported and unpunished.

The liabilities of indentured servitude were temporary, not permanent, and courts in all of the colonies rigorously enforced these labor agreements, freeing servants whose masters attempted to keep them beyond the term of their service. A Maryland servant who had been duped into signing a fifteen-year contract, successfully petitioned the governor and council for relief on the basis that it was "contrary to the laws of God and man that a Christian subject should be made a slave."[20] Nor did the condition of servitude apply to the progeny of the servants.

John Rolfe of Virginia brought the first blacks ("twenty Negars") to the American mainland in 1619. By 1641 blacks numbered only 250, and as late as 1680 there were only about 3000 in Virginia and fewer than 7000 in all the mainland colonies. Thereafter, the number of black slaves grew rapidly, and so too did the laws governing their status. The laws affecting blacks were gradually gathered into compilations called slave codes. The colonies settled in the late seventeenth and the eighteenth centuries borrowed heavily from earlier colonists. The Georgia Code of 1755 incorporated wholesale a ready-made body of law from the South Carolina Code of 1690.

On the eve of the American Revolution every colony legally sanctioned slavery, but some of the earliest provisions concerning slavery aimed to abolish or limit it. Rhode Island, Georgia, New Jersey, New York, and Massachusetts all passed legislation designed to curtail the peculiar institution. The trustees of Georgia, for example, agreed to exclude slavery for a decade after the founding of the colony out of a fear of racial upheaval. These and other concerns eventually yielded to powerful economic pressures. When South Carolina rice planters began to encroach on Georgia's lands, the Georgia proprietors decided to accept slavery lest their residents lose an opportunity to capture a part of the vibrant rice market.

Racial hatred, fear of social chaos, and economic necessity animated the laws governing slavery. The English held powerful assumptions about the cultural inferiority and sexual promiscuity of blacks that stirred a racially based paranoia. This sense of dread combined with a shift in agricultural patterns toward the staple crops of tobacco and rice, as well as declining mortality rates, made investments in slaves rewarding. In the Chesapeake and southern colonies, the planters accumulated large tracts of land that made possible the economics of scale on which slave labor depended.

The main features of slave law appeared in the slave codes. They defined slavery as a lifetime condition, distinguishing slaves from indentured servants. With the brief exception of Maryland, slave status was made inheritable through the mother. The codes were racially specific, because only blacks qualified for slavery. Thus, while white indentured servitude quietly disappeared (some blacks and Indians had also been servants), black slavery rushed forward to save the English colonists from the dilemma of having to enslave their own race. The law also deemed the slave to be an interchangeable commodity that could be bought and sold. The southern colonies, where the trade in slaves was most brisk, fumbled for almost half a century until finally concluding that they were "chattels personal" rather than real property.

The mother country knew no category of permanent slavery. The colonists concocted slave law in disregard of English authority. Virginia in 1661 formally adopted the whole of English law except where "a difference of condition" made it inapplicable.[21] The presence of blacks and the possibilities of the tobacco culture constituted such a difference, and the exceptions in the law had profound consequences for society. The racial animus that made slavery possible was only strengthened by the presence of ever greater numbers of black slaves. Legal degradation fueled social degradation, and under such circumstances the rights of blacks lost most of their substantive meaning. It was not necessary to extend the rights of Englishmen to Africans, because Africans were a "brutish sort of people." And because they were brutish, it was "at least convenient" to enslave them.[22]

Reconciling the rule of law with human slavery occupied Americans from the beginning of this peculiar institution. Colonists attempted, as would later generations, to preserve legal legitimacy by placing form over substance. Regular quarter sessions and justice of the peace courts proved too slow for the kind of expedited justice that masters wanted when their slaves were accused of criminal acts. Special slave-trial courts, composed of two to three justices and several local freeholders, permitted masters to defend their slaves, to bring charges sometimes in writing, and to call witnesses. In Virginia and New York, the system "was often harsh, but it was uniform and not arbitrary. And it was rapid."[23]

The emerging law of slavery bound whites as well as blacks. While colonial society was largely self-policing, the presence of large numbers of black slaves in the Chesapeake region and further south imposed on whites the irksome liability of mounting slave patrols. South Carolina's patrol acts of 1737 and 1740, for example, subjected white males to enlistment for terms of twelve months without pay. Patrolers had to contribute not only their time (usually at night, at that), but also weapons and mounts. Since opulent planters were few in number, the task fell most fully on small planters and nonslaveholders.

There was nothing inevitable about slavery. It was a product of human choice, and colonial law legitimated rather than created it. Virginia offers a compelling example. Before 1660 in Virginia there were both free and slave blacks, and the status of the latter apparently equaled that of white indentured servants. In one case brought in 1646 the sale of a slave from one master to another was made to depend on the slave's consent. In 1649 William Watts, a white man, and Mary, a black servant, were required to do penance for fornication like any other couple—by standing at Elizabeth River, Virginia with the customary white sheet and white wand. The rise of tobacco prices after 1660 and then the development of the rice culture in South Carolina and Georgia in the eighteenth century obliterated any possibility of racial harmony. In these colonies settlers from Barbados, where slavery had long existed as a customary practice outside the regular administration of English law, honed a hard legal edge on the peculiar institution. Colonial Americans bequeathed not only a socially bankrupt institution but a body of law to support it that would prove divisive (even disastrous) for centuries to come.

Law and the Colonial Economy

We quite properly think of the colonists as deeply concerned with matters of morality, sin, and crime, but legislators devoted much of their lawmaking power to rules affecting basic economic activities. So too did the courts. The majority of cases docketed involved civil rather than criminal matters, and the bulk of these disputes centered on economic issues.

The colonists did not believe that government that governs least governs best, nor did the rulers of Tudor and Stuart England from which they came. A quest for economic opportunity motivated many colonists, and they expected government to facilitate their economic security and growth amid a harsh environment. As the colonies moved from settlements to societies and from colonies to provinces, an indigenous American capitalism emerged. It was characterized by market-oriented production, specialization, accelerated accumulation of capital, and an end to most price and wage regulation by the mid-eighteenth century.

Economic Regulation

Colonial economic regulation, while pervasive, was limited by the resources available to enforce compliance. It was most effective at the local level. To ensure the success of their markets, town officials oversaw the quality and price of goods and services. Edward Palmer, the carpenter who built the stocks in Boston, was the first person clamped in them because he charged an excessive fee.

Colonial legislators also sought to regulate the marketplace, especially where staple crops were involved. During the 150 years before the Revolution, the Maryland legislature promulgated statutes covering the growth, sale, and price of tobacco. The goal was to attain the maximum return to individual planters by limiting the flow of substandard tobacco while keeping a balance in the marketplace between buyers and sellers. In some instances authorities adopted drastic measures. The Maryland legislature once again ordered a halt to tobacco cultivation for a year in 1667–1668, although the colony's proprietor, Lord Baltimore, voided it for fear that the act would hurt the English.

Nonagricultural business was also subjected to regulation. In Massachusetts, for example, the *Lawes and Libertyes* of 1648 set forth in substantial detail the proper manufacture of leather goods. It empowered towns to appoint "searchers of leather" to inspect and to seize leather not tanned according to the law.[24]

Services also received attention. Legislative regulation of taverns in Virginia offer a particularly good example of the interaction of economic and moral imperatives. The Virginia House of Burgesses in 1638 passed the first tavern statute. It required the licensing of all tavern owners and fixed the rates that they could charge. The ensuing 150 years of legislative intervention reflected how changing social attitudes affected colonial regulation quite apart from economic considerations. The short-lived government of radical Nathaniel Bacon, Jr., concluding that taverns contributed to "idleness and debaucheryes," outlawed all taverns except for those in James City and at the terminals of the York River ferry.[25] When Bacon was overthrown in 1677, a new tavern statute appeared. It expanded the limit on the number of taverns to two per county ("except where the general court shall be held"), toughened licensing standards, fixed rates, and then added that anyone operating a tavern also had to provide "for travellers good dyett, lodging, and horse meate."[26] This last requirement increased the capital necessary to open and operate a tavern, and it threatened the livelihood of small operators of "loathsome and unwholesom" tippling houses who sold only liquor by the drink.[27] In the eighteenth century, the legislature added new statutory provisions attacking gambling in taverns and ordering them closed on the Sabbath.

The enforcement of these measures through county courts produced often mixed results. Tippling houses remained open, gambling became a common feature of tavern life, and owners often flaunted legislative directions to close on Sundays and to renew their licenses yearly. Travelers deluged officials in Williamsburg with complaints about price gouging, both for drinks and rooms. In sum, Virginia legislators proved better able to devise than to implement their economic regulatory measures, at least when county officials—sensitive as they were to local sentiments—ignored abuses they perceived as unimportant, or unenforceable.

Throughout the colonies, the employers set maximum wage rates through the law. The same feeble machinery of the law that undermined tavern regulation in Virginia proved equally incapable of keeping labor from reaping the advantage of a market in which labor was dear. Wages were estimated by contemporaries to be two to three times greater than in England, leading Judge William Allen to conclude: "You may depend on it that this is one of the best poorman's countries in the world."[28] But even with higher wages the costs of land were so low that farming was a powerful attraction. Some of the southern colonies passed laws forbidding skilled laborers (such as carpenters and masons) to leave their trade for agriculture. The measures proved wholly unenforceable. By the early eighteenth century wage–price regulation was virtually at an end in most of the colonies, largely confounded by labor scarcity.

Regulatory measures were most effective in New England and the middle colonies. The nuclear settlements and strong communal habits of seventeenth-century New England made local control not only possible but desirable; it established as well the precedent of active participation by the government in the commercial growth of the economy. In the Chesapeake region, planters with vast stretches of land and control over county offices often went their own way. Regulation of the tobacco trade only became feasible beginning about the third decade of the eighteenth century. A long period of stagnation in tobacco prices finally convinced leading planters to accept a system of public warehouses, the inspection of plant quality and packing practices, and some regulation of prices. These planters understood that, in the face of widening economic competition in the eighteenth century, they could benefit from a formal certification of the quality of their goods by a seemingly independent colonial authority. Even in the low-level commercial economy of prerevolutionary America, legislators perceived the law as an essential instrument by which to further growth.

The English mercantile system (in which the colonies produced for the exclusive advantage of the mother country) operated increasingly at odds with colonial economic ambitions. The imperial system taxed colonial business transactions, regulated supply and demand, and dictated to whom the colonists could export. Mercantilism benefited the colonists because it guaranteed an overseas market. It also shackled creative entrepreneurs, who were quite prepared to make their own way in the growing world of commerce. Bad feelings ensued on both sides.

Typical was the furor raised in New England by the White Pine Acts. Parliament in 1722 and 1729 passed these measures that set aside timberlands in New England for the Crown's naval use. Some settlers, perhaps innocently enough, entered these lands and illegally felled trees. When the Crown confiscated the processed boards, residents took extralegal measures to restore what they believed to be their natural economic rights. In Exeter, New Hampshire in 1734, for example, a riot occurred when English officials seized contraband boards covered by the White Pine Acts. Like vigilantism, rioting carried the conduct of law and politics into the open, giving colonists an incentive to develop a popular will theory of law.

Land Law

The agrarian character of colonial America gave the legal questions of ownership and alienation of land compelling economic significance. The Crown was in theory over-lord of all lands in British North America, but it effectively disposed of this claim through the gift and sale of lands to proprietors and chartered corporations. These new claimants, in turn, redistributed the lands. "They were wrestling," Richard Hofstadter has written, "with the laws of wilderness economics."[29] Claims meant nothing if their holders could not induce settlers to work the land and to fortify vulnerable borders. The abundance of land facilitated these objectives by driving prices down within reach of men who could occupy, manage, and cultivate it.

The resulting law of real property was not uniform. It departed significantly from practices in England, and it varied from colony to colony depending on differing social and economic arrangements.

The communitarian values of the early settlers in New England, for example, figured prominently in the way they invoked their legal tradition. Land law there had the overriding purpose of maintaining a cohesive community free of the vestiges of feudalism. Under the town system in New England, legislatures allotted lands collec-tively to church congregations or groups of new settlers. This scheme of distribution initially provided for mutual ownership of common and pasture lands, but commu-nitarianism in early New England quickly disappeared, being replaced by a system of individual landholding on a generally equal basis.

New Englanders expanded on their legal tradition by establishing the public recor-dation of land titles. A rudimentary system of land recording developed in sixteenth-century England, but the New England settlers expanded on it both quantitatively and qualitatively. The New England system required that the records of all land transac-tions be kept in one place, which was generally in a town clerk's office. Deeds recorded in this way took precedence over any other. Litigants indeed brought unre-gistered land claims as evidence, but the formally registered documents carried pre-sumptive weight.

Recordation had three important objectives. First, it facilitated the transfer of land by eliminating uncertainty. Second, in the absence of a trained bar in the seventeenth century, it avoided the problem of an insufficient number of lawyers incapable of conveyancing land under the traditional common law methods. And, third, in New England it encouraged social harmony by quieting discord over land.

The New England recordation scheme became more rather than less important in the eighteenth century, when a trained bench and bar began to appear. As David Konig has shown, seventeenth-century New England town officials were notoriously careless in keeping track of land distributions. They often remedied their errors by granting disputing parties additional lands. This solution began to fail as town lands grew scarce as a result of increased population and aggressive accumulation by some residents. Previously informal disputes over land could only be resolved through formal appeal to the judicial process.

New Englanders initially favored simplified forms of land actions that involved only questions of trespass. In Connecticut, for example, the courts required that an action of "Surrendry of Seizin and Possession" be brought, but it was little more than a greatly modified form of the old common law action of ejectment stripped of the fictions.[30] Throughout the colonies, the simpler forms of pleading land cases prevailed, although by the eighteenth century the presence of increased numbers of lawyers trained in the common law brought about the appearance of the fictitious John Doe and Richard Roe. These names were used by common law lawyers to obscure the identity of the real plaintiff and defendant and to rest the case on its technical merits. Despite this drift toward greater technicality, American land law never became as cumbersome as that in England.

Landholding in the middle colonies was more diverse. In New York the early Dutch patroon system resulted in a few huge grants of land. The pattern was similar in New Jersey. In both colonies, quit rents were enforced by landlords, often provoking riots and encouraging squatting. The upheaval was hardly surprising. A carpenter could earn approximately three shillings a day, roughly the cost of one acre of land. Only in Pennsylvania, Maryland, and Virginia were quit rents collected with anything resembling peaceful regularity.

In the Chesapeake and southern colonies, land was also widely available, but a commitment to staple agricultural production dictated a still different land law. The standard way of bringing labor to the land in these colonies was the headright system. Under it, a newcomer was given fifty acres of land in return for transporting himself unencumbered to the colony. The practice was transmuted into one that rewarded people for bringing others with them, such as indentured servants. The headright system was intended to promote compact settlement, but fraud and the vagaries of the market made it work in a nearly opposite fashion. Newcomers and planters often made double or triple claims for the same persons. Headrights became negotiable instruments: sea captains, for example, sold them to planters. A conscious need to extend landholdings in order to expand staple crops production drove this behavior. The resulting social order was more hierarchical than elsewhere in the colonies because land was less equally distributed. By the time planter capitalism had emerged triumphant in the early eighteenth century, the headright system was officially ended in Virginia, Maryland, and Georgia. These colonies sought to raise revenues by selling their remaining lands. Well-heeled planters and their offspring were active buyers, both for speculating and for increasing staple production.

The colonists broke dramatically from the English in their attitudes toward the succession of heirs. Primogeniture and entail were pervasive doctrines in English land law. The former provided that an estate went to the eldest male son in case the father should die intestate (without a will); the latter reinforced this practice by requiring that lands could not be distributed beyond male family members. The American colonists gave significantly less heed to these traditions in the English common law. To some extent the middle-class character of the colonies, in which land ownership was pervasive, contributed to this development. Furthermore, the seventeenth-century English middle class was accustomed to writing wills, and this experience was transferred to the American colonies. Like the quit rent, primogeniture and entail did not work well in the New World.

New England readily abandoned primogeniture. Every colony, except Rhode Island, formally ended it by the late seventeenth century. In its place, these colonies substituted an equal division of property to all sons upon the death of an intestate father, except that the eldest son received a double share. Partible inheritance permitted an ever-widening distribution of land to holders, but it also made certain that all of the sons in a family were provided the means to make their way in the world.

In the Chesapeake and southern colonies, as well as New York, primogeniture in cases of intestacy persisted down to the American Revolution. In practical terms, however, it had long since ceased to be of importance. The gentry class recognized that maintenance of their social positions depended not only on holding land but also ensuring its effective use after their death. Virginia planters, like middle-class New Englanders, were writers of wills. For example, George Washington's father, Augustine Washington, confronting unexpected death in 1743, passed his final hours anxiously dividing up his huge estate among his children and relatives. He devised a significant portion to his eldest son, Lawrence, but he distributed handsome parcels to others as well. Even if primogeniture had been adopted, as C. Ray Keim found for Virginia, "widespread land ownership would still have developed rapidly, since younger sons could accumulate holdings of hundreds of acres of land in a few years."[31]

The practice of male entail persisted somewhat longer. Only two colonies, South Carolina and Delaware, had abolished entail before Thomas Jefferson in 1776 persuaded the Virginia Assembly to end it. Ten years after the Declaration of Independence all of the states, except Massachusetts and Rhode Island, had followed suit.

The experience with entail in Virginia offers a good example of the way in which land law acquired distinctively American qualities. It reveals, as well, that as land increasingly took on value for what it could produce rather than for the mere holding of it, the law kept step.

English parliamentary legislation had made it possible to devise lands through wills, through primogeniture, in case of intestacy, and through entail by conveyancing. The entailing of lands was recognized by parliamentary legislation in 1685; it also provided that entailed estates could be docked with relative ease through a process known as common recovery and fine. Virginia was typical of most colonies in following this transplanted legal tradition until the early eighteenth century. The House of Burgesses in 1705 made it nearly impossible to dock an entailed estate. The statute of that year required that an exception could be made to an estate already entailed only by special legislative act. Why Virginia took this action remains the subject of hot debate, although the action seems to have confirmed the aristocratic bias in early Virginia society at a time when the tobacco trade was under substantial pressure. The new legislation worked a hardship on small landholders as well as on large planters who owned small pieces of land that they wished to dispose of by sale. The Burgesses dealt with these annoyances in 1734 by allowing landholders to dock small pieces of property without legislative approval.

But the informal reaction was more telling than the legislative response. Parents, such as Augustine Washington, were careful to prepare detailed wills and, when time permitted, to pass parcels of land in fee simple to their children through deeds. Land descended in fee simple without restraint to any particular class of heirs, as contrasted to the fee (en)tail provisions. An estate in fee simple came as close as possible to absolute ownership. Moreover, the Virginia legislature increasingly broadened the exceptions made by special legislative act, although the wealth and social connections necessary to gain legislative attention limited the practice to large planters.

Ultimately social and economic necessity prevailed. Entail was a burden that stalled economic growth. Ownership of several pieces of land was quite common in Virginia (and the Chesapeake and southern colonies generally), where securing the most productive lands was essential to the success of staple crops production. An eighteenth-century planter owned as many as ten tracts, varying in size from 100 to 500 acres. Those tracts held in fee tail could not be disposed of to buy other and potentially more productive tracts. Moreover, families of planters sought to escape the often exhausted soils of the eastern tidewater by moving to better land further west, and unencumbered holdings made such a move economically more feasible.

Virginia in 1776 ended entail. It did so, in the words of Thomas Jefferson, because the practice "is contrary to good policy, tends to deceive fair traders, . . . discourages the holder thereof from taking care and improving the same, and sometimes does injury to the morals of youth, by rendering them independent of and disobedient to their parents."[32]

The bias against development was quite strong in early American law. It flowed from the assumption that property owners had the right of absolute dominion over their land. An owner had the power to prevent any use of his neighbor's land that conflicted with his own quiet enjoyment. Sir William Blackstone, the greatest English commentator in eighteenth-century common law, asserted the principle forcefully in his *Commentaries on the Laws of England*, published between 1765 and 1769. Americans snapped up copies.

By the late eighteenth century, however, American experience and English common law principle had produced two contradictory theories of property rights. The first was explicitly against development. It limited property owners to what courts regarded as the natural uses of their land, and what was "natural" was usually equated with what was "agrarian."[33] The second theory of property rights on which courts drew amounted to a rule that priority of development conferred a right to arrest a future conflicting use. This rule of priority use, or "first in time is first in right," was more compatible with economic development. But in actual operation the doctrine tended to limit economic growth, because it effectively gave the first person to establish a use on land an essential monopoly over it, barring others in the future from advancing from initial low-level development to something more sophisticated. Only in the nineteenth century, however, did the quest for development become sufficiently strong that the potential conflict between the doctrines of prior right and natural use receive close attention, and resolution, from the courts and legislators.

Contract

As an independent and substantive body of law, contract scarcely existed in colonial America. American lawyers read Blackstone, and he confirmed what they knew by experience: the law of contract was subordinated to the law of property. The preindustrial colonial economy operated on a modest level; business transactions tended to be executed instantaneously, rather than on a future basis. Thus, contract was an instrument for exchanging title to property rather than for securing some future money payment. This title theory of exchange meant that the remedy for a broken agreement would be the actual property bargained for, rather than payment for damages. Under these circumstances, colonial Americans worried less about expectation damages (damages given in money if the contract failed in execution), and more about specific performance, the passing of title of the particular good.

Colonial contract law lagged behind that in England. The English as early as the sixteenth century recognized that mutuality of promises could be sufficient consideration to sue for a broken contract, although not all contracts were treated as bilateral promises in the modern sense. This notion indeed took greater hold in the mother country in the eighteenth century. As A. W. Brian Simpson has observed, "the award of expectation damages was the norm" by the end of the century.[34]

In the colonies this development was substantially retarded. True enough, by the mid-eighteenth century, colonial Americans had entered into trading and commercial arrangements that joined center with periphery, town with farm, and provinces with larger world. But the first American instance of any consequence in which a court applied expectation damages occurred in *Lewis* v. *Carradan,* a Pennsylvania case decided in 1786.

The immature state of the American legal profession in the eighteenth century contributed to this lag. Juries exercised important influence in contract cases, interjecting their own evaluation of the substantive fairness of contractual dealings rather than heeding closely reasoned legal arguments. In the Massachusetts case of *Pynchon* v. *Brewster* (1766), a jury returned a verdict in which it diminished damages because it thought the plaintiff had already partially benefited by the contract. Jury intervention added equity to the decision but it contributed significant uncertainty to the expanding marketplace of prerevolutionary America. Modern notions of commercial contract law awaited full development in the nineteenth century, when the pace of economic activity dramatically quickened.

Negotiable Instruments and Commercial Exchange

The colonists moved significantly ahead of the mother country in fostering a legal environment supportive of negotiable instruments. These are a class of documents that included bills of exchange, checks, promissory notes (including bank notes), drafts, and other types of securities. Their function in the mercantile world is to provide a means of transferring wealth from one person to another and, as important, to a third party by the holder of the note. The negotiability of such instruments facilitated commerce and trade. They were of special value in the money-scarce economy of colonial America.

The colonists recognized out of necessity the value of having negotiable instruments that were broadly accepted. Massachusetts in 1647 set the pattern with a statute that provided that assignments of debts to others could be made as long as they were properly signed on the back and not based on fraud. The Massachusetts act was widely copied in New England and the middle colonies. The Chesapeake and southern colonies also adopted a lenient attitude toward negotiable paper, largely because of the heavy business they did in staple crops and slaves. Thus, business relations in Maryland and Virginia depended on tobacco and chattel notes, and both circulated broadly.

In the eighteenth century an influx of English lawyers and greater commerce between the colonies and England imposed a somewhat stricter view on negotiable paper than in the mother country. But these changes were superficial. The emerging commercial middle class in colonial America simply found the stuffy regulation of English negotiable instrument law unnecessary and unworkable.

Liability and Fault

Neither the English nor the colonists used the word tort to describe the law that they developed to deal with civil wrongs; both understood that fault and liability went hand-in-hand, but the concepts were still murky. Implicit was the notion that each person owed a standard of due care to others, and with this concept went an unarticulated notion of assumed duty. Like contract, however, the law of tort did not begin to develop its modern character until the nineteenth century.

Americans accepted the English notion of no liability without fault, but they twisted this transplanted legal tradition in ways meant to fit their own circumstances. In England, for example, with its limited lands, the rule emerged that owners of animals had responsibility to keep them fenced. Cattle and hogs had to be enclosed and, if they escaped and damaged the property or crops of another, the owner was held liable for the damages. In North America the doctrine was reversed. Owners of agricultural lands were charged with the duty to fence their crops from wandering domestic animals.

What underlay this rule was a consensus throughout the colonies that grazing animals were more valuable than were crops. The American rule of fencing animals out reflected a community wish to protect animals and to place the burden of care on those who might be damaged by them. In a sense, the fencing-out rule was an early form of contributory negligence in which the plaintiff could not impose liability on another if he himself had contributed to the wrong.

In other areas Americans abided by traditional English notions of strict liability. People, for example, who used fire were held accountable for their actions under all conditions. Fire was an inherently dangerous commodity, and it was to be strictly regulated by imposing a heavy responsibility on those who used it. Most American colonial jurisdictions also accepted the view that the owners of proven dangerous domestic animals could not escape liability for destruction caused by their animals just because a fence proved incapable of keeping them out of a farmer's crops.

The Legacy of Substantive Law

Early American law, like early American legal institutions, was shrouded in ambiguity. It is a misnomer to speak of "American" colonial law, because the colonies were fundamentally reshaping their legal traditions and, at best, shared only broad tendencies. Those tendencies included an emphasis on simplicity (abetted by a modest bench and bar), a commitment to humane and rational approaches to the law, a strong sense of equity in practice if not in form, a respect for due process, an antidevelopmental bias in the treatment of real property, and a propensity to erect legal rules that served the interests of the top of the social order. The widespread distribution and easy alienation of real property attenuated blatant class conflict.

The colonists learned through experience that a legitimate rule of law required constant adaptation. Adaptation sometimes became invention; the law of slavery was colonial America's most radical and troubling departure from its transplanted legal tradition. Colonial law had another important tendency in that it was consensual. Early Americans did not articulate a popular will theory of law, but most of their substantive law rested on the practical assumption that wide agreement with rules would promote their legitimacy. The crisis of imperial authority that surfaced in the mid-eighteenth century ignited these latent presumptions, culminating in revolution, a new nation, and the Americanization of the ambiguous tendencies of colonial law.

3

The Law in Revolution and Revolution in the Law

The Ambiguity of the American Revolution

There is no doubt that the American Revolution was indeed a revolution in that British colonies transformed themselves into sovereign states and later into an independent nation. The new American states also eradicated the few vestiges of feudalism, such as the practice of primogeniture, that had persisted in the colonies. There is no denying, as well, that the revolutionary leaders suffused their rhetoric with powerful social possibilities. Thomas Jefferson's assertion in the Declaration of Independence that ''all men are created equal'' presented a startling specter of social change to a world accustomed to unquestioned social hierarchy.[1] Extensive landholding and frontier conditions before the Revolution lent substance to this rhetoric of social leveling, especially in comparison with England. Benjamin Franklin, for example, insisted on v'earing a simple republican black coat, even when he represented American interests in the fashionable courts of Europe.

Yet the American Revolution was an ambiguous affair as revolutions go. It presented few scenes of revolutionary crowds pitted against a besieged upper class; the battle over who should rule at home was less dramatic than the struggle to secure home rule from the English. The Declaration of Independence aimed to free Americans from the control of the British monarchy, not to free all Americans, as the perpetuation of slavery made clear. The King, not the American upper class (such as it was), Jefferson wrote, was the object of revolutionary ardor because ''He has plundered our seas, ravaged our coasts, burnt our towns, and destroyed the lives of our people.''[2] Americans were not angry at one another, by and large; they were angry at their British rulers. An elite class, one anxious to partake fully in the emerging commerce of the

era, remained firmly in control. The Revolution hardly touched the way of life carved
out by country nabobs south of Pennsylvania. Planters not only kept their black slaves,
but they maintained control over tidewater society and local government, partly because their less affluent neighbors willingly deferred to their leadership. Most of the
northern colonies indeed brought an end to slavery, because the economic justification
for it was dubious in any case. In Boston, New York, and Philadelphia, a coalition of
merchants, landowners, and (most significantly) lawyers dominated patriot leadership.
They preserved property rights and generally retained a secure hold over state government after the Revolution.

The leadership of lawyers in the Revolution perhaps explains why the entire affair
exuded a legal pungency. No heads rolled in America; loyalists were tarred and
feathered but not hung. Patriot leaders permitted them to flee with their lives and they
confiscated their lands only after proper legislative and judicial proceedings. The
revolutionary pamphleteer Thomas Paine, in *Common Sense,* captured the conservative and legal cast of events begun in 1776 when he wrote that in "America the law
has become king."[3] If the Revolution produced no massive social upheaval, it did
compel Americans to rethink their assumptions about the nature of law, and it was in
this way that the Revolution had its greatest impact.

Changes in law flowed from the Revolution on two levels and in two different
chronological spans.[4] Although the history of private law during the Revolution remains unwritten, the evidence suggests that only modest change occurred. The newly
free American states, through so-called reception statutes, formally embraced that part
of the English common law that did not contradict prior colonial practices. Revolutionary violence, it seems, did little to nourish any profound change in private law. Yet,
when viewed over the long haul, the Revolution had enormous consequences for
private law, because it permitted Americans in the following century to engage in the
kind of experimentation that was impossible within the empire. The forces of acquisitive capitalism and the Enlightenment's emphasis on individual reason and human
worth stimulated not only the revolutionary generation but fueled the explosive outburst of nineteenth-century American lawmaking.

In the short haul, though, the Revolution's impact was most pronounced on public
law. Americans of this generation scrutinized the relationship of fundamental principles of government to the legitimacy of legal action as they never had before and never
would again. The did so because the essentially conservative nature of the Revolution
posed for them a profound predicament: they had to "break the law while remaining
legal."[5] Throughout the years from 1760 to 1787, the revolutionaries repeatedly
assessed their place under the British constitution, the relationship of written to unwritten law, the basis of sovereign authority for American law, the proper instrument for
invoking that authority, and the ties that would bind the new states to one another and
to central authority. Sovereignty, representation, federalism were the constitutional
issues with which the generation of the Revolution wrestled.

The solutions came in fits and starts. What Americans believed to be the basis of
constitutional authority in 1761, in 1776, and in 1787 were different; what we think of
today as the essence of our constitutional tradition emerged only gradually.

The British Constitution in Trouble

The colonists' chief legal problem was to determine the extent to which they were represented in and protected by the British constitution. The first major rumblings of constitutional discontent emerged near the end of the French and Indian War in 1763 when the English government abandoned its policy of "salutary neglect" in favor of a vigorous program of customs enforcement and taxation. The English wanted the colonists to help pay for the huge debts accumulated as a result of the war and to contribute directly to the defense provided them by British troops. The administrations of Lord Grenville and his successors had no constitutional qualms about imposing such demands and in invoking the doctrine of virtual representation to justify it. This concept held that all persons in the empire were represented in Parliament, regardless of whether they had actually voted for a member, so long as there were members whose interests were similar to theirs. The colonists, for their part, remained committed to the British constitution, but they became increasingly disillusioned with the way in which Parliament denied them what they believed to be the rights of all Englishmen: protection from arbitrary government and direct representation of their interests. Direct or actual representation meant that the people actually voted for their representatives. That is what the colonists had in mind when they repeatedly invoked the phrase, "no taxation without representation."

The nature of the British constitution contributed to the disjunction between authorities in London and the colonists. That constitution was different from what emerged in Philadelphia in 1787; it was neither a written nor a single document. Instead, the British constitution was a collection of documents—Magna Carta, the Bill of Rights, and the Act of Supremacy, for example—as well as customary practices that had historically limited the government's exercise of arbitrary power. Make no mistake: the British constitution was one of the great achievements of eighteenth-century Enlightenment political science. Yet the rise of an international commercial economy created pressures that ignited a sustained theoretical debate in England, the colonies, and the Continent about the proper character of public law generally and the British constitution specifically.

By the mid-eighteenth century the political opposition in England had formed into a coherent faction called the Whigs. The shortened term derived from Whiggamores, the seventeenth-century Scottish insurgents against the Crown. The Whigs felt estranged from the centers of power that (with the rise of empire) increasingly centered on government bureaucracy, the development of a money economy, and the growing power of the urban, merchant class. Prominent Whig leaders had a social and economic agenda as well. They wanted the English nation to return to the virtues of agriculture, simple government, honest labor on land and craftsmanship in the cities, and direct trade among individuals.

Pamphleteers broadcast the Whig opposition to the government, initially in England and eventually in the colonies. John Trenchard and Thomas Gordon were perhaps the most influential of the opposition pamphleteers. They argued in *Cato's Letters* (1713–1719) that Britain had sunk into corruption because of the activities of the Bank of England. Trenchard and Gordon charged that the bank had conspired with certain members of Parliament to foster economic monopolies that promised eventually to subvert the traditional constitutional protections accorded English citizens. These polemical essays were important in America after 1750, because they provided patriot leaders with a ready-made rhetoric of opposition.[6]

Whigs viewed the British constitution as an assembly of parts, with Parliament independent of the Crown and of political factions. They also stressed that while the Glorious Revolution had ended the divine-right rule of monarchs, sovereignty had not shifted to the Parliament, as government leaders insisted in the eighteenth century. Whigs rejected the idea that Parliament was absolutely sovereign. Instead, they insisted that Parliament's authority was limited by the same customs and practices that had historically restrained the monarchy from the arbitrary exercise of power. But those constitutional understandings were nowhere written down as part of the organic law. For all of its genius, the British constitution was impossible to find in all of its parts, a condition that handicapped the Whig opposition in England and the colonies.

Whig thought shaped American patriots' understanding of their place within the empire. As the Reverend Jonathan Mayhew explained in commenting on the impact of Whig ideology on the coming of the Revolution, "many things much to the present purpose . . . look almost like prophecy."[7]

The Whigs directed their opposition against the so-called court party. Its leaders believed that Britain had given birth to a modern, dynamic, expanding imperial economy predicated on mercantilism, a system of political economy that developed in postfeudal Europe. Its primary interest was the establishment of overseas colonies from which to extract raw materials and to which to sell finished goods. The court party insisted that the British constitution was an engine of economic expansion, and that the Glorious Revolution, in making Parliament the source of sovereign authority, had established a framework to harness that power better than any other known to history. The court party's broad reading of parliamentary powers did not mean traditional liberties were at an end; rather, its leaders stressed that, if England wanted to enter the world of commerce, Parliament had to have sufficient discretion to pass laws that would enable it to reach that end.

Sir William Murray, Lord Mansfield, chief justice of King's Bench (1756–1788), and Sir William Blackstone provided the constitutional justification for that position. Mansfield was eighteenth-century England's greatest commercial lawyer and a proponent of parliamentary sovereignty. His support of an expanding commercial economy reinforced his belief in absolute parliamentary sovereignty.

Blackstone was equally preeminent, and no other legal figure equalled his impact on the colonies. His *Commentaries on the Laws of England,* published between 1765 and 1769, sold almost as many copies in America as England. Blackstone was to the eighteenth century what Sir Edward Coke, also chief justice of King's Bench (1613–1616), had been to the seventeenth: the source of organizing authority of the English law.

He also supported the new constitutional monarchy, extracting from English law the proposition that Parliament was the source of sovereignty for the English nation and its increasingly extended empire. "If the parliament will positively enact a thing to be done which is unreasonable," Blackstone wrote, "I know of no power that can control it."[8] He preached an inherently conservative message, and it was one that a great number of lawyers in the colonies adopted, either in outright loyalty or in patriotic insistence on conducting a legal revolution.

The Bar and the Movement toward Revolution

The arguments of Blackstone and the Whig opposition infected American thinking just as the colonial bar gained greater professional competence. The growing economic vitality of the colonies in the mid-eighteenth century sparked this transformation in the bar. It became more numerous, more prestigious, and more jealous of its prerogatives. This escalation in the importance of lawyers, moreover, occurred throughout the colonies. Thus, twenty-five of the fifty-six signers of the Declaration of Independence, and thirty-one of the fifty-five delegates to the Constitutional Convention in 1787 were lawyers.

American lawyers were hardly of one mind about the British constitution; some were loyalists and others patriots. But the patriot lawyers were important because of their tutoring in the British constitution and the common law.[9] They were the natural leaders of a highly legal revolution. Their knowledge provided an intellectual basis for unity until they could manufacture their own nationalism to take its place. Arguments about the nature of property and liberty under the British constitution gave colonies as disparate as New York, the Carolinas, Virginia, and Pennsylvania a basis for common action and thought. These colonies might well have revolted in any case, although it is doubtful that they would have without the presence of the bar. Until independence generated its own revolutionary substitute, British law and constitutional thought remained the only common denominator among Americans, who in other respects differed from each other far more radically than they differed from Great Britain.[10]

The patriot lawyers applied their Whig beliefs in America not England. They took the opposition arguments about the nature of rights and property from the mother country and tailored them to fit colonial expectations of the British constitution. Lawyers did not cause the American Revolution, but they did define its intellectual boundaries and its essentially conservative cast. This was so primarily because they were essentially attempting to define the nature of the rule of law as it applied under colonial circumstances.

Lawyers figured prominently on both sides in the revolutionary struggle that extended from 1761 to 1776. Each initiative taken in London, such as the infamous Stamp Act, provoked a colonial legal response and resulted in violence. Popular action paralleled legal argument. Two of these episodes provide insight into the unique role played by the patriot bar in seeking to adjust the received constitutional tradition of England to the colonies. The first was the Writs of Assistance Case begun in 1761; the other was the standing-army controversy and the Boston Massacre. Neither, by itself, propelled a break with England; but both, in the flow of developments within the colonies, pressed American patriots to measure the future of the rule of law as they understood it under the British constitution.

Writs of Assistance

John Adams, who made extensive notes on the Writs of Assistance Case of 1761, observed that, "Then and there was the first scene of the first Act of Opposition to the arbitrary Claims of Great Britain. Then and there the child Independence was born."[11] The case was the first articulate expression of what became an American tradition of constitutional hostility toward the general powers of search. It was also the opening salvo in the colonists' legal resistance to the new English mercantile policy.

The customs writ of assistance was an odd creature. Both it and a search warrant, in the name of the Crown, provided the bearer with legal authority to enter and search a premises. The search warrant was an exercise of jurisdiction in which a justice, upon a showing of cause, went through a minimal process of deliberation. The customs writ of assistance, on the other hand, was issued by a functionary in the English Court of Exchequer as an administrative act. It was entirely ministerial and by itself conferred no power on the bearer; it provided only that a constable was to assist the customs officer in making a specific search of a given building.

This distinction was lost on Charles Paxton, surveyor and searcher of customs in Boston. As a zealous official, he used a writ obtained in 1756 from the Massachusetts Superior Court to invade the warehouses of uncooperative merchants, ignoring the requirement that he give oath that probable cause existed to suspect that illegal goods were being hidden. Paxton treated the writ as if it was general in nature, rather than special and specific. The merchant community retaliated by accusing him of customs racketeering, of using his position and the writ to force merchants to pay him protection money, and of being "no man's friend."[12]

Two events in 1760 and 1761 precipitated a crisis. The first was the death of King George II, in whose name all writs had authority. Within six months of the king's death those persons holding writs had to apply to the new sovereign. Second, in September 1760 Chief Justice Stephen Sewall of the superior court died, and Governor Francis Bernard, bent on a vigorous customs enforcement policy, appointed his lieutenant governor, Thomas Hutchinson. The new chief justice, who was not a lawyer, was well on his way to becoming "the most hated man in Massachusetts." "Virtuous but not stylish, intelligent but didactic, heavy-spirited and self-absorbed," the historian Bernard Bailyn has explained, "he judged people, and often found them wanting."[13] He was also a "good friend" of Paxton.[14]

Hutchinson immediately ran afoul of James Otis, Jr., who appeared before the superior court to argue against renewing Paxton's writ of assistance. Personal and political rivalry tinged the legal confrontation. Otis believed that Hutchinson had usurped a seat on the court that Governor Bernard had supposedly promised to the senior Otis.

Otis transformed the technical legal issue of whether the customs writ was general or specific into an intense debate over the nature of the British constitution and the place of colonists under it. The customs writ of assistance, Otis argued, was merely a device for the enforcement of the Navigation Acts. Otis had made a decisive turn, linking the political question of control over the colonial economy to the right of the English to exercise such control. As Peter Oliver, himself a judge on the court, subsequently recalled, Otis's assertion "broke down the Barriers of Government to let in the *Hydra* of Rebellion."[15] He argued that the issuance of the writ ran counter to the "fundamental principles of law" that composed the original British constitution of the seventeenth century.[16] To substantiate the idea that fundamental principles of law would prevail over acts of Parliament, Otis cited Lord Coke's celebrated judgment in *Bonham's Case* (1610) that "it appears in our books that in many cases the common law will control acts of Parliament, and sometimes adjudge them to be utterly void."[17]

Otis's actions demonstrated how *legal* the growing colonial opposition to English control was. Yet the arguments he made were ancient rather than modern. He claimed the rights of Englishmen, not the rights of colonists. He made no attempt to assert that the American colonists could of their own will make law to suit themselves; instead, he insisted only that they be extended the same privileges as they would otherwise receive in England. He clung to the notion that English constitutional law was more than adequate to serve the interests of the colonists, and that it rested on reason and discoverable natural law principles. The rights of the colonists, Otis wrote, were guaranteed "by the law of God and nature as well as by the common law and the constitution of their country."[18] He did not need a written document to state the existence of such liberties; they were already understood within the great tradition of the English common law. He agreed, in short, with Hutchinson: the Parliament was the constitution, a source of authority complete unto itself. Like Hutchinson, he shared a belief in the British constitution and the notion of Parliament as the source of sovereign authority, although Otis reached quite different conclusions about its meaning.

The writs of assistance cases changed little from a strictly legal point of view. Hutchinson did grant Paxton a new writ, but the British attorney general in 1766 informed the colonial customs service that the writ was illegal, because the power of the exchequer to issue it did not run by implication to colonial common law courts. By then the damage was already done. Otis had set loose the principle of natural law as a means of limiting arbitrary governmental action otherwise uncontrollable by the constitution. Otis's sharp attacks through the Boston press on Hutchinson following the decision and the subsequent mob violence directed against the chief justice and later governor of Massachusetts revealed how this principle could be turned into a direct manifestation of popular will. If Otis did not quite appreciate the implications of his natural law theorizing, other and more radical figures were more than willing to embrace the legal issues through political action.

Standing-Army Controversy

The British decision to station a standing army in the colonies following the French and Indian War raised constitutional questions just as serious as the writs of assistance case. Traditional seventeenth-century English notions of restraint on power had positively forbidden the presence of a standing army. The decision by the government of Robert Walpole in England to quarter such an army raised cries of alarm from Whigs in England and their colonial counterparts. The latter charged, as had Otis in the writs of assistance cases, that the Parliament had violated a customary right under the British constitution.

The standing-army controversy ratcheted constitutional discourse up a notch from Otis's natural law arguments. Americans began to assert that they could chart their own future. "A military force," the Massachusetts House of Representatives protested, "if posted among the People, *without their express Consent,* is itself, one of the greatest Grievances, and threatens the total subversion of a free Constitution."[19] A popular will theory of law appeared to support colonial assertions on behalf of customary protections of liberty embodied in the unwritten British constitution.

The British troops in their fine red uniforms initially inspired a sense of awe, even terror in the colonial public. Familiarity gradually bred contempt, especially as the bored troops engaged in whoring and petty thievery. Whig agitators took glee in carrying out demonstrations against supporters of the King right in front of the troops, a practice inadvertently aided by English officers, who exercised restraint because they were uncertain of their constitutional authority to perform as police, and who often kept their troops out of town. In Boston, for example, no person was tarred and feathered by patriot leaders until the soldiers were stationed within the town limits.

The standing-army controversy initiated two enduring themes in American legal history. The first was that the use of soldiers as police endangered liberty. As a colonial pamphleteer argued, "What is got by Soldiers, must be maintained by Soldiers."[20] Second (and related to the first theme) any law that required enforcement by soldiers was not properly law. That is, law had to resemble something based on a notion of contractual agreement between government and the governed and in which the command of the government derived authority from a legitimate source of sovereignty. Extralegal, direct popular action growing out of opposition to writs of assistance, standing armies, and the entire British commercial policy became the most direct assertion of popular sovereignty.

Mob Violence and Popular Sovereignty

By the middle of the eighteenth century mob violence had become "a purposive weapon of protest and dissent in both Great Britain and America."[21] Moreover, the colonies had experienced substantial insurrectionary behavior, most notably in Bacon's Rebellion in Virginia (1676–1677) and the overthrow of Governor Edmund Andros of Massachusetts (1689). Patriot leaders after 1760 resorted to "politics out of doors" in their struggle for independence. Richard Matwell Brown has counted at least thirty instances of coordinated riots between 1760 and 1775 aimed directly at the British and most especially at enforcement of customs laws.[22]

Mob action was often quite spectacular. Following passage of the Stamp Act in 1765, for example, a mob attacked the home of Thomas Hutchinson, whose decision in favor of his old friend Paxton in the Writs of Assistance Case was remembered. The Boston mob attacked with such fury that it battered down the walls, burned the furniture, destroyed the library, tore windows and doors from their frames, and cut down the trees in the Hutchinson yard. Yet there was also an understanding that mob action, as deplorable as it might be, had validity within the constitutional order. Hutchinson himself in 1768 noted that "mobs a sort of them at least are constitutional."[23] Hutchinson was not pleased with the destruction of his home, but he nonetheless recognized, as even did the House of Lords, that "rioting is an essential part of our constitution." Popular impatience constituted a necessary force in the maintenance of free institutions. "Anarchy," John Adams observed, "can never last long, and tyranny may be perpetual."[24]

The patriots justified revolutionary violence as an expression of "popular sovereignty" and the will of the majority. Civil disobedience, mob action, collective protest, and vigilante action against individuals became the connective tissue that gave substance to constitutional notions of rights requiring protection. Yet this violent basis for legal change exposed the "demonic side of our national history."[25] The rule of law might have a popular base but "popular justice" had to be balanced by regard for procedural regularity.

The Boston Massacre

Evidence of this quest for a principled rule of law appeared in two ways during the late eighteenth century. The first was in the passage of antiriot statutes by the colonies. The second was a considered effort by even revolutionary leaders to inculcate what Samuel Adams in 1784 declared to be "Decency and Respect due to Constitutional Authority." "[T]hose Men," Adams continued, "who under any Pretence or by any Means whatever, would lessen the Weight of Government lawfully exercised must be Enemies of our happy Revolution and the Common Liberty."[26]

Revolutionary leaders, with all of their growing commitment to popular will, appreciated that principles of natural law and constitutional authority had to be maintained. Taunting citizens of Boston, for example, had precipitated the famous Boston Massacre in 1770, after one of them had suggested to a British soldier that he could "go clean my shithouse."[27] The British troops responded by killing several of their tormentors; tempers were sufficiently frayed that the whole city might have exploded. Governor Hutchinson displayed calm leadership, but even more important were the roles of John Adams and Josiah Quincy in providing the accused soldiers with a brilliant defense in court. "The eyes of all are upon you," Quincy told the jurors. It is "of high importance to your country, that nothing should appear on this trial to impeach our justice or stain our humanity."[28] Some soldiers were convicted of manslaughter, but the punishments were light. The trial had done little to settle fundamental differences, but it did reinforce the underlying commitment to breaking the emerging popular will theory of law with a belief in a rule of law.

Extralegal, direct popular action against the British authorities seemed suitable, even necessary for the preservation of colonial rights. The law took shape in response to events; the colonists moved further and further away from the notion that they could adequately protect themselves exclusively through the British constitution. Rebellion offered the means of breaking from the English hold, but the revolutionary leaders also needed, in their continuing concern to be legal, a means of legitimating that break.

Rise of Modern Constitutional Consciousness

The Writs of Assistance Case, the standing-army controversy, and imperial policy as a whole sharpened American thinking about the differences between what was legal and what was constitutional. There seemed little doubt that the actions of Parliament during the 1760s and 1770s were legal; that is, Parliament did what it was lawfully empowered to do. Colonial revolutionaries, in reacting to these measures, developed a modern constitutional consciousness that differentiated the fundamental principles of government from the institutions of government. The patriots, in short, concluded that Parliament was not the embodiment of sovereign authority and that the fundamental principles of government had to be in writing if they were to have meaning.

Written Law, Natural Law, and Social Contract Theory

American Whigs by 1776 doubted that the unwritten British constitution could check Parliament's expansive powers. As John Reid has shown, they embraced the ideals of that document and the ancient customs that went with it, but they also concluded that an unwritten constitution was inadequate to check Parliament's expansive powers. Thomas Jefferson, for example, complained that Parliament had undertaken "to make law where they found none, and to submit us at one stroke to a whole system no particle of which has its foundation in the Common law."[29]

Beginning in the 1760s, Americans separated ideas about the principles of government from the product of its actions: the law. They did so by tying the idea of a written constitution to two related notions, natural law and social contract. Otis in the Writs of Assistance Case had injected natural law theory into revolutionary discourse, and it grew in breadth thereafter. Natural law theory held that the positive law of a state, in order to be regarded as worthy of being obeyed, had to embody or affirm certain eternal principles inherent in the structure of the universe. In the seventeenth century several English writers—notably John Locke, James Harrington, and Algernon Sidney—joined this idea to the concept of the social contract. The social contract held that an agreement existed between ruler and ruled, between government and the governed. The rulers, for their part, were obligated to secure to the people their rights and to provide for the common good; the ruled owed loyalty to the state and obedience to the specified rules. The notion of mutual bargaining, which was itself gaining authority with the rise of the commercial economy of the last half of the eighteenth century, added credibility to social contract theory. So, too, did Calvinist covenant theology.

Natural law theory and the social contract gave American public law its emphasis on limiting governmental power. If government violated the social contract and if it denied natural rights and abused public trust, the people retained a right to overthrow it. The polemical writings of Trenchard and Gordon fueled the colonists' Whiggish perspective on limited government.

On the level of formal theory, the work of John Locke did the same. Locke wrote in the immediate wake of the Glorious Revolution, and his work aimed to refute the ideas of absolute monarchy of Thomas Hobbes and Sir Robert Filmer. More than any other single work, Locke's *Second Treatise on Civil Government* (1690) enunciated two critical principles of modern law. The first was that under social contract theory the ruled enjoyed a right of revolution against an arbitrary ruler. Second, Locke defined law as the command of the sovereign that depended on a concrete charter or constitution. The chief problem involved in the formulation of this tradition in the American colonies was identifying the proper basis of sovereign authority for the written document that would check the exercise of power. The final phase in the intellectual development of American public law in the days immediately preceding the Revolution turned on settling in practice the issues of sovereignty and republicanism identified by Locke's theory.

Republicanism, Democracy, and Sovereignty

The American preoccupation in the early 1770s with written restraints on political power actually masked a peculiar confusion in the American mind about the nature of law. That confusion involved the problem of sovereign authority: the basis on which the government could command the actions of those who entered into the social contract. American revolutionaries from 1776 to 1787 groped their way toward several solutions, the most important of which was popular sovereignty.[30]

Locating sovereign authority for government turned on perhaps the most important concept of the revolutionary era: republicanism. The term derives from the Latin *res publica,* or "public thing." It refers to the conduct of the people's affairs for their interest and well-being rather than for the benefit of the ruler. Accordingly, republican government had its origin in the people.

There was no one document, such as Locke's *Second Treatise,* that set forth the American scheme of republicanism. Until the Declaration of Independence the terms republican and democrat were hurled as epithets back and forth across the Atlantic. But by 1775 a body of republican thought began to emerge, first among anonymous writers and then in full flower in Thomas Paine's *Common Sense* (1775). Paine made the use of invective into a positive good. As John Adams explained, Paine had done nothing less than "write down the ideas that were in the air."[31]

Paine thrust a public will theory of law on the revolutionary generation. He called for independence based on actual representation and a written organic law, while rejecting out of hand the standard line of the King's ministers that, under the system of virtual representation, the colonists were already represented by every member of Parliament. He also spurned monarchical authority, parliamentary sovereignty, and the unwritten British constitution by claiming that if law was the command of the sovereign, then it had to be based directly on the fully represented interests of the people in the lawmaking body. Republican government, to Paine, promised a rule of law that would be more legitimate for the American people than that enacted by the English Parliament.

Existing political theory limited the scope of Paine's republicanism. American Whigs subscribed in 1776 to the theory of the French legal philosopher, Charles Louis de Secondat, Baron de Montesquieu that a republic could exist only in a small and socially homogeneous geographic area. Even defenders of British authority like Thomas Hutchinson conceded that popular rights necessarily diminished as the distance from the seat of government grew. "I doubt," he wrote in 1773, "whether it is possible to project a system of government in which a colony 3,000 miles distant from the parent state shall enjoy all the liberties of the parent state."[32] When the break with England finally did come, Americans quite naturally established their new republican governments at the state level. They did not think of creating a national republican government, because to have done so would have been theoretically absurd and contrary to the local interests they had consistently championed.

The Declaration of Independence

The Declaration of Independence provided the bridge over which colonial Whigs crossed into their new world of republicanism and independence. It was a classic exposition of legal argument set to political purposes. Thomas Jefferson and his colleagues on the drafting committee of the Continental Congress pleaded a legal case intended to accord them political freedom and enjoyment of the ancient rights of the British constitution that Parliament had so often ignored. Here was the decisive example of the revolutionaries breaking the law while remaining lawful.

Jefferson's declaration owed something to Locke and to Scottish commonsense philosophers, the latter of which both Jefferson and James Madison counted among their teachers. The document articulated a limited concept of natural law and social contract theory, but in so doing it took aim at George III and not Parliament. On first glance this seems anomalous behavior because it was Parliament that had claimed absolute sovereign authority, enacted legislation taxing and regulating the colonists, and pressed the notion of virtual representation. The King, however, presented an easier and safer target. The Declaration listed grievances against George III and used these as the basis by which to withdraw from the empire. The right of revolution was asserted against a tyrant and not against the British constitution that Parliament represented. Jefferson's claim on existing British constitutional authority gave the revolutionaries the right to remove themselves from Parliament's direct control. To the end, the revolutionaries believed that they understood the British constitution more fully than their masters.

The Declaration's attack on the King also satisfied republican theory. Revolution had been forced on the King's reluctant subjects, and the bonds of allegiance between George III and each one of his American subjects had been destroyed. The Declaration's appeal to "reason and good Conscience" was crucial, for Congress was asking the King's American subjects to judge, by their own authority, whether or not he was still entitled to their allegiance. The subject who disavowed his allegiance to the Crown transformed himself into a republican citizen. Once this was done Americans could proceed to form their own governments in order to preserve "internal peace, virtue, and good order."[33]

The Declaration's insistence on a legal break with England was fortified by its social conservatism. Locke had included in his famous trilogy of inalienable rights life, liberty, and property. Jefferson altered the last of these to read the pursuit of happiness. This new phrase, which Jefferson borrowed directly from Scottish commonsense philosophy, blunted the document's potentially radical threat to existing property holders (save loyalists) and the social upheaval that would have accompanied genuine internal rebellion. As important, it established that for government to succeed it had to be based on the pursuit of happiness—the doing of good for the commonwealth—through the ongoing promotion of virtue, the chief tenet of commonsense philosophy.

The Declaration was an equivocal document in other ways. Although it was a legal brief based on the ancient British constitution, it also contained natural law principles, the idea of the social contract, and a hazy commitment to popular sovereignty. The failure of Jefferson to sketch any of these in detail stemmed from the need to hold moderate support. The Continental Congress invoked the failure of the monarchical government to justify the popular assumption of authority: the sovereignty of the people is not directly asserted. Yet Congress, outside the Declaration, was more direct, advising the thirteen colonies to organize themselves as states based on "the authority of the people."[34] The Declaration emphatically underscored what delegates to the Congress had already decided: to fashion a new constitutional order based on the will of the people and organized on the basis of states.

The First State Constitutions

The founding fathers of the American states originated the modern written constitution. They have not received, as Peter Onuf has argued, the credit they deserve for the boldness of their actions in putting theory into practice.[35] In a world dominated by monarchy and aristocracy, where the traditional authority of government was taken for granted, there were few precedents for the Americans' central claim that they were entitled to make their own governments. The states, then, as today, were great laboratories of constitutional experimentation, and their early organic laws reconciled the revolutionary idea of popular sovereignty with a commitment to a rule of law under limited, constitutional government. The founders of the new states responded to their novel situation by empowering special conventions to draft written constitutions: this was their most important contribution to constitutional theory and practice. Yet the earliest of these constitutions also reflected the ongoing confusion in American life between what was constitutional and what was legal.

Phases of Early State Constitutional Development

Early state constitutional development passed through two distinct phases. The first began in 1775. Provincial legislatures, responding to calls from the Continental Congress, drafted and then ratified constitutions in the same way they drafted and passed bills. The legislators, in framing these first organic laws, believed that they constituted the "full and free representation of the people."[36] The people did not ratify their labors; the distinction between fundamental and statutory law remained blurred. There can be no doubt, however, that the drafters of these first state organic laws believed that popular will was the basis of sovereignty. The first North Carolina constitution, for example, stated that the legislature that drafted it was "chosen and assembled . . . for the express purpose of framing a Constitution."[37]

A second phase came a few years later, and it involved a clear distinction between statute and constitution making. Astute contemporaries realized that state governments that operated under the earliest constitutions (organic laws neither drafted by constituent conventions nor ratified by the people) were not fully compatible with the idea of popular sovereignty *and* limited government. Thomas Jefferson, for example, complained in his *Notes on Virginia* (1781) that under the Virginia Constitution of 1776, "the ordinary legislature may alter the constitution itself."[38] While the legislature represented the people of a state, that did not mean that the legislators could act for the people in a constituent capacity, even when authorized to do so by a special vote. The inhabitants of Beverly in Essex County, Massachusetts voted against the 1778 constitution proposed for their state because "some other Body, distinct from the General Court, [should] be delegated from among the People for the sole & entire purpose of forming a Bill of Rights & Constitution of Government."[39]

Americans met this challenge by creating constituent constitutional conventions. This device was chosen "for a specific purpose, not to govern, but to set up institutions of government."[40] Americans were determined to separate the extraordinary act of creating a government from the ordinary act of legislating. The constituent convention of popularly elected members established a distinct source for fundamental, constitutional law, and provided the theoretical basis for separation of powers and judicial review in a republican government where all power flowed from the people.

Massachusetts was the first new state to use successfully the convention technique. Many of that state's town meetings, fearful that they were not sufficiently represented in the legislature, had blocked ratification of the 1778 constitution. They then successfully demanded adoption of the convention procedure, and the result was the constitution of 1780, the world's oldest written fundamental frame of government. Political necessity in early Massachusetts influenced constitutional decision making, a pattern that subsequent generations would repeat again and again.

The Legislative Bias of Early State Constitutions

The transition to republican constitutionalism varied from colony to colony. Connecticut and Rhode Island, for example, clung to their original charters with only minor modifications. Elsewhere new ruling documents were adopted.

The constitutions of the first phase embodied a ''Whig-republican'' ideology that blended republicanism, popular sovereignty, distrust of executive authority, and communitarianism through social contract theory. The documents were based on the theory of actual representation, although they abetted political inequality as we would understand it today, because they excluded women and blacks from political participation and required a modest freehold of males to vote and hold office. These organic laws placed great authority in the legislative branch to determine community goals. In this corporatist scheme of republicanism, the commonwealth took precedence over the individual, but the new state constitutions also drew on natural law principles to limit the states' coercive powers through formal bills of rights.

The Whig-republican tradition flourished especially in New England. It included such constitutional devices as small electoral districts, short tenure in office, many elective offices, and constituent instruction of representatives. The documents that contained these provisions were, like the soon-to-be created federal Constitution, of modest length; they were charters of broadly sketched principles the implications of which subsequent generations would work out.

The second phase of early state constitution making somewhat limited this Whig-republican tradition by distinguishing the people from their representatives. The American predilection for written constitutions that blended popular sovereignty and fundamental law devalued legislation: state constitutions were ''higher'' laws and legislation was by definition limited in scope. The controlling idea was that the people were set apart from their representatives essentially to keep a watch over them. Once again, Jefferson's hostility toward the Virginia Constitution of 1776 was based on the fear that legislators would overreach themselves. ''If the present assembly pass any act,'' Jefferson wrote in 1785, ''and declare it shall be irrevocable by subsequent assemblies, the declaration is merely void, and the act repealable, as other acts are.''[41] By the mid-1780s, a written constitution created by a constituent convention and the doctrine of separation of powers emerged as the two most important restraints on the excesses of legislative authority.

Separation of Powers

State constitutions repudiated the organizing principle of English constitutionalism, the theory of mixed government. This meant that the branches of government mixed together the three important social estates (monarchical, aristocratic, and democratic), guaranteeing each a voice that would check the other. Montesquieu explored the doctrine in *Spirit of the Laws* (1748), a work based on observation of the English government and society. He argued that a separation of the branches of government would prevent any one of them from becoming tyrannical, but he continued to join this separation to the traditional notion of social estates rather than governmental function exclusively.

The colonial experience roughly paralleled Montesquieu's theory of separation of powers. The monarchy consisted of the executive authority through the colonial governor; the aristocracy of large landholders filled the upper house of the assembly; and the democratic elements controlled the lower house. The fate of the judiciary reveals the fuzzy nature of this separation doctrine. It was subordinate to the legislature; in many colonies the upper house (often acting with the governor) functioned as the highest court, while the lower assembly discharged apparently judicial functions, such as granting divorces and settling local disputes. The judiciary exercised no coercive powers over the other branches, and it had little in the way of protection against encroachment by these branches on its prerogatives.

Still, in every colony, the sharing and limiting of power based on separation of governmental functions had real vitality. The broad distribution of property among the colonists and great distance from England attenuated the social model of estates upon which mixed government rested. The picture was far from uniform, however; something resembling modern separation theory was stronger in some colonies, such as Massachusetts and Virginia, than in others, such as Georgia and Rhode Island.

The emergence of popular sovereignty and republicanism prompted the framers of state constitutions to formulate a modern scheme of separation of powers. In a democratic republic, no social divisions justified the division of governmental power: by definition, the sovereign "people" subsumed all social groups.

The new state constitutions replaced mixed with balanced government and they "disembodied government from society."[42] Balanced government abolished the concept of social estates; instead, each branch was identified by its function—administrative, lawmaking, and judging—not its social constituency. The switch to balanced government also meant that the judiciary emerged independent and coequal with the executive and legislative. Behind this change was the notion that the people could and should be represented in each of the branches. Separation of powers nicely complemented the theory of popular sovereignty, because it made the people, as a constituent power, into a force that "remained outside the entire government, watching, controlling, pulling the strings for their agents in every branch or part of government."[43] In theory at least, no single branch could, separated and checked as it was by the others, claim sufficient authority to become tyrannical.

True separation was achieved only gradually. The state judiciaries, once again, provide the best evidence. Those state constitutions proclaimed before the Declaration of Independence (e.g., New Hampshire, South Carolina, and New Jersey) had incomplete modes of separation, especially where the judiciary was concerned. Virginia in June 1776 became the first state to define the judiciary as a distinct third branch of government, and five other states followed this radical scheme. Even in these states the legislature retained an element of accountability over the courts, because judges of the highest appellate courts received their offices through legislative election. Most states, however, encouraged judicial independence by providing tenure during good behavior, something that English judges had enjoyed but colonial judges had not.

Separation of powers and balanced government granted the judiciary an expanded role in the implementation of the rule of law. Yet the highest appellate courts of the new states exercised their new powers warily, as the early history of state judicial review suggests.

Judicial review is the practice by which courts are empowered to strike down on constitutional grounds legislative and executive acts. Although a source of controversy, judicial review today is largely taken for granted. Such was not the case during the first two decades of state constitutional history, when state courts struck down fewer than a dozen legislative measures. The most famous of these were the cases of *Trevett* v. *Weeden* (1786) in Rhode Island and *Bayard* v. *Singleton* (1787) in North Carolina. In the former, the Rhode Island Superior Court came close to declaring a recently passed paper-money force act unconstitutional because it violated property rights guaranteed under the old charter. In the latter, the North Carolina Supreme Court actually declared unconstitutional an act that denied "every citizen . . . a right to a decision of his property by trial by jury."[44] As few in number as they were, these early cases demonstrated that the new American scheme of constitutionalism rested on the simple premise that legislative power had to be checked by the judiciary as well as the electorate.

The legislatures retained preeminence within these new balanced state constitutions. The Pennsylvania Constitution of 1776 was the most "radical" manifestation of this ascendancy. It provided for a plural executive, a unicameral legislature, and a "supreme court of judicature" whose judges served seven-year renewable terms. The emphasis on legislative authority appeared in every other state constitution, although no other state went quite so far as Pennsylvania. The technical parliamentary powers acquired over the course of the colonial struggle with England and with royal executives in each of the colonies meant that the new legislatures had secure control over their internal operations. In the nineteenth century, however, judicial and executive power steadily expanded at the expense of legislative authority.

A Nation of States

The lessons of colonial life that had sparked the Revolution in the first place worked against the extension of state constitutional innovations to a central government. The revolutionaries conceived of the states as separate political entities banded together out of necessity to secure their independence. The experience of empire had provided a rough introduction to the concept of federalism, a system of government in which powers are apportioned between a central government and provincial or state governments. The empire was at best an incomplete model, however; it was a unitary government in which the colonies had no distinctive body of powers that they exercised unchecked by Parliament. Most important, through the 1770s and the first half of the 1780s, revolutionary leaders continued to believe that a republican government could succeed only in a small geographic area. They equated localism and decentralization of power with republicanism, a perspective on early American public law that reinforced the local and agrarian character of the economy. The failure to extend immediately balanced government and popular sovereignty to the national level was not an oversight, because such an action would have made no sense in then existing theory and, in any case, a strong central government would have threatened the very goals for which most revolutionaries fought.

Articles of Confederation

When viewed in this way the Articles of Confederation, which became effective in 1781, made sense. They represented at that time the best thinking in the colonies about how to organize a national government based on a written document and spread over a large geographic area.

Were they a true constitution? That all depends. If we mean that they sketched a basic frame of government that took into account the relationship of the states to the national government, then they were. But if we mean by the term constitution an organic form of government founded on the consent of the people and characterized by separation of powers, then they were not. The Articles derived their existence directly from the states, and the states, in turn, made claim to their own sovereignty based on the will of the people that resided within their boundaries.

The Articles were exactly what they said they were: a confederation of sovereign states. They indeed provided for a "president" and a "judiciary" to hear cases arising out of the wartime capture of vessels, but neither of these offices was independent (even, for that matter, identifiable) to the same extent as their counterparts in the states. Nor, moreover, was Congress either sovereign, as Parliament had been, or a true lawmaking body, as were state legislatures. Congress, according to the Articles, could make resolutions, determinations, and regulations, but not laws. Only the states, in which the people as constituent power were represented, had legislatures—and executive and judicial establishments as well. Questions of naturalization, too, were left entirely to the states. The Articles indeed permitted Congress to carry out certain activities that Parliament had exercised under the old regime, such as making war, sending and receiving ambassadors, and coining money, but the lawmaking function resided squarely in the states.

The Articles reflected how most American revolutionaries thought that the empire should have been organized all along. There was no provision for a bill of rights in them because they posed no threat to individual liberty, the protection of which, in any case, properly belonged in republican theory to the states. Compared with the Constitution of 1787, the Articles were weak. But that is what was expected of them; the patriots wanted the rule of law to flow from the bottom up, not the top down.

The Excesses of State Power

In hindsight the articles seem like a way station on the road to the Constitution. That perspective lends an unfortunate air of inevitability to the way the "critical period" culminated in the Philadelphia convention in 1787. The Treaty of Paris in 1783 broke the binding ties of wartime cooperation among the states, leaving each of them to pursue their interests, both on the North American continent and in the larger world. Events and ideas, much as they had in 1761 and 1776, again began to accumulate in patterns that divided Americans in their thinking about the nature of public law, the scope of republican government, and the meaning of federalism.

A crisis indeed existed, but it was not one of material condition, at least not altogether. Most parts of the country rebounded nicely from the postwar recession caused by the rapid resumption of large-scale imports from England. Important problems nonetheless remained, most notably confusion about the jurisdiction of the states over interstate matters, internal challenges to existing state authority, and growing threats of disunion.

The new republican governments encountered numerous challenges. Separatists in Massachusetts schemed to break off and create the new states of Maine and Nantucket, settlers in the Wyoming Valley wanted their own state outside of Pennsylvania, and proponents of a ''lost state'' of Franklin sought independence from North Carolina and possible alliance with Spain or Britain.

There was also substantial internal upheaval. Indebted farmers well remembered the value of revolutionary mob action, and they rekindled the tradition of directly challenging the rule of law in most of the new states. In central and western Massachusetts, for example, Captain Daniel Shays and an army of debtors symbolized the crisis of republican government when they closed the local courts. Popular sovereignty seemed out of control, and the ''national'' government of the Articles stood powerless to assist the states. ''There are combustibles in every State,'' George Washington wrote while the outcome of Shays's Rebellion was unclear, ''which a spark might set fire to.'' Washington's solution was simple: ''a prompt disposition to support and give energy to the federal system.''[45]

These pressures rendered inviable the idea that the Articles could be gradually reformed through the adoption of carefully drawn individual amendments.[46] Some persons did react to Shays's Rebellion by demanding a return to monarchy, but most influential leaders agreed with Washington that the solution lay properly with a stronger national government. For most Americans, as well, the solution was not to undo republican government in the states, but to extend its principles to the national level. What became obvious was that the existing theory of American public law, as youthful as it was, had to be further elaborated. The delegates to the Philadelphia convention in 1787 provided just such a reprise through a federal Constitution that gave truly national implications to Tom Paine's observation that in America ''the law has become king.''

4

Law, Politics, and the Rise of the American Legal System

The Postrevolutionary Struggle over Law and Politics

Public law in the United States from 1787 to 1815 involved an extended struggle over the proper relationship between law and politics. All Americans could agree with the editor of a Boston newspaper who wrote in 1804 that "that which is not regulated by law must depend on the arbitrary will of the rulers, which would put an end to civil society."[1] They disagreed, however, about the content and the implementation of the rule of law.

Their differences stemmed from competing visions of the proper role of government in an emerging capitalist economy. Nationalist exponents of commerce and manufacturing, principally in the northern states, clashed with representatives from agrarian regions, generally in the southern states. The former emerged as the Federalist party; the latter became, by about 1800, the Jeffersonian Republican party. Neither accepted what subsequently became a cachet of American politics: the legitimacy of opposition by the party out of power to the government and its leaders. This fear of opposition owed something to the lessons of English dissenters who had taught that factions were destructive of republican government. It also derived from a sense of insecurity nurtured by almost constant conflict between the world's two major powers, England and France. Under such circumstances Federalists resorted to the power of the state to impose their vision of the public good. Their actions stimulated not only opposition but a sustained debate over critical legal issues raised by it; among them were the organization and independence of the judiciary, the legitimacy of the common law, the limits of popular dissent, and the definition of treason.

By the end of these two decades, the moderate Jeffersonian opposition had itself become the political majority, and in that position it had to fit its principles to the exigencies of governing, in both the federal and the state governments. The resolution it struck between the competing values of law and politics involved nothing less than the framing of the nineteenth-century legal system.

Novus Ordo Seclorum—A New Order for the Ages

"We have only finished the first act of the great drama," Benjamin Rush wrote in 1786. "We have changed our . . . government, but it remains yet to effect a Revolution in our principles. . . and . . . to accommodate them to [new] forms of government."[2] The constitutional convention that met the following year in Philadelphia began that process of accommodation, although it took almost three decades to complete it.

The Constitution broke from both the principles and the form of government embodied in the Articles of Confederation. The framers authored a "*novus ordo seclorum*" (a new order for the ages) not just for America but for the world.[3] The framers were already experienced in fashioning organic laws, and many of the seeming innovations in the federal document, such as separation of powers and popular sovereignty, derived from state constitutional practices. The Constitution was nonetheless ingenious (even revolutionary) because it extended these principles over a vast geographic area with a diverse population, and it divided authority between a central government and the states. In 1787 the United States became the world's largest constitutional republic ever.

Divisions in the Convention

The delegates to the Philadelphia convention were a mixed lot. All of them were nationalists in the narrow sense of that term, accepting the necessity of some new arrangement to strengthen central authority. They differed, however, over the scope of that reformation and, in every case, they remained deeply attached to their respective states. Public creditors and representatives of commercial interests were overrepresented (there were only four farmers), but many small farmers and large slaveholders were also dissatisfied with the Articles. Above all, the delegates thought of themselves as patriots.

Divisions existed among these patriots, and reconciling these political divisions ultimately affected the character of the nation's new fundamental law. George Washington, the convention's presiding officer, led the nationalist proponents of a strong central government. Alexander Hamilton, Gouverneur Morris, James Wilson, and (to a lesser extent) James Madison joined him. These nationalists, or Federalists as they came to be known, were drawn from the big states; they came from areas of good communications and commercial activity. They were cosmopolitan in outlook and education, admiring of the English system, elitist in social views, and experienced in the Revolution, as military or high civilian officials.

The Federalists assumed that, on balance, passions of self-interest drove humanity. The purpose of public law was to harness this passion for self-promotion to the common good through an active government, one capable of representing domestic interests abroad and stimulating the development of trade, commerce, and manufacturing at home. Federalists proposed, in sum, to place the new land in the mainstream of acquisitive capitalism.

Elbridge Gerry of Massachusetts and George Mason of Virginia led the convention's other major division, the republican ideologues. Although called Antifederalists by convention's end, they recognized that something had to be done to strengthen national authority. They were supporters of regional interests and were not necessarily democrats. Gerry explained to the delegates that "the evils we experience flow from the excess of democracy."[4] They uniformly believed that concerns for public welfare rather than the baser passions of self-interest guided human behavior, and that this quality should be depended on as the operating principle for the new government.

The Antifederalists came from areas away from the seaboard, where agriculture was more important than commerce and where lines of communication were often weak. They wanted authority to be exercised on the local level, believing as they did that a republican form of government could succeed only in a small geographic area. They were older, less well organized, and less imaginative than the Federalists; yet they were capitalists just the same, frequently pursuing their economic fortunes through agriculture rather than commerce.

The delegates also differed over the relationship between power (the ability to bring about change) and liberty (freedom from restraint). The Federalists were young, ambitious men of the Revolution, who (though fearful that power might overwhelm liberty) were so certain in their own abilities that they believed a new national government would succeed if it were under their control. The Antifederalists, on the other hand, were "men of little faith," who worried that power would obliterate liberty and did not trust themselves completely to exercise it through republican government.[5] Therefore, they did not trust it to any other hands.

Other issues cut across these major factions. Delegates from the small states worried that their large-state counterparts would give them short shrift. Northern and southern delegates also disagreed, first about the extent to which the national government should support commercial over agricultural capitalism and, second, about the future of slavery. Southerners, while often uncomfortable with their rôle as masters, recognized that their slaves and the wealth produced from slave labor constituted an important property right that required protection from a potentially encroaching national government. They feared, as well, the social consequences of freeing the slaves—not to mention the economic costs.

These ideological, social, and economic divisions necessitated compromise. The Federalists, who largely dominated the proceedings, relied on compromise and innovation—the basic arts of the political process—to mold a new scheme of public law and, with it, a new form of government.

The Problem of Sovereignty

Projecting the doctrine of popular sovereignty onto a national constitution raised practical and theoretical problems. Antifederalists believed that a republic could exist only in a small geographic area and that only one sovereign could exist in a state. William Grayson of Virginia, for example, observed that "I never heard of two supreme coordinate powers in one and the same country before."[6] The term sovereignty had historically required that authority reside in one place, and the Federalists knew that this could not be the states because such an arrangement would frustrate their economic agenda. Both groups of delegates entered the convention convinced that excessive democracy, as exemplified by Shays's Rebellion, threatened property rights and social stability. Placing the authority for a new national government in the hands of the people seemed unlikely and unadvisable.

In a pattern that became familiar over the next two centuries, a political elite (the Federalists) legitimated their goals through an appeal to popular will. The "authorities of the general government and state government all radiate," James Madison explained as he tipped existing theory on its head, "from the people at large."[7] Madison pressed this popular will theory of national public law because it offered a practical means of reaching an objective—a stronger national government supportive of economic and social stability—that was otherwise denied to the Federalists. Once the Federalists perceived " 'the great principle of the primary right of power in the people,' they could scarcely restrain their enthusiasm in following out its implications."[8]

Madison countered fears of excessive democracy by formulating a kinetic theory of government. Popular sovereignty, he explained, would "enable the government to control the governed; and in the next place oblige it to control itself."[9] The people would energize each branch of the new government, creating a tension that would prevent any one branch, and government as a whole, from becoming tyrannical. Madison, as had the states before, rejected Montesquieu's theory of mixed government and estates; the new Constitution disembodied government from society, making the people as a whole, rather than in separate estates, a check on government. But the people's authority also enabled national government to act on behalf of national interests. The framers adopted, as well, a scheme of checks and balances that further diffused and restricted power.

Popular sovereignty also supported two other Federalist goals of binding the several states into a national republic and preventing the rise of political factions, or parties. Madison, in *Federalist* No. 10, argued that the United States was a republic and not a democracy; this meant that the people delegated "government to a small number of [elected] citizens" rather than allowing each citizen to decide and act directly on government. "Extend the sphere and you take in a greater variety of parties and interests," he counseled, and "you make it less probable that a majority of the whole will have a common motive to invade the rights of other citizens."[10] The resulting tension would prevent arbitrary restraints on liberty through majority tyranny (a constant problem in small republics and democracies). Also, a large republic promised to prevent a political faction from selfishly controlling government for its own rather than the public purpose. The framers not only failed to foresee the rise of political parties as a legitimate form of opposition to government, but they positively worked to prevent them.

Federalism

The Federalists accommodated existing state governments by dividing the indivisible. Blackstone and other English commentators had held that it was "a solecism in politics for two coordinate sovereignties to exist together."[11] What emerged from the convention was "a system hitherto unknown," which was a plan for "a perfect confederation of independent states."[12]

Federalism is a system of government under which there exists simultaneously a federal or central government and several state governments as contrasted with a unitary government. The "original understanding" of federalism reached in 1787, according to the historian Harry Scheiber, rested on a "compound principle" that was both structural and operational.[13] It grafted a system of national government onto existing states by giving the states direct and equal representation in the Senate and by leaving with the states the major reponsibility of controlling the process of elections and establishing the criteria of citizenship. The Constitution granted the national government, mostly in Article I (the legislative), only enumerated powers, but with the proviso that Congress retained authority "to make all laws necessary and proper for carrying [them] into execution."[14] The new government could, for example, levy taxes, raise armies, and regulate commerce among the states. Those powers not specifically enumerated remained with the states.

Federalism cut the other way as well. Fear of state legislative authority persuaded the delegates to place certain prohibitions on the states, such as restricting their authority to coin money and interfere with private contracts. Such prohibitions, according to James Wilson, were necessary because in the states the people did not delegate enumerated powers but rather "invested their representatives with every right and authority which they did not in explicit terms reserve."[15]

These were modest limitations. The states retained the important power to provide for the morals, health, safety, and welfare of their citizens. These police powers, as they were known, enabled each state to act directly on persons without fear of interference by the national government.

The framers refrained from putting a bill of rights in the Constitution on the logical grounds that the document established a government of limited, enumerated powers. As Hamilton observed, there was no point declaring "that things shall not be done which there is no power to do."[16] Antifederalists did win a victory of sorts when they obtained pledges from several state conventions that their ratification depended on Congress subsequently amending the Constitution to include a bill of rights. The first Congress, followed by ratification of three-fourths of the states, added ten amendments. The first eight affirmed basic rights; the ninth provided that the people retained rights not otherwise enumerated; and the tenth granted the states those "powers" (not rights) not given to the national government or denied to the states by the Constitution. This Bill of Rights applied only against the national government. The framers simply did not envision the federal government as mediator in the conduct of the states in matters of individual liberty. That modern concept only emerged after adoption of the Fourteenth Amendment in 1868 and the revolution in federalism that followed it.

The original concept of American federalism meant that in the final analysis the resolving of conflicts between the states and Congress would have to be decided by an "informal political process."[17] The principle of federalism was established, but future generations would settle on the exact terms by which the indivisible would be divided.

The Judiciary

The framers also defined the new judicial branch in equally broad terms, leaving to Congress the responsibility of adding most of the detail. Article III stirred far less debate than did either Article I (the legislative) or Article II (the executive).

As in so many other areas, the framers drew upon state experience in establishing the federal judiciary. Most of the framers, with the notable exception of James Wilson, embraced the departmental theory of constitutional interpretation that underlay the organization of the state judiciaries. This theory held that each department or branch of government was capable within its sphere of responsibility of interpreting the state's organic law. State constitutions, while fundamental law, combined elements of a strictly legal nature such as trial by jury, with matters of political significance such as the powers of the executive and legislative branches. Under the departmental theory, the political branches had responsibility for political-constitutional controversies, and the judicial branch assumed the role of settling legal-judicial questions, overseeing the rule of law. State appellate courts emerged in the 1780s and 1790s as institutions designed to fulfill the republican function of preserving the common good through legal authority while protecting themselves from legislative and executive encroachments.

The delegates in Philadelphia wanted to strike a balance between law and politics. They expected the judiciary to curb popular excesses while preserving minority rights of property holders. They had no understanding of the judiciary (as some persons do today) as a political and lawmaking body. That function belonged exclusively to the political branches. That is what Alexander Hamilton meant when he described the judiciary as the "least dangerous branch" because it had access to neither the purse nor the sword.[18] "If judges should be disposed," Hamilton wrote in *Federalist* No. 78, "to exercise *will* instead of *judgment,* the consequences would equally be the substitution of their pleasure to that of the legislative body."[19] The requirement of the judicial process that judges could not act until a controversy was presented to them in proper legal form further restrained their discretion.

Creation of the Federal Courts

Article III secured two of the great structural principles of the Constitution: federalism and separation of powers. Section 1 provided for two types of courts: a "Supreme Court" and "such inferior Courts as Congress may from time to time ordain and establish."[20] The former became the nation's highest appellate court (it heard cases brought on appeal from other federal and state courts); the latter were to operate as the trial courts of the federal system. Federalists wanted to specify the structure of the lower federal courts explicitly; Antifederalists proposed that state courts administer federal trials. They agreed by not agreeing, leaving the entire matter of the lower federal courts to Congress.

Article III conferred jurisdiction (the authority by which a court can hear a legal claim) in two categories. The first was based on subject and extended to all cases in law and equity arising under the Constitution, laws, and treaties of the United States, as well as cases of admiralty and maritime. The second category depended on the nature of the parties in legal conflict. This jurisdiction included controversies between citizens of different states, between a state and citizens of another state, between states, and between a state and the nation.

Most of the delegates appreciated that the rule of law in a republican government required an independent judiciary that was only indirectly accountable. The president was given authority to appoint federal judges with the advice and consent of the

Senate. Once commissioned, these judges would hold office during good behavior, and their salaries could not be diminished. The framers had not the slightest intention of making the judges *democratically* accountable; on the contrary, they had to be shielded from popular impulses because under the departmental theory, they dispensed justice, rather than made law. Should judges, however, engage in "high Crimes and Misdemeanors," the framers specified that they could be removed through impeachment by the House and conviction by the Senate.

The Matter of Judicial Review

The words *judicial review* do not appear in the Constitution, and their absence has confounded generations of Americans. The convention delegates agreed to the establishment of a Supreme Court only after they had rejected proposals for a Council of Revision to scrutinize congressional legislation and another to allow Congress to veto state legislation. That the delegates debated these methods of constitutional oversight in the context of the judicial power indicates that they assumed the Supreme Court would oversee the constitutionality of acts of Congress and state legislatures. Experience in the states had already confirmed that such a power was indispensable in republican government to the maintenance of the rule of law.

There seems little doubt that the framers anticipated that judicial review would be exercised; the only unknown was its scope. Luther Martin, an Antifederalist, for example, observed during the convention that "As to the constitutionality of laws, that point will come before the Judges in their proper official character. In this character they have a negative on the laws."[21] It did not follow that they could do what they wanted; delegates of every ideological stripe posited a sharp distinction between constitutional interpretation necessary to the rule of law and judicial lawmaking. "The judges," John Dickinson, a Federalist, concluded, "must interpret the laws; they ought not to be legislators."[22]

There was also a textual basis for the exercise of federal judicial review, especially of state laws. Article VI made the Constitution the "supreme Law of the Land," and in Article III the courts were named as interpreters of the law.[23] The same conclusion can be reached by combining Article I, section 10, which placed certain direct limitations on the state legislatures, with the supremacy clause and Article III. Simply put, judicial review of state legislation was an absolute necessity under the framers' compound system of federalism. The Supreme Court could also inquire under the departmental theory into acts of Congress that encroached on the judicial branch. The scope of this power remained to be worked out. "That the Framers anticipated some sort of judicial review," the great constitutional scholar Edward S. Corwin wrote during the 1930s, "there can be little question. But it is equally without question that ideas generally current in 1787 were far from presaging the present vast role of the Court."[24]

A Compromised Document for a Government at a Distance and Out of Sight

The ratified Constitution rendered most existing republican theory obsolete. It did so in little more than 6000 words, giving new meanings to federalism, separation of powers, popular sovereignty, representation, and judicial authority.

Two features distinguished the nation's new organic law. The first was that the United States was not one republic or even thirteen; it was a multitude of several thousand insular political communities that would continue for the next sixty years to view the national government as "at a distance and out of sight."[25] The national government had become federal, but decentralization and local authority remained pervasive. The local jury, not the new Supreme Court, provided citizens with their most immediate contact with the rule of law. The militia, not a national army and navy, protected public safety.

Second, the Constitution was also compromised. Federalists and Antifederalists accommodated their differences. That the Federalists got the better of the matter meant that, over the next two centuries, the national government would afford advantages to commerce.

Such an advantage had long-term consequences because of the sectional compromises over slavery on which the document rested. What was left unsaid in the new document was as important as what was explicit. The words "slavery" and "slaves" do not appear in the Constitution, but concern about the peculiar institution nonetheless shaped the document. If the Federalists, some of whom were slaveholders themselves, generally prevailed, they did so only by granting significant concessions to southern slave and agricultural interests. Slaveholders were overrepresented in Congress by having three-fifths of all slaves counted for the purpose of apportioning House seats. They were protected from direct taxes on their slaves, they enjoyed a pledge of aid from the national government to return escaped slaves, and they were guaranteed a steady flow of imported slaves until 1808. Political compromise came wrapped in constitutional language, even though the framers understood that law and politics had to be separated.

The compromises over slavery seeded long-term conflict, but the generation of the framers fell into disagreement over other more immediate matters. One of the most troubling involved the proper role of law, parties, and political opposition: a balance would have to be struck between law and politics in the new republican governments, both in the nation and the states. Federalists and Jeffersonian Republicans struggled with these matters for a quarter-century after ratification of the Constitution.

Establishing the National Legal Order: The Federalist Persuasion

"We are all Republicans, we are all Federalists," newly elected President Thomas Jefferson proclaimed in his 1801 inaugural address.[26] But these words of reconciliation concealed powerful differences that had split the Federalists of the Philadelphia convention into rival political groups, something that the framers had hoped to prevent. Parties appeared because the kinetic form of government adopted by the framers begged for leadership, both to organize the internal actions of government and to forge ties between the citizenry and their representatives. The Federalist party and its Jeffersonian Republican opposition developed from the top down; conflict over the conduct of the national government carried over into the states where local issues fueled political division. As the party in power, the Federalists viewed the growing Jeffersonian Republican opposition as a threat not only to themselves but, given their view of the pervasiveness of human self-interest, to the existence of the republican government.

This suspicion of opposition meant that law and the courts (the instruments of government coercion and of the protection of individual rights, respectively) were central to the outcome of the political struggle between Federalists and Jeffersonian Republicans. Political skirmishing over judicial and legal authority took place across a broad front, involving national and state courts and the law, and culminated in precedents of enduring significance for the legal system of the United States.

Judiciary Act of 1789

A Senate committee headed by Oliver Ellsworth of Connecticut drew the Judiciary Act of 1789. It established a federal court organization that lasted almost unchanged for a century, and its outlines remain quite recognizable today. Yet the act was a product of its times. It was framed in a "political context as an instrument of reconciliation . . . to quiet still smoldering resentments."[27]

The act embodied two policy decisions that made it politically acceptable. First, Congress exercised its powers to create lower federal courts, something that the Federalists had wanted; however, it lodged the new courts squarely in the states. The 1789 act divided the country into thirteen districts and made the boundaries of the courts in these districts coterminous with those of the states. (Massachusetts and Virginia received two each, Rhode Island and North Carolina none because they were still not members of the Union.) The district courts in the coastal states became especially important through the exercise of their jurisdiction over admiralty and maritime cases. They also heard civil cases and some minor criminal matters. The act also divided the country into three circuits in each of which a circuit court, consisting of two justices of the Supreme Court and one district judge in the circuit, sat twice a year. The circuit courts entertained appeals from the district courts below and held jury trials involving the most serious criminal and civil cases involving the federal government.

The act made Supreme Court justices into republican schoolmasters whose presence in the circuits symbolized the authority of the remote national government. Circuit riding also exposed the justices, in their capacity as trial judges on circuit, to local concerns. The inculcation of republican virtue exacted a stiff price from members of the Court. Horseback and stage riding made Justices Samuel Chase and Oliver Ellsworth martyrs to gout and renal stones. Justice William Paterson suffered so extensively while traveling the Vermont circuit in the spring of 1794 that he complained to a fellow justice that "[I] nearly went out of my head."[28]

The 1789 act also confirmed Congress's full control over lower federal court jurisdiction, which the act set in limited terms. It consisted of admiralty cases (allotted exclusively to the district courts) and cases concerning the diversity of citizenship, with a limited appellate jurisdiction in the circuit courts over district court decisions. Federalists indeed succeeded in section 25 of the act in allowing federal courts to review state court decisions involving federal laws and the Constitution. That provision stirred controversy for the next forty years as first Jeffersonian Republicans and then Jacksonian Democrats sought, in the name of states' rights, to have it repealed.

Local influence remained pervasive in the decentralized federal courts. District judges, for example, not only lived among the people they served, but section 34 of the 1789 act directed that on comparable points of law federal judges had to regard the decisions of state courts as the rule of decision in the federal courts.

The Struggle over the Federal Courts: States' Rights and Treason

The federal courts during the 1790s gained a measure of respect, but great prestige lay in the future. John Jay, the nation's first chief justice who had earlier resigned his post, declined reappointment in 1801 because he had no faith that the Supreme Court could ever acquire enough "energy, weight and dignity."[29] The justices heard only about one hundred cases during the first decade of the Court's existence. The lower courts were busier. Even in Kentucky, on the edge of American civilization, the federal courts competently handled a large volume of casework.[30]

Efficiency and prestige aside, the emerging Jeffersonian Republican opposition flayed the federal courts for their conduct. For example, the Supreme Court in *Chisholm* v. *Georgia* (1793) rekindled fears that federal judges would undermine state authority. Two citizens of South Carolina brought an action in federal court against the state of Georgia to recover a debt. Georgia refused to appear, contending that as a sovereign entity it could choose the time and the forum in which it would be sued. There is little doubt that the states had played fast and loose with their debt, and that active enforcement by the federal courts would have brought a swarm of creditors down on them. The Supreme Court ruled against Georgia, and Justice James Wilson's ruling sent a shudder through emerging Republican ranks. "As to the purposes of the Union," the Federalist Wilson concluded, "Georgia is not a sovereign state."[31] The Eleventh Amendment, which went into effect in 1798, affirmed that states could not be sued by nonresidents without their permission. The quickly adopted amendment repaired constitutional understandings, but it did not curb the growing political clamor against the federal courts.

Divergent attitudes toward the course of U.S. economic and foreign policy exacerbated the political controversy surrounding the courts. Federalists wanted strong commercial ties with England and a prosperous trading economy, and, as the leaders of an insecure nation in a hostile world, they developed something of a bunker psychology that assumed that the rule of law had to buttress their claims. They treated opposition to their policies from the pro-French and agrarian Jeffersonian opposition as treasonous and those persons who refused to cooperate as traitors deserving of severe punishment.

There was reason for concern, because some Americans decided to take the law into their own hands. Settlers in western Pennsylvania in 1794 and 1795, for example, forcefully opposed collection of an excise tax (a tax placed on domestic consumption of goods) on distilled whiskey, their principal cash crop. Many small farmers, locked in competition with large producers, refused to pay the federal excise tax collectors who inspected their stills. The government then forced the recalcitrant farmers to make the arduous journey across the mountains to stand trial in the federal circuit court in Philadelphia. The small farmers rebelled. They menaced exciseman, wrecked the stills of those large producers who did cooperate, and even threatened to burn Pittsburgh.

Federalists organized a national army larger than that which had fought the Revolution in an effort to make an example of the rebellious farmers. Within three weeks the uprising ended. A federal grand jury in Philadelphia indicted more than thirty men for treason. Two were convicted, although President Washington ultimately pardoned both on the dubious grounds that they were mental incompetents.

Their trials nonetheless dramatized the insensitivity of the Federalists to political opposition. These trials were the first instances in which the meaning of treason under the Constitution was defined. In *United States* v. *Vigol* (1795) and *United States* v. *Mitchell* (1795), Justice William Paterson charged the jury that treason amounted to "levying war" against the United States by widespread armed opposition to the execution of a U.S. statute. The blatant partiality of the Federalist judges during the trials promoted the very behavior that Federalists sought to prevent: the rise of organized opposition to the national government. Some members of the emerging Jeffersonian Republican party, for example, denounced Justice Paterson for blithely charging the jury in the *Mitchell* case that "[u]pon the whole, . . . the prisoner must be pronounced guilty."[32]

Federalist judges flashed their political teeth four years later when the same federal circuit court in Pennsylvania heard yet another case of alleged treason. In this instance, John Fries, a former revolutionary war soldier, had led a local militia that released prisoners held by a federal marshal. The Fries' rebels protested a federal tax imposed on houses to pay for the costs of putting down the Whiskey Rebellion. Fries was tried twice, and in both instances the *Vigol* and *Mitchell* precedents were invoked. At the second trial (the first had ended in conviction, but Fries won a new trial because of alleged bias by one of the jurors), Justice Samuel Chase, an ardent Federalist, acted from the bench as counsel for Fries. The defendant's attorneys, correctly concluding that both judge and jury were hostile to their client, withdrew from the case. Chase "proceeded in . . . a steamrolling manner" that culminated in a guilty verdict.[33] "The end to all punishment," Chase informed Fries as he sentenced him to death, "is example; and the enormity of your crime requires that a severe example should be made to deter others from the commission of like crimes in the future."[34] Subsequently, President John Adams, who was troubled by the political excesses of the trial and the broad definition given to treason, pardoned Fries.

Chase, like other Federalist jurists, believed that the new national courts had to coerce political stability. If the laws could not be obeyed, Chase concluded, "there must soon be an end to all government in this country."[35] But Chase's actions merely confirmed for Jeffersonian Republicans that the Federalists had turned to the courts in order to crush their political opponents.

Seditious Libel and the Sedition Act of 1798

The Federalists resorted to other forms of legal action to suppress political opposition. Even before Chase condemned Fries to death, the Federalist-controlled Congress passed the Sedition Act of 1798. Historians have divided over the meaning of the measure, with some suggesting it was a blatant instrument of oppression and others arguing that it was a reasonable response by a government seriously concerned about the country's survival.[36]

It certainly contained enough political purpose to make moderate Federalists like John Adams hold their noses. The measure, which imposed a penalty for publishing material creating distrust of the federal government, did not apply to any statements made against Thomas Jefferson, Adams's vice-president. Moreover, it was timed to expire the day before Adams's term ended. But the measure was progressive in the sense that sedition was no longer a strict liability crime, as it had been in England. That is, merely printing seditious statements was not proof of sedition. The act allowed truth to be entered as an "affirmative defense." What was a breakthrough in the history of free speech was less significant than it might seem, because the defendant had the difficult task of proving that a public officer was corrupt, incompetent, or ineffective. In any case, open political discourse did not lend itself to a strict true-and-false test, and criticism of the people's representatives seemed vital in a republic.

Federalist prosecutors invoked the law with fervor and Federalist judges gave jury charges in seditious libel cases that made conviction practically inevitable. Thomas Cooper, for example, found himself on trial in 1800 before Justice Chase and District Judge Richard Peters for having published comments that accused President John Adams of borrowing money at too high a rate during peacetime, of keeping a standing army and navy, and of interfering with the judiciary. Justice Chase told the jury that the accused had to prove the truth of his charges against President Adams "beyond a marrow," rather than that the prosecution had to establish guilt beyond a reasonable doubt (the emerging American standard).[37] Cooper was convicted and sent off to jail, preferring martyrdom to accepting a pardon.

The Sedition Act was the first national experiment in using legal authority to reap political benefit. John Adams's administration directed prosecutions against Cooper and other editors and political leaders. The owners of four leading opposition papers were indicted, and three were convicted of violating the Sedition Act. Matthew Lyon, a Republican congressman from Vermont, who was something of an excitable personality, was convicted of libeling President Adams and hustled off to jail for four months.

Judiciary Act of 1801

A decade in power made the Federalists acutely aware of the value of the federal courts to the political goals (and power) that they embraced. When the election of 1800 assured the ascendancy of the Jeffersonian Republicans, the Federalists responded with the Judiciary Act of 1801, a measure that combined political purpose with needed reform. Gouverneur Morris explained that the Federalists had found it necessary to reorganize the federal judiciary because they "are about to experience a heavy gale of adverse wind; can they be blamed for casting many anchors to hold their shipe through the storm?"[38]

The 1801 act had two key provisions. First, it created sixteen new circuit judgeships and ended the practice of circuit riding for Supreme Court justices. This provision was both a reasonable reform and a political gimmick that gave the outgoing Adams administration the opportunity to appoint several "midnight judges." Second, the Federalists sought to establish a genuinely national court system capable of bringing coherence to federal land policy and commercial relations. The Jeffersonians blasted the legislation and, once in power, they moved swiftly to repeal it.

The Jeffersonian Crisis

William Branch Giles, a radical Jeffersonian Republican congressman from Virginia, warned in 1801 that "what concerns us most is the situation with the Judiciary as now organized."[39] With Jefferson in the White House, a Republican majority in Congress, and Republican control of several state legislatures, the radicals intended to humble federal and state judges while working a wholesale plan of legal reform. Radicals distrusted lawyers and believed that local democracy in an agrarian society based on "common sense and common honesty between man and men," not the technicalities of the common law, offered the surest road to justice.[40]

Moderate Jeffersonian Republicans, like President Jefferson, stood poised between the extremes of Federalism and radical Jeffersonianism. Like the radicals, the moderates were troubled by the behavior of the federal judiciary, but like the Federalists they saw the national courts as a vital instrument for the maintenance of the republican experiment. They wanted, in short, to restrict the federal judiciary, and even to teach sitting Federalist judges a lesson in republican accountability, but they had no desire to disable the federal court system. Jefferson also had a "darker side," and he resorted to the federal courts to coerce political opponents, especially after 1807 when he imposed an embargo on American commerce with the Continent, driving Federalist merchants to criminal acts.[41]

Moderate Triumph in the States

This Jeffersonian crisis over the judiciary also extended into the states where divisions existed between radicals and moderates. The former envisioned a judicial system that would be under the direct control of the people, that abolished appellate courts, and that relied on readily accessible trial courts uncluttered by common law pleading. They had a particular animus toward the common law. Radicals regularly cited Benjamin Austin, an artisan from Boston, whose pamphlet, *Observations on the Pernicious Practice of the Law by Honestus* (1786), condemned the common law as too technical and urged that, "for the welfare and security of the Commonwealth" lawyers "should be ANNIHILATED."[42] The radicals wanted to replace the common law, which they often described as a "hodge-podge of mystery," with a simple code drawn up by the legislature, the people's branch of government.[43] Deeply democratic and inherently localistic, they proposed to wed the law to the ebb and flow of daily communal life.

Federalists in the states took a contrary position. They not only supported the common law as a historic protection for "liberty" and property, but they believed that only persons trained in it could successfully administer the rule of law. Where the radical Jeffersonians in states like Pennsylvania, Kentucky, and Virginia proclaimed that appellate courts were a distant and unaccountable check on popular will, Federalists argued that such courts prevented juries from disturbing the purity and reason of law. Moreover, Federalists expected that a multilayered state court system would ensure that property rights would never be sacrificed to legislative majorities and juries. That juries in the federal treason cases had proved remarkably pliable in sustaining the government seems to have been either lost on or ignored by the Federalists. They were, in any case, more prepared to trust in the judiciary than in the people.

Moderates agreed with radicals on the need for judicial and legal reform, but they also agreed with the Federalists that courts had to check popular will. From the time of the Revolution through 1815, every state except two modified its constitutions in ways that restricted the legislative branch and enhanced judicial authority and legal organization. The two states that did not engage in constitutional reform modified their judiciaries through statutes. The moderates prevailed almost everywhere. Only in Kentucky did the radicals have a significant impact; only in Massachusetts did the Federalists hold sway.

Most states adopted expanded and inexpensive trial courts. Each trial court possessed an original criminal and civil jurisdiction, and each was staffed by three or more judges. Most states expected that these judges would have some legal training, and in most instances these new courts eclipsed in importance the old justice-of-the-peace courts, long a favorite of radicals. New intermediate courts of appeal appeared that sat in specific locations throughout the year, thus bringing appellate justice closer to all state residents. A high appellate tribunal capped the court structure. Most state appellate judges held office during "good behavior," and the principle of judicial review survived, although these judges did not begin to exercise significantly this power until the mid-nineteenth century. The common law also survived, although distrust of it remained pervasive, and throughout the rest of the century legal reformers repeated demands for codification of state law.

Taken together, these state reforms meant that the administration of justice was somewhat decentralized yet organized in a hierarchical form. The new structure promised a measure of certainty, uniformity, and predictability in legal decision making, qualities that benefited the budding capitalist economies of most states. The moderate triumph, moreover, was every bit as sweeping at the national level.

Federal Judiciary Act of 1802

On the national level, the Jeffersonian Republicans' first target was the Judiciary Act of 1801 and John Adams's midnight appointees. Moderates worried about the constitutionality of any measure that would abolish courts and thereby remove judges without impeaching them. Radicals wanted root-and-branch change that would not only eliminate the Federalist appointees but reduce the federal courts' influence. The final product was the Judiciary Act of 1802, a measure that "probably really satisfied no one in the Republican party."[44]

The 1802 act repealed the Judiciary Act of 1801, eliminating the sixteen circuit judgeships. The Federalists condemned the measure as an unconstitutional, and partisan, removal of judges who enjoyed tenure during good behavior. Some moderate Jeffersonians were also skeptical, but they acquiesced, agreeing to abolish the judgeships because of what they stood for in origin—a patently partisan exercise of the appointing power—and not to reverse or penalize decisions of the sitting judges.

The 1802 act contained two other important provisions. First, it narrowed the scope of power granted to the courts under the 1801 act, reaffirming that local pressures would continue to influence enforcement of federal laws. Second, the act restored the practice of circuit riding, forcing the justices of the Supreme Court to resume regular contacts with the citizenry in federal trial courts.

The Republicans also put the Supreme Court on notice. The Congress passed the Judiciary Act of 1802 in April, and one of its provisions abolished the June session of the Supreme Court, directing the justices not to reconvene until February 1803. The Republicans worried, of course, that the Federalist-controlled high court might declare the new act unconstitutional. As well, the Court already had before it an important case, *Marbury* v. *Madison* (1803), that tested the Republican policy of refusing to grant commissions to Federalist appointees who had not received their commissions during the last frantic hours of the Adams administration. The purpose of the act, taken in its entirety, was quite clear. It was, according to Jefferson, designed to "restore our judiciary to what it was while justice & not [F]ederalism was its object."[45]

Impeachment

The radicals then turned their attention to those sitting Federalist judges whom they could not reach through the Judiciary Act of 1802. The only provision in the Constitution for a judge's removal is "impeachment for, and Conviction of, Treason, Bribery or other high Crimes and Misdemeanors."[46] During the previous two decades impeachment in the states had evolved into a political process, and congressional radicals, as in so many other early constitutional episodes, mimicked state practices. They insisted that a judge need not have committed an indictable crime in order to be removed from office. Such a position had momentous consequences, because it threatened the assumption that in a republican government the judiciary was independent of direct political interference. The radicals, for their part, believed that the Federalist judges had already surrendered their independence through politically motivated actions, a position that moderates did not entirely accept. This division within the Jeffersonian party framed the crucial constitutional decisions involved in the impeachments of John Pickering of the Federal District Court for New Hampshire and Justice Samuel Chase of the Supreme Court.

Judge Pickering had been a distinguished lawyer and respected New Hampshire Federalist. He was also an alcoholic with a nervous disorder in which saliva drooled constantly from his open mouth. Although deranged beyond recovery, Pickering remained faithful to his Federalist ideals and refused to leave the bench. The actual articles of impeachment charged that he had improperly discharged a federal customs suit involving the brig *Eliza,* but he had violated no federal law. The articles indeed cited his bizarre behavior (they charged, for example, that he "did appear on the bench . . . in a state of total intoxication"), but neither his dismissal of the suit nor his conduct constituted a "high crime" or a "misdemeanor."[47] This did not matter. The radical Jeffersonians had little trouble (even moderates and some Federalists were aghast at Pickering's condition) in disposing of the judge. The Senate trial in 1804 lasted only two weeks and concluded in Pickering's conviction. The implication seemed clear: if the radicals could impeach and convict a madman, they could certainly bring to task the prime Federalist bully on the Supreme Court: Justice Samuel Chase.

The Chase impeachment in 1805 was something altogether different from that of Pickering. Chase was not only fully in command of his senses but was anxious, in his usual combative style, to prove the correctness of his actions. The radicals charged the justice with a long list of violations, including his conduct at the treason and sedition trials. In 1803, he had sealed his fate when he delivered a harangue to a Baltimore grand jury against Jefferson and the Republicans in Congress who had passed the Judiciary Act of 1802. The president reacted bitterly, urging Congress to make certain that such a "seditious and official attack on the principles of our Constitution" did not "go unpunished."[48]

Chase was certainly guilty of bad judgment, of a wretched political sense, and of a haughty attitude toward the discharge of his duties. However, he was not guilty of a crime, even though the radicals in Congress, who secured a vote of impeachment in the House, proceeded on that basis. Divisions within the Republican party over the issue of criminal conduct proved fatal, and moderate Republican senators deserted in sufficient numbers to acquit Chase.

The Chase impeachment marked a decisive shift from the experimental republicanism of the late eighteenth century to a burgeoning political democracy of the nineteenth century. Impeachment in the states had been viewed as a practical way (in a world that condemned political parties) to remove self-interested, disorderly, and arbitrary officials. Moderate Republicans, like the Federalists, worried indeed that organized opposition to *their* political rule in government might threaten the constitutional order as a whole, and they certainly cracked the legal whip over the Federalists' heads. But they were also different in this regard from the Federalists. They seem to have benefited both from the lessons of their own opposition and from a recognition that they might become the victims of the impeachment process. Political interference with the judiciary also ran counter to the moderates' avowed commitment to an unpoliticized legal order. Political matters, Jeffersonian moderates recognized (although they did not always act accordingly), properly belonged to the legislative and executive branches of government. This rule freed the federal judiciary from the fear of intrusive, carping, and inexpert criticism from the legislature. The Chase episode meant that impeachment would not be used thereafter as "a means of keeping the Courts in reasonable harmony with the will of the nation."[49]

Yet the Chase impeachment, taken together with the Judiciary Act of 1802, further limited the federal judiciary. The full nationalizing potential of the lower federal courts remained unfulfilled over the next seventy-five years; Congress refused to implement the remedies required (and that had appeared in the Judiciary Act of 1801) for truly effective federal justice. With limits placed on the jurisdiction of the lower federal courts, state judges and legislators had the initiative to develop the major substantive areas of civil and criminal law.

The Chase impeachment also delivered a palpable warning to other members of the high court, especially to Chief Justice John Marshall, whom John Adams in 1801 had appointed shortly before leaving office. Marshall seems to have believed (probably correctly) that if Chase had been convicted, he would have been the next target. This realization contributed to Marshall's already strong tendency to appear above political controversy, and to avoid, where possible, the resolution of issues bound to plunge the Court into the political thicket.

The Supreme Court and the Growth of Federal Judicial Power

Despite the radical Jeffersonian attack on the federal judicial system, the influence of the Supreme Court grew steadily during the period 1801–1815. Its growing prestige owed much to the leadership of John Marshall, a Virginian, a Federalist, and an able lawyer. The chief justice blended a gifted intellect, modest and unpretentious behavior, and "the rare faculty of condensation; he distilled an argument down to its essence."[50] He had a vision of greatness based on the belief that the new nation needed strong institutions through which people of ability could exercise authority to the benefit of all. Marshall believed that the judiciary should separate the majesty of the law from politics. That did not mean, however, that Marshall was nonpolitical—far from it. He well understood that the Court purchased its success by not intruding on those responsibilities that clearly belonged to the elected branch. He devoted more than three decades to establishing the basic principle that law embraced certain core values free from overt political considerations and that the justices had to treat constitutional disputes, while certainly ripe with political consequences, as matters for legal judgment.

The Rise of Federal Judicial Review

Marshall's most notable achievement during these years was to establish that the high court could review both federal and state laws. "If Congress were to make a law not warranted by any of the powers enumerated," Marshall had argued at the Virginia convention to ratify the federal Constitution in 1788, "it would be considered by the judges as an infringement of the Constitution which they are to guard. . . . They would declare it void."[51] Marshall supplied a practical meaning to these words in the classic case of *Marbury* v. *Madison* (1803) and then, seven years later, he demonstrated the importance of judicial review to American federalism by striking down a state law in *Fletcher* v. *Peck* (1810).

Marshall himself contributed to the chain of events that culminated in *Marbury*. Shortly before his appointment to the Court in 1801, Marshall, as secretary of state, failed to deliver a commission as justice of the peace in the District of Columbia to William Marbury, a loyal Federalist and one of Adams's midnight appointees. Marbury subsequently requested that James Madison, the new Republican secretary of state, issue the commission. Madison refused, and Marbury went directly to the Supreme Court, claiming that section 13 of the Judiciary Act of 1789 gave the Court original jurisdiction to issue writs of mandamus. (The writ was a command by a court to a ministerial officer ordering certain actions.) Marbury expected the Federalist-dominated Supreme Court to issue a writ of mandamus ordering the Jeffersonian Republican-controlled executive branch to deliver his commission.

Marbury's request coincided with the radical Jeffersonian attack on the federal judiciary. Marshall certainly appreciated the political exigencies involved, but he was also determined to demonstrate that on matters of constitutional and legal interpretation the Court had an authoritative voice.

The first part of the chief justice's opinion sustained Marbury's claim on the basis that there were certain rights in nature, called vested rights, with which government could not tamper. Marbury had been granted a species of property through his commission and, by law, he was entitled to receive it. The Court, Marshall continued, had the authority to reach such a conclusion because it was obligated under the Constitution to protect rights based in fundamental law. Marshall distinguished between political and other rights, finding that the former was the exclusive domain of the elected branches while the latter, which included Marbury's claim to his commission, was the responsibility of the Court.

What Marshall gave to Marbury in the first part of the decision he took away in the second part. Having stated the basis for judicial review (maintaining fundamental rights), he then found that the Court could not provide a remedy to Marbury. Why? Because, Marshall said, Congress in section 13 had improperly augmented the original jurisdiction of the Supreme Court. The Constitution in Article III stated *fully* what the Court's original jurisdiction was to include, and it did not include issuing writs of mandamus.

Marshall worried that an expansion of the Court's original jurisdiction would thrust the justices into political disputes. The chief justice enunciated the principle that under the doctrine of separation of powers, the justices would not enforce unconstitutional acts of Congress. "It is emphatically the province and duty of the judicial department," he wrote, "to say what the law is. . . . If two laws conflict with each other, the courts must decide on the operation of each."[52] Interpreting law was not synonymous with making it; Marshall saw legal principles as omnipresent and immutable.

Marshall's *Marbury* opinion was important in several ways. First, it fixed the idea of vested rights and made the Court a protector of them. Second, it propounded the same departmental theory of judicial review that the state appellate courts were developing in dealing with state legislatures. Third, it was only one of two instances before the Civil War when the Court did strike down a federal law, the other coming in the famous slave case of *Dred Scott* v. *Sandford* in 1857. The Court was far more active, when unencumbered by the departmental theory, in reviewing state legislative acts that raised a federal constitutional issue or conflicted with a federal law or treaty.

In *Fletcher* v. *Peck* (1810) Marshall affirmed the sanctity of contracts and expanded their meaning to include grants made by state governments to individuals. The *Fletcher* case involved claims to millions of acres of land in the present-day states of Alabama and Mississippi that the Georgia legislature had sold to speculators. Money had greased the skids of legislative action; almost every member of the legislature had been bribed. A subsequent legislature, amid great public fanfare, repealed the original legislation, although by this time the speculators had unloaded most of the land on innocent third parties.

Marshall's opinion in *Fletcher* declared the repeal act in violation of the contract clause of the Constitution. The chief justice also held that states, even though they were sovereign for some purposes, had to abide by their contractual agreements. Marshall supported property rights, a major tenet of Federalist policy, and threw behind them the power of the federal judiciary. The decision was in many ways more important than that in *Marbury,* because the Court demonstrated that through judicial review of state acts it could have a distributive effect on competing national economic interests. Although the Federalists had lost the political battle, John Marshall secured through public law their vision of a growing commercial empire.

The Federal Common Law of Crimes

The Marshall Court proceeded more cautiously with the issue of whether there was a federal common law of crimes. The justices refused to embrace this potentially large source of jurisdiction because they doubted the constitutional bases for doing so and, just as important, they recognized that such jurisdiction would potentially thrust the Court into an overtly political role.

During the 1790s the existence of nonstatutory federal crimes, or common law crimes, was hotly debated. The Judiciary Act of 1789 gave the federal circuit courts jurisdiction over "crimes and offenses cognizable under the authority of the United States."[53] The statute did not specify what those crimes were nor did it indicate the extent of federal authority. Congress in 1790 indeed passed the Crimes Act, defining seventeen crimes ranging from obstruction of legal process to treason, and it also provided for certain procedural safeguards, such as guaranteeing the accused a copy of the indictment brought against him or her. The list of violations was remarkably short, an indication either that Congress wanted to leave the major functions of policing to the states or that it expected federal judges to fill in the vacant spaces.

Federalists supported the idea of a common law of crimes; Republicans objected to it. John Randolph of Roanoke, a leading radical, observed that "if the courts below can at once saddle us with the common law of England, there is no necessity for prohibiting the abridgement of the freedom of speech or press. We know what the common law of England is—an almost . . . unlimited license to punish.''[54] Federalists, on the other hand, thought that the national courts required just such powers, and during the 1790s Federalist judges, with the ironic exception of Justice Samuel Chase, conducted themselves as if they enjoyed such a common law jurisdiction. In 1793, for example, the Federal Circuit Court in Pennsylvania accepted a common law indictment against Gideon Henfield for engaging in acts hostile to the United States by assisting the French in the capture of an English vessel. The jury, however, delivered a verdict of not guilty.

The issue became more clearly drawn in 1797 when Robert Worrall, a businessman, was indicted for having attempted to bribe the U.S. commissioner of the revenue. While Congress had by this time added bribery of federal officers to the Crimes Act of 1790, it did not specifically enumerate among the list of officers the commissioner of the revenue. The English common law, however, made bribery a crime, and the federal prosecutor proceeded against Worrall on that basis. A jury in the Federal Circuit Court of Pennsylvania found Worrall guilty, but his counsel, Alexander J. Dallas, immediately moved to prevent judgment on the basis that the court had no jurisdiction to decide the case. Dallas argued, among other things, that the public expected that all prosecutions in federal courts had to rest on statutes. He also claimed that "the nature of our Federal compact will not . . . tolerate this doctrine.''[55] The federal government, by virtue of the Tenth Amendment, which had reserved to the states all powers not given to the federal government, was one of limited, enumerated, and delegated powers. The federal courts, Dallas asserted, could only act on the basis of a specific statute that made bribery of the commissioner of the revenue a crime.

The judges in the *Worrall* case, Chase and Richard Peters, divided. Chase agreed with the defense counsel; Peters took the side of the government. Chase concluded that the federal government, unlike the states, had not brought the common law from England, because neither the Constitution nor a federal statute had adopted it. Peters, on the other hand, concluded that the provision in the Judiciary Act of 1789 giving federal circuit courts jurisdiction over "all crimes and offences cognizable under the authority of the United States" had done precisely that. The split between the judges offered the possibility of appealing the case to the Supreme Court, but Worrall refused, and he was sentenced to three months' imprisonment and a $200 fine.

The Supreme Court did eventually get the opportunity to decide on the constitutional basis of a federal common law of crimes in *United States* v. *Hudson and Goodwin* (1812). The case involved an indictment for libel brought against the *Connecticut Courant* for an article it had published in May 1806 that accused President Jefferson and Congress with conspiring to pay Napoleon Bonaparte $2 million to make possible the acquisition of the Louisiana Purchase. Republicans, on the eve of the War of 1812, were just as susceptible to turning to the federal courts to silence political opponents as the Federalist had been earlier.

The Supreme Court, however, rejected conclusively the idea of a federal common law of crimes. Justice William Johnson, a Jeffersonian appointee, held that it had "long since been settled in public opinion" that there was no federal common law jurisdiction.[56] The decision meant that, in the absence of a legislative act, the federal courts were without power to hear and punish criminal violations. The decision reiterated the will theory of law and reaffirmed the principle that individual liberty required strict control of judicial discretion. It also made clear that the states would retain their extensive police powers unfettered by a competing federal common law jurisdiction over crimes.

The Legal System

By 1815 the moderate Jeffersonian Republican point of view about the relationship of law to politics, state to nation, and commerce to agriculture had triumphed. The moderates had found a middle ground in the struggle between Federalists and radical Jeffersonians in implementing the broad principles and institutions crafted by the framers in Philadelphia. The notion that republican government spread over a large geographic area could also tolerate opposition grew more slowly, and both Federalists and Jeffersonian Republicans harbored genuine suspicions about each other's motives. But the moderate triumph carried with it the idea that opposition to government was legitimate and that conflicts over public policy would be settled through legal *as well as* political processes. The law became an extension of political discourse, a development that the French visitor to the United States, Alexis de Tocqueville, captured in the observation that "scarcely any political question arises in the United States that is not resolved, sooner or later, into a judicial question."[57]

Moderates created from the spare language of national and state constitutions a truly hybrid legal system. That system incorporated both elite and democratic impulses; it was decentralized yet hierarchically ordered. It emphasized the Enlightenment's rationality and American capitalism's quest for stable economic arrangements based on uniform and certain laws. The moderates' legal reforms "democratized business enterprise, . . . for in the years immediately following independence most people generally believed that business enterprise and democracy were incompatible."[58] The judiciary won its independence, but it was to be responsive but not directly accountable to the people. So, too, the new system depended on lawyers and judges— the trained technicians of the law—rather than on either a formal legislative codification of the common law or informal schemes of conciliation and arbitration among laymen that the radicals touted.

The "new order for the ages" had a decidedly state-centered cast. The moderate resolution of the conflict between law and politics left substantial discretion to local juries, but it also envisioned state appellate courts with great authority to interpret the substantive common law and state legislatures in full possession of their police powers (powers to provide for health, safety, morals, and welfare). The moderate triumph fixed the most critical decisions about the allocation of economic resources and social policy before the Civil War in the states. The federal courts, with their jurisdictional wings clipped, held at best a limited check over the states' authority. The federal Supreme Court had demonstrated the importance of judicial review, but the heyday of federal judicial and legislative authority lay in the future. State judges and legislators orchestrated the creative explosion in the law that came after the Jeffersonian crisis and before the Civil War.

5

The Active State and the Mixed Economy: 1789–1861

Distributive Justice

Americans achieved with independence one of the crucial goals of the Revolution: control over their economic destinies. They exploited their new economic opportunities with a vengeance. In the late eighteenth century, Hector St. John de Crevecouer, in *Letters from an American Farmer,* reported that the aim of "industrious" farmers was to produce enough goods "to sell" rather than on which to subsist.[1] Americans did not want to get by, they wanted to get ahead. Alexis de Tocqueville in the 1830s observed that the quest for "profit" had become "the characteristic that most distinguished the American people from all others."[2] Seemingly, Adam Smith, the great English economist who wrote *Wealth of Nations* (1776), had prepared the script: the invisible hand of individual material gain would guide the collective economic progress of the new nation.

The profit motive flourished amid the abundant resources of a virgin continent. Small towns and rural life characterized America in the seventy years before the Civil War, but the signs of economic transformation dotted the landscape. Smoke belched from locomotives and steamships, the great technological wonders of the mid-nineteenth century. The personal, informal, and local dealings that typified the colonial economy gave way to an increasingly impersonal national and international commercial market economy based on regional specialization.

Markets are places where sustained patterns of private trading for profit occur. During the antebellum years they expanded dramatically. It was as if someone had pulled the east coast up and tilted it toward the Pacific, spilling people across a continent. One of every two and one-half persons lived west of the Appalachian Mountains when the first shot was fired at Fort Sumter. Existing population centers became denser, swelled by immigration and a high birthrate. New York City contained one million inhabitants on the eve of the great conflict and Philadelphia almost as many. The foreign export and domestic markets expanded sharply, providing cotton planters in the slave South, commercial and manufacturing interests in the Northeast, and food producers in the Midwest with great opportunities. By 1850 for the first time in American history, the value of manufactured goods surpassed that of agricultural production.

This transformation of the economy was based on trading among private individuals for profit. Privatization of economic decision making was one of the most important features of the antebellum marketplace. The market was not the creation of law; it was the product of actions taken by merchants, bankers, lenders and borrowers, and farmers and planters. Privatization meant that the distribution of economic rights flowed from agreements reached among private individuals rather than from the command of government, either federal or state. Privatization perfectly fitted republican theory. The history of the British empire had taught Americans that unrestricted governmental power threatened economic liberty. The enhancement of private economic bargaining was a necessary check on governmental authority. "A wise and frugal Government," proclaimed Thomas Jefferson at his first inaugural in 1801, "which shall restrain men from injuring one another, shall leave them otherwise free to regulate their own pursuit of industry and improvement."[3]

Economic development harmonized as well with another theme of republican theory, the idea of the public interest. Antebellum Americans did not embrace "a dogmatic laissez-faire faith."[4] This term means to "let alone," and it is usually invoked to describe an open or free-market economic system, like the one envisioned by Smith in *Wealth of Nations* (1776), in which the impersonal forces of supply and demand operate unrestrained by government. The idea of mixed economic activity, however, in which government intervenes in the private marketplace to serve the public good, better captures the law's impact on the antebellum economy than does strict laissez-faire.

Congress and state legislatures enacted statutes either to promote or to regulate the marketplace. In legislative bodies, decisions about economic issues are political matters; indeed the rise in the 1830s of the nation's first mass two-party system, composed of Jacksonian Democrats and Whigs, partly stemmed from contending views about the economy. These political parties emerged as devises that could be used (among other things) to consolidate majorities in state legislatures and Congress capable of shaping public policies to the social interests with which those parties were identified. The notions of deference and social consensus that had dominated the earlier political culture disappeared.

The critical question about law in the antebellum economy (and for that matter in American economic history generally) is not whether lawmakers intervened in the marketplace, because they did. Rather, the issue is one of distributive justice. This concept means the way in which legislative and judicial bodies allocated through law the costs, benefits, and risks of economic growth. Assessing distributive justice is difficult because it occurred within a federal system, across a continent with a moving frontier, and through both legislative and judicial bodies. In this chapter we examine the contributions of positive law—statutes enacted by legislatures—to the antebellum mixed economy; the next chapter will devote attention to the common law—judge-made law—and judicial interpretation of statutes.

Positive Law and Mixed Economic Enterprise in the Federal System

The history of law in the United States is the history of legal institutions broadly conceived. Congress and state legislatures were the most important "lawmakers" of the nineteenth century.[5] They distributed economic justice through positive laws that promoted and regulated the marketplace. Federalism gave differing scope to their actions, with the states intervening more frequently and forcefully than Congress. In neither instance did the level of promotion or regulation match the depth of governmental involvement that has come to characterize the administrative state in the late-twentieth-century United States. Legislative decisions were political decisions, made with a view to serve the "rights of the public."[6] This concept meant that the commonwealth, the public as a whole, had certain rights that had to be placed above private self-interest. In legislative bodies, partisanship, sectionalism, and intrastate regional rivalries defined the public interest. Following a burst of activity in the first part of the century, legislative promotion and regulation waned. It was the victim of its own initial enthusiasm, of political stalemate in Congress, and of charges that state legislatures had unevenly distributed economic justice. The populist and antigovernmental stirrings of the late 1840s and 1850s climaxed in an outburst of constitutional reform that diminished legislative power.

Congress and the Promotion and Regulation of Enterprise

Congress displayed an early enthusiasm for intervening in the private marketplace. Federalist Secretary of the Treasury Alexander Hamilton persuaded Congress during the 1790s to adopt a program that favored commercial and manufacturing interests. It included funding the federal and assuming the state Revolutionary War debts in order to improve the credit rating, passing taxes and tariffs to pay the debt and protect infant domestic industries, and chartering a national bank to stabilize the currency. After the election of 1800, all but the most radical southern states' rights wing of the Jeffersonian Republican party embraced the main features of the Hamiltonian program. Jefferson ordered the planning of the National Road, the nation's first involvement with a large-scale internal improvement. Subsequently, James Madison approved bills establishing the Second Bank of the United States and the Tariff of 1816, James Monroe signed a measure authorizing Congress to subscribe $300,000 to the stock of the Chesapeake and Delaware Canal Company, and John Quincy Adams secured grants of land for canals to be built in Illinois and Indiana while signing other legislation that pleged financial involvement of the federal government in the Louisville and Portland Canal, the Dismal Swamp Canal, and the Chesapeake and Ohio Canal.

Congress used the law as an instrument to promote private economic enterprise. A strong sense of public purpose influenced these actions. The federal government's promotion of private enterprise, either by creating conditions that encouraged commercial and manufacturing activity or by directing subsidies to transportation improvements, was intended to serve all of the people. These congressional policies created the foundation upon which a national commercial market in agricultural goods and manufactured items grew.

These national economic initiatives did not benefit everyone equally. Congress in the Indian Removal Act of 1832, for example, displaced thousands of native Americans from their ancestral lands in the Southeast to poorer lands in the Indian Territory of present-day Arkansas and Oklahoma. Their "trail of tears" was a lawfully mandated policy designed to open the Indians' former lands to what the whites considered more profitable forms of farming and planting.

Other congressional policies stirred controversy within the white community along sectional and class lines. What was wanted in the West was not always best for the East; what served the interests of manufacturers did not necessarily benefit small farmers and laborers. After 1820 a higher tariff on imported manufactured goods to many southerners meant only that they were footing the bill to construct canals and roads over the Appalachian Mountains. Moreover, as John Randolph observed during a debate in Congress over internal improvements during the 1820s, "If Congress possesses the power to do what is proposed in this bill they may emancipate every slave in the United States."[7]

Sectional conflict formed the political fault lines that disrupted the lawmaking role of Congress. The most dramatic evidence of sectional tension over federal economic policy surfaced in the Nullification Crisis of 1832, when a South Carolina convention adopted an ordinance declaring null and void a federal tariff. The nullifiers were motivated as much by fear about the disruption of the institution of slavery, whose fate they believed was tied to the strength of their economy, as by the direct economic effects of the tariff. Throughout the antebellum years the specter of slavery was always near the surface of the debate about the national economy. President Andrew Jackson reacted forcefully to the Nullification Crisis, denouncing the theory of secession it embraced and forcing the nullifiers to retreat.

During the 1830s charges also began to appear that the promotional role of Congress abetted class distinctions. The Democratic party of Andrew Jackson challenged the doctrine of vested rights, claiming that Congress had inequitably distributed the benefits and costs of promoting economic growth by granting special privileges, sometimes in the form of monopolies, that enabled a few entrepreneurs with existing capital to grow rich at the expense of less well-capitalized but equally ambitious men-on-the-make. At the same time, the Whig party, led by Senator Henry Clay of Kentucky, insisted that the federal government had to encourage well-capitalized entrepreneurs to take risks. Clay told his colleagues in Congress that there was little choice. Capitalists, he insisted, "must be patronized, by the general government," or internal improvements "so necessary to the public good . . . never could be accomplished."[8] The combined fate of the Second Bank of the United States, the tariff, public land policy, and patents for new inventions reveals how the Jacksonian Democrats, through political control of the national government, gradually reduced the direct promotional role of Congress in the economy.

Banking was an economically important and politically controversial business. State banks provided the antebellum economy with bank notes as its principal medium of exchange and bank loans as its most important source of credit. The first supported the second. The more notes a bank could issue, the more loans it could make. The worth of the notes, however, depended on the value of the gold and silver specie held in the bank. If a bank's notes got too far out of proportion to its specie reserves, the public ceased to trust the specie as currency, they depreciated in value, and business transactions occurring in distant markets suffered from the attendant uncertainty.

When Congress in 1816 chartered the Second Bank of the United States, it fashioned a classic model of mixed economic enterprise. Congress capitalized it at $35 million, of which the government put up $5 million. Its twenty-five directors included five public members appointed by the president.

Congress blended promotional and regulatory goals in the bank. The bank and its several branches served as a repository for the federal government, and federal funds, along with those invested by foreign countries, provided the basis on which it could issue its own notes. The bank stabilized the currency by refusing to accept weak state bank notes in payment of debts owed to it, forcing the state banks to act more cautiously.

Perceptions of the bank's usefulness depended on a person's economic position. Debtors and speculators charged incorrectly that the bank was nothing more than a "monster" that kept money tight and then foreclosed when payment became impossible. Senator Thomas Hart Benton of Missouri made the case for western farmers against the bank, which had its headquarters in Philadelphia. "All the flourishing cities of the West," Benton roared in Congress, "are mortgaged to this money power, they are in the jaws of a monster! A lump of butter in the mouth of a dog! One gulp, one swallow, and all is gone!"[9] The bank enjoyed support among creditors, who expected future payment in undepreciated currency, and merchants and manufacturers, who depended on a stable currency.

When the charter of the Second Bank of the United States came up for renewal in 1832, a political storm ensued with lasting consequences for the promotional role of Congress. "The Bank is trying to kill me," Andrew Jackson proclaimed, "*but I will kill it.*"[10] And so he did. When Congress sent a bill rechartering the bank to the president, he vetoed it. Jackson rejected the legislation on several grounds, claiming, for example, that Congress had no authority to pass such legislation and that the Supreme Court, in the case of *McCulloch* v. *Maryland* (1819), had ruled incorrectly when it held that Congress did have such power under the "necessary and proper" clause of the Constitution. Jackson and his Democratic followers rejected as well the idea that Congress through its lawmaking power should attempt to serve the public interest by serving special interests. "There are no necessary evils in government," Jackson informed the Congress. "Its evils exist only in its abuses. If it would confine itself to equal protection, and, as Heaven does its rains, shower its favors alike on the high and the low, the rich and the poor, it would be an unqualified blessing."[11]

Andrew Jackson did not try to set himself above the rule of law, and his vision of distributive justice left an important role for the states. He argued that he too had the constitutional right to chart the course of economic development. Jackson understood that banking was crucial to the economy, and throughout his second term he supervised the removal of the federal deposits to state banks, many of which his partisans controlled. The battle over the Second Bank of the United States eventually took its toll, however; throughout the remainder of the antebellum period the promotion and regulation of banking was an exclusively state function. Decisions about distributive economic justice gravitated to the state legislatures. Initially the benefits weighed on the side of speculators, debtors, and stockjobbers, but the costs of laissez-faire became apparent in the Panic of 1837. It burst the speculative bubble in paper money that the national bank's death had encouraged, in many instances ruining the small businessmen and farmers that Jackson had professedly hoped to aid. The states never filled the regulatory void.

The Democratic party's disdain for granting special privileges to encourage economic development also shaped early patent law. The Constitution, in Article I, section 8, gave Congress power "to promote the progress of science and useful arts, securing for limited times to authors and inventors the exclusive right to their respective writings and discoveries."[12] Justice Joseph Story in an 1825 case in a federal circuit court had enunciated what became the Whig position, when he held that an inventor had only to demonstrate that an object was "new," rather than a work of "genius," in order to receive a patent.[13] Democrats believed that such a doctrine encouraged monopoly, and in the Patent Office Act of 1836 they tightened the requirements necessary for obtaining a patent, providing that one would only be issued when the applicant could prove that it was "useful and important" and had not been previously "invented or discovered."[14] Democrats concluded "that the disincentive costs of monopoly could well outweigh the incentive benefits of patents."[15]

The Democratic party retained political control of the national government for the remainder of the years before the Civil War, and the policies it pursued diminished the promotional role of Congress. Conflicting economic interests expressed through political parties gave Congress little opportunity to exert full national authority, and the divisiveness of sectionalism merely added to governmental inertia. The federal tariff, for example, held the promise both to protect domestic manufacturers and to raise revenues, but a partisan consensus was possible only on the second of these. Southerners, who consumed large amounts of manufactured goods, claimed that they were discriminated against. New Englanders, on the other hand, approved the tariff, although the evidence suggests that it was probably more important to the textile industry than to any other business in the section. Political leaders in both sections, however, did accept the redistributive consequences of the tariff as a revenue measure, because the collections by it maintained the nation's credit worthiness, making the United States an attractive place for the investment of foreign capital. What government had done was to "tax one group of people (chiefly, buyers of imported goods) . . . for the immediate benefit of a smaller group of people (securities holders [and investors])."[16]

Public land policy was similarly hamstrung. The public domain was the federal government's single most important asset, and the use of it had important social and economic consequences. For example, Congress under the Articles of Confederation had passed the Northwest Ordinance of 1787, which set terms for the purchase of lands from the national government and promoted the advancement of education by requiring that one section in each county be set aside for a common school. But as the domain of the United States expanded thereafter, partisan and sectional wrangling in Congress contributed to a confused public land policy that benefited speculators able to purchase lands rather than settlers who were able to invest only sweat equity in return for developed land. Manufacturing interests in the Northeast initially resisted any liberal land policy for fear that easy terms of settlement would mean a loss of labor and consequently higher wages. Southerners, too, disapproved of easy terms, because any revenues not raised through the sale of public lands would have to come through a higher tariff. They also realized that a force of free white farmers in the West, where slavery would have a difficult time flourishing, would be hostile to the peculiar institution.

Partisan and sectional contention did not stop the rush westward, however; each spurt in the price of agricultural commodities produced a surge of westward migrants. But it did mean that would-be settlers had either to buy their land from speculators or simply to squat on it in the hope that the federal government would eventually recognize their ownership. Congress gradually did make the terms of purchase easier, but the South blocked homestead legislation that would have given lands to settlers who had lived on and improved them.

Congress and Regulation: The Steamboat

While partisan and sectional tensions gradually stalemated the promotional role of the national government, Congress before the Civil War "never assumed an extensive regulatory role."[17] Unlike the British empire, the new Constitution created a government that stressed promotion and distribution of grants and that encouraged mixed economic enterprise rather than strict regulation of individual economic conduct. Its most difficult tasks were the collection of small revenues generated by the tariff and excise taxes. Congress regularly deferred to local and state control in most matters, refusing, for example, despite repeated pleas from local authorities, to pass federal quarantine laws to stop the spread of cholera. In the case of steamboating, however, the social costs of technological innovation became so great that national regulation became essential. Congress's actions provided a glimpse of a future in which federal lawmakers would become unwilling to leave the distribution of the social costs of enterprise exclusively in private hands.

The steam boiler revolutionized the market economy of the United States by contributing directly to the "transportation revolution."[18] First on steamboats and later on railroads, Americans put the scientific advances in boiler construction to the quiet practical goal of turning a profit. The new technology was far from perfect, and the builders and operators of it were sometimes less than competent. The result was death and suffering among passengers and crews of riverboats where most of the boiler explosions occurred prior to the Civil War. In 1838 alone, for example, at least 496 lives were lost as a result of steamboat explosions, a number that exceeded on an absolute and per capita basis losses in similar accidents in England and France where government regulated the new technology.

Congress in that year attempted to deal with the problem, but Democrats would only agree to weak legislation that did nothing to halt the slaughter. In 1850 and 1851 alone some 764 persons died in boiler explosions aboard steamboats. Even confronted with these staggering numbers, some Democrats were reluctant to act. "A man's property," proclaimed Senator Robert Stockton of New Jersey in opposition to an 1852 bill to regulate steamboats, "cannot be said to be his own, when you take it out of his control and put it into the hands of a Federal Officer."[19] The magnitude of the crisis had become sufficiently great that bipartisan and bisectional sentiment grew in favor of placing the rights of the public above private profit. "I consider that the only question involved," argued another Democratic senator in reply to Stockton, "is this: Whether we shall permit a legalized, unquestioned, and peculiar class in the community to go on committing murder at will, or whether we shall make such enactments as will compel them to pay some attention to the value of life."[20]

Congress in 1852 passed the nation's first major regulatory act. It governed the operation of steamboats, set standards for boiler construction, and established boards to inspect, license, and investigate steamboat operators. It also contributed to a dramatic decline in steamboat accidents.

The 1852 act was a straw in the wind rather than the harbinger of a vast new role for Congress. The trend before the Civil War was for economic promotion and regulation to devolve to the states. The Democratic majority subscribed to a policy of limited national government, and conflicting sectional class attitudes contributed to a political stalemate in Congress that made privatization and decentralization major themes in public policy. When Congress did act it usually did so in ways that fulfilled the existing constitutional mandate to enhance commercial relations, and to this extent business interests and persons holding capital probably fared better than laborers and farmers. The pattern was hardly clear. These latter groups may well have benefited, as Andrew Jackson and his Democratic followers proclaimed, as much by federal inaction as they would have by action. Still, there is no doubt that, while it could have done more, Congress did facilitate the rise of a national market economy. Only, however, after the southern states seceded in 1861 did the new Republican party have a sufficiently commanding voice in Congress that it could orchestrate a public policy that re-energized federal promotion and regulation of the private marketplace.

State Promotion and Regulation of the Antebellum Economy

As in Congress and in the state legislatures, the popular foundations of political power guided mixed economic activity. Parties contended over state intervention in the economy with as much if not greater vigor than on the national level. The pattern of events in the states was much like that in Congress: a burst of legislative activity early in the nineteenth century followed by a decline in the wake of the Panic of 1837. Intrastate rivalries generated competing demands on each state's limited resources for legislative support of economic development. When some of these mixed economic schemes collapsed, the Democrats, who had themselves argued in favor of many of the programs, seized on the political possibilities presented by a disillusioned public to slap restrictions on legislative authority. Throughout, the Democrats charged that active government favored the few at the expense of the many.

Each legislature enacted its own distinctive promotional and regulatory statutes. The division between what was a regulatory and a promotional measure blurred, in part because the scope of these activities was much broader in the states than at the federal level. As well, in the 1840s and 1850s, the states admitted to the Union in the area west of the Mississippi had frontier economies, while those in the settled East were entering a period of mature economic development.

Even though the laws governing each state's mixed economy were unique, general patterns did appear. Of these, one of the most important was the singularly American vision of the state as a "commonwealth." The commonwealth idea "was essentially a quasi-merchantilist concept of the state within a democratic framework."[21] The state existed to ensure that the "rights of the public" took precedence over any individual or group interest. The commonwealth idea fitted well with federalism, because it left the states, as sovereign entities based on their own organic laws, to act directly on the citizenry. The federal Constitution reserved to the states the police powers to provide for the health, safety, morals, and welfare of their citizens. The dominant partisan majorities in the state legislatures invoked these powers both to regulate and to promote private bargaining on a scale far more intense than anything undertaken by Congress.

Regulation and Promotion

Regulatory legislation was one of the most important ways in which legislatures breathed life into the commonwealth idea. They enacted a veritable blizzard of economic regulations under the guise of enhancing the rights of the public. Most of this legislation involved low-level economic relationships, much as had been the case in the colonies. The Georgia legislature in 1791, for example, enacted a law that stipulated the proper packaging of tobacco in "hogsheads or casks"; the Massachusetts General Court (that state's legislature) in 1833 specified that "pure spermaceti oil" could only be sold under the names "sperm, spermaceti, lamp, summer, fall, winter and second winter oils."[22] In both states, failure to comply was punishable by a fine.

Every state had laws regulating the sale of food products, setting standards for the conduct of peddlers and vendors, and directing manufacturers to include the name and place of manufacture. These measures had two major purposes. First, they were mercantilist. That is, they guaranteed the quality of goods produced within the state, making that state's economy competitive with every other state in the national marketplace. Second, such measures also provided a modicum of protection to consumers against fraudulent commercial practices. Much nineteenth-century regulation, therefore, while driven by an economic purpose, also carried forward from the colonial era an ethical commitment to fair dealing.

State legislatures were much better at passing regulatory measures than they were at funding the expenses of enforcement. Ensuring compliance with regulation of low-level economic activities was left almost completely to private initiative, another example of the privatization of economic decision making. Ferry operators in New York during the years before the Civil War were required by statute to maintain a record of the tolls they charged and collected, but only when a private citizen complained were the records checked.

Where the scope of regulation involved higher level economic activities such as banking, railroads, and insurance companies, the legislature devised commissions. Ohio, for example, established a canal commission in 1831 to oversee the building and operations of the state's most expensive internal improvements. It had limited enforcement powers and its actions were, in every case, always subject to second-guessing by the General Assembly, which most often responded to constituent concerns about tolls and the location of new canals instead of abstract matters of economic efficiency. Legislative interference in Ohio and elsewhere was constant but almost always ad hoc and based on investigations that came after the fact.

These antebellum state commissions relied on persuasion to accomplish their duties, hardly a sufficient means to meet the challenges of expanding corporate enterprises, such as the railroads. Rhode Island in 1839 established the nation's first railroad commission, and legislatures in the New England states, where the commonwealth idea was particularly strong, embraced regulatory commissions more quickly than any other section of the nation. As with steamboats on the national level, concerns about safety motivated state legislatures. Connecticut, for example, established a commission that in the 1850s had the right to inspect the physical equipment of the railroads and to recommend needed repairs, although it had no power to fix rates or suspend service. Furthermore, the railroads (in a pattern that held through the remainder of the nineteenth century) were themselves influential, controlling both the commissions intended to regulate them and the state legislatures. In perhaps the most flagrant example, the railroads in New York bought off the commissioners, who in 1857, after only two years of existence, persuaded the legislature to abolish their offices.

Promotion was the most important mixed economic activity undertaken by state legislatures. They increased grants of aid to private enterprise, transforming government's primary responsibility from one of ensuring the maintenance of uniform standards of moral and economic behavior to one of allocating valuable resources among contending social interests. These initiatives came in all shapes and sizes. Vermont, for example, granted tax exemptions to local manufacturers between 1812 and 1830. New York in 1817 excluded textile workers from jury duty and militia service. Other states offered land grants and bounties, or they sponsored agricultural and industrial fairs.

The states fell along a spectrum in their promotional endeavors. The formation of public policy in some states, such as Wisconsin, was characterized by "drift and default."[23] In Wisconsin and other "frontier" states during the antebellum years, government was "underdeveloped," lacking the resources, personnel, and expertise necessary to evaluate fully the proper direction of the public interest. There was a broad consensus that the market should be allowed to function through private decision making aimed at encouraging economic development. In other states, however, a public enterprise model prevailed. The legislatures of New York, Ohio, and Pennsylvania adopted comprehensive plans for public construction of transport facilities, and established the rudiments of bureaucratic administration, through commissions and boards, to oversee these programs. In still other states, especially in the South, these styles of "drift and default" and "public enterprise" blended together.

Within this "moving kaleidoscope" there were nonetheless trends in the development of positive law that channeled the distribution of the costs, benefits, and risks of economic development.[24] The most important of these involved corporations, the power of eminent domain, and debtor-creditor relations.

Corporations

A corporation is an artificial person created under the laws of a state for either a public or a private purpose. All corporations are public in the sense that the authority of the state creates them, but some, such as the business corporation, exist to promote the private wealth of its members, while others, such as transportation companies, fulfill a public service. Depending on the terms of its charter, a corporation may exist for a specified number of years or in perpetuity, and it does so irrespective of changes in number or composition of its members. During the antebellum period the corporation assumed its modern form, although its greatest growth and legal development occurred in the late nineteenth and early twentieth centuries as industrial America matured.

The first American corporations were charities, municipalities, and even churches. Some early corporations were deemed public even when they were engaged in activities that we might consider private today. For example, the colony of New York in 1735 passed separate acts making the owners of wharves, water-powered mills, internal improvements, and community service enterprises public corporations. Although colonial governors enjoyed some authority, to charter corporations (as had the king in England), the practice developed in the new states after the Revolution that only state legislatures, as the repository of the will of the people, could create corporations.

Most of the corporations chartered from 1789 to 1861 engaged in improving public transportation, followed by banking, insurance, and manufacturing which comprised most of the rest; of these, only manufacturing concerns were treated as private. The others were known as franchise corporations. A franchise corporation was granted a special privilege—for example, in return for providing a valuable public service, collecting tolls or issuing circulating bank notes as a medium of exchange. These corporations were expected to follow provisions in their charters treating matters of public interest, such as the amount of tolls and the liability of shareholders. Franchise and benevolent corporations were viewed as having equal social utility. A turnpike and a church building "were both visible and useful public improvements and all communities needed them."[25]

State involvement with franchise corporations was often extensive. For example, when the Pennsylvania legislature chartered the First Bank of Pennsylvania in 1793, it subscribed one-third of the capital stock. The State Bank of South Carolina was designated the fiscal agent of the state, making loans to further economic development based on revenues paid into the state coffers.

The monopoly privileges granted by state legislatures to early national franchise corporations also had antidevelopmental consequences that stirred political controversy and fomented competing claims by business competitors. The successful application of new technology required that old grants of corporate monopoly had to give way. Yet the original incorporators, who had assumed a risk premised on future exclusive control, claimed that they had what amounted to a vested right. The doctrine of vested rights held that there existed certain rights (the guarantee to property and life, for example) that so completely accrued to a person that they could not be arbitrarily disturbed, either by another private person or by government.

The role of the Massachusetts General Court (that state's legislature) in encouraging bridge building over the Charles River illustrates the way in which corporate monopoly rights collided with the rights of the public to the benefits of improved technology. The General Court in 1785 granted a charter to the Charles River Bridge Company to operate a toll bridge between Charlestown and Boston. Then in 1827 the state legislature, amid demands for cheaper and easier means to cross the Charles River, granted another charter to the Warren Bridge Company with the proviso that as soon as the costs of construction were paid the bridge would become free. The Warren Bridge incorporated several new design and engineering techniques that facilitated the flow of traffic between the two cities. The proprietors of the Charles River Bridge claimed that the legislature lacked the authority to grant a charter to a rival bridge company that would reduce significantly the value of their investment. The U.S. Supreme Court in 1837 settled the controversy, finding that the right of the legislature to provide for a new bridge outweighed the claim of the original bridge incorporators.

The private corporation also emerged as a device by which to stimulate and organize economic activity. Throughout the antebellum period, however, the partnership, in which individuals contracted with one another to arrange their business affairs, was the preferred method of private entrepreneurial organization. The corporation was "not indispensable to the growth of market activity."[26] Still, the corporate form gained some acceptance because it offered several distinct advantages: helping protect collective ownership of real property, facilitating the mobilization of capital, offering a means of limiting risks in speculative enterprises, and allowing easy access to courts.

Antebellum state legislatures evolved a substantive body of rules dealing with private corporations. The two in particular that were important were limited liability and general incorporation.

Until about 1820, charters for most private corporations were founded on the principle of unlimited liability. Each shareholder was responsible for all of the debts of the corporation should it go bankrupt. An ethical principle lay behind the rule. Persons who engaged in business activity for profit were morally responsible to compensate their creditors completely. Many state governments by the 1820s recognized that unlimited liability posed a daunting impediment to the accumulation of capital necessary to meet growing business demands. Legislators, therefore, began to enact corporate charters that specified limited liability, a rule that proved the single greatest lure to would-be investors. Shareholders were liable for the corporation's debt only in proportion to the amount of the stock they owned. Limited liability made the corporate form a device by which individuals could pursue profit far in excess of the amount of their investment without fear that, should the venture fail, they would be held responsible for all of its debts. State legislatures crafted a public policy that encouraged people to enhance their economic well-being—and that of the state as well—by offering them a known limited risk that could be measured against their own resources.

State legislators also made the formation of corporations easier. This entailed a movement from special to general charters. As long as the pace of business activity remained low, state legislatures could accept petitions and act on them in an orderly fashion. Under the special charter scheme each corporation had its own charter. The rapid growth in the market in the 1820s and 1830s made this system unwieldy. As economic rivalry among the states increased, the most competitive states were those that offered a cheap legal means of encouraging participation by their citizens in the growing market.

Special charters for private business corporations also stirred claims of legislative manipulation, favoritism, bribery, and corruption. People able to win special charters were viewed as the beneficiaries of political access to the legislature that the average person could not command. Just as Jacksonian Democrats blasted the Second Bank of the United States, so they claimed that state legislatures had engaged in similar monopolistic practices in granting special charters. "If corporate powers are necessary," the *Racine* [Wisconsin] *Advocate* proclaimed in 1848, "let them be made as limited as possible in extent, and as available as possible to all. Let general incorporation laws alone be passed, even for villages and cities, so that . . . all may avail themselves of them."[27]

Every state adopted general incorporation laws. These acts made the advantages of incorporation available to all people. The New York legislature in 1811 passed the first general incorporation law for manufacturing businesses, and the practice spread with great rapidity during the 1830s and 1840s. These laws standardized the means of obtaining a charter and doing corporate business, and they added continuity and predictability to corporate affairs. The measures specified standard practices, such as proxy voting, the duration of corporate life, modes and times of meetings, and the extent of liability. In most states, either by legislative act or constitutional provision, the actual responsibility for distributing the charters was given to an executive officer, usually the secretary of state.

The adoption of general incorporation laws proceeded from several assumptions. First, they equalized the opportunity to secure the legal advantages of incorporation while encouraging economic growth through private dealings. Second, general incorporation laws democratized entrepreneurship during the early stages of industrial growth. Third, these laws "also equalized the opportunity for different sections of [a] state to undertake local improvement projects with their own resources without having to bargain politically for the privilege."[28]

General incorporation laws were evidence of the laissez-faire thread that ran through the antebellum economy. State legislatures were left with little direct control over the formation and conduct of private corporations, although they continued to regulate various aspects of franchise corporations through commissions and charter provisions.

State involvement was nonetheless important. Most charters of incorporation before the Civil War were special, not general. In theory, special charters were only to be used when the object of the corporation could not be realized under the general laws. In operation, many people in business went to the legislature with the hope of gaining through a special charter some advantage that the standardized working of the general incorporation statutes could not provide. Most of these special provisions reveal that there were few instances of sinister private gain at the expense of the public welfare. Rather, legislatures used them as bargaining chips, giving new corporations certain benefits but exacting from them limitations on corporate life, on landholdings of the corporations, and on its capital. Distrust of corporations was great, although it was certainly true as well that access to legislative authority was an undoubted benefit throughout the antebellum period, and most legislatures expended considerable energy and time dealing with the unending round of jockeying by various corporations.

Antebellum state legislatures relied on the corporate form to organize and discipline credit, transportation, and manufacturing businesses. Corporate statutes yielded great private and social profits by promoting the rapid expansion of regional markets and by forging the infrastructure of a truly national market. But political pressures democratized corporate business opportunities with only minimal provisions for regulation. The democratic model that evolved from 1830 to 1860 assumed a competitive marketplace. When business consolidation began after the Civil War, the old forms of corporate law and the narrow regulatory base created to oversee them simply were inadequate to the needs of an industrial economy experiencing rapid business consolidation.

Eminent Domain

A turnpike, canal, or railroad corporation traversed property owned by private individuals. In doing so they exhibited one of the fundamental changes in thinking about property: its value derived from wealth that could be created by using it rather than the social status that accrued from its mere possession. This dynamic view of property was especially important in the case of franchise corporations whose activities were justified because they served the public interest. The idea of vested property rights collided with the commonwealth notion that state government had to take an active role in promoting the rights of the public. Antebellum legislatures attempted to balance these tensions of security in property and the public's right to economic growth through eminent domain law.

Eminent domain means the power of government to take private property for a public purpose, subject to reasonable compensation. It emerged only after the Revolution, and in the new republican nation it was a power to be jealously guarded. The colonial practice had been to seize property with compensation provided at the discretion of the legislature. The notion that the public had certain rights that exceeded those of individual property holders was widely accepted, and the framers of the Constitution in the Fifth Amendment added the doctrine of just compensation, although only by the 1830s did this provision become a familiar part of state public law.

The major developments in the antebellum law of eminent domain came through the actions of courts, but state legislatures played an important part in two ways. First, they established through statutes the basis on which the eminent domain power could be exercised. Second, they gradually granted this power through special charters to franchise corporations, such as canals and railroads, as a means of subsidizing their expansion.

The Milldam Acts were the earliest examples of state legislatures interfering through their police powers with vested property rights. Falling water was crucial to both agriculture and nascent manufacturing because it provided the energy by which to turn a turbine to mill grain or spin cotton into cloth. As late as 1870, falling water generated about one-half of the power for American industry.

Beginning in the late 1790s, state legislatures enacted statutes that allowed a mill operator to flood land that he did not own. They designated mills as quasi-public businesses that the state had an interest in promoting. Legislatures reversed the common law rule that flooding the land of a neighbor created an injury and that the dam itself was a nuisance. Most acts granted to affected property owners a right to sue, but only for statutory damages (those damages specified in the statute). If a landowner adjacent to a mill incurred a loss greater than the statute covered, he had no basis on which to seek additional damages. The Milldam Acts not only granted a special privilege to a few persons to operate mills, but they fixed for them the costs of a significant risk.

The Milldam Acts introduced the basic features of public expropriations for public purposes into U.S. law. State legislatures elaborated on the practice by permitting franchise corporations to exercise the power. They did so for practical reasons. The corporations were better suited to make efficient economic decisions about the course to be followed by a railroad or canal than was the state legislature. Eminent domain power was also an inducement to private individuals to invest in public improvements. Canal, turnpike, and railroad companies, for example, could take the land that promised the maximum return on invested capital. In return, they were compelled to submit to some minimal public scrutiny, through initial hearings about granting a franchise and subsequently through regulation by a commission or a legislative committee.

Antebellum legislatures embraced eminent domain because it was a means of protecting venturing capitalists who could achieve a public purpose through private profit. The public purpose doctrine, in this respect, complemented the belief that the state should encourage the development of property over an older view of property that stressed its quiet enjoyment. These same eminent domain provisions in the charters of antebellum franchise corporations produced innumerable lawsuits as property holders pressed courts to define their rights and the meaning of just compensation. The responsibility of balancing the inherent tension between private and public rights fell to courts, and the result was a luxuriant growth of eminent domain law.

Debtors, Creditors, and Bankruptcy

State legislators also had to balance conflicting interests in another controversial area: debtor–creditor relations. In a cash-scarce economy, credit was a necessity for economic expansion, but the boom-and-bust cycles of the years before the Civil War inevitably produced insolvent debtors. What to do with them was politically divisive. Democratic legislators pushed for rules easing the burden on debtors; their Whig counterparts usually wanted creditors protected. States gradually adopted the position that insolvency was not a sin, as had been the colonial understanding, but the inevitable outcome of an impersonal market economy in which there were winners and losers.

Consistency was hardly the humbug of state debtor–creditor laws. Senator Robert Y. Hayne of South Carolina observed in 1826 that each state had a distinctive system, "each differing from all the rest in almost every provision intended to give security to the creditor, or relief to the debtor—differing in every thing which touches the rights and the remedies of one, or the duties and liabilities of the other."[29] Because each state defined creditor rights in its own way, "anyone engaged in far-ranging ventures, whether maritime trade, back-country commerce, or buying and selling across state lines, had to conduct his affairs with these differences in mind."[30] State legislatures, which acted in other areas to bring order to business dealings, added uncertainty in the national marketplace through their debtor–creditor laws. This condition was not relieved until Congress in 1898 passed meaningful national bankruptcy legislation.

Bankruptcy is a proceeding in which government through a court takes possession of the property of a debtor so that it may be distributed among creditors in some equitable manner. It prevents creditors from exercising undue influence over a debtor, makes certain that there is fairness among creditors, and discharges the debtor from all liabilities, providing a fresh start. Only a few colonies provided for the outright discharge of debts, and even those that did seldom extended it to all freeholders.

In the English law, the creditor's ultimate weapon was to imprison the defaulting debtor until the obligation had been paid. The practice was widely accepted in the colonies, and every state continued it after the Revolution. The regimen was meant to be harsh. The words of Sir Robert H. Hyde, a mid-seventeenth-century English jurist, were still applicable at the end of the eighteenth century. "If a man be taken . . . in prison for debt," Hyde wrote, "he must live on his own, or on the charity of others; and if no man will relieve him, let him die in the name of God, says the law; and so say I."[31]

Imprisonment for debt indeed rested on some meaningful economic assumptions that were best suited to low-level economic activity. First, it was based on an anti-developmental premise that discouraged risk taking. The rule was "borrower beware"; if a person borrowed recklessly, then he would be punished severely. Second, imprisonment for debt in a predominately agrarian economy, in which land was the most important resource, made some sense. Land, it must be remembered, could remain productive even while a debtor was imprisoned. If, however, he entered into bankruptcy he then lost his land and his productive capacity. Bankruptcy was a more desirable way of dealing with insolvent debtors in a maturing market economy where maintenance of the credit system and the return of persons to nonagricultural production was considered desirable.

Progress toward abolishing the practice of imprisoning debtors was slowed by the requirements of a dynamic marketplace, by a lingering sense that indebtedness—if not morally wrong—was certainly suspect, and by humanitarianism. The ethical proposition that honest people did not default died hard. As late as the Panic of 1857, Rhode Island, a state with an admittedly harsh posture toward debtors, imprisoned 607 individuals for insolvency. In many states, including Rhode Island, complete abolition of imprisonment for debt did not come until the twentieth century; however, practices changed more quickly than statutes, as the dwindling list of imprisoned debtors suggests.

Imprisonment for debt lost its ethical underpinnings at the same time that impersonal market forces began to shape the economy. State legislatures responded to the bursts of insolvency brought on by the boom-and-bust cycles in the economy with bankruptcy, stay, and mortgage moratorium laws.

Responsibility for bankruptcy legislation fell to the states by federal default. During the years before the Civil War, Congress passed two major acts: one in 1800 and the other in 1841. Both survived briefly, and the first, which applied only to tradespersons rather than the citizenry as a whole, was repealed because it was "partial, immoral . . . impolitic . . . and anti-republican."[32] The 1841 act, which followed on the heels of the Panic of 1837, was more important because it reflected the new attitude of trying to be fair to both debtors and creditors, while restoring the health of the credit system without which further economic expansion was impossible. Debtors and creditors objected to the act in operation, and the quickly improving economy hastened its repeal in 1846.

The states were free to act without fear of congressional preemption. The result was confusion. Some states passed stay laws, which were particularly popular with farmers. These laws suspended debt collection until such time as business conditions permitted the resumption of ordinary rules of debtor–creditor relations. Mortgage moratorium acts worked in the same way. Several states also adopted bankruptcy acts, and some of these passed during the early national period were retrospective, applying to debts contracted *before* the act had gone into effect. The U.S. Supreme Court in 1819 shut the door on this practice as a violation of the contract clause of the Constitution. Even prospective state bankruptcy acts, which the Supreme Court did hold constitutional, raised a political clamor, because in the minds of many creditors they represented an attempt to redistribute the risks of previous private bargains.

The long-term trend was clear. With the growth of corporations and the rise of the banking system, the entire scheme of debtor–creditor relations became more impersonal and accountable. Loans were made not on the basis of personal assessment, but on a measure of the borrower's record and future prospects for profit. The growing geographic scope of business activity further depersonalized credit relations, and the absence of a federal bankruptcy statute added an element of uncertainty to national creditor–debtor relations. As in other areas of promotional and regulatory action, state legislation treating debtor–creditor relations generated a political reaction that resulted in constitutional restrictions that limited legislative power.

Erosion of Faith in the Active State

In the last two decades of the antebellum period, increasing restrictions were applied to the lawmaking role of state legislatures, especially in such public enterprise states as

Ohio, New York, and Pennsylvania. The wish to curb legislative authority was strong everywhere. It took expression in state constitutional conventions that rewrote existing organic laws or, in states like California, that framed new documents that blunted legislative power while giving greater responsibilities to the judicial and executive branches. There was an "erosion of faith in the active state."[33]

The experience of Ohio illustrates the withdrawal of public support for legislative intervention in the economy. The General Assembly in 1825, spurred by the example of New York's success with the Erie Canal, plunged headlong into promotion of transportation. The legislators pledged the state's full faith and credit to build the Miami Canal and, four years later, the Ohio Canal. Even this prodigious effort failed to satiate demand; sections of the state not served by these projects demanded further legislative action.

The General Assembly responded to these demands in 1837 by passing the "Loan Law." It typified the way in which most other states approached the problem of financing costly internal improvements. The law required the state to give financial aid to franchise corporations building canals, turnpikes, and railroads. In effect, the state committed itself to an open-ended investment in private transportation development. The state's debt by 1840 tripled to more than twelve million dollars, and Democratic critics fastened the pejorative title "Plunder Law" onto the 1837 act.

Ohio was a rich and growing state that might well have sunk even further into debt had not the Panic of 1837 struck. The state met its commitments under the 1837 act, but the General Assembly repealed it outright in 1842 amid a wave of popular indignation toward mixed economic enterprise. The legislature then adopted a new plan, responding to improving economic conditions in the mid-1840s and renewed demands from those parts of the states that had not participated fully in the previous improvement binges. The General Assembly, like many other state legislatures, devolved responsibility for the proposed new improvements on local governments. They did so through "loan of credit" legislation, a device widely used in the nineteenth century that restricted state involvement in transportation improvements without slamming the door completely shut on the idea of mixed economic enterprise.[34] Unlike a direct loan, a loan of credit involved the local government as an underwriter that issued bonds, the proceeds of which went to canal or railroad companies. Ohio's local governments snatched the opportunity given to them by the General Assembly and plunged heavily into debt.

The results were disappointing and politically explosive. In a pattern repeated throughout the nation, some rail lines were never built; others proved uncompetitive because they duplicated existing service; still others were only partially constructed. Mixed economic enterprise had gone sour.

State Constitutional Reform

Democrats responded with a populist, antigovernmental, and anticorporation attack on the active state. State legislatures by the late 1840s and early 1850s had become "deeply mired in party politics and changing social and economic interests."[35] The constitutional convention emerged as the device by which to overcome a seemingly unresponsive political system. As one delegate to the Ohio constitutional convention of 1850–1851 explained, "I wish to see the State government brought back to its simple and appropriate functions, [leaving] railroad, canal, turnpike and other corporate associations, to get along upon their own credit, without any connection or partnership with the State whatever."[36]

More than one-half of the states by 1860 either had rewritten existing constitutions or had written new documents. These new organic laws attempted to rein in legislative power by limiting state indebtedness and prohibiting state and local governments from aiding private enterprise through the "loan of credit" or the purchase of private stock. The new documents also placed stringent restraints on capital expenditures. These were logical responses to the failures of the inflated promises that were made at the time the states built internal improvements. Many of the new state constitutions crafted in the fifteen years before the Civil War included provisions for general rather than special charters of incorporation, made just compensation a constitutional principle, and either abolished or limited the practice of imprisonment for debt.

The postindependence republican faith in legislative bodies disappeared, and in its place two new themes surfaced. First, state constitutions, which had been viewed as fundamental laws half a century earlier, became codelike documents intended to limit governmental action. The Ohio Constitution of 1851, for example, was almost double the length of the state's previous organic law, and everywhere delegates seized on their organic laws to check what state legislators could do in economic matters. Second, the roles of state officials began to change significantly. Governors gained increased authority in these documents through the veto power, the pardoning power, and the ability to make appointments, once the exclusive province of the legislature.

Perhaps the most dramatic change came to the judiciary. The practice of electing trial court judges for limited terms had gained acceptance in many states by the 1820s, but it failed to spread to the appellate bench. The idea persisted that appellate judges should remain free from direct partisan and popular influence as they went about mechanically discovering the law. Mississippi in 1832 was the first state to elect all of its judges for limited terms of office (typically six to eight years), and after New York adopted the new selection process in 1846 many states, including Ohio, followed in quick order. The only notable holdout was Massachusetts, where a fierce struggle over the judiciary in 1852 culminated in a victory for supporters of the appointive method and tenure during good behavior.

The motives behind this change were complex. The same populist and antigovernmental pressures that were directed against the legislatures were also aimed at the judiciary. Charles Reemelin, a farmer and delegate to the constitutional convention in Ohio, claimed that popular election would reduce the "aristocratic tendencies of the [judiciary]."[37] But equally, if not more important, many members of the bench and bar, who controlled the convention committees that crafted the judiciary articles, embraced popular election as a counterweight to legislative authority. Michael Hoffman, a delegate to the New York constitutional convention in 1846, encapsulated the position when he explained: "In reorganizing the legislative department we have given it less power for general legislation, [and thus] a large share of judicial legislation will be inevitable, and we must endeavor to supply it" through the popular election of judges.[38] The new method of selection put judges in the position of being able to overturn through judicial review the acts of the popularly elected branches without facing the charge that they were undemocratic.

Popular election was also backward looking. It took account of what was an already well-perceived change in the role of the appellate judiciary. These judges had emerged since 1789 as mediators of conflict among competing social and economic interests. It was not mere happenstance that the decision to make them elective came at the end of a great wave of state legislative involvement in mixed economic enterprise. The convention delegates confirmed through their actions that appellate courts had become, on questions involving distributive economic justice, lawmaking as well as lawfinding institutions.

6

Common Law, the Economy, and the Onward Spirit of the Age: 1789–1861

"The Americans," Alexis de Tocqueville wrote in the 1830s, "have given their courts immense political power."[1] Judges, who were increasingly trained lawyers, proceeded gradually between the Revolution and the Civil War to claim an extended sphere of operations, one in which they exerted political force as well as legal authority. A new vision of law and an explosion of economic activity precipitated the redefinition of the judicial role. The legal profession "began to observe with frequency that all law, whether promulgated by a court or a legislature, was an essentially mutable and transitory product of sovereign command."[2] Legal instrumentalism—a pragmatic and utilitarian view of law—competed with an older conception of it as precedent-bound rules that judges applied mechanically. Judges continued to declare rights based on law, but in the emerging market economy affirming the rights of one party and denying those of another often amounted to mediating between competing visions of economic progress. Sometimes the choice was between private parties, at other times between a private individual and the state, and at still other times between the states and the national government.

Judges invoked concepts of both private and public rights in allocating economic costs, risks, and benefits among different social interests within the federal system. The doctrine of vested rights retained some validity, but complete security for private property rights was contrary to the republican principle that the power of the state had to be used to enhance the commonwealth. Antebellum judges concluded that private rights had to yield to "the rights of the public."[3] This doctrine held that the commonwealth enjoyed certain rights that the courts were duty-bound to protect against self-interest.

Changing Roles of Jury and Judge

Jury

One of the most important consequences of the increased instrumentalism of U.S. law "was the dramatic shift in the relationship between judge and jury that began to emerge at the end of the eighteenth century."[4] Until that time the jury had exercised power over questions of law as well as fact. Today, these responsibilities are divided, with the judge treating matters of law and the jury left to decide on issues of fact. The judge, once the trial ends, instructs the jurors on the relevant points of law, and his or her instructions are considered binding. In the eighteenth century, the lines of authority ran in a different way. "The jury may in all cases," wrote William Wyche in his 1794 treatise on New York practice, "where law and fact are blended together, take upon themselves the knowledge of the law."[5] Jury instructions, which are highly regularized today, tended in the early years of the republic to be informal and nontechnical.

The typical eighteenth-century jury was free to accept the judge's instructions uncritically, modify them, or even reject them. While in theory the jury had to accept the law as given, in reality it often did as it pleased, because the jury's secret deliberation was beyond the court's immediate oversight. In the famous case of John Peter Zenger, a printer accused of libeling the governor of the colony of New York in 1735, the trial judge ordered the jury to disregard the law as argued to it by Zenger's counsel. The jury, however, took its own view of the law, which matched that of Zenger, and ruled for the printer. The jury gave a "general verdict," which reflected its evaluation of the validity of the facts and the law.

Through the nineteenth century the division of labor between judge and jury sharpened. The jury had historically functioned as an appendage of the community, and even though qualifications of race, sex, and property holding made it an unrepresentative body, it was still a democratic force. Americans intended to keep it that way by limiting direct judicial influence. States, for example, began passing statutes that restricted judges in commenting on the evidence. A North Carolina statute of 1796 made it unlawful, "in delivering a charge to the . . . jury to give an opinion whether a fact is fully or sufficiently proved," because that was "the true office and province of the jury."[6]

The autonomy gained by the jury over matters of fact was lost over questions of law. This development was much more pronounced in civil than in criminal cases, but even in the latter there was concern that jury discretion would promote injustice. Because criminal proceedings always held the potential to deny a person's liberty or life, the ideal of uniform application of the law was at war with the belief that the jury should impose the community's understanding of guilt or innocence based on fact instead of law. Some states, such as New Jersey in 1844, went so far as to write into their constitutions provisions that required juries to be judges of fact and law "in prosecutions or indictments for libel."[7]

In civil cases the jury became a finder of fact in the service of the court. Nineteenth-century trial courts adopted several procedural devices that limited the scope of jury autonomy. The growth of a commercial market economy made order and stability necessary in jury verdicts. Writers on law and counsel for commercial interests concluded that greater judicial control over the law in a case would produce the kind of stable legal climate in which business would flourish. Moreover, as the nature of law practice shifted from the settlement of disputes over land to issues of commercial law, the rising American legal profession, from whose ranks judges were almost exclusively drawn, concluded that a uniform system of commercial law complemented their personal and professional ambitions.

Commercial lawyers in the United States, for example, began in the late eighteenth century to expand the "special case" or "case reserved." This device allowed them to submit points of law to the judge while avoiding the jury's intervention. The special case involved obtaining from a judge a decision on a point of law based on a mutually agreed statement of facts. English and Scottish judges had permitted extensive use of the special case in marine insurance cases, and commercial lawyers in the United States seized on its advantages.[8] The special case permitted counsel, upon receiving a judgment from the court on the legal issues, to settle the dispute out of court without exposing his clients to an uncertain jury deliberation.

Another major procedural reform was the award of a new trial for verdicts "contrary to the weight of the evidence." This device enabled judges to second-guess the jury's verdict, and before the late eighteenth century it was hardly known in American law. With independence and a coequal status with the other branches, the judiciary began to reconsider jury verdicts, especially in cases where the evidence was often complicated. Not only did judges order new trials, but in doing so they impinged on the jury's supposedly exclusive fact-finding role. In New York and South Carolina, for example, the practice of granting new trials based on a judge's weighing of the evidence was well established by the early nineteenth century.

Judges, of course, never brought juries wholly under control; jury discretion remained then, as now, an important democratic feature of the American legal system. Yet the trend was clear: this development made it possible for "American courts after 1790 [to] overthrow particular anticommercial doctrines of the eighteenth century."[9]

Judiciary

The judiciary also extended its influence over legislative policies, although judges continued to respect legislative authority. The immediate postrevolutionary view held that judges exercised judicial review as agents of the rule of law rather than popular will. The measure of their integrity was the extent to which they fulfilled this role through the mechanical application of precedent. Judges had discretion, of course, but constitutions and precedents (higher law and history) were palpable limits on that discretion. Judges were legal and not political actors.

By the mid-1830s, however, some lawyers and judges began to advocate a new conception of judicial power that altered this traditional dichotomy between law and politics. Courts, they insisted, should become active participants in resolving conflict among social interests. Francis Hilliard and William Duane, two of the nation's most prominent lawyers, insisted that judges had an overtly political as well as judicial character. In 1831 a writer in the *American Jurist,* one of the nation's first law journals, proclaimed that law was "essentially variable, extending and contracting itself according to the condition of the nation, accommodating its flexible character to the manners, habits and employments of the people."[10] The new basis of law, according to Hilliard, was "generally expediency, public policy"; judges made law, as opposed to merely finding it, because they were often "governed . . . by ideas of political expediency."[11] Judicial review, the Pennsylvania Supreme Court added in 1830, equipped judges with a "latitudinarian authority" that was "great and . . . undefined."[12]

Although the incidence of judicial review by state and federal appellate courts increased most dramatically after the Civil War, its exercise by antebellum judges nonetheless fortified their growing role as economic policy makers. In the case of the federal judiciary, and especially the Supreme Court, judicial review also swept away state impediments to the emerging national market economy.

Common Law and Economic Development

Antebellum judges dethroned the English common law by Americanizing it. In the process, they added certainty to the ambiguity that had shrouded much colonial law. Corporation, labor, property, contract, and tort law emerged by 1861 as significantly different from what they had been in 1787. State courts played a dominant role in this transformation of American law, but federal courts and judges also contributed, giving truly national scope to legal development. The ethical yardstick employed by colonial courts was replaced by a new measure that asked judges to consider how legal rules encouraged economic growth, individual risk taking, and the accumulation of capital.

Judicial decisions require cases and controversies. "The characteristic of judicial power is that it can act only when called upon or in legal language, when it is seized of the matter." Tocqueville concluded, "[t]here is nothing naturally active about judicial power; to act, it must be set in motion."[13] Issues of economic development set the judiciary "in motion."

Capital and Labor

Corporations

The corporation was the form of business organization that carried the nation into the new economic age. State legislatures "arm[ed] associations of private individuals with a portion of its sovereign power so that they could accomplish collectively what they wanted but could not do privately."[14] Antebellum judges contributed to this creative legal process in three areas: the doctrine of *ultra vires,* the concept of limited stockholder liability, and the protection of corporate charter rights under the Constitution's contract clause.

The doctrine of *ultra vires* ("beyond the powers") was the most notable judicial manifestation of hostility toward the corporate form. And there was more than a little hostility. Judge Spencer Roane of the Virginia Court of Appeals in 1809 expressed the fears of conservative agrarian interests. In *Currie's Administrators* v. *The Mutual Assurance Society,* Roane wrote that "no . . . set of men, are entitled to exclusive or separate emoluments or privileges from the community" when they were "merely" engaged in "private or selfish acts."[15] Subsequently, Jacksonian Democrats attacked corporations as "having no souls or consciences" and possessed of a powerful "accumulating character."[16]

State courts invoked *ultra vires* to limit the exercise of corporate power by declaring certain acts as void and incapable of ratification. Contrary to the general role played by courts in the economy, this doctrine contributed an element of uncertainty to business dealings, because it meant that a person who entered into a contract with a corporation did so at some risk. If the contract were declared *ultra vires,* it could not be enforced and damages could not be collected. The highest courts of Pennsylvania and Maryland during the 1850s, for example, declared the acts of corporations *ultra vires,* because they exceeded the powers granted in their charters by the state legislature. After the Civil War, as the corporation became indispensable, the doctrine withered away.

On balance, however, antebellum state courts encouraged the development of the corporate form, especially by recognizing the principle of limited shareholder liability. The experience of Massachusetts was typical. In the 1809 case of *Andover and Medford Turnpike Corporation* v. *Gould,* the Supreme Judicial Court held that a person who had voluntarily become a member of a business corporation could not be sued for unpaid corporate assessments unless he had expressly promised to pay them. The court's decision diminished some of the risk of shareholders joining a corporation, because they could abandon the enterprise if the assessments became onerous.

A decade later the same court pushed this disposition to favor investment in corporate activity even further. In the cases of *Spear* v. *Grant* (1819) and *Vose* v. *Grant* (1819), the judges were asked to rule on whether the shareholders of a bank that had been dissolved were still liable for the debts owed by the bank. Judge Isaac Parker held that they were liable only if the charter explicitly provided so.[17] If the charter contained no such provision, the shareholders were absolved of the burden of the corporation's debt. The court took the same tack with regard to shareholders of manufacturing corporations, and the state legislature, anxious to attract investors to the state, had by 1830 enacted comprehensive legislation that established the modern rule of limited liability. Thereafter, the "people were free to join [corporations] largely to further their own economic well-being."[18]

Establishing the scope of corporate charter powers was a crucial function of antebellum courts. While state judges generally held that corporate charters should be narrowly construed, the federal Supreme Court embraced a more expansive doctrine in the landmark case of *Dartmouth College* v. *Woodward* (1819).

The case involved the issue of whether the New Hampshire legislature could alter the terms of a charter originally granted to the college by King George III in 1769. The college claimed that the contract clause of the federal Constitution prohibited the legislature from impairing the terms of the charter. A charter was merely a contract, and the corporation could lay claim to the same property rights as private individuals. Much was at stake. Although Dartmouth College was a philanthropic institution, the case was widely perceived as having profound implications for the extent to which the states could interfere with the conduct of private business. The case arose at a time when the corporate form of organization was gaining favor with private investors.

Marshall's opinion further encouraged them. He held that a charter granted by a legislature was a contract protected under the terms of the Constitution's contract clause. The states, while sovereign, were also held to the same standard in contractual relationships as were private individuals. Marshall reached this conclusion with the policy implications of his actions clearly in mind. "The objects for which a corporation is created," Marshall wrote, "are universally such as the government wishes to promote. They are deemed beneficial to the country; and this benefit . . . would . . . perhaps [be] unattainable without the aid of a corporate charter."[19] Marshall's opinion invoked federal constitutional authority to promote voluntary risk taking by creating a stable legal environment for the formation of private corporations.

Justice Joseph Story's concurring opinion reinforced Marshall's commitment to stable corporate arrangements and advanced the distinction between a private and a public corporation. Story reiterated what Marshall had also made clear: legislatures retained control over private corporations. "A corporation cannot be controlled or destroyed by any subsequent statute," Story wrote, "unless a power for that purpose be reserved to the legislature in the act of incorporation."[20] A legislature merely had to reserve the right to alter the terms of the charter—the contract—in order to take future action. In following years legislatures began to write such clauses into corporate charters, and in some states an article was included in their constitutions giving legislatures this power. As well, the Supreme Court in the 1830s modified *Dartmouth,* holding that charters of incorporation were to be interpreted in favor of the state.

Story's concurrence also established the legal basis for distinguishing a public from a private corporation. Critics of corporations argued that, because they were chartered by the state and fulfilled a responsibility that reached into society, they were inherently public. The notion of a wholly private corporation contradicted the commonwealth ideal that corporations existed to fulfill a public need. As a North Carolina judge put the matter, "it seems difficult to conceive of a corporation established for merely private purposes."[21] If that view had prevailed, the door would have been opened to extensive legislative interference with corporate activity.

Story slammed the door shut. Instead of defining corporations based on their function, he defined them based on the nature of their endowments. A private corporation, he ruled, was one whose capital stock was privately subscribed. Story's doctrine was "a practical response to a major aspect of corporate development"—the rise of the private business corporation.[22] In Story's own New England, the *Dartmouth College* decision placed a secure legal floor under would-be entrepreneurs, and the corporation became a major force in the transformation of manufacturing in that region.

Antebellum judges contributed to the long-term transformation of the corporation. Judges, like legislators, assumed that the public good was most readily achieved when private individuals were encouraged to pursue their own economic endeavors. This assumption conformed with the antebellum reality of small corporations engaged in often keen competition in a developing national market economy. In the late nineteenth century, however, as corporations became giant businesses, Story's distinction between private and public corporate activity lost its meaning. The antebellum fascination with stimulating growth was replaced by the problem of how to restrain powerful industrial businesses.

Labor

The same state courts that approved the development of the corporate form of organization for investors rejected for most of the years before the Civil War efforts by workers to protect their earning power through collective organization. The pattern in a developing economy is for the savings necessary for capital formation to be accumulated at the expense of labor by forcing low wages and the social costs of development on the work force. In the antebellum legal struggle between capital and labor, capital usually prevailed.

Industrialization and the creation of a wage-earning class occurred gradually. Like the corporation, the full economic and legal development of the labor organization was incomplete by the time of the Civil War. The numbers tell the story. In 1800, only about 10 percent of the white labor force was categorized as an "employee"; most "laborers" were self-employed, predominantly in agriculture. That number had risen to about 20 percent by 1860, but even in urban areas, such as New York City and Philadelphia, workers there did not begin to regard their position as wage earners as permanent until the 1850s. Furthermore, on the eve of the Civil War, manufacturing, which was the largest employer of wage earners, accounted for only about one-third of the output of the entire economy. The legal rules affecting labor touched only a small portion of a still basically agricultural and rural population. Furthermore, early labor organizations were little more than primitive price-fixing combinations that reflected the semientrepreneurial status of the skilled artisans who organized them.

The English common law doctrine of criminal conspiracy shaped the early American law of labor organization. Conspiracy is an agreement between two or more individuals to effect some unlawful purpose, and the mere act of agreeing is enough to bring an indictment. The labor conspiracy doctrine held that collective as opposed to individual bargaining would interfere with the natural operation of the marketplace, raise wages to artificially high levels, and destroy economic competitiveness. The prevailing wage fund theory held that there was only a fixed part of the national income available for wages. If labor organized, this economic theory provided, it robbed unorganized workers of what was due to them naturally.

The labor conspiracy doctrine was carried to North America largely intact, and it was first applied in Philadelphia in the 1806 case of *Commonwealth* v. *Pullis,* also known as the Philadelphia Cordwainers' Case. (The name Cordwainer was taken from the Cordovan leather that shoemakers worked.) The case involved the explosive issue of whether labor unions were illegal under the common law. Federalists in Philadelphia argued that they were; Jeffersonian Republicans took the opposite position. The case raised other issues: the extent to which the English common law would be accepted by Americans, the liberty of individuals to contract for their own economic arrangements, and the economic future of Philadelphia.

Philadelphia shoemakers in 1794 organized the Federal Society of Journeymen Cordwainers for the purpose of improving their economic lot. They demanded that the master craftsmen hire only association members. The journeymen, in essence, attempted to create a closed shop. The master craftsmen retaliated, not only by forming their own association, but when the association's members struck for higher wages in the fall of 1805, they persuaded the city government to prosecute the journeymen for engaging in a criminal labor conspiracy.

The trial lasted three days before a jury composed of nine merchants and three master craftsmen, hardly a balanced panel. The prosecution argued that the association represented a "state within a state" and that its operation threatened the liberties of all persons, denying those workers who did not wish to join the association the opportunity to sell their labor freely. "If any one of the defendants," the prosecutor explained, could "charge $100 for making a pair of boots, nobody would interfere, if he could get his employer to give it." Once that same individual organized in order "to regulate the price of the labour of others as well as [his] own," then the labor conspiracy doctrine applied.[23] The prosecutor also conjured up a vision of the economic decline of Philadelphia, with investors fleeing to other cities where the legal climate supported competition and low wages. Liberty and the public interest, all put in the context of Adam Smith's free-market economics, demanded conviction. The judge in the case made certain that the jury understood as much. His blatantly one-sided charge gave the already biased panel little reason to reconsider their assumptions.

Between 1806 and 1842 the conspiracy doctrine was applied in at least a half-dozen cases. Most of the time, prosecutors and judges cloaked economic necessity in terms of individual liberty. Justice John Savage of the New York Court for the Correction of Errors explained in *People* v. *Fisher* (1835) that workers' "extravagant demands for wages" would interfere with the beneficent, natural operation of the free market. "It is important," Savage observed, "to the best interests of society that the price of labor be left to regulate itself, or rather, be limited by the demand for it."[24] The reporter of the Pittsburgh Cordwainers' Case of 1815 offered a more straightforward analysis. "The [guilty] verdict of the jury," he said, "is most important to the manufacturing interests of the community for it puts an end to these associations which have been so prejudicial to the successful enterprise of the capitalist."[25]

By the 1840s U.S. courts began to retreat from the labor conspiracy doctrine. Chief Justice Lemuel Shaw, of Massachusetts, a central figure in adjusting the law to the changing economy, led the way in the case of *Commonwealth* v. *Hunt* (1842). Shaw sought to strike a balance between the interests of labor and capital, seeking to promote community interests as a whole by reducing social strife.

In 1840 Jeremiah Horne, a disgruntled employee, persuaded District Attorney Samuel D. Parker of Boston to bring suit against the Boston Journeymen Bootmakers' Society. The union had fined Horne for having done some extra work without pay, but the fine was removed when Horne's employer paid it. Horne was shortly fined again for another infraction, and despite the urging of his employer to pay, Horne refused. The union then expelled him, providing that he could gain reinstatement by paying the fine and signing a pledge to obey the union rules. When Horne refused, the union demanded that he be fired, and the employer complied. At that point, Horne turned to Parker, who successfully argued his case before Judge Peter O. Thacher in the Boston Municipal Court. Thacher informed the jury in his charge that coercion by the union of a fellow worker would, if widespread, "tend directly to array [laborer and employer, and the rich as well as the poor] against each other, and to convulse the social system to its centre. A frightful despotism would soon be erected on the ruins of this free and happy commonwealth."[26] The jury required only twenty minutes to convict, and the defendants (seven journeyman shoemakers) then appealed to the Supreme Judicial Court of Massachusetts.

Shaw's opinion, written for a court composed of Federalists and Whigs, significantly modified the labor conspiracy doctrine in overturning the lower court conviction. Shaw had a "hard-headed insight into the workings of a competitive economy."[27] The best interests of the commonwealth would be furthered through competition, and unions were one means of stimulating just such competition. Shaw did not rule that all labor combinations were legal, but he did find that as long as the means used by unions were legal they were free to make demands on employers. He held that a closed shop was not itself illegal, nor was the act of achieving it through a boycott.

Shaw founded his decision on the commonwealth idea. He believed that benefits to the public might accrue from the contest between unions and employers. The same notion of the rights of the public also influenced the development of judicial attitudes toward property.

Property

Antebellum judges furthered the tumultuous economic growth of the era by redefining property law. Eighteenth-century Americans thought of property as an institution "merely of security," in which its possession defined social status.[28] Two other important ideas were part of this static conception, and both of them derived from Blackstone's *Commentaries*. The first, absolute domain, was summed up in two phrases from Blackstone: "Use your own property in such a manner as not to injure that of another," and "the owner of the soil owns to the sky."[29] Absolute domain gave to every property owner a veto over the acts of others that might disturb the quiet enjoyment of his land. The second idea was vested property rights, which guaranteed to every individual the right to enjoy ownership of land free from arbitrary governmental interference.

Absolute domain and vested rights made sense in an economy characterized by low-level activity. But, as the tempo of economic activity quickened in the early nineteenth century, these concepts came under growing scrutiny. Americans increasingly adopted a dynamic conception of property, one that stressed property as an "institution of growth."[30] This dynamic view of property complemented the needs of growing communities. The economic success of the commonwealth depended on government intervention in the marketplace through devices such as eminent domain to foster economic expansion. To put property to new uses, yet "simultaneously preserve a reasonable measure of security for vested rights, became a critical task for the [judiciary]."[31]

Antebellum property law moved through two distinct phases. During the first phase, the doctrine of priority and prescription held that the best way to promote initial economic activity was to give a monopoly over the uses of land to those persons willing to undertake the risks of development. The rights they enjoyed were prescriptive; that is, because they were there first others could not interfere with the uses they made of the property. By the 1830s this doctrine yielded to a second, instrumental concept of property law, known as the reasonableness or balancing doctrine. It stressed the efficient use of resources based on competition and rejected as inefficient the monopolistic features of absolute domain. The rule permitted courts to choose among competing economic interests based on their assessment of the proper balance to be struck between the rights of the individual and the rights of the public.

The judicial transformation of property law was extensive. For example, courts either abandoned or modified the common law tradition of "ancient lights," which had prevented the erection of buildings that cast a shadow or blocked the view of an adjoining property owner. Judges also weakened the doctrine of "waste," which had required a tenant to tear down any improvement he had made to the land at the end of his lease. The judicial acceptance of a dynamic view of property law based on economic efficiency and public rights doctrine was especially evident in three areas: water rights, eminent domain, and nuisance.

Riparian Water Rights

The English common law of riparian rights was forged in a humid environment with numerous streams and abundant rainfall. A riparian right accrues to a person who owns the bank of a stream and has access to water by virtue of that position. Riparian owners were entitled to equal shares of whatever water they needed for "natural uses." They did not enjoy a similar right for artificial uses. The artificial, or extraordinary, uses differed from the natural ones in about the same way as desired uses differed from absolute necessity. Farmers had to have water to drink and for domestic stock, but other competing users wanted water for the purposes of manufacturing and mining. The English common law doctrine of natural flow severely restricted the amount of water that a riparian proprietor could take for such artificial purposes.

In the antebellum era the doctrine of natural flow came under attack in two ways. First, in the states east of the Mississippi River, where water was abundant, judges applied the reasonableness and balancing test to reduce the restrictions on artificial uses. Their decisions worked to the benefit of certain business users, such as textile producers, who needed large amounts of falling water to power their factories. This new emphasis in the law hurt old-mill operators, who found the flow of water reduced, and farmers, whose lands were often flooded as a result of the increasingly tall dams needed to back up ever larger amounts of water. Second, as the nation expanded beyond the Mississippi, the requirements of irrigation and mining forced a reversal in thinking about what, in an arid climate, constituted an artificial use.

Typical of developments in the East was the New York Supreme Court's decision in *Palmer* v. *Mulligan* (1805). A closely divided court held for the first time that an upstream owner could dam up water for mill purposes, even though he had failed to establish a prescriptive right to do so and his actions caused "little inconveniences" to other owners. Under the then existing doctrine of priority and prescription, courts had previously held that a blockage in the flow of water had to be long-standing (usually twenty years) in order to enjoy common law protection. The majority offered an explicit policy basis to justify its action. Judge Brockholst Livingston observed that without such a rule "the public, whose advantage is always to be regarded, would be deprived of the benefits which always attend competition and rivalry."[32] The rights of private property holders had to be balanced against the rights of the public to improve facilities created through competition. *Palmer* v. *Mulligan* began a long line of cases in which U.S. judges accepted the idea that the ownership of property implied the right to develop that property for business rather than natural, agricultural uses.

The antidevelopmental doctrine of natural flow declined gradually. There was strong opposition to *Mulligan,* as the sharply divided court that decided it suggests. Even in the 1820s several state appellate courts in the East refused to extend riparian rights to mill and factory owners on an unlimited basis, clinging instead to priority and prescription. Joseph Angell in 1824 lent support to their action in *Watercourses,* the leading antebellum treatise on riparian rights. Angell denounced the New York decision as "contrary to authorities and obviously unjust."[33] He asserted the traditional common law, based on the doctrine of natural flow, that the only test for the use of water by an upstream owner was the absence of all but the most trivial injury to those living downstream.

The utilitarian position eventually prevailed, and Chief Justice Lemuel Shaw was its principal architect. Massachusetts depended heavily on the cotton textile business, and cotton factories required larger and higher dams than those erected to process grain. Between 1820 and 1830, for example, the productive capacity of all mills in New England expanded by more than 60 percent.

The legal and economic issues that came to Shaw's court were intertwined. The size of the new mills was such that they often interfered with existing mill owners who claimed a prescriptive right over the water's flow. If these prescriptive rights stood, existing mill operators would have had a virtual state-sanctioned monopoly over the water's use. Such a monopoly stymied the introduction of new and more powerful mills that depended for their successful operation on an ever-greater diversion of water. The question presented was not just whether the builders of a new and technologically more advanced cotton mill could interfere with the natural flow for an artificial purpose, but whether in doing so they could diminish the monopoly rights of existing mill operators for the benefit of the entire community.

Shaw's opinion in *Cary* v. *Daniels* (1844) invoked the rights of the public and limited private property rights. The case involved a new cotton mill that significantly diverted water from existing users. Shaw shifted the test away from the injury done to them and toward what he called "the usages and wants of the community." "One of the beneficial uses of a watercourse," he explained, "and in this country one of the most important, is its application to the working of mills and machinery; a use profitable to the owner, and beneficial to the public."[34] The state could not stand in the way of progress. Some existing property holders had to suffer losses without a legal remedy in order that the community as a whole could benefit.

Judicially enforced riparian rights west of the Mississippi River were also utilitarian, pragmatic, and prodevelopmental. Much of the legal development of riparian property law in the West occurred after the Civil War as the pace of settlement quickened. But as early as the 1850s the issues were drawn as settlers moved into semiarid and arid regions. Economic expansion into the Southwest encouraged the Anglo-American values of predictability and individualism, values that collided with the already well-established Spanish civil law tradition of placing communal over individual needs. The common law not only overwhelmed the civil law but it also changed itself to accommodate the new environmental circumstances. The traditional common law rule of equal apportionment among all riparian owners led to grave consequences in much of the West because water was insufficient to divide equally among all users. Furthermore, according to traditional property doctrine, a riparian owner was one who actually owned land fronting on a watercourse. If this practice had been followed in the West, landowners who lived far from the source would have been denied water for irrigation and mining.

The western states and territories organized before the Civil War received the existing common law. Eastern legal principles quickly broke down in the West, even in Texas and along the Pacific slope where the climate was more humid than on the Great Plains. Western appellate judges replaced the doctrine of natural flow, which was already crumbling before the demands of manufacturers in the humid East. These judges realized that the climate and geography of the West made the doctrine of prior appropriation (first come, first served) a necessary legal innovation. An individual who got to the water first, no matter that he was not a riparian owner, had priority before all others to the amount of water he had first appropriated, whether for irrigation or mining. In most western states, appropriative water rights were regarded as a class of property that could be sold in whole or in part.

This new judicial formulation of riparian rights had grassroots support. In California, for example, extralegal miners' clubs devised codes that established the doctrine of prior appropriation. The California Supreme Court subsequently ratified it. In the 1855 case of *Irwin* v. *Phillips* the high court ruled, in one of its earliest decisions on resource law, that "[c]ourts are bound to take notice of the political and social condition of the country, which they judicially rule."[35] As in the East, the judicial interpretation of early riparian rights in the West was pragmatic and intended to hasten economic development. The pursuit of wealth and enterprise took precedence over equity. Geography and climate might alter the substance of the law, but judges kept it resonant with developmental economic purposes. The western doctrine of prior appropriation "encouraged entrepreneurs to scramble for water, quickly construct works, and apply the asset to the industry of the region."[36]

Vested Rights and Eminent Domain

In the antebellum period no state constitution affirmatively granted the eminent domain power. Instead, the federal Constitution and most revised state constitutions after 1820 placed limitations on its exercise. The Fifth Amendment, for example, read: "[N]or shall property be taken for public use without just compensation."[37] Although the federal amendment was adjudged in *Barron* v. *Baltimore* (1833) not to apply against the states, state courts regularly invoked it along with clauses in their own constitutions to restrict the power of eminent domain. State court judges developed two important limitations that protected property rights: first, that property might be taken only for a "public purpose"; and second, that the owner had to be given fair, or just, compensation.

Judges, however, also adopted a utilitarian perspective on vested rights by interpreting the power of eminent domain in such a way as to foster economic growth.[38] First, judges gave wide play to the coercive feature of the power of eminent domain. They accepted, for example, the practice of offsetting. Numerous legislatures mandated that the calculation of the presumed benefits to an individual attributable to construction of a canal, road, or railroad be used to "offset" the value of losses suffered as a result of having property taken.

Second, judges agreed that franchise corporations could exercise the power of eminent domain as long as they did so for a public purpose. Lacking sufficient fiscal resources from taxation to meet all the demands of their citizenry for improved communication, the state legislatures chartered franchise corporations to raise capital to operate public enterprises. Eminent domain became an indirect subsidy without which promoters of public developments would have been left at the mercy of any single property owner who "decided to hold out for an extortionate price."[39] The public had certain rights to economic development and prosperity that judges were required to enforce.

The worst fears of the proponents of vested property rights were given national expression in the 1836–1837 case of the *Charles River Bridge*. Chief Justice Roger B.

Taney, a Jacksonian Democrat recently appointed to the Court, endorsed the new pragmatic attitude that vested rights had to give way before new technological advances that promised economic growth.

Charles River Bridge involved the application of the Contract Clause of the federal Constitution to an action taken by the Massachusetts legislature. In 1828 it chartered the Warren Bridge Company to build a new bridge to satisfy the needs of commercial traffic between Boston and Charlestown. The new toll-free bridge was only a few yards from an older, less technologically advanced toll bridge chartered by the legislature in 1785. Beneath these prosaic actions a political, legal, and economic storm raged. The Jacksonian-controlled state legislature was pitted against the Supreme Court in a contest in which "[c]apitalism itself was at issue: what it meant and who would set economic policy."[40]

Daniel Webster, appearing for the old bridge company, argued that, if legislators went back on their promises to investors, no one would invest in future improvements. Property rights had to be strictly protected or economic development would collapse.

Justice Taney, however, offered for the Jacksonian majority on the Court a different vision of how to achieve economic progress. He held on the narrow legal issue that, contrary to *Dartmouth College,* no monopoly or other power should be viewed as implied in a corporate charter. But the opinion was even more important for the dictum (a judicial statement without legal precedent) that Taney added. Only by preventing established capital from entrenching itself could economic growth based on new corporate development occur. While private property was still to be "sacredly guarded," Taney also argued that "the community also have rights," and the "happiness and well-being of every citizen depends on their faithful preservation." Recognizing that the Charles River Bridge Company had an implied monopoly over bridge building on the Charles River would be bad economic policy. The chief justice concluded by warning that "modern science" would be throttled and transportation would be set back a century, if such monopoly powers were recognized.[41] Taney, through his judicial office, struck a blow for democratic capitalism. Justice Story argued in dissent not only that Taney was wrong on the law, but that his decision would "arrest all public improvements, found[ed] on private capital and enterprise" by jeopardizing the security of all such investments.[42]

The vested-rights position that Webster and Story advocated failed to persuade most antebellum judges. The authority of the state to provide for the public interest expanded, and eminent domain was one example. The justices in *West River Bridge* v. *Dix* (1848), in which Webster once again asserted his view of vested property rights, spoke in sweeping terms, finding that eminent domain was "the single power, under which . . . the whole policy of the country, relative to roads, mills, bridges, and canals rests."[43]

Nuisance and the Decline of Quiet Enjoyment

The utilitarian character of antebellum property law also appeared in the law of nuisance. Nuisance suits became more numerous from the mid-1830s to the end to the Civil War as the pace of technological change quickened. Most of these suits sought injunctive relief based on equity principles in which a judge would enjoin a person from some activity, such as operating a steam engine over a particular portion of track.

Property owners in the path of economic expansion claimed that their right to the quiet enjoyment of their property had to be sustained against the sparks, noise, and filth belched forth by railroads and factories.

A nuisance can be either public or private. Typically, relief was provided only for private rather than public nuisances, and the way in which courts fitted certain kinds of economic activities into these categories substantially affected the susceptibility of risk-taking entrepreneurs to the costs of lawsuits.

Courts favored the defendants in these suits. They often invoked the doctrine of prescriptive rights to protect what was a private nuisance at the same time they used the same doctrine in riparian and eminent domain cases to fuel economic development. The Massachusetts Supreme Judicial Court in 1842, for example, rebuffed home-owners' claims that the owners of a soap and candle factory, which had burned down, should be enjoined from rebuilding because its "noisome, noxious and offensive vapors, fumes and stenches" had made their homes unlivable and unsellable.[44] The court held that because the plaintiffs had countenanced the factory before it burned down, they could not subsequently demand that it not be rebuilt. The factory, despite its offensive nature, had by its previous operation created a prescriptive right to operate.

Antebellum courts also applied balancing tests to weigh the social utility of an alleged nuisance against private rights. Judges invariably limited private rights if the nuisance involved the slightest hint of using property in an economically efficient and publicly beneficial way. In *Grey* v. *Ohio & Pennsylvania Railroad Co.* (1856), for example, the Pennsylvania Supreme Court was asked by a farmer to enjoin the construction of a railroad. The court refused to do so, concluding after balancing "the inconveniences . . . incurred by the respective parties" that the railroad was more important than the farmer.[45]

State judges also regularly denied injunctive relief by declaring that what seemed to be a private nuisance, such as the sparks generated by a railroad engine, was actually public. Lemuel Shaw took the position that a railroad, even though privately owned and financed, was "no less a public work; and the public accommodation is the ultimate object."[46] Only the legislature could provide compensation for the damage created by a public nuisance.

Antebellum judges treated property as a dynamic commodity to be employed for productive uses deemed in the interest of the public. By the 1840s a reasonableness and balancing test had displaced the older doctrine of absolute domain. Vested property rights and quiet enjoyment suffered as a result, although they were not completely extinguished. The judicial formulation of the common law of property hastened economic growth in the name of the public good.

The Will Theory of Contract

Contract law was the most potent set of rules by which participants in the marketplace ordered their economic relationships. Before the Revolution, contract scarcely existed. Colonialists treated bargained-for agreements as an aspect of property law, and they used it to transfer title to goods rather than to guarantee future performance. They also followed a theory of "sound" or "just" price that required judges and juries to evaluate an agreement on the basis of its terms and consequences. The just-price theory of contract embodied standards of fairness and equality that offered protection against overreaching by social superiors against their inferiors.

The "will theory" of contract that emerged after the Revolution fitted with republican rhetoric about the popular basis of law and the privatization of economic decision making. It assumed, incorrectly, an important degree of social and economic equality. Modern contract law was "thus born staunchly proclaiming that all men are equal because all measures of inequality are illusory."[47]

The "will theory" of contract was a body of rules, not for transferring property (although it continued in many instances to play that role), but for enforcing agreements in a marketplace of fungible goods. What counted was that the wills, or minds, of two independent and free individuals had met and that they had settled between themselves on the terms of the bargain. The equitable character of their agreement was not for the courts to consider; judges had only to establish that the agreement had been made.

Judges, lawyers, and legal writers all participated in the transformation of the law of contract. No other area produced such a robust legal literature. Daniel Chipman, Nathan Dane, Joseph Story, and Guilian Verplanck published major treatises on the law of contract before the Civil War. The capstone of this literature appeared in 1844 when William Wetmore Story, the son of Justice Joseph Story, published *A Treatise on the Law of Contracts*. "Every contract," the younger Story wrote, "is founded upon the mutual agreement of the parties."[48]

Three features of the new contract theory had important implications for the economy. First, it stressed the significance of expectation damages in the context of national markets. Expectation damages are based on what cash return the plaintiff anticipated if the bargain had been completed. So long as merchants dealt in specific goods, a suit for specific performance or full restitution of the amount entered into the bargain met business needs. But by the early nineteenth century, agreements turned increasingly on the realization of a future return, the value of which would be dictated by the marketplace.

Sands v. *Taylor* (1810), a New York Supreme Court case, was among the first to award expectation damages. A buyer, after accepting part of a shipment of wheat, refused to accept the rest. The seller, worrying that the remaining grain would rot, decided to sell it on the open market, doing so at a price lower than the original buyer had agreed to. The seller sued based on the difference between the original contract price and the price he had realized in the open market. Obviously, both parties had speculated on the future price of grain, and the buyer had backed out when he realized that he could get a better price on the open market.

A second economic implication was that an objective approach to contract theory made interpretation a matter of law rather than fact, sharpening the division of labor between judge and jury. Objectivity meant that judges ensured that agreements adhered to the usages of the marketplace rather than strictly considering equality of price. The question of whether a contract existed was for the judge and not the jury to decide. Furthermore, a judge was to instruct jurors about the range of possible damage awards based on his assessment of the value of the agreement in the marketplace.

Theory and practice never blended fully in antebellum contract law. The idea that judges objectively analyzed contracts was illusory, because they continued to examine the terms of the contract. They had ample opportunity to infuse their beliefs into the law. But the nature of judicial inquiry was different from that undertaken in the colonial era.

A third impact of the new contract theory on the economy was its revision of the doctrine of consideration. Consideration is that element in a contract that shows through the exchange of something of worth that a meeting of the minds has taken place. Under the sound-price doctrine of the eighteenth century, with its emphasis on the exchange of title to goods, consideration had to be adequate for the bargain to be made. In the nineteenth century, with the rise of an active futures market, goods themselves were not necessarily exchanged. The issue facing judges was not the value of the consideration (it could be a dollar), but whether it had actually been transmitted. If so, the judge (and hence the jury) had no reason to inquire further about the equality underlying the agreement. Courts were to leave the parties to themselves.

Sales and Caveat Emptor

In the eighteenth century, most sales occurred in local markets in which title to specified goods passed from one hand to another. A small knot of merchants dominated the law of sales; buyer and seller "in a typical transaction" were "both . . . middlemen, who understood the business background and were familiar with documents and customs."[49] The expanding commercial market economy of the nineteenth century changed these close relationships. No longer did one party necessarily know either the other party or the accepted market customs. In these circumstances, judges interpreted the law of sales to favor the seller.

The doctrine of *caveat emptor* demonstrates the impact of the theory of contract on the law of sales. *Caveat emptor* means buyer beware. The doctrine, which had its roots in the English common law, provided that in the absence of fraud or breach of an express or implied warranty, the buyer buys at his own risk, relying on his own estimate of the quality and suitability of goods. In colonial America, the sound-price doctrine undermined *caveat emptor,* and judges subscribed to the view that "a sound price warrants a sound commodity." Simply put, in colonial America, if one paid a reasonable price for a good that proved defective, it followed that *caveat emptor* would not apply.

The "will theory" of contract increased the importance of *caveat emptor*. The leading case was *Seixas* v. *Woods* (1804) decided by the New York Supreme Court. That court held that there could be no recovery against a merchant who unknowingly sold defective goods. The U.S. Supreme Court in *Laidlaw* v. *Organ* (1817) embraced the doctrine, in one of the first cases decided by the justices involving a contract for the future delivery of a commodity, in this instance tobacco. John Bannister Gibson of the Pennsylvania Supreme Court in 1839 summed up the reasoning behind *caveat emptor* and extended its scope. A buyer of a horse, despite a "defluxion from the [horse's] nose at the time of the bargain," accepted assurances from the seller that the animal was fit. The horse was not, and the buyer sued to recover the price. Gibson, however, overturned the jury's decision, declaring that "he who is so simple as to contract without a specification of the terms, is not a fit subject of judicial guardianship." Any other rule, Gibson concluded, "would put a stop to commerce itself in driving everyone out of it by the terror of endless litigation."[50]

Caveat emptor imposed a stern regime of contract law in an expanding capitalist economy. Its ascension was incomplete, however. The sound-price doctrine continued to flourish in South Carolina and Louisiana thanks to the civil law tradition. Moreover, Guilian Verplanck, in *An Essay on the Doctrine of Contracts* (1825), posed moral objections, arguing that individuals too often entered into bargains with unequal knowledge. He urged that an ethical sense should inform what were becoming decisions left to private agreement and market forces. Skill, shrewdness, and experience were all acceptable talents in the competitive new market economy, but special knowledge that permitted fraud was not.

Judges adapted the law of sales to an expanding economy and provided through *caveat emptor* an indirect subsidy to its operation. Any particular buyer or seller was in all likelihood a middleman as well, a link in the chain of distribution from original producer to the ultimate consumer. *Caveat emptor* allowed an end to the transaction rather than permitting endless suits to decide who knew what when. Persons were left free to make their own agreements, and that was what the nineteenth-century law of contract was all about.

Negotiable Instruments and the Federal Common Law of Commerce

Judges also applied the new contract doctrines to the law of negotiable instruments. A negotiable instrument is a document by which one party promises to pay either money or goods to another, called the bearer. A check written on your bank account is a negotiable instrument, but commercial contracts—called commercial paper in the legal vernacular—were the most important form of antebellum negotiable instruments. They circulated as currency, because specie (gold and silver) was in short supply and paper currency was often unsound. The most perplexing area of the law of negotiable instruments involved the right of assignment. This word simply means that the instrument, which was prepared by the first person and represents a debt, is given to a third person, who can collect on it in payment of an obligation owed by the person giving it to him. The negotiation of commercial paper was vital to the web of commercial agents and the trading network they controlled.

The long-term pattern was toward full negotiability of commercial paper and the establishment of a uniform set of principles to govern its flow. In 1800 only five states provided for full negotiability, but by the Civil War every state had accepted that position. The federal courts were particularly important in molding this uniformity, and the role of Justice Joseph Story was especially significant.[51] Story was the nation's leading authority on negotiable instruments, a position he claimed through his influential treatise, *Commentaries on the Law of Promissory Notes* (1845).

Story delivered the opinion of the Supreme Court in *Swift* v. *Tyson* (1842), a case that developed the federal common law of commerce. *Swift* involved the application of a New York court decision that held that a person could not give a bill of exchange (a document drawn on the account of one person and given to another for something received of value) to satisfy a preexisting debt. In essence, a bill of exchange could not be assigned. The New York law limited the circulation of commercial paper and produced great uncertainty for people engaged in commercial dealings.

Justice Story used *Swift* as an opportunity to begin the development of uniform rules for the negotiability of commercial paper where the parties were in diversity—

that is, where they were from different states. To do so, he had to resolve the question of the basis on which federal court judges ruled. Was the Federal District Court sitting in New York obliged to follow the common law of that state on a commercial law question? Or, could it decide on some other basis? Section 34 of the Judiciary Act of 1789 provided that "the laws of the several states . . . shall be regarded as rules of decision in trials at common law in the courts of the United States, in cases where they apply."[52] What this meant was unclear, because "law" could be a statute or a court ruling. Story decided that the word "law" in the 1789 act meant the "positive statutes of the state, and the construction thereof adopted by the local tribunals, and . . . rights and titles to real estate." Negotiable paper was not real property and it lay outside local control, when the parties were from different states. Therefore, Story said, federal judges in commercial cases were free to turn for their decisions to "the general principles and doctrines of commercial jurisprudence."[53]

Story aimed to replace the indeterminacy in commercial law with a unified body of rules promulgated by federal courts that could be broadly applied. The decision was a milestone in the rising authority of the federal courts and law. While the Supreme Court rejected a federal common law of crimes as an inappropriate interference with the states and with individual rights, it proved willing, in the face of a chaotic marketplace, to develop a federal common law of commerce.

Antebellum judges shaped the market economy through their interpretation of the law of contract. The Supreme Court, for example, broadened the meaning of a contract, first in holding in *Fletcher* v. *Peck* (1810) that a grant made by a state was a contract and then in *Dartmouth College* v. *Woodward* (1819) that a charter granted by a state was a contract. Along with state judicial decisions, the law of contract became a utilitarian device that fostered technological development, gave stability and uniformity to commercial dealings, and hastened the growth of a national market economy. But the "will theory" of contract law also opened a great divide between traditional precepts of morality and equity on the one hand, and objective formal rules on the other.

Tort

The same issues of economic efficiency and moral conduct appeared in tort law. A tort is a civil wrong. Judges employ legal principles associated with it to distribute the costs of accidents among social interests. Accidents associated with the advent of new technology, such as the application of steam power to transportation by railroad and steamboat, created potentially debilitating costs. One way to reduce those costs in an already capital-scarce economy was to relieve risk-taking entrepreneurs of responsibility for them. The victims of accidents produced by the machinery of the Industrial Revolution, on the other hand, suffered both physical damage (and often death) and financial loss, both in earning power and in the costs of regaining their health. Historians differ sharply about which of these groups—capitalists or victims—benefited from judicial mediation of disputes among them rising out of accidents, but the courts seem to have maintained something of a middle ground in tort law (as they did in other areas of antebellum law).

Tort law in the United States only began to develop as a separate body of law during the 1840s. Until then most tort principles had been considered a part of the law of contract. The first major treatise was not published until 1859, with Francis Hilliard's *The Law of Torts, or Private Wrongs*. The case law only swelled after the Civil War, when industrialization had its fullest impact. Still, antebellum developments were significant, both as a precursor of the future and as evidence of assumptions that judges of that era held about the proper relationship of law to economic growth.

The establishment of the fault principle was the most important tort law development before the Civil War. The English common law followed the doctrine of strict or absolute liability, which meant that all a plaintiff (the injured party) had to do was show that the defendant had committed the injury. There was no attempt to assess blameworthiness. Judges also accepted through the action of "trespass on the case" that an injury could be done on an indirect basis. Trespass on the case meant that if a person could be shown to have indirectly caused an accident he was just as responsible as if he had directly caused it. Absolute liability placed the burden, and hence the costs of the accident, squarely on the person who perpetrated it, whether or not he did so either intentionally or indirectly.

Antebellum judges, however, reexamined the meaning of tort liability within the context of a market economy dependent on new and often dangerous forms of technology and a society in which strangers increasingly came into contact with one another. The fault standard replaced strict liability. *Brown* v. *Kendall* (1850), decided by Lemuel Shaw, was the leading case. The defendant, in attempting to break up a fight between two dogs, inadvertently damaged the eye of the plaintiff. The plaintiff sued on the basis of absolute liability. Shaw concluded that this traditional standard was no longer applicable, finding that the plaintiff had to "show either that the [defendant's] intention was unlawful, or that the defendant was in fault; for if the injury was unavoidable, and the conduct of the defendant free from blame, he will not be liable." Shaw held that the defendant was required only to exercise a standard of "ordinary care," which meant the degree of care that a prudent person would exercise.[54]

Shaw virtually created a new field of law. He introduced the principle of blameworthiness: that there could be no liability without fault. Injured people could no longer win damages merely by showing that a person had perpetrated the injury. They had to show as well that the action had been negligent. Furthermore, Shaw permitted a defendant to escape liability if he could show that his act had not directly caused the accident.

Shaw's decision contained another innovation: the idea of contributory negligence. Under it a plaintiff could not collect damages if he was in any way responsible for (if he contributed to) the accident. The plaintiff's own negligence, even if slight, acted as a barrier to his recovery.

The results of this prodefendant bias were stark, even chilling, in the area of employer–employee relations. Traditionally, the English common law had placed an employee in the position of a servant for whom his employer (as his master) was responsible for all of his civil wrongs. New technology, the factory system, and expanding markets undermined this relationship by creating both physical and psychological distance between employer and employee.

Courts accepted the new reality of the workplace through the fellow-servant rule and the doctrine of assumption of risk. As with the law of labor organization, the emerging law of industrial accidents favored capital over labor, augmenting the costs of accidents on the work force through these doctrines. They were found in an English case, *Priestly* v. *Fowler* (1837), and accepted into American law shortly thereafter. In *Murray* v. *South Carolina Railroad* (1841), the South Carolina Supreme Court overturned a jury verdict given to a fireman on a railroad line who had lost a leg in an accident. But the leading case was *Farwell* v. *Boston and Worcester Railroad* (1842), decided by Lemuel Shaw, who limited the labor conspiracy doctrine the same year in *Commonwealth* v. *Hunt*. The same insistence on a competitive marketplace that prompted Shaw to accept labor organization also explains his insistence that risk-taking capitalists not be fettered by what he considered an unreasonable level of liability for their actions.

Farwell involved an engineer whose right hand was crushed when the engine tipped over on him as a result of another employee improperly throwing a switch. Shaw, for a unanimous court, invoked the fellow-servant rule and the doctrine of assumption of risk to deny Farwell any recovery. A person "takes upon himself," Shaw wrote, "the natural and ordinary risks and perils" of a job when he hires on.[55] Farwell, Shaw argued, should have realized that he was assuming the risk of just such an injury. Furthermore, because the employer was removed from the direct supervision of Farwell, the engineer had two choices: he could warn the employer of any potential danger or he could quit. Shaw's opinion placed the costs of the accident on the victim—except under the most demanding standards—rather than on the corporation and its management. Farwell, of course, could sue his fellow servant, but such a person was unlikely to have the resources necessary to pay full compensation. Shaw freed some capital for further business investment and, thereby, provided through the law an indirect subsidy for early industrial expansion.

The thesis that courts used the fault standard to subsidize capital development must be advanced with care. Gary Schwartz, for example, has found that for the jurisdictions of New Hampshire and California, the trial and appellate judges often showed great solicitude for the victims of accidents, especially passengers. There was a long-standing common law rule that public carriers were fully responsible for the safety of the passengers they transported. "Railroad passengers," he found, "were only rarely denied a recovery on account of contributory negligence."[56] The judiciary was also sensitive to the victims of boiler explosions. In *Spencer* v. *Campbell* (1845), the Pennsylvania Supreme Court rejected a defense plea that any negligence in the explosion of an engine at a grain elevator was due to the plaintiff's own negligence. The court ruled that the owner of a public trade or business, which required the use of a steam engine, owed a duty to the public it served to be responsible for any injury resulting from its deficiency. The case became a precedent for future lawsuits involving boiler explosions.

The U.S. courts continued to apply the doctrine of absolute liability to ultrahazardous activities, although the fault principle was regularly applied to actvities, such as steamboats and trains, that had perilous accident records. The New York Court of Appeals in 1852 decided the leading American case of absolute liability. *Thomas* v. *Winchester* involved a drug manufacturer who had provided a potentially fatal poison, belladonna, instead of extract of dandelion to a druggist. The druggist then sold the compound to the plaintiff. The case was important because a decade earlier an English court, in *Winterbottom* v. *Wright* (1842), had held that an action for damages could only be brought if there was a direct connection (i.e., privity of contract) between the plaintiff and defendant. Arguably, in *Thomas* v. *Winchester*, the plaintiff, whose wife had nearly died, was not in privity of contract with the drug manufacturer.

The New York court decided otherwise. It held that the production of drugs was so inherently dangerous that manufacturer responsibility extended into the marketplace. The court likened the role of the drug manufacturer to "[t]he owner of a loaded gun who puts it into the hands of a child by whose indiscretion it is discharged" and thus is "liable for the damage occasioned by the discharge."[57]

Antebellum judges devised rules that shaped the law of tort for the remainder of the nineteenth century and well into the twentieth. They accepted that some injuries would go uncompensated and that a fault standard (removed from jury supervision) would facilitate economic development by insulating entrepreneurs from the costs of accidents. Tort principles fell with special harshness on the growing industrial work force, although judges in cases involving public transportation accidents showed some solicitude to passengers.

Codification

The codification movement, like the far more successful movement to elect judges, was a critical response to the judicial creation of an American common law. The codifiers drew part of their inspiration from Jeremy Bentham, an English philosopher, criminal justice reformer, and critic of the common law. Codifiers ridiculed both the practicality and suitability of judicial interpretation of the common law, and they proposed to replace it with a scheme of entirely written law, in which (like the civil law system) all of the pertinent laws would be contained in a code that judges would apply rather than interpret and adapt. They insisted that the tasks of creating and adapting the law belonged, in a republican government, to elected legislators.

The American codification movement, which was strongest from the 1820s through the 1840s, was composed of two groups. The first were social reformers, represented by Robert Rantoul, a Jacksonian Democratic lawyer from Massachusetts. Rantoul believed that judicial interpretation of the common law was "an evil sprung from the dark ages" that hurt the poor, who could not obtain legal counsel and thus were always at the mercy of the judiciary.[58] Rantoul also complained that the common law was encrusted with technicalities that so mystified common people that they never knew for certain what the law was. Under the common law system, Rantoul observed, litigants found out what the law was only after judges had made their decisions. Codification promised, therefore, to restore a sense of legitimacy to the law based on fair dealings, certainty, and popular will.

Legal reformers like Timothy Walker, editor of the *Western Law Review* during the 1840s, and Justice Joseph Story made up a second block of codifiers. They were unconcerned about the effects of codification on the poorer classes, stressing instead the lack of uniformity and certainty in U.S. law, especially in matters involving commercial relations. A code promised to simplify and unify this body of law, to reduce the growing bulk of reports, and to speed the processing of commercial disputes by freeing lawyers from the technical encumbrances of the common law. Such a reform, Walker and Story argued, would propel the economic development of the new nation.

Enthusiasm for the codification movement waned in the 1850s, although there have been recurrent bursts of activity ever since. In part, the success of other law reforms short-circuited it. The broad adoption of the popular election of judges, which was a lawyers' reform, took away from social reformers the argument that judges were not popularly accountable. Furthermore, several state legislatures did undertake law revision, culling their statutes and forming what remained into legislative codes.

Besides Louisiana, which was a civil law state, the most important center of codification was New York. It was in New York that David Dudley Field (whose brother Stephen became a justice of the U.S. Supreme Court and whose other brother Cyrus invented the transatlantic cable) emerged as the nineteenth century's most important advocate of codification, acting from the tradition of Walker and Story. Field in 1848, at the direction of the New York legislature, prepared the Field Code of Civil Procedure. Based on the earlier work of Edward Livingston in Louisiana, Field directed his efforts at civil procedure: the way in which lawyers brought and pleaded cases before the courts. The code aimed to simplify this process and to make for a more just system, giving greater weight to the substantive issues in a case rather than the manner in which lawyers presented them. The Field Code was adopted in Missouri (1849) and California (1851), and several other western states also embraced it after the Civil War.

The common law, however, was undisturbed. Most significantly, a large and potently influential group of practitioners (the most able and successful members of the emerging antebellum bench and bar) stood implacably against the full-blown schemes of codification advanced by Walker and Field. They were motivated to oppose it by "an attachment to what they considered a tried and true legal system, and a fear that change would produce legal uncertainty destructive of established rights."[59]

Onward Spirit of the Age

Some historians, especially Morton J. Horwitz, have argued that U.S. law was transformed during these years, and that this transformation served the wealthy by indirectly subsidizing through new common law doctrines the costs of economic expansion. The courts became politicized instruments of economic progress whose benefits spilled over to only a small portion of the population. There is no doubt that the nation's infatuation with economic progress infected many judges as well as legislators. "The onward spirit of the age," wrote a Kentucky appellate judge in 1839, "must have its way. The law is made for the times, and will be made or modified by them."[60] The law had become, another judge concluded, "a practical system, adapted to the condition and business of society," and "suit[ed to] the local conditions and exigencies of every people."[61] The legal culture certainly adapted to social change, and judges (and legislators also) played a vital role.

Yet Horwitz's argument seems overdrawn in two ways. First, the judiciary certainly facilitated economic development through legal instrumentalism, but it clung to the idea that the public enjoyed certain rights that it was required to protect. Vested rights declined in importance as the new notion of public rights and popular authority over the judiciary increased, but judges continued in their historic role of protecting individual rights. Even in cases involving labor, the judiciary accepted that unionization was not a criminal activity.

Second, Horwitz underestimates the extent to which the idea of the rule of law had penetrated into American culture, as the experience of immigrants on the Overland Trail from St. Louis to the Pacific Coast in the 1840s and 1850s reveals. Although the immigrants were beyond the reach of any legal authority during their journey, they behaved in ways that underscored their law-abiding nature. When circumstances forced the dissolution of a company of sojourners, they resolved the issue by cutting their wagon into parts, each part going to an individual in the amount of the share he or she had in the enterprise. Far from being violently lawless, the immigrants displayed a remarkable degree of equanimity in settling disputes. By respect for "their neighbor and their neighbor's property they were, more often than not, adhering to a morality of law."[62]

Judicial power steadily expanded during these years and its growth had profound consequences for U.S. law. By the time of the Civil War, federal and state courts had reduced the lawfinding role of the jury in civil cases, fashioned a distinctive American common law that included a federal common law of commerce, established the principle of judicial review, and (as a consequence of doing all of these) emerged as economic policy-making institutions. In this regard, Horwitz is right in concluding that economic growth was hastened by making formal legal concern with morality and equity seem subversive to the rule of law itself. Similar developments also shaped the nineteenth-century law of crime and personal status.

7

Race and the Nineteenth-Century Law of Personal Status

Racism ran like a fault line through the nineteenth-century United States, appearing in constitutions, legislative enactments, and common law proceedings. The legal status of nonwhites had a long and convulsed history as nineteenth-century white Americans struggled to reconcile a professed national commitment to equality before the law with a fear of cheap nonwhite labor and strange cultures. The relative legal positions of blacks, native Americans, and the Chinese differed, but one common theme gave unity to the law of personal status where race was involved: the assumption of white racial and cultural superiority.

The Law of Slavery

The antebellum law of slavery established a system of both labor and racial control. After the American Revolution that system operated almost exclusively in the southern states, although vestiges of it persisted in the North until the 1830s. In the North the absence of a compelling economic need and the libertarian ideology of the American Revolution extinguished the peculiar institution. Beginning with Pennsylvania in 1780, the northern states provided for the gradual legal abolition of slavery. Even in the South, where the number of slaves was greater and where their role in the economy was more extensive, sentiments in favor of emancipation appeared. The North Carolina legislature, for example, passed laws in the eighteenth century that eased the way for slaveholders to free their human property.

Social and economic necessity eventually overrode these abolitionist sentiments. Southern whites lived in fear of the consequences of freeing the slave population. Thomas Jefferson, in his famous *Notes on the State of Virginia* (1781), objected to a proposal that called for the emancipation of all slaves born after a certain date. "Deep-rooted prejudices entertained by the whites; ten thousand recollections, by the blacks, of the injuries they have sustained," Jefferson wrote, "[and] the real distinctions which nature has made . . . will divide us into parties, and produce convulsions, which will probably never end but in the extermination of the one or the other race."[1] While Jefferson (a symbol of liberty in the nineteenth century) believed in human freedom, he thought, like many southerners, that it was impossible and wrong to achieve a racially egalitarian society through the law.

Economic necessity also prompted white southerners to throw a wall of legal protection around the peculiar institution. In the years immediately following the Revolution, the South suffered through an economic depression. Prices of slaves dropped; abolitionist sentiments rose. The introduction of Eli Whitney's cotton gin in the 1790s reversed southern economic fortunes, making cotton and gang slave labor highly profitable. Humanitarian concerns faded; a powerful planter class, whose wealth depended on slavery, turned to the law to legitimate it. Slavery survived in the South "not as an act of brute power and not as a discredited social habit," but "by the cataloguing power, the rule-making capacity . . . of . . . the law."[2] Southern lawyers and judges depersonalized the slave system, pulling on professional masks that obscured the slave's humanity and the master's moral responsibility.

A web of constitutional, common law, and statutory provisions framed the legal structure of slavery. The framers of the federal Constitution did not officially recognize slavery; the words slave and slavery nowhere appear in the document. Slavery nonetheless insinuated itself into the nation's new ruling document through North–South compromises struck in Philadelphia. James Madison believed that these compromises were so important that the Constitution would never have been agreed to without them. In total, the framers took into account the slaveholder interests in eight provisions.

Three of these provisions were of particular importance, and their inclusion set a pattern followed until the Civil War in which sectional accommodation depended on a delicate balancing of constitutional authority. The first was the fugitive slave clause in Article IV, which declared that persons held to service or labor under the laws of a state had to be returned to the person claiming that service. The second was a nonamendable denial of congressional power to prohibit the slave trade for a twenty-year period. The third was the three-fifths clause in Article I, which included slaves in the reckoning of population for the purposes of representation and direct taxation.

The silence of the Constitution on slavery affirmed the framers' view that it was a local rather than a national institution. This position had strong support in the English common law. The leading case was *Somerset* v. *Stewart* (1772), decided by Lord Mansfield. A slave brought to England by his master had escaped, but was recaptured. Antislavery activists then sought a writ of habeas corpus demanding the slave's release on the grounds that, because England had no law of slavery, Somerset was free. Mansfield agreed with the abolitionists, freeing Somerset with the observation that slavery was "so odious, that nothing can be suffered to support it but positive law."[3] The *Somerset* decision promptly passed into U.S. law, where it shaped the operation of the federal system and left slavery vulnerable to legal challenge. Slavery in the United States resulted directly from state, not federal, statutory law. It either existed by local, positive law, or it did not exist at all.

Slave Codes

Because slavery was a local institution, the law that supported it displayed great variety. Every slave state had a slave code, and that code (a body of statutes defining the institution) spelled out the property rights of masters to their slaves, the duties owed by slaves to masters, the safeguards available to the community to protect against slave rebellions, and the treatment that masters could exercise over their slaves. The codes were monuments to the idea that law could mold human behavior, order society, and fix personal status.

The codes shared certain basic assumptions and they had considerable continuity with their colonial counterparts. By the end of the eighteenth century, for example, slaves were generally treated in state codes and in court decisions as personal rather than real property. Because they were "chattels personal," slaves could be bought, sold, leased, used as collateral, bequeathed to subsequent generations, and even freed. In its crudest form, the slave law of the antebellum South simply categorized black human beings as property assets.

As in the colonial era, slave status was perpetual and inherited through the mother. This second condition was unique, because under English common law the status of children depended on the father. Slave codes expressed the truth of southern sexual practices: white men invariably engaged in sexual relations with black slave women. To have extended freedom to the progeny of these relations would have been a tacit acceptance of slave humanity and race mixing, a practice that troubled southerners almost as much as the threat of slave insurrections. Jefferson, for example (who many historians believe had his own black paramour), refused to free his slaves, insisting that freed slaves had "to be removed beyond the reach of mixture" lest they "stai[n] the blood of [the] master."[4]

The codes commanded absolute obedience by slave to master. "The condition of the slave being a merely passive one," the Louisiana Slave Code of 1806 proclaimed, "his subordination to his master and to all who represent him is not susceptible of modification or restriction. [H]e owes to his master . . . a respect without bounds."[5] Many southern appellate judges embraced this absolute view of slavery. Judge Thomas Ruffin, of North Carolina, explained in *State* v. *Mann* (1829) that under the law of slavery "the power of the master must be absolute to render the submission of the slave perfect."[6] A master was free to do as he wished, short of murdering his slave. He was restrained only by common sense, community approval, and any laws passed by the legislature. Ruffin worried about the corrosive effect of slave law on the general morality of the South, believing that absolute subjugation of the slave "constitutes the curse of slavery to both the bond and the free portion of our population." But he grimly concluded that "it is inherent in the relation of master to servant."[7]

Beginning in the early 1830s, the severity of the codes increased as slavery matured into a system of race as well as labor control. By 1820 the number of slaves had doubled from 1790, and the problem of managing them grew apace. In addition, slaves themselves worked within the institution to find forms of resistance, ranging from simple malingering to outright rebellion. The latter was suicidal, but enough incidents occurred to force whites to seek greater security. When Nat Turner, a slave preacher, led a band of armed followers in 1831 on a bloody rampage through Virginia's Southampton County (killing sixty men, women, and children), terrified whites retaliated, first by slaughtering at least 100 blacks and then by writing into the Virginia Slave Code harsh penalties for slaves who rebelled and whites who encouraged such behavior. The Virginia Code of 1849, for example, provided fine and imprisonment for any person who maintained "that owners have no right of property in their slaves."[8] "If a free person," the Alabama Code stated, "advise or conspire with a slave to . . . make insurrection, . . . he shall be punished with death, whether such rebellion or insurrection be made or not."[9]

Despite the emphasis in the law on the slave as property, white southerners understood perfectly well that slaves were human beings capable of perpetrating criminal acts. They had volition, will, and personality, all of which the law had to mute. Southern slave and criminal codes enforced slavery as it was, and southern lawmakers seldom worried about the theoretical coherence of the law they fashioned. They uniformly dealt more severely with slaves and free blacks than with whites. Certain felonies committed by blacks, free or slave, were otherwise treated as misdemeanors if perpetrated by whites. At a time when penal reformers were reducing the incidence of capital punishment, southern states broadened the scope of the death penalty for slaves guilty of murder in any degree, poisoning, robbery, rape or attempted rape of a white woman, rebellion, and arson. Furthermore, incorrigible slaves were singled out. In Louisiana, for example, a slave convicted three times of striking a white person was to suffer death.

What was on the books, both in punishments and protections for slaves, often differed from behavior. J. D. B. De Bow, a prominent southern publisher and writer, thought that the real law of slavery was on the plantation. "On our estates," he wrote, "we dispense with the whole machinery of public policy and public courts of justice. Thus we try, decide, and execute the sentences in thousands of cases, which in other countries would go into the courts."[10] Before the Civil War the law of slavery and race relations in the South was generally "indwelling." "The southern consensus on race," Daniel Boorstin writes, "was so pervasive and constraining" that the law merely ratified rather than channeled attitudes about slaves and free blacks.[11]

Contradictions of Slave Law in Operation: Sentiment and Interest

The law of slavery maintained social consensus at the expense of moral authority. The master's paternalistic sentiments toward his or her slaves was always in tension with an economic need to exploit their labor. This contradiction was profound, because white southern society was itself stratified. The law of slavery supported a powerful master class, but it had also to accommodate the needs of nonslaveholding whites, who constituted the majority in southern society.

A master's economic self-interest often mitigated the harshness of the codes. Slaves were capital assets; their injury and death was a direct loss to their owners. What was on the statute books did not necessarily find expression in the operation of the legal system. The Virginia legislature in 1732, for example, legalized benefit of clergy for slaves; in 1801 it began the institution of the reduced sentence and transportation (putting the slave out of the state by sale), and in 1848 it abolished benefit of clergy as the legal system ostensibly toughened. Yet in the 1850s, only 14.6 percent of condemned slaves were actually hanged, whereas between 1785 and 1791, only one of the 131 slaves sentenced to death escaped the gallows.[12]

Much slave justice occurred beyond the reach of the rule of law. The nature of slavery as a total institution contradicted notions of due process of law. The results were often barbaric, as in the case of *Souther* v. *Commonwealth* (1851). A Virginia slave accused of a petty offense was tied to a tree by his master, Souther. After growing exhausted with whipping his slave, the master "applied fire to the body of the slave; about his back, belly and private parts. He then caused him to be washed down with hot water, in which pods of red pepper had been steeped. This sort of punishment was continued and repeated until the negro died under his infliction."[13] Souther suffered only a five-year term in the penitentiary for second-degree murder. As a Virginia judge explained in a similar case, "[w]here the battery was committed by the master himself, there would be no redress whatever, for the reasons given in Exodus 21:21, 'for he is his money.' The powerful protection of the master's private interest would go far to remedy this evil."[14]

The clash between sentiment and interest in the law of slavery also appeared in the procedural protections that antebellum state appellate judges extended to slaves accused of crimes. Southern legislatures and courts "were in many respects astonishingly considerate of slaves' procedural rights in major criminal cases."[15] The older states had the most draconian criminal codes for slaves. Virginia, for example, which is uniformly believed to have had the most humane slave system on a day-to-day basis, maintained the most repressive system of criminal law regarding slaves. However, in Alabama and Mississippi, which had healthy and expanding slave economies, slaves enjoyed substantial statutory protections and appellate courts were solicitous of their procedural rights. "[I]t is the crowning glory of our 'peculiar institutions'," wrote the chief justice of Florida in 1860, "that whenever life is involved, the slave stands upon as safe ground as the master."[16] Georgia in 1850 extended full procedural equality to slaves, and during the ensuing decade proslavery advocates gleefully reminded northern abolitionists that slaves were protected by law.

This paradox of equality within slavery was summarized by Chief Justice Joseph Henry Lumpkin of the Georgia Supreme Court in 1852. Confronted with an appeal by a slave from a rape conviction, Lumpkin explained that "a controversy between the State of Georgia and a *slave* is so unequal, as of itself to divest the mind of all warmth and prejudice, and enable it to exercise its judgement in the most temperate manner."[17] Nonetheless, Lumpkin sustained the slave's guilty verdict, and he was hung.

Some southern appellate judges took the humanity of slaves so seriously that they founded their decisions on it, especially in the newer slave states. In 1846 Nathan Green, of the Tennessee Supreme Court, underscored the humanity of a slave in deciding *Ford* v. *Ford,* a case in which the family of a deceased master challenged his decision to free a slave by will. Judge Green not only found in favor of the slave, but wrote that "[a] slave is not in the condition of a horse or an ox, . . . he is made in the image of the Creator" and "the laws under which he is held as a slave have not and cannot extinguish his high-born nature nor deprive him of many rights which are inherent in man."[18] Although *Ford* v. *Ford* was a civil case, Green extended his concern about slave humanity to criminal proceedings as well. Moreover, postmortem manumission cases like *Ford* were significant, because they raised directly what criminal cases did not: immediate freedom for the slave.

Southern judges were part of the noble tradition of the common law. Their decisions gave meaning to it; their actions revealed a commitment to law as an autonomous body of rules that *could* work in favor of the slaves committed by positive law to abject subjugation. But there is a danger in making too much of the seeming liberalism (of the equality-within-slavery paradox) of some jurists. Southern appellate judges operated within a proslavery mentality, and the common law tradition provided a mask that concealed their humanity and that of the slaves. The indwelling character of slave law was such that judges, when given a legislative mandate of equality to build upon, could recognize a slave's humanity in a criminal trial without endangering either the master's property rights or the South's economy or system of racial control. Judges were able, as a result, to reconcile fairness for slaves (and even a degree of legal equality) with a system of perpetual racial bondage.

Too much also can be made of fairness to slaves in the criminal trial courts of the antebellum South. The criminal procedure accorded whites let alone slaves was primitive, especially in rural areas. In South Carolina in 1831, for example, an appellate court ruled that slaves could not be tried twice for the same crime, but twenty years later a slave was executed for a crime for which he had already been whipped. The decision prompted John Belton O'Neal, the state's most respected jurist, to observe: "If the prisoner was a *white man and not a Negro* could such a course receive the countenance of anyone?"[19]

The Business Law of Slavery, Slaveholders, and Nonslaveholders

The law of slavery had implications for matters other than race relations. Slavery also figured significantly in the development of the common law and in the conduct of business relations in the South. Slaves were in many ways the South's most important commodity and antebellum southern business law took account of that reality. Tens of thousands of cases crowded the dockets of southern trial and appellate courts involving slaves as subjects in some business arrangement. They were the center of disputes over the warranty of fitness given by sellers to buyers, and as property they were regularly mortgaged, hired, stolen, bartered, wagered, seized for debt, and fought over in succession and divorce contests. Matters of tort, contract, and consumer protection involving slaves were everyday facts of legal life in the region.

The law of slavery also had implications for nonslaveholding whites. Slave patrols, for example, were typically composed of nonslaveholders whose duty it was to guard the slave system against runaways and arrest slaves suspected of violating the law. The patrols exercised extraordinary authority in the rural and lightly populated southern states that had no official police forces. The patrol's power often caused consternation among masters. The patrol offered the nonwealthy whites the opportunity to destroy and abuse the property of their social superiors. Slaveholders repeatedly went to the courts with charges that patrollers had invaded their plantations and whipped their slaves excessively. But masters "looked upon the patrol as an essential police system, and none ever seriously suggested abolishing it."[20]

But it was in business dealings that the interests of slaveholders and nonslaveholders were most fully joined. In tort law, for example, the English common law held masters absolutely liable for the negligence of their servants. Slaves were not servants; they were chattels under the absolute legal dominion of the master. The social and the legal position of the slave "simply was not the social and legal position of the English servant."[21] The tension created by the slave's personality in the criminal law matched the anomaly of a slave being held liable for accidents by any provision in the law of torts. The question arose: who would pay for slave accidents? Obviously, slaves could not.

Emerging concepts of nineteenth-century tort law freed employers of responsibility for accidents involving their employees through the fellow-servant rule, contributory negligence, and assumption of risk. Southern courts, like their northern counterparts, applied these doctrines to white workers, and the South Carolina Supreme Court was the first to invoke the fellow-servant rule. The extension of these principles to slaves would have posed questions about the scope of the master's control, a matter on which the slave system was not interested in compromising.

Yet compromise it did. The way in which southern courts treated the matter of masters' liability for slave wrongs depended on whether jurists worked within a system defined by statutes, the civil law, or the common law. In Louisiana, for example, appellate judges applied the civil law standard of absolute liability. The Louisiana Supreme Court held that ownership of slaves carried as one of its "burthens" responsibility for the actions of slaves owned by the master, although the law also provided the means by which masters could limit their damages.[22]

In the common law jurisdictions, the problem was more acute and the solutions to it depended on the extent of nonslaveholder power. As with procedural fairness in slave criminal proceedings, the scope of masters' liability was greatest where nonslaveholders were politically strongest. While southern appellate judges paid close attention to developments in tort law in the North, they were nearly unanimous in declaring that slaves could never be elevated to the status of "fellow servants." Courts generally allocated the costs of industrialization in the South by siding with the masters and placing the burden of accidents on the industries that hired the slaves.

White nonslaveholders had a direct interest in receiving compensation for slave wrongs. The legislatures of Arkansas and Missouri, for example, made masters civilly liable for a specified series of trespasses. The Tennessee legislature provided that masters would be liable for injuries that resulted from certain stipulated offenses, but that the damages could not exceed the value of the slave. The notion that masters could and should control their slaves was particularly strong. Judge Nathan Green, for example, urged the Tennessee legislature to impose by statute a broad rule of liability on masters for the actions of their slaves, observing that such a law "would be fair and equal among the slaveholders themselves; and, in relation to a large majority of the people of the state, who do not own slaves, it is imperiously required."[23]

The law ironically accommodated the South's system of social deference to the "indwelling" character of slavery by legally imposing extralegal solutions. For example, an Arkansas statute provided that "in all [torts], and offences less than felony" committed by a slave, the master could "compound with the injured person and punish his own slave, without the intervention of any legal trial or proceeding; but if he refuse to compound, the slave may be tried and punished, and the damage recovered by suit against the master."[24]

Southern judges also protected the slave-buying public from attempts by slave dealers, auctioneers, and individuals who were seeking to unload a diseased, disabled, or refractory slave. In Louisiana the Civil Code regulated the sale of slaves in much the same way as the sale of any other commodity. During the antebellum period, the state's supreme court heard more than twelve hundred appeals involving slavery and the most numerous of these concerned provisions of the state's code regulating the sale of slaves defective in mind or body. The Louisiana Supreme Court strictly followed the letter of the code, which favored slave buyers over sellers. In common law jurisdictions protection for slave buyers was equally strong. The best example was South Carolina, the state with the highest percentage of slave population and a history of intensive slave buying from the colonial days to the Civil War. While the doctrine of *caveat emptor* had strong support in the North, it was explicitly rejected in matters involving slaves by the South Carolina courts. In effect, judges in South Carolina held, beginning with *Timrod* v. *Schoolbred* (1793), that sellers gave all buyers who paid a sound price an implied warranty as to the fitness of the slave. Once again, where slavery was strongest was where the protection for slave buyers was greatest. In the upper South, the South Carolina approach was not adopted, although judges and legislators were still solicitous of slave buyers and far more skeptical of the doctrine of *caveat emptor* than were northern judges and legislators. More generally, the favorable stance to the buyer of most southern lawmakers shows that they had little trouble treating slaves like ordinary articles in commerce.

Economic Contradictions of Slave Law

Sentiments of humanity and economic self-interest were expressed in powerful contradictions that ultimately worked to the detriment of the southern economy. John Archibald Campbell, a justice of the U.S. Supreme Court from Alabama, who resigned to join the Confederacy, appreciated the tension between paternalism toward the slave and the imperatives of the market. "The connection of husband and wife, and parent and child," Campbell explained in discussing the law of slavery, "are sacred in a Christian State." But in the business world practical considerations necessarily limited the emotional energy that a master could expend on his slaves. The law was supposed to keep such sentiments from developing. "[T]he liability of the slave to change his relation on the bankruptcy of his master, and the frequency with which [it] occurs," Campbell observed, "has . . . deprived the relation of some of its patriarchical nature."[25] Maintaining legal control over the slave as property was the essence of the southern law of slavery, regardless of the contradictions it raised, both within the region and in the nation as a whole.

The emerging market economy of the nineteenth-century United States bore down upon the law of slavery. Even the closest human bond was subject to market pressures, and the law did nothing to ameliorate this reality. The recognition of the market realities of slavery did not mean that the economy of the South matured in the same ways as that of the free states. The opposite may well have been the case. A myriad of social relations was necessary to the maintenance of the peculiar institution; sanctioning these by law hindered the construction of an economy competitive with the North. Political and social stability "were maintained at the expense of efficient economic arrangements."[26]

Masters needed slaves, and the South's legal system, as an extension of the social system, protected and perpetuated slavery. An aggressive slave system went unchallenged from within by a legal system wedded to a dispassionate rule of law founded on virulent racism. Outside the South, however, a different cultural ethic prompted a different legal response to human bondage.

Antislavery and the Legal Order

Slavery was an extension of local law with national implications. The vast majority of residents in the free states were as racist as their southern cousins. Even most antislavery political leaders in the North harbored racist sentiments. Representative David Wilmot of Pennsylvania, whose famous proviso in 1846 sought to block the expansion of slavery into territories gained through the Mexican War, explained that he urged the measure because "the negro race already occupy enough of this fair continent; let us keep what remains for ourselves, and our children . . . for the free white laborer."[27] Public facilities, including schools, were segregated. The idea of free soil and free labor animated most northern antislavery politicians, who believed that free whites should not have to compete against slave labor in the vast new territories acquired by the United States. As a matter of practical politics, the Republican party of Abraham Lincoln had no plan to destroy slavery where it existed, although with Lincoln's election in 1860 many southerners were ready to secede for fear that Republican control would mean precisely that result.

Southern concerns were well founded. Beginning in the 1830s, slaveholders confronted a vital antislavery movement that resourcefully appealed to legal and constitutional arguments. The antislavery critique of the legal order's support for slavery involved more than just an attack on the peculiar institution. It included, as well, "moralistic arguments about the law of God and the rights of man" coupled with a resolve that in the United States the law "should [be] decid[ed] . . . consistently with standards of what, in some ultimate sense, was right and wrong."[28] In short, antislavery advocates expected through the law to persuade Americans to adopt a new commitment to morality. If the formal legal process should prove unavailing, then some antislavery leaders urged civil disobedience based on higher law principles.

By the time of the Civil War, three different approaches to the legal and constitutional problems of slavery emerged in the antislavery movement. For shortened purposes they can be referred to as radical, moderate, and Garrisonian.

The radicals' most important legal figures were Alvan Stewart of New York and Lysander Spooner of Boston. Both of these lawyers rejected the essential principle of *Somerset,* that slavery could exist by local positive law, and insisted that the institution was everywhere illegitimate. They demanded abolition of slavery based on the Fifth Amendment's due-process clause and the guarantee in Article IV that the federal government would ensure a republican form of government to every state. These were genuinely radical constitutional and legal positions, and only a small portion of the organized antislavery movement embraced them.[29]

Moderates occupied the legal and constitutional mainstream of antislavery. Their most important spokesman was Salmon P. Chase, a Cincinnati lawyer. Where the radicals had argued that the federal government had the power to destroy slavery everywhere, the moderates insisted that the federal government lacked any power over slavery. They subscribed to *Somerset,* insisting that it prevented the federal government from extending slavery into the new territories and returning escaped slaves to their masters. If slavery were divorced from the national government, the moderates believed, then it would eventually wither. The moderate position, in essence, became the position of the Republican party on the eve of the Civil War.

The Garrisonian abolitionists developed yet a third position. Their most important legal spokesman was Wendell Phillips, a Boston patrician animated by a belief in religious perfectionism. The Garrisonians believed that slavery was above all else a sin, and that any institution that supported it was immoral. Not only did they reject *Somerset* as meaningless, but they also insisted that the Constitution was, in the words of their leader William Lloyd Garrison, "a covenant with death and an agreement with Hell . . . and should be immediately annulled."[30] In 1854, Garrison dramatized his opposition by publicly burning a copy of the nation's ruling document, setting off a riot that forced him to flee for his life. Phillips argued that a "higher law," based on overriding moral principles, should be substituted for the fatally compromised Constitution, and that each person had a duty to exercise civil disobedience aimed at toppling the established rule of law.

Such arguments stirred a level of suspicion of political dissenters not seen since the end of the eighteenth century, and Democrats leveled charges of treason against abolitionists just as Federalists had at their Jeffersonian opponents. The few treason prosecutions undertaken by the federal government against abolitionists during the late 1840s and 1850s failed.

Legal and Constitutional Issue of Fugitive Slaves

The legal status of escaped slaves emerged as the chief concern of the antislavery bar, and it was in state and federal courtrooms that its members honed their legal arguments. Congress implemented the fugitive slave clause of the Constitution in the Fugitive Slave Act of 1793. Under the act, an owner or his or her agent could seize a suspected runaway and, after obtaining a certificate from a federal judge or local magistrate, haul the person back to the owner's state. The measure depended on the willingness of state and local authorities to cooperate, because the federal legal presence was limited. The measure was also subject to criticism, because it extended no due-process protections to individuals seized under it, making free blacks as well as fugitive slaves easy targets for ambitious slave catchers.

By the 1830s the antislavery bar began a sustained campaign against the constitutionality of the Fugitive Slave Act. Salmon P. Chase and James G. Birney, a former Alabama slaveholder who was converted to the antislavery cause, fired the first salvo in 1837 in the case of an escaped slave, Matilda Lawrence. When Lawrence was dragged before a local magistrate, Chase condemned the 1793 act. The Cincinnati lawyer, who came to be known as the "attorney general for runaway negroes," maintained that the law was unconstitutional, because it failed to provide due-process protections to the fugitive and because, in any event, the national government lacked power to pass the act in the first place. Moreover, Chase asserted that the principle of *Somerset* had to hold, because when Matilda Lawrence came into Ohio, a free state, she became free. Slavery could only exist on the basis of positive law, and once she left the immediate jurisdiction of a slave state its power no longer controlled her. Chase made the essential point that freedom was national and supported by natural law. The local judge rejected these arguments; Matilda Lawrence's owner shipped her to the New Orleans slave market for sale.

The clamor over the Fugitive Slave Act mounted during the 1840s. Several northern states, for example, had earlier passed "personal liberty" laws that extended to accused fugitive slaves certain procedural safeguards, including jury trial and the writ of habeas corpus. These measures complicated the operation of the federal act that relied on state courts and officers to make it work. There was also the issue of whether states could impose these conditions on the execution of a federal law, and many southerners, though usually viewed as proponents of states' rights, protested as unconstitutional these exercises in local autonomy.

The question of state authority and the application of the *Somerset* principle converged in the 1842 case of *Prigg* v. *Pennsylvania*. Edward Prigg, a slaveholder's agent from Maryland, had seized a runaway in Pennsylvania and returned her to Maryland in violation of an 1826 Pennsylvania personal liberty law. When Prigg returned to the state he was arrested under that statute and charged with kidnapping. The matter quickly moved to the U.S. Supreme Court.

Justice Joseph Story wrote the opinion for the Court, although six other justices entered opinions as well. Story, as we have already seen, was a strong nationalist and an advocate of uniformity in national legal standards. His opinion held the Fugitive Slave Act of 1793 constitutional and the Pennsylvania personal liberty law of 1826 unconstitutional. The power over fugitive slaves, in the name of uniform national treatment and specified constitutional authority, rested exclusively with Congress. The decision was a major victory for the slave interests, and Story left no doubt about the power of the federal government to provide for the recapture of fugitive slaves. He described that power as "absolute and positive . . . pervading the whole Union with an equal and supreme force, uncontrolled and uncontrollable by State sovereignty or State legislation."[31] Story refused to apply *Somerset,* avoiding completely the issue of whether a slave entering free territory became free.

The antislavery bar seized from seeming defeat an innovative approach to the fugitive slave issue that Story's opinion had left open. Story was unclear about whether the states, given the exclusive authority of the federal government over fugitive slaves, could refuse to aid in implementing the federal law. The antislavery bar argued that if federal authority was exclusive, then the federal government would also have to provide the means of enforcement. Many northern states, at the urging of the moderate wing of the antislavery bar, passed new personal liberty laws that prohibited state officials from enforcing the federal fugitive slave law and denied the use of state facilities for that purpose. The national government bore not only the constitutional burden but also the administrative costs of recapturing fugitive slaves.

Southerners attempted to seal this loophole in the Compromise of 1850. Congress passed as part of that measure a new fugitive slave act that provided for the appointment, by federal circuit courts, of commissioners to decide whether a fugitive should be returned. The act did not require a jury trial, nor did it permit the alleged fugitive slave to testify, and the determination of the commissioner was conclusive against any writ of habeas corpus by a state. As an added incentive, the commissioner received a larger fee for returning the fugitive to slavery rather than freedom. The measure made the rendition of fugitives a ministerial rather than a judicial process, throttling continued direct legal intervention by antislavery moderates such as Chase.

Problem of Comity and Conflict of Laws

The fugitive slave cases raised the legal principle of comity. The term means the courtesy or consideration that one jurisdiction gives by enforcing the laws of another, granted out of respect and deference rather than obligation. Judges often have to decide which conflicting body of laws will be applied. Comity had enormous implications for the system of racial control exercised in the South, for as long as free states continued to respect the legal rights of masters to exercise dominion over their slaves while sojourning or in transit, then slave property remained mobile. Until the 1830s a "sectional accommodation" existed, in which northern courts accepted that southern laws protected masters sojourning with their slaves in free states.[32]

This accommodation broke down in the 1830s and it was Justice Story, who later wrote the opinion in *Prigg,* that contributed intellectual force to its collapse. Story in 1834 published *Commentaries on the Conflict of Laws,* and in it he argued that the practice of comity was strictly voluntary and rested on no moral compulsion. Every state, according to Story, had complete control over what law should be enforced within its boundaries. The Story doctrine confirmed the jurisdictional supremacy of the forum state, which is the place where the case was heard. The implications were far-reaching, because the new doctrine permitted courts and judges in the free states to refuse to return slaves to their masters, because they were not commanded by the law of their state to do so. The new conflict-of-laws principle also meant that, except for the federal Fugitive Slave Act, there was no necessary legal basis for the return of slaves. The new legal principle tightened already taut sectional lines.

The significance of the new doctrine of comity first appeared in *Commonwealth* v. *Aves* (1836), in which Lemuel Shaw wrote the opinion. The case involved Med, a six-year-old girl brought by her mistress into Massachusetts on a visit. Abolitionist women in Boston secured counsel, who sought a writ of habeas corpus for her release.

Shaw explicitly rejected an appeal made on the principle of comity as the basis for the interstate rendition of the girl. Instead, Shaw followed Mansfield's earlier argument in *Somerset* and the view of comity asserted by Story. Slavery, Shaw declared, was contrary to natural right and dependent on local law for its "existence and efficacy." To extend comity in such cases would mean permitting any amount of slaveholding residence short of outright domicile, and that, according to Shaw, was repugnant to "sound policy."[33] Shaw found that comity might apply on a regular basis to property, but (in a clear swipe at one of the cardinal features of southern slave law) slaves were not property and therefore comity would not extend to them. Because Massachusetts had failed to enact a "sojourning statute" (an act that permitted masters to have their slaves with them), it followed that, except for accidental and brief intrusions by masters with slaves into the state, slaves would become free under Massachusetts law once they reached the state. Southerners disapproved of this new arrangement, and one Georgia judge described the new comity principles formulated by Story and Shaw as "the foul spirit . . . of modern fanaticism."[34]

Neither the decision in *Aves* nor the approach of most northern judges to the legal status of slaves brought into free territory was so sweeping. Shaw did not apply his decision to fugitive slaves nor did he apply it to any slave who voluntarily returned home with his master. Shaw was a conservative, and he and other judges—in both the North and South—were unwilling to use judicial power to declare that slavery was illegal. The antislavery bar charged that free-state judges were too willing to buckle under to slaveholders.

Northern Judges and the Masks of the Law

Slavery posed for northern judges issues about their role in the legal system every bit as perplexing as those confronted by southern judges. We know that in the distribution of economic justice, the antebellum appellate judiciary was often instrumental, giving discretion to human will in framing the legal bounds of economic decision making. But many of these same northern judges, though openly hostile to slavery, pulled on the masks of the law and resorted to a highly formal approach to issues of personal status, morality, and race.

By the 1850s, opponents of slavery sought to awaken northern moral sentiment through civil disobedience and dramatic rescues of escaped slaves. Judges were confronted with popular efforts to free people who would, under the letter of the law, be returned to slavery. The judiciary sustained the rule of law over emotion and mob action, but judges did so by placing their legal masks on in ways that ignored the humanity of individual slaves. Typical was Lemuel Shaw's action in the case of Thomas Sims.

Sims was a fugitive slave captured in Massachusetts and hauled before a federal commissioner under the 1850 act. Sims's antislavery lawyers then sought a writ of habeas corpus from the Supreme Judicial Court of Massachusetts, arguing that the Fugitive Slave Act was unconstitutional and that by virtue of being in free territory Sims had become a free person. Tensions ran so high that the courthouse was encircled with chains and ropes to prevent disruption of the proceedings.

Shaw's opinion confirmed the worst fears of antislavery advocates. Shaw not only denied the writ but upheld the Fugitive Slave Act of 1850 in what was "the preeminent judicial determination on that issue from any court, federal or state."[35] Shaw held the fugitive slave clause had been necessary for the ratification of the Constitution and that subsequent generations could not disturb it through judicial interpretation. Congress had power to enact a fugitive slave law under that clause and the necessary and proper clause of Article I. In short, as offensive as slavery might have been to Shaw, he decided, as a matter of law, to return Sims to slavery.

Similar scenes were played out in other courtrooms in the North, as judges with antislavery sentiments refused to use their offices to strike at the immorality of slavery. Henry David Thoreau, for example, extolled resistance to this law and chided judges for upholding it even when they knew full well that the ends were evil. "The law will never make men free," Thoreau wrote in his essay, "Slavery in Massachusetts," "[I]t is men who have got to make the law free." He stigmatized Shaw and other judges as "organ grinders" who were incapable of distinguishing the mechanical act of churning out opinions based on the law with what he believed was a greater duty to the higher law of moral conscience.[36]

Northern judges repeatedly pulled on their judicial masks, placing law over sentiment and precedent over innovation. The judicial role exercised a powerful influence. "The law is our only guide," wrote Justice John McLean, one of the two dissenters in the famous *Dred Scott* case. "If convictions of what is right or wrong," he insisted, "are to be substituted as a rule of action in disregard of the law, we shall soon be without law and without protection."[37]

Higher Law and the Dred Scott Case

The antislavery bar offered the higher law principle as a response to judicial formalism. Senator William Henry Seward grabbed public attention with the concept in a political speech in 1850, although he was merely voicing a proposition that went back to the American Revolution. "There is higher law," Seward intoned to Senate colleagues with quasi-religious fervor, "than the Constitution."[38] Even if the Fugitive Slave Act of 1850 was constitutional, an issue that Seward and other moderate antislavery proponents rejected, the law of conscience overrode it. Such sentiments, of course, posed a direct challenge to established authority and, given the delicate nature of the sectional balance, threatened to divide the Union.

The Supreme Court thoroughly refuted higher law notions in *Dred Scott* v. *Sandford* (1857). The case required more than a decade to work its way through state and federal courts. Scott with his wife and children had traveled with their master, an army surgeon, to the Minnesota territory (where slavery was forbidden by the Missouri Compromise of 1820) and then returned with him to Missouri, a slave state. The precise legal issue before the Court was whether Scott could sue for his freedom in a federal court based on being a citizen of Missouri. Counsel for John Sanford, Scott's owner by the time the case reached the Court, insisted that a black had no capacity to be a citizen, either of the state or the nation. The justices could have settled the issue of pleading without ever reaching the merits of Scott's case—especially the question of whether Scott and his family had become free as a result of having sojourned in territory declared free under the Missouri Compromise.

Although each of the nine justices wrote separate opinions, that of Chief Justice Roger B. Taney was authoritative. Taney rejected every argument made in Scott's behalf, denying him citizenship in both the United States and Missouri. Neither free nor slave blacks, according to Taney, could be citizens. "[In 1776]," the chief justice explained, "they had for more than a century before been regarded as beings of an inferior order, and altogether unfit to associate with the white race, either in social or political relations; and so far inferior that they had no rights which the white man was bound to respect."[39] Taney held that the Missouri Compromise of 1820 was unconstitutional and asserted that Congress had no power to deny slaveholders control over the use of their peculiar property. Rather, the federal government had a positive duty to protect the property rights of all citizens, including masters, and the mere sojourn of a slave in free territory did nothing to disturb those rights. Taney, in effect, directly refuted *Somerset* and all of the constitutional principles upon which the moderate antislavery bar had stood.

Taney did not blunder into the *Dred Scott* decision, even though his opinion was filled with historical errors and flawed reasoning. He invoked federal judicial power to assert the right of slaveholders to their property and, even more important, to establish conclusively in the law the degraded legal position of blacks. For the first time in their history, "the American people had to consider the meaning and consequence of judicial review actually executed at the federal level."[40] Taney's opinion threw the weight of national legal authority squarely on the side of slaveholders, effectively nationalizing what had previously been a local institution. Taney attempted to substitute the force of law for political accommodation, but once the Court made clear that it favored the interests of one section over another, the remaining ties of political unity snapped, leaving the sectionally based northern Republican party to claim control of the national government in 1861.

Race Relations after the Civil War

The Civil War freed one sixth of the U.S. population from bondage. A small number of free blacks had lived in both the North and the South before the war, and they were everywhere denied by law full social and political equality. Only Massachusetts permitted them both to serve on juries and to give testimony. Lemuel Shaw, in *Roberts* v. *City of Boston* (1849), summarized their condition in an opinion dealing with the authority of the school board of Boston to segregate children by race. He conceded that "all persons without distinction of age or sex, birth or color, origin or condition, are equal before the law," but he also found that the legislature through its police powers could arbitrarily give or withhold rights on the basis of race, because "those rights must depend on laws adapted to their respective relations and conditions."[41]

Union victory in the Civil War presented an unparalleled opportunity to redefine the legal basis of race relations. The greatly enlarged free black population was a source of potential political power for Republicans, a means of realizing the moralistic objectives of antislavery advocates, and the basis on which to adjust the scope of federalism. By establishing the ascendancy of the Union, the war opened possibilities for the exercise of federal power over the law of personal status, an area previously the exclusive legal domain of the states.

The most striking early example of Republican efforts to secure protection of the black minority in the South was the Freedmen's Bureau. Created by Congress in 1865, it did not receive full powers until the following year and its effective operation ceased in 1868. Congress endowed the bureau with "control of all subjects relating to refugees and freedmen in the rebel states."[42] The bureau's director, General Oliver O. Howard, construed this statute to authorize local bureau agents working in southern localities to try minor civil and criminal cases. The purpose of the bureau was to "set the law in motion."[43] The bureau's agents attempted to create enough familiarity among blacks with the law that southern whites would continue with a program of equal justice after the federal military presence had left. These bureau agents adjudicated hundreds of thousands of complaints each year, most of them involving common law matters of contract, tort, and property that were traditionally the preserve of state courts. Bureau courts became another layer a federal layer of legal authority, and their decisions usually went in such a way as to favor blacks.

Republicans turned to other devices to press the authority of the national government on the South. For example, military courts in the days immediately following the end of the war contributed significantly to the restoration of law and order. Congress also expanded the jurisdiction of the federal courts, making it easier for blacks to remove cases from often hostile state courts, and enlarged the number of federal courts in the region, making federal judicial power more readily available.

Black Codes

These measures were inadequate to the task of protecting blacks under the law. Southern states almost immediately passed Black Codes to curtail the newly won liberty of freedmen, while white-supremacist nightriders sought to intimidate blacks through violence. The codes recognized that blacks were human beings and free persons. Blacks could buy, sell, own, and bequeath real and personal property. They could also make contracts (including marriage contracts with other blacks, but not whites), sue and be sued, and testify in courts in cases in which blacks were a party.

The codes, on the other hand, were instruments of racial control that, while acknowledging the freedmen's new status, imposed a kind of quasi slavery. For example, blacks were forbidden from pursuing certain occupations (e.g., skilled artisans, physicians, and merchants) and were restricted in the areas in which they could live. They could not own firearms, and—in a nod to the social etiquette of slavery days— they were forbidden to direct insulting words at white people. Blacks could not serve on juries, vote, or hold office. They were, in sum, political ciphers and social pariahs.

Several northern states passed similar laws at the same time. These states also strengthened their rules against black migration in an effort to prevent race mixing and to preserve free white-labor markets. Northern political leaders, including conservative members of the Republican party, clung to a strong states' rights policy, believing that the legal basis of social policy should be formed locally. Yet, in the period immediately following the war, many of these same northerners believed that southerners deserved to be punished, and that the Black Codes embodied an unacceptable reassertion of a political and social system supposedly destroyed by the war.

Civil War Amendments

Beginning in 1865 and continuing for the next decade, congressional Republicans invoked the lawmaking authority of the federal government to reconstruct the social basis of southern politics. Until the Civil War, the Constitution had been interpreted as primarily a system of negatives. The prodigious effort necessary to fight that conflict transformed the nation's ruling document into an engine for change. The antislavery bar's stress on the positive responsibility of the national government to advance individual rights converged with the nationalism of Marshall, Story, and Abraham Lincoln. The resulting new view of the Constitution held that it imposed duties on the national government "to act positively, as an instrument, to realize purposes that had inspired the creation of the nation."[44]

The three Civil War amendments—the Thirteenth, Fourteenth, and Fifteenth— embodied the spirit of this new constitutional order, redefining through federal authority the social and political position of blacks and the relationship of the central government to the states. The Thirteenth, ratified in 1865, not only abolished slavery but gave Congress, for the first time in any amendment, "power to enforce this article by appropriate legislation."[45] Some scholars even argue that the amendment, which was unique in having a direct social objective, provided the necessary basis on which every incident of racial discrimination, such as segregation, could be eliminated. Whatever the merit of that argument, in practice the Supreme Court interpreted the amendment narrowly.

The Fifteenth Amendment was ratified five years later. It did not grant blacks the right to vote, but it outlawed federal and state governments from denying or abridging the right to vote based on "race, color, or previous condition of servitude."[46] The amendment was an attempt by Republicans to establish a legal basis by which to proceed against southern whites who intimidated black voters. As with the Thirteenth Amendment, the Court applied an exceedingly restrictive meaning, limiting federal enforcement of black voting rights.

The Fourteenth Amendment, ratified in 1868, had the greatest influence on the long-term development of the law of personal status and, more generally, the nature of the federal system. Of the amendment's five sections, three dealt with punitive measures directed against the South; a fourth gave Congress the power to pass necessary legislation to enforce the amendment.

The first section was the most far-reaching. It established national citizenship and declared that equal protection of the laws, privileges and immunities, and due process of law extended to all persons against state action. In so doing, the amendment worked a powerful revolution in federalism, making the national government ascendant over the states. The amendment also overturned Chief Justice Taney's *Dred Scott* opinion, making blacks national citizens eligible for federal protection of their civil and political rights.

The specific intent of the amendment's framers remains subject to speculation, and the historical record of its congressional debate has left twentieth-century interpreters divided. One principal area of disagreement involves the question of whether the framers of the amendment meant to incorporate the Bill of Rights against the states. Until that time, the Supreme Court had held that the Bill of Rights applied only against the national government. The theory of incorporation holds that the Fourteenth Amendment worked such a profound revolution in the federal system that the rights and liberties contained in the Bill of Rights were meant to apply to the states as well. They had been incorporated in the broad guarantees of due process, equal protection, and privileges and immunities. Although some lower federal court judges accepted the doctrine of incorporation during Reconstruction, the Supreme Court rejected it, and not until the twentieth century did the justices begin selectively to incorporate most, but not all, of the Bill of Rights provisions into the Fourteenth Amendment.

The new amendment provided Republicans in Congress with authority to implement a full-blown plan of reconstruction. Congress provided for a reformation in governance of the South, effecting the repeal of the Black Codes, stemming the violence of the Ku Klux Klan, and asserting federal military, judicial, and legal power. The result was a temporary revolution in the South's political and social character. Whites were disfranchised, blacks were elected to public office, and the legal systems of some of the Confederate states fell under black influence. In South Carolina, where Klan violence was epidemic, J. J. Wright, a black man, became a justice on that state's supreme court.

Limits of Social Change through the Law

The embedded racism of the Reconstruction era limited the scope of social change through the law. The Republican party grew weary of the costs associated with reconstruction, and as the memory of the war slipped away the northern white public, which had little real interest in the fate of blacks to begin with, also lost interest. As the southern race demagogue "Pitchfork" Ben Tillman of South Carolina explained to the North: "You do not love [blacks] any better than we do. You used to pretend that you did, but you no longer pretend it."[47]

The Supreme Court was skeptical of Republican initiatives, because they reversed the traditional relationship between the states and the national government. Congress, for example, passed the Civil Rights Act of 1875, a far-reaching measure whose flowery preamble proclaimed "the equality of all men before the law" as well as the duty of government "to mete out equal and exact justice to all, of whatever nativity, race, color, or persuasion." The act gave to "all persons within the jurisdiction of the United States" the "full and equal enjoyment" of facilities.[48] These words seemed to permit the government to prosecute violations in quasi-public and even private accommodations that served the public, such as theaters, hotels, and railroad cars.

Many congressmen during the final debate on the measure claimed it was unconstitutional, and the Supreme Court, in *The Civil Rights Cases* (1883), agreed. By a vote of eight to one, the justices struck down the law. Justice Joseph Bradley explained that "[w]hen a man has emerged from slavery, and by the aid of beneficent legislation has shaken off the inseparable concomitants of that state, there must be some stage in the progress of his elevation when he takes the rank of a mere citizen, and ceases to be the special favorite of the law, and when his rights as a citizen, or a man, are to be protected in the ordinary modes by which other men's rights are protected."[49] The decision spelled the end to the positive use of federal law to promote equality among the races; it began a long cycle in which federal and state law discriminated against not only blacks, but native Americans and Chinese.

Black Involuntary Servitude, Segregation, and Political Exclusion

Once the Redeemer governments of the South regained political control in the late 1870s, they resurrected the labor control features of the earlier Black Codes and imposed new limits on black social and political participation. The "indwelling spirit" of southern race relations law surfaced with a vengeance. Southerners knew "that the laws were intended to maintain white control of the labor force."[50]

A system of involuntary servitude replaced the shattered law of slavery. Involuntary servitude was not peonage, however. Peonage had a precise and narrow legal meaning: it was the condition that existed when individuals had to work against their will even without a claim of debt. Peonage existed in the South after the Civil War, even though outlawed by the federal Peonage Act of 1867, but it was not widespread.

Involuntary servitude facilitated both the recruitment and the retention of black labor. Like slavery, it was both a social and an economic system. The variety of statutes enacted by southern legislators testifies eloquently to the complexity of the system. Enticement statutes established the property claims of employers to "their" blacks by making it a crime to hire away a laborer under contract to another person. Emigrant-agent laws assessed prohibitive license fees against those persons who made their living by moving labor from one state to another, and a variety of contract-enforcement statutes virtually imposed peonage. Some contract legislation made breaking a labor contract a criminal offense even when no debt was involved. Vagrancy statutes of great breadth permitted police to round up idle blacks in times of labor scarcity and also gave employers a coercive tool that kept workers on the job. Blacks jailed on charges of vagrancy or any other petty crime were then vulnerable to the criminal-surety system, which gave the offender an "opportunity" to sign a voluntary-labor contract with his former employer or some other white who agreed to post bond. Convict-labor laws began where the surety system ended, and blacks who had no surety often joined the chain gang.

Legally imposed social segregation by race developed in cadence with involuntary servitude. When Reconstruction collapsed, the southern states gradually imposed formal segregation. To some extent, the economic degradation of blacks through involuntary servitude settled their social position as well. Yet, even when blacks could make use of public facilities, by the letter of the law they seldom did. The segregation statutes that appeared in the late 1880s and 1890s did not replace a scheme of social integration, but rather one in which blacks were excluded by customary understanding. Legal segregation formalized existing social arrangements rather than creating new ones.[51]

Southerners reimposed white supremacy on every front. State legislatures, for example, mandated segregation on railroads, even though many railroad companies objected to the practice because it added to their operating costs. Arkansas went so far as to segregate voting places. Private citizens, in both the North and the South, placed racial covenants in deeds that prohibited the sale of real property to nonwhites.

Everywhere in the South, black political participation was proscribed. The most common devices were literacy and understanding tests that excluded illiterate and poorly educated blacks, and poll taxes that made black poverty a legal barrier to the enjoyment of political rights. These measures, which were often touted as reforms to promote good government, applied to lower-class whites as well, but states made provision for their exemption, often through so-called grandfather clauses. The Oklahoma version, which was so racially motivated that even the Supreme Court struck it down in *Guinn* v. *United States* (1915), required voters to be able to read and write any section of the Oklahoma Constitution. But it exempted anybody who was entitled to vote on January 1, 1866, in any country—and anybody descended from such a voter. Of course, blacks could not qualify.

The various exclusionary tests dealt a staggering blow to the black electorate. In Louisiana, for example, the number of registered black voters fell from 127,000 in 1896 to 3300 in 1900.

The Supreme Court approved all but the most racially blatant of these measures. The justices decided by a vote of eight to one in *Plessy* v. *Ferguson* (1896) that separate but equal facilities were constitutional under the Fourteenth Amendment, upholding a Louisiana statute titled an "Act to promote the comfort of passengers," that prescribed segregation on trains and boats. Justice Henry Billings Brown's opinion for the Court found that laws were "powerless to eradicate racial instincts or to abolish distinctions based upon physical differences."[52] The Court had officially vanquished for the next half-century the antislavery vision of an instrumental rule of law sensitive to higher law principles.

Native Americans, the Chinese, and the Definition of Status

Two other racial minorities, native Americans and Chinese, were also affected by changes in the law of personal status. In both instances the ideal of equality before the law was never fulfilled.

Where the law of black personal status was based on local and state control, that of the native American was federal. The Supreme Court, in *Cherokee Nation* v. *Georgia* (1831), had declared the Indians a "dependent domestic nation," and Congress had acted accordingly, pursuing a policy of separatism through the reservation system.[53]

By the end of the nineteenth century, Congress reversed itself, embracing a new policy of assimilation and destruction of Indian culture. White economic self-interest explains part of the change; western farmers, ranchers, and railroad men hungered for reservation lands. There were less materialistic impulses as well. Well-documented abuses on the reservations had an impact on public opinion, and white reformers sought to solve the Indian problem by simply absorbing the native American population.

The high point of this movement was the Dawes Severalty Act of 1887. It permitted native Americans to obtain homesteads and become U.S. citizens, losing their status as members of a particular tribe. The act had strong support in the West, for it promised a rapid opening of valuable reservation lands to white development.

The Indians resisted assimilation and so too did southern racists concerned with preventing any kind of race mixing. Secretary of the Interior L. Q. C. Lamar, a Mississippian who took the scientific racist theories of his day seriously, thought the black experience relevant to that of native Americans. "The tribal system must be adhered to," Lamar proclaimed, "[i]t is the normal condition of the existence of this race."[54] Although Congress ceased making formal treaties with Indians in 1871, the courts continued to treat the tribes as distinct alien nations of quasi-sovereign people. As a result, native Americans before the law had a shadowy form of nationality as domestic subjects without genuine citizenship. That was not extended until 1924. The criminal jurisdiction of the federal territorial courts did not reach the reservation until 1885, and in many noncriminal matters, the reservation Indians remained "a people without a law."[55] This condition applied even after 1898, when the Curtis Act ended tribal courts and brought the reservations under the full jurisdiction of the federal judicial system.

The Chinese

The Chinese were the most exotic of the wave of nineteenth-century immigrants. The press and "scientific" racists characterized them as purveyors of drugs and prostitution; the white working class viewed them as a threatening source of cheap labor.

As the numbers of Chinese increased, their status before the law declined, especially in the American West where they were concentrated. The California constitutional convention of 1879, for example, was a hotbed of Sinophobic sentiment. Dennis Kearney, the leader of the state's Workingman's party, persuaded the delegates to exclude all resident Chinese from the suffrage and to forbid their employment on public works. Earlier in the decade the state had authorized segregation of Chinese and Japanese in public schools. State and local governments engaged in an orgy of restrictive measures. These included laws penalizing corporations that hired Chinese labor, empowering municipalities to remove them from city limits, and forbidding them from obtaining occupational licenses. The San Francisco Board of Supervisors prohibited any person to conduct a laundry business in a building constructed of wood, the common building material of the Chinese.

The federal Ninth Circuit Court of Appeals and the Supreme Court struck down most of this legislation. In *Yik Wo* v. *Hopkins* (1886) the high court held that such discrimination was an illegal "denial of the equal protection of the laws and a violation of the Fourteenth Amendment."[56] But Justice Stephen J. Field, who presided over the Ninth Circuit Court in California and was also a member of the Supreme Court, had little concern for Chinese equality. "Our institutions," he said, "have made no impression on them during the more than thirty years they have been in the country. . . . They do not and will not assimilate with us."[57]

Organized labor in the West persuaded Congress to restrict the Chinese influx. The Chinese Exclusion Act of 1882 proclaimed that "the coming of the Chinese laborers to this country endangers the good order of certain localities." Justice Field, who voted in 1889 to uphold the act, confessed to "a well-founded apprehension—from the experience of years—that a limitation to the immigration of certain classes from China was essential to the peace of the community on the Pacific Coast, and possibly to the preservation of our civilization."[58] Congress renewed the act in 1892 and in 1902 suspended all Chinese immigration indefinitely. The results were dramatic: the population of Chinese dropped from a high of 104,000 in 1880 to 85,000 in 1900.

The first Chinese Exclusion Act coincided with the collapse of Reconstruction. Both seem to have been watersheds in the treatment of Chinese before the courts. As territories became states, a new legal system went into place, one staffed by local rather than national personnel. Until about 1882 the Chinese often received support from the appellate judiciary. In the case of *Charley Lee Quang* (1879), for example, the Oregon Supreme Court overturned the conviction of three Chinese defendants found guilty of murder, because the trial judge failed to inform the jury that the Chinese, who did not believe in the sanctity of Christian oaths, might be lying. Counting both civil and criminal cases, Chinese won a majority of cases brought on appeal in the Pacific Northwest before 1883. Thereafter, their position before the law steadily eroded, and from 1883 to 1902 they lost nearly 70 percent of their appeals in criminal cases and almost 60 percent in civil actions. State supreme courts joined in "the wave of anti-Chinese sentiment following the Exclusion Act of 1882."[59]

Race and the Shift from Status to Contract

"The movement of progressive societies," the Englishman Sir Henry Maine concluded in 1861, "has hitherto been a movement from Status to Contract."[60] Maine believed that the modern legal order would make talent and ability more important in determining personal status than such ascribed characteristics as race, sex, and family. Maine's vision was hopeful and unfulfilled. Yet change was under way, and the Civil War was a watershed. Until then racial minorities were subject to the vagaries of local majorities, but after the Civil War the federal government had the constitutional basis for a potentially far-reaching role in defining their legal status. The moral imperative of the antislavery movement was expressed in legislative enactments and constitutional amendments.

Change and progress were not synonymous. If slavery was dead, legally enforced segregation, involuntary servitude, paternalism, and political exclusion replaced it. From the perspective of 1787, the changes made in the law of personal status were dramatic, but even when the law recognized equality it did not guarantee it.

8

The Nineteenth-Century Law of Domestic Relations

Rise of the Republican Family

The eighteenth-century American family was a vital link in the chain of social authority. Households, in the words of historian John Demos, were "little commonwealths" tightly integrated into the community.[1] Within the family, as in the larger political society, patriarchy ordered social relations. Fathers dominated, with wives and children yielding to their authority. Demos, for example, found in his study of the Plymouth Colony that patriarchy (the rule of the family by its male head) rested on a "deep and primitive kind of suspicion of women, solely on account of their sex."[2] The birth of a child in rural colonial America was welcomed as the arrival of a future laborer and as security for parents later in life. While affection certainly existed in family relations, colonial Americans placed authority over liberty, stability over change, and community values over individual self-interest.

The ideological and economic forces that flowed from the American Revolution challenged these traditional arrangements. Republicanism fostered a family order in which authority was accountable, property rights were equated with independence, and human relations were set in contractual terms. The new republican family was a private, inward-looking institution, in sharp contrast to the community-oriented little commonwealths of the colonial era.

Market capitalism also shaped the republican family. As the nation's economy was transformed from an agricultural to a commercial base, the relative values of family members changed as well. Fathers went away from home to work and earn a wage, while mothers assumed responsibility for the domestic sphere. Children became precious to families in the middle and upper classes, losing some of their economic value as workers. During the nineteenth century each family member gradually assumed a new identity, and together they sought refuge from a competitive and materially acquisitive world by their individual hearths.[3]

These ideological and economic changes bred a cult of domesticity and companionate marriage. The gradual separation of the work place from the home granted wives new autonomy in the domestic sphere, but they also assumed the burden of being the moral guardians of the nation. Companionate marriage complemented this cult of domesticity. Marriage emerged as an institution in which love, affection, and companionship were valued. Nineteenth-century writers on the family, for example, urged husbands, who were often absent for long days at work, to develop closer emotional ties with their wives, to treat them as equals in the home, and to place themselves and their children under the wife's moral guidance.[4]

The rise of the republican family was accompanied by the development of a new body of substantive law, that of domestic relations. At the beginning of the century, questions involving the legal status of the family were scattered through several different categories of law: contract, property, and tort, for example. By the end of the century, however, a unified body of domestic relations law had emerged that involved courtship, marriage, property rights of wives, adoption, divorce, and child custody. An increasingly technical treatise literature accompanied it, and one of its pioneer authors, Joel P. Bishop, wrote in 1868 that "a practitioner familiar with every other department of law, yet is unread in [family law], cannot give sound advice on questions coming within this department."[5]

Creating the Family: The Law of Courtship and Marriage

The Breach-of-Promise Suit

Courtship was traditionally a stage of bargaining about the economic terms of a marriage rather than an interlude in which the two parties tested their affection for and compatibility with one another. English law treated marriage as a property transaction in which the bride represented a property asset whose disposition, especially among the wealthier classes, often entailed arduous bargaining between the father-in-law and the suitor. With marriages thus arranged, the future husband and wife did not, in the modern sense, fall in love.

In the postrevolutionary republican legal order, the breach-of-promise suit came to reflect the new assumptions that accompanied the companionate marriage. A suitor who spurned a woman faced an action that combined elements of both contract and tort. These suits were invariably brought against men who then had to calculate not just the direct economic costs to be borne by breaking the agreement but also other more open-ended costs that could be imposed, under tortlike doctrines, for acting deceitfully in depriving a woman of her opportunity to be a mother and wife. The breach-of-promise suit was the principal means by which private parties policed courtship, although its importance declined through the course of the nineteenth century, eventually falling into social and legal disrepute.

The leading early nineteenth-century case on breach of promise was *Wightman* v. *Coates* (1818), decided by the Supreme Judicial Court of Massachusetts. After a long engagement, Maria Wightman charged Joshua Coates with refusing to consummate his marriage promise. Coates denied that he had ever asked her to marry, although Maria produced love letters that suggested otherwise. Chief Justice Isaac Parker's opinion for the court conceded that previously such suits had turned on matters of finance. Parker deemphasized the financial aspects of courtship and stressed instead the loss of emotional well-being that an unanticipated end of courtship brought when a promise of marriage had been made. Parker tipped the scales of judicial scrutiny in favor of women. "A deserted female," he wrote, "whose prospects in life may be materially affected by the treachery of the man to whom she had plighted her vows, will always receive from the jury the attention which her situation requires; and it is not disreputable for one, who may have to mourn for years over lost prospects and broken vows, to seek such compensation, as the law can give her."[6]

Breach-of-promise suits were actions brought by women and were premised on an understanding that women needed to marry and to become mothers in order to fulfill their social responsibilities. Judges held out to women through breach-of-promise actions not equality but special treatment based on women's peculiar condition. Males incurred greater liability for their actions because their social position and their innate qualities made them superior to women. Appellate judges, for example, accepted circumstantial proof of a breach, even though similar evidence in economic and criminal cases involving only male parties would have been rejected. In the context of courtship, the "will theory of contract" was less binding on women than men, because women were of such a disposition that they could be taken advantage of and hence required the protection of the state. The end of traditional patriarchy only meant that a new judicial patriarchy grew to replace it.

Male youthfulness and the bride's unfitness for matrimony and motherhood were the only major impediments to female-initiated breach-of-promise suits. Judges indulged the youthful experimentation of males, usually refusing to hold males under the age of twenty-one to promises of marriage that they made and then broke. Males could also escape the consequences of their promises by showing that they had been misled about their fiancée's moral or physical fitness. A women who brought a breach-of-promise suit usually did so with the full knowledge that her previous sexual conduct might become a matter of public record. But judges also applied a strict standard of proof of female sexual indiscretion, recognizing that false allegations would destroy a woman's reputation unfairly.

Although courts extended special protection to women, they also expected that women would exercise sound judgment. Chief Justice John Bannister Gibson of the Pennsylvania Supreme Court, for example, held that a woman who had been seduced and impregnated under a false promise of marriage could not collect any greater award as a result. "Every girl who is silly enough to surrender her citadel of virtue to her lover," Gibson proclaimed, "must not [forget] that professions are not promises."[7]

Tort principles also guided the U.S. law of courtship, enabling jilted and defiled women to strike back against seducers. Contract principles limited the plaintiff's damages to the value of the immediate loss, but in the case of virtue such damages were difficult to calculate under contract theory and, in any case, the loss was literally beyond repair. The punitive and exemplary damages (those that applied to punish the seducer and to warn off others by the magnitude of the damages) available in tort created more open-ended costs for seducers. Yet courts were slow to accept these principles, and in the first half of the century most jurisdictions clung to the old common law rule that women who had been seduced could not bring suit. Only a father or guardian, who had ostensibly suffered a property loss, could do so.

By midcentury, state appellate courts had begun to reconsider seduction. Victorian Americans stressed the passionless nature of women, and some authorities even argued that women were incapable of experiencing sexual sensation. They were merely empty vessels waiting to be filled by their husbands with the germ of a new generation. Seduced women were innocent victims of the lust and deceit of men. The Victorian view of female nature and the character of seduction prompted judges to recognize that women possessed distinct rights that required redress. The judiciary shifted fault to men, permitting women to seek remedies against them as a matter of both right and the maintenance of a truly companionate marriage.

The same Victorian principles that made seduction easier for women to prove also made it socially riskier for them to pursue in court. Social reformers, for example, charged that the women who filed these suits were mercenaries who lured men into relations and then turned on them for financial gain. Although precedent affirmed that statements made by a would-be bride to her friends could be entered as evidence to show the intent of the suitor, the Michigan Supreme Court, in the leading case of *McPherson* v. *Ryan* (1886), rejected that doctrine. The old rule, the judges held, placed "almost every man at the mercy of an evilly disposed and designing woman."[8] Further, as the circle of economic opportunity for women widened ever so slightly at the beginning of the twentieth century, the loss of a suitor was less damaging than it had been a hundred years before.

The state appellate judiciary policed nineteenth-century courtship, although its control diminished as the breach-of-promise suit appeared as a legally sanctioned form of blackmail. Women had carved out just enough of a niche in the expanding industrial marketplace that they could literally afford to abandon the suit. The decline of the breach-of-promise suit was evidence of the waning significance generally of contractualism in the late-nineteenth-century law of domestic relations.

Marriage, the Contract Ideal, and the Public Interest

Unlike England, where ecclesiastical courts had jurisdiction over marriage, in the United States nuptials were a thoroughly secular rite, though one shaped by prevailing moral values. The blending of moral authority and the public interest was particularly important in two areas: the regulation of the wedding ceremony and the designation of persons considered fit to marry. In the nineteenth century, "state after state shifted from an initial promotion of individual rights through eased matrimonial regulations to the imposition of greater controls over those seeking matrimony."[9]

Celebration of Marriage

Colonial fathers regulated their children's marriage behavior, because children were a form of property and their marriage raised direct economic interests. Marriage was also important for the community as a whole, which depended on successful unions for growth and stability. Engaged couples were required by law to initiate a community informational system by publishing banns, which are declarations of an intent to marry that were posted in a conspicuous place. Some colonies also required couples to secure a license, a measure that not only alerted the community of their impending action but, because a fee was required, also gave evidence of their financial capacity.

Marriages were celebrated in two secular forms. The first was a civil ceremony (though sometimes performed by a religious official as an agent of the state); the other was irregular or common law marriage. Today, the popular meaning of common law marriage implies an immoral practice, but in early American law irregular marriage had a different meaning. It was a verbal agreement between two people to consider themselves husband and wife, followed by cohabitation. Almost all nineteenth-century states recognized it, and it was as legally binding as a ceremony carried out before an official authorized by the state.

In the fluid, frontier environment of the new nation, common law marriages were crucial to establishing property rights and the legitimacy of births, and judges extended full recognition to them. The leading case was *Fenton* v. *Reed* (1809), decided by James Kent, chief justice of the New York Supreme Court. Kent subsequently became chancellor of the state and, along with Joseph Story, the century's most influential law writer. In the suit, Elizabeth Reed sought judicial validation of her second common law marriage so that she could collect her husband's Revolutionary War pension. Her first spouse, John Guest, had deserted her, and, believing him dead, she moved in with Reed. Some time later Guest returned, but he died without reclaiming Elizabeth. Elizabeth continued to live with Reed until his death.

Kent declared that Elizabeth had lived in bigamy during the time she was married to both Guest and Reed. But he held that after Guest's death, Elizabeth and Reed were husband and wife. "No peculiar ceremonies are requisite," Kent subsequently explained in his *Commentaries,* "by the common law to the valid celebration of the marriage. The consent of the parties is all that is required . . . by natural or public law."[10] Kent believed that through voluntary action couples were most likely to bind themselves successfully, and he regarded marriage as a private rather than a public act that appellate judges were especially well equipped to superintend. Only a minority of courts in New England and the upper South rejected Kent's ruling.

Most state appellate judges before the Civil War accepted the economic necessity of common law marriage, and they readily embraced the *Fenton* principle. They refused to upset established patterns of cohabitation and to entangle family property rights in order to uphold public regulatory authority. Colonial Pennsylvania, for example, had established rigid marriage laws, that included an admonition to the citizens of the state to marry and bear children. But in 1833 Chief Justice Gibson ruled that they were "ill adapted to the habits and customs of society as it now exists," and that to end common law marriages "would bastardize the vast majority of children which have been born within the state for half a century."[11]

The behavior of antebellum legislators had the long-term effect of undermining common law marriage by making a civil ceremony easier to obtain. They lowered fees and authorized a widening number of religious leaders, municipal officials, and judicial officers to perform marriages. The marriage license remained the primary method of public regulation, but it was interpreted by courts to be an administrative aid "to register, not to restrict marriage."[12]

Social reformers after the Civil War claimed that the absence of state regulation of nuptial rights had contributed to a marriage crisis that massive immigration and industrialization had aggravated. Common law marriage had worked, they concluded, only because the population was relatively homogeneous and agrarian.

The scientific eugenics movement, which had its heyday between 1880 and 1920, contributed a sense of urgency to demands for marriage reform. Eugenicists claimed that crime, mental illness, and social disorder generally had biological bases. They promised that, through the scientific control of heredity, it was possible to eliminate these problems eventually. Eugenicists cloaked prevailing fears about racial and ethnic pollution of the population in neutral, scientific language. The attorney Joseph Chamberlain, an avid proponent of greater state supervision of the marriage ceremony, declared that the efforts to regulate marriage practice were "not based on historic rules or race feelings but on scientific fact."[13]

State legislators coupled the eugenicists' arguments with the concept of the rights of the public to justify intervention with the traditional private contractual basis of marriage. Licensing reemerged as one important means of social control. Couples had not only to submit themselves to a public official, but they had also to provide vital information for statistical purposes. Although licensing requirements varied from state to state, their effect was to discourage irregular marriage by denying property and birth rights. Mississippi in 1892 enacted the stiffest law. It held marriages void if celebrated without a license, and thereby eliminated a long-standing statutory basis for common law marriages. By 1906 only New York and South Carolina lacked code provisions requiring a license before a wedding.

The traditional practice of publishing banns had all but died out by the early twentieth century. Legislators replaced them with new laws that required couples to give notice followed by a waiting period, usually three days, before a license would become valid. Maine, in 1848, was the first state to prescribe this practice, and a century later more than one-half of the states had adopted it.

Common law marriage remained an option in most states, although code provisions made it unattractive and appellate judges chipped away at its once-secure foundations. Couples could no longer openly defy legislative dictates and expect the judiciary to support them based on common law principles. The Kansas Supreme Court, in the leading case of *State* v. *Walker* (1887), concluded as much. The judges sustained the conviction of E. C. Walker and Lillian Harman for illicit cohabitation because the bride and groom had openly denied "the right of society, in the form of church and state, to regulate" marriage.[14]

Regulating Fitness for Marriage

The eugenics movement had an even more dramatic impact on laws regulating fitness for marriage. At the beginning of the nineteenth century the traditional English limitations on fitness for marriage had molded the republican family. The disabilities named included physiological, mental, moral, and contractual liabilities that, depending on their degree and kind, prevented one of the parties from entering into legal matrimony and provided the grounds, if a marriage did exist, to annul it.

Postrevolutionary marriage law assumed that there was an age below which a marriage could not be consummated through sexual union leading to procreation. The English common law conferred nuptial rights at age twelve for women and fourteen for men; paternal control, however, continued until age twenty-one. These common law minimums were seldom approached; most brides and grooms throughout the nineteenth century married in their early twenties, although the age dropped slightly toward the end of the century. Effective policing was difficult in any case, especially as patriarchy eased and the participants themselves claimed under the companionate ideal that they were best able to judge the appropriate marriage age.

Sexual incapacity, like age, was more a basis for terminating a marriage than for blocking it, although the colonial precedents for annulment were murky. Only when legislators began to regulate these matters did significant numbers of cases appear. Most impotence statutes treated the failure to disclose the condition before marriage as a fraud, because a party had offered themselves for marriage knowing that they could not consummate it.

There were problems of proof and emotion, as the case of *Devanbaugh* v. *Devanbaugh* (1836) demonstrated. Chancellor Reuben Walworth of New York was asked to consider whether a marriage should be annulled because a husband claimed that his wife was incapable of sexual intercourse. Walworth ordered a physical examination of the woman, and the medical examiner testified that the wife had an especially strong hymen that could only be breached surgically. Walworth decided that the woman was not incurably impotent and that surgery would remedy the problem. The wife resisted the procedure, and she refused to live further with her husband. Walworth would go no further. "[It] is," he wrote, "a matter to be settled with her own conscience and her lawful husband, as this court has no jurisdiction in any case to enforce the performance of her marital vows."[15]

Marriage partners had a legal right to a sexually complete union. Legislators provided as much; judges enforced these requirements. Most of the cases, as the *Devanbaugh* example indicates, involved suits brought by men against women, suggesting perhaps that more women than men in the Victorian era were willing to accept an unconsummated marriage.

Judges before the Civil War also liberalized taboos against marriage of kin. As a general rule, U.S. common law, in a departure from English practice, banned only truly incestuous marriages: between parent and child, brother and sister. The approach in the United States through midcentury was to leave the matter of regulation to individual conscience and the church, although there were regional variations. In New England and the older South a "biblical system" evolved that permitted first-cousin unions but banned marriages among other kin. At the same time, a "western system" developed in the new states of the American frontier that proscribed first-cousin marriages but authorized unions among non-blood-related kin. These differences stemmed from a policy of encouraging the full distribution of family wealth in lightly populated areas.

Mental competence was another standard of fitness for marriage. A person with an impaired mind could not meet the contractual standard of knowingly consenting to enter into a nuptial agreement. In the absence of a scientific definition, statutes and common law rulings before the Civil War groped to distinguish between mental incapacity and insanity. Courts tended to act only when the evidence was beyond dispute. For example, the New Hampshire Supreme Court in 1850 decided in *True* v. *Raney* the fate of a twenty-two-year-old woman. She had been abducted and married, and her parents sued to have the union dissolved. They testified that their daughter could not wash or dress herself, spell or read, use money, tell time, knit or sew. Chief Justice John J. Gilchrist dissolved the marriage, concluding that "there is every reason to believe that no person so lamentably imbecile as this young woman appears to be, could have the remotest idea of the meaning of a contract for the performance of any of the ordinary duties of life, and still less of a contract of marriage."[16]

Lawmakers after the Civil War engaged in more vigorous regulation of fitness for marriage than their predecessors. For example, the Supreme Court in *Reynolds* v. *United States* (1878) declared Mormon polygamy "an odious practice" that would "make the professed doctrines of religious beliefs superior to the law of the land, and in effect permit every citizen to become a law unto himself."[17] Congress applied additional statutory pressure thereafter, ultimately forcing the Mormon leadership to abandon the practice in order to win statehood for Utah in 1890.

Race was yet another criteria that postwar lawmakers invoked to justify standards of nuptial fitness. Law in the United States was unique in its prohibitions of interracial marriage; the English common law had no such requirement. Maryland was the first colony to place a statutory ban on marriages between individuals of different races, and in the antebellum period many states and territories added to the list. Even where there was no explicit ban, private prejudice was effective. The law formally ratified rather than imposed one of society's most powerful social taboos.

Emancipation stirred new fears, especially in the South, where Black Codes contained clauses prohibiting miscegenation (the intermarriage of persons of different races). Similar bans directed at the Chinese appeared in western states, but the brunt of the antimiscegenation statutes fell on blacks. The North Carolina Supreme Court in 1869, for example, overturned the marriage of a black man and a white woman, finding that "[t]he emancipation of the slaves had made no alteration in our policy, nor in the sentiments of our people."[18] The Texas Court of Appeals in 1877 rejected efforts by Charles Frasher to reverse his conviction for marrying a black woman based on the Fourteenth Amendment and the Civil Rights Act of 1866. "[M]arriage is more than a contract," the Court proclaimed, "it is a civil status, left solely by the Federal Constitution and the law to the discretion of the states under their general power to regulate their domestic affairs."[19]

By 1916, twenty-eight states and territories prohibited interracial marriage. More statutes banned miscegenation than any other form of racially related conduct, and James Schouler, the nineteenth century's leading authority on the law of domestic relations, observed that while "the manifest tendency of the day" was toward removing all "legal impediments of rank and condition," the "race barrier" continued to have "a strong foundation in human nature, wherever marriage companionship is concerned."[20]

The eugenics movement also contributed to the new standards of marriage fitness, and its biological and hereditary foundations lent scientific credence to racism. Even legal writers such as Christopher Tiedeman and Thomas M. Cooley, who criticized state efforts to regulate the marketplace, accepted that biology and medicine made interference in personal and family relations necessary. The new legislation aimed, in the eyes of its proponents, to prevent the degeneration of society by imposing scientific controls on marriage. Connecticut in 1895, for example, banned marriage of feeble-minded, imbecile, and epileptic men and women under forty-five years of age, and imposed a minimum three-year prison term on violators. By 1900 every state prohibited marriage between blood relations.

Victorian beliefs made medical controls essential curbs on lustful males who, through their contacts with prostitutes, were believed to spread venereal diseases to faithful brides. By the 1930s, twenty-six states and territories had enacted statutes similar to an 1899 Michigan law, the first in the nation, which authorized criminal penalties for people who had gonorrhea or syphilis and married. Wisconsin in 1913 became the first state to require medical examination of the groom for veneral disease before a license could be issued.

The eugenics movement achieved its greatest success in the passage of laws that permitted marriage of social dependents and deviants only after sterilization. Indiana in 1907 was the first state to provide that idiots, habitual criminals, imbeciles, and rapists could marry only if they consented to sterilization. By 1931 twenty-seven states had adopted similar measures. In some instances, notably Indiana and New York, state appellate courts held that these measures violated due process and equal protection of the laws. The U.S. Supreme Court, however, granted the states significant discretion. In *Buck* v. *Bell* (1927), for example, Justice Oliver Wendell Holmes, Jr., approved the sterilization of eighteen-year-old Carrie Buck, whose mother had also been feeble-minded, under a Virginia statute. Holmes explained that it was "better for all the world, if instead of waiting to execute degenerate offspring for crimes, or to let them starve for their imbecility, society can prevent those who are manifestly unfit from continuing their kind."[21]

Operating the Family: Married Women's Property, Birth Control, and Children

The law of domestic relations involved the distribution of rights and resources between parents and among parents and children. Nineteenth-century lawmakers intervened in the republican family to redirect the property rights of married women, to set standards for birth control and abortion, and to regulate the adoption of children.

Married Women's Property Acts

Market capitalism, not republican ideology or feminist protest, produced the first major reforms in the legal rights of married women to control their property. The speculative economy of the early nineteenth century offered risks and rewards, and by the 1830s state legislators sought to protect the viability of the family and the advancement of the economy through "married women's property acts." These laws were designed to protect wives from the pecuniary embarrassments of their husbands. Various legal practices existed at the end of the eighteenth century that anticipated these laws and attenuated the full harshness of coverture, especially for upper-class women with property. For example, dower, the practice of guaranteeing to wives one-third of the property of their husbands upon their deaths, secured a measure of protection. Where dower rights were involved, husbands had to obtain the agreement of wives for conveyance of property.

Married women also received protection through a separate equitable estate. Establishing such an estate was a fairly easy procedure; it required no attorney. The amount of property in question was of little importance, although where large amounts were involved this trust agreement made sound financial sense. The estate could be created before the wedding by marriage contract (called a prenuptial agreement) or later. It could also be established by will, deed of gift, or deed of sale. Whatever the arrangement, the document designated a trustee who was charged with holding the property for the separate use of a particular married woman. Some documents gave wives blanket control over the property held in trust for them; more typically, the agreements provided them only limited control. In any case, the sole purpose of the trust was to exempt the woman's property from liability for the husband's debts.

Most married women did not have a prenuptial agreement. Instead, wives received separate estates only when it became apparent that the property they brought into the marriage was threatened by creditors. The growth of separate estates "constituted a major advance for women of the middle and upper classes, but it began in expediency, a response to the failures of scores of individual men."[22] The purpose of the separate estates was not to place women in an equal position with men, but to provide security against financial ruin.

In states with a strong civil law tradition (e.g., California, Texas, and Louisiana), the community property system prevailed. It provided that husband and wife each owned one-half of the property, although just as in common law jurisdictions the husband had an exclusive right to manage the property. A wife's property, moreover, could be seized by creditors for the debts created by her husband. The system nonetheless gave security to a wife's property inheritance, because she automatically came into possession of her half upon her husband's death.

Legislators in states with either a common or a civil law tradition decided to enact married women's property laws in response to the periodic upheavals in the economy. These measures provided equity rather than equality to women by breaking the doctrine of coverture.[23]

Legal protection for the property rights of married women came in three waves. The first began in the late 1830s and lasted until the mid-1840s. The legislatures of Arkansas and the territory of Florida in 1835 first passed married women's property legislation, although they did so to protect women's rights that existed under former civil law regimes as these jurisdictions adopted the common law. The 1839 Mississippi law, which is usually touted as the first in the nation, was more significant because it was the product of the economic collapse produced by the Panic of 1837, and, as such, it became the model for other states anxious to keep wives' property free from the clutches of their husbands' creditors. This first wave of married women's property acts therefore freed wives' estates from the debts of their husbands, leaving the traditional marital estate and coverture rules intact.

The uncoordinated lobbying of feminists, such as Elizabeth Cady Stanton in New York, contributed to the passage of the second wave of acts. This generation of legislation was concentrated in the North and it created separate estates for wives. The acts were modest incursions on patriarchy and the free market through their interference with traditional coverture and dower rights.

The New York law of 1848, which replaced that of Mississippi as the national model, typified the narrow scope of this second generation of legislation. It insulated a married woman's property from her husband's debts and dictated that it "shall continue her sole and separate property, as if she were a single female."[24] Property that came in the future to a woman covered by the law was also to be held in her sole possession and control, just as would be the case for a single woman. The statute, however, provided that property received directly from her husband would not be free from his debts. Thus, a husband could not protect *his* property from creditors by giving it to his wife. The New York law disrupted neither the credit markets nor companionate relationships in households.

The third wave of legislation after the Civil War took account of the changing work place that women were entering in small but growing numbers. These laws protected women's earnings from the institution of coverture. Massachusetts passed the first statute in 1855, followed by several other states in the 1860s and 1870s.

The married women's property acts fitted the domestic role assigned to women in the republican family. They granted women special treatment under the law; they provided equity not equality. Domesticity supplied an ideological base for these laws, but nineteenth-century market capitalism was the driving force behind them.

Abortion and Birth Control for Married Women

At the same time that legislators granted narrow property protections to women, they also restricted the freedom of wives to control the size of their families through contraception and birth control. A dramatic decline in family size was one of the central demographic facts of the nineteenth-century United States. White female fertility declined during each decade of the century, falling from 7.04 to 3.56 children per family. By the beginning of the twentieth century the United States had one of the lowest fertility rates in the Western world.

Americans purposefully limited family size, through either birth control or abortion. The exact reasons for these actions (i.e., wives exercising greater control over the family by regulating pregnancy, the companionate family dictating greater attention to fewer children, husbands calculating shrewdly the costs of children, or all of these) are uncertain. Whatever the motivation behind their use, abortion and birth control raised the most controversial issues within domestic relations law. Developments followed a pattern similar to other areas of family law. Beginning in the middle of the century, state legislatures intervened with growing frequency, and the judiciary balked at accepting completely these incursions into previously private matters.

Birth Control Becomes an Obscenity

The reduction in family size coincided with greater social awareness and scientific understanding of birth control. Eighteenth-century couples engaged in age-old and largely inefficient methods, such as delayed marriage, breast-feeding, abstinence, and *coitus interruptus*. In the nineteenth century, however, birth control became associated with radical social reform, espoused most fully by Robert Dale Owen and John Humphrey Noyes. This connection contributed to the nineteenth-century middle-class perception that the practice was a mark of social degeneracy. At the same time, new methods of control appeared, the most popular of which was douching after intercourse. Charles Knowlton, a Massachusetts family physician and student of Owen's writings, described the method in the first treatise on medical jurisprudence, *Fruits of Philosophy,* published in 1832. By 1881 the book had sold more than 277,000 copies, and it was the most authoritative tract available in English on contraception.

Knowlton's graphic descriptions offended church and community leaders. Several towns in Massachusetts charged him with peddling obscene material, even though neither the common law nor statutes made the distribution of birth control material illegal. Knowlton pleaded that he sought merely to improve public health, but the prosecution successfully charged that he had fomented obscenity. Only in his hometown, after two hung juries, was he acquitted. Massachusetts in 1847 declared that publishing obscene material was illegal, although *Fruits of Philosophy* continued to circulate.

Explicit restrictions on the dissemination of birth control information first appeared in the 1870s as a moral purity movement took hold. Its leaders succeeded in linking birth control to obscenity in the atmosphere surrounding the family in the Victorian United States. They also received strong national support. Anthony Comstock, a failed New York City businessman, mobilized the reform effort. He denounced the few state laws dealing with obscenity as too weak and turned to the federal government. Along with Vice-President Henry Wilson and Supreme Court Justice William Strong, Comstock drafted the first national obscenity statute that, after little debate, became law on March 1, 1873.

The Comstock Act banned the circulation and importation of obscene materials through the mails. The list of banned items included goods designed, adapted, or intended "for preventing conception or producing abortion."[25] It punished violators with a $5000 fine and a period of one to ten years at hard labor, or both. Vice-President Wilson rewarded Comstock's efforts by securing for him the office of special postal agent to enforce the act.

Several states promptly passed "little" Comstock acts, the harshest of which was in Connecticut. In 1879 Phineas T. Barnum, the great circus promoter, persuaded the legislature to make illegal the *use* of contraceptive materials. Barnum and his supporters recognized the enforcement problems raised by the law, but they expected a vigilante citizenry to report on the habits of neighbors and friends. The author Dio Lewis, who campaigned for the new regulations, insisted that "any friend of virtue, male or female, may quickly bring to justice these whelps of sin. It seems hard that decent men are not allowed to shoot them on sight as they would shoot a mad dog."[26]

Judges shared Comstock's enthusiasm for state regulation of morality. The Supreme Court in *Ex Parte Jackson* (1877) endorsed the Comstock Act and added to it the broad definition of obscenity developed by Lord Chief Justice Cockburn in the English case of *Queen* v. *Hicklin* (1868). Cockburn held that "the test of obscenity is this, whether the tendency of the matter charged as obscenity is to deprave and corrupt those whose minds are open to such immoral influences, and into whose hands a publication of this sort might fall."[27] Justice Stephen J. Field's opinion in *Jackson* connected these sentiments to an active role for the state in the maintenance of moral authority. "[T]he object of Congress," Field wrote in explaining passage of the Comstock Act, "[had] not been to interfere with the freedom of the press, or with any other rights of the people; but to refuse its facilities for the distribution of matter deemed injurious to the public morals."[28]

Comstock personified the excesses that flowed from the Victorian quest for moral purity. Posing as an impoverished father, Comstock pleaded with Madame Restell, a wealthy operator of a New York City bordello close to St. Patrick's Cathedral, for birth control information. Hundreds of women yearly flocked to the clinic that Restell operated, seeking information about contraception and abortion. When Restell provided the information, Comstock arrested her, and facing imprisonment, the sixty-seven-year-old woman slit her own throat with a carving knife. Comstock was without remorse: "a bloody end to a bloody life."[29]

In the early twentieth century a new generation of reformers, led by Margaret

Sanger, attacked the Comstock acts as unwarranted intrusions on the privacy of family decision making. Sanger pioneered the strategy, later adopted by the civil rights movement, of bringing test cases in order to stir public and professional support. Most state appellate courts countenanced legislative intervention, easing rather than overturning restrictions on information about and use of contraceptive materials. The New York Court of Appeals in 1918, for example, accepted that doctors could give birth control advice for the "cure and prevention of disease" of most any kind.[30] Such decisions merely equated sexual rights with medical authority, and proponents of birth control such as Sanger were dismissed as radicals who threatened the medical security of the family and the nation.

Abortion

Abortion carried a far heavier moral and legal burden than did birth control. Colonial women had relied on it, along with infanticide, to rid themselves of the offspring of rape or seduction. Abortion carried no legal penalties under the common law so long as it was performed before "quickening," the period at about four or five months when the fetus began to move in the womb. The term originated during the Middle Ages with Thomas Aquinas, who concluded that movement in the womb indicated that a soul had entered it.

The justices of the Supreme Judicial Court of Massachusetts in 1812 first plumbed the legal depths of the issue. *Commonwealth* v. *Bangs* involved the fate of Isaiah Bangs who beat and administered a drug to his pregnant lover in an attempt to prevent the birth of their bastard child. The court held that Bangs had not acted illegally because the state failed to produce evidence that the fetus had quickened. Other jurisdictions followed the *Bangs* decision, giving the quickening doctrine a firm hold in the common law.

Legislatures gave statutory authority to the quickening doctrine. Connecticut in 1821 enacted the first abortion statute, incorporating the common law principle that a crime could only be ascertained if quickening had occurred. The act was directed against abortionists and not against the women on whom it was performed. A mother, in short, could not be her own abortionist, even though, unlike other sex crimes (incest and rape), her cooperation was almost always given. Other state legislatures through the 1830s and 1840s followed the quickening rule, even at a time when the English were doing away with it by parliamentary act. A few states, most notably New York in 1828, also recognized that an abortion might be legal after quickening if performed "to preserve the life of [the] woman" upon the advice of two physicians.[31]

Abortions increased significantly during the 1850s and 1860s, rising from approximately one in every twenty-five to thirty live births to one in every five or six births by the 1860s. The surge in abortion seems to have been concentrated among middle-class white women, and their behavior drew increasing condemnation from religious leaders. A Boston minister, for example, described abortion as nothing more than "fashionable murder."[32]

The medical profession had the greatest influence in redirecting courts and legislatures toward an increasingly antiabortion position. The American Medical Association, founded in 1847, made an end to abortion one of its chief tasks, and its leaders viewed abortion law reform as a means by which the profession could enhance its influence.

State legislatures responded to these demands in various ways, but the general direction was toward more comprehensive acts that imposed stiffer penalties. Massachusetts in 1845 passed the first separate abortion statute, but as late as 1860 thirteen states had no provision in their laws making abortion a crime, and those that did continued to rely on the quickening rule.

By the 1880s, however, medical and religious leaders swung legal authority decisively against abortion. They did so by invoking the states' police powers to make abortion a criminal act against public health and safety, a plausible enough position because abortion was a risky procedure that subjected women to death and sterility from hemorrhage and infection. The antiabortion statutes of the late nineteenth century, like the little Comstock acts and measures to regulate the industrial marketplace, were further evidence of the expansion of legislative authority into previously private matters.

Abortion became a crime in most states and the quickening doctrine lost much of its vitality. The New York legislature in 1881, for example, made prequickening abortion a criminal act, but it provided lesser penalties for the destruction of an unanimated fetus. The New York law, like statutes in California, Minnesota, Indiana, and the territory of Arizona, also subjected women seeking abortions to criminal penalties.

Abortion statutes limited the discretionary rights of women over their bodies, as a matter of both moral concern and public health. Male legislatures had made control of the woman's womb a matter for public concern and determination. The law's impact was certainly felt among married women, who turned by the end of the century to contraception rather than abortion as the principal means of birth control. The practice continued to flourish in the early twentieth-century United States, even though it was a criminal act in most states. Frederick J. Taussig, a physician and opponent of abortion, concluded that in 1910 as many as 80,000 abortions were committed each year and that only a very small percentage of those who administered them were ever convicted.

Children and Adoption

The social and legal status of children also changed in the nineteenth-century republican family. In premodern society, children were rarely differentiated from adults; they were simply smaller versions. In the modern era, childhood became a recognizable stage of human development; children were innocent, delicate, and malleable human beings with a psychology and emotion all their own. The companionate marriage and the inward-looking quality of the family accentuated these qualities, making children individuals with an identity removed, but not separate, from their parents.

The economic importance of children changed as well, although the extent of that transformation depended on the child's social class position. By the mid-nineteenth century, the conceptualization of the "economically worthless child" had been in large part developed among the U.S. urban middle class.[33] Concern shifted to children's education as the determinant of future marketplace worth. Far from relying on his child as old-age insurance, the middle-class father began insuring his own life and setting up other financial arrangements such as trusts and endowments, to protect the unproductive child. However, the economic value of the working-class child increased rather than decreased in the nineteenth century. Rapid industrialization after the 1860s introduced new occupations for poor children, and according to the 1870 census about one of every eight children was employed. Only by about 1930 did children of the working class join their middle-class counterparts in a new nonproductive world of childhood.

State encroachment on the once exclusive power of parents over their children rested on the English common law doctrine of *parens patriae*. It meant that the judiciary was empowered to intervene to protect the child's property from waste by parents or guardians. Courts in the United States expanded this doctrine in several ways, extending greater protection, for example, to children in custody proceedings. The concept of protecting a public trust was also embedded in the doctrine, and state legislatures relied on it and the police powers to justify their intervention. They were encouraged to act by mid- and late-nineteenth-century educators, physicians, and reformers, all bent on saving children from themselves and their parents. Legislators, for example, began to treat youth as a separate category. Except in the South, legislatures passed compulsory school attendance laws. They provided, by the end of the century, special juvenile courts, and they limited the nuptial freedom of young people by raising the marriage age.

The economic interests of the middle class figured in another way. Given the large number of middle-class property holders, the establishment of a child's legitimate parents and the passage of wealth from generation to generation were vital economic concerns. Nineteenth-century family law in the United States provided clarity in both areas.

Bastards in the English common law had been *filius nullius*. This term meant that the child was the heir of no one and that he or she had no claim on their parents' estate. First by judicial decision and then by legislation, U.S. lawmakers softened the harsh English doctrine. Unwed mothers and their illegitimate children gained reciprocal rights of custody and inheritance, although only Arizona and North Dakota declared all children the legitimate offspring of their natural parents and thus entitled to support and education as if they had been born in legal wedlock. Far more important was the growing role of social workers and welfare bureaucrats at the beginning of the twentieth century, a development pioneered by Minnesota in 1917 when it established a state board to safeguard the interests of illegitimate children.

Adoption was a more far-reaching innovation in the domestic relations law of the United States. In the postrevolutionary republican family, adoption was handled privately, and those parents interested in securing the legal rights of their new children did so by private legislative acts. Courts, however, also began to recognize that adopted children had limited rights to parental property. By midcentury, legislatures replaced these private arrangements with general statutes that sketched the legal obligations owed by parents to their adopted children. Alabama in 1850 passed the first measure, followed the next year by the more famous Massachusetts statute. By the beginning of the twentieth century an elaborate bureaucratic network had emerged, partly to deal with illegitimate children, that established guidelines covering the fitness of would-be parents. The new laws cut both ways, however; children taken from their natural parents could be removed by the state to a "better" home, thus severing by state action what had been at the beginning of the century the most intimate relationship. Children were separate, if naturally dependent, individuals whose needs and interests public officials could best protect.

Dissolving the Family: Divorce and Custody

Divorce

Divorce in colonial America was extremely rare. It could be obtained only through legislative action, a time-consuming and costly enterprise that required the legislative body to pass a private act. Many couples divorced from "bed and board"; they simply separated without legally dissolving their relationship.

The extent of divorce changed more slowly than did its form. Legal divorce remained uncommon into the early twentieth century, especially in the South, although recent studies have shown that even there, wives were quite willing to divorce their husbands, despite a social stigma greater there than elsewhere. As late as 1851, legislative divorce was the only way out of a marriage in Virginia and Maryland. Northern legislatures much more quickly relieved themselves of the task of granting private divorce acts. Massachusetts in 1780 was the first state to allow judicial divorce, and by the end of the nineteenth century every state except South Carolina provided for it.

Marriage and the family were widely perceived as anchors of social stability, yet the companionate form of marriage invited dissolution when expectations of love and affection proved unreachable. Just as the act of marriage established property interests and legitimated procreation, so divorce severed those ties. Divorce was essentially an economic matter, like so much else of the emerging domestic relations law. The devolution and disposition of property rights along rational lines among millions of small property holders depended on a simple legal mechanism, and judicial divorce provided it.

Even as divorce law became rationalized, it remained deeply conflicted. Organized religion, for example, was a formidable opponent of divorce. The Catholic Church damned it as sin; Protestant denominations portrayed it as an act of personal and national moral degeneration. The same social reformers who argued for tighter standards of marital fitness and limits on birth control also pointed to the increasing incidence of divorce as evidence of social decay. Judges and legislators imbibed these social assumptions and, despite the pressures for greater change, they were unwilling to make divorce too easy and too efficient.

The adversarial process was itself an impediment. The concept of consensual divorce was not known in the law of the nineteenth-century United States; one party had to prove that the other had committed a wrong of sufficient magnitude that existing legal relations warranted rearrangement. Legislators surrendered the task of issuing divorce decrees, but they continued to write statutes that spelled out the terms on which judges could grant them.

The statutory grounds for divorce exhibited the mix of moral and economic interests raised by marriage. Every state legislature placed adultery on the list, and the most conservative states, like New York, included no other. Elsewhere desertion was a common ground, but so too were fraud, impotence, conviction of a felony, and habitual drunkenness.

By the end of the century, cruelty emerged as the most common ground. Its legal definition meant different things in different places. Initially, state legislatures defined cruelty as physical harm or coercion, invariably by the husband against the wife. It proved a flexible concept. In California in 1863 the Supreme Court, in *Powelson* v.

Powelson, rejected the idea that only physical assault constituted cruelty. "[W]e think that any conduct sufficiently aggravated to produce ill-health or bodily pain," the court concluded, "though operating primarily upon the mind only, should be regarded as legal cruelty." By 1890 the judges had gone so far as to hold that because companionate marriage in "advanced civilizations" was based on "mutual sentiments of love and respect," indignities could destroy the basis of marriage even if there was no threat of physical harm. Two years later the legislature ratified the court's action, providing that "mental suffering" could be proven even if there was no evidence of deterioration in a spouse's physical health.[34]

What seemed an adversarial process was often consensual. Husbands, wives, lawyers, and even judges colluded in order to circumvent hidebound rules and to diminish the costs of an already expensive process. The legal system "winked and blinked and ignored."[35] In New York, for example, divorce required proof of adultery. An industry of sorts sprang up to meet this demand, and some lawyers, for a fee, would hire women to pose with husbands for incriminating photographs in hotel rooms.

The legal system encouraged the end to unhappy marriages, although a less cumbersome body of rules would have doubtless permitted even more. The divorce rate grew steadily through the nineteenth century, and it rose more than 70 percent between 1860 and 1900. There were 7380 divorces in 1860, or 1.2 per 1000 marriages; in 1920 there were 167,105 divorces, or 7.7 percent per 1000 marriages. More than two-thirds of all of these divorces were granted to women.

Child Custody

The increasing incidence of divorce raised the related issue of child custody. Traditionally, fathers had retained custody of children, but this practice went into gradual decline in the nineteenth century as patriarchy weakened and the public trust concept in the doctrine of *parens patriae* strengthened.

State appellate judges forged two important doctrines in nineteenth-century child custody cases. The "best-interest-of-the-child" doctrine was first developed by Chancellor Henry De Saussure of South Carolina in *Prather* v. *Prather* (1809). The case involved a South Carolina mother who sued for custody of her child on the grounds that the father was a known adulterer. De Saussure broke from the common law rule that children belonged to their father and granted custody to the mother on the grounds that the child's best interests would be served. Custody disputes in the new republic became discretionary hearings in which the judge balanced a newly recognized right of the mother to the child against the assessment of the needs of the child.

The "tender years" doctrine also biased custody decisions in favor of mothers and contributed to judicial discretion at the same time that it institutionalized Victorian gender commitments. Under it, mothers gained a presumptive claim to their young children, and in the era after the Civil War many state courts insisted daughters of all ages were best cared for by their mothers. The Alabama Supreme Court in 1876, for example, explained that "no greater calamity can befall an infant daughter, than a deprivation of a mother's care, vigilant precept, and example."[36] The tender years doctrine provided legal recourse to mothers based on their special status rather than any acknowledgment that they were as well equipped as men to provide for their children.

From Patriarchy to Judicial Maintenance

"[E]xperience proves," explained Joel P. Bishop, one of the pioneers of U.S. domestic relations law, in 1871, "that the habits make the law, and not the law the habits."[37] Market capitalism and republican ideology blended in the nineteenth-century United States to transform the status of husband and wife, parent and child. The century's lawmakers took account of these changes, leaving behind them an inheritance of significance to today's generation. A persistent belief that the private family was the foundation of national morality and that the law had to protect it amidst sweeping social change lent urgency to their efforts. Domestic relations law assured continuity within change, transforming "what at the beginning of the century had been the most private of public law into the most public of private law."[38]

Judicial maintenance replaced patriarchy during the course of the nineteenth century, and the fate of the family, like the fate of the economy, became a matter of public regulation. Judges and legislators emerged as custodians of the family, carving out a new legal status for children and married women. The former by 1900 had distinct rights, including the right not to be abused, mistreated, neglected or exploited, or denied support and education. The latter attained an equitable claim to property, the possibility of escaping an unhappy marriage, and a presumptive claim to their offspring. Their new position depended almost entirely on social assumptions that were translated into a special legal status rather than on any underlying belief that as a matter of human right they should be equal before the law with men.

9

The Dangerous Classes and the Nineteenth-Century Criminal Justice System

The social reformer Charles Loring Brace in 1872 described what he called the "dangerous classes." These were, according to Brace, people "hidden beneath the surface of society" who formed the "great masses of the destitute, miserable, and criminal persons."[1] Controlling the most fearsome element of the "dangerous classes," the criminal, absorbed the energies of nineteenth-century lawmakers and raised fundamental questions about the relationship between individual liberty and social stability. Criminal law involves the *power of the state* to deprive individuals of their liberty (through imprisonment, even death) and property (through fines and confiscations). Social stability requires that the liberty of some persons, whose behavior the state judges criminal, must be checked in the interests of the public.

Americans of the postrevolutionary era sought to reconcile these competing demands of liberty and social stability. They hedged state power in criminal prosecutions while founding the criminal law on a popular, decentralized basis. New state constitutions, the federal Constitution of 1787, and the Bill of Rights established explicit substantive and procedural safeguards against the abuse of criminal law. Efforts by Federalists to permit federal judges to try common law crimes collapsed with the Supreme Court's decision in *United States* v. *Hudson and Goodwin* (1812). The states, however, retained, through the police powers, ample authority to define and punish crime, but this authority was rooted in popular legislative bodies and not judges.

By the end of the nineteenth century this decentralized and popularly based approach to criminal justice had been displaced. The jolting social transformations that accompanied immigration, urbanization, and industrialization created pressures for a systematic and scientific approach toward the problem of crime, an approach that was not fully realized until the mid-twentieth century.

Creating the Antebellum Criminal Justice System

Postrevolutionary Republican Attitudes toward Crime

Colonial Americans equated criminal behavior with sin, and they had no conception of rehabilitation. The purpose of the criminal law was to punish and deter. While colonial lawmakers believed that crime was endemic, they "did not interpret its presence as symptomatic of a basic flaw in community structure or expect to eliminate it."[2]

The Revolution, however, unleashed powerful forces of market capitalism and individualism, and republican values began shortly thereafter to reshape Americans' understanding of the criminal law. The economic forces of the Revolution, for example, placed great value on holding and using private property for individual gain. Criminal law and the apparatus of criminal justice adapted to this change. Statutes dealing with economic crimes (theft, burglary, and such) began to appear in greater numbers. Prosecutors devoted less and less time to traditional moral offenses, leaving these matters to private discretion and judgment, even though laws against fornication, adultery, and Sabbath breaking remained on the books. At the time of the Revolution, for example, in Middlesex County, Massachusetts, two-thirds of all prosecutions were for immorality, and crime was regularly described as a sinful act. By 1800 more than 50 percent of all prosecutions were for theft, and only 0.5 percent were for moral offenses.[3] The dominant use of the criminal law in the early republic was "as defender of an economic and political order, and much less as guardian of a code of sexual and social behavior."[4]

Enlightenment political thought also shaped postrevolutionary theories about crime and punishment. Although the evidence about the actual incidence of crime is contradictory, there is little doubt that Americans at the end of the eighteenth century believed themselves to be caught in an epidemic of crime and that bringing it under control was essential to the success of their republican experiment.

The Italian nobleman Cesare Bonesana, Marquis of Beccaria, presented to late-eighteenth-century Americans the most coherent explanation of the classical or rational school of criminology. Beccaria in 1764 published *Essay on Crimes and Punishments*. The first English translation appeared in Charleston, South Carolina in 1777, but two years before John Adams had invoked Beccaria in defending the English soldiers involved in the Boston Massacre. Thomas Jefferson's *Commonplace Book* contained twenty-six extracts from the *Essay*, and Jefferson drew extensively from it in formulating his proposed reforms of Virginia penal law in 1776. Jefferson even included *Essay on Crimes and Punishments* as one of the six most important works on civil government.

According to Beccaria the criminal law was an instrument of liberty not a tool of repression. Liberty, he asserted, could only prevail by curbing the "despotism of each individual" from plunging society into chaos.[5] The legitimacy and the efficiency of the criminal law were intertwined, and Beccaria insisted that its success depended on its humane and rational qualities. Punishment had to be proportional to the crime; justice required the swift and predictable administration of punishment. Disproportionate penalties, vague criminal statutes, and unwritten judge-made law undermined the effective administration of the criminal law. Beccaria also opposed the death penalty, unlike most other thinkers of the Enlightenment, because it afforded an "example of barbarity" that actually encouraged rather than deterred wrongdoing.[6]

Beccaria's thoughts about the nature of criminal justice struck a responsive chord among postrevolutionary authorities, who confronted the dual tasks of formulating republican governments based on consent while curbing individual licentiousness. As one observer noted in 1784, "it must give every man of feeling [sic] the most sensible pain, when he observes how insufficient our penal laws are to answer the end they were designed to."[7] In Virginia at this time, the entire criminal justice system seemed incapable of bringing wrongdoers to justice. For example, one-third of those examined at the county level for felonies were discharged and one-third of those tried were acquitted.[8] Lawmakers confronted an actual crisis in criminal justice, a crisis in which republican government seemed susceptible to destruction not from foreign powers but from domestic criminals.

First Burst of Criminal Law Reform, 1787–1820

Lawmakers responded to this crisis by tailoring criminal law and the administration of punishment to republican ideals. Pennsylvania, where the Quaker religion was strong, was a hub of reform activity. The framers of the Pennsylvania Constitution of 1776 directed future legislators to compose a new and more humane criminal code "as soon as may be, and punishments made . . . in general more proportionate to the crimes."[9] Reaching that goal required more than a decade, but in 1786 the legislature abolished the death penalty for robbery, burglary, and sodomy. Eight years later the legislature advanced an even more radical proposition, establishing the principle of degrees of criminal activity. In the case of murder, for example, the new statute declared that the "several offenses, which are included under the general denomination of murder, differ . . . greatly from each other in the degree of their atrociousness." The law then proceeded to distinguish between two "degrees" of murder: the "first," which was premeditated or committed in the course of a felony and the "second," which included all others. Only first-degree murder was punishable by death.[10]

Benjamin Rush, a Philadelphia physician, was the strongest voice for reform in the new nation. Rush set his ideas down in two important works, *Enquiry into the Effects of Public Punishments upon Criminals and Society* (1787) and *Considerations on the Injustice and Impolicy of Punishing Murder by Death* (1792). Rush insisted that republics were prone to disorder and licentiousness, and only through the exercise of public virtue (the sacrificing of the individual to the common good) could the republican experiment succeed. He fitted Beccaria's ideas about humane and proportionate punishment to American circumstances, making capital punishment the focus of his attention. "Capital punishments," he insisted, "are the natural offspring of monarchical governments."[11] The gallows eroded rather than strengthened republican values and behavior. Severe and excessive punishments marked monarchies; mild and benevolent ones characterized republics.

Most reformers stopped short of Rush's opposition to the death penalty for all offenses. They wished only that capital punishment be withdrawn for crimes such as robbery, burglary, counterfeiting, and rape. The Pennsylvania legislation, in this regard, was a model of the moderate purposes of law reform.

Other states adopted similar reforms. Rush's writings circulated widely among state legislatures including Massachusetts and Virginia. In the latter, George K. Taylor implored the legislature to "imitate and adopt" Pennsylvania's scheme of criminal law.[12] Not every effort succeeded. Edward Livingston of Louisiana, for example, was the early republic's first advocate of a thorough codification of law. He achieved some success when the state, with its strong civil law tradition, embraced his civil code that was patterned after the famous French Code Napoleon. Legislators brushed his criminal code aside as too radical. Still, change was pervasive. South Carolina, the most traditional of the southern states on matters of crime and punishment, reduced the number of crimes that carried the death penalty from 165 to 22 between 1813 and 1850.

The decline in the use of the death penalty raised a practical problem: what was to be done with criminals who would otherwise have been executed? Once again Pennsylvania set the pace. Reformers there and Quaker activists in England urged the construction of penitentiaries to house criminals. A complex set of ideas about human nature and the possibilities of individual change animated the penitentiary movement. Where the colonists had emphasized innate sin, the postrevolutionary generation stressed the environment as a breeding ground of criminality. The Quakers approached the problem from a religious perspective, but ideas of the Enlightenment, expressed through Beccaria's classical theory of criminology, reinforced and complemented the proposition that law was a tool of individual rehabilitation and social reformation. Tunis Wortman, a New York reformer, explained in 1796 that "the doctrine of *innate ideas* has long since been exploded" and man was now viewed as "the creature of education and the child of habitude."[13]

What has come to be called the penitentiary was known at its inception by different names, most commonly "house of repentance" or "house of reformation." Pennsylvania in 1788 commissioned the Philadelphia Society for Alleviating the Miseries of Public Prisons, of which Rush was a charter member, to report on the existing facilities and practices of jails. The society's report was sharply critical, observing that punishment that was *"more private or even solitary labour,* would more successfully tend to reclaim the unhappy objects."[14] The society's report fixed for the next half-century the optimistic republican belief that all persons were capable of self-reformation if placed in the proper environment and given, through solitary confinement and the discipline of hard labor, the opportunity to reflect on and correct their wayward habits.

Critics of the penitentiary denounced incarceration as either contrary to republican ideals or simply impractical. Samuel Adams, for example, concluded that the only way to sustain the new republic was through measures that provided that those "who dare rebel against the laws of [the] republic ought to suffer death."[15] Stephen Burroughs, a convict incarcerated at the Castle Island facility in Massachusetts, wondered in his memoirs how it was "that a country which has stood the foremost in asserting the cause of liberty should so soon after obtaining the blessing themselves, deprive others of it?"[16]

This opposition made little headway. In the last decade of the eighteenth century, a majority of legislatures adopted the penitentiary as a substitute for the gallows and embraced the idea of institutional rehabilitation of criminals. The New York legislature in 1796 appropriated funds for the Newgate facility in the Greenwich Village area of lower Manhattan. New Jersey in 1797 completed its first penitentiary and Virginia, Kentucky, Massachusetts, Vermont, New Hampshire, and Maryland followed suit shortly thereafter. In most southern states, the peculiar institution of slavery solved the problem of controlling the dangerous class.

By the 1820s this initial burst of criminal law reform and penitentiary building faded, although the goals associated with it persisted. Mounting expenses, overcrowding, and the prevalence of repeat offenders suggested that changing codes and building prisons alone would not halt the spread of crime. Yet the failure of the first wave of criminal law reform energized a new generation of reformers who extended the concepts of environmentalism, human perfectibility, and institutional discipline beyond the scope imagined by Rush.

Antebellum Criminal Justice Institutions

The institutions of the criminal justice system began to take on a modern form in the antebellum years. The most important developments involved the jury, the penitentiary, the juvenile house of refuge, and the police.

The Grand and Petit Jury

The grand and petit juries brought the force of community will to bear on the legal process. The criminal jury underwent significant changes, of which the most dramatic was the "increasing restriction placed on the jury's right to decide law."[17] This development paralleled a similar decline in the civil jury's law finding role.

A grand jury inquires into complaints and accusations brought before it and, based on evidence presented by the state, issues bills of indictment. It is called a "grand" jury because it involves a greater number of jurors (in common law no less than twelve and no more than twenty-three) than an ordinary trial or "petit" jury. The grand jury was originally conceived in English law as an institution in which jurors disclosed whatever personal knowledge they had of crime. Early in the history of the United States, the grand jury had evolved the somewhat different role of relying on the sense of the community to prevent indiscriminate prosecutions. The grand jury was also an administrative body that inquired into the condition of highways, taverns, and jail facilities. It was an investigatory body that checked corruption and laxness in local government at the same time that it posted indictments against members of the community for alleged criminal violations.

The grand jury was a source of controversy. Jeffersonian Republicans, for example, charged that Federalist judges used grand jury charges to further political objectives. Even Chancellor James Kent, the great conservative common law jurist of New York, believed that judges should restrict themselves in charging grand juries "to the business of the penal law."[18]

The secrecy that surrounded grand jury proceedings fueled additional agitation, especially after the franchise democracy of the Jacksonian United States gained hold in the 1840s and 1850s. Several state constitutional conventions debated its fate, with critics charging that secret proceedings in criminal matters were contrary to the spirit of the new nation's democratic institutions. Defenders of the grand jury, who were overwhelmingly Whig, subscribed to the traditional republican notion of community control; opponents, who were overwhelmingly Democrats, argued that only through open proceedings was it possible to place responsibility for upholding the community's morality where it belonged—on the individual.

The grand jury weathered this onslaught because of the absence of a workable alternative. Democratic reformers, for example, urged that public examination replace the grand jury's secret deliberations. Antebellum lawmakers, however, concluded that, important as individual virtue and responsibility were, property, life, and personal reputation were better protected through the grand jury's institutionalized secrecy. The clamor indeed prompted some changes, the most important of which was the decision in most states to broaden the authority of prosecutors to bring an information (which was an accusation of wrongdoing) independent of the grand jury.

The petit jury also changed. Jeffersonian Republicans advocated an active and unchecked jury solidly anchored to democratic principles. Jacksonian Democrats in the 1830s and 1840s echoed this earlier belief that the trial jury was merely an instrument of popular justice. Alexis de Tocqueville explained as much when he wrote that "the jury is pre-eminently a political institution; it should be regarded as one form of the sovereignty of the people."[19] Yet lawmakers also recognized that freewheeling juries sapped one of the most valuable components of the rule of law: consistent and uniform decision making based on precedent.

Two issues structured the antebellum debate over the criminal jury. The first was its power to decide questions of law; the second was the method by which its members were selected. Prior to about 1800 a consensus existed that an unfettered jury served the interests of justice by linking the criminal law to community morality. Juries issued general verdicts that stated either the innocence or guilt of a defendant. John Adams, for example, concluded that general verdicts allowed a juror "to find the verdict according to his own best understanding, judgment, and conscience, tho in opposition to the direction of the court."[20] Jurors did not operate totally at will, and the same limitations on jury discretion that appeared in early nineteenth-century civil proceedings also emerged in criminal trials. Counsel, for example, could use special pleading before a court, a technique that framed a factual question in such a way that jurors had either to answer yes or no, leaving the matter of law strictly to be settled by the presiding judge.

Nineteenth-century criminal trial judges gradually eroded the jury's dominance, although their actions generated substantial controversy. Legislators aided this shift through statutes that specified, for example, tighter rules for the admissibility of evidence. Uniformity in adjudication became more important than unrelieved democratic sentiment. Moreover, the declining influence of the jury flowed directly from the growing technical character of law over which judges, as the heads of the rising legal profession, exercised increasing command.

Because the jury was an instrument of popular control and an accepted feature of Anglo-American law was that every defendant deserved a trial before his peers, the issue of jury composition (i.e., how to select jurors) also stirred debate. We know tantalizingly little about this process of selection. Women and blacks, of course, because they were not considered part of the political community, were excluded. Most states relied on the tax roles to compose the venire (the pool of potential jurors), and widespread property holding probably made American juries more representative of the community on the whole than their English counterparts, where the sheriff had exercised great authority in composing them. Lawmakers provided that both the prosecution and the defense could exercise some number of challenges, either preemptorially (usually limited in number) or for cause (usually with no limit on the number, but with constraint by the judge).

Throughout the nineteenth century, pressures for economy and efficiency in government narrowed the bases on which juries were composed. State legislatures, for example, passed laws that reduced the number of jurors needed to compose the venire and increased the number of challenges allowed by both sides. Even more important, this legislation permitted the use of "bystander jurors." If the venire was exhausted, then the clerk of the court could turn to bystanders. Clerks broadly interpreted the term bystander to include persons well beyond the confines of the courtroom. The practice, critics rightly charged, diminished the quality and representativeness of the jury. In Indiana, for example, bystander juries were composed of a class of "idle and dissolute persons" and "loafers and drunkards," who were predisposed to allow the guilty to escape and whose presence "destroy[ed] the good effect of jury trials, as well as impair[ed] public confidence and acquiescence in their decisions."[21]

Discovery of the Asylum

During the 1820s one generation of prison reformers gave way to another. The first generation lacked "any clear idea what these structures should look like or how they should be administered."[22] The early reformers, such as Benjamin Rush, had argued that incarceration was more humane than hanging, but they had only a vague idea of how the prison should promote rehabilitation.

The new generation offered the prison as *the* solution to the problem of criminal disorder. They had "discovered the asylum" as an institutional solution to fundamental social dislocations, including insanity and poverty as well as crime. Like their predecessors, prison reformers of the Jacksonian era had strong religious ties, especially to evangelical denominations that stressed the perfectibility of humankind, and they were also deeply involved in other social reform causes, such as antislavery and prohibition. Perhaps their single most important voice was that of Louis Dwight, leader of the Boston Prison Discipline Society, the most influential prison reform group from 1825 to 1854.

The prison rested on two interrelated concepts. The first was the idea, associated with Beccaria, that crime was the product of an unhealthy environment and that a person placed in a healthy one would eventually reform. This idea flowed from a second proposition: human beings were rational creatures capable of self-reformation. Environmentalism, rationalism, and optimism fused in the prison. It offered a refuge of rehabilitation in which hard work, discipline, solitude, silence, and religious study supposedly altered old patterns of behavior in favor of new, socially acceptable ones.

What distinguished prison reformers of the Jacksonian era from their predecessors was a grand vision that molded architecture and administrative control into a total institution. Within this general framework two competing systems emerged: the Auburn, or congregate system, and the Eastern State Penitentiary, or separate system.

The Auburn system took its name from the prison in the town of Auburn, New York. Opened in 1819, the facility initially imposed a regimen of solitary confinement for the worst offenders, leading to nervous breakdowns, disease, and suicide. Four years after it opened, and after an inspection by state authorities that revealed shocking conditions, Warden Elam Lynds devised a new system of prison discipline. Prisoners slept in individual cells but worked and ate together. The design of the prison, in the form of a fortresslike castle with a large central gathering area and separate cells, was ideally suited to Lynds's program. The warden imposed total silence, doing so in the belief that inmates would contemplate their own rehabilitation and that they would not have the opportunity to learn additional evil ways from other inmates. Discipline and order were reinforced by making prisoners move in a lockstep shuffle, with eyes downcast and one hand on the shoulder of the man next to them. Those prisoners who refused to cooperate were subjected to rigorous punishments, including whipping and torture. Alexis de Tocqueville reported, after visiting Auburn in 1831, that "the silence within these vast walls . . . is that of death. We felt as if we traversed catacombs."[23]

The rival system in Pennsylvania was built at the Eastern State Penitentiary at Cherry Hill, opened in 1829. The architecture of the building captured its approach to corrections. The Eastern State facility was designed in the form of spokes that radiated from a central administrative hub with small cells forming a honeycomb up the sides of the spokes. Each prisoner had his own exercise yard, denying him contact with other prisoners. More so than in the Auburn system, the Eastern State scheme denied prisoners access to outside influences, curtailing mail and visitors. It had fewer recidivists (repeat offenders) than Auburn, but it also took a greater toll in human life through suicide.

The faults and advantages of both systems were evenly distributed, but the costs were not. State legislators favored the congregate prison not only because it was cheaper to build and administer than its separate counterpart, but also because the Auburn plan offered the additional feature of prison industries, which held the never-realized promise of making the prisons self-supporting. The Auburn plan "provided the best of both worlds, economy and reform."[24] By the time of the Civil War, however, these remained elusive goals, as prisons, like insane asylums and poorhouses, evolved into holding facilities rather than the institutions of rehabilitation that their optimistic founders had so fervently sought.

House of Refuge

Houses of refuge and youth reformatories appeared at about the same time that the second wave of prison reform took hold. They too promised to rehabilitate individual children by placing them in an environment free from corrupting influences.

The origins of reformatories for disobedient children lay, to some extent, with attempts in the colonial and revolutionary eras to care for the orphaned poor. George Whitefield in 1740 organized the first orphan asylum in Savannah, Georgia. Overseers of the poor following the Revolution regularly dispatched children to another rising public institution, the almshouse. Troublesome and disobedient children, however, were frequently dispatched to jails. Because children were considered highly impressionable, reformers made removing them from direct contact with adult offenders a priority. If the young were vulnerable to corruption, they were also eminently teachable.

What began as a private philanthropic effort early in the nineteenth century evolved into a state-supported enterprise by midcentury. The experience of New York was typical. The first separate reform organization, the Society for the Reformation of Juvenile Delinquents, appeared in 1825. Reformers connected juvenile crime to poverty, and the leaders of the New York City society concluded that instead of relieving the conditions of poverty directly they had to take children from their families and place them in an environment that emphasized discipline and training. In the spring of 1825, the New York legislature chartered the New York House of Refuge as a private charity. Within three years philanthropists founded houses of refuge in Boston and Philadelphia.

The legislatures that chartered these houses of refuge also forged a policy that facilitated commitment. Children were incarcerated by order of a judicial body, by a recommendation of local overseers of the poor, and by the personal inclinations of a parent. There was little in the way of due-process protections for children, a consequence that grew quite naturally out of the belief that the state, through the doctrine of *parens patriae,* had a direct and growing responsibility for the care of children.

From its inception in the Jacksonian era, the ''crime'' of juvenile delinquency was a vague category of antisocial behavior. A child, for example, could be classified a delinquent because his or her parents failed to provide proper support. Children could also be placed in a reformatory for status offenses; that is, they were susceptible to incarceration because of some personal condition (e.g., vagrancy) rather than some action they had taken, such as stealing.

The refuge attempted to infuse the child with middle-class values: thrift, industry, and social responsibility. Release came either with age or, more often, with an apprenticeship; this program worked well until the 1850s, when the emerging industrial economy reduced the need for apprentices and thus the opportunities for adolescent laborers. Children were returned to society with the proviso that they could be re-institutionalized if they became unruly or uncooperative. The policy of conditional release developed in the houses of refuge was extended later in the century to adult offenders through parole and probation. The house of refuge seldom achieved the more noble purposes for which it was designed, and by the time of the Civil War it had become, like the penitentiary, a ''warehouse for the unwanted.''[25]

Police

Historians generally cite the establishment of a day watch in Boston in 1838 as the first urban police force, but Philadelphia had experimented with a similar arrangement as early as 1833. Whatever the first date, the antebellum police differed from their counterparts after the Civil War, and the nineteenth-century police, taken as a whole, were far removed from modern urban law enforcement institutions. The police changed from ''an informal, even casual, bureaucracy to a formal, rule-governed, militaristic organization.''[26] Duties changed along with organizational structure. The first police forces were charged with maintaining the orderly functioning of cities, a small part of which involved catching criminals. In the era after the Civil War they undertook to control the dangerous classes, with a growing emphasis on crime. Today, they are exclusively associated with crime and traffic control.

The slave patrol in the South and the night watch in the North and South were the antecedents of the police. The slave patrol in Charleston, South Carolina, in 1837 had a force of 100 officers. In rural portions of the South, patrolmen exercised control over slaves who were away from their plantations as well as aiding in catching and returning escaped slaves.

The night watch, which had its origins in England during the thirteenth century, was a preventative patrol meant to give out the hue and cry when an offense had occurred. The watch worked reasonably well in small communities where personal and direct control based on an underlying social consensus existed. This informal consensus waned as U.S. cities grew in size and as their populations included greater numbers of strangers with socially and ethnically divergent origins. Urban riots, a commonplace event in the nineteenth-century United States, revealed the growing social tensions. Clashes between Anglo-Saxon Protestants and Irish Catholics, for example, exploded in several nineteenth-century cities. The slavery controversy fueled additional lawlessness, with attacks on white abolitionists in Boston, Cincinnati, Philadelphia, and other major cities. The most deadly riot occurred in 1863 in New York City where police and state militia units subdued draft rioters only after federal troops joined them in the fourth day of the upheaval.

Early police forces in the United States drew their inspiration from the English, whose experience with the impact of industrialization and urbanization preceded that in the United States by almost a half-century. Parliament in 1829 passed the London Metropolitan Police Act, which emphasized the prevention of crime. The police exercised social control by developing a continuous presence throughout society, with officers walking patrol over regularly assigned routes, known as "beats." The act's architect, Sir Robert Peel, required that beat officers be uniformed and supervised through a system of military-style ranks.

Lawmakers in the United States owed much to the English model, but they also departed from it in significant ways. First, the English police were a national organization controlled by a member of the king's cabinet. In the United States, however, the police emerged as a local force responsive to local political demands. Police administration in England was imposed from the top down; in the United States it was created from the bottom up. Second, the English police, free from the people's direct control, fashioned high standards of professionalism. In the United States, police work was a job for amateurs who owed their posts to political rather than professional considerations. Third, early American police forces did adopt a strategy of crime prevention, like the English, but they initially rejected both uniforms and military-style management as antidemocratic.

Police forces in the United States professionalized at a slower pace than their English cousins. The New York City police, for example, only became uniformed in 1853 and only after considerable debate. James W. Gerard, a prominent New York reformer, argued that the "great *moral* power of the policeman of London in preventing crimes lies in his coat." Uniformed officers prevented crime by striking fear and dread in the hearts of the "criminally-disposed population . . . by their well-known intelligence, activity, unflinching firmness, and incorruptible *honesty.*"[27]

Antebellum police forces were deeply enmeshed in local politics, a condition that persisted into the late nineteenth century. An individual with the right political connections could be hired despite the lack of obvious qualifications, and good officers could be discharged from their jobs with the shift from the administration of one party to the next. There was no formal training for recruits; supervision of beat officers was weak. The police were just one more element in the emerging urban machine that the development of mass political parties in the mid-nineteenth century fostered.

Early police forces played a small role in detecting crime, leaving that task to the thief catcher, an individual who was seldom a police officer and who, despite the title, did not actually catch thieves. Instead, the thief catcher recovered stolen goods, operating in the capacity of a modern-day fence. The most famous of these individuals, who were far more numerous in England than the United States, was George Reed, a constable in Boston during the 1820s. "The secret of his wonderful success," wrote a contemporary about Reed, "was in his having in his employ parties who were in his power, whose liberty and in some cases, it was intimated, their permission to ply their vocation, depended on the value of the information they were able to furnish him."[28] During a brief period in the mid-nineteenth century, the police often functioned as intermediaries between thieves and victims, negotiating cash payments in exchange for stolen goods. In New York, for example, the police might have charged as much as seventy-five dollars to secure the return of a watch.

Criminal Justice System after the Civil War

Stagnation, disillusionment, and decline plagued the institutional framework fashioned by lawmakers before the Civil War. The government-sponsored mobilization required by the Civil War renewed belief in the efficacy of institutional solutions. On every level of the federal system, "American governments and private associations, or quasi-public ones, were the globe's pioneers in efforts to institutionalize the public good."[29] Lawmakers after the Civil War, who were usually portrayed as committed to the cause of social and economic laissez-faire, actually laid the ground for reforms—including parole, probation, and the indeterminate sentence—that are typically ascribed to the Progressive era (see Chapter 10). As with economic policy making, the robust state-based federalism of the Gilded Age emphasized local and state solutions to industrialization and urbanization.

The Problem of Crime

The crime rate is the incidence of *reported* crimes per 100,000 population. Because much crime is never reported, the *real* crime rate is doubtless higher than the reported rate, and some experts believe that as much as one-half of all crime is never reported. Until the 1850s the crime rate grew steadily. Thereafter, however, the pattern changed abruptly, and at virtually every level and in a startling variety of regions in the late nineteenth-century Western world (not just the United States), the rate of felony offenses declined. The absolute numbers of crime indeed increased, but not as quickly as the population. Crimes of public disorderliness (drunkenness and disturbing the peace) also declined; unlike the felony rate, however, these crimes continued to decline well into the twentieth century.

A declining crime rate in the last half of the nineteenth century has important implications. Scholars have long argued that industrialization and urbanization contributed to the development of serious crime. They have insisted that teeming cities filled with immigrants and a growing wage-labor force caused crime. They also argue that criminal justice reforms mounted after the Civil War were ineffective and frequently contributed to class antagonism and repression.

Not only do falling crime rates contradict these assumptions, but so too does the most intensive study of the operation of a single criminal justice system, that of

Alameda County, California from 1870 to 1910. There the "crime rates probably declined in the county. Apparently, in the late nineteenth century, Oakland [the major city in the county] became less violent, more orderly."[30] What happened in Alameda County likely happened elsewhere. The criminal justice system probably became more effective, as professionalization took hold, and, at the same time, urbanization and industrialization imposed a social discipline that slowed the rate of criminal activity.

Quite apart from the statistical evidence, Americans after the Civil War were convinced that crime plagued their lives. Lawmakers responded by reasserting traditional institutional solutions at the same time that they broke new ground through measures that combined individualized treatment, bureaucratic organization, and professionalization.

Prison, Individualized Treatment, and the Scientific Basis of Crime

Enoch Wines and Theodore Dwight in 1867 prepared the first comprehensive survey of prisons in the United States. Their *Report on the Prisons and Reformatories* concluded that "there was no prison system in the United States . . . which would not be found wanting."[31] Prisons, Wines and Dwight argued, had failed to fulfill the optimistic promise held out for them by prewar reformers. They trumpeted a new round of institutional reform that began three years later at the National Conference of Penitentiary and Reformatory Discipline in Cincinnati.

The Cincinnati Congress was the most important event in the history of penology in the United States. Organized by Enoch Wines, the convention covered virtually every major issue of prison reform. Particularly influential was a paper by Zebulon R. Brockway, then superintendent of the Detroit House of Corrections, and in 1877 warden of the Elmira Reformatory, the model penal institution of the late nineteenth century.

Brockway advocated the indeterminate sentence and individualized treatment within an institutional setting. He affirmed the traditional role of the prison in imposing new habits through rigorous discipline, agreeing with antebellum penal reformers that religious instruction, secular education, and hard labor were essential to rehabilitation. Brockway, however, placed far more stress than earlier reformers on individualized treatment. He believed that existing sentencing practices, by establishing a foreseeable period of detention, gave inmates little incentive to improve and operated, in any case, on the false premise that each person could be rehabilitated in the same amount of time. According to Brockway, who favored sentences with no maximums or minimums, indeterminate sentences were essential for one simple reasons: the offender had complete control over his or her improvement.

Brockway's insistence on an individualized approach to the rehabilitation of criminals had broad appeal, not just to reformers, but also to lawmakers and prison administrators. The former believed that Brockway's plan would make existing facilities work better without significant additional costs. The latter embraced the greater discretionary control that the indeterminate sentence promised. Wardens, for example, could coerce cooperation from recalcitrant prisoners by certifying that they were not making acceptable progress toward rehabilitation.

Science lent credibility to the new emphasis on individualized treatment. At the same time that the eugenics movement was stimulating a reassessment of the law of race relations and the family, the research of an Italian army physician, Cesare Lombroso and an American, Richard L. Dugdale, were reshaping assumptions about crime, criminal law, and institutions.

Lombroso developed the science of anthropometry, which means the study and techniques of human comparison. His ideas were set forth in *The Criminal Man* (1876), in which he purported to show, through systematic measurements, that criminals were invariably "born" as biological "throwbacks" to an earlier and lower form of life. He concluded that there were several categories of criminals (born criminals criminals governed by passions, criminals who acted only occasionally) and that each of them bore distinctive physical characteristics. Black and frizzled hair, a sparse beard, oblique eyes, a small skull, a retreating forehead, and voluminous ears were all evidence of inherited criminality.

Dugdale also drew his inspiration from the science of heredity, and his *"The Jukes"*: A Study in Crime, Pauperism, Disease and Heredity (1877) became a popular sensation. Dugdale found that since the seventeenth century one Ada Jukes had produced offspring whose numbers included habitual thieves, murderers, and prostitutes. Dugdale's study lent the then-accepted standards of science to the proposition that a bad seed, once planted genetically, would echo through generations of criminals.

Sorting out those individuals who bore the mark of Cain from those who did not was one of the reasons for adopting an individualized approach to criminal rehabilitation. The prison remained at the center of the rehabilitation process, but lawmakers added enough new elements in the last quarter of the nineteenth century to forge the outlines of a genuine correctional system. These included probation, parole, revised sentencing practices, plea bargaining, and the juvenile court.

Probation

Probation provides that an offender can be freed to the community as long as he or she meets certain specified conditions. The practice filled many of the idealized goals of the Cincinnati Congress, and it had a long common law history. First English and later American judges had given suspended sentences to criminal offenders deemed good risks, on the provision that, should they fail to maintain their good behavior, they would have to serve the full term of their sentence.

Massachusetts in 1878 was the first state to enact a probation statute. The legislature formalized what had been a long-standing informal practice. John Augustus, a Boston shoemaker, began functioning as a volunteer probation officer in 1841. Augustus visited criminal courts and took up the causes of those individuals he believed capable of redemption. He was apparently motivated by a sense of compassion, paying fines for drunks, posting bail for indigent offenders, and even helping to find employment for the charges he took under his wing. The Boston criminal court eventually took official notice of Augustus's activities; judges assigned convicted offenders to his care instead of committing them to correctional institutions. The exact number of persons aided by Augustus is in dispute, but he asserted that by 1858 he had served some 1152 men and 794 women.

The Massachusetts statute was a model for the rest of the nation. It authorized probation officers for Suffolk County (Boston) only, but in 1880 the legislature extended this provision to the entire state. As in most other states, the probation officer, though originally controlled by municipal officials, was subsequently placed under the supervision of the courts. By 1900 four other states (Missouri, Rhode Island, New Jersey, and Vermont) had established probation systems.

Parole and the Indeterminate Sentence

Parole is the practice by which inmates are released after having satisfied certain conditions. The assumption is that parole offers an incentive for good behavior, one that motivates prisoners to hasten their own rehabilitation. The indeterminate sentence provides that convicted offenders are incarcerated until such time as they demonstrate that they are capable of reentering society. No state adopted open-ended sentencing; instead, state legislatures rewrote the punishment portions of criminal statutes, requiring that convicts had to be released after they reached the maximum term of years under their sentence.

Discretionary early release of prisoners was well established in both England and the United States before the Cincinnati Congress. Captain Alexander Maconochie, who in 1840 became superintendent of the penal colony on Norfolk Island in Northeastern Australia, is usually called the father of parole. Maconochie's plan was subsequently adopted by Sir Walter Grofton, director of Irish Convict Prisons, whose work was well known to Americans. Grofton invented the "ticket of leave" program through which prisoners moved up grade by grade until they finally earned permission to leave.

Lawmakers after the Civil War also drew on their own experiences. For example, delinquent children placed in houses of refuge had gained early release through apprenticeship. In adult prisons, wardens devised programs that rewarded well-behaved prisoners by reducing their sentences. The pardoning power, by which a governor intervened to release a prisoner before his or her sentence ran its course, was pervasive. In Massachusetts between 1828 and 1866, 12.5 percent of all prisoners were released by pardon. The practice made administrative sense (as did parole and discretionary release under indeterminate sentences) because it abated overcrowding, placing the most deserving convicts on the streets while making room for more dangerous and recently convicted felons. New York in 1817 was the first state to have a "good time" or commutation law that reduced sentences of inmates serving more than five years by as much as 25 percent. By 1869 twenty-three states had some form of commutation law.

Brockway campaigned to make conditional release a formal part of the U.S. correctional system. After becoming warden of the Elmira Reformatory in 1877, he made that institution into a national model. Supported by legislation that imposed a modified form of the indeterminate sentence, Brockway introduced a grading system that allowed prisoners to lower their sentences by earning credits for good behavior.

By 1900 eleven states had some form of indeterminate sentence and another twenty states had some form of parole. The sentencing statutes varied widely, and they had somewhat contradictory effects. Legislatures specified longer maximum penalties and inmates spent somewhat longer periods of time behind bars than they had under the old sentencing system. Most prisoners won release before they completed their maximum sentence, but overcrowded facilities rather than massive rehabilitation dictated the release of those inmates who had served the longest terms.

New Prison Facilities for Specialized Offenders

Reformers after the Civil War were particularly concerned with the treatment of women and youthful offenders. The prevalent cult of domesticity created special concerns about female felons, whose behavior seemed to threaten the moral foundations of the nation. Reformers like Dwight and Wines had another concern: widespread accusations of sexual debauchery in prisons and jails. Because one of the cardinal features of the rehabilitative ideal was instilling a moral code in prisoners, sexual immorality in prison was considered especially corrosive. In early prisons, men and women were not fully separated, and such segregation as did exist was usually by departments (separate wings of a main prison facility) rather than separate institutions. Massachusetts was the lone exception in the mid-nineteenth century, ordering that all female offenders be confined in county houses of correction, a practice that spread rapidly after the Civil War.

Separate female facilities developed slowly because there were so few female offenders. Nineteenth-century crime was a man's world that women seldom entered. In Oakland, California between 1872 and 1910, nine of ten arrests were of men. At least in Oakland, women most often were arrested for drunkenness and public disorder rather than for serious felonies or morals charges, such as prostitution. Women who did behave in disorderly ways incurred far more public wrath than did men, of whom such behavior was almost expected.

Lawmakers after the Civil War gradually realized that successful rehabilitation of female offenders required separate facilities. Indiana in 1873 opened the nation's first women's prison, followed by Massachusetts four years later and then New York in 1881. In each instance a private philanthropic movement committed to the well-being of women persuaded legislators to establish the new institutions. Prisons for female offenders mirrored in their programs the larger assumptions of society, seeking to inculcate in women convicts Victorian attitudes toward sexuality, personal discipline, and the proper habits of mother and wife.

State lawmakers also became sensitive to the plight of young adult offenders, who were often thrown into prison with more experienced criminals. New York in 1825 provided that male first offenders under the age of twenty-one were to be confined in local houses of correction if the space was available. Michigan in 1861 opened the Detroit House of Corrections with the objective of providing a supportive environment to young adult offenders. The most famous response was Brockway's Elmira Reformatory, into whose plans the New York legislature wove "all the best ideas of the day."[32]

The Elmira Reformatory became a national model. The New York legislature mandated that the facility was to house only individuals between the ages of sixteen and thirty who had been convicted of their first felony. Elmira practiced conditional-release programs, and its regimen of work and education sought to equip inmates for productive lives. Brockway pioneered the use of prison industries as vocational training grounds. His goal was total rehabilitation of the individual.

Juvenile Court

The juvenile court crystallized the main features of corrections after the Civil War: individualized treatment, indeterminacy, and expanded discretionary decision making.

Providing juveniles with their own court system was an extension of discretionary commitment practices long associated with houses of refuge. In this light, the nation's first juvenile court, established in Chicago under an Illinois law of 1899, was further evidence of the way in which succeeding generations built upon rather than discarded earlier practices.

As was so often the case, private civic groups initiated reform. The Chicago Women's Club had taken an active interest in the Cook County jail during the 1890s, pressing for changes in the treatment of juveniles. An 1898 grand jury investigation of youthful offenders added credibility to the club's accusations of mismanagement, corruption, and maltreatment. Armed with this evidence, the club persuaded law-makers in Springfield to establish a separate juvenile court for Chicago.

The act was further evidence of judicial regulation of child welfare under the concept of *parens patriae*. The court was a "child-saving" institution.[33] It extracted children from unsavory home environments while sparing them the stigma of a criminal record. The juvenile court was purposefully designed to circumvent the traditional procedural protections accorded the accused, substituting in their place the beneficent discretion of judges, who theoretically tailored justice to the needs of each child. The juvenile court was not a place to punish but to help children who, with proper assistance, could achieve useful, middle-class lives.

Plea Bargaining

The growing discretion of an increasingly bureaucratic criminal justice system also surfaced in plea bargaining, a practice that further undermined the community's most important voice in the system—the jury. Plea bargaining involves a prosecutor and a defense attorney reaching agreement about the plea to be entered to a crime and the sentence to be meted out in return. The origins of this practice remain obscure, but it seems certain that it was functioning by the mid-nineteenth century. In the 1860s the district attorney for New York City encouraged defendants to plead guilty to lesser offenses and that such bargains were "always under the table."[34] The rise of probation seems to have stimulated additional plea bargaining. Studies of individuals granted probation in the late nineteenth century indicate that they often changed their plea from innocent to guilty of a lesser charge.

The pressure of heavy caseloads and crowded prisons are often cited as a primary factor in encouraging plea bargains. Yet bargained pleas were as frequent in busy urban courts as in rural areas. Plea bargaining seems rather to have been an instance of the increasingly specialized and bureaucratic treatment of offenders. It had the advantage of conveniently settling cases where guilt was obvious. In other instances, the plea bargain was useful if the prosecutor could not prove fully all the elements of the crime that was charged, such as first-degree murder, but could satisfy the requirements for a lesser charge, such as manslaughter.

Plea bargaining also made sense from the defendant's point of view, if he or she was guilty. Nineteenth-century criminal trials were freewheeling, cursory affairs that invariably ended in conviction. During the 1890s, for example, trials for serious crimes in Leon County, Florida took about one hour, and in the overwhelming number of cases the defendants were found guilty. In late nineteenth-century Georgia, eight of ten blacks were found guilty and six of ten whites.[35] Going to trial offered guilty defendants little hope of success, whereas pleading to a lesser charge let them charter their own fates.

By all available evidence, the incidence of plea bargaining has grown significantly since the late nineteenth century. Between 1880 and 1910 in Alameda County, for example, about 8 percent of all pleas were bargained; today, that percentage has nearly tripled.

Police and Late-Nineteenth-Century Social Welfare

The police in the nineteenth century experienced two transformations. The first was from approximately 1850 to 1885, the second in the 1890s. During the first period, the police abandoned the constable and watch system in favor of a centralized military organization and uniforms. The second transformation involved a change in police behavior rather than organization. Until the mid-1880s the police were as much social welfare agents as crime preventers. Thereafter, the scope of their dealings with the "dangerous classes" narrowed as they became agents against crime rather than for class control.

Police forces after the Civil War were arms of municipal administration, and their duties included tasks quite different from what they do today. The police, especially after their uniforms made them visible, performed what were then considered pressing social responsibilities: finding and returning lost children, discovering open sewers, and providing lodging for tramps overnight. In small communities children were never really lost unless physically away from the community, but in the sprawling and impersonal urban world of the era after the Civil War, a child could quite easily wander a short distance from home and become lost. Parents and friends did search on their own, but the police became active in these matters. The introduction of uniformed police in New York City, Chicago, St. Louis, Washington, D.C., Detroit, and Pittsburgh coincided with a sharp rise in the demand for help in finding lost children.

After about a generation in uniforms, the police were increasingly expected to perform the specialized function of preventing crime and enforcing criminal law, rather than offering social welfare services. Furthermore, by the 1890s specialized municipal agencies appeared whose duties included recovering lost children, freeing the police to engage in crime control.

Another important task of the early uniformed police was providing overnight lodgings for the homeless. When times were bad, tramps and poor people appeared at the doors of police stations, and the police accommodated them with a place to sleep and, in some instances, a meal. The police acted as agents of social class management, not just as preventers of crime. By the 1890s, however, this activity was attacked as incompatible with the more important function of crime prevention. As with lost children, the management of the dangerous classes passed from the police to new social welfare agencies. The police became just one more agency of government in which separate bureaus dealt respectively with recreation, planning, health, and welfare.

As the police withdrew from management of the problems of everyday urban life, they also became less active in arresting people. The overall police arrest rates dropped, and so too did the rate for public order arrests. Police ceased to take the initiative to deal with disorderly persons; they acted only when called on by the citizenry. Their energies flowed increasingly into solving "serious" crimes, such as homicide and burglary.

The concepts of police professionalism and of rational administration took hold in the 1890s, a forerunner of even more sweeping developments in the Progressive era. There were two stimulants to greater professionalism. First, with police corruption a matter of public agitation, police leadership sought to put their own houses in order. The Lexow Commission in 1894 and 1895, for example, revealed that New York City police officers were complicit in vice operations, extortion of confessions through torture, and haphazard procedures for the accounting of public monies. Police chiefs banded together amid such revelations, founding in 1893 the National Chiefs of Police Union, which quickly became the International Association of Chiefs of Police (IACP).

Second, the police began to look beyond their own jurisdictional borders, seeking through cooperation to gain a hold on criminal activities that were nationwide in scope. The IACP, for example, had by the late 1890s established a central bureau of criminal identification, supported by subscriptions of individual police departments. There were even efforts in Congress, urged by leading chiefs of police, to establish a federally funded bureau that would coordinate and disseminate information. These efforts paved the way for the subsequent creation in 1935 of the Federal Bureau of Investigation.

Substantive Law of Crime

Lawmakers responded to the growing interdependency of nineteenth-century society and economy by passing more laws. They retained a fundamental commitment to the idea that statutes could guide human behavior. In 1822, for example, Rhode Island listed only 50 criminal acts; by 1872 the number had increased to 128. Indiana in 1881 specified more than 300 crimes, and they covered a panoply of human activities. After the Civil War especially, the states turned to criminal penalties to regulate economic and moral behavior, passing statutes that criminalized economic monopolies, abortion, and gambling. Downturns in the economic cycle spawned great numbers of unemployed people, and legislatures and city councils, seeking to preserve municipal order, passed a variety of vagrancy statutes, which the police in hard times enforced with special enthusiasm.

Despite the explosion in the numbers of statutes, the substantive criminal law changed less than did the institutional apparatus of apprehension and punishment. For example, antebellum reformers sought to abolish the death penalty. A wave of anti-capital punishment activity swept the nation in the 1830s, supported by such diverse figures as President John Quincy Adams and abolitionist William Lloyd Garrison. Michigan in 1846 abolished the punishment for all crimes and by 1849 fifteen other states had abolished public executions. But the effort stalled with the Civil War, and a new attack on the death penalty did not come until the Progressive period.

McNaghten Test and the Law of Criminal Insanity

The belief that insanity or mental illness might excuse criminal behavior produced important changes in the substantive criminal law. The so-called insanity defense reflected the influence in the nineteenth century of scientific naturalism, a body of thought that held that physical and emotional causes, rather than moral wickedness, explained human behavior. The eugenics movement, studies of heredity, and the infant discipline of psychiatry all stemmed from scientific naturalism.

The common law had historically treated people as rational, autonomous beings responsible for their actions. It required that in order to convict a criminal a *mens rea* (a criminal intent, in simple terms) had to be established. A person who was demented could not, of course, fulfill that requirement. But the common law imposed a stiff test: the defendant had to show that he or she lacked the basic, fundamental ability to tell right from wrong. A person could not be partly crazed; it was all or nothing.

The common law, however, ran counter to the naturalistic view of human behavior advanced by nineteenth-century students of medical jurisprudence, such as Isaac Ray, the author of *Medical Jurisprudence of Insanity* (1838). Ray was an international authority on insanity who was at the forefront of the movement to erect asylums for the insane. Ray insisted that physical disease of the brain compelled people to act contrary to their own moral standards, and that the traditional common law test (that a person had knowledge that an act was right or wrong) was unduly strict and contrary to scientific knowledge.

Ray indirectly influenced the most important nineteenth-century case involving the insanity defense: *Regina* v. *McNaghten* (1843). Daniel McNaghten shot and killed Edward Drummond, the personal secretary of British Prime Minister Robert Peel. McNaghten suffered from a delusion that members of Peel's Tory party were persecuting him, and after stalking the prime minister and his party for the better part of a day he placed a pistol at Drummond's back (mistakenly thinking it was Peel) and fired. Counsel for McNaghten attempted to circumvent the common law test by invoking Ray's writings. The jury, guided by the presiding judge, found McNaghten not guilty by reason of insanity.

A storm of protest followed and, in response to it, the House of Lords forced Queen's Bench to define the insanity defense. Ironically, the same court that had encouraged the jury to find the defendant not guilty retreated, formulating the McNaghten or "right or wrong" rule, which amounted to only a slight liberalization of the common law test. The McNaghten rule provided that a defendant's actions could be excused if he was "labouring under such a defect of reason from disease of the mind as not to know the nature and quality of the act he was doing; or, if he did know it, that he did not know what he was doing was wrong."[36] The McNaghten rule "completely obliterated the McNaghten precedent."[37]

Yet the rule was also a step toward acceptance of mental impairment as a defense to criminal responsibility, because the previous test had held that the accused had to prove that he did not know the difference between right and wrong any more than a "wild beast."[38] *McNaghten* allowed either "defect of reason" or "disease of the mind" to be introduced into evidence as the cause of the accused's failure to distinguish between what was right and what was wrong.

A few jurisdictions in the United States embraced a more liberal standard, notably the irresistible impulse test, to which Ray subscribed. "There are," Ray wrote, "an immense mass of cases where people are irresistibly impelled to the commission of criminal acts while fully conscious of their nature and consequences."[39] The majority of states, however, retained the McNaghten test well into the twentieth century.

Declining Significance of Intent

The acceptance of the insanity defense was one way in which nineteenth-century lawmakers whittled away at the concept of intent. The common law had long recognized that intent could not be established in a person with impaired or underdeveloped faculties of reasoning. Thus, drunks and children under age could not be held accountable for their criminal acts because they could not be shown to have had a state of mind, a *mens rea,* that would account for their behavior. During the nineteenth century, however, the importance of intent was diminished in matters outside these traditional areas.

The declining importance of intent stemmed from two developments. First, the purposes of criminal law shifted from punishment to regulation of antisocial behavior. The operation of a dangerous machine, such as a steam engine and by the early twentieth century an automobile, created new social responsibilities. The concept of criminal negligence was extended to cover these and other activities as a means of discouraging reckless behavior. After the 1850s, for example, lawmakers began to hold corporations, which had previously been viewed as unreachable through the criminal law, susceptible to criminal prosecution.

Second, criminal law became increasingly important as a means of protecting property. The common law had historically required that prosecutors had to establish an accused's intent to steal or destroy property. Early American statutes, for example, specified that injury done to property had to be malicious in order to be criminal. By the end of the century new statutes, designed to protect the wealth of the community, made criminal those acts that did not involve malicious injury. The phrase "intent to defraud" was dropped from one property crime after another. Selling mortgaged property, passing bad checks, obtaining property under false pretenses, embezzlement by public officers, and willful misapplication of funds were added to the list of criminal actions that did not require the prosecutor to prove intent.

Social Control of the Dangerous Classes

By 1900 the broad outlines of the modern criminal justice system had appeared. The social control exercised through this system was compatible with the disciplined labor force and stable social order that accompanied industrialization and urbanization. The rate of crime dropped rather than increased amidst these profound changes. The term "dangerous classes" and the idea of moral wickedness became anachronistic, superseded by scientific explanations of criminality founded on a naturalistic view of humanity and backed by the science of the day. Professionalization and bureaucratic institutions (the police, prison, and probation and parole apparatus) displaced, but did not altogether replace, the traditional means of securing social stability through family, friends, and the church.

The word "system" suggests too much, however; it conveys a sense of order, routine, and efficiency that was not present. Popular control, local decision making, and corruption persisted. So too did vigilantism, which amounted to "popular justice with a vengeance."[40] More than 300 separate vigilante movements—ranging from the anti-Irish San Francisco Vigilance Committee of 1856 (with its strong ties to business), to the Negrophobic Ku Klux Klan of the Reconstruction era—appeared in the nine-teenth-century United States. In the last sixteen years of that century, there were 2500 recorded lynchings, mostly of blacks in the South and the remainder in the West. Such behavior mocked the rule of law and the inability of the decentralized and poorly funded criminal justice system to strike a meaningful balance between individual liberty and social stability. It was precisely such conditions to which reformers of the Progressive era addressed their efforts, not only in criminal justice but in the broad role of law in society and the economy.

10

Law, Industrialization, and the Beginnings of the Regulatory State: 1860–1920

From the Civil War through World War I, startling change characterized every aspect of life in the United States. Massive immigration altered the cultural and ethnic mix of the nation. This stream of newcomers merged with a steady flow of Americans leaving the farm to form a mighty river of urbanization. On the eve of the Civil War urbanites (persons living in communities of 2500 or more) represented about 20 percent of the total population. In 1920 more than 50 percent of the population lived in towns and cities. The city symbolized the most dramatic change sweeping the nation: the transformation of the economy from commerce and agriculture to manufacturing and industry.

An explosion of economic growth rocked the United States. The gross national product, which represented the value of all the goods and services produced each year, leaped by $7 billion to over $35 billion. Every possible measure of industrial activity soared. The production of iron and steel jumped from about 900,000 tons at the end of the Civil War to 24 million by World War I. Textile manufacturers in 1860 used about 845,000 bales of cotton; by the turn of the century they consumed more than 4 million bales. Railroad track mileage increased from about 30,000 miles in 1860 to about 240,000 in 1910. Nowhere in the late nineteenth century was economic growth so spectacular as in the United States, already among the very richest nations.

Lawmakers responded to these sweeping economic changes during two broad periods of political development. The first was the "party period," which had its origins in the first mass two-party system of the 1830s and remained vital until the end of the Gilded Age in the late 1890s.[1] These years were characterized by massive voter participation and, among the major parties, a perpetuation of the traditional distributive role of the legal and political systems. The second era was the Progressive period that began about 1900, when Theodore Roosevelt replaced the assassinated President William McKinley, and ended in the conflagration of World War I. The Progressive era was characterized by declining voter participation and a change in emphasis in the law from promotion of economic activity, based on a traditional scheme of distributive justice rooted in politics, to one of regulation based on an increasingly bureaucratic and apolitical model of public policy.

Governmental Promotion of Economic Enterprise

Laissez-Faire and Social Darwinism

The antebellum ideology of individualism and laissez-faire composed an important part of the late-nineteenth-century legal response to the Industrial Revolution. These concepts provided that the greatest and cheapest productivity would occur only if the individual employer and employee were left to compete in a free market. Some economists waxed eloquent on the subject, describing the free market as the work of "God's laws" that not only benefited individuals on earth but prepared them "for the life that is to come."[2] Governmental interference with the economy, so the argument ran, threatened production and, ultimately, the public interest. The concept of "freedom to contract" (the ability of individuals to arrange, free from government, their individual economic fates) became a catchword for the era. In 1887, President Grover Cleveland, a Democrat, vetoed a small appropriation for drought-stricken Texas farmers with the remark that "though the people support the Government, the Government should not support the people."[3] Senator Roscoe Conkling, a New York Republican, observed about the same time that all that the state could do was "to clear the way of impediments and dangers, and leave every class and every individual free and safe in the exertions and pursuits of life."[4]

Free-market ideology and freedom to contract were complemented by the theory of Social Darwinism. Political and sociological philosophers, most notably in the United States the Yale sociologist William Graham Sumner, applied the evolutionary biological theory of Charles Darwin to society. Social Darwinists insisted that the advancement of the economy depended on competition among human beings, with the fittest surviving. Hence, the role of government was strictly limited. "Minimize to the utmost the relations of the state to industry," Sumner urged.[5] In such circumstances the benefits of economic growth would shower on the most productive and therefore the most deserving.

There are problems in explaining legal development solely in terms of laissez-faire concepts. The question that stirred this generation was not whether there should be economic growth (there was a wide consensus that there should be), but how that growth should be managed and for the benefit of which social interests. Nor was the debate concerned with whether government should be involved in the economy, but instead whether government's role, both in Congress and state legislatures, should emphasize economic promotion or regulation. Industrialization and urbanization generated enough social pressure to cause a divergence of the theory of laissez-faire and the practice of lawmakers.

Federal Promotion of Economic Enterprise

With the secession of the South, northern Republicans gained control of the Congress, and they embraced a view of the Constitution that enhanced the traditional distributive economic role of the legislative branch. Republicans blended the abolitionists' stress on the positive responsibility of the federal government to advance individual rights with economic nationalism. In theory, at least, the bounty of government activity was to fall broadly over the nation; in practice, early Republican policies laid the foundations for big business.

The riches that Congress bestowed were varied and generous. Congress, for example, was directly responsible for stimulating the growth of the railroads, the nation's single most important, and most feared, business during the Gilded Age. Congress extended massive subsidies to transcontinental railroad developers through land grants. The Pacific Railroad Bill of 1862 granted enormous amounts of federal land to the Union Pacific–Central Pacific Railroad, the first of the transcontinentals. Two years later Congress made an even more generous land grant to the Northern Pacific. In all, Congress handed over 131 million acres of federal land to private railroad promoters, and the states chipped in an additional 49 million acres. By 1900 the amount of land given for the purpose of subsidizing railroads was as large as the state of Texas.

Congress was active in other ways as well. In 1862, for example, it created the Department of Agriculture, a subcabinet agency that brought national attention to agricultural issues, and passed the Morrill Land-Grant Act, a law that donated thirty thousand acres of federal land to every state for each of its senators and representatives. The land supported at least one agricultural college, furthering scientific agriculture while encouraging the production of general knowledge vital to the economy as a whole. A quarter-century later, Congress passed the Hatch Act, which set aside funds on an annual basis for agricultural experiment stations.

The promotional role of Congress also included tariff and banking legislation. The former protected emerging industries, such as steel, by placing a duty on imported goods. The Republican-backed McKinley tariff of 1890 far surpassed the revenue tariffs (tariffs passed to raise money to pay for government operations) of the years before the Civil War. Even the Underwood Tariff, passed in 1913 at the beginning of the Democratic administration of Woodrow Wilson, while dropping rates considerably on many industries, maintained the general concept of protecting emerging businesses. National banking legislation facilitated credit arrangements and therefore the availability of capital necessary to the expansion of manufacturing. The National Banking Act of 1863 created so-called national banks, whose circulating notes provided business with a sound and uniform medium of exchange. By the Progressive era, however, promotional legislation often had a strong (and sometimes overriding) regulatory component. The Federal Reserve Banking System, created in 1913, was typical. It further strengthened credit markets, thereby stimulating business activity, but significantly enhanced federal oversight of the economy through a central bank and twelve regional banks.

Congress also passed homestead legislation that was intended to encourage permanent settlement of the national domain by clearing the West of native Americans with the army and by authorizing extensive work on rivers and harbors to facilitate water-borne commerce. These and other promotional activities were dramatic evidence of federal intervention in the economy. Congress promoted the release of individual creative economic energy by placing the nation's natural wealth at the people's disposal, but with often uneven results. The railroad, for example, meant new towns, new jobs, and new businesses; it also brought enormous personal wealth to private entrepreneurs who bet and won.

State Promotion of Economic Enterprise

The release of creative economic energy that characterized state economic policy in the prewar years grew stronger after Appomattox. State mercantilism, in which each state sought through the law to bolster its economic fortunes, remained vital, but so too did prewar memories of fiscal debacles brought on by overly generous state aid. Mid-nineteenth-century state constitutional restrictions on public aid to private enterprise persisted well into the twentieth century, but in spite of these every state legislature devised legal means to compete with the equally ambitious efforts of other states anxious to attract new enterprise.

State legislatures crafted new ways to subsidize railroad development. One of the favorite methods was the local aid bill. These laws empowered municipalities and counties to underwrite through tax-secured bonds the stock subscriptions of railroad companies. In other instances local governments simply subsidized developers, on the promise that a rail line would reach them. Entrepreneurs went where capital was available. The New York & Oswego Railroad, for example, "meandered over the upstate New York countryside in search of local aid, finally touching (in both senses of the word) some fifty communities with 250 labyrinthine miles of track."[6]

Local aid came in other forms. For example, Illinois in 1869 gave tax advantages to local governments that issued railroad bonds. Between 1866 and 1873, twenty-nine state legislatures approved over eight hundred proposals to grant local aid to railroad companies. The three leaders (New York, Illinois, and Missouri) authorized over $70 million worth of aid.[7] In some instances, state governments undertook internal improvements that directly benefited the railroads. Massachusetts in 1865 financed the five-mile-long Hoosac Tunnel through the Berkshire Mountains that gave Boston a direct line running to the West.

During the 1870s, however, most direct and local aid came to an end. Laissez-faire ideology had little if anything to do with this change in policy. Rather, state legislators responded to public sentiments that linked hard economic times with overly ambitious state programs. Large-scale bankruptcies, swindles, and defalcation on bonds following the Depression of 1873 punctuated state promotion of railroads. When times were bad, legislators withdrew from promotional activity; when times improved, they returned, although direct aid became less and less significant. The railroads continued to grow, of course; they expanded from 93,000 miles in 1880 to 260,000 miles in 1920. All of this growth was brought about from company earnings and private investment, although earlier direct state support was crucial to the economic takeoff of railroads.

State promotional activity came in other forms. Bureaus to gather data on various aspects of the marketplace flowered in the late nineteenth and early twentieth centuries.

Massachusetts in 1869 created the nation's first bureau of labor to gather statistics in order to monitor social conditions among workers, but corporate managers, enamored with the concept of scientific management, snapped up these same data to evaluate the labor market. Promotional and regulatory goals in the states were far more complementary in practice than laissez-faire theory suggested.

Distribution of Economic Privileges: Eminent Domain

State promotional activity was also significant in distributing privileges, the two most important of which were eminent domain and incorporation. The heyday of public expropriation of private property, one of the most glaring exceptions to laissez-faire ideology, lasted from about 1870 to 1910.[8] Before the Civil War, state legislatures, drawing on authority in state constitutions, empowered private corporations to take private property (subject to due-process and just-compensation provisions) for public purposes. These expropriations redounded to the benefit of the entire community and placed the "rights of the public" above private property interests.

Beginning in the 1870s, state legislatures, especially in the developing West, put a new wrinkle in eminent domain law. They authorized private corporations to take private property for *private* purposes. Delegates to the Colorado constitutional convention of 1875–1876 blazed the way, framing the first fundamental law in the nation to contain such a provision. This portion of the constitution was of particular importance to mining companies chartered in the state.[9]

Most western legislatures formulated the eminent domain power in ways that mirrored the diverse economic interests that sought to invoke it. Eminent domain, in this sense, was a distributive public policy that resonated with economic pluralism. The political and legal furor that surrounded the eminent domain power in the western states suggests as much. The clash among farmers, ranchers, and miners typically had more to do with who would benefit from the power (either via irrigation to raise crops and livestock or via extraction of minerals) than whether the power should be used. Most western states took an eclectic approach, giving a little bit to every interest. The Idaho legislature prepared an extensive list of economic activities that private individuals could pursue through the eminent domain power. These included "wharves, docks, piers, chutes, booms, ferries, bridges, toll-roads, by-roads [and] supplying mines and farming neighborhoods with water."[10]

The eminent domain power in the dry portions of the West facilitated irrigation, which hastened settlement and economic development. An instrumental vision of law animated economic progress, doing so in ways that rendered laissez-faire theory obsolete. The doctrine of prior appropriation, the controlling principle of western water law, held that the first to get to water had the exclusive use of it; however, this doctrine made little sense if, having acquired it, a user could not take advantage of it. Obviously, the property rights of some landholders suffered. In most western states, private individuals could invoke state eminent domain laws in order to convey water to their own lands.

By 1910 this burst of activity ended amid complaints that corporations had abused the privilege. Eminent domain did not vanish, however; legislatures stiffened the requirements to invoke it, including statutory provisions that juries try all cases of expropriations by private corporations. During the remainder of the twentieth century

municipalities increasingly invoked eminent domain in its new, more publicly accountable form, to plan and renew cities, while the national government relied on it to
develop major regional economic enterprises, such as the Tennessee Valley Authority.

Business Corporations

States before the Civil War had used the privilege of incorporation as a spur to
economic activity. By 1860 most states had enacted general incorporation laws, even
though the vast majority of businesses still preferred to organize under special charters.
In the late nineteenth century, Democratic and Republican state legislators recognized
that they could create a more appealing business environment by affording a high
degree of freedom to corporations. West Virginia, Delaware, and New Jersey made
themselves attractive by granting corporations broad powers. A revision in 1899 to the
already liberal corporation law of New Jersey, where John D. Rockefeller's powerful
Standard Oil Corporation had reincorporated after leaving Ohio, provided that "the
conduct and condition of [a corporation's] business are treated as private and not public
affairs."[11] New Jersey law also made it possible for corporations chartered there to
own stock in foreign corporations, which made the holding company legally viable. A
Massachusetts legislator in 1903 captured the new spirit of corporation law by insisting
that "the modern theory [held] that an ordinary business corporation should be allowed
to do anything that an individual may do."[12]

Corporation law changed because it had to. Many states, buffeted by demands
from local producers, attempted before the Civil War to enforce antidrummer legislation aimed at out-of-state sales personnel. For example, in 1845 Missouri passed a
statute that required agents of nonresident corporations to pay a license fee for the right
to sell commodities "not the growth, produce, or manufacture of [Missouri]."[13] After
the Civil War, the Singer Sewing Machine Company, which had set up a nationwide
sales force to distribute its new invention directly to the public, successfully fought the
legislation in federal courts. Similar laws in other states either atrophied for lack of
enforcement or were repealed, because they discouraged new business formation.

Municipal Corporations

The states also facilitated economic growth by easing the terms on which municipal
corporations operated. Special charters gave way to general charters; municipal corporations gained greater independence and authority to manage their affairs. Swelling
urban populations and the growing economic importance of cities as centers of manufacturing necessitated greater local autonomy. Under the traditional special charter
provisions, legislatures had to recast and remodify the operating documents of the
cities. Even general charters called for legislative oversight from time to time, denying
municipalities flexibility in dealing with myriad problems, including often massive
corruption in city administration. The quest for municipal reform was coupled to
municipal self-rule, and both of these were critical to the economic health of the cities.

By the last quarter of the century, home rule appeared as the solution. The
Missouri Constitution of 1875 was the first to include a home-rule provision. Under it,
a municipality was given control over its local affairs in return for a pledge to abide by
certain legislative provisions. The most important of these involved the borrowing

power of the municipality. Home rule applied usually to the largest municipalities, although California in 1890 extended the privilege to communities of 3500 or more people. Home rule freed busy legislatures from the time-consuming task of overseeing the day-to-day operations of local government, while aiding municipalities in planning and administering local government.

Attack on Distributive Politics

Behind this promotional activity were political parties that channeled the distribution of resources and privileges and that dominated political participation during the party period. Each state had party bosses such as the Republican Thomas C. Platt and the Democrat David B. Hill in New York during the 1890s. Urban party machines organized the swarms of recent immigrants and provided them with badly needed services. The parties aggregated the electorate and organized governmental functions, most notably the legislatures, which distributed resources and privileges to individuals and groups. In return, these groups rewarded their chosen party at the polls. Industrialization and urbanization, however, unleashed social changes that this traditional distributive scheme was incapable of accommodating. Third parties and social reform movements burst on the scene to urge a new view of law and legal institutions designed to serve disaffected social constituencies.

Populists, Mugwumps, and the Law

The Populists delivered the initial blow to laissez-faire ideology and traditional distributive politics. The Populist party, which began as social and mutual-aid societies known as the Grange, by the late 1880s and early 1890s had a distinctly political form and a platform that aimed to assist farmers (black and white), laborers, and in some places people with small businesses. The Populists traced the severe economic distress caused by industrialization to the growing control of "moneyed interests" (large corporations and especially railroads) over government. Only radical solutions, Populists argued, could subdue the power of concentrated wealth.

Populists urged government to switch its role from distribution to regulation and administration. Government was encouraged to pursue an active public policy of improving the conditions under which citizens lived. The Populists, for example, in their national platform of 1892, called for nationalization of the railroads, protection of public lands, an end to industrial monopoly, regulation of freight and railroad shipping rates, a graduated income tax, and the abandonment of the gold standard in favor of paper money that would aid the debtor interests with which they were identified. The Populists on the state level won political control of the Nebraska and Kansas legislatures in 1890 and had strong representation in the 1880s in other predominately rural state legislatures; they also clamored for administrative bodies (free from direct political influence) to regulate the rates charged by railroads and grain elevator operators.

Opposition to the traditional distributive role of government and to partisan control of it also came from the social elite of the cities, including professionals, intellectuals, well-to-do businessmen, and old-money families. In part, these groups were unhappy that they were being forced from their former leadership roles, that political operators and their legions of immigrant voters had seized political control from the "best men." They stressed values of "disinterestedness," "independence," and "expertise." In the mid-1880s these reformers became a national movement known as the Mugwumps, and throughout the country they pushed for reform of urban politics, the introduction of the secret ballot (from Australia), and the scientific rather than partisan management of government.

As has been true throughout the political history of the United States, much of the Populist and Mugwump program was eventually absorbed by the two major parties, especially when Democratic and Republican leaders concluded that failure to do so would lead to political losses. The borrowing was never complete and often incidental, but the Panic of 1893 was sufficiently shocking that a major realignment of politics followed in the presidential election of 1896. The paralyzing equilibrium of politics in the United States ended with a sweeping Republican victory in 1896; during the subsequent period both parties moved to accept many of the once-radical goals of the Populists.

Progressives and the Law

Lawmakers responded to industrialization, but the forces unleashed in the economy during the late nineteenth century were not *fully* confronted on the national level until the first two decades of the twentieth century. Developments proceeded somewhat more rapidly in most states, with experimentation in the 1880s involving what subsequently became known as "Progressive" reforms in the first two decades of the twentieth century.

The Progressive movement, with its emphasis on scientific and rational solutions to public policy issues, also brought about an erosion of popular participation in government. The importance of discordant social groups (blacks, poor southern whites who had supported the Populist movement, and immigrants, who fueled the great political machines and flirted with socialism) was reduced in the political equation by Progressive "reforms" such as registration requirements, nonpartisan ballots, and other devices that restricted the suffrage and weakened the discipline of party machines. These changes helped to make government more responsive to well-organized economic interests, a pattern that continued to develop through the twentieth century.

Electoral participation declined at the same time that the function of government switched increasingly to regulation and administration. With this change the necessities of grounding public policy in an active electorate, as had been the case in the "party period," faded. Expertise rather than popular legitimacy provided the rationale for many of the laws intended to reorder American society and economy. In the presidential election of 1904, voter turnout fell below 70 percent for the first time since 1836; eight years later turnout again dropped sharply, to below 60 percent.

Progressivism was not a single unified movement, but a collection of often disparate groups with differing (even contradictory) motivations. Some Progressives pursued the goal of economic efficiency. The business community, for example, recognized that the excesses of industrialization had to be curbed in the interests of a more efficient and profitable marketplace. Civic leaders within the Progressive movement wanted an end to the economic burden they associated with old-fashioned party rule. They urged reforms, such as at-large election districts, whose effects were to undermine the political strength of immigrant voters. Other Progressives were animated by a spirit of social justice for many of these same immigrants. Jane Hull, for example, wanted to uplift the lives of the homeless and poor and to end social disharmony, which itself seemed to threaten political stability and belief in a rule of law.

Progressives indeed shared much in common. Most significantly, they possessed an attitude of knowing and confronting social reality. A new "disposition of calculation" came into the formulation of public policy, one that included a "new inclination to think in matter-of-fact terms about cause and effect in social relations and to cast up balance sheets of profit and loss in matters of community-wide effect."[14] The traditional "rights of the public," which had influenced early nineteenth-century American legal development, became coupled to a political reform movement that stressed the regulation and administration of economic activity. Such calculation required not only new and expanded methods of government, but greater penetration by law and legal institutions into day-to-day life. What was important was scientific expertise capable of rationally solving major issues of public interest rather than the traditional resort to the distributional party politics of the nineteenth century.

Progressivism, composed as it was of impulses of economic efficiency and social justice, embraced many separate but parallel movements: antitrust, railroad regulation, the reform of municipal government, women's suffrage, hours and conditions of work, and the abolition of child labor, to name but a few of the most prominent. The Progressives, in a much more complete and direct way than the Populists and Mugwumps, enlisted legal authority to reach all of these ends. They sought to reshape institutions in ways that would make them more responsive to a growing urban, industrial society. As Richard Hofstadter has concluded about the Progressives, "it was expected that the [neutral] state, dealing out evenhanded justice, would meet the gravest complaints. Industrial society was to be humanized through the law."[15]

State Regulation of Economic Enterprise

The states' historic police powers furnished the constitutional support for legislative efforts to regulate industrialization. No other area of state activity was more controversial; no other legislative actions ran more fully in opposition to the doctrine of laissez-faire. Through the last quarter of the nineteenth century, the states were the center of regulatory activity, limiting corporate enterprise, throwing up a shield of protective legislation for women and child laborers, and pioneering the development of bureaus and independent regulatory commissions. Given the national character of economic change, however, authority gravitated from the states to the nation, culminating in the federal government's intervention in the economy during World War I.

State Regulation of Railroads

State regulation grew in response to the railroad. Farmers, merchants, and laborers urged railroad regulation, and by the early twentieth century they were joined by railroad managers, who viewed regulation as a means of reducing cutthroat competition. Massachusetts pioneered the way in 1869 with legislation that substantially revised its prewar railroad commission. The revised body was given "general supervision of all railroads," with authority to examine them and to make certain that they complied with the law.[16] The commission, as was typical of most early state regulatory bodies, had no power to set rates or to enforce what it deemed reasonable rates. Its role was strictly advisory.

In the Midwest, where Grange and Populist agitation was significant, legislators fashioned somewhat more powerful regulatory bodies. Illinois in 1871 passed Grange, laws that established a commission with authority to ascertain whether railroads and warehouses were complying with the laws. If not, the commission could seek prosecution of the violators. The commission lacked rate-setting authority, but its hand was strengthened considerably by tough legislation that set down strict rules about the maximum charges that the railroads could levy. Other midwestern states followed a similar pattern, and somewhat later Virginia (1877), South Carolina (1878), and Georgia (1879) also added commissions.

Every state commission was buffeted by forces that it could not fully resist. Legislatures were jealous of their own powers and therefore unwilling to give broad authority to the new regulatory bodies. These early bodies, moreover, were formed during the "party period," which meant that the key decision in the regulatory process, the setting of rates, remained subject to political alteration in the legislatures. The railroads were hardly docile creatures, because state regulations could influence their profits and the way in which they conducted business. And they were also possessed of the financial resources to orchestrate the political process with the quite predictable result that the regulated became the regulators. In California, for example, Leland Stanford and Collis P. Huntington of the Central and Southern Pacific Railroads influenced the state's late-nineteenth-century political and administrative machinery. No sooner had delegates to the California constitutional convention of 1879 fashioned a commission to regulate railroads than the railroads took control of it.

The state commissions also labored under the burden of having to apply legislatively mandated rates on a day-to-day basis in a highly competitive marketplace. In practice, "this meant that commissions learned—if not already so disposed—to be gentle and sympathetic with their railroads." Commissioners had "to chastise [railroads] but not kill them."[17] State commissions were generally incapable of doing either. The railroads, for their part, gravitated toward the position that federal supervision was an attractive alternative to a tangled web of state regulation.

State Regulation of Other Corporations

Although the most dramatic examples of state regulation applied to railroads, legislators also exercised their police powers on behalf of other regulatory causes. Economic expansion, for example, fostered a middle class anxious to obtain life and accident insurance. Insurance companies rushed to meet this new business with aggressive marketing and sales programs that often promised far more than they delivered. The states responded with a torrent of legislation that touched every aspect of the business, and, as with railroads, they frequently turned to commissions to regulate the insurance business, with about the same results. What both the companies and the policyholders wanted, however, was some uniformity in underwriting practices, but Congress refused to encroach on an area that the states had historically controlled. Only late in the nineteenth century did the movement toward uniformity receive support when the Wisconsin legislature, with the support of the American Bar Association, in 1895 enacted the Standard Fire Insurance Policy, a model statute widely copied by other states.

State legislatures also invoked the police power to regulate the activities of foreign corporations (corporations chartered outside the state). The United States was still a nation of states, and each state regarded itself as a community of interest operating in a hostile environment of rival states. State and local officials, under the prodding of their constituents, passed laws that discriminated against out-of-state corporations. These included measures prescribing marketing and sales practices, imposing discriminatory licensing and taxation policies, preventing the entry of certain articles of commerce, and setting inspection standards for goods shipped into and out of the state.

The meat-packing business is a case in point and a demonstration as well of the way in which technological advances in the late nineteenth century reformulated traditional relationships within the federal system. Until the late 1870s, cattle were driven along major western trails to railheads in places such as Cheyenne, Wyoming and Ogallala, Nebraska. The live animals were then shipped by rail to the East, where they were slaughtered and sold. When fresh meat was available, consumers knew that it had been slaughtered nearby.

The introduction of refrigeration on railroad cars not only extended the potential market for dressed beef but, because unsalable parts of the animal could be disposed of before shipping, it also permitted the processor to save up to 35 percent on freight costs. By combining refrigeration with mass-processing technology and a strategic location amidst the Chicago stockyards, "the . . . packers were able to ship dressed beef thousands of miles and still undersell local butchers by a substantial margin."[18] Senate hearings in 1888 revealed unscrupulous practices by a few large meat packers to control the meat market, but these revelations produced few demands by local butchers for national regulation.

Instead, the Butcher's Protective Association in the following year successfully lobbied several state legislatures to pass acts that prohibited the sale of dressed beef, mutton, or pork unless it had been inspected by state officials twenty-four hours before slaughter. In many states these efforts failed, because the large packers threw all of their resources against the proposed legislation. Where lobbying proved ineffective, the companies broke the law, engaging corporate counsel to challenge these police-power measures in the federal courts as unconstitutional limitations on interstate commerce. The states eventually lost, overwhelmed by the dictates of an expanding national market.

The legislatures also undertook to regulate various occupations through licensing procedures. Between 1890 and 1910, occupational licensing first achieved a firm foothold in the statute books of most states, although lawyers, doctors, and school-teachers had been covered by statutes even earlier. The new laws extended to such diverse callings as plumbers, barbers, funeral directors, nurses, electricians, horse-shoers, and dentists. Frequently, the granting of the license was delegated to a commission or board that had to pass on the qualifications of the candidate. Moreover, much of this regulation was friendly. It was passed at the urging of the regulated occupational groups in order to "rationalize the trade and eliminate 'unfair competition'."[19]

Regulation of Labor and the Work Place

In 1860 relatively few people worked for a wage. By 1900, however, more than two-thirds of the labor force sold their labor or skills to others for a daily or weekly wage. Children and women (most unmarried) formed an important part of the new economic order. By 1900 more than 700,000 children between the ages of ten and fifteen were at work in nonagricultural jobs, and more than 3.7 million women had entered the wage-earning labor force. The world of work in which they and their male counterparts toiled was often squalid, dangerous, and subject to the fluctuations of the business cycle. Downturns in the economy in 1873–1879, 1884–1886, and 1893–1897 threw hundreds of thousands of people into unemployment. In the Depression of 1893–1897 more than 18 percent of the labor force was unemployed, the greatest collapse in the labor market before the Depression of the 1930s.

These enormous changes in the work place and in the structure of the labor force were translated into two separate developments. The first was an increasing incidence of violent confrontation between labor and capital. A cut in wages, for example, by the Baltimore and Ohio Railroad in 1877 precipitated nationwide rioting that culminated in the destruction of millions of dollars worth of railroad property.

Unionization was the second response to industrialization. Just as capital sought to mobilize its resources, labor gradually accepted that it too would have to bring its collective power to bear. The early unions, such as the Knights of Labor, established in 1871, clung to a republican conception that stressed the individual worth and dignity of workers and that resisted full collectivization. But as labor increasingly became a commodity to be traded in the new world of industrial work, workers' combinations became tighter and more authoritative, a development that culminated in the formation of the American Federation of Labor (AFL) in 1886. Samuel Gompers, the first leader of the AFL, concluded that capitalism was in the United States to stay and that wage earners would have to gain their benefits within the existing system. Part of what labor wanted was legal recognition and protective legislation designed to improve working conditions.

State legislatures responded to developments in the labor market in often contradictory ways. On the one hand, the violence associated with the labor movement was translated into often harsh antiunion statutes. An 1885 Alabama law banned boycotts and picketing that blocked strikebreakers. The measure was entitled "An Act to protect and encourage industry within the State."[20] Rhode Island imposed penalties on strikers who obstructed the movement of streetcars. Illinois, in the wake of Chicago's Haymarket Riot in 1886, passed the first state criminal syndicalism law. These laws, which became pervasive after World War I, established criminal penalties for people who attempted to bring about a change in industrial ownership.

The fear of social disorder that attended the labor movement was also a stimulus to reform. Several states outlawed the blacklist, which employers used to keep union members, once fired, from being rehired. The "yellow dog" contract, which pledged a worker as a condition of employment not to join a union, was also outlawed in several states but persisted in others until the New Deal. Other statutes forbade paying workers in scrip (a certificate constituting a kind of money) and required regular paydays.

Protective Legislation

Protective legislation designed to shield children, women, and males in hazardous occupations was the most dramatic and controversial form of state intervention. By the end of the Civil War, the nation's rising urban middle class had created the "economically worthless child."[21] Middle-class fathers began insuring their own lives and setting up other financial arrangements such as trusts and endowments designed to protect children who no longer had to labor on the farm. However, the same process of industrialization that freed the middle-class child increased the value of the labor of working-class children, whose families depended on their wages.

The idea that child labor was a preventable evil took hold in the mid-nineteenth century. Connecticut in 1842 had a rudimentary wage and hour law for children, and New Jersey in 1851 passed the first comprehensive statute that prohibited children under ten from working and set limits of ten hours a day and sixty hours a week for older children. By 1900 some twenty-eight states, most of them in industrialized areas of the North and Midwest, had some kind of legal protection for child workers. Organized labor supported these measures, but more out of expediency than altruism. Labor leaders appreciated that child labor undercut the wage structure of adult male workers and impaired organizing efforts.

Even in the major industrialized states, regulations covering children were vague and enforcement was lax. Child labor laws typically only protected children in manufacturing and mining, and often contained so many exceptions and loopholes that they were ineffective. For example, children could obtain poverty permits that allowed them to work if their earnings were necessary for self-support or to assist their widowed mothers or disabled fathers. Compulsory education laws in most states did more than child labor acts to keep children out of the mills and factories. There were never enough inspectors to enforce the laws. New Jersey in 1900 had a force of four child labor inspectors to oversee more than seven thousand manufacturing establishments.

The special recognition accorded by the law to working children opened the door for regulation of the hours women worked. All-male legislatures relied on cultural stereotypes to guide public policy. Legislators believed that the "inferior" physical condition of women meant that they could not endure the rigors of the industrial work place for periods as long as men and that, because women were the "mothers of the race," their right to contract could be limited based on the state's interest in maintaining the women's reproductive abilities. Massachusetts in 1874 set the legal workday for women "in any manufacturing establishment" at ten hours, and sixty hours a week.[22] Illinois in 1893 went even further, passing model legislation prohibiting women in factories and workshops from laboring more than eight hours in any one day and forty-eight hours in a week. These same legislators, however, never presumed to invoke their powers to ensure that women could enter professional and managerial positions.

Advances made on behalf of children and women also spilled over into the male work force, especially in the West. Delegates to state constitutional conventions often directed the people's representatives to protect workers in hazardous occupations. The Colorado Constitution of 1876 and the Idaho document of 1889, for example, provided specific protections for miners. The Utah Constitution of 1895 ordered the legislature to prohibit women and children from working in the mines and required the legislature to "pass laws to provide for the health and safety of the employees in factories, smelters, and mines."[23] The legislature a year later passed an eight-hour law for workers in smelters and mines. The New York legislature in 1888 required that street-railway workers could not work more than twelve hours at a stretch, and in 1892 a ceiling was placed on the hours that could be worked by all railroad employees. Taken together this legislation reflected a basic assumption: long hours of labor were, as a whole, dangerous in an industrial society for employees, fellow servants, and the public.

There were limits to state intervention in the work place, even in the Progressive era. State legislatures, except where women workers were involved, ignored the most sensitive element of the capital–labor equation: minimum wages. The legislatures of New York, Indiana, and Nebraska established wage guidelines, but these applied only to workers on public projects. The Oregon legislature adopted the most progressive approach, one that became a model for other states, creating in 1912 an Industrial Welfare Commission to fix minimum wages and maximum hours for women and minors.

Legislative Erosion of the Fellow-Servant Rule

State legislatures affected labor and the economic circumstances of the new industrial work place by fastening statutory limitations on the existing common law of industrial accidents. Death and dismemberment were one of the social and individual costs of industrialization. New technology wrought human havoc. By the 1890s, for example, railroads alone were killing 6000–7000 and injuring 30,000–40,000 people *each year*. About one-third of the killed and two-thirds of the injured were railroad employees. Such bloodletting prompted demands from labor that legislatures reform the common law doctrines (the fellow-servant rule, assumption of the risk, and contributory negligence) that applied to industrial accidents, all of which courts had forged earlier in the century when industrialization was only beginning and when its casualties were few.

The English anticipated developments in the United States, but only by a few years. Parliament in the Liability Acts of 1880 and 1887 increased employer liability for on-the-job accidents. Legislatures in the United States moved more cautiously. Georgia in 1856 became the first state to modify the fellow-servant rule, allowing railroad employees to recover for injuries caused by the acts of fellow servants, provided they themselves were free from negligence. Iowa passed a similar act six years later, followed by Wyoming (1869) and Kansas (1874). The distributive nature of the political system during the "party period" meant that the winds could blow in both directions, as the example of Wisconsin suggests. That state in 1875 abolished the fellow-servant rule for railroads; in 1880, however, when conservative political forces regained control of the statehouse, the act was revoked.

The long-term trend was toward legislative repeal of the fellow-servant rule. By 1911 twenty-five states had laws modifying or abolishing the rule. Railroad accident law "reached a state of maturity earlier than the law of industrial accidents generally; safety controls were imposed on the roads, and the common law tort system was greatly modified by removal of the employer's most effective defense": the fellow-servant rule.[24] By 1900, even though the number of industrial accidents had increased, the costs of managing them seemed far more possible than a half-century before. Moreover, shifting liability from employee to employer was not enough, because the legal remedies might well prove too costly for workers who were injured, out of a job, and with few resources to pursue a lengthy court battle. Corporate leaders were also ready for a change, because they wanted a rational scheme of compensating injured employees that would end the chaos and uncertain costs associated with jury trials in industrial accident litigation.

By 1910 six states had passed compulsory worker compensation laws. Although these varied in substance and content, they shared several common features. They established a government-operated insurance pool, and all employers were required either to pay into it or to purchase comparable private insurance. The laws made employers immune from liability for specified accidents. Schedules of payment were established for injured workers who needed only to file for an administrative hearing before a state commission. By 1920 more than half of the states had established compensation plans.

The experience of the states was vital in shaping the federal response to industrialization. For more than half a century, Americans had been absorbed in the furious development of their country and the distributive politics of their mass two-party system. Industrialization, however, fostered economic and social conditions, the regulation of which exceeded the grasp of the states' police powers.

National Regulation of Economic Enterprise

The regulatory efforts of Congress after the Civil War were tentative and often contradictory, pulled as they were, on the one hand, by the nationalizing forces of the economy and, on the other, by a traditional respect for the rights of the states and the majoritarian democratic impulse of the era's mass two-party system. Because Congress was a political institution in an era in which party-structured political activity dominated, it (like state legislatures) was often guided by the principle that the best regulatory measures were ones that "every legislator could take back to his district with some evidence of dutiful service."[25]

This traditional distributive approach to regulation, in which contending political interests received some recognition, was gradually, but not completely, displaced in the Progressive era by a new model of regulation. That new model emphasized a scientific, rational, and nonpartisan approach that depended on the professional expertise of the regulators rather than the political attachments of members of Congress.

Administrative Law Agency

The late-nineteenth-century response to economic consolidation was the administrative law agency, a hybrid governmental institution that combined executive, legislative, and judicial functions. These bodies were separate from both the legislature and courts. Yet they legislated, in that they adopted regulations that had the force of law; they also adjudicated, in that they held hearings and rendered quasi-judicial opinions. This "fourth branch" of government, nowhere mentioned in the Constitution, exercised delegated powers from the legislature, fulfilling on a day-to-day basis the oversight functions of regulation that a legislative body was incapable of doing.

The impetus for this new administrative approach to regulation came from several sources. The experience of the Civil War, for instance, had shown the value of agencies and bureaucratic organization as a means of solving large-scale problems. The Union Army moved increasingly toward a bureaucratic form of organization during the war. The Sanitary Commission, which was an unofficial auxiliary of the army, invested its major efforts in achieving sound public-health practices in army installations located in the North as well as evacuating the dead and wounded from battlefields. The commission became a prototype of how an agency staffed with competent people could efficiently perform important functions free from direct political manipulation. The Freedmen's Bureau during Reconstruction provided another example.

The abolitionists also abetted the impulse toward administrative regulation by affirming the principle that government should be bound by moral authority, and that its decisions about public policy should be free from partisan taint and strict majority control. Although abolitionists never dominated either Congress or the Republican party (let alone state legislatures), their emphasis on morality and impartiality in government countered the distributive political principles of majoritarian democracy.[26] With political scandals of unprecedented proportions rocking the nation in the late nineteenth century, intellectuals connected the abolitionists' stress on morality to the idea that emerging principles of science would provide an apolitical foundation for independent regulation. The writer and reformer E. L. Godkin, for example, predicted in 1868 that the nation would be rescued from its "moral anarchy" by "mental culture" and that "the next great political revolution in the Western world" would give "scientific expression to the popular will, or, in other words place men's relations in society where they never yet have been placed, under the control of trained human reason."[27] The independent regulatory agency became the instrument of human reason over politics.

The national scope of economic change, the clamor of reformers, and the pressures of third parties eventually produced significant action. It came in two phases. The first, during the party period, was tentative and uneven; the second, during the Progressive era, was more extensive. The two most important early federal regulatory measures were aimed at the new economy's most vital elements: railroads and manufacturing. The Interstate Commerce Commission (ICC) of 1887 and the Sherman Antitrust Act of 1890 reveal the mix of political and administrative solutions to the problems created by economic growth. Congress kept one foot in the old world of distributive politics, while stepping haltingly into a future of administrative regulation. The result was an "incoherent, unworkable policy from which no one stood to benefit."[28]

Interstate Commerce Commission

The rise of a national railway network linked geographic areas into a system of economic interdependence, exposing the inadequacies of the existing system of *state* regulation. The ICC became the instrument by which Congress attempted to rationalize national markets and the rail transportation system.

The political motivation behind the ICC is frequently told in terms of a struggle between radical western farmers and ruthless eastern railroad moguls. While dramatic, this interpretation seriously underestimates the variety of economic interests touched by the national rail network. Eastern merchants, midwestern wholesalers and merchants, and western farmers had an interest, though not necessarily the same interest, in having federal regulation of railroad freight rates. So too did the railroads. There was fierce competition on the trunk lines (lines connecting western agricultural regions, midwestern trade centers, and eastern manufacturing and port cities) at the same time that extensive monopolies existed in localities served by branch and feeder lines. The railroads attempted to deal with these problems through pooling arrangements, which were private agreements among carriers to serve particular areas and to charge fixed prices. The pooling agreements were constantly breaking down, and the companies could not seek judicial relief because the agreements lacked the force of law. The rail carriers also engaged in discriminatory pricing practices based on the length of haul, with shorter hauls, where local feeder lines were involved, often costing more than trips across several states on the more competitive trunk lines. To encourage some larger customers, railroads gave rebates while charging the posted rate to smaller customers.

Congress debated the creation of the ICC for a decade. It finally acted only after the Supreme Court, in *Wabash, St. Louis & Pacific Railroad Company* v. *Illinois* (1886), struck down an Illinois railroad regulation statute as an unconstitutional interference with the exclusive power of Congress to regulate interstate commerce. The *Wabash* case sounded the death knell for most state regulation of railroads moving in interstate commerce and invited congressional action.

The Interstate Commerce Act treated the major discriminatory practices undertaken by the railroads. The act provided that all customers had to be treated in a similar fashion. It declared rebates illegal, forbade pooling, and ended long-haul, short-haul discrimination by requiring that "all charges . . . be reasonable and just."[29]

Congress created a commission of five members to hear complaints about railroad practices and to undertake investigations on its own initiative. The president appointed the members of the commission with the advice and consent of the Senate, and they served staggered terms at the pleasure of the president for a maximum of six years. No more than three commissioners could come from the same political party, diminishing fears of partisan control of commission policy, but falling short of the reformers' demands for a body of apolitical experts. President Grover Cleveland appointed Thomas M. Cooley chairman of the the commission. Cooley was a former judge of the Michigan Supreme Court and one of the nation's most influential writers of legal treatises that advocated laissez-faire.

The law was a compromise among competing interests, and it languished for two decades. To some extent, Cooley's leadership, which was favorable to the railroads, worked against the commission's authority. The Supreme Court, furthermore, sliced away at the few initiatives that the commission did take. Even more important, however, was the measure itself, which put the commission in the untenable position of having to balance too many interests with too little authority to do so. Congress had been unable, in creating the commission, to transcend the pluralism of U.S. politics with the principle of independent regulation by experts, and the result was that the conflicting interests within society that had prompted passage of the legislation to begin with were translated into the commission itself.

The commission began to attain real significance during the Progressive era when

Congress enhanced its enforcement and oversight functions. President Theodore Roosevelt had made greater authority for the ICC a major goal, and he obtained some of it from Congress in the Hepburn Railway Act of 1906. That measure gave the ICC the power to set and put into effect maximum rates upon complaint of a shipper and also the authority to examine railroad books and prescribe uniform bookkeeping. The need to mobilize the economic resources of the United States during World War I carried the regulatory impulse farthest. In December 1917 the Railroad War Board, which Congress had created to bring order to the nation's sprawling transportation system, nationalized the railroads.

Despite its shortcomings, the original ICC was an important event in the history of nineteenth-century law in the United States. It provided the building block upon which the administrative state of the twentieth century subsequently rose.

Sherman Antitrust Act

Even as Congress created regulatory commissions, the alternative of direct legislative action persisted. On matters of economic competition, Congress chose not to delegate its authority to an administrative body but to enact a regulatory statute, the Sherman Antitrust Act. As with the ICC, the passage of the Sherman Act illustrates the ambivalence with which "Americans have regarded competition, cooperation, and corporate growth," as well as their perhaps too great a confidence in the powers of legislation to produce changed behavior.[30]

Monopoly power emerged as a genuine threat to economic order in the late nineteenth century. Fierce competition among maturing industries created pinched profit margins that prompted corporate managers to consolidate control over greater portions of the market. To do so, they turned to new legal devices—first the trust and, in the 1890s, the holding company—that permitted a single company to control the pricing and market structure of several "foreign" corporations. The new national corporate structure of the economy depended heavily for its growth on law and legal institutions.

The Sherman Antitrust Act, named after Senator John Sherman of Ohio, was passed amid great public uproar over corporate consolidation. Antimonopoly sentiment had a long history in the United States and the Sherman Act was merely its latest manifestation. It declared that "every contract, combination in the form of trust or otherwise, or conspiracy, in restraint of trade or commerce among the several States or with foreign nations, is hereby declared illegal."[31] The act created no administrative structure, as had the Interstate Commerce Act; instead, the task of enforcement fell to the Department of Justice and the federal courts. Violators were susceptible to fine, imprisonment, and, in the case of corporations, dissolution.

The key provisions of the act were ambiguous at best and the policy sentiments underlying it at odds with the promotional role (the release of creative economic energy) that Congress was pursuing elsewhere. In the highly competitive atmosphere of the late nineteenth century, all businesses had to restrict trade and consolidate the marketplace if they expected to remain viable. Despite the wording, the framers of the statute did not intend to ban *all* combinations, revealing that "both fear *of* competition and fear *for* competition were important factors in bringing about" the Sherman Act.[32]

The statute's vague wording simply captured the contradiction of a public policy that sought both to promote and to regulate in ways that did not always complement one another.

The Sherman Act was problematic in another way. While the act covered transportation of goods across state lines, there was at least reasonable debate about whether manufacturing (the production of goods, even by a corporation that operated in several states) was encompassed within the statute and the commerce clause of the Constitution. Manufacturing had traditionally been treated as a local enterprise, the control of which properly belonged to the states. But the rise of an industrial market economy of transcontinental proportions posed difficult regulatory problems for the states.

The overwhelming support for the measure, which passed the Senate by a vote of fifty-two to one and by voice vote in the House of Representatives, suggests that critics thought that the Supreme Court would nullify it. In any case, in a pattern repeated throughout the legal history of the United States, members of Congress were willing, given the diverse political pressures that played on them, to permit the federal courts to pour meaning into the hollow phrases of the nation's first—and to this day most important—antitrust act.

In the Progressive period, Congress (this time at the urging of Woodrow Wilson) sought to infuse greater regulation into antitrust policies. The Clayton Antitrust Act of 1914 added the following phrase to the prohibited business practices: "where the effect may be to substantially lessen competition or tend to create a monopoly in any line of commerce."[33] The act also excluded labor unions, which the federal courts had held to be included under the Sherman Act. The additional wording, however, handed greater rather than less discretion to the courts. In the same year, Congress also created the Federal Trade Commission (FTC) with broad powers to investigate companies and to issue "cease and desist" orders against unfair trade practices that violated antitrust law. These measures, however, depended for effective enforcement, like the ICC, on a bipartisan board of commissioners whose orders were subject to review in federal courts.

Bankruptcy Legislation

Congress also formulated new bankruptcy legislation in the wake of the Civil War. Once again, the legislation reflected the often competing demands of different economic interests. Debtors wanted to free themselves of commitments that they could not meet; creditors wanted to ensure that, in hard times, they would receive back the money they had lent out in flush times. Northeastern businessmen, moreover, expected any new bankruptcy act to allow them to reclaim some portion, no matter how small, of the debts lost to southerners as a result of the Civil War.

The Bankruptcy Act of 1867 therefore satisfied no one entirely and failed to bring the uniformity in debtor–creditor relations demanded by expanding interstate commerce. Merchants disliked the law because courts construed its somewhat vague provisions to mean that "insolvency" occurred not when a firm lacked assets to pay debts but when it was impossible for it to pay in the course of ordinary business. Once a merchant failed to meet a commitment, a creditor could push him into involuntary bankruptcy. The 1874 revision of the act permitted debtors to submit a plan for working out their debts over a period of years, thus preventing creditors from seizing assets of a viable company. The law remained controversial, however, and Congress repealed it four years later.

New legislation in 1898 stemmed directly from frustration within the business community over uniform national standards of bankruptcy. National bankruptcy legislation was also a reform pressed by the new American Bar Association, whose founding charter in 1878 dedicated it to "advance . . . uniformity in legislation."[34] The professional bar and the business community by century's end had a mutual interest in a uniform system of national laws that promised a stable economic environment. The Panic of 1893, which visited heavy damage on debtors, awakened them to the value of national legislation.

The 1898 act provided that a wage earner or "a person engaged chiefly in farming or the tillage of the soil" could not be forced into involuntary bankruptcy.[35] The law was particularly important in establishing the priorities to be followed in the distribution of assets. Although it permitted federal judges to follow long-established state priorities, it set forth certain federal requirements, the most important of which was that "workmen, clerks, or servants" were to have first claim based on wages due them within three months of the commencement of bankruptcy proceedings.[36] The new law took into account the interdependent nature of the maturing industrial economy and the need to restore promptly the purchasing power of insolvent debtors.

Income Tax, the Federal Police Powers, and the Precedent of World War I

Congress undertook other regulatory and protective legislation that belies the laissez-faire label so frequently attached to the era's legal history. Some measures, such as the federal income tax passed in 1894, combined elements of both regulation and promotion. The Union government had passed an income tax to finance the Civil War, but it was abolished at the end of the conflict. Populists in the 1880s and early 1890s urged passage of a new tax, both as a means of reducing the tariff, which fell most fully on consumers, and as a device to redistribute corporate wealth. Historically, the federal government had paid its bills through the tariff, but in the 1890s the government was running large surpluses, a condition that heightened demands for the income tax as a means of reducing the tariff. The states had long relied on taxes on property to finance government, but the federal income tax was a dramatic and controversial innovation that many members of Congress voted for in the expectation, as with the Sherman Act, that the Supreme Court would declare it unconstitutional. This time the justices did not disappoint them, striking down the law a year after it was passed. Agitation for a new law carried over into the Progressive era, and in 1913 the Sixteenth Amendment to the Constitution was ratified, granting Congress power to impose an income tax.

The national government also responded to complaints for greater regulation of the working and living conditions of labor. In 1884, for example, it mimicked the state experience by establishing a Bureau of Labor, which issued reports about the impact of industrialization on workers. The demands of window-glass workers in 1885 resulted in a prohibition on the importation of contract labor. Safety practices on interstate railroads also came in for scrutiny, and Congress in 1893 imposed a clutch of regulations on interstate carriers that provided, among other things, for grab irons and handholds in the ends and sides of each car and couplers that worked automatically upon impact. In 1898 Congress, in the aftermath of the Pullman Strike, made it a criminal offense for railroads engaged in interstate commerce to discharge workers under "yellow dog" contracts that pledged them as a condition of employment not to join a union. The Federal Employers Liability Act of 1908 did away with the fellow-servant rule for interstate railways.

An important component of the Progressive movement involved a resort to federal authority on a large scale. In part, Progressives relied on the commerce power, creating from it the concept of federal police powers. For example, Congress invoked this authority to pass the 1906 Pure Food and Drug Act, which forbade the manufacture, sale, or transportation of adulterated or fraudulently labeled foods and drugs in interstate commerce; during the same year Congress also passed the Meat Inspection Act, which provided federal inspection of all companies selling meats in interstate commerce. The Keating–Owen Child Labor Law of 1916 barred from interstate commerce the products of child labor, although the act was ultimately declared unconstitutional by the Supreme Court.

The Progressives greatly extended the legal and constitutional bounds of national involvement in the economy and, more generally, in social relations. The Progressive amendments (the Sixteenth, Seventeenth, Eighteenth, and Nineteenth) to the federal Constitution testify eloquently to this change. The Sixteenth in 1913 granted Congress power to impose an income tax. The Eighteenth Amendment, which became part of the Constitution in 1919, prohibited the manufacture, sale, or transportation of alcoholic beverages. The other Progressive constitutional amendments aimed to weaken the hold of political parties over the body politic. The Seventeenth, ratified in 1913, broke one of the strongholds of the party bosses by requiring the popular rather than the state legislative election of U.S. senators, and the Nineteenth, ratified in 1920, prohibited discrimination in voting based on gender.

World War I enhanced the Progressives' faith in bureaucracy, administrative agencies, and expanded federal lawmaking authority. Just as had the Civil War seventy years earlier, the nation's entry into world conflict provided the rationale on which to escalate federal involvement in the economy. Congress, for example, clothed the War Industries Board (1917) with broad powers to determine economic priorities and to allocate resources. The Lever Food and Fuel Control Act of the same year empowered the president to make regulations and issue orders to stimulate production and control the distribution of foods and fuels necessary to the war effort. These and a host of other wartime regulatory measures were repealed or lapsed after the conflict ended, but they were powerful precedents for the future penetration of federal lawmaking authority into the day-to-day lives of Americans.

A Bridge into the Future

Legislators between 1860 and 1920 were affected by and contributed to the era's massive economic transformation, and their behavior defies the characterization of laissez-faire so frequently stamped on them. The transformation of the economy was accompanied by more not less legislative intervention, by more not less law in the lives of individual citizens. This activity was undertaken both to promote economic growth and to regulate some but certainly not all of its consequences. The distributional policies that characterized the party period gradually gave way to a scheme of administrative regulation in the Progressive era that held forth the promise (only partly unrealized) that impartial experts would solve problems on a neutral, scientific basis.

The historical domination by the states of economic promotion and regulation also faded before an increasingly national and interdependent economy. Given the nature of the federal system, the states lacked sufficient constitutional authority to adapt through the law to the forces of industrialization. The nationalization of the economy held different implications for Congress; its authority increased as that of the state legislatures waned. Legislators at all levels, however, succeeded during the party period and the Progressive era in building a legal bridge over which the rural and agricultural nation of the era before the Civil War crossed into the urban and industrial twentieth century.

11

The Professionalization of the Legal Culture: Bench and Bar, 1860–1920

The economic and social transformation of the late-nineteenth-century United States spilled over into the legal culture. The bench and bar played an active role in the development of corporate capitalism, emerging by 1920 in their modern forms as professional arbiters of an apolitical and "scientific" body of rules. Yet cleavages existed. Some judges and lawyers advanced a "formal" and conservative legal approach to the problems of the industrial United States. These formalists believed that judges had to restrict themselves to abstract reasoning rooted in laissez-faire economic principles. Other members of the bench and bar urged a sociological and liberal approach to industrialization, drawing on social scientific evidence rather than abstract legal principles to support legislative and regulatory intervention in the economy. These proponents of "sociological jurisprudence" were invariably identified with the Progressive movement.

Each generation has struggled with the question of whether the judicial role fits more properly in one or the other of these categories. From the Civil War to about 1900 the trend favored the formalistic and conservative judicial approach, but from then through World War I sociological jurisprudence and liberalism gained credibility. Amid this give-and-take, a larger trend emerged: the steady movement toward the professionalization of legal education and law practice. Whatever their ideological disposition, lawyers adjusted to industrialization by replacing religion with law as the controlling element of society.

Rise of the Legal Profession

The growth of an urban, industrial society after the Civil War molded the composition, structure, and training of the bar. The practice of law became professionalized at the same time that other middle-class occupations such as engineering, medicine, and education were developing their own "professional cultures." A profession was "a full-time occupation in which a person earned the principal source of an income. During a fairly difficult and time-consuming process, a person mastered an esoteric but useful body of systematic knowledge, completed theoretical training before entering a practice or apprenticeship, and received a degree or license from a recognized institution."[1] A professional person insisted on objective standards of technical competence, superior skill, and high-quality performance. A professional held out service to the public and could not refuse a client without explanation.

The professionalization of the law had its roots in the antebellum era. Until about 1830, the lawyer class had been guildlike, based on local control and built on a restrictive system of personal alliances including marriage, paternal occupations, and extended apprenticeship. Beginning in the 1830s, local authorities lost control over the certification of lawyers to state government and, at about the same time, sons from white Protestant middle-class families, whose fathers tended to be clerks, tradesmen, and artisans, began entering the profession in significant numbers. But it was not until the post-Civil War era that professionalization of law practice surged. Banks, railroads, and industry, which were anxious to enlist skilled professionals to provide specialized legal services, increasingly hired lawyers away from the courtroom and the office.

Changing Nature of Law Practice

"The chief forum of the lawyer," proclaimed an article in the *American Lawyer* of 1893, "has been transferred from the court house to the office. Litigation has declined, and counsel work has become the leading feature of practice."[2] Prior to the Civil War, law offices had been small, composed of an attorney and one or two clerks. Even as late as 1930 most lawyers still practiced alone or with one partner, but fifty years earlier a new path of professional practice had appeared. The careers of lawyers shifted at the end of the nineteenth century from solo practice and partnership to the law firm.

The rise of the law firm was a response to industrialization. Through the mid-nineteenth century the problems raised in the law had been relatively simple, and the situations that surrounded them could be understood by the lay public. The best lawyers were generalists, and their role was to provide legal representation in court in response to a variety of legal problems.

By the 1870s, however, the traditional features of law practice faded, beginning in the industrializing Northeast and Midwest and extending, eventually, to the entire nation by 1920. The role of the lawyer evolved from advocate to counsel, and lawyers began to specialize, doing so out of the necessity of being competitive in a legal culture that was demanding increasing knowledge of practitioners.

Nowhere was this change more dramatic than in the growth of what were for that time large law firms, those with five or more members. The appearance of these firms changed the overall shape of the legal elite. Although the lawyers in these firms were an infinitesimal percentage of all lawyers in the country (less than 0.5 percent in 1898 and only 1.3 percent in 1915), the growth of large firms far exceeded that of the profession as a whole. For example, in the cities of New York, Boston, and Chicago between 1900 and 1915 the growth rate for all lawyers was 1.7 percent, whereas lawyers in large firms in these cities increased at an annual rate of 6.7 percent.[3]

The trend toward large firms was a response to industrialization and urbanization.

Large firms filled the needs of corporations that were increasing in complexity and number. The fastest rate of growth in large firms occurred during the 1890s, the same period in which business corporations underwent sweeping consolidation through mergers. Although every large firm had corporate clients, not all large firms specialized in corporate law. Many listed themselves as engaged in general practice, noting on their letterheads the clients whom they served as references. And within these large firms the individual practitioners still counted for a good deal. Elihu Root, one of the turn-of-the-century's most famous Wall Street lawyers, earned between $50,000 and $110,000 per year, personally supervising a variety of legal operations for a host of corporate clients that his firm served. That firm, however, consisted of three to five partners and no associates throughout the 1890s.

The trend toward bigness also encouraged the creation of the factory system of law practice, which the firm of Paul D. Cravath in New York City pioneered. In the 1890s Cravath brought his organizational genius to the practice of law. He hired only young lawyers who had graduated from both college and law school, preferably with high scholastic marks from elite universities. The young lawyers, who had driving and forceful personalities, were paid a salary as associates of the firm. In addition, Cravath organized the office routine of the firm, creating files, ordering typewriters, and hiring stenographers and copyists. Once organized, the Cravath system, which by the 1920s was solidly entrenched in the United States, "churned out anonymous organization men, steadfastly loyal to the firm that had hired them."[4] After a five-year probationary period, the brightest advanced to partnership, which entitled them to take a share of the firm's profits. The returns were lucrative. While two-thirds of the lawyers practicing in New York City at the end of the nineteenth century earned about three thousand dollars annually, those practicing in the large firms molded on the Cravath system could expect to earn triple that amount. But barriers to access became "more formidable as the desirability of access increased."[5] Perseverance and integrity were not enough; the best opportunities in the new-learned profession of the law depended on Anglo-Saxon, upper class, Protestant, and Ivy League educational credentials.

Even though relatively few lawyers joined law-firm factories, this new mode of organization dominated the professional landscape of twentieth-century cities such as New York, Chicago, and San Francisco, which offered lucrative opportunities in corporation and finance law. As these firms grew in number the traditional view of law practice faded. The nineteenth-century image of the law as a learned profession, with all that it implied in personal deference and respect, social prestige, and cultural power, dissolved before the new and impersonal system. The leading lawyers of the new regime were negotiators and facilitators, and practical men of business who knew the uses and the means of wealth.

While large law firms and law factories became the paradigm of practice, great diversity existed among practitioners. If Elihu Root earned $100,000 a year on Wall Street in 1900, most of his contemporaries earned between $2000 and $5000. In California, for example, the bar during the late nineteenth century steadily moved from a frontier to an urban setting, with lawyers following "the practice of the dollar and some specializ[ing] to meet the needs of a rapidly urbanizing and industrializing population."[6] The pattern in California was the pattern of developing legal practice everywhere. First land, then laws and administrative regulations, and later corporations and industry provided lawyers with opportunities for profitable practices.

Wherever they were, lawyers adapted to new social and economic circumstances.

Even in the South, where an idealized past held sway, the bar responded to the new currents of change. Virginia lawyers, for example, between 1870 and 1900 remained "provincially oriented and steeped in the rural-planter tradition."[7] The solo practitioner and dual partnership that provided general legal services to the agriculture-based economy remained dominant throughout the period, but attorneys in the region were also responsible for the growing consensus about nonagricultural economic development. The first four-person firm did not appear in Virginia until 1901. Yet by the turn of the century in Virginia and elsewhere in the South, lawyers were clustering in cities, and the demands of corporations invited them to specialize in their practices.

Rebirth of Bar Associations

The push toward professionalization and the growing social importance of lawyers and the law explain the rebirth of the bar association movement in the 1870s. During the first half of the nineteenth century the bar had been a "very loose, very open" mass.[8] There were a few primitive clubs or associations, but these organizations, except in Massachusetts, had little authority to discipline their members, to set criteria for admission, or to impose ethical standards. The leading members of the bar during these years also harbored a suspicion about the involvement of lawyers in political activity and the unregulated nature of law practice.

The post-Civil War movement to professionalize the bar involved standards of professional conduct. Leaders of the bar formed themselves into associations whose purpose was to encourage a sense of professional distinctiveness among fellow practitioners. Part of the motivation behind the bar association movement was the stigma of political activity that had been attached to lawyers from the beginning of the republic. Isaac F. Redfield, judge of the Vermont Supreme Court, wrote in 1871 that "a lawyer in the legislature is no more in the profession than a merchant, a banker, or a mechanic."[9] Partisan involvement with the judiciary was often direct. In Redfield's Vermont in 1874, the Democratic party reorganized the state supreme court and, in the process, threw out all of the incumbent Republican judges. Moreover, concerns about the baneful consequences of political activity paralleled a deepening concern on the local level that the judiciary had become, through elective politics, an often corrupt and incompetent handmaiden of the parties. Big-city politicians often made heavy demands on the judiciary. In New York City, for example, Judges George G. Barnard and Albert Cardozo (the father of U.S. Supreme Court Justice Benjamin Cardozo), were imprisoned for taking bribes.

In February 1870 the bar association movement got under way in New York City, where changes in the bar and allegations of corruption were greatest, with the founding of the Association of the Bar of the City of New York. Attorneys in the city were worried that the threat posed by machine politics to the legal process would soil the business climate on which they increasingly depended. "[I]t is impossible for New York to remain the center of commerce and capital on this continent," roared Samuel J. Tilden, a Democrat and prominent attorney, "unless it has an independent Bar and an honest judiciary."[10] One of the founders of the new association in New York concluded that "I think I can express the idea of this association, and the purpose for which it is to be formed, by saying that we shall aim to make ourselves . . . a *profession*."[11]

More than corruption and a fear of political intervention with the bar stirred the association movement. Competition was also important. In the late nineteenth century, trade groups rapidly organized in order to gain some control over the market they served, and occupational groups as diverse as plumbers and funeral directors sought the same goal through licensing laws. Bar associations joined the movement, urging state legislators, who were themselves overwhelmingly lawyers, to establish qualifications for entry into the profession. Between 1870 and 1890, requirements for admission to the bar tightened noticeably, especially the replacement of the traditional oral with a formal written examination. By 1917 some thirty-seven states had centralized boards of bar examiners. In the view of the bar associations, public service and self-interest were mutually reinforcing.

The association movement spread rapidly throughout the country, although small-town lawyers in lightly populated rural states often successfully resisted. In Mississippi, for example, continuing efforts between 1886 and 1892 to form a statewide bar association ended in failure. Although a few of the "brightest and best [Mississippi] lawyers might have wanted it, Mississippi was not yet ready to join modern industrial America."[12] In states like Mississippi, the bar as an entity had little impact on the formulation of state constitutions and rules of practice and procedure, although individual lawyers with access to political power rather than professional authority usually did.

The theme of professionalization also figured in the rise of the American Bar Association (ABA). The first national bar group, the American Legal Association, had been formed in 1849 by John Livingston, and its most notable achievement had been the publication of a national directory of lawyers. But it quickly disappeared, the casualty of the parochialism of the bar that viewed itself in local rather than national terms. Twenty-nine years later, in 1878, Simeon E. Baldwin, a judge of the Connecticut Supreme Court, launched a more successful effort with the founding of the ABA. The initial meeting was attended by 100 lawyers at Saratoga Springs, a posh resort in upstate New York. At the time there were more than sixty thousand lawyers in the country. The charter of the new group set forth its purpose clearly: to "advance the science of jurisprudence, promote the administration of justice and uniformity in legislation . . . uphold the honor of the profession . . . and encourage cordial intercourse among the members of the American Bar."[13] The new association, which in its first decade was as much a social as a working group, grew slowly. By 1902 it had 1718 members and by 1920 that membership had only doubled. A rival national federation of state and local bar associations, the National Bar Association, was established in 1888, but it failed within a few years.

The size of the ABA's membership should not obscure either its importance or the motives behind its creation. The new organization, like local and state bar associations, was purposefully exclusionary. It literally sought to enlist the best *men* in a crusade to reform the bench and bar. The ABA has historically been connected with the opponents of late-nineteenth-century reform, but on closer study a somewhat more complex estimate is in order. Rather, the ABA "was itself a manifestation of that spirit to which its founders were highly sympathetic."[14] These elite lawyers worried about the changes sweeping the practice of the law. The expansion of the bar had allowed "ambulance chasers" and ethnic immigrant lawyers to join the profession. At the same time, the forces of industrialization had made corporate clients important, and they placed demands for loyalty to the company over loyalty to the profession. The leaders of the ABA also recognized that the profession of law had to share its prestige with others of the new "scientific" professions, such as economics, political science, and history. Until the organization of the ABA, the American Social Science Association (1865–1909) had tended to the scientific interests of lawyers. Thus, the creation of the ABA was an effort on the part of the most prestigious element of the bar to differentiate itself from other professional groups, while fostering a sense of professional consciousness all its own.

The ABA succeeded because it advocated a limited agenda with a moderate theme. The ABA's stress on professional standards was readily translated into a number of standing committees with responsibility to oversee developments in various areas of the law, such as judicial administration, legal procedure, and commercial law. These committees met, wrote reports, and offered recommendations that carried no official weight but did bear the stamp of approval of the nation's leading law association. Moreover, the ABA's concern with a more scientific approach to law and its study, as well as its stress on greater uniformity of laws, fitted nicely with the demands of a consolidating national economy. Beginning in 1892 the ABA met concurrently with the National Conference of Commissioners on Uniform State Laws, which was an offshoot of a group originally organized by the state of New York. Their combined efforts produced recommendations on uniform laws that were offered to the states in the form of model legislation. Finally, the ABA was conscious of the need to take a middle course in reform, because it wanted to upgrade the caliber of the bar, increase the pay of lawyers, and make the practice of law a decent (by its lights) calling.

Changing Social Composition of the Bar

In the early nineteenth century the bar tended to be inbred, with its members drawn from the upper classes. Lawyers in Philadelphia in 1800, for example, were recruited "predominately from families of wealth, status, and importance."[15] Even in these early years, however, the pattern was far from uniform, and by the 1830s the bar became increasingly open as earlier formal restrictions to entry were either repealed or disregarded. By the 1860s both lawyers and judges displayed considerable variety in their family backgrounds. Before 1840, for example, most lawyers in Massachusetts were drawn from families where the fathers were professional and where the new lawyers went on to marry the daughters of professionals. After the Civil War a new pattern had emerged, with the children of businessmen taking an ever-greater part in the law and with them frequently marrying the daughters of businessmen. This lateral broadening of the profession appeared elsewhere, especially in the Northeast, Midwest, and to a lesser extent, the Far West. Diversity in the bar was a by-product of urbanization and industrialization. Elsewhere the social composition of the bar changed more slowly, especially in the South where the recruitment of lawyers remained in professional families well into the twentieth century. The bulk of the bar, however, was drawn throughout the nineteenth and early twentieth centuries from the middle class.

By 1900 the social transformation of the legal profession was occurring in another way. Foreigners, women, and blacks were gaining a modest representation. In the case of ethnic lawyers there was a generational lag as the children of immigrants were schooled and then entered the legal profession. For example, ethnic lawyers remained a small part of the legal profession in Massachusetts until as late as 1900, even though Boston was a magnet for Irish and Italian immigrants. In 1870 there were only forty (3.3 percent) foreign-born lawyers in Massachusetts, and half of these were Irish, and as late as 1896 people with Irish ancestry (that included those born in the United States) composed only 1 percent of all the profession in Boston. But ethnic lawyers were on the increase, and the pressure on law schools was so intense that they routinely created quotas for Jewish, Catholic, and East European students.

Most of the ethnic lawyers admitted to the bar through 1900, in Massachusetts and elsewhere, had less education and parents with lower social status than their counterparts who were from native stock. They lived and practiced in urban industrial areas, where they served a ready-made ethnic clientele. A few immigrant lawyers achieved distinction. Louis D. Brandeis, from a Jewish immigrant family in Louisville, Kentucky, became one of Boston's most successful corporate attorneys in the 1890s, later reaching the U.S. Supreme Court. But in most instances, even after gaining admission to practice, ethnic lawyers seldom achieved parity with the native elite that controlled the bars of every state.

Women suffered significant disabilities in attempting to practice law, reflecting their second-class political status. Women had a political role only when matters of public policy were deemed appropriate to their sex. Between 1875 and 1890, for example, seventeen states permitted women to vote in school board elections and three allowed women with property to vote on tax and bond referenda. Efforts by suffragettes to expand further political participation for women foundered. Between 1870 and 1910 seventeen states held referenda on giving women the right to vote, and only Colorado in 1893 and Idaho in 1896 were successful.

Women were further stigmatized when it came to the practice of law. They were excluded from the bar before the 1870s, and their ranks grew only at a glacial pace through the 1920s. Before 1920, for example, no woman was licensed to practice law in the state of Virginia, and in 1900 there were only fifty women with law practices in Massachusetts. But a few women wanted access to the bar. The most celebrated case was that of Myra Bradwell, who had married a lawyer in 1852. Bradwell studied law and passed her examination, but was refused admission to the bar of Illinois in 1869. She appealed to the U.S. Supreme Court, arguing that the equal protection clause of the Fourteenth Amendment prohibited state legislation excluding her from practice. The justices unanimously disagreed. Justice Joseph P. Bradley explained for the Court that the traditional family was "founded in the divine ordinance, as well as in the nature of things." Women's place was, according to Justice Bradley, inherently in the "domestic sphere" and not in the courtroom or the boardroom.[16]

The Supreme Court held fast to this position, granting the states broad powers to exclude women from law practice (or, of course, to include them). Perhaps the most important case was *Ex Parte Lockwood* (1894). The justices were asked by Belva Lockwood, a nationally known feminist, to consider the refusal of the state of Virginia to admit her to law practice. The statute regulating admission to the bar provided that "any person" could be licensed, but public sentiment and cultural understanding clearly excluded women. The high court rejected Lockwood's appeal on the grounds that the term "persons" did not extend to women and that the right to practice law was not a privilege or immunity of a citizen of the United States. The next year, the Virginia statute was amended to permit "any male citizen" to be licensed to practice law.[17]

Women did make inroads, however, largely through the efforts of sympathetic state legislators. In the same year as the Bradwell case, Arabella Mansfield was admitted to practice in Iowa. The first woman lawyer in Illinois was Alta M. Hulett, who was single, and broke the barrier in 1873. Clara Foltz gained admission to the bar after successfully campaigning to have a California statute rewritten that restricted the practice of law to "any white male citizen."[18] The University of Michigan Law School decided to admit women in 1870; Yale's law school followed in 1886 and Cornell's in 1887. Yet the bar stayed a male preserve. As recently as 1960, less than 3 percent of the country's lawyers were women.

Black males enjoyed only slightly greater access to the bar than did women. As late as 1934, there were only about twelve hundred black lawyers. The 1870 census listed only three in Massachusetts; there were fourteen in North Carolina in 1890, and something slightly above two dozen in Texas in 1900. These black lawyers played an important role in the black communities they served, although they were less influential than ministers. In Galveston, Texas from 1895 to 1920, black attorneys, while restricted by the system of Jim Crow, "served their community and the law far more efficiently than conventional mythology suggests. As spokesmen for racial justice, they sometimes used their legal skills in creative ways to attack the institutionalized racism of the New South."[19]

Black lawyers had a broad legal practice, handling both civil and criminal cases, although the most profitable cases (that of banks, industrial corporations, and trusts cases) went to white attorneys. Blacks, like the bar generally, reflected in their behavior the kinds of clients whom they served and who, as important, turned to them for legal counsel. Black lawyers were out of the mainstream of the legal profession in large measure because they represented a black clientele.

Educating Lawyers for the Science of the Law

The establishment of higher standards of legal education hastened the development of professionalism. Through the first half of the nineteenth century legal education had been casual, providing training to would-be lawyers through the apprenticeship system. A few law schools had existed before the Civil War, but there was little uniformity in either the method or the substance of the teaching of law. Some judges and lawyers, like Tapping Reeve (founder of the famous Litchfield Law School in Connecticut), operated private schools, and a few colleges created law departments. By about 1850, however, the emphasis in legal training shifted decisively away from the office and apprentice system and toward professional education. Between then and 1900 the number of law schools increased from 15 to 101, with an enrollment of over ten thousand. The University of Michigan Law School, which was the largest in the nation, alone had 883 students in 1900. By 1920 the student population in law schools had almost doubled again. By 1895 twenty-four states required from one to four years of study (or a college degree) before a candidate could take the bar examination, and this number grew steadily thereafter.

These institutions of legal education displayed considerable variety. Night law schools, for example, flourished in the late nineteenth and early twentieth centuries. The Iowa Law School, in Des Moines, granted twelve degrees to its class of all night students in 1866. By 1900 there were twenty night law schools and five other institutions that mixed day and night training. These night schools were particularly important in training practitioners; they gave their students a practical education in the law that equipped them to practice in their ethnic communities. Immigrants found these schools particularly attractive, and much of the ethnic bar of major cities, as well as local political and judicial figures, were recruited from them.

Blacks also had separate institutions, although in the South the "separate but equal" doctrine of *Plessy* v. *Ferguson* (1896) invariably produced inferior facilities and faculties. The most important institution of black legal education was the Howard University Law School, which opened its doors after the Civil War. Its influential and forceful dean, John Mercer Langston, the son of a white plantation owner and a slave woman, trained a small corps of black lawyers, many of whom went on to spearhead the fight for black civil rights in the first third of the twentieth century. Langston became the first head of the law department at Howard, where he developed a curriculum that relied on the lecture method with moot court practice to teach black students both the law and confidence in themselves. Despite discrimination and a continuing lack of professional opportunities, black lawyers had made "slow but steady progress, for which Langston and his Howard-trained disciples deserved much credit."[20]

The growth of legal education generated demands by legal educators in the ABA for a separate association to serve law schools. The ABA had established a section on legal education, but legal academics finally pressured the ABA in 1899 to issue a call for the establishment of an organization of "reputable" law schools.[21] The American Association of Law Schools (AALS), composed of twenty-five charter members, was open to schools and not individuals, and to gain admission institutions had to meet certain minimum standards. The AALS became a watchdog of legal education, invoking its private accreditation powers to push law schools, and the state legislatures that controlled the bar admissions process, to adopt a more professional view of legal education. The AALS made the increasing number of night law schools a special object of attack. But through the first quarter of the twentieth century, it had mixed success. It represented a steadily smaller proportion of the law school population, partly because its standards were unrealistically high and partly because its membership was so small that it could not bring effective pressure on legislatures.

Christopher Columbus Langdell and the Case Method

The upper levels of the educational hierarchy dominated AALS and shaped the course of legal education. Trends were set from the top down, and none was more important than the introduction in the 1870s of the casebook method at Harvard Law School. The traditional method of legal education, though varying from place to place, demanded that students memorize assigned portions of a text and then repeat that material when quizzed by the instructor. Students were not, as a rule, required to have any college education, and the course of instruction varied from a few months to a year or two. Methods were dogmatic, even among the best instructors.

Christopher Columbus Langdell, who served as dean of Harvard Law School from 1870 to 1895, introduced radical reforms that altered the course of legal education. His changes met with often considerable resistance. Students and faculty protested—the former often by refusing to attend class—and some of the reforms did not take firm hold until after Langdell left the deanship a quarter-century later. Yet, Langdell left a lasting mark; in its broad outlines, his scheme continues to dominate legal education today.

The new dean tightened admissions standards by requiring students without a college degree to take an admissions test. Langdell lengthened the period of law training from one to three years and devised courses appropriate for students in each year of their work. He also introduced final examinations that students had to pass at the end of each year in order to move to the curriculum of the next year and ultimately graduation.

These reforms were a prelude to Langdell's most important change, which was the case method of instruction. Casebooks were nothing new; the first had been prepared in 1810. They were collections of actual cases on a given subject that were arranged in such a way as to show the principles of the law and how they had developed. John Norton Pomeroy at New York University Law School in the 1860s had used the casebook and with it the case method. The latter simply meant that instead of lecturing to the students, the professor led them through a process of inquiry into the cases. Each case became an example of a real-life experience from which the students could learn.

Langdell shifted the emphasis in the case method, however. He moved it away from a tool for vocational training and into a means of developing a scientific approach to the law. The object of the law department at Harvard under Langdell was ''not precisely and only to educate young men to be practicing lawyers, though it [was] largely used for that purpose. It [was] to furnish all students who desire it the same facilities to investigate the science of human law, theoretically, historically, and thoroughly as they have to investigate mathematics, natural sciences, or any other branch of thought.''[22] Langdell blended science with law in the service of the emerging industrial nation. Langdell's approach to legal studies was based on his insight that in order best to serve their corporate and nationally oriented clients, lawyers had to be more skilled in the process of legal thinking and in brief preparation than in the technical vocational skills that were invaluable to the solo practitioner.

Langdell in 1871 published the first casebook on contracts, and he used it extensively in his classes. It consisted mostly of English decisions, underscoring Langdell's belief that the system of law in the United States needed to return to its English roots and to emphasize a more formal approach to the study and implementation of law.

This new scheme placed new demands on law teachers. Previously, they had been practitioners, valued for their practical knowledge and firsthand experience. Langdell, however, sought out new Harvard graduates already trained in the casebook method and sympathetic to the concept of legal science. The role of the law professor was to teach basic principles and leave the application of the law to later experience. Law schools became truly professional schools. They were scientific laboratories in which students and teachers were engaged in a quest for the enduring truths of the law through rigorous analysis of a selected body of cases from which could be adduced enduring legal principles.

By 1920, Langdell's system became the model for legal education throughout the nation. Few educational reforms have enjoyed such rapid and complete acceptance, and Harvard graduates accepted positions at other important law schools around the country, spreading Langdell's message. As a result, the structure and content of legal education on the national level took on an important degree of uniformity. The familiar modern law school emerged: formal entrance requirements, the case method of teaching, course organization built around certain core subjects, large libraries filled with state and national reporters, and law reviews edited by law students who practiced their craft as junior scientists of the law.

Langdell's revolution in legal education succeeded because it presented the law as a science, as an enterprise distinct from its old nemesis of politics, and equal in weight to the other emerging disciplines of the social sciences. The law, according to Langdell, was not just a vocation (something tawdry that craftsmen practiced) but a genuine branch of higher learning that required rigorous formal training. It was, in a word, a profession, and a scientific one at that. The approach nicely complemented the search being undertaken by bar associations, especially the ABA, to find a professional basis for the law, and it also well served emerging corporate capitalism.

But the new science of the law was really no science at all. Langdell's model "of science was not experimental, or experiential; his model was Euclid's geometry, not physics or biology."[23] Langdell endorsed empirical research but limited its scope to law reports—that is, reported cases. Even those cases were limited, and Langdell, in his own subject speciality of contracts, spent much time uncovering the principal cases that settled conclusively particular legal problems. The life of the law was logic, and a dry logic at that. The new scheme gave the law schools a position of scholarly equality in universities, something that Langdell believed was essential to the success of law education; but it was also segregationist in that none could enter its practice save those who had trained in it. The law school was part of the university world and the flood tide of scientific inquiry that was sweeping over it, without being in that same world.

Legal Formalism, Laissez-Faire, and Sociological Jurisprudence

Legal Formalism

The acceptance of the case method and a scientific approach to law were part and parcel of broader intellectual trends associated with the term legal formalism. The movement from legal instrumentalism to legal formalism was "uneven in pace and coverage," and the Civil War became a rough dividing point for these differing approaches to the law.[24]

Instrumentalism was the older path, and its heyday was in the antebellum era. Instrumentalists argued that law should be applied as a tool to promote economic growth without resort to regulation. Judges engaged in instrumental activity by using their common law authority to fashion doctrines that expedited and enhanced private business activity and entrepreneurship generally. Instrumentalism was a flexible, adaptive, and freewheeling view of the law that relied extensively on the states' police powers. This instrumentalist approach never died away, either on the bench or in state legislatures and Congress, whose members invoked the law to promote and, later, to regulate economic activity.

Formalism, on the other hand, sounded a retreat from the concentration on results and emphasized instead formal procedures that led to a result. Formalism was antilegislative, favorable to judicial review, and symptomatic of the increasingly wordy state constitutions that appeared in the late nineteenth century. As a doctrine it held that law had universal truths rather than transitory legislation as its base. The law was a whole body of knowledge that scientific legal thinkers could discern and properly trained judges could apply. Formalism, however, did not imply inactivity; to the contrary, it gave judges reason to act. Appellate judges were supposed to be oracular, to propound impartially a set body of doctrine. When legislative activity, carried out in the name of popular and partisan majorities, interfered with formal legal doctrine, then judges were supposed to strike it down mechanically. In this sense, judge-made law was superior to legislative enactments, which were sporadic and molded by popular whim rather than being based on enduring scientific truths. Legal formalists stressed the importance of federal courts because their appointed judges held tenure during good behavior, freeing them, unlike elected state appellate judges, to find and apply legal truths.

The concept of legal formalism connected smoothly with the concept of laissez-faire after the Civil War. Protective and regulatory legislation, for example, became a special object of attack. Christopher Tiedeman, one of the era's most influential law writers, observed in 1886 that "[g]overnmental interference is proclaimed and demanded everywhere as a sufficient panacea for every social evil which threatens the prosperity of society. Socialism, Communism, and Anarchism are rampant throughout the civilized world."[25]

Thomas M. Cooley, Tiedeman, and John Forrest Dillon combined laissez-faire and legal formalism in such a way as to equip appellate judges with a thorough rationale on which to limit legislative action. Cooley was chief justice of the Michigan Supreme Court from 1864 through 1885, when the electorate rejected him because of his close attachment to railroad interests. Cooley was a great judge and one of the nineteenth century's most prolific writers of legal treatises. His most important work was *Treatise on the Constitutional Limitations Which Rest upon the Legislative Power of the States of the American Nation*. Never has the title of a book revealed more about its contents. First published in 1868, and appearing in twelve subsequent revised editions, *Constitutional Limitations* was the most authoritative treatise written about the relationship between state legislative and state and federal judicial power. Cooley's message was simple: legislatures were to steer clear of any regulatory efforts, and the courts, when legislatures did act, were bound to strike down laws as unconstitutional that violated the free use of property. Such a view was reactionary, in as much as it placed property rights above human interests as defined by legislative authority. But Cooley was also a spokesman for civil liberty, arguing that the individual use of property was a sacred right and that judges were duty-bound to protect it.

At the end of the century, Christopher Tiedeman echoed Cooley's ideas. A professor of law at the University of Missouri and a prolific author, Tiedeman's reputation rested most fully on *A Treatise on the Limitations of Police Power in the United States* (1886). He went even further than Cooley, denouncing any governmental regulation, even usury laws that limited the interest charged by lenders. Tiedeman believed that state legislatures should invoke their police powers only to "provide for the public order and personal security by the prevention and punishment of crimes and trespasses."[26] Justice David J. Brewer of the U.S. Supreme Court summarized Tiedeman's sentiments when he wrote in an 1892 decision: "The paternal theory of government is to me odious. The utmost liberty to the individual, and the fullest possible protection to him and his property, is both the limitation and the duty of government.''[27]

John Forrest Dillon was a judge of the Iowa Supreme Court (1862–1868) and the author of the late nineteenth century's most authoritative work on municipal bonds, *Law of Municipal Corporations* (1872). This arcane branch of law was nonetheless important in an era when cities clamored for the legal means by which to encourage economic development only to see their efforts culminate in debt levels that they could not manage. Dillon, who later became a federal circuit court judge and a highly successful Wall Street lawyer, gave national stress to formalism and laissez-faire. He spread the gospel that national judicial constraint on city bond policies was essential when state-elected judiciaries failed to control cities and towns. ''Dillon's Rule'' held that cities were totally subject to the will of their states and that the federal courts were fully empowered to enforce these requirements when the states refused to do so.

Sociological Jurisprudence

Legal formalism and laissez-faire promoted an interventionist role for judges, underscored the worth of legal science, and treated law as frozen, with its principles and values set and its rules determined for all time. But even while these views held sway in the late nineteenth century, they came under attack from members of the legal community who doubted the rejection of both experience and social facts that legal science implied and who urged a close tie between law and the practice of social science. These proponents of sociological jurisprudence took the position that judges ought not, as a matter of course, to use their power to interfere when the legislature, acting on sound evidence, had decided to pursue a certain policy. The most important voices were those of Oliver Wendell Holmes, Jr., Roscoe Pound, and Louis D. Brandeis.

Oliver Wendell Holmes, Jr., wrote at the end of the nineteenth century that "certainty . . . and repose," the elements that formalists deemed most valuable, would not be "the destiny" of U.S. law in the years to come.[28] Holmes was a wounded veteran of the Civil War who had studied and taught at Harvard Law School, where he became a critic of Langdell's methods. Holmes went from Harvard to the bench of the Supreme Judicial Court of Massachusetts in 1882 and served as chief justice from 1899 to 1902, when he was appointed by Theodore Roosevelt to the U.S. Supreme Court.

He published *The Common Law* in 1881, and it was nothing less than a thorough history of the English common law and its development. The work contrasted sharply with the ideas of Langdell, Cooley, and Tiedeman because it reminded its reader that social and economic facts had to be taken into consideration in determining law. Holmes concluded that the greatness of the law was in its ability to adapt to changing circumstances and that this adaptive quality did much to give authority to the entire idea of the rule of law. Holmes wrote in *The Common Law* one of the most famous phrases of U.S. legal history. ''The life of the law,'' he observed, ''has not been logic: it has been experience. The felt necessities of the time, the prevalent moral and political theories, institutions of public policy, avowed or unconscious, even the prejudices which judges share with their fellow-men, have had a good deal more to do than the syllogism in determining the rules by which men should be governed."[29] Holmes, unlike the formalists, was willing to grant legislatures considerable authority to develop laws that fitted the circumstances of the new era of industrialization.

Roscoe Pound added his voice to the practical and social scientific view of law associated with Holmes. It was Pound who invented the term "sociological jurisprudence." He received a doctorate in botany from the University of Nebraska in 1897 after briefly studying law at Harvard, where he never received a degree. He was admitted to the Nebraska bar and practiced law while teaching botany at the University of Nebraska. Pound became a law professor at Harvard in 1910 and served as dean of the school from 1916 to 1936. A prolific author of legal scholarship, his essays and books ranged over a wide number of topics including criminal law, prison reform, and the organization of courts. Pound was especially critical of Langdell's approach to legal education if not his exact method, and he raised objections to the pinched view of science that Langdell and the legal formalists held. In 1912 Pound published an influential series of articles in the *Harvard Law Review* under the general title, "The Scope and Purpose of Sociological Jurisprudence." The term had little to do with the then-rising academic discipline of sociology. Rather, Pound meant by it an approach to law under which judges could and should weigh in the balance the social and economic consequences of their decisions. Pound's notions had implications for lawyers as well, because he urged on them the role of gathering and presenting evidence that would help a judge in reaching a determination about those consequences.

Louis D. Brandeis showed the bar how these notions could be given practical expression. Brandeis was the son of German-Jewish immigrant parents who had settled in Louisville, Kentucky. After graduating from Harvard Law School in 1878, he founded a highly successful corporate practice in Boston. Brandeis, however, was a Progressive to the core, and in the late nineteenth and early twentieth centuries he sought to promote his vision of an efficient and democratic society through two means. First, he was one of the original "prophets of regulation," believing that regulatory bodies, whose personnel were committed to scientific methods and empirical studies, would free the economy from the traditional distributive influences of political parties.[30]

Second, Brandeis advanced his social agenda through legal advocacy. Reform groups retained him as counsel, and he offered "sociological briefs" on their behalf before both state and federal courts. These briefs were composed of extralegal materials "drawn from government labor statistics, reports of factory inspectors, and testimony from psychological, economic, and medical treaties."[31] Sources such as these had rarely been invoked in legal arguments before the twentieth century, and their large-scale use by Brandeis began a long-term trend in which judges and juries increasingly took into account certain social and economic facts surrounding a case as well as considering the law. President Wilson in 1916, over the outcries of legal formalists, elevated Brandeis to the Supreme Court, where he served as an associate justice until retirement in 1939.

New High Priests

Between 1860 and 1920 the practice of law in the United States became a profession whose basic tenets were congruent with the demands of an industrializing and urbanizing society. Lawyers accommodated and accepted these developments; they did not resist them. The elite of the bar, through law associations and influential law schools, turned toward a professional model that made legal culture more impersonal, scientific, and lucrative. The legal profession joined with the business community on many levels and consequently shared in both its socioeconomic advances and its national outlook, emerging as the "new high priests" of an increasingly legalistic, industrialized society.

12

The Judicial Response to Industrialization: 1860–1920

Legal formalists, such as Tiedeman and Cooley, denounced regulatory and protective measures as "class legislation." They insisted that government should not use its power to improve the condition of one social group at the expense of another, or to alter the relative bargaining power of laborers and employers or consumers and producers. Their motives were mixed. They were concerned that popularly elected majorities would ravage the property of the rich and middle classes, undermining their wealth and the nation's economic expansion. As important, they also sought to "preserve liberty."[1] As a matter of constitutional right, they insisted that governmental policies should not redistribute justly earned wealth. On both the matter of public policy and constitutional liberty, they looked to the appellate judiciary, through the practice of judicial review and formalist legal doctrines, for support.

The courts during these years are often portrayed as reactionary and formalistic organs of laissez-faire. The behavior of the judiciary was more complex than this stereotype would suggest. Appellate judges did invoke laissez-faire principles in a few celebrated cases, but in most instances state and federal courts "moved consistently toward approval of a wide range of reform legislation" which, "although occasionally delayed in the courts, [was] not blocked there."[2] Furthermore, some time after 1880, statutory legislation began to "grow prodigiously," becoming "the most dynamic sector of American law."[3] As a result, the task of appellate judging changed from its traditional emphasis on examining common law rules to assessing the intentions of legislators in passing a particular statute. Invariably, attorneys like Louis Brandeis pressed sociological briefs on judges, urging them to consider new types of information that bore upon these intentions.

Judicial System

State Courts

The economic transformation of the United States after the Civil War prompted a growing recourse to the law. The range and scale of judicial activity expanded well beyond the bounds of the prewar years, with courts deciding an ever-increasing number of private disputes as well as determining public policy. Judges had a large and active hand in the governance of a rapidly changing society.

The system of federal, state, and local courts grew denser and more complex after the war. In 1900, for example, the federal courts included six territorial courts, special judicial commissions, the Court of Claims, sixty district and nine circuit courts of appeals, and the Supreme Court. The states had equally elaborate judicial structures. California had a state supreme court, twenty district courts, fifty-three county courts, numerous probate courts, justices' courts (in rural areas), and municipal courts. The pattern was much the same elsewhere: a high appellate court, with an intermediate court of appeals, then trial courts at the local level.

The lower courts bore the brunt of the growing recourse to law, and the composition of their dockets mirrored the social and economic changes that accompanied industrialization. The civil trials courts of Boston between 1880 and 1900, for example, "entertained the problems of about 20,000 plaintiffs a year."[4] These municipal courts served as forums in which the populace tried to settle problems relating to business, residence, finances, and injury associated with the growing complexity and anonymity of urban life. The courts became safety valves, taking on mediating functions that could no longer be provided by social institutions and conventions that had characterized the United States before the Civil War. The vast majority of cases were cut-and-dried. Debt collection was the main theme: grocers, clothing stores, and doctors asked the court to make their debtors pay.

The civil business in other trial courts was as impressive. New Hampshire's county circuit courts had 4400 cases continued (held over to the next year, not settled) in 1876; another 6000 were added the following year. Ohio's courts of first instance in 1873 handed down over 15,000 civil judgments, involving monetary transfers of more than $8.5 million. In December 1903, there were over 5100 cases on the dockets of Kansas City's courts, and about 60 percent of these were liability claims against companies. Under these circumstances, dockets became crowded and delays were the norm. A special committee of the American Bar Association in 1885 studied the problem and found that under then-existing conditions a lawsuit took from one and a half to six years to be decided.

Business grew throughout the rest of the judicial system. By 1900, the work of the nation's appellate courts alone amounted to about twenty-five thousand cases (reported in some four hundred volumes) each year. New York's Court of Appeals, perhaps the most influential final appellate court in the nation, handed down between five hundred and seven hundred decisions a year. The Illinois Supreme Court did about seven hundred to nine hundred a year. The California Supreme Court in 1860 published about one-hundred fifty opinions. In 1890 that number had more than tripled to about five-hundred fifty opinions, but in 1920, thanks to various reforms in court operations and jurisdiction, the court published only about two-hundred fifty opinions.

The highest appellate courts of the states were not only busy, but, as Table I reveals, they were deeply involved in the economy. From 1870 to 1900 more than one-third (36.2 percent) of the cases decided in these courts dealt with business matters, such as contract, debt, corporations, and partnerships. Another one-fifth (21.4 percent) involved issues of real property. The courts were significant forums for the resolution of business disputes.

Over the next century, the courts decided proportionately fewer business disputes. Litigants simply decided that alternative ways of handling business suits (such as arbitration) were preferable to the courts, which were slow, expensive, and relatively technical, even with a variety of reforms that aimed to simplify pleading and streamline the flow of litigation. In the mature industrial age, "the [state supreme courts] appear to do *less* work on commercial and industrial transactions, not more."[5] In the early years of industrialization the courts participated in economic and commercial regulation, but, as the industrial economy matured, that responsibility gravitated increasingly to the other branches of government, especially independent regulatory and administrative commissions. State supreme courts became more concerned with problems arising out of the confrontation between citizen and state and the collision of human bodies and motor vehicles, which replaced the railroad locomotive as the most important source of accident litigation. As Table I indicates, tort, constitutional, and criminal cases have increasingly filled the dockets of modern state supreme courts.

The leaders of the state bar associations after the Civil War pressed for reforms that would ease the burden of mounting judicial business. Many states increased the number of high court judges. California began in 1850 with three justices, expanded that number to five in 1862, and then expanded it again to seven in 1879. A few states, like California, divided the justices into separate departments, with only the most difficult or important cases decided by the full court. A number of states created special bodies to assist their overburdened tribunals. New York's Commission of Appeals, established in 1870 with a five-year tenure, disposed of about a thousand cases. Nebraska in 1895 set up a State Board of Irrigation with judicial powers: this body handled about a thousand claims that would have otherwise been treated in the regular

TABLE 1. Percentage of State Supreme Court Cases by Law Category, 1870–1970

Category	1870–1900	1905–1935	1940–1970
Debt and contract	33.6	29.3	15.0
Real property	21.4	15.4	10.9
Corporations/Partnerships	2.6	2.4	1.4
Torts	9.6	16.4	22.3
Criminal	10.7	11.6	18.2
Public law	12.4	13.0	19.4
Family and estates	7.7	9.7	11.8
Not known	2.3	1.8	0.7

Source: Taken from Robert A. Kagan, Bliss Cartwright, Lawrence M. Friedman, and Stanton Wheeler, "The Business of State Supreme Courts, 1870–1970," *Stanford Law Review* 30(November 1977):133–35.

courts. Texas in 1891 divided its supreme court into two distinct bodies with separate elected judges: a criminal court of appeals and a civil court of appeals.

Reformers also tried to restrict the flow of cases to the highest courts by creating intermediate courts of appeal and either limiting the jurisdiction of the high court or giving it greater control over the kind of cases that it could hear. In Illinois, for example, the newly created intermediate court of appeals in 1877 became the last stop for contract and damages cases where the amount in controversy was less than $1000. By about 1920 these and other court reforms inspired by the Progressive era had reduced the number of cases reaching the highest appellate courts, allowing their judges to concentrate on what they deemed important cases. But the courts were the products of political decision making, and most reforms were never sufficiently thorough to make a fundamental difference.

Federal Courts

The business of most lower federal courts had been modest before the Civil War, but from 1860 to 1920 cases flooded these courts. In 1871, the U.S. district courts disposed of 8187 criminal cases; in 1900, 17,033; and in 1920, 34,230. In 1873, these same courts settled 14,527 civil cases; in 1900, 22,520; and in 1920, 32,240. There were 52,477 civil cases pending in all of the district courts in 1900 compared with the 38,194 on the dockets of district and circuit courts only twenty years before. The Supreme Court docket expanded as well. The high court between 1862 and 1866 averaged about 240 cases per term; from 1878 to 1882 about 855; and from 1886 to 1890 about 1124.

The enormous increase in the population of the United States, and in the power and reach of the federal government after the Civil War, made it inevitable that the caseload of the federal courts would expand from their humble origins.[6] Between 1850 and 1875, for example, the expense of operating the federal judiciary soared from $500,000 to $3 million and by 1900 that figured had tripled again. The federal circuit court in Chicago on January 1, 1878 had 3045 suits pending, ten times the number heard in the average antebellum circuit court. These lower federal courts became "forums of order" in which interstate businesses could secure a hearing free from the local interests that dominated state courts.[7] That process began in 1842 with Justice Joseph Story's decision in *Swift* v. *Tyson,* which established a federal common law of commerce. It gathered momentum after the Civil War and continued unchecked into the New Deal.

Congress nationalized both the organization and jurisdiction of the lower federal courts. The Judiciary Act of 1869, for example, established nine new circuit court judgeships, each of which was filled by a judge who presided over both trials and appeals from the district courts. The new circuit judges relieved Supreme Court justices of much of their traditional circuit-riding duties, enabling the high court to devote more attention to its growing business in Washington. The Circuit Court of Appeals Act of 1891, which was meant to unclog the justices' dockets, ended their circuit riding and reorganized the old federal circuit courts, creating new circuit courts of appeal. The judges of this intermediate court of appeals received some of the business that had previously gone to the Supreme Court. This reform somewhat diminished the high court's business. In 1900, there were 723 cases docketed and from then through 1920 the Court's docket contained an average of about 930 cases each year.[8]

The Circuit Court of Appeals Act fixed two important new principles, both of which mirrored experiences in the states and both of which have continued ever since to influence the Court's jurisdiction: that there should be a powerful intermediate appellate court (the Circuit Court of Appeals); and that the Supreme Court should have broad discretion, through the grant of the writ of certiorari, to decide which cases were of such importance that they deserved review by the high court. A writ of certiorari (meaning "to be informed of") is issued in order that the Supreme Court may inspect the proceedings conducted in a lower court to determine whether there have been irregularities. In expanding the use of the writ of certiorari, the Congress reduced the historic right of appeal to the Supreme Court based exclusively on an error committed by a lower court. The statute thus expressed "a radically new principle concerning the Supreme Court's function: that the business of the Supreme Court was, not to see justice done in every case, but to decide . . . more important policy issues."[9]

Of even greater importance, Congress ordered changes in federal court jurisdiction. These changes fell into two broad categories: the power to remove cases from state to federal courts and the diminished scope of appeals to the Supreme Court as a matter of right.

The Removal Act of 1875 was a milestone in the history of the lower federal courts' relationship with the business community.[10] The act hastened the removal of suits from state to federal courts, from local to national forums of law. It provided that either party could remove a case to federal court; it permitted removal of all diversity suits, even when one of the parties did not live in the "forum" state (i.e., they were not resident in the state where the federal court proceeding was to be held). Most important, it permitted removal of all suits raising a question of federal law. The act was intended to permit newly freed slaves to circumvent the prejudice of state courts, but corporations engaged in interstate business benefited most from the removal provisions. They could engage in forum shopping: that is, they could find the court, federal or state, that offered them the best opportunity of winning their case. The act also promoted uniformity in corporation law, especially among big businesses with national markets.[11]

Judicial Review

Appellate courts extended the scope of their powers at the same time that their dockets swelled. The power of courts to strike down legislative measures contrary to constitutional authority was acknowledged by the framers of federal and state constitutions. The subsequent development of this practice was never clear nor simple, and it was always plagued by controversy. First, there was lingering suspicion that judges, in a republican form of government, had no right to second-guess legislators, a position that received strong support from Jeffersonian Republicans and later Jacksonian Democrats. The problem was less critical in the states after the 1850s when the method of judicial selection changed from legislative and executive appointment to popular election.

Second, because of the federal nature of the legal system in the United States, judicial review took place in different forums and with appeal to different bodies of constitutional authority. State appellate courts established early that they could interpret their constitutions and, if necessary, overturn legislative acts. Yet the federal

Supreme Court, because of the supremacy clause in the federal Constitution, was also capable of interpreting state legislative acts and court decisions that involved federal constitutional issues and legislative acts. Thus, the high court could inquire into state activities but the state courts could not, in turn, limit the actions of the federal Congress or courts by passing conclusively on the meaning of the federal Constitution.

Judicial review of state statutes by state courts was "a rare, extraordinary event" before the Civil War.[12] By 1861, for example, the Virginia Court of Appeals, the state's highest appellate court, had decided only thirty-five cases in which the constitutionality of a law was in question. Of these, the judges overturned only four.[13] The Supreme Judicial Court of Massachusetts, one of the two or three most prestigious appellate courts in the nation before the Civil War, had by 1860 considered the constitutionality of sixty-two laws and found only ten of them unconstitutional.[14]

From the beginning of the nation, the Supreme Court reviewed state laws and court decisions to ensure that they did not violate certain specific federal constitutional prohibitions on the states, such as the ex post facto, contract and commerce clauses. Between 1789 and 1864 the justices held forty-one acts of state legislatures unconstitutional, although this was less than 0.5 percent of all cases brought before them. The justices were less active in dealing with Congress, voiding only two federal statutes before the Civil War.

By the 1850s, however, the appellate judiciary had already emerged as a major force in public policy, and its decisions were widely understood to have distributive economic and social consequences. Furthermore, critics of overextended legislative authority expected that popularly elected judges would restrain this legislative authority, and that meant exercising the power of judicial review. Judges by the eve of the Civil War not only administered the rule of law but they served the important function of mediating among the growing number of conflicting interests that crowded the political scene in the United States.

The appellate judiciary after the Civil War built upon this legacy, expanding and enhancing its power in response to the distributive political decisions of the party period. By 1920 judicial review had become an accepted, if still controversial, feature of public life. The Virginia Court of Appeals found against 1 in 3 of the statutes that came before it during the late nineteenth century; Ohio's court held 15 state laws unconstitutional in the 1880s, 42 in the 1890s. The Minnesota Supreme Court between 1885 and 1899 struck down approximately 70 state statutes; the Utah Supreme Court in the period between 1893 and 1896 threw out 11 of the 22 statutes brought before it. Much the same occurred in the federal Supreme Court. Of the 217 state laws struck down by the Court from its start in 1920, 48 were voided in the peak decade of the 1880s, and the justices, while displaying deference to Congress, still struck down 32 federal acts between the Civil War and 1937. The Court overwhelmingly upheld, however, state and federal enactments.[15]

Judicial Response to Regulatory Legislation

In the late nineteenth century, this surge in judicial review involved judicial scrutiny of legislative regulation of the social and economic consequences of industrialization. The *American Law Review,* for example, claimed in 1894 that "it has come to be the fashion . . . for courts to overturn acts of the State legislatures upon mere economical theories and upon mere casuistical grounds."[16] Upon close examination, in instances of both regulatory and protective legislation, and in both state and federal courts, judicial behavior was far more complex and less doctrinaire than once believed.

State Courts and Economic Regulation

Courts employed several constitutional hooks on which to impale economic regulatory measures. The most important was substantive due process of law, which was "the most formidable doctrine in the judicial arsenal of antilegislative weapons."[17] Due process before the Civil War had essentially one meaning: procedural. The due-process provisions in state constitutions and the Fifth Amendment to the federal Constitution provided that every person was entitled to an orderly proceeding that afforded an opportunity to be heard and to be protected in his or her rights. But due process began about the time of the Civil War to take on another substantive meaning that derived from the old doctrine of vested rights. Substantive due process meant that there existed an irreducible sum of rights that vested in the individual and with which government could not arbitrarily interfere. In short, there were substantive, not just procedural limitations on legislative power. The New York Court of Appeals in 1856, in *Wynehamer* v. *People,* gave the first significant decision involving the doctrine, and a year later Chief Justice Roger B. Taney, in *Dred Scott,* weakly argued that the due-process clause of the Fifth Amendment protected slave property from federal regulation.[18]

Substantive due process had two purposes. First, it had certain antiredistributive economic effects. When legislatures attempted through regulatory measures to redistribute the costs of economic development, high state courts objected on substantive due-process grounds, thereby favoring the wealthy at the expense of the poor.

Second, it was a means of voiding special legislation that aided one group over another. Thus, substantive due process was not used exclusively, or even predominately, in state appellate courts to protect the rich from the poor. For example, in *People* v. *Gillson* (1888), the New York Court of Appeals invalidated an act that prohibited the Atlantic and Pacific Tea Company from giving a teacup and saucer to consumers who purchased its coffee. What was at stake in this litigation had nothing to do with the redistribution of wealth but instead involved the right of "citizen traders" to sell and consumers to buy a cup, a saucer, and coffee, rather than coffee alone, for the price of the coffee.[19] The Iowa Supreme Court in 1900 struck down legislation that permitted the use of oil for lighting purposes only in lamps made by a particular manufacturer, but not in other lamps. The judges reasoned that as a matter of right any producer capable of manufacturing the required oil should be able to sell it.[20]

State courts upheld the vast majority of economic regulatory measures, leaving intact legislation that demonstrated a proper use of the police powers to promote health, safety, morals, and welfare. Typical was the fate of most occupational licensing laws, where only a whisper of constitutional conflict was heard in the courts. Appellate judges overturned these statutes only when they granted some advantage to one occupational group over another. In *People* v. *Ringe* (1910), for example, the New York Court of Appeals considered the constitutionality of an "undertaker–embalmer" statute that mandated that all undertakers be duly licensed embalmers. The judges made clear that the legislature had authority to regulate the profession, but that it had gone too far in combining the two jobs in one person. It was common knowledge that undertakers had not always been embalmers and that most rural undertakers were not embalmers at the time the case was decided. The law was simply a way of giving undertakers a monopoly over the funeral business, cutting out embalmers, and having little to do with the health, morals, or safety of the community. What bothered the court in *Ringe* was that the statute vested monopoly power in an occupational group, interfering with the "common law right to engage in a lawful business" and involving an "unnecessary and unwarrantable interference with constitutional rights."[21]

Federal Courts and Economic Regulation

The Supreme Court's invocation of substantive due process of law to strike down state legislation stirred great controversy. In the case of state legislation, the Court relied on a substantive interpretation of the due-process clause of the Fourteenth Amendment to calibrate the extent of the states' police powers. The Court also considered the scope of state and congressional regulatory authority under the commerce clause, an issue of special importance given the increasingly interdependent character of the industrial market economy.

The first important federal judicial test of state regulation came in the *Slaughterhouse Cases* (1873). The Republican-controlled legislature of Louisiana in 1869 passed a law giving one major slaughterhouse in New Orleans a virtual monopoly over the slaughtering of all beef, hogs, and other livestock. Unsanitary conditions in the meat preparation industry, not only in New Orleans but also elsewhere in the nation, led the legislature to act using its police powers. Yet the measure had political overtones, because rival Republican and Democratic entrepreneurs were competing to control the lucrative flow of Texas cattle to New Orleans and the subsequent distribution of the processed beef. The Republican legislature awarded its political friends in the Crescent City Live Stock Handling and Slaughterhouse Company the franchise, making the erstwhile Confederate and Democratic butchers conspicuous losers.

The Democratic butchers sued. They had two principal claims, both made under the recently adopted Fourteenth Amendment. First, they charged that the legislation abridged their privileges and immunities (their rights, in simple terms) as citizens of the United States. Second, they claimed that the legislation also violated the due-process clause of the Fourteenth Amendment. Behind these assertions rested assumptions about what Congress had intended when it passed the amendment and the states ratified it. Counsel for the Republican monopoly claimed that not only did Louisiana have sufficient authority under the police power to enact that law but that, in any case, the fundamental rights in controversy remained under the control of the states. Furthermore, they contended that the protections accorded by the due-process clause applied *only* to blacks, because Congress passed the amendment to protect newly freed slaves. The plaintiff Democrats argued that the due-process clause had created a substantive national right to pursue whatever lawful calling an individual wished, unfettered by state legislative restrictions. The new amendment, they insisted, gave them greater security than had existed before the war, because there was no doubt—the Fourteenth Amendment said as much—that the due-process clause applied to the states.

By the narrow margin of five to four, the Court sustained the Louisiana statute. Justice Samuel Miller, whom President Abraham Lincoln had appointed, wrote for the majority. The Fourteenth Amendment, Miller said, did nothing to change state control over fundamental rights included in the privileges and immunities clause. Moreover, the states' regulatory powers were paramount, even if they led to a monopoly. To apply the Fourteenth Amendment in the present case, Miller observed, would "constitute the Court a perpetual censor upon all legislation of the States on the civil rights of their own citizens," and thus interfere with licensing acts, liquor regulation, hours of labor, and child labor laws.[22] The Court "joined the other sectors of the postwar polity in affirming the principle that government might act . . . positively . . . in the realm of economic policy."[23]

Four years later the justices decided another police powers case, and they once again affirmed state economic regulatory authority. *Munn* v. *Illinois* (1877) involved one of five state laws, so-called Granger laws, which stipulated the amount of money that a grain elevator operator could charge for storing grain and provided penalties if these rates were exceeded. Ira Munn was one of the largest and most unscrupulous elevator operators in Chicago, and he had been found guilty in state court of violating the act. His counsel appealed to the Supreme Court, arguing that the Fourteenth Amendment's due-process clause prohibited such regulation because it interfered with Munn's practice of his vocation.

The Court decided for Illinois by a decisive margin of seven to two. Chief Justice Morrison R. Waite, writing for the majority, ignored the Fourteenth Amendment issue and concentrated instead on the scope of state regulatory authority. Waite applied the "public interest doctrine," which had flourished in antebellum state supreme courts and legislatures, to sustain the Illinois act. "When private property is devoted to a public use," Waite wrote, "it is subject to public regulation." The owner of property "affected with a public interest . . . must submit to be controlled by the public for the common good, to the extent of the interest thus created." If legislatures abused their police powers, Waite insisted that "the people must resort to the polls, not to the courts."[24]

Even though Ira Munn lost his case, the Court may well have accepted his major premise: that the Fourteenth Amendment banned certain kinds of state-imposed regulations of private business. The decision left open the possibility that wholly private businesses (those that used property not directly affected with a public interest) would not be subject to regulation by the state. Furthermore, Waite concluded that where the commerce involved was of an interstate character, the commerce clause of the Constitution would override the police powers of the state to regulate even a business affected with a public interest. The responsibility for regulating those businesses belonged to Congress, Waite observed, and not to the state legislatures.

Lawyers with business clients unhappy with state regulation seized on these openings. Their task was facilitated by two developments. First, the Removal Act of 1875 permitted them to remove regulatory cases from generally hostile state courts into the federal courts where they could advance the substantive due-process and commerce clause arguments. Second, the Supreme Court in *Santa Clara County* v. *Southern Pacific R.R. Co.* (1886) held that a corporation was a person under the meaning of the Fourteenth Amendment.

In the remaining decades of the nineteenth century the justices became increasingly innovative in their approach to the due-process and commerce clauses, often borrowing liberally from the briefs of attorneys who argued against state regulation. In one sense, the Court turned more conservative: the decisions that followed *Munn* had the distributive consequence of favoring capital. But the direction of the Court after *Munn* can also be understood as an affirmation of individual rights over special privilege conferred by the states. In both instances, the justices carved out for themselves an ever-widening role in formulating public policy and in exercising a monopoly over interpretation of the Constitution.

The Court's actions were so far-reaching that Congress was forced to act. The crucial case was *Wabash, St. Louis, and Pacific Railway Co. v. Illinois* (1886). The justices had previously held that the states, through their police powers, could exercise jurisdiction over interstate commerce in the absence of congressional legislation. State regulation had considerable support in a federal system that continued, even amidst explosive economic growth, to cherish local control. In *Wabash,* however, the Court severely curtailed state regulation, finding that even when a state regulated commerce (e.g., railroads) that operated within its boundaries, it might still indirectly affect some interstate commerce. The states, according to Justice Miller speaking for the Court, had attempted to do what the Constitution explicitly prohibited, that is, to regulate interstate commerce. The decision was so sweeping that the following year, Congress, which had been wrangling over the issue for a decade, created the Interstate Commerce Commission (ICC).

The Court accepted the constitutionality of the ICC but steadily sliced away at its powers. The justices by the beginning of the twentieth century had held that the ICC lacked power over determining rates and restricted its investigatory powers. Justice John Marshall Harlan, who was often critical of the work of his colleagues, observed in 1897 that the Court had gone "far to make the Commission a useless body for all practical purposes."[25] Between then and 1906, the agency won only one major case out of sixteen before the high bench. When Progressives, in the Elkins Act (1903) and the Hepburn Act (1906), strengthened the power of the ICC to set maximum freight rates, the Court retreated, and the ICC, while still somewhat hamstrung in its authority, entered a period of considerably greater activity.

The justices also invoked due-process arguments to curb state regulatory agencies. The turning point was *Chicago, Milwaukee and St. Paul Railway Co. v. Minnesota* (1890). The state of Minnesota adopted legislation establishing a railroad and warehouse commission, with power to determine the maximum a railroad could charge for hauling freight within the state. The railroad had no choice but to charge the rate established by the commission and the railroad had no opportunity to appeal the matter to a court if it disagreed with the rate finding. The case reached the Court at a time of great labor and farmer unrest, and conservative elements charged that the Minnesota legislation fostered "socialism."

The Court struck down the law by a vote of six to three. The justices' decision was in some ways unexpected, because they had previously sustained state legislation that permitted administrative bodies to determine what constituted a reasonable rate. The lawyers for the railroads, however, appealed to the Court not only on the basis of the due-process clause of the Fourteenth Amendment but also on the grounds that only courts could make a determination of reasonableness and that the new state administrative agencies were usurping judicial authority. The argument persuaded the justices, who may have felt that—given the social upheaval of the times—they had a special duty to protect property, albeit the property rights of railroads.

Justice Samuel Blatchford, a former New York railroad lawyer, spoke for the

Court. "The question of the reasonableness of a rate," he wrote, "is eminently a question for judicial investigation, requiring due process of law for its determination. If the company is deprived of the power of charging rates for the use of its property, and such deprivation takes place in the absence of an investigation by judicial machinery, it is deprived of the lawful use of its property, and thus, in substance and effect, of the property itself, without due process of law."[26] Blatchford's decision was not a strict invocation of substantive due process, but rather an appeal to the traditional procedural safeguards attached to public expropriations of private property. Still, it cleared the ground for the Court's subsequent affirmation of that doctrine. Blatchford's opinion also exhibited the broadened scope of judicial review, in which the Court not only inquired into the constitutionality of a measure (did it square with the letter of the Constitution) but also measured the effect of legislation. In this case, the Court judged the worth of a statute based on whether the user of property, a railroad, was receiving a reasonable return.

The Court's transformation of the due-process clause of the Fourteenth Amendment was completed in *Allgeyer* v. *Louisiana* (1897), the first case in which the justices relied fully on a substantive interpretation of due process to strike down a state law. This case involved a statute that prohibited residents of the state from doing business with a New York life insurance company. Louisiana was effectively blocking the transaction of interstate business activity, something that the Supreme Court had consistently championed since before the Civil War. The justices invalidated the Louisiana law, however, on substantive due-process grounds. The distributional effect of the decision was hardly to protect the rich from the poor, because the measure opened to citizens of the state the opportunity to engage an effective competitor to insurance companies within the state.

Judiciary: Trusts and Monopolies

In the last quarter of the nineteenth century, state governments undertook, amid great public clamor, to regulate the "trusts." The Granger laws of the 1870s and the more detailed legislation passed in the 1880s invoked the states' police powers to restrict monopoly practices in several areas of business, with the greatest attention given to industrial combinations. By 1890 about ten states had passed antitrust laws and six state supreme courts had found trust agreements illegal as monopolies, conspiracies in restraint of trade, or against public policy. In several other states, attorneys general brought suit against monopolies as being *ultra vires* (i.e., acting beyond the scope of their powers). State appellate judges were willing both to accept legislative regulation of trusts and, when legislation was absent, to allow states to proceed on grounds of public policy against the trusts.

These state court decisions reflected two different sentiments. On the one hand, the courts clearly imbibed the historical resentment against monopoly power. On the other hand, their decisions against interstate monopolies constituted one way of sustaining local businesses in an increasingly competitive marketplace. The Singer Sewing Machine Company, which held an exclusive patent on the sewing machine, created a nationwide distribution and sales system in the 1870s that bypassed local merchants and salespersons. In *State* v. *Welton* (1874), the Missouri Supreme Court sustained the conviction of M. M. Welton, an agent of Singer, for failing to pay a license fee for the privilege of engaging in local business.

Control of interstate monopolies and efforts to protect local business from nonresident corporations was simply beyond the scope of state legislative or judicial authority. The Singer Company, for example, purposefully violated state law in order to gain a hearing on constitutional grounds in the federal courts. The major trusts dodged the consequences of state court antitrust decisions by incorporating in other states, such as New Jersey and Delaware, that had more liberal incorporation statutes.

The Supreme Court encouraged the efficient conduct of business affairs across state lines. In *Welton* v. *Missouri* (1876), it broke with precedent by reversing the earlier decision of the Missouri Supreme Court against the Singer Company and overturning the state statute upon which it rested as an illegal restraint on interstate commerce. The decision was an initial step in the creation of a judicially supervised national market that was "spacious enough for the most ambitious growth which private individuals or groups could contrive."[27] Moreover, as with the application of substantive due process to state economic regulation, the Court "eagerly embraced the opportunity to deduce from the commerce clause a new and fundamentally important constitutional right: the right of nonresident corporations, even without express congressional license, to engage in interstate transactions on terms of equality with local firms.[28]

The economic nationalism of the Court was restrained in one important way, however. The justices had historically given the states broad discretion to regulate the behavior of nonresident corporations engaged in production (mining and manufacturing) rather than marketing activities. The states had made little use of this authority. The reason was simple expediency: mining and manufacturing, which grew rapidly after the Civil War, constituted a base of taxes, employment, and wealth. Even amid the great antimonopoly crusade of the 1880s, many states followed a pattern of allowing nonresident corporations engaged in these businesses to do what they wanted relatively unrestrained from direct state supervision.

The historical precedent for regulation of these businesses was with the states. But the states did not uniformly undertake that responsibility, with resulting confusion and uncertainty. The Sherman Antitrust Act offered a vaguely drawn national solution to the problem, but its implementation rested entirely with the federal courts.

The justices accepted the constitutionality of the Sherman Act, but they limited the power of Congress to regulate manufacturing monopolies. The leading case was *United States* v. *E.C. Knight* (1895). The American Sugar Refining Corporation controlled 90 percent of the nation's sugar refining capacity. The government charged that the agreements used to secure this monopoly substantially restrained trade and imposed higher prices on consumers. The Supreme Court concluded otherwise. Chief Justice Melville W. Fuller held that commerce and manufacturing were completely different activities and that the Sherman Act applied only to the former. "Commerce succeeds to manufacturing," Fuller wrote, "and is not a part of it."[29] Remedies to the problems created by manufacturing monopolies belonged where they had traditionally rested: with the states. States, and not the federal government, issued corporate charters, and states therefore had the authority to revoke these licenses if the companies acted *ultra vires*. Fuller sincerely believed that, in the federal system of the United States, the responsibility for regulating manufacturing monopolies properly belonged with the states. The decision restricted federal antimonopoly efforts just as the justices had circumscribed administrative regulation of the national marketplace in the ICC cases.

The justices were unequivocal in their hostility to clearly redistributive legislation, such as the federal income tax passed by Congress in 1894. The following year the Court, in *Pollock* v. *Farmers' Loan and Trust Co.*, declared the tax unconstitutional. That decision stuck until it was voided by the adoption of the Sixteenth Amendment in 1913.

In matters of economic regulation, state and federal judges interjected themselves into the formulation of public policy. They did so through doctrinal devices, most notably substantive due process, that permitted them to substitute their policy choices for those of legislators. The traditional practice of judicial review assumed a more expansive meaning that contributed directly to the increasing monopoly exercised by judges over constitutional interpretation. Their decisions, however, also involved concern with rights. While the courts trimmed many regulatory efforts, they left in place the major pieces of federal legislation and retained for the state legislatures important, if somewhat hollow, authority to deal with economic matters.

Judiciary and Protective and Labor Legislation

Freedom to Contract and Legislative Paternalism

"[T]he unwritten law of this country," wrote Christopher G. Tiedeman in 1900, "is in the main against the exercise of the police power."[30] Historians of an earlier generation accepted Tiedeman's analysis, and they concluded that state and federal courts, influenced by laissez-faire social and economic theory, savaged the paternalistic efforts of legislators to redistribute the costs of industrialization through protective legislation for women, children, and workers in hazardous occupations.

Between 1870 and 1920, the public and the legal community devoted great attention to the thousands of decisions made by appellate judges involving protective legislation. Judges fashioned a new doctrine of freedom or liberty to contract, which echoed the laissez-faire and property rights sentiments of the era. Liberty to contract, which was closely tied to the concept of substantive due process, meant that an individual was free to obtain through private bargaining the best possible terms of employment. The New York Court of Appeals, for example, explained in *In Re Jacobs* (1885) that the state legislature could not impede "the application of the [worker's] industry and the disposition of his labor, and thus, . . . depriv[e] him of his property and some portion of his personal liberty."[31] Freedom to contract sprang from the private-contract paradigm that so influenced nineteenth-century law. The doctrine was never absolute, and by the late nineteenth century, at the very time liberty to contract began to have authority in constitutional law, the contract paradigm in private law matters began to erode, because it was ill-suited to large-unit economic development.

Freedom to contract was the major constitutional hurdle that all protective legislation had to negotiate. The results of sustained judicial inquiry produced the same results as in the economic regulation cases: judges in a few spectacular instances, such as *In Re Jacobs*, overturned legislation, but in the vast majority of cases they left these measures and the police powers upon which they rested intact. Only in matters involving unions were the courts consistently hostile.

Child Labor and the Courts

In the last quarter of the nineteenth century, child labor statutes became widespread, with much of the support for them coming from labor unions anxious to protect the wages of their adult members. Appellate judges approached these statutes from two traditions. First, the English common law had historically given the father an almost unlimited right to the earnings of minor children, and the parents also enjoyed full powers to contract out the labor of their children. Second, however, because children were not possessed of full legal rights, they also came under the powers of the state as *parens patriae* (i.e., persons requiring the legal guardianship of the state). By the end of the century judges were relying on this doctrine to exercise fuller control over children in family matters and to approve legislative regulation of child labor.

Even the highly conservative New York Court of Appeals accepted this legislation. In *Marino* v. *Lehmaier* (1903), for example, the court endorsed a law that forbade the employment of children under sixteen in certain occupations and made it a misdemeanor for parents to consent to such employment. Every child labor regulation brought before the New York court was sustained, and in every other state judges rejected arguments based on freedom to contract, parental rights, and class legislation.[32] "It is competent for the state," wrote the Oregon Supreme Court in 1906, "to forbid the employment of children in certain callings merely because it believes such prohibition to be for their best interest. . . . Such legislation is not an unlawful interference with the parent's control over the child or right to its labor, nor with the liberty of the child."[33]

The Supreme Court was equally accepting of state legislation. Only one case even made it to the Court for review, and in *Sturges & Burns Manufacturing Co.* v. *Beauchamp* (1913) the justices gave an expansive reading of the police powers in relation to child labor and rejected due-process arguments by the plaintiff. When it came to protecting children, "the legislative judgment carried very far."[34]

The Court, however, was not prepared to permit the Congress, based on the commerce power, to undertake national regulation of child labor, something that reformers wanted because they believed that existing state statutes were laxly enforced. In *Hammer* v. *Dagenhart* (1918), Justice William Rufus Day, speaking for the Court, overturned a two-year-old statute that prohibited the movement of goods in interstate commerce that were produced by child labor. Nine months later the Congress passed a new statute, which levied a tax on goods produced by child labor, but the Court in *Bailey* v. *Drexel Furniture Company* (1922) voided it on the grounds that it invaded powers reserved to the states. Subsequent efforts to pass a child labor amendment to the Constitution foundered for lack of votes in the states to ratify it.

Women Workers and the Courts

The courts accorded state legislatures significant discretion under the police powers to write protective legislation for women. Most of this legislation dealt with hours of work and flowed from the assumption that the inherently delicate physical condition of women, and their special place in society as the bearers of the next generation, justified state intervention.

The earliest case involved a Massachusetts law that prohibited the employment of

women for more than sixty hours per week. In *Commonwealth* v. *Hamilton Manufacturing Company* (1876), the Supreme Judicial Court sustained the law in a brief
opinion that found that "[t]he principle has been so frequently recognized in the
Commonwealth that reference to decisions is unnecessary."[35] By late in the nineteenth
century, when the tide of opposition to such legislation was fullest, other courts were
more hostile. The most famous case was *Ritchie* v. *People* (1893), in which the Illinois
Supreme Court considered the constitutionality of an 1893 statute limiting women's
hours in factories or workshops to no more than eight in any one day and forty-eight in
a week. The court held that the measure violated freedom to contract. Judge Benjamin
D. Magruder, one of the late-nineteenth-century stalwarts of freedom to contract,
concluded that the legislation, because it discriminated against women based on sex,
actually harmed them by interfering with their ability to contract for the best possible
job arrangements.[36]

The *Ritchie* decision stirred public condemnation. So too did two other prominent
judicial decisions striking down hours legislation for women. In *People* v. *Williams*
(1907), Judge John C. Gray of the New York Court of Appeals adopted Magruder's
line of reasoning, concluding that a statute prohibiting employment of women in
factories between 9:00 P.M. and 6:00 A.M. "overstepped the limits set by the constitution of the state to the exercise of the power to interfere with the rights of citizens."[37]
The Colorado Supreme Court in the same year voided a similar statute, although its
decision was based on technical grounds rather than freedom to contract.[38]

In every other state, the courts sustained women's hour legislation as an appropriate exercise of the police powers. "Surely an act which prevents the mothers of our
race from being tempted to endanger their life and health by exhaustive employment,"
wrote the Pennsylvania Supreme Court in 1900, "can be condemned by none save
those who expect to profit by it."[39]

The Supreme Court added its endorsement in 1908. The case was *Muller* v.
Oregon. Curt Muller, the owner of a laundry in Portland, appealed a decision by the
Oregon Supreme Court that had upheld a law limiting the hours of women workers in
factories and laundries to no more than ten per day. Louis D. Brandeis prepared a
"sociological brief" that demonstrated through statistics the harm done to women as a
result of long hours of work. A unanimous Supreme Court accepted Brandeis's argument, rejecting the argument by Muller's counsel in favor of freedom to contract, and
endorsed the long-standing paternalistic attitude toward women by all-male legislatures. Thereafter, state courts consistently upheld this legislation, and both Illinois and
New York reversed their previous positions.[40]

Males and Hours of Work

Where children and women were not involved, the courts held state legislatures more
tightly to the well-defined limits of the police powers of health, safety, morals, and
public welfare. For example, state courts were initially hostile to legislation that set
maximum hours of work on public projects. The California Supreme Court, in *Ex
Parte Kuback* (1890), struck down a Los Angeles ordinance establishing eight hours as
a day's work when performed under contract to the city. Judge Irving G. Vann of New
York in 1903 explained that the legislature of that state could not limit the hours of
work on city projects because "[we] cannot see that [this law] bears any reasonable

relation to the public health, safety or morals."[41] The same year, however, the Supreme Court, speaking through Justice John Marshall Harlan, affirmed the decision of the Kansas Supreme Court that had upheld a state law limiting to eight hours work on public projects. "[I]t cannot be deemed part of the liberty of any contractor," Harlan concluded, "that *he* be allowed to do public work in any mode he may choose to adopt, without regard to the wishes of the State."[42] Thereafter, state laws regulating hours of public works were upheld by the vast majority of state courts.

State and federal courts even accepted statutes regulating the maximum hours of work of male laborers in the private sector as long as they were engaged in hazardous undertakings. The Utah Constitution of 1893, for example, contained a provision directing the legislature to "pass laws to provide for the health and safety of the employees in factories, smelters and mines."[43] Such a constitutional provision was itself indicative of the ends to which reformers would go to provide a basis of constitutional legitimacy for the exercise of the police powers. The legislature promptly passed an eight-hour law and in 1896 the Utah Supreme Court, noting that working conditions in smelters filled with noxious gases constituted a health danger, upheld it. The state supreme court dismissed freedom-to-contract arguments with the observation that even without an explicit constitutional provision the legislation would doubtless have been constitutional under the state's inherent police powers.

The U.S. Supreme Court accepted this position in reviewing the Utah decision. In *Holden* v. *Hardy* (1898), the justices by a vote of seven to two set forth "the paradigmatic [position] for approving protective legislation, with its holding that special and dangerous conditions justified the intervention of the state."[44] The Court dismissed the right-to-contract argument because employer and employee did not stand in a position of bargaining equality. The state could intervene to protect the welfare of whichever party had significantly less bargaining power. The opinion in *Holden* provided that the legislature had extensive power to decide when such an imbalance existed. Because the police powers were not limitless, however, some degree of judicial inquiry was always necessary, even though the justices did not say so. Their subsequent actions suggested as much.

Many state courts turned to *Holden* v. *Hardy* to sustain legislation directed at such groups as street railway workers and miners. Yet there was also resistance. The Colorado Supreme Court in 1899 rejected an eight-hour law for miners as class legislation that violated freedom to contract. The judges found, contrary to *Holden,* that it was up to the judiciary "to determine what are the subjects upon which the [police] power is to be exercised, and the reasonableness of that exercise."[45]

The U.S. Supreme Court agreed as well in the most famous (or infamous) of the protective legislation cases, *Lochner* v. *New York* (1905). The case involved an act that established a ten-hour day and a sixty-hour week for bakery workers. Bakers suffered from "white lung" disease, caused by constantly breathing flour, and baker's leg, which resulted from long hours of standing. The statute, however, presented the Court with as much a union case as an hours case, because the objective of the legislature, among other things, was to bring the wages of nonunion bakers into line with union bakers. Although Justice Rufus Peckham did not broach this issue in his opinion for the Court's bare five-to-four majority that struck down the law, it may help to explain why the Court acted in a way that seemed contrary to its earlier holding in *Holden* v. *Hardy.*

The Court's decision demonstrated that the justices were fully prepared to inquire into the nature of working conditions as a basis on which to second-guess legislative action. The New York law was impermissible as an exercise of the police powers because, according to Justice Peckham, it was an effort "simply to regulate the hours of labor between the master and his employees, in a private business, not dangerous in any degree to morals or in any real and substantive degree, to the health of the employees."[46] Peckham shifted the traditional emphasis in judicial review from a concern with the kinds or classes of governmental powers under review toward the consequences that flowed from the exercise of the police powers. This new formulation of judicial power was intended to aid the Court in sustaining individual rights, in this instance liberty to contract. Just as substantive due process in economic regulation cases permitted the invocation of judicial power to protect the right to hold and use property, so liberty to contract in *Lochner* emphasized the right of individuals to contract free of state interference.

Of the four dissenters in *Lochner,* Justice Oliver Wendell Holmes, Jr., was the most important. He was coldly cynical in his evaluation of both human nature and his colleagues on the bench. Holmes argued that over the generations human ideas and the relationship of interests in society changed, and that the law, including the Constitution, had to evolve accordingly. Judges, in Holmes' view, could not mask their preferences by insisting that they mechanically applied law; nor could they merely read their social views into constitutional law. "[T]he Fourteenth Amendment does not enact Mr. Herbert Spencer's Social Statics," Holmes insisted, "[a] constitution is not intended to embody a particular economic theory, whether of paternalism and the organic relation of the citizen to the State or of *laissez faire.*"[47]

The *Lochner* decision was in many ways an aberration with limited impact. Judges in places as different as Montana, New York, and Mississippi sustained various hours laws, many of which by the second decade of the twentieth century applied generally to all workers in manufacturing, not just people laboring in hazardous occupations. Even the Supreme Court distanced itself from *Lochner,* although it refused to overrule itself. In *Bunting* v. *Oregon* (1917), the high court sustained the opinion of the Oregon Supreme Court that had approved a ten-hour statute that applied to both men and women, even though it had a time-and-a-half requirement for overtime pay, making it a wage regulation.

Wages and the Courts

Hours legislation reflected the belief that some work was so unhealthy or dangerous as to require restrictions on the time that a laborer spent at it. Such statutes were justified on the grounds that certain classes of workers, such as women and children, required state protection. Minimum-wage legislation, however, stirred lingering fears of governmental redistribution of wealth and violation of freedom to contract. "[A]ny wages are 'fair'," wrote conservative critic W. A. Croffut, "which are as high as that sort of work commands in the open market."[48]

The courts indeed accepted some degree of legislative prerogative, and, as with hours legislation, an initial judicial assault on wage statutes was followed by acceptance of most of them. Many mines and factories, for example, paid in scrip. These were certificates, not legal tender, redeemable only in company-owned stores, which charged premium prices. Payment in scrip forced workers to buy through the company store and bound them to their employers. Labor groups successfully pushed for the legislative abolition of scrip payment and, even more, for laws that regularized the time and place at which workers were paid.

Godcharles & Co. v. *Wigeman* (1886) was the first important scrip case. The Pennsylvania Supreme Court invoked liberty to contract in overturning a statute that outlawed scrip payment. The judges described the law as "an insulting attempt to put the laborer under a legislative tutelage which is not only degrading to his manhood, but subversive of his rights as a citizen of the United States. He may sell his labor as he sees fit."[49] Through the 1880s and the early 1890s state supreme courts regularly cited *Godcharles*. Judge Adam Snyder of the West Virginia Supreme Court in 1889 condemned all scrip laws as attempts "to degrade the intelligence, virtue, and manhood of the American laborer, and hoist upon the people a paternal government of the most objectionable character, because it assumes that the employer is a knave, and the laborer an imbecile."[50]

By the turn of the century, however, courts had reversed themselves, recognizing, as in other areas of protective legislation, that scrip laws were acceptable because the parties in the contractual relationship were not on equal ground. State judges in Indiana, Tennessee, West Virginia, Rhode Island, and Massachusetts approved a variety of payroll-regulating measures. The U.S. Supreme Court, in *Knoxville Iron Co.* v. *Harbison* (1901), contributed additional impetus to the movement by validating the legislative power to set standards for paying and computing the wages of workers.

State courts eventually embraced minimum-wage legislation for women but not men, with the most intense litigation during and after World War I. After initial reversals in New York (1901), Indiana (1903), and Nebraska (1914), the pendulum swung in the other direction. As judges accepted the principle that legislatures could fix the hours of women's work, which obviously affected wages, they gradually acknowledged that women's wages could be fixed directly. Judges in Oregon, Minnesota, Arkansas, Washington, and Massachusetts between 1914 and 1920 sustained minimum-wage laws for women, on the basis that the physical condition of women required special legislative protection through the police powers. No such provisions extended to men, however.

The U.S. Supreme Court, in *Bunting* v. *Oregon,* accepted tacitly that states might indirectly regulate wages by placing a penalty of extra pay for overtime work, but when the issue of wage regulation was posed directly to them, they were intransigent. The majority on the high court clung to the doctrine of freedom to contract in minimum-wage cases, and in *Adkins* v. *Children's Hospital* (1923) the justices struck down a federal wage provision for women. Only at the end of the New Deal did the Court reverse its position and did state and federal minimum-wage laws for male and female workers pass constitutional muster. Still, "in the field of minimum-wage regulation, as in regulation of child labor and hours, state courts, after initial hostility, proved more than receptive to the arguments of reformers."[51]

Industrial Accidents and Workers' Compensation

Workers' compensation statutes were the final area of protective legislation treated by the courts. By 1910 some six states had passed some form of compulsory workers' compensation. These laws established government-operated workers' compensation insurance pools that required employers either to subscribe to the public plan or to provide comparable private insurance coverage. Employers were immune from liability for those accidents covered under the plans.

The initial response to these measures was harshly critical. In the most famous case, *Ives* v. *South Buffalo Ry. Co.* (1911), the New York Court of Appeals overturned that state's workers' compensation statute, denying that the police powers of the states permitted such legislation. Progressive reformers denounced the decision, and the business community, now persuaded of the value of the legislation, protested lustily as well, going so far as to urge Congress to pass a federal compensation statute.

The *Ives* decision, however, was an isolated event. A few months later the Washington Supreme Court upheld a statute nearly identical to the one overturned in *Ives*. The supreme courts of Wisconsin, Massachusetts, Montana, and Ohio quickly ratified additional legislation. Even in Texas (1915), where part of a plan was held invalid, the judges of the Court of Civil Appeals, did not deny the state legislature's authority to pass it. In 1915, the New York Court of Appeals, following the passage of an amendment to the state constitution by an angry electorate, upheld a law virtually identical to that struck down in *Ives*.

The U.S. Supreme Court in 1917 added its support. The high court in 1908 had invalidated the first Federal Employer Liability Act as overly broad, then four years later resoundingly approved a revised measure. The justices, moreover, accepted arguments made by the states that they had sufficient authority under the police powers to pass compensation acts. In three separate cases, the Court in 1917 sustained state laws and rejected arguments made against them based on freedom to contract and substantive due-process doctrines.

Unions and the Courts

Judge Lemuel Shaws' opinion in *Commonwealth* v. *Hunt* (Massachusetts, 1842) held that labor unions were not criminal conspiracies, but most courts continued to cast a jaundiced eye on unions and their major activities of picketing, striking, and boycotting. Unions became associated with radicalism (even anarchism), and courts tended to treat them as ongoing threats to public order, even when legislatures recognized them as legitimate.

The judiciary applied two important legal tools against organized labor. First, courts consistently invoked liberty to contract in striking down legislation supportive of unions. For example, Judge Magruder of Illinois declared unconstitutional a law that required contractors on public-works projects to hire only laborers belonging to unions. The U.S. Supreme Court added its voice. In *Adair* v. *United States* (1908), the justices overturned the Erdman Act, which declared illegal "yellow dog" contracts (in which employees promised as a condition of employment not to join a union) on railroads. In *Coppage* v. *Kansas* (1915) the justices invalidated a similar state law, with Justice Mahlon Pitney declaring that "there must and will be inequalities of fortune. [I]t is from the nature of things impossible to uphold freedom of contract and the right of private property without at the same time recognizing as legitimate those inequalities."[52]

The injunction was the second device employed by the courts to limit union power. An injunction is an order by a court to some person to stop them from doing something. Injunctions operate on persons and not things, and the injunction can be issued quickly and, because it is an equitable instead of a legal remedy, without a jury trial. Union members who failed to obey an injunction to cease picketing or other activities were subject to summary punishment, including imprisonment, for acting in contempt of court.

The first labor injunction was probably issued in 1880 by a New York court against strikers at the Johnston Harvester Company. Thereafter, the cases "grew in volume like a rolling snowball." [53] The most celebrated labor injunction case involved Eugene V. Debs, president of the American Railway Union, and the leader of the great Pullman strike of 1894. Debs refused to heed an injunction issued by federal District Court Judge Peter Grosscup of Illinois to desist from obstructing the nation's railroads. The bloody rioting surrounding the strike only subsided when federal troops took charge of the railroad yards in Chicago. Debs went to jail for six months, and the Supreme Court, in *In Re Debs* (1895), affirmed Grosscup's contempt action, making Debs a martyr to the cause of labor and fomenting great agitation within the organized labor movement against the federal judiciary.

Some states attempted to pull the teeth of the injunctive power by passing legislation prohibiting its use. A 1915 Massachusetts statute, which the American Federation of Labor considered a "model labor law," provided that a person's labor should be construed as a personal rather than a property right and that no injunction should issue in labor matters. [54] The Supreme Judicial Court of Massachusetts in *Bogni* v. *Perotti* (1916) invalidated the law, relying on liberty to contract to do so. "The right to make contracts to earn money by labor," the judges declared, "is at least as essential to the laborer as is any property right to other members of society." [55]

Federal judges also invoked injunctive authority under the guise of the Sherman Act, which they applied to unions as well as corporations. Judge Edward C. Billings, of the federal District Court of Louisiana, in *United States* v. *Workingmen's Amalgamated Council of New Orleans* (1893), was the first judge to grant a labor injunction under the Sherman Act. Although the Sherman Act nowhere mentioned labor unions, Billings inferred, probably correctly, that its framers had intended for it to include labor. Other federal judges extended Billings's approach, and the Supreme Court held in *Lowe* v. *Lawlor* (1908) that secondary boycotts (in which a union blocked the sale of goods to nonunion members) was an illegal restraint of trade. Although the major Progressive antitrust law, the Clayton Act (1914), specifically limited the use of injunctions against labor and provided for trial by jury in contempt proceedings, subsequent judicial rulings weakened its authority.

Judicial Response to Industrialization

The common law typically operates after the fact. It resounds to, rather than anticipates, new situations and new institutions. Litigants have to bring cases; counsel for them have to offer arguments about how to square precedents with new social conditions. In this sense, industrialization brought about a dramatic surge in the demands placed on the federal and state appellate judiciaries. The business of the courts mirrored the economic and social changes wrought by industrialization, and appellate judges continued to fulfill their historical role of allocating the costs, risks, and benefits of economic development while protecting individual property rights under a written constitution. They also, however, acquired new authority, invoking it through a revamped power of judicial review by which they considered the substantive consequences of legislation as well as the issue of whether legislative bodies had the constitutional authority to act, especially through the police powers, to adjust the effects of industrialization.

The courts exercised their more extensive authority with some ambivalence, and judges on the same courts often mixed formalist and instrumentalist conceptions of the proper judicial role. The industrial world was a reality, and judges gave far broader discretion to legislatures than historians have usually recognized. As important, judges began to recognize that extrajudicial materials could be useful in understanding the intentions of legislators and in coming to grips with the social implications of the law in action. But the judiciary clung to the notion that they had a special responsibility to protect traditional economic rights and, with the help of counsel and law writers such as Cooley and Tiedeman, they fashioned the doctrines of substantive due process of law and freedom to contract. These doctrines were judicial expressions of the laissez-faire mentality that pervaded, but never completely controlled, American social and economic thought between the Civil War and World War I. The judiciary before the Great Depression of the 1930s only gradually and incompletely recognized the breadth of social and economic change that swirled about it. Yet the currents of change in legal thought, in sources of authority for judicial opinions, in the nature of the judicial role, and in economic organization that were underway during these years culminated with the New Deal at another turning point in the legal history of the United States.

13

Cultural Pluralism, Total War, and the Formation of Modern Legal Culture: 1917–1945

In the first half of the twentieth century, the United States burst onto the world stage. The nation in World Wars I and II plunged into armed conflicts of such magnitude that the federal government completely mobilized the nation's human, economic, and patriotic resources. Developments abroad complemented the Progressives' insistence that, in many areas of domestic affairs, the federal government was best able to formulate public policy for an increasingly interdependent and culturally diverse society. The nation had become culturally pluralistic at the same time that it became more deeply involved in world affairs. Between 1870 and 1914, the nation's ethnic and religious makeup became increasingly rich. More than 25 million immigrants from southeastern Europe and Russia spilled ashore; most of them were unskilled laborers destined for the nation's industries. The political, personal, and religious practices of these new immigrants frightened much of the native-born white population. Their anxiety fueled a nativist movement that sought to perpetuate existing cultural values against the foreign born and, during the 1920s, in a revived Ku Klux Klan. The Klan broadened its attack to include Jews, Catholics, and the foreign born and proclaimed a slogan of "native, white, Protestant supremacy."[1]

During World War I and, to a lesser extent World War II, cultural tensions and national security converged. Faced with an unprecedented military threat, national and state lawmakers censored political discourse and quashed dissenters and radicals. During World War I, these measures fell with particular severity on ethnic groups, which had become closely identified in the public mind with labor agitation and un-American political "isms": socialism, anarchism, and communism. Following the attack on Pearl Harbor in 1941, the federal government directed its power toward the Japanese-Americans.

Modern civil liberties were born in these years. Civil liberties refers to legal guarantees, mostly under the First Amendment to the Constitution, that protect individuals against governmental interference with religious belief, speech, press, and association.

Modern civil rights also had their origins in the racial conflict of these decades. Civil rights refers to the legal protection that individuals enjoy against injury, discrimination, and denial of rights by private persons and by government. Civil rights are usually thought of in terms of the social and economic pursuits of everyday living.[2]

Like nativism, racism had been an established feature of life in the United States. The two great wars, however, spurred demographic changes with broad implications for race relations. The growth of defense industries in the North and the West drew blacks out of the agricultural South. Between 1915 and 1918, some 450,000 blacks trekked to northern cities in search of industrial jobs that they seldom had access to in peacetime. Blacks also served in the armed forces, albeit in segregated units, and their participation, especially in World War II, gave them a claim written in blood to fuller political and social equality.

Nativism, racism, and national security converged in such a way as to raise anew the meaning of the rule of law and to reshape values within the legal culture. By the end of World War II, that culture was cast in its modern form, which featured private associations (the American Civil Liberties Union and the National Association for the Advancement of Colored People) seeking to promote civil liberties and civil rights, a professionalized bar and criminal justice system, and a federal government significantly more involved than ever before in the lives of its citizens.

Cultural Conflict and Social Control

Immigration Restriction

The adoption of federal restrictions on immigration in the early twentieth century was a dramatic departure from past practices. Congress passed no significant immigration legislation until after the Civil War. In 1875 it barred the entry of "women for the purposes of prostitution" and "criminals whose sentence has been remitted on condition of emigration."[3] Seven years later the Chinese, at the urging of Western labor leaders, were excluded, and in 1902 the ban on both Chinese immigration and citizenship became permanent. Congress in 1891 had imposed additional requirements on all immigrants, excluding the insane, criminals, polygamists, paupers, and "persons suffering from a loathsome or dangerous contagious disease."[4]

In 1903 immigration policy took a decidedly political turn from which it has never retreated. Congress reacted to the assassination of President William McKinley by a foreign-born self-proclaimed anarchist by requiring an inspection of the political opinions of applicants. The law permitted immigration inspectors to exclude "anarchists, or persons who believe in or advocate the overthrow by force and violence of the Government of the United States . . . or the assassination of public officials."[5] Concerns about political radicalism fused with fears of racial pollution of the native population, a theme trumpeted by the eugenics movement at the turn of the century. Even the respected Progressive labor economist John R. Commons warned that stricter immigration policies were in order, because the traditional open door to European immigrants threatened the United States with "race suicide."[6]

Nativist sentiments and national security anxieties begat additional restrictions during World War I. In 1917 Congress imposed a literacy test for all immigrants, but the requirement proved insignificant; would-be immigrants willingly learned enough of a language to pass the examination. The high unemployment immediately following World War I encouraged further restrictive measures, culminating in the most important immigration measure of the twentieth century, the National Origins Act of 1924. This racist statute limited immigration to 2 percent of each nationality as reflected in the 1890 census, a cutoff date that hit hard at immigrants from southeastern Europe and Russia. The annual rate of immigration fell to 164,000 in 1924 in comparison with more than 800,000 who had entered in the fiscal year ending 1921. These ceilings were lowered even further in 1929, and in 1931, with the Depression underway, more foreigners left the United States than entered.

Control of Radicals

Equally far-reaching consequences for the civil liberties of all Americans flowed from the convergence in wartime of nativist sentiments with fever-pitch patriotism. During the nineteen months of U.S. participation in World War I, the administration of President Woodrow Wilson sought to curb dissent directed toward the government's wartime policies. These policies struck a sympathetic public chord, in part because they connected political radicalism to the foreign born. The administration justified these measures, as would its successors, by insisting that a war had to be won, and temporary limitations on civil liberties would hasten victory.

The administration relied on the Espionage Act of 1917 and the amendment made to it in early 1918, the Sedition Act. The Espionage Act contained two principal censorship provisions. First, the act made it a felony to attempt to cause insubordination in the armed forces, to interfere with the operation of the draft, and to convey false statements about the military with the intent of disrupting their operations. Second, the act permitted the postmaster to ban treasonable or seditious material from the mail.

Congress directed the Sedition Act against pacifist groups, vocal labor leaders, and radicals, especially members of the Communist party. The law made it a felony, among other things, to "disrupt or discourage recruiting or enlistment service, or utter, print, or publish disloyal, profane, scurrilous, or abusive language about the form of government."[7] The law threw a legal collar around radicals, and granted broad enforcement powers to the attorney general.

The states also developed loyalty programs, and these too rested on nativist sentiments. When World War I broke out, state leaders, "[a]ware of the value of public identification with patriotism and loyalty in a period of national hysteria," rushed through measures directed at radical labor and religious groups long considered troublesome by the native-born majority. Eleven states passed sedition statutes that punished various kinds of opposition to the war, and state leaders applied these laws with special zeal against the foreign-language press.[8] Four other states, where the Industrial Workers of the World (a radical labor group with strong connections in the foreign community) was active, passed criminal syndicalism laws. These statutes made it a crime to advocate or to bring about the overthrow of the industrial order.

Through the enforcement of these and related "security" measures, government poked its nose into the behavior of native as well as foreign-born opponents of the war. Postmaster General Albert S. Burleson, for example, required all foreign-language newspapers to submit for the Post Office Department's approval literal translations of all news and editorial articles that contained material on the government, the policies of the belligerent powers, or the conduct of the war. When an editor, such as socialist Victor Berger of the *Milwaukee Leader,* refused to cooperate, Burleson revoked second-class postage privileges and undertook prosecution in the federal courts. The editors of German-language papers quickly learned to print nothing but praise for the government's wartime policies.

Wartime hysteria etched with nativism encouraged extralegal violations of civil liberties. Some were silly, but others were deadly. The Austrian-born violinist, Fritz Kreisler, and the famous Swiss-born conductor of the Boston Symphony, Dr. Karl Muck, were denied access to American music halls. In Columbus, Ohio schoolteachers met after school to paste into school music books blank sheets of paper covering "The Watch on the Rhine" and "The Lorelei." Five hundred citizens of Collinsville, Illinois, who had decided that a fellow townsman, Roger Prager, was a German spy, dragged him into the street, wrapped him in the American flag, and then murdered him.[9]

The Red Scare, Sacco and Vanzetti, and Prohibition

In 1919 and 1920, the fear of foreign radicals reached a fever pitch in the so-called Red Scare. The Communist International, an organization established in the Soviet Union in 1919 to export revolution to the rest of the world, made Americans begin to see radicals everywhere.

Wilson's attorney general, A. Mitchell Palmer, established an antiradicalism division in the Department of Justice and assigned a young attorney, J. Edgar Hoover, to oversee its operation. Based on intelligence gathered by Hoover, Palmer in late 1919 and early 1920 raided the headquarters of suspected revolutionaries and subversives, most of whom were not U.S. citizens. The largest of these raids occurred on January 2, 1920, in which Palmer rounded up over six thousand radicals, searching homes and offices without warrants, holding persons without specific charges, and denying them access to legal counsel. Lacking the protection of U.S. citizenship, hundreds were deported from the country.

Other events in the 1920s kept alive the fear of foreign subversion and radicalism. For example, in May 1920 at the height of the Red Scare, Nicola Sacco, a shoemaker, and Bartolomeo Vanzetti, a fish peddler, were arrested for the robbery and murder of a shoe company paymaster in South Braintree, Massachusetts. Both were Italian aliens; both had evaded the draft and were self-proclaimed anarchists. Although the guilt of Sacco and Vanzetti is still hotly debated, there is little doubt that their fate symbolized the cultural conflict of the era. The unjust conduct of their trial was a source of international controversy for the next seven years, with Harvard Law School Professor Felix Frankfurter, among others, providing legal aid to the convicts. Their appeals exhausted, both men were executed in the electric chair on August 23, 1927.

Like the fate of Sacco and Vanzetti, national prohibition had great "symbolic" importance amid the cultural conflict of the era.[10] It was an extravagant appeal to legal authority and governmental machinery in the interests of cultural hegemony. Behind prohibition were old-line, rural, and Protestant Americans bent on imposing their cultural values on newly arrived immigrants, the working class, Catholics, and urbanites. The Eighteenth Amendment to the Constitution went into effect on January 16, 1920. It did not forbid people from drinking, but prohibited the manufacture, transport, and sale of intoxicating liquor. In the intense anti-German hysteria of World War I, the fact that many breweries had German names (e.g., Pabst and Busch) contributed to the amendment drive.

The amendment was a classic example of the interaction of state and federal constitutional development. By 1919 two-thirds of the states had already passed bans on liquor, but the ultimate success of liquor restriction depended on national control through the federal government. Prohibitionists believed that the national government alone could bring order out of cultural diversity. Historically, the police powers had been reserved to the states, but the prohibition amendment intruded so fully on that established pattern that critics unsuccessfully urged the U.S. Supreme Court to declare it unconstitutional as a violation of the Tenth Amendment. Congress in the Progressive era had already asserted the concept of a federal police power, and the Supreme Court in *Rhode Island* v. *Palmer* (1920) upheld the amendment and the Volstead Act, which implemented the amendment, as fully encompassed by the emerging concept of the federal police powers.

The "noble experiment" of prohibition was at once evidence of the growing role of the federal government and of its limits as an agent of national social control. Prohibition was a costly failure, and the onset of the Depression hastened its repeal. With the economy faltering badly, a revitalized Democratic party, which depended on ethnic voters, embraced repeal. Furthermore, the federal government was simply unable to enforce the measure effectively. Proponents of repeal also argued that liquor production would provide new jobs, and on December 5, 1933 the Twenty-First Amendment, the only amendment ever to be directly ratified by popular conventions (which circumvented state legislatures apportioned in favor of rural areas), supplanted the Eighteenth.

The Smith Act and the Relocation of Japanese-Americans

Yet cultural tensions, if somewhat dampened, remained an important source of social conflict and a basis on which the federal government extended its authority. Typical of developments were the Smith Act (1940) and the relocation of Japanese-Americans following the bombing of Pearl Harbor.

With war raging in Europe, Congress in March 1940 reenacted the Espionage Act of 1917, with increased penalties for peacetime violation. Congress added additional muscle, however, through the Alien Registration Act of June 1940, also known as the Smith Act, after its author, Congressman Howard Smith of Virginia. The measure was directed primarily at Communists, because Communist sabotage (Hitler had not yet invaded the Soviet Union) of defense industries was considered a genuine threat. The measure made it illegal not only to conspire to overthrow the government but to advocate or conspire to advocate its overthrow. Nearly five million aliens were registered and fingerprinted within a few months, although Attorney General Robert H. Jackson exercised "great caution and tact in insisting that such actions be taken sympathetically and with solicitude for the rights and feelings of those so handled."[11] Still, by the end of the 1940s, the Smith Act became the backbone of the federal government's efforts to root out communism.

A combination of racism, nativism, and wartime security concerns combined to bring about the forced removal of Japanese-Americans from their homes in 1942. On the afternoon of the Japanese attack on Pearl Harbor on December 7, 1941, President Roosevelt issued a proclamation that made German, Italian, and Japanese aliens "deemed dangerous to the public peace or safety of the United States" subject to "summary apprehension."[12] By mid-February 1942 at the end of the alien roundup under this proclamation, more than three thousand Japanese on the mainland and in Hawaii had been arrested. (The better-assimilated German and Italian ethnic communities were left untouched.) This number included almost 10 percent of the adult males among Japanese aliens on the West Coast. One of the reasons the government was able to act as quickly as it did was that since 1932 the agency that became the Federal Bureau of Investigation (the same agency that had overseen the Palmer Raids) and military intelligence had maintained surveillance over Japanese deemed "subversive."[13]

The program might have stopped there had it not been for the continuing military setbacks suffered by the United States in the Pacific and the anxiety of the white elite business and political establishment of California. A tougher policy toward the remaining Japanese-Americans emerged gradually and amid considerable opposition during the first six months of the war. For example, General John L. De Witt, the commander of U.S. forces on the West Coast, thought that the initial roundup and the establishment of restrictive areas around military facilities would suffice. The Department of Justice thought a strategy of total removal was unnecessary and constitutionally flawed.

Prejudice existed against the 112,000 people of Japanese descent living on the West Coast. Two-thirds of them were citizens, and "more would clearly have been, if they had not been barred by the federal naturalization laws."[14] The Japanese in California were successful and skilled agricultural workers, truck gardeners, and small-business operators; their prosperity, in the midst of general economic depression, bred white resentment. California political leaders, including Governor Earl Warren (later to become chief justice of the United States), joined with white pioneer fraternal groups, such as the Native Sons of the Golden West, to mount a vigorous campaign for immediate evacuation. The War Department agreed, General De Witt changed his mind, and in the name of national security they successfully urged on President Franklin D. Roosevelt a massive program of forced relocation. Without discussion with his cabinet and based on his inherent presidential powers, the president on February 19, 1942 issued Executive Order 9066, directing the relocation of all Japanese-Americans (including U.S. citizens) from the West Coast to relocation camps in such places as Jerome, Arkansas and Heart Mountain, Wyoming.

The relocation of the Japanese-Americans was "the most drastic invasion of the rights of citizens of the United States by their own government . . . in the history of the nation."[15] They suffered not only great personal trauma and hardship, but frequently heavy financial losses. They were forced to dispose of their land, homes, stores, and personal property almost overnight. Some of the young men among them joined the armed services and went to fight with great valor in Europe.

The Crime Control Decades

The ethnic and racial diversity of U.S. cities, prohibition, and high unemployment brought on by the Depression posed new challenges to the criminal justice system. The period from World War I through World War II comprised the "crime control decades," and here too the federal government expanded its legal authority.[16]

Racial Rioting and the Criminal Justice System

The influx of blacks into northern cities often created racial tensions that sometimes exploded into violence. In 1919 and, less so, in 1943 urban race rioting spread across the nation. These riots stemmed from competition between blacks and white ethnic groups for jobs, housing, and recreational facilities. White aggression was followed by black retaliation. One of the worst disorders of the World War I period occurred in Chicago in 1919 when a white mob killed a black youth who had crossed the unofficial color line that divided swimming areas on Lake Michigan. Over the next four days a general melee ensued, with gangs of white youths, many of them Irish, sweeping into the black ghettos. Thirty-eight people (twenty-three black) died. In the case of the Chicago riot, as well as others at about the same time in Omaha, East St. Louis (Illinois), Knoxville, and Washington, D.C., the police carried out "[d]iscriminatory law enforcement" that "contributed to racial tensions leading up to the outbreak of violence."[17] In the face of overwhelming police racism, nothing was done in the wake of these World War I riots to improve police–community relations.

Similar rioting occurred during World War II in northern, midwestern, and western cities. In Los Angeles, for example, the so-called Zoot Suit riot, named after the fashionable teenage dress of the day, involved a three-way clash between Mexican-Americans, white servicemen, and the Los Angeles police. The worst riot, however, was in Detroit in 1943, where since 1940 the white population had grown by 440,000 persons and the black population by 50,000. Competition for jobs, housing, and public transportation was intense and often fought along racial lines, even in the midst of war. The Detroit riot began on a hot summer afternoon and lasted two days, throwing the entire city into chaos and leaving thirty-four people dead and more than $2 million worth of property destroyed.

Police and community leaders determined in the wake of the World War II riots to improve race and community–police relations. Racism persisted, but the need for social cooperation during wartime, a growing sense of police professionalism, and the new strength of black leaders in northern cities contributed to the movement. The program received a particularly strong boost in California, where Governor Earl Warren sponsored an official inquiry into the rioting and the means to better race relations. One of the products of Warren's efforts was *A Guide to Race Relations for Police Officers* (1946), which became a model for other states and cities trying to improve race relations, riot control, and the police role in the ghetto. These enlightened programs, which seemed to promise that the rule of law had to be enforced on a color-blind basis, fell short of success. Departments were reluctant to hire black officers, and, as suburbanization after the war left the core of major cities to blacks, predominately white police forces became estranged from the people who suffered most from crime.

Ethnicity, Crime, and the Criminal Justice System

The ethnic composition of U.S. cities also had an impact on the criminal justice system. Urban crime and the criminal justice system were rooted in the city's "ethnic neighborhoods and were means of social mobility for persons of marginal social and economic position in society."[18] In Chicago in 1930, for example, ethnic groups dominated the city's underworld, and they also filled important criminal justice posts. Of the police captains 76 percent were Irish, and almost all pickpockets were Jewish. Municipal and criminal court judges were drawn predominately from Catholic, Jewish, and European immigrant groups. They had taken advantage of the opportunities offered in night law schools in the city to gain admittance to the bar and they ascended to the bench in party-controlled judicial elections.

The criminal justice system most frequently snared unorganized offenders such as juvenile delinquents, wife beaters, and drunkards. But organized crime, with its ethnic identification, captured public attention.

Organized crime involved labor racketeering and the distribution and sale of illegal goods and services, such as narcotics, gambling, and prostitution. It was a business. Crime leaders had to make a substantial capital investment, organize a regular payroll, and build customer loyalty. In the more corrupt cities, such as Chicago, illicit earnings poured into the campaigns of city officials and the bank accounts of police officers. There was nothing new about this connection between vice, crime, and political and police corruption. Similar practices had flourished in every major U.S. city during the nineteenth century. The difference was that what had been a small business then became a big business in the first third of the twentieth century.

The key to this transformation was the Eighteenth Amendment. Passed with the best of intentions, the amendment made illegal something that millions of Americans wanted, and may actually have made alcohol more attractive by making it forbidden. It worked, at least to the extent that it dramatically cut per capita alcoholic consumption. That success was purchased at a steep price. Prohibition opened up a business of enormous profit potential, and organized crime rushed in to provide the service. By the late 1920s, urban crime syndicates enjoyed revenues of more than $100 million a year. With the rewards so great, urban warlords engaged in mind-numbing violence. Between 1923 and 1926, for example, "Chicago criminals murdered an estimated 215 of their colleagues, . . . while the police killed another 160 suspected gangsters."[19] In 1929, Al Capone, the most famous mobster of the twentieth century, consolidated his control of the city's crime syndicates with the brutal St. Valentine's Day massacre.

The exploits of Capone and other mobsters, along with the fear engendered by the Great Depression, heightened the public sense of a collapse in law and order. Crime rates grew gradually during the 1920s, and accelerated more briskly during the 1930s, prompting the federal government, states, and cities to form crime commissions. In 1921, for example, Cleveland recruited Roscoe Pound, a proponent of sociological jurisprudence, and Felix Frankfurter to assist in a far-reaching study of the criminal justice system. *Criminal Justice in Cleveland* (1922) drew on sociological insights in reporting that the system was nearly in collapse. It concluded that a discretionary system of justice, in which plea bargaining was a central feature, had undermined public confidence. Similar studies in Missouri (1926) and Illinois (1929) reflected disillusionment, with most of the criticism leveled at parole and the basic assumptions behind the ideal of individual rehabilitation.

Most reformers came from outside the ethnic and racial ghettos in which crime was rooted. They only dimly grasped the dynamics of crime in an increasingly heterogeneous society. Their moral values "were not shared by a number of their fellow citizens and their legal values were not shared by politicians and officials."[20] Gambling, liquor, and even prostitution were accepted in many ethnic and black neighborhoods, and the police were under relatively little pressure to enforce vice laws on a daily basis. These conditions did not mean that there was an absence of concern with commercialized vice, saloons, crime, and official corruption. There was concern, but the criminal underworld (by virtue of its secure position in the social structure of major cities) was simply better equipped to manipulate the criminal justice system than were reformers (who were from outside that social structure) to impose change on it.

Federal Government and Crime

The seriousness of the crime problem combined with the inability of local officials to cope with it led to increased involvement by the national government. President Herbert Hoover in 1929 created the Wickersham Commission (named after Attorney General George Wickersham, who chaired it) to conduct the first "comprehensive survey of American criminal justice at the national level."[21] Roscoe Pound was also a member of the commission, and he once again brought his sociological perspective to bear on the problem of crime. The commission was charged, among other tasks, with determining whether, given the level of gangland violence, repeal of Prohibition was in order. The commission failed to resolve the Prohibition issue and most of its fourteen volumes received little attention as the effects of the Great Depression rolled over the country.

The commission's findings were nonetheless important in two ways. First, by directing public and police attention to the use of "third-degree" interrogation tactics against criminal suspects, the commission lent the imprimatur of federal authority to more professional (and legal) police practices. Second, in the midst of skepticism heaped at the local level on the rehabilitative ideal, the commission endorsed a sociological perspective on criminal behavior that reaffirmed the importance of individualized correctional treatment. The commission condemned the existing prison system and urged probation and parole as the only rational and humane solution to the problems of crime. The Wickersham Commission's report marked the beginning of yet another cycle of correctional reform, one that peaked in the 1960s.

The penetration of the federal government into criminal justice matters occurred in other ways. For example, through the efforts of Sanford Bates, whom President Hoover in 1929 appointed to head the new U.S. Bureau of Prisons, the federal correctional system set the standard by which state programs were judged over the next half-century.

Growing populations in federal prisons resulted from expanded federal jurisdiction and enforcement. A mobile society made crime a national problem that local and state governments alone were helpless to solve. Progressives relied on an enhanced conception of the federal police power to permit Congress to criminalize the movement of lottery tickets and stolen automobiles in interstate commerce. During the 1930s, for example, it passed the "Lindbergh Law" (1932) making kidnapping a federal offense, the Fugitive Felon Law (1933) making it a federal crime to cross state lines to avoid prosecution, the Interstate Theft Act (1934) expanding federal control over the interstate transportation of stolen goods, and the Marijuana Tax Act (1937) establishing penalties for the sale and possession of the drug.

The FBI in Peace and War

New and vigorous enforcement machinery accompanied this expansion of federal criminal jurisdiction. President Theodore Roosevelt in 1908 asked Congress to create a federal detective force within the Department of Justice to enforce federal gambling and prostitution statutes. Congress refused to act, fearing, among other concerns, that its members would become subject to intimidation through investigation. Roosevelt, when Congress adjourned, created the new Bureau of Investigation (it became the Federal Bureau of Investigation in 1935) by executive order. In 1924, Attorney General Harlan Fiske Stone named J. Edgar Hoover, a little-known bureaucrat, director of the bureau, and under his leadership it flourished.[22]

Hoover had a genuine gift for promoting the bureau by enhancing the federal role in police matters. He won a major victory in 1930 when Congress gave the bureau responsibility for administering the new Uniform Crime Reports (UCR). These yearly reports on criminal activity composed the first national crime records system. It suffered from serious flaws, most notably its emphasis on "crimes known to police" and the lack of auditing procedures so serious as to present "a distorted picture of criminal activity."[23] Nonetheless, the UCR became the authoritative source of information on criminal activity for the next four decades, and through it the FBI called public and professional attention to the behavior of local police forces.

The FBI contributed to the professionalization of local police operations in other ways. It set a national standard for law enforcement officers by intensively training its own agents in the most modern police methods. In 1935, the bureau opened the National Police Academy training center, and since then tens of thousands of police officers have received training much beyond that provided by local forces. The bureau also gave great emphasis to scientific criminal detection, and the crime laboratory it opened in 1932 accepted samples of blood, cloth, and hair for analysis from throughout the country. The crime lab became the center of criminal identification through the use of fingerprints. This system had reached the United States in 1904, but the FBI in the early 1930s embarked on a campaign to collect and centralize as many fingerprints as possible. Between 1930 and 1974, the bureau gathered more than 158 million separate prints.

The bureau also reinforced the tendency in local police operations to rely on a military leadership structure. Police departments from throughout the nation copied the strong executive style of leadership Hoover exercised over the bureau. To be compared favorably with the FBI was for local police forces a high and much sought-after compliment. The military style laid heavy stress on weapons training, and "for the first time in their history the American police fully embraced a military mentality, complete with the ideology of a 'war' on crime and the weaponry to carry it out."[24]

The bureau also became deeply involved in dealing with matters of internal subversion. In 1934 President Franklin D. Roosevelt ordered the FBI to investigate various German-American groups. As in World War I, concern about "internal security" rationalized investigation and surveillance of suspect groups with ethnic and racial ties. Hoover correctly understood that the bureau's role in coordinating antiespionage and counterintelligence work would further enhance its reputation publicly and its power within the growing federal bureaucracy. The passage of the Smith Act in 1940 allowed the FBI to target Communists as well as Fascists. These intelligence gathering activities furthered the development of the national security state initiated during World War I.

The necessity of the bureau was beyond dispute, but Hoover badly abused the sensitive power entrusted to him. He developed extensive files on the personal lives of senators, congressmen, cabinet officers, and even presidents, exploiting them in ways that perpetuated his own control over the agency. Hoover became, as some members of Congress feared at the bureau's creation, an "institutional vigilante—a government within the government."[25]

The Bar and Pluralist Culture

As with the criminal justice system, the bar was also shaped by the social tensions associated with national security, nativism, and racism. Lawyers were at once part of the larger world of social and economic change and of a smaller subculture preoccupied with narrow professional concerns. The elite of the bar, through the ABA and state bar groups, pounded on the theme of reform, but their proposals had differing consequences depending on one's ethnic, racial, and economic standing. The organized bar, as the professional embodiment of the rule of law, also had a special responsibility to provide leadership when civil liberties and civil rights were under attack, a challenge that it seldom met. At the same time, other lawyers, animated by a strong sense of rights consciousness, attempted to deal with the new threats to individual liberty, carrying forth the tradition of moral and social change pioneered through the legal instrumentalism of the antislavery bar.

Professionalism and Its Implications

During the 1920s, "a sprawling, stratified [legal] profession" was transformed in structure and values: from individualism to organization, from apprenticeship to formal training, from advocacy to counseling, and from the "disruptive fluidity of the late nineteenth century to the uncertain stability of the twentieth century."[26] The ABA and the AALS, while often disagreeing on substantive reforms, encouraged these developments. Yet the most important powers to set educational and bar examination standards rested with state legislatures. The organized bar, with its elite of corporate lawyers, could urge reforms, but state legislatures were usually sensitive to the demands of their ethnic constituencies for an open and diverse bar. At no time were bar groups permitted to control admission.

The organized bar had a mix of motives in lobbying for tighter standards. Their actions were part "of the far larger movement toward institutionalization, and . . . leaders of the bar . . . were committed to an ethical, educated bar."[27] At its annual meeting in 1921, the ABA first committed itself to a substantial declaration in favor of higher standards. In that year, only fourteen states had any requirements for preliminary general education, and only ten required the equivalent of graduation from high school as a condition of eligibility for bar admission. Improvement was "fast after the

Association's action''; the organized bar's influence counted for something.[28] By 1940 all states required some professional study preparatory to bar admission, and in that year forty states mandated a minimum three years of professional preparation, some of which, depending on the state, could be satisfied through an apprenticeship or clerkship. By 1940, as well, two-thirds of the states required at least two years of college study or its equivalent.

State legislatures, again with the urging of the organized bar, also tightened the bar examination process. By 1940 every state had some system of formal bar examinations, and the National Conference of Bar Examiners, created in 1930, prodded state examiners toward national standards. The bar examinations did exclude impressive percentages of applicants on their first attempt; for example, during the 1930s about 50 percent failed the first examination. But every state permitted reexamination, and when allowance was made for repeaters, about 90 percent of all applicants eventually passed.

Exclusionary sentiments, rooted in racial and ethnic prejudice, lay behind many of these actions. In 1921 Alfred Z. Reed, a nonlawyer member of the Carnegie Foundation, issued a far-reaching report on the status of legal education in the United States based on an extensive survey of day and night law schools. Reed found that the United States of the 1920s was a pluralistic society with diverse legal needs. He also observed that law, like medicine, was a "public profession" in which "practicing lawyers do not merely render to the community a social service, which the community is interested in having them render well. They are part of the governing mechanism of the state.''[29] From this conclusion, Reed argued that the existing diversity in legal education was a strength to be built upon, and that the "public trust" accorded the legal profession could be best realized through lawyers of differing skills and qualifications drawn from and capable of serving the diverse legal constituencies of society.

ABA and AALS leaders received Reed's report coolly, and their actions demonstrated that "professionalism" involved more than improving bar standards. In the first third of the twentieth century, it was a code word that justified racial exclusion and the imposition of quotas on law school admissions. Recent immigrant groups (especially Jews and Italians) and blacks faced obstacles that white and Protestant applicants did not. Through the 1930s, for example, Jews were excluded from the most prestigious of the increasingly powerful (and increasingly large) Wall Street law firms. John W. Davis, perhaps the most influential attorney in the 1930s and 1940s and a managing partner in the New York firm of Davis, Polk, described himself as one of those people "who resent all immigration in general and that of the Russian Jew in particular.''[30] Even the most elite law schools, which did grant admissions to a few Jews, other ethnic Americans, and even a very small number of blacks, suffered from a continuing burden of prejudice. Dean Thomas Swan of the Yale Law School in 1923 argued against using grades as the basis of limiting enrollment to the law school, because such a development would admit students of "foreign" rather than "old American" parentage, and Yale would become a school with an "inferior student body ethically and socially.''[31]

Attempts to impose ethical standards also cut in two directions. The ABA in 1908 adopted its first canons of professional ethics. These canons were an attempt to upgrade the professional and public credibility of lawyers by asking them to affirm their commitment to certain practices. These included canons, widely copied by state bar associations, that prohibited the solicitation of business by circulars and advertising.

These self-regulatory measures doubtless kept the public safe from some unscrupulous attorneys, but they also hindered less well-connected ethnic and black lawyers in establishing themselves. The ban on advertising also kept the practice of law wrapped in mystery and retarded the broad availability of legal services.

Bar integration (compulsory bar association membership) and judicial reform also mixed professional goals and social biases. Progressive reformers, notably Herbert Harley (a lawyer turned newspaper editor), wanted the bar to correct abuses in practice by having the power to discipline their members, including disbarment. The only way to attain a self-policing profession was to require all practicing attorneys to be members of the state bar association, which could then exercise discipline over them. Bar integration, moreover, promised to limit professional competition, and thereby mitigate unethical conduct, and to provide a strong voice by which the bar could lobby for judicial and court reforms. Harley in 1913 organized the American Judicature Society with the twin goals of promoting bar integration and judicial reform.

Cultural conflict plagued both reform measures. For example, the New York state legislature during the 1920s twice considered the matter of enacting laws requiring bar integration, but most elite corporate lawyers from the state's major metropolitan areas, especially New York City, successfully opposed the legislation. William D. Guthrie, a powerful Wall Street lawyer who led the opposition, complained that bar integration only meant that control of the bar would pass to the "large numbers of undesirable members" recruited from the state's "teeming population of recent immigrants." The result, Guthrie concluded, would be "a public clamity."[32]

Bar integration, under these circumstances, made slight headway. The earliest converts were those states—North Dakota (1921), Alabama (1923), Idaho (1923), and New Mexico (1925)—that had a small homogeneous bar unaffected by severe cultural conflict and the rural–urban tension that accompanied it. By 1960 more than one half of the states had adopted an integrated bar, although in most instances state supreme courts, rather than the bar associations, continued to exercise their historical responsibility for disciplining the bar.

Judicial reform of state courts blended a long-standing concern about the role of party politics in judicial elections and a continuing concern that ethnic voters, under the tutelage of party bosses, unduly influenced the composition of the bench. The ideas of Harley and others (most notably Albert M. Kales, a distinguished Chicago lawyer) gradually won acceptance in state legislatures, which saw in the reform of the judicial selection process an opportunity to cleanse the bench.

In 1937, the ABA finally added its endorsement to a proposal by the American Judicature Society for a plan of "merit" judicial selection that combined features of both the elective and appointive systems. Missouri in 1940 was the first state to adopt the plan. It provided for executive appointment for an initial period of service at the end of which the judge stood for election, not against an opponent, but on his or her record. The so-called Missouri plan only gradually made inroads in traditional partisan judicial elections.

The organized bar suffered from the racism that permeated the rest of society. In 1912 the ABA mistakenly admitted three blacks, and when the error was discovered attempts were made to rescind their membership. Moorfield Storey, a past president of the ABA and the first president of the NAACP, denounced the move to oust the black members. A compromise was struck that permitted the three to remain in the association, but required all future applicants to identify themselves by race. The association thereby committed itself to a lily-white membership for the next half-century, "elevating racism above professionalism."[33] The ABA, moreover, maintained silence in the wake of the Palmer raids and the relocation of Japanese-American citizens. The ABA and state bar associations clung with great consistency to the belief that "the rule of law was rooted in a common religious and moral order. This inferred a clear relationship between law and community and a willingness on the part of citizens to subordinate personal interests to the 'common good'."[34]

Challenges to the elite practitioners of the organized bar came on several fronts. The diffuse and diverse American bar, for all of its racism, nativism, and anti-Semitism, had the capacity for growth and change. The ABA included only about one-fifth of the bar during these years (its membership has never risen above one-half of all practicing lawyers), and the new immigrant lawyers as well as many native-born Protestant attorneys believed that the profession had a responsibility to rise to the challenge of defending unpopular and beleaguered individuals. Felix Frankfurter, a Harvard-educated German-Jewish immigrant, declared war on the corporate bar. The ambience after World War I that had permitted the Palmer raids and the executions of Sacco and Vanzetti "pained him."[35] Frankfurter ridiculed ABA President John W. Davis for failing to commit his prestige to "sanity and reason" amid the postwar "lawlessness and intolerance."[36]

Some of the most dissident members of the bar in 1936 formed the National Lawyers' Guild, the first association to challenge the ABA's attempt at professional hegemony. Guild members committed themselves to the realization of civil liberties and civil rights through the affirmative use of legal institutions and government power. The guild was "a true child of the thirties," drawing into its membership black and ethnic lawyers who resented their marginal status and the parochial concerns of the bar.[37] The guild was closely identified with the Communist party, and later the ABA and anticommunist politicians hounded its members so diligently that by the mid-1950s its energies were dissipated in an unsuccessful effort at self-preservation.

The ACLU, the NAACP, and the ILD

An awakening sense of civil rights consciousness lay behind the creation of special-interest litigation groups, which turned to the judicial process to reach goals otherwise denied to them through the regular political process. The American Civil Liberties Union (ACLU) had its origins among the opponents of World War I, who in 1914 had organized the American League for the Limitation of Armaments, which was soon renamed the American Union Against Militarism. Roger Baldwin, a social worker and one of the founders of the union, gave particular attention to the legal needs of conscientious objectors who refused military service. Conservatives in the union objected to Baldwin's activities, and in 1920, after several reorganizations, Baldwin founded the ACLU.

The ACLU organized legal talent on a systematic basis to safeguard individual liberties. The abolitionists of the 1840s and 1850s had undertaken such activity, but they lacked the central organization and careful attention to the legal process that characterized the ACLU's work. The ACLU became a prototype of public-interest litigation groups after World War II. It had in-house counsel to argue important national cases, while it enlisted local members to provide legal assistance and to monitor violations of speech, press, religious freedom, and the rights of the accused.

The NAACP applied a similar scheme to the promotion of black civil rights. The association had its origins with the Niagara Movement, which famed black leader W. E. B. Du Bois founded in 1905. Four years later, a band of blacks and whites, including Moorfield Storey and Du Bois, founded the NAACP. Storey's skills as a litigator and his national prestige proved invaluable. The NAACP organized local branches, as had the ACLU, and relied on them to conduct investigations and to furnish local lawyers who would make preliminary arguments. Storey provided directions about constitutional strategy. He also frequently handled cases on appeal to the Supreme Court, either directly by arguing the case himself or in filing *amicus curiae* (i.e., as a friend of the Court) briefs to support other counsel actually making the argument.

The NAACP adopted a strategy of gradualism, working in steps to build fuller protection of black rights by incremental expansion of the equal-protection clause of the Fourteenth Amendment (against the most blatant forms of segregation) and the Fifteenth Amendment (against state laws disfranchising blacks). Louis Marshall, a prominent Jewish lawyer from New York City who had fought against anti-Semitism in the legal profession, joined Storey as the association's leading litigators.

Storey and Marshall both died in 1929, and their deaths opened a new phase in the history of the NAACP's legal campaign against racism. The association adopted a more aggressive litigation strategy, one based on establishing that separate facilities had to be truly equal. To support its expanded efforts, the association's legal advisory committee, composed of the most distinguished white civil rights and civil liberties lawyers of the era (Clarence Darrow, Arthur Garfield Hays, and Morris Ernst), appealed to the American Fund for Public Service, whose chief administrator was Roger Baldwin, for more than $400,000. Although Baldwin was sympathetic to the NAACP's cause, he also believed that the NAACP placed too much emphasis on change through the law and not enough on direct social action. As a result, the fund awarded the NAACP only a quarter of its request.

With this modest donation, the NAACP created a Legal Defense Fund and hired attorneys to undertake a systematic attack on segregation and disfranchisement. Nathan Margold oversaw the Legal Defense Fund's operations until 1933, when he left to join Franklin Roosevelt's administration. Charles Houston, Jr., the Harvard-trained son of a prominent black attorney from the District of Columbia, then took charge. Houston was dean of the Howard University Law School, where he upgraded the quality of legal education for blacks. Houston, unlike Storey, brought more black lawyers into NAACP cases, including such notable figures as Thurgood Marshall, who became in the 1940s and 1950s the NAACP's chief litigator. Houston and Marshall turned law practice for these black civil rights lawyers into "a mission of consuming social and personal significance."[38]

Like Baldwin, radical lawyers within the Communist party judged the gradualist policies of the NAACP inadequate. The party's concern with blacks was a mix of pragmatism and sentiment. Blacks were a fertile ground for recruitment and the discrimination directed against them was evidence of the nation's corrupt capitalist economy. Blacks were, according to the party, "class war prisoners."[39] The party was never fully persuaded of the wisdom of legal action against the existing political order, but, like the ACLU and the NAACP, it recognized the value of proceeding to its objectives through the courts and laws. In 1925, the party formed the International Labor Defense (ILD) based on support from Communists and non-Communists alike. William L. Patterson, a black attorney from Harlem who had participated in the defense of Sacco and Vanzetti, became the ILD's director in 1932. Patterson's objective was to secure immediate, tangible results for blacks, and many of them found this message appealing in comparison with promises made by other left-wing groups about racial change *after* the class revolution.

Origins of Judicial Protection of Civil Liberties and Civil Rights

Civil Liberties

A majority of public and private leaders of the late nineteenth and early twentieth centuries believed that civil liberties "were only to be protected for those citizens who had demonstrated, both by their attitudes and their behavior, that they were prepared to utilize those freedoms in positive and constructive ways."[40] Growing cultural and racial pluralism, when combined with national security concerns, tested this consensus. Federal and state efforts to muster the nation's patriotic resources during World War I posed unprecedented questions about the constitutional protections accorded civil liberties. The federal judiciary before the war had heard only a few cases, and the case law in the state courts, based on state bills of rights, was only slightly larger. The courts in these few cases had fashioned a restrictive tradition, but the sweep of government efforts in World War I was so extensive that it drew the attention of a small academic elite, most notably Zechariah Chafee, Jr., a Harvard Law School professor and prolific author. Chafee left an indelible stamp on the area of free speech and his major work, *Freedom of Speech* (1920), was perhaps the most influential single book published on the subject in the twentieth century. Through the writings of Chafee and the decisions of federal courts during World War I, the modern law of civil liberties began to take form.

Chafee and other advocates of civil liberties recognized that the entry of the United States into World War I exposed a tension between the rights of citizens, under the First Amendment, to oppose that conflict and the necessities of fighting the war. The American common law adhered to the principle of no prior restraint on speech or writing. After publication, however, the government or a private person (relying on the law of libel) could seek through a lawsuit to demonstrate injury. In order to prove injury it was necessary to show a "proximate" (i.e., a direct relationship) between what was spoken and written and the damage done. In theory, simply proving that the material had a "bad tendency" was not enough. In practice, however, judges had taken a broad view of proximate causation and had been sensitive to protecting the public welfare. It was against this tradition that Chafee argued. Justice Oliver Wendell Holmes, Jr., for example, held in *Patterson* v. *Colorado* (1907) that anyone uttering words dangerous to the public interest was susceptible to punishment.

During and after World War I, the Supreme Court had to take account of not only the First Amendment's meaning but also the extent of its application. Since the early nineteenth century, the Supreme Court had held that the Bill of Rights applied only against the federal government and not the states. The ACLU and Chafee wanted to expand the protection of the Bill of Rights through incorporation of it in the due-process clause of the Fourteenth Amendment. Incorporation meant that the national authority of the federal judiciary could be brought to bear in supporting unpopular minorities (such as dissidents and radicals) against local majorities. Incorporation, of course, had no relevance where a federal statute was in question.

The Court endorsed the federal government's wartime security measures. In *Schenck* v. *United States* (1919), the justices upheld the military censorship provisions of the Espionage Act. Schenck, the secretary of the American Socialist party, had circulated antidraft leaflets among the armed forces. He appealed his conviction in a lower federal court on the grounds that the Espionage Act violated the First Amendment. The Supreme Court unanimously rejected Schenck's position, and Justice Holmes concluded that the right of free speech was not absolute. "Free speech," Holmes explained in one of the most memorable lines of legal history, "would not protect a man in falsely shouting fire in a theatre, and causing a panic."[41] The government might do in wartime that which it could not do in peacetime. Holmes went on to spell out a test (the clear and present danger test) by which to measure violations of the right to free speech. "The question in each case," Holmes wrote, "is whether the words used are used in such circumstances and are of such a nature as to create a clear and present danger that they will bring about the substantive evils that Congress has a right to prevent. It is a question of degree and proximity."[42]

Holmes's clear and present danger test was the old bad-tendency test wrapped up in new judicial wording. The Court drew on it to sustain the convictions of radicals in two other cases, *Frohwerk* v. *United States* (1919) and *Debs* v. *United States* (1919).

The Court also sustained the Sedition Act in *Abrams* v. *United States* (1919), but in this instance Holmes, who had come under withering criticism from Chafee and other civil libertarians for his *Schenck* decision, dissented. Along with Justice Louis D. Brandeis, he urged a more generous interpretation of the clear and present danger test. The case involved the publication of pamphlets attacking the government's dispatch of an expeditionary force to Russia to aid the forces fighting the Bolsheviks. Justice John H. Clarke wrote for the majority that the purpose of the pamphlets was to "excite, at the supreme crisis of the war, disaffection, sedition, riots, and . . . revolution."[43]

Holmes and Brandeis disagreed. "Nobody can suppose," Holmes insisted, "that the surreptitious publishing of a silly leaflet by an unknown man, without more, would present any immediate danger that its opinions would hinder the success of the government arms or have any appreciable tendency to do so."[44] Beginning with this decision, the clear and present danger formula became a device to protect rather than restrict future civil liberties. It made little headway with the majority of the Court, whose justices clung to the bad-tendency test.

When the Court turned to state criminal syndicalism and sedition laws it encountered a somewhat different set of issues. These state measures simply did not have the same compelling national-security rationale as federal legislation. The ACLU pressed the attack on the state laws with special vigor, but, in doing so, it and the justices encountered a fundamental and highly controversial issue of whether the Fourteenth Amendment's due-process clause had incorporated the First Amendment's provisions against state action. The First Amendment provided that "Congress shall make no law . . . abridging the freedom of speech, or of the press."[45] The Court, in *Hurtado* v. *California* (1884), had decided that the Fourteenth Amendment had not incorporated the Bill of Rights, leaving advocates of nationalizing the Bill of Rights (i.e., applying it to the states) with a significant barrier to scale.

The Court in the 1920s gradually eroded the *Hurtado* precedent. In *Gitlow* v. *New York* (1925) the justices considered a New York criminal anarchy law under which Benjamin Gitlow, a Communist party leader, had been punished for publishing a "Left Wing Pamphlet" calling for the overthrow of the state government. The ACLU took Gitlow's appeal to the high court, and its attorneys argued that the concept of liberty in the Fourteenth Amendment included the exercise of speech and press free from state interference. The majority disagreed and upheld Gitlow's conviction, but it did so with a bow to the idea of incorporation. Justice Edward Sanford declared for the Court that "we may and do assume that freedom of speech and of the press—which are protected by the First Amendment from abridgement by Congress—are among the fundamental rights and 'liberties' protected by the due process clause of the Fourteenth Amendment from impairment by the states."[46] The Court made this affirmation to show that the First Amendment could be used to *uphold* the New York law, but in practical operation its decision meant that the Court could also strike down a law.

ACLU lawyers pressed this potential advantage. Not until *Stromberg* v. *California* (1931) did the Court accept that the joining of the First and Fourteenth Amendments could be used to strike down a state law. The California General Assembly had passed a law prohibiting the display of the red flag as an emblem of anarchism or of opposition to organized government. Chief Justice Charles Evans Hughes, whom President Hoover appointed in 1930, wrote in overturning the statute that "the conception of liberty under the due process clause of the Fourteenth Amendment embraces the right of free speech."[47] In the same year, the Court in *Near* v. *Minnesota* extended the protection to the press, in ruling unconstitutional a Minnesota statute that permitted prior restraint, because state courts could permanently enjoin any publication they found to be a "nuisance."[48]

Civil Rights

The NAACP and ILD also made limited gains in laying the foundation for modern civil rights law. When the NAACP was formed, civil equality in public policy was limited by two doctrines: "state action," which appeared to exempt private discrimination and intimidation from the prohibitions of the Fourteenth Amendment, and "separate but equal," which required proof of actual inequality of facilities to show that the equal protection of the laws guaranteed by the Fourteenth Amendment had been denied. Moorfield Storey and Louis Marshall worked within the confines of these doctrines, whereas NAACP counsel after World War II sought to overturn them. Storey and Marshall were forming the first part of the association's beachhead strategy that culminated in *Brown* v. *Board of Education* (1954), striking down the separate-but-equal doctrine. In the first three decades of the twentieth century, however, the NAACP barely had its feet on the beach. All that Storey and Marshall had to work with by way of precedent was a West Virginia case (*Strauder* v. *West Virginia,* 1880), affirming the right of blacks to sit on juries, and a California case (*Yick Wo* v. *Hopkins,* 1886), nullifying building codes for laundries that effectively excluded Chinese from the laundry business.[49]

Through either direct or indirect participation, Storey managed to move the black civil rights agenda forward. In *Guinn* v. *United States* (1915) the justices ruled that the "grandfather clause" of the Oklahoma constitution, which permitted illiterate whites with relatives voting before 1866 to vote without passing a literacy test, discriminated unconstitutionally against blacks, whose relatives had been nonvoting slaves. In *Nixon* v. *Herndon* (1927), the justices held that all-white party primaries, in which blacks were prohibited from voting, violated the equal-protection clause of the Fourteenth Amendment. The NAACP over the next two decades claimed a string of high court victories that cracked open the voting process in southern states. Finally, Storey personally argued the case of *Buchanan* v. *Warley* (1917), which involved a Louisville, Kentucky ordinance that classified certain blocks of the city "white" and others as "colored." The justices struck the measure down on equal-protection grounds.

During the 1930s, Charles Houston's aggressive leadership of the newly formed Legal Defense Fund pushed the cause of black rights even further. But the NAACP was often locked in bitter conflict with the ILD to gain control of cases. Typical was the struggle over the appeals taken from the famous Scottsboro, Alabama cases, in which the ILD won its greatest victory and in which the Supreme Court accepted that other provisions of the Bill of Rights could be nationalized.

The case involved the arrest in March 1931 of nine black boys charged with the rape of two white girls, and the unseemly haste with which the accused were doomed to the electric chair. The ILD enlisted the services of several distinguished authorities on constitutional law, most notably Walter H. Pollak. He argued, in *Powell* v. *Alabama* (1932), that the right of access to counsel (a right specified in the Sixth Amendment) should be extended against the states through the due-process clause of the Fourteenth Amendment. Justice George Sutherland, while not specifically overruling the *Hurtado* precedent, spoke for the Court in holding that the right to counsel was protected nationally in capital cases.

Yet significant barriers remained to full equality for blacks and other racial minorities. When, for example, the justices were pressed to decide the constitutionality of the federal government's wartime relocation of the Japanese, a majority of them acquiesced. In *Hirabayashi* v. *United States* (1943) and *Korematsu* v. *United States* (1944), the Court sustained the actions of the Roosevelt administration. The Court was not in the position, as has often been true during war, of second-guessing a policy that was predicated on a "pressing public necessity."[50] Nonetheless, the Court's behavior was a "disaster" that smacked to many of supporting Nazi-like actions, of hiding behind legal technicalities as a way of avoiding constitutional conflict, and of creating a precedent of menacing proportions should the nation find itself locked in a third world conflict.[51]

Race, Ethnicity, and Rights Consciousness

Between 1917 and 1945 cultural and racial diversity challenged the values and assumptions of the legal culture. The presence of massive numbers of foreign born and their children, demographic shifts caused by internal black migration, and total war left white, native-born, Protestant Americans scrambling to maintain their cultural values and social practices. Racism, nativism, and national-security hysteria shaped the legal culture in ways that mocked the rule of law.

But these years bequeathed other important (and contradictory) lessons. American legal culture mirrored the rich diversity of the general culture, displaying a continuing capacity to adapt, though sometimes imperfectly, general principles of equality and fairness to social change. Even if incompletely realized, the promotion of ethical and moral conduct in the profession, the administration of a criminal justice system based on individual rehabilitation, a commitment to openness in political discourse, and a belief in equality before the law persisted. Equally important, the magnitude of social change generated within the federal system a growing tendency toward centralization of authority, a belief that the national government should promote individual rights and equality, and an awakening realization of the instrumental relationship between legal and social change. Despised minorities realized for the first time the potential for securing protection against local majorities through the nationalizing authority of the federal courts.

14

The Great Depression and the Emergence of Liberal Legal Culture

The Great Depression

The Depression, which lasted from 1929 to 1941, was an economic plague so sweeping that it altered expectations about the proper relationship of law to society, of government to the governed. The white middle class had historically provided the bedrock support for the legal culture, but it experienced perhaps the most wrenching changes. That economic calamity should befall poor blacks and whites made sense in light of the laissez-faire individualism associated with the late nineteenth and early twentieth centuries, but that prosperous and hardworking citizens should be flung into unemployment and uselessness was something else altogether. The Great Depression sorely tested old assumptions, which held that voluntary rather than governmental regulation was best, that economic well-being flowed from personal virtue, and that government had a limited role in promoting the collective social welfare. The New Deal, which President Franklin D. Roosevelt initiated in 1933, stood for the proposition that lawmakers should provide a social and economic security net to catch the victims of an impersonal industrial order and that administrative agencies should bring a scientific coherence to the economy. Old assumptions gave way only grudgingly, however; a struggle ensued between the political and judicial branches with far-reaching implications for the substance of law, the conduct of legal institutions, and the character of American legal culture.

Law Reform and Legal Thought between the Wars

During the years between the wars, new patterns of legal reform and thought emerged, of which the American Law Institute and the legal realist movement were the most important. Both drew strength from the Progressive legacy of an efficient and moral administration of public affairs, and both wrestled with the problem of how law should respond to social change. They diverged, however, in the means of reaching those goals, underscoring once again the persistent diversity in American legal culture.

American Law Institute and the Quest for Uniformity and Certainty in Law

The burgeoning corporate economy of the early twentieth century compounded the historical problem of uncertainty in the law. Mid-nineteenth-century legal reformers, most especially David Dudley Field of New York, had won only limited acceptance for codification as a means of ordering the profusion of case law. The federal system had ordained multiple state approaches to common law matters, and the industrialization of the economy expanded the scope and complexity of the case law that spewed forth from a host of tribunals. State legislators added further to the bulging materials on the shelves of law libraries. The West Publishing Company beginning in 1879 had brought a rough, if complicated, order to this Niagara of law, but its National Reporter system only made contradictory precedents more available to both sides in a dispute. What the law was remained uncertain. The National Conference of Commissioners on Uniform State Laws, founded in 1892, convinced some states to adopt several uniform statutes, but these measures barely touched the great bulk of the common law. The American Bar Association, which founded a standing committee in 1888 to create a system of "legal classification," fared little better. The problem did not go away; the volume of law reports increased inexorably. The number of volumes of appellate court cases increased from about thirty-five hundred in 1885 to almost nine thousand by the beginning of World War I, "thus making the sheer bulk of the case law almost overwhelming."[1]

The American Law Institute (ALI), founded in Washington, D.C. in 1923, was the modern response to the complexity and uncertainty of the common law. The founders included the elite of the legal establishment; the *New York Times* reported that they were "probably the most distinguished gathering of the legal profession in the history of the country."[2] William Draper Lewis, professor of law at the University of Pennsylvania and an old Progressive ally and personal friend of Theodore Roosevelt, was the driving force behind ALI, although it was also closely associated with the Harvard Law School.

The motives behind the formation of the ALI reflected the mixed sentiments of the Progressive movement, from which it drew inspiration. Some of its conservative members, like Elihu Root, harbored nativist and antiradical sentiments; for them, ALI held forth the promise of increased legal and political stability in a world rocked by war and, in Russia, by communist revolution. At the other end of the political spectrum, Roscoe Pound believed that the new organization would bring social science methods to bear in restoring precision to the administration of justice. In method and substance its work was essentially formalistic and within the tradition of legal science associated with Christopher Columbus Langdell.

The founders agreed on one important matter: the need for greater certainty in the law. One commentator at the founding meeting expressed the sentiments of most delegates with the observation that "the uncertainty, the confusion, [are] growing worse from year to year. . . . Whatever authority might be found for one view of the law upon any topic, other authorities could be found for a different view. . . . The law [is] becoming guesswork."[3]

The principal work of the ALI was issuing restatements of the law. It hired prominent law school faculty, many from Harvard, to rearrange and reorganize the major common law fields (i.e., torts, contracts, property, agency, business corporations, and conflict of laws) and to provide a sparse commentary. The first of the restatements (on contracts) appeared in 1932 under the authorship of Samuel Williston, a Harvard Law School professor in the mold of Langdell. By 1945 the institute had issued eight other restatements.

The restatements marked the culmination of the Langdellian tradition, because they reflected the ALI's belief that through scientific study the principles of the law could be condensed into a powerful logic that would persuade bench and bar of the law's inherent unity. Lawyers began to cite the restatements as legal authority (which they were not and never have been), and appellate judges made increasing reference to them. On balance, however, the ALI's work never achieved the kind of influence that Lewis, Pound, and others had anticipated. Appellate judges simply were not willing to give up their discretion because a Harvard law professor thought they should. Furthermore, while the founders of the ALI had expected that the restatements would not only unify the common law but also connect it to social change, they were eventually forced to lower their sights, making "legal certainty the institute's only objective, a goal underlined by its decision to print the rules in especially bold black letters."[4]

Legal Realism

The legal realists during the 1920s and 1930s agreed with the ALI's diagnosis that the law was too uncertain, but most of "them disagreed sharply with the remedy advocated by the Institute."[5] The realists proposed to place facts, social analysis, and psychological insight into the operation of the judiciary ahead of the ALI's effort to create a "theology" of the common law by restating its fundamental principles. Legal realism stressed the functions of law rather than the abstract conceptualization of it, to which Langdell had been wedded. It also acknowledged that human idiosyncrasies and will often framed legal conduct, but without resort to social scientific methods, the law could not be understood and proper social policy could not be framed.

The roots of realism stretched back to Oliver Wendell Holmes, Jr., and the sociological jurisprudence of Roscoe Pound. As an intellectual movement, "legal realism was a fairly unoriginal contribution."[6] The realists adopted Holmes's skepticism about the nature of law and his cynical view of the role of human will in judicial decisions.

New currents of intellectual development and the changed face of Progressivism in the 1920s pushed legal realism beyond Holmes. Much of the Progressive accomplishment (e.g., social welfare legislation, administrative regulation) continued and even expanded in the 1920s. The great slaughter on the battlefields of World War I, however, undermined Progressive faith in human perfectibility and standards of morality. Progressives came "to question the inviolability of their own moral principles."[7] At the same time, the behavioral sciences, especially psychology and anthropology, stressed the unique and often irrational quality of human behavior. This insight tended to undermine the existence of overarching moral and religious beliefs, a development that proponents of sociological jurisprudence rejected but legal realists accepted.

The case of Benjamin N. Cardozo is instructive. Cardozo was judge of the New York Court of Appeals from 1917 to 1932, at which time President Herbert Hoover elevated him to the Supreme Court, where he served until 1938. Cardozo was the most respected state appellate judge of the twentieth century and one of the nation's most influential commentators on judicial behavior. However, he was not a realist, although, in the mold of sociological jurisprudence, he was critical of the prevailing belief that judging was merely a mechanical exercise.

Cardozo in 1920 delivered the Storrs Lectures at Yale Law School, which were published the following year as *The Nature of the Judicial Process,* the most perceptive book written about judging in this century. Cardozo confessed that judges were more than simple machines; they often made law rather than simply declared it. "I have grown to see that the [judicial] process in its highest reaches is not discovery, but creation; and that the doubts and misgivings, the hopes and fears, are part of the travail of [the judicial] mind . . . in which principles that have served their day expire, and new principles are born."[8] Yet Cardozo remained convinced, as the realists were not, that justice demanded respect for precedent. Otherwise, he believed, litigants would lose faith in the courts.

The legal realists sought to move beyond Cardozo's commonsense psychological understanding of judging toward a behavioral approach to law. The popularity of the behavioral sciences soared during the 1920s, and the faculties of the Yale and Columbia Law Schools, which were the hotbeds of the realist movement, turned to them in an effort to lead American jurisprudence away from the strictures of formalism and beyond the limits of sociological jurisprudence.

Karl Llewellyn and Jerome Frank were the most outstanding of the realists. The former served on the law faculties of both Yale and Columbia, while the latter, who became an administrator in the New Deal and a judge on the U.S. Court of Appeals, was a research associate on the Yale faculty. In 1930 Llewellyn published "A Realist Jurisprudence—The Next Step," in the *Columbia Law Review,* and the same year Frank brought to press *Law and the Modern Mind,* the most important book written about American law from the realist perspective. Like Llewellyn, Frank stressed the impermanence, flexibility, artificiality, and uncertainty of legal rules and principles. Frank went even further, because he gave particular stress to judicial psychoanalysis, arguing that the "law may vary with the personality of the judge who happens to pass upon any given case."[9] Realists like Frank rejected formalistic and deductive logic, which, they argued, merely concealed a judge's prejudices and preferences. The realists indeed believed in general legal principles, but they insisted that the traditional deference accorded to precedent was merely a screen that shielded the inherently conservative biases of most judges.

During the 1930s, Pound and the realists exchanged barbed criticism. The most serious differences involved the worth of legal rules and the place of moral values in the law. In 1931, Pound and Llewellyn traded charges in the *Harvard Law Review.* In "The Call for a Realist Jurisprudence," Pound claimed that Llewellyn and Frank had failed to bring a "theory of values" into a "program of relativist-realist jurisprudence."[10] Llewellyn, with Frank's assistance, responded that society was always in flux and that the law was always racing to catch up. Under these circumstances no single theory of moral values was ever adequate.

Pound and the realists never settled their differences, and historians disagree about the persistence and impact of realism. The commitment to innovative research by the mid-1930s had worn thin, in part because the Depression dried up sources of potential funding for empirical studies, and the New Deal agencies absorbed the talents of many of the realists' strongest voices, such as Frank. Llewellyn in the 1940s joined the formalists in the ALI to become the chief intellectual parent of the Uniform Commercial Code, which summed up all of the statute laws of commerce. The rise of Nazi Germany and the advent of World War II further undermined the realists, because their approach to moral and ethical values seemed to deny the legitimacy of a consistent rule of law.

The traditional Langdellian approach itself was undergoing change from within at its most influential center, Harvard Law School; moreover, Felix Frankfurter and several other faculty members, while eschewing Frank and Llewellyn, had worked some of the insights of sociological jurisprudence into their teaching, even though they clung to the casebook method. Frankfurter, for example, who taught one of the first courses in administrative law, was impatient with the realists because they "think they are adding something to current legal thinking when Holmes said it all two generations ago, and said it much better."[11]

Despite their shortcomings, the realists played a significant role in forging an alliance between "legal theory and empirical analysis . . . that had begun forty years before and that was to become a commonly accepted part of American law in the years after the Second World War."[12] Legal realism was not at all a direct consequence of the Great Depression, but it did capture symbolically the repudiation of stock assumptions about the prevailing culture on which jurisprudential ideas rested: prosperity was transitory, the capitalist system was not omnipotent, and men were quite capable of incompetently managing the economic order. The New Deal, while not directly connected to the realist movement, nonetheless displayed in action the kind of pragmatic and instrumental approach to law with which the realists were identified. Yet a massive generational gap existed between lawyers and politicians of the New Deal and federal and state judges, many of whom by political disposition and training looked to sustain the very values that were slipping away.

The New Deal

The Great Depression was as much a legal as an economic crisis. It raised in sharp relief two enduring historical problems. The first was the proper relationship between law and politics. The public interest in economic recovery and alleviating human suffering had to be balanced against the traditional protection of individual property rights and the separation of powers among the three branches of government. The second was the degree of government intervention in the economic and social order. The critical question before lawmakers in the 1930s was not whether they should intervene but the method of their intervention.

During the 1920s, the direct role of the federal government in the economy declined. Yet the Progressive ideal of an efficient and orderly economy based on planning persisted in the government-sponsored trade association movement. These associations were voluntary organizations of business competitors who joined together to share information. Herbert Hoover, first as secretary of commerce and then as president from 1929 to 1933, gave vigorous support to the movement, drawing on the resources of the Department of Commerce to sponsor trade conferences and publish statistics for each of the major industrial and agricultural groups. The trade associations were also an important source of business for the corporate bar, because the cooperative agreements among business in the same industry had to be carefully worded in order to pass scrutiny under existing antitrust laws. The Republican-controlled Federal Trade Commission and the Department of Justice relaxed antitrust enforcement as a further means of stimulating the trade associations. During the 1920s, the Supreme Court was generally supportive of the trade association movement, although it refused to accept association agreements that created "legal obligations on individuals or groups who might not be fairly represented by the agreement."[13]

The New Deal, therefore, was hardly unique in its instrumental approach to lawmaking. However, the New Dealers foresaw a far more active and direct role for government than had the Progressives. The Roosevelt administration assumed that the federal government was responsible for virtually every important phase of the national economy, and it took the traditional concept of distributive justice and turned it into a positive duty. Government was responsible for promoting the individual well-being of each citizen. The emergency actions of the New Deal era subsequently became permanent changes in the relationship of the federal government to the states and to individual citizens.

State and Federal Legislative Response to the Great Depression

The states fashioned their own New Deal programs. Legislators enacted relief and regulatory measures, including price regulations, social welfare programs, minimum-wage legislation, and moratoriums on foreclosure of mortgages. The federal courts subjected these laws to serious scrutiny on substantive due-process grounds of state interference with freedom to contract and private property rights. The magnitude of the Depression made state efforts wholly inadequate in dealing with the profound disruptions that beset the highly interdependent industrial economy. Solving the chaos of the Depression was indubitably a federal problem. For example, on the eve of Roosevelt's inauguration, thirty-eight states had closed their banks; moreover, banks in the rest of the country operated on a restricted basis. Yet only the federal government could gain national control of the banking crisis, and two days after his inauguration, Roosevelt declared a bank holiday, shutting the doors on every bank. Congress then rapidly passed new banking legislation at Roosevelt's direction, and confidence was subsequently restored in the banking system.

The banking bill was one of fifteen measures passed in the first one-hundred days of the New Deal. In one of the most creative and active periods in the history of the Congress, the national government dramatically broadened its involvement in American life. Congress created the Home Owners Loan Corporation to refinance home mortgages, the Federal Deposit Insurance Corporation (FDIC) to insure bank deposits up to $2500, the Civilian Conservation Corps to put unemployed youth to work in conservation and reforestation projects, and the Tennessee Valley Authority (TVA) to combine regional development with rural electrification in the South. The TVA and the

New Deal generally exemplified the way in which the expanded role of the federal government served over time to consolidate society, with electricity, highways, and educational aid chipping away at the historical localism and agrarianism of the South. Much the same occurred in the West, where federal irrigation and dam projects undertaken during the New Deal contributed to that region's rapid development after World War II.

Experimentation was the hallmark of Franklin Roosevelt's New Deal. "I have no expectation of making a hit every time I come to bat," the president disarmingly told critics. "What I seek is the highest possible batting average."[14] The pragmatic and flexible approach of the Roosevelt administration was reflected in the changing course of the New Deal itself. The so-called first New Deal lasted from about 1933 to 1935, ending amid Roosevelt's concern that his measures had not gone far enough to satisfy the public and that, at the same time, the justices of the Supreme Court believed that he had stretched constitutional authority too far. The second New Deal, which began in 1935, stressed commission regulation and the importance of administrative lawmaking to reorder the economy and economic relations between labor and business.

Roosevelt built upon the cooperative methods that lawyers and businessmen had experimented with in the 1920s, such as trade associations and cooperation among government, labor, and business. The first New Deal relied on business–government cooperation and executive–bureaucratic administration in restoring business and agricultural profits, in strengthening labor's position to bargain and consume, and in providing for the unemployed. Each of these goals found expression in major early New Deal legislation: the Agricultural Adjustment Act, the National Industrial Recovery Act (which created the National Recovery Administration), and the Public Works Administration.

The National Industrial Recovery Act

The National Industrial Recovery Act (NIRA) provides a case study of the legal and constitutional assumptions behind the early New Deal. The NIRA, which drew its constitutional authority from the commerce clause of the Constitution, set up a system of industrial self-government to manage the problems of overproduction, cutthroat competition, and price instability. The statute authorized the president "to establish such agencies . . . as he may find necessary" and to "delegate any of his functions and power" to officials appointed by him.[15] The measure provided for the creation of codes of fair competition with the purpose of preventing the practices that had driven prices downward, but this national experiment in government by trade association began without the barest semblance of an administrative structure through which to draft and implement these codes. Members of industrial groups doing business in interstate commerce drafted their own codes, which had the force of law, and their decisions were seldom subject to review under existing antitrust laws. The framers of the codes had to make provision for working conditions, including minimum wages and maximum hours. Child labor was outlawed and (under section 7[a]) workers received the right to organize and bargain collectively "through representatives of their own choosing."[16]

The president charged the National Recovery Administration (NRA) with the responsibility of implementing regulatory control over more than three million large and small businesses. The president appointed Hugh Johnson as head of the agency, and Johnson in turn hired Donald Richberg, a prominent labor lawyer during the 1920s, to the post of general counsel. Richberg then assembled his own legal staff.

Among other immediate consequences, early New Deal legislation brought a flood of lawyers into the nation's capital to take charge of operating the new administrative machinery. These New Deal lawyers were almost uniformly born in the twentieth century, and over one-half of them were in their late twenties or early thirties. They were, according to a critic dismayed as they swooped down on Washington, "boys with their hair ablaze," bringing a new spirit of active government involvement in every aspect of public life.[17] They were also disproportionately recruited from the elite law schools; fully 60 percent came from Harvard, Yale, and Columbia. Some received their training from realists; most were schooled in the modified Langdellian scheme of legal education that became prevalent in the 1920s and 1930s. Most of the New Deal lawyers "emerged from law school with a veneer of progressive liberalism over a foundation of doctrinal orthodoxy and apolitical professionalism."[18] Felix Frankfurter, a close adviser to Roosevelt, sent a steady stream of his students, known as "Happy Hot Dogs," to Washington, where they were stuffed into the New Deal agencies. These young lawyers were politically liberal, and they were urban in upbringing and Jewish and Catholic in heritage. The New Deal created such a demand for skilled lawyers with the proper political credentials that it opened the corridors of political power to people previously excluded by reason of their ethnicity or religion.

The lawyers assembled to administer the NIRA codes quickly found themselves often at odds with the practices and behavior of the business community whose voluntary and cooperative regulation they sought to cultivate. The NIRA depended for its success on efficient administration and a respect for the standards of due process. Neither of these conditions was realized. Both small producers and labor failed to receive significant protection under the legislation. A profound disregard for due-process standards as well as the spirit and letter of the law frustrated early regulatory efforts inside the NRA and other New Deal agencies. Many businessmen, as well as a few of the lawyers within the NRA, considered that traditional concerns with due process only led to an overemphasis on legal methods that promoted delay in decision making. Businessmen used their authority to dominate industries they were supposed to protect, and they abused their power by interfering with union organizational efforts. Donald Richberg concluded that "private enterprise was not only generally intolerant of interferences by organized labor and by the government, but sought continually to exercise public authority to discipline its own ranks."[19]

The NRA, like almost all of the early New Deal agencies, suffered from two major defects. First, it rested on an ill-defined constitutional foundation, which the Supreme Court used in 1935 to strike it down. Second, and as important to the future of administrative law and regulation, the trade association model of the NRA precluded the kind of vigorous enforcement and rational planning that made administrative agencies attractive. Many of the New Deal lawyers pressed for a more vigorous commission system of administrative oversight. Under this scheme, the government administrators would cease to be middle men who would ensure cooperative and voluntary acceptance of commission findings and become active participants basing their judgments on a neutral and impartial investigation of the facts.

National Labor Relations Act

Labor had long had a lower priority than business under the law. While lawmakers had done much to rationalize corporate and business activity, labor had received little protection to bargain and organize collectively. The labor movement was itself divided between elite craft workers and unskilled industrial laborers; therefore, the expectations of these two groups regarding government involvement were significantly different. The American Federation of Labor (AFL), which represented craft workers, had painstakingly established over the previous quarter-century a network of private agreements. Industrial workers, on the other hand, had increasingly resorted to strikes, sit-ins, and outright violence to coerce business into accepting their right to bargain and organize.

Even before the Roosevelt administration came to office, Congress had granted labor unions distinct legal personalities. The Norris–LaGuardia Act in 1932, for example, recognized that individual workers were unable to deal effectively with employers under prevailing economic conditions and, therefore, that they should be able to bring their collective strength to bear in support of themselves. The act treated unions as entities with rights and interests of their own, and it permitted them greater legal authority to engage in economic conflicts (e.g., strikes) and narrowed the grounds on which employers could obtain injunctions. The Norris–LaGuardia Act, however, contained no means of enforcing provisions for labor representation, leaving the unions to seek relief through the courts, where often in the past they had been treated hostilely.

The Depression produced increasing labor militancy. In 1934 alone there were about eighteen hundred strikes involving 1.5 million workers. This labor upheaval, coupled with the weak administration of the NIRA provisions governing labor, placed enormous pressure on the administration. Roosevelt only decided to accept stronger legislation when it became apparent that the NRA had collapsed administratively and that, in any case, the Supreme Court would likely declare the measure unconstitutional.

At the very last moment, the administration threw its support behind the Wagner Act, named after Senator Robert F. Wagner of New York. The National Labor Relations Act, ultimately passed by Congress in 1935, drew its authority from the commerce and due-process clauses of the Constitution. Wagner's constitutional reasoning was significant, for upon it rested the modern-day authority for federal labor law. He insisted that unfair labor practices, which the act enumerated, were actually burdens on interstate commerce that Congress was fully empowered to regulate and that restriction of those practices was not contrary to a substantive reading of due process of law. Although a friend of labor, Wagner cleverly operated on the premise that industrial peace, rather than the best interests of laborers, supported the legislation.

The act placed the weight of the federal government on the side of labor in the struggle to organize. It upheld the right of workers to join unions by outlawing many unfair management practices, such as blacklisting workers for union activities or failing to join a company union. The act established the nonpartisan National Labor Relations Board (NLRB) to protect workers from employer coercion, to oversee elections for union representatives, and to enforce collective bargaining agreements. The NLRB, unlike the NRA, was given punitive powers to enforce its findings.

The act was a milestone in the history of U.S. labor law, but it had mixed implications for labor. Its passage meant that collective bargaining was guaranteed in a wide range of industries. Organized labor, for the first time, was permitted to participate directly in decisions about the shape of the U.S. economy, a goal it had been seeking since the beginning of the century. The Congress of Industrial Organizations (CIO), which was established the same year as the Wagner Act, was directly aided by the new law. The CIO undertook a highly successful, if sometimes violence-ridden organizing effort among the nation's unskilled workers; it drew, as well, unprecedented numbers of black and women workers into the ranks of organized labor. In this regard, the tangible social benefits of the Wagner Act were great indeed.

The act also reconstituted the practice of collective bargaining, "bringing this hitherto private activity fully within the regulatory ambit of the administrative state."[20] The national government lent its authority to aid employees in creating the unions that could bargain collectively with employers. Federal involvement, however, was undertaken in the name of industrial peace and harmony, requiring the unions to act within the guidelines established by the NLRB. The effect of the New Deal legislation in changing actual working conditions was not revolutionary; collective bargaining, while surely an important gain, did not redistribute power in U.S. industry. The administrative regulations of the NLRB legitimated the role of labor in the economy without fundamentally altering the distribution of either wealth or authority.

The Second New Deal and the Problem of Delegation of Legislative Power

The Wagner Act was only one of several legislative initiatives undertaken during the second New Deal that involved the rise of administrative authority and the penetration of federal law into the daily lives of Americans. The Social Security Act, signed by Roosevelt on August 14, 1935, provided old-age assistance through a federal–state pension fund, administered by the Social Security Administration, to which both employers and employees contributed. The act also established a joint federal–state unemployment compensation system, providing further evidence of the growing importance of cooperative federalism. The Fair Labor Standards Act established a minimum wage and entrusted to the Department of Labor the responsibility of overseeing its operation. The Food, Drug, and Cosmetics Act of 1938, one of the last major pieces of domestic New Deal legislation, significantly strengthened the Pure Food and Drug Act of 1906, giving new enforcement and investigatory powers to the Food and Drug Administration. Still another statute permitted the secretary of agriculture to set standards of quality and condition for certain agricultural commodities moving in interstate and foreign commerce.

The fulfillment of the administrative and social welfare state during the New Deal raised issues about the scope of administrative authority and the place of the administrative agency within the traditional scheme of separation of powers. While New Deal measures enjoyed great popular support, an increasingly suspicious business community questioned the extent to which Congress could delegate to agencies and bureaus the authority to conduct legislative and judicial-like actions. Congress was surely within its powers to direct agencies to carry out defined tasks, but critics of the New Deal (and of administrative regulation since) have charged that such agencies should not engage in the formation of policy, because that power cannot be delegated by Congress, under the concept of separation of powers, to an agency that is also part of the executive branch. The political opposition to the legal experimentation of the New Deal was translated into a string of Supreme Court decisions.

The Supreme Court and the New Deal

The public had the opportunity through electoral democracy in the 1930s to reshape only two of the three branches of government. Armed with the judge-made weapon of judicial review and shielded by the doctrine of *stare decisis,* federal judges tenured during good behavior constituted "the most formidable barrier to the New Deal."[21] After twelve years of Republican control, the federal courts were filled with judges schooled in legal formalism and committed to a conservative political philosophy. The 140 federal judges appointed by Roosevelt's three Republican predecessors made up three-fourths of the district court bench and two-thirds of the appellate bench when Roosevelt took office.

The far-reaching Judiciary Act of 1925 had done much to enhance the policy-making role of the Supreme Court. This measure, which was the most important piece of judicial legislation passed in the twentieth century, continued the process begun in the Judiciary Act of 1891 of allowing the Supreme Court to concentrate its energies on constitutionally or nationally significant issues. The act was maneuvered through Congress by then Chief Justice William Howard Taft, who, more than any other chief justice in the Court's history, fulfilled his administrative role energetically. The measure entailed a "drastic transfer of existing Supreme Court business to the circuit courts of appeal."[22] It provided that appeals from most district court decisions would be shunted to the circuit courts of appeals, whose decisions, in most instances, were to be final. The only notable exceptions were cases of national importance, such as those involving interstate commerce or antitrust statutes, suits to enjoin enforcement of either Interstate Commerce Commission (ICC) orders or state laws, and appeals by the federal government in criminal cases. Supreme Court review was made overwhelmingly discretionary through the writ of certiorari, which gave the Court significant control over its docket. In sum, the Judiciary Act of 1925 was still another example of the attempt by lawmakers to bring coherence and consistency to the federal legal system.

The Supreme Court was, if anything, a bit more sharply divided in its political and ideological composition than was the federal judiciary as a whole. The conservative wing of the Court was composed of the so-called Four Horsemen (Justices Willis Van Devanter [1911–1937], James McReynolds [1914–1941], George Sutherland [1922–1938], and Pierce Butler [1922–1939]), named after the ancient horsemen of the apocalypse. On the other wing were three generally liberal justices: Benjamin N. Cardozo (1932–1938), Louis D. Brandeis (1916–1939), and Harlan Fiske Stone (1925–1941). Between the two wings was the chief justice, Charles Evans Hughes (1930–1941) and the mercurial Owen J. Roberts (1930–1945).

State Legislation

The justices turned their initial attention to state legislation because almost a year passed before the most important of the federal New Deal measures reached the Court.

One of the earliest cases involved an Oklahoma statute that declared that the manufacture of ice was a public utility subject to state regulation. The statute required ice operators to obtain a certificate before they began business. The measure was intended to raise prices by limiting competition, and the state acted on the basis of its police powers and the view that ice making was effected with a public interest.

The Supreme Court in *New State Ice Company* v. *Liebmann* (1932) took exception to the Oklahoma statute. The majority held that ice manufacturing was not a public utility and that the legislation fostered monopoly. Justice Brandeis dissented vigorously, arguing that it was up to the Oklahoma legislature to decide whether a business was effected with a public interest, and that under depression conditions the Court had no business second-guessing the legislature on these matters. Given the enormity of the economic crisis, Brandeis urged his colleagues to adopt a position of judicial restraint that would encourage the states to experiment.

Two years later, the Court went off in another direction. In *Home Building & Loan Association* v. *Blaisdell* (1934), the justices were asked to rule on the constitutionality of the Minnesota Mortgage Moratorium Law. This emergency measure sought to deal with the plight of farmers faced with losing their property through mortgage foreclosure. The act permitted courts to expand the interval from foreclosure to sale in order that farmers might have additional time to raise the money to pay their indebtedness. By a five-to-four majority, the Court sustained the law. Justice Hughes wrote that under emergency conditions the states had authority to ensure the well-being of their citizens. Because the measure only delayed rather than prevented foreclosure, Hughes argued that the contract clause of the federal Constitution had not been violated. Conservatives argued the opposite. Justice Sutherland concluded that the contract clause was most applicable under just such emergency circumstances, and that the Minnesota law violated the clause because it rearranged the terms on which the parties had originally agreed.

In *Nebbia* v. *New York* (1934), the Court upheld still another state emergency statute. In this instance, New York state had created a control board to regulate the entire milk industry. The board had power to set minimum wholesale and retail prices, a measure intended to diminish cutthroat competition. Leo Nebbia, a Rochester grocer, was convicted of selling milk below the legal price, and he argued on substantive due-process grounds that his Fourteenth Amendment rights had been violated and that the milk business was not effected with a public interest.

The Court split badly once again, with a five-to-four majority sustaining the New York law. Justice Roberts spoke for the Court in holding that the measure was a reasonable effort by the state to deal with an emergency. With the marketplace in upheaval, the state legislature was clearly within its police powers to try to restore order. Justice McReynolds, for the dissenters, argued that the public interest was not what the legislature said it was. At the same time, he gave a stirring endorsement to the concept of the Court as a superlegislature. The justices, McReynolds wrote, "must have regard to the wisdom of the enactment."[23] The modern expression of extensive and interventionist judicial power, ironically, lay with the conservatives on the Court, who wished to overturn on grounds of policy as well as constitutional law the actions of the states.

A year later, in *Morehead* v. *New York ex rel. Tipaldo,* the conservative wing prevailed. In that case, the justices, with Sutherland writing for the Court, overturned a

1933 New York model minimum-wage law. In this instance, the Court relied on its earlier decision in *Adkins* v. *Children's Hospital* (1923). The Court's action stirred sharp criticism from proponents of the New Deal in the states, and even the Republican platform of 1936 approved of state regulation of hours and wages for women and children.

The Court gave a mixed reading to state New Deal legislation. The conservatives opposed any measures that either regulated market conditions or undermined principles of contract, but they were unable to command consistently a majority of the Court. The decisions were usually close, with Roberts and Hughes providing the swing votes. These same divisions appeared when the justices considered federal legislation, but they more frequently struck these measures down. Roosevelt grew disillusioned with the Court, and he orchestrated the most important confrontation between it and the political branches during the twentieth century.

Federal Legislation

The early New Deal legislation was fraught with problems. Much of it had been drafted hastily. For example, the committee that wrote the NIRA overhauled the nation's business structure in one week. Members of Congress and the lawyers who aided them were often cavalier in their attitudes about the basis of constitutional authority upon which the measures rested. The commerce clause, the general welfare clause, and the taxing power were invoked in pell-mell fashion. There was a national crisis under way and the national government had to do something about it, and quickly. The breadth of many of the statutes and the fulsome claims made for constitutional authority by the New Deal raised real problems for all of the justices because, whatever their political sympathies, they had shown great resistance to state statutes that were vague and overly broad. Even the liberal members of the Court, who preached judicial restraint when state statutes were involved, balked at the centralizing tendencies of the New Deal. Finally, the New Deal lawyers who filled the new administrative agencies often disagreed with one another, and the administration's legal representation before the federal courts was often unsympathetic or, even worse, unfamiliar with the programs.[24]

The Court exploded whatever hope the New Deal had for the constitutional integrity of its program. The entire Court was convinced that Congress had violated the separation-of-powers standards by indiscriminately delegating legislative power to executive agencies. The NIRA was the subject of special scrutiny. The lawyers who administered it through the NRA believed that economic nationalism based on an expansive concept of the commerce clause had made such broad delegation "constitutionally . . . unassailable," but they quickly learned that "the Legal Realists of the 1930s had more perceptively plumbed the judicial mind."[25]

The delegation question surfaced in the two cases in which the Court struck down the NIRA. The New Deal first appeared before the Court in *Panama Refining Company* v. *Ryan* (1935). The Court considered section 9(c) of the NIRA, which permitted the president to ban the interstate shipment of petroleum produced in excess of quotas set by the states. In 1933 the price of wholesale gasoline had fallen to two and a half cents per gallon, of crude oil to ten cents per barrel. National controls seemed a plausible solution. Eight of the nine justices disagreed, and for the first time in U.S.

history, the Court held unconstitutional an act of Congress because it improperly delegated legislative powers to the president without specifying adequate guidelines. The decision removed the oil industry from national controls.

The delegation issue also surfaced in *Schechter Poultry Corp.* v. *United States,* which the Court decided on "Black Monday," May 27, 1935. On that day, the justices not only struck down the entire NIRA in *Schechter,* but they also held unconstitutional the Frazier–Lemke Mortgage Act, on grounds that it deprived creditors of property without due process of law. *Schechter* involved the New York City kosher poultry business, the largest in the country. This $90 million industry employed some sixteen hundred workers in over five hundred small shops. Some 96 percent of all chickens were imported from other states. The Schechter brothers were wholesale slaughterers of chickens, and they were bound under the Live Poultry Code of the NIRA to abide by certain business practices involving minimum wages, maximum hours, sanitary working conditions, and the sale of only healthy fowl. The Schechters openly violated the codes in an effort to boost their profits. They sold diseased and uninspected poultry at cut-rate prices, causing "Brooklyn to become the dumping ground of sick chickens for the whole United States."[26]

The *Schechter* case presented the Court with two questions. First, was Congress's delegation of codemaking power to the president constitutional? The justices answered unanimously that it was not. Because Congress had provided no guidelines for the content or operation of the codes, the NIRA had put the president in the position of being able to create a governmentally sanctioned system of industrial cartels. Justice Cardozo, in an opinion concurring with that of the Court by Chief Justice Hughes, concluded that the absences of standards in the law amounted to "delegation run riot."[27]

The second question before the justices was whether the commerce power granted Congress authority to regulate manufacturing activities? Chief Justice Hughes concluded that it did not. Hughes returned to the traditional distinction, first articulated in *E. C. Knight* (1895), that the commerce power did not reach to manufacturing activities. Because the chicken-processing business in which the Schechter brothers engaged was outside of the commerce power, then Congress could not regulate it. This view of the commerce clause made no substitute constitutionally feasible, and it effectively ended efforts by the New Deal to develop a broad-scale national program of centralized industrial regulation and planning.

These two cases were important not only for striking down a vital piece of New Deal legislation, but for putting Congress on notice about the manner in which it delegated legislative power. Since these two cases, the Court has not invalidated a congressional delegation of power, suggesting that later acts delegating power were better written. After the New Deal years, the Court ceased to express doubt about the place of administrative agencies in the divided federal system of government. The *Panama Refining* and *Schechter* decisions also induced Congress to indicate clearly the goals, means, and processes it intends for an agency to follow.

The year following these cases the justices struck down another pillar of the New Deal, the Agricultural Adjustment Act. In *United States* v. *Butler,* the Court, by a six-to-three vote, concluded that a tax applied to agricultural producers was not for the purpose of raising revenues, but of purchasing compliance with a program that paid farmers not to produce. Justice Roberts, writing for the majority, found that the general welfare clause did not invest the Congress with authority to do whatever it wanted. Roberts asserted that in making these judgments he had not allowed personal or policy considerations to enter. "[T]he judicial branch of the Government," he explained, "has only one duty,—to lay the article of the Constitution which is invoked beside the statute which is challenged and to decide whether the latter squares with the former."[28]

Both the opinion and Roberts's formalistic view of the judicial process struck a sore nerve. Proponents of legal realism condemned the opinion as further evidence of the intrusion of judicial values into the decision-making process, and the administration took it to be a condemnation of much of the constitutional authority on which its response to the Depression rested. Justice Stone, moreover, in his dissenting opinion, in which Brandeis and Cardozo joined, chided Roberts for his narrow view of the taxing power and attacked the notion that judging was simply a matter of squaring the law and the constitution in a mechanical fashion.

The Court in mid-1936 had not pronounced the constitutional fate of the most important of the laws passed in the early phases of the second New Deal. Still waiting consideration were the Wagner Act, the Tennessee Valley Authority, and Social Security. Roosevelt was upset with the Court's actions and he began to consider plans by which to reverse its decisions. But in the 1936 presidential campaign he avoided directly assaulting the Court, running instead on a platform of economic improvements that he attributed to the success of the New Deal. The public gave him a thundering round of approval, and, based on this mandate, he launched a direct assault on the Court and the formalistic values with which it had been identified.

The Court Packing Plan

Throughout U.S. legal history, presidents have sought to mold the federal courts in their political image. On balance, they have fitted political considerations to professional needs, and the federal courts have had an impressive record of judges with high quality and character. From time to time, however, presidents have also become frustrated with the federal bench, especially the Supreme Court. But never had any president attempted to do what Franklin Roosevelt sought to do: remake the Supreme Court by changing the rules of the game by which vacancies became available. Neither death nor resignation by early 1937 had created any vacancies for Roosevelt to fill. The president, frustrated by his inability to appoint new justices, proposed to change the political cast of the federal courts by adding new judgeships.

The president clothed his plan with an apparent concern about the judicial workload. "The simple fact is that today," Roosevelt informed Congress in a message accompanying his proposed bill in February 1937, "a new need for legislative action arises because the personnel of the Federal judiciary is insufficient to meet the business before them."[29] He quite inaccurately claimed that the Supreme Court had a congested docket. As he later admitted publicly, he was much more concerned about the reactionary nature of the justices' opinions, a problem he attributed to their age. "Modern complexities call . . . for a constant infusion of new blood in the courts," he observed. "Little by little new facts become blurred through old glasses fitted, as it were, for the needs of another generation; older men, assuming that the scene is the same as it was in the past, cease to explore or inquire into the present or the future."[30] He went on to accuse the Court, composed of "nine old men," of "acting not as a judicial body, but as a policy-making body" that had "thwart[ed] the will of the people."[31] The argument about age was a canard that Roosevelt invoked to mask his ideological motivation. The eighty-year-old Brandeis was not only vigorous but the source, through Felix Frankfurter (a friend of Roosevelt), of suggestions for the course of New Deal policy.

Roosevelt's plan, which was greeted with mixed enthusiasm in a Congress dominated by members of his own party, called for appointment of additional judges in all federal courts where there were incumbent judges of retirement age who did not choose to resign. With regard to the Supreme Court, Roosevelt proposed that once a justice reached age seventy, he would be given six months to retire. If he failed to do so, the president would be permitted to appoint an additional justice, up to a maximum of six new appointees. At the time the bill was proposed six justices would have qualified: the "Four Horsemen," Brandeis, and Hughes. Congress held hearings on the plan during the spring of 1937, but even ardent New Dealers recoiled at the president's willingness to bend judicial authority to political necessity. The measure therefore languished in Congress.

The Court-packing plan was a vivid demonstration of what the legal realists had been arguing about and what Holmes had said in *Lochner*. Law was clearly related to the political interests of the judges who passed on it. The measure broke the myth that judges were merely mechanics whose oracular decisions revealed some enduring truths. Even those supporters of the president who objected to the Court's decisions, found in the Court-packing plan a dangerous assault on the idea that law was a neutral body of principles that could be impartially administered.

Judicial Restraint and the Acceptance of the Administrative and Social Welfare State

In April 1937, the Court handed down decisions in several important cases involving state and federal legislation from the second New Deal. The two swing votes on the Court (Justices Roberts and Hughes) joined the liberals, providing the basis for the derisive contemporary comment that, in view of the pending Court-packing measure, their actions were a "switch in time that saved nine." In *West Coast Hotel* v. *Parrish,* the court by a five-to-four vote sustained a Washington State minimum-wage law, abandoning the substantive due-process arguments that it had previously invoked to strike down state regulatory measures. Shortly thereafter the justices granted labor a significant victory, upholding the Wagner Act in *National Labor Relations Board* v. *Jones and Laughlin Steel Corporation.* The Court discarded the rule against manufacturing as commerce that it had relied on only two years before in *Schechter*. Justice Hughes, speaking for another five-to-four majority, found that the unfair labor practices outlawed by the Wagner Act were detrimental to interstate commerce. "When industries organize themselves on a national scale," Hughes concluded, "making their relation to interstate commerce the dominant factor in their activities, how can it be maintained that their industrial labor relations constitute a forbidden field into which Congress may not enter when it is necessary to protect interstate commerce from the paralyzing consequences of industrial warfare?"[32]

The Court's changed direction undercut the little congressional support still remaining for the Court-packing plan. Charitably, one could say that Roosevelt had lost the battle but won the war. The justices proceeded to endorse the other major parts of the second New Deal. These included Social Security in *Steward Machine Co.* v. *Davis* (1937), the Fair Labor Standards Act in *United States* v. *Darby* (1941), and the second Agricultural Adjustment Act (AAA) in *Wickard* v. *Filburn* (1942). Moreover, by 1941, Roosevelt had placed his own stamp on the Supreme Court with seven new appointments. Among the new justices were Felix Frankfurter, a Roosevelt crony and adviser, Hugo Black, a senator from Alabama, and William O. Douglas, chairman of the Securities and Exchange Commission during the New Deal. Together they composed the heart of the Roosevelt Court that dominated American constitutional law through the 1960s.

The Court-packing scheme and the Court's changed direction climaxed a long struggle by legal and economic progressives to force the justices to accept the social welfare and administrative state. The New Deal between 1933 and 1940 created fourteen new agencies whose duties it was to manage rather than police the various aspects of the economy. A significant part of the economic regulatory business of the nation, over which the federal courts had presided since the 1880s, was finally in the hands of administrative agencies that exercised powers granted to them by Congress. Administrative regulations, moreover, replaced judicially applied common law principles as the most important rules governing the conduct of the national economy. This constitutional revolution also destroyed the last barriers to the welfare state and embraced the "transformation of the presidency into an instrument of virtually permanent emergency government."[33]

The constitutional developments of the New Deal had somewhat contradictory consequences for the Supreme Court. On matters of economic regulation the justices eventually adopted a position of judicial restraint. One of the most important demonstrations of this was its decision in *Erie* v. *Tompkins* (1938). This case involved an injury sustained by a man hit by a train while walking along the tracks of the Erie Railroad in Pennsylvania. In that state the common law rule held that he had no cause of action because he was negligent for walking on the tracks. Instead, he brought suit in federal court based on grounds of diversity of citizenship between himself and the railroad. He won damages of $30,000, but the railroad appealed to the Supreme Court.

Since the late nineteenth century, liberal critics of federal judicial power had complained that the diversity jurisdiction of the federal courts had given its judges too much power. They aimed their criticism specifically at the Court's earlier decision in *Swift* v. *Tyson* (1842), in which Justice Joseph Story had tried to establish the basis for a consistent and uniform body of commercial law supervised by the federal courts. In practice, the result had been two sets of common law, one state and one federal, and a disposition by the lower federal courts (which, ironically, was not followed in *Erie*) to favor interstate corporations.

Justice Brandeis wrote for the majority of the Court in remanding Tompkins's case back to the federal court for trial on the basis of Pennsylvania law. For the first and only time in U.S. history, the Court in *Erie* declared one of its own decisions (*Swift* v. *Tyson*) unconstitutional. Brandeis held that the Constitution had made no provision for a federal common law of any kind, whether commercial or criminal. The decision was a ringing affirmation of the independence of state courts and state law within the federal system.

In operation, however, the decision did not diminish the power of the federal judiciary and no new authority was allocated to the states. Moreover, the federal courts retained an important hand in matters of economic regulation, because an increasingly large part of their responsibilities entailed interpretation of congressional statutes delegating broad powers to administrative bodies.

The Supreme Court also had substantial authority, thanks to the expanded certiorari jurisdiction in the Judiciary Act of 1925, to reset its agenda. In the highly fluid society of the emerging modern United States, special-interest litigation groups, such as the NAACP and the ACLU, pressed the justices to blaze new paths of constitutional law. The New Deal, for example, had treated blacks paternalistically, and the NAACP recognized as a result that important civil rights breakthroughs would have to be imposed by the judicial rather than the political process. The ACLU was already seeking fuller protections for the civil liberties of various minority political and religious groups. The New Deal had demonstrated that the law and legal institutions could be positive, active forces. With the matter of economic regulation largely settled, and with Roosevelt appointees filling judgeships, the federal courts were primed to consider a range of new civil liberties and civil rights issues.

Emergence of Liberal Legal Culture

The New Deal culminated a long-term trend toward greater centralization of lawmaking power in the national government and a declining role for the states as primary centers of policy making. Economic crisis, the legacy of Progressivism, and the experience of World War I encouraged the development of a relativistic and instrumentalist view of law. The emergency of the Great Depression justified programs that, in short order, became the central features of the American version of the social welfare state. More so than ever before in U.S. history, lawmakers emerged as social engineers, who believed that government had a positive responsibility to fix a basic standard of living and to smooth out the erratic swings in the business cycle. The concept of distributive justice, which stretched back into the nineteenth century, took on a new meaning, one in which government under law was supposed to diminish economic risk taking and to heighten individual economic opportunity. Lawmakers had an affirmative duty to provide for rights and liberties, not just to refrain from interfering with their enjoyment. If the courts were to restrain themselves in considering economic regulatory measures, the new configuration of rights consciousness encouraged them to act assertively to promote individual rights and liberties. This new approach raised powerful expectations among groups long disadvantaged, such as blacks, ethnics, native Americans, and women, that judicial institutions were on their side and that through them old wrongs could be legally righted.

The Great Depression was the catalyst of liberal legalism, the dominant force in the U.S. legal culture after World War II. Liberal legalism is an inchoate and largely unarticulated concept, but in its essence it fused the social reformist impulse of Progressivism, the relativism and instrumentalism of legal realism and sociological jurisprudence, and the regulatory responsibility of the state associated with the New Deal.[34] The traditional liberal doctrine of laissez-faire and individualism, which had been in tension with the concept of an active state since the founding of the nation, finally gave way to the new orthodoxy of liberal legalism. It held forth the promise of broad-scale social justice by relying on the administrative-legal process and judicial power to resolve conflict among contending social interests.[35] Yet, as the Wagner Act fore-shadowed, the roots of liberal legalism in the New Deal stressed social stability and harmony; rights protected by the state were exercised subject to how the public interest might best be served. The New Deal's commitment to state responsibility for curing social and economic ills was a final break from traditional laissez-faire assumptions, but, in both public and private law, the course of the new liberal legalism in the forty years after World War II was as uncertain and fraught with contention as that which it replaced.

15

Contemporary Law and Society

Consensus, Social Change, and the Law Explosion

Following the carnage of World War II, the world's richest and most powerful nation locked ideological horns with its former ally, the Soviet Union, in a new kind of conflict called the Cold War. Americans in the 1950s settled into a period of political consensus in response to the threat of communism. This consensus upheld the idea that the United States was a free, moral society, and a political democracy that cherished individual equality and public discourse. Republicans and Democrats, while differing on specific policies, embraced a bipartisan foreign policy, the social welfare state, and the scheme of government–business relations forged by the New Deal.

Lyndon B. Johnson, who became president in 1963 following the assassination of John F. Kennedy, attempted to build upon this consensus. Johnson was a New Deal Democrat whose Great Society program was the embodiment of liberal legalism. It proposed to use legal authority to foster equality of opportunity by promoting racial harmony and by fighting, through the largess of the federal government, a War on Poverty that involved urban renewal, job training, public housing, education, and health and legal services for the poor.

This political consensus crumbled during the late 1960s and early 1970s under the weight of the Vietnam War and social, technological, and scientific change. As Martin Luther King, Jr., the leader of the black civil rights movement in the 1960s, explained, the Great Society was ''shot down on the battlefield of Vietnam.''[1] Antiwar protesters began with the nonviolent tactics of the black civil rights movement, but peaceful resistance turned to political rebellion and a counterculture of drugs, free love, and rock music. Drug freaks and antiwar protesters were lumped together in the minds of the majority of Americans, many of whom were fed up with the war but clung to the traditional values of hard work, the nuclear family, good manners, and patriotism.

The rebels of the 1960s, products of the baby boom of the postwar era, became in large part the "me" generation of the 1970s and 1980s. At the height of the baby boom, the average family had more than 3 children. By 1980, that figure had fallen to less than 1.6 children. The declining birthrate of the 1960s and 1970s reflected changing attitudes toward gender roles and women's new economic aspirations as well as the availability of oral contraceptives. Attitudes toward marriage, childraising, and the family also changed. The divorce rate surged, climbing 100 percent during the 1960s, and premarital sex and homosexual relationships between consenting adults became socially acceptable.

The baby-boom generation also ushered in a new crime wave. The ranks of the most crime-prone age group, that of fifteen to twenty-four, swelled by more than a million persons a year during the 1960s. Between 1960 and 1974, the year with the highest crime rate in the twentieth century, the crime rate soared 203 percent with violent crimes against people rising even faster. The assassinations of John F. Kennedy (1963), Robert F. Kennedy (1968), and Martin Luther King, Jr. (1968), as well as the attempted assassination of George C. Wallace (1972), contributed to a sense of un-bounded lawlessness, as did the great urban riots in New York, Newark, Los Angeles, Cleveland, and Detroit from 1964 to 1968.

The United States seemed to be "unraveling."[2] The wisdom of the leaders, either in business or politics, was no longer taken for granted. Even the "silent majority," to which Republican President Richard M. Nixon successfully appealed in 1968, had its faith shaken. Nixon, a longtime proponent of law and order, resigned in 1974 after revelations that he had attempted to cover up a break-in by his political henchmen at Democratic national headquarters in the Watergate complex in Washington, D.C.

The loss of faith in leadership encouraged an atmosphere of impatience with previously ignored social and environmental issues. Feminists, environmentalists, and consumer rights advocates, while different in many ways, shared an instrumental view of the legal system, borrowing from the courtroom tactics pioneered by the NAACP. Its lawyers in 1954 won a landmark victory in *Brown* v. *Board of Education,* which overthrew the doctrine of separate but equal in public facilities. The decision nourished the sense of rights consciousness that had begun in the World War I era and, as important, demonstrated the possibilities of social change through litigation. Special-interest litigation became a fixed feature of the contemporary United States.

Rapid technological and scientific advances also placed new demands on the legal system. The computer, jet flight, robotics, in vitro fertilization, and complex life support systems made possible undreamed-of feats that afforded Americans control over "time, distance, and destiny" to a degree unparalleled in the nation's history.[3] These developments furthered a trend that had originated with the Industrial Revolution: social interdependence. Strangers increasingly relied on strangers to perform the myriad tasks of a complex modern society.

By the late 1970s, observers of the U.S. legal system had concluded that the combination of a brittle social order and rapid technological change had produced a "law explosion." "Americans in all walks of life," reported a popular weekly news magazine in 1978, "are being buried under an avalanche of lawsuits."[4] The quantitative evidence suggests a rise in the number of civil and criminal cases *filed* in state trial courts, and between 1960 and 1980 the number of cases *filed* in the federal courts of appeal almost quintupled, and during the same period *filings* in the Supreme Court more than doubled.[5]

Whether this increase in court *filings* constituted an explosion (an unprecedented and unwieldy increase in the appeal to the courts to settle problems at a greater rate than in the past) remains in hot debate. But there is no doubt that important qualitative changes did occur in the legal culture that involved the legal profession, substantive private law, the criminal justice system, and the federal administrative and regulatory apparatus. In the next chapter we shall examine the ways in which these changes appeared in public law.

The Legal Profession, Education, and Thought

Growth and Diversity of the Contemporary Bar

Since 1950 the ranks of lawyers have swollen dramatically, far outstripping population growth. The legal profession became increasingly financially attractive and its services correspondingly more in demand. In 1960 there were 286,000 lawyers; in 1987 there were about 690,000 men and women practicing law, or about one lawyer for every 350 people in the nation, a ratio unrivaled in the rest of the world. The entrance of women into the profession contributed more than anything else to this growth. Women in 1987 constituted about 14 percent of all lawyers, up from 2.5 percent in 1950.[6] The great upsurge in female law students came in the 1970s, a reflection of women's raised professional consciousness and a strong job market for lawyers. In 1968 about one-tenth of the law students were women; by 1982 women composed close to one-half of all law students. Yet in 1987 women remained dramatically underrepresented in major law firms.

Blacks made only marginal gains. By 1969 they composed 12 percent of the national population but only 1 percent of the bar, and they were grossly underrepresented in law schools. The civil rights activism of the 1960s made only a slight difference; by 1984 only 2.6 percent of the bar was black.[7] Furthermore, once they gained admission to the bar, blacks continued to experience discrimination. "While the ethics of the profession support the ideal of equal justice for all," a report on black lawyers in Chicago during the early 1970s concluded that "black Americans meet both direct and indirect discrimination when they seek to obtain legal training and later attempt to establish themselves within the metropolitan bar."[8]

Racial and gender distinctions still have validity, but religious and ethnic taboos have disappeared. Jews and Catholics by the late 1960s became fully integrated into law practice and legal education. "There was still a hint of anti-Semitism among the larger firms in the 1960s. By the 1970s, no such discrimination was generally thought to exist; moreover, the majority of law students at many elite schools were Jewish."[9]

The demands for a more open profession emanated from younger and less established lawyers, from liberal activists of the 1960s who were anxious to extend legal services to the poor and minorities, and from public-interest lawyers associated with the consumer movement who wanted to reduce legal costs by encouraging competition. The ABA and state bar groups responded to these demands by attempting to balance the economic self-interest of the bar against the undisputed existence of "a vast neglected public for whom legal services were unavailable."[10] The ABA in 1969 adopted a new Code of Professional Ethics, which repudiated many of the laissez-faire, guildlike assumptions of earlier codes. The new code nonetheless asserted that the obligation to provide legal service remained a matter of individual responsibility; it discouraged most group practices by salaried lawyers in clinics, and it strictly limited advertising.

The Supreme Court did what the bar refused to do. In *Goldfarb* v. *Virginia* (1975), the justices held that minimum-fee schedules imposed by state bar associations violated antitrust laws, clearing the way for the establishment of cut-rate law clinics.[11] Two years later, in *Bates* v. *State Bar of Arizona*, the Supreme Court ruled that the bar association codes against advertising violated First Amendment rights to "commercial" free speech.[12] The decision inspired the creation of many more legal clinics, some even in local department stores and shopping malls. The decision also prompted the ABA and local bar groups to acknowledge that "competition and professionalism" were compatible.[13]

The Johnson administration directly involved the federal government in the delivery of legal services, an activity long advocated by the National Lawyers' Guild and steadfastly resisted by the ABA. Congress in 1964 created the Office of Economic Opportunity (OEO) to fight the War on Poverty, and under it the administration launched a small program that made grants to lawyers willing to establish storefront neighborhood law offices. Two years later, Congress created the Legal Services Office within OEO, which later became the Legal Services Corporation.

Federally sponsored legal aid became the cutting edge of the public-interest law movement, which was composed of lawyers who pursued civil rights, poverty, consumer, and environmental issues. The objective of the public-interest law movement was to make the United States more democratic by making the law more responsive. Public-interest law meant more than safeguarding rights; it meant direct legal action to bring about social change. At its peak, OEO scattered nearly twenty-five hundred lawyers in three hundred communities to provide representation to more than one million clients. By the 1980s, after sustained attack by the Republican administrations of Richard Nixon and Ronald Reagan, federal legal services had shrunk considerably, blunting the cutting edge of one of the Great Society's most effective (and controversial) programs.

Conventional legal practice also changed. A large firm at the turn of the century had been composed at most of ten members. By 1983 there were 183 firms with more than one hundred lawyers. Solo practice remained an important aspect of the profession, but one that gradually lost ground. In 1951 60 percent of all practicing lawyers practiced alone; twenty-six years later, however, only one-third of a much swollen bar was in solo practice. The consolidation of law practice also meant that increasingly larger firms commanded an ever-greater portion of the dollars spent on legal services. The market share of firms with gross receipts of more than $1 million increased from 14 percent in 1967 to 20 percent in 1972, and to 38 percent by 1985.

Law became a gigantic business served by a larger, more competitive, and more socially representative bar than a century before. As a study of Chicago lawyers reported in 1982, "one could posit a great many legal professions, perhaps dozens."[14] Lawyers worked for huge firms, they practiced alone in small groups, and they served business in legislative and regulatory bodies.

Legal Education

Law schools after World War II were flush with students studying under the G.I. Bill, a federal measure that was the beginning of the national government's expanding role in all levels of postwar education. The law rewarded veterans for their military service while easing their transition back into the peacetime economy. With student numbers up, state legislatures finally overcame their concern "that Abraham Lincoln had not been to law school."[15] Throughout the nation an almost uniform pattern of statutorily mandated education appeared, requiring an undergraduate degree followed by three years of legal education.

Law schools became much more selective in the late 1960s and 1970s as applicants lined up in unprecedented numbers. Students leaving undergraduate schools in the midst of civil rights, consumer, environmental, and antiwar activism expected that a career in law would equip them to meet the many injustices of U.S. society. The experience of the University of California at Berkeley School of Law was particularly instructive. In 1954 the law school at that institution accepted 70 percent of all applicants; in 1968 the acceptance rate dropped to 34 percent. By 1977 there were 126,000 law students, a figure larger than the total number of practicing lawyers in 1900. By the early 1980s the numbers flattened and then even dropped. A significant weakening in the economy combined with a widespread belief that there were too many lawyers made the increasingly expensive investment in legal education less attractive. In the wake of Watergate, moreover, the earlier correspondence between law practice and social justice appeared quaint. By 1988, however, applications once again soared, rising as much as 25 percent at prestigious law schools.

Once in law school, students often suffered from "intellectual ennui."[16] The traditional case method retained its hold, although many law teachers, influenced by legal realism, resorted to social scientific and noncase materials. Courses in legal ethics assumed more respectability in the wake of Watergate.

The most important curricular developments involved skills training and hands-on experience as supplements to the abstract case method. John Bradway in 1928 pioneered the legal aid clinic at the law school of the University of Southern California, and the program became so successful that he was invited to establish a similar program at the Duke Law School. Not until the radicalized 1960s did clinical work gain a foothold. However, in recent years, internecine warfare between "scholars," interested in pursuing in-depth research on legal topics, and "clinicians," anxious to equip students with skills, deadened the full and enthusiastic adoption of the law clinic concept.[17]

Legal Thought and Theory

The tension between practice and theory also pervaded the postwar debate among legal scholars about the appropriate agenda for research and teaching. The consensus ideology of the era snubbed legal realism, although some scholars retained an interest in the relationship between social and legal change. But nothing emerged to replace realism in the 1950s and 1960s. Instead, legal thought of the period was "derivative and incorporative; previous assumptions were modified rather than rejected."[18] The emerging strands of legal thought returned to doctrine, gave emphasis to the policy-making function of lawyers, and stressed that law was based on "reason" rather than fiat.

The postrealist era dates from the publication in 1943 of a significant article by Yale Professors Harold Laswell, a political scientist, and Myres McDougal, a property law teacher. "Legal Education and Public Policy: Professional Training in the Public Interest" appeared in the *Yale Law Journal*. Laswell and McDougal integrated developments in legal thought since World War I into a "policy science" approach.[19] They sought to consider the need for moral values in both teaching and practice while retaining the realists' devotion to social science. Their emphasis on doctrine was a return to Langdell, but they also insisted that, because law students would someday become policy makers, legal educators had a duty to imbue in them a sense of social responsibility. The ideas of Laswell and McDougal laid the groundwork for the rise of the public-interest law movement in the 1960s.

Laswell and McDougal were, at best, able to "influence rather than restructure" law teaching and legal thought generally.[20] Their approach was too abstract, too academic, and too costly to implement. It also ran counter to the nature and goals of the majority of law students and teachers, who persisted in viewing themselves as engaged in practical professional training.

The social upheavals of the 1960s were accompanied by conflicting trends in legal thought. At the University of Chicago, a "law and economics" school of thought, led by Richard Posner, held that law should be based on the efficient operations of the marketplace. The classical economic theory that lay behind the new school of legal thinking gave it a sense of certainty, which the realists had jettisoned, and a unity of purpose that had not been present since Langdell. At the same time, the critical legal studies movement of the 1970s and 1980s attacked both the ideology of New Deal liberal legalism, the consensus "policy science" approach, and the ideas of Posner. Its major figure was Roberto Unger at Harvard University, although the Conference of Critical Legal Studies, founded in 1977, gained a significant following throughout the country. "Class bias" and "gross disparities of bargaining power," critical legal studies scholars insisted, lurked behind a facade of "neutral and formal rules."[21] Though seemingly connected to legal realism, the critical legal studies movement was quite different in that it took seriously the idea (far more than the realists) that politics and the law were inseparable and that there was no autonomous rule of law.[22]

Substantive Private Law Development since World War II

Substantive private law responded to the same social trends that affected the bar. In the trial courts, a pronounced shift occurred from civil to criminal matters, and on the civil side there was a shift from cases involving market transactions (e.g., contract, property, debt collection) to family, criminal, and tort cases. A similar change occurred in the makeup of appellate case loads of state supreme courts and federal courts of appeal. Judges increasingly construed statutes and administrative regulations that treated areas once the exclusive preserve of the common law. The absolute increase in the numbers of statutes and rules was a manifestation of the law explosion. A single fat volume could encompass the laws of a state in the nineteenth century; a whole book shelf was often necessary by the 1980s. The Supreme Court's constitutional revolution of 1937, which dethroned substantive due process and freedom to contract, enhanced legislative and administrative intervention into society and diminished the sanctity of property and contract rights. The traditional lines demarcating private law categories blurred, leading to the creation of protean bodies of new law, such as products liability, which gave judges extensive new policy-making authority.

Property: Entitlements, Zoning, and Landlord–Tenant

The welfare state introduced a new form of property called entitlements. The federal government (and to a lesser extent state governments), beginning in the New Deal, became a source of wealth. The entitlements that government created came in many forms. They were direct income and benefits, such as social security, unemployment compensation, aid to dependent children, veteran's benefits, and state and local welfare. They also included government jobs and contracts, licenses to practice a profession or engage in a trade, franchises to operate certain services (such as taxis), the use of public lands and resources, and access to services (such as technical information about some aspect of agriculture, labor, or waste disposal).[23]

The question of whether these entitlements composed a body of property rights was argued before the Supreme Court in the 1960s and 1970s. Liberal public-interest lawyers claimed that the high court should shield the recipients of these entitlements from the capricious activities of the bureaucratic state by granting certain of them (e.g., the poor, veterans, unwed mothers, dependent children) special constitutional protection. The justices refused to equate these entitlements with traditional property rights, finding in the leading case of *Dandridge* v. *Williams* (1970) that most entitlements were the product of social and economic regulation that state and federal government were free to exercise as long as they did so on a reasonable basis. Simply being poor, for example, did not grant a person any special claim to constitutional protection. More generally, the Court has held that what government granted, the bureaucratic state could revoke or modify without compensation. In most instances, an agency investigated, tried, and heard appeals from its decisions about claims to these entitlements. Even in instances, such as veterans' benefits, where courts heard appeals, a party first had to exhaust all administrative channels, a time-consuming process.

Zoning

Zoning was an activity derived from the police powers of the states, which usually delegated it to local municipalities. Industrialization and urbanization at the end of the nineteenth century presented issues so complex that the traditional common law action of nuisance proved unavailing in dealing with them.

New York City in 1916 passed the first comprehensive zoning ordinance, and it became a model for the rest of the country. The ordinance divided the city into residential, commercial, and unrestricted-use zones. The framers of the measure sought to save this elaborate system of controls from "legally fatal rigidities" by empowering an appointed administrative board to grant relief in cases where the new law created unnecessary hardships.[24]

The tangled web of motives behind this first exercise in land-use planning characterized the subsequent history of zoning. Advances in building materials and architectural design had made the skyscraper a reality, and these buildings acted as magnets that drew ever-larger populations into the cities and poured thousands of workers onto the streets. More than population control was involved, however. Fifth Avenue merchants wanted the new ordinance in order to prevent ethnic workers in the adjoining garment district from encroaching on their elegant sidewalks and wealthy clientele. From the beginning, therefore, in zoning law ''[t]he nugget of the idea of stability was not a concern over the quality of urban life nearly as much as a preoccupation with real estate values.''[25]

Zoning evolved as a matter of state and local concern. The Supreme Court in the landmark case of *Village of Euclid* v. *Ambler Realty Co.* (1926) upheld local zoning control as a rational extension of traditional public-nuisance law, with the advantage of alerting all owners before the fact of what they could and could not do with their land. ''A nuisance,'' the justices concluded, ''may be merely a right thing in the wrong place, like a pig in the parlor instead of the barnyard.''[26]

Zoning laws after World War II went hand-in-hand with suburban development. The automobile opened the countryside, low land values put housing within reach of many people, and the suburbs offered the prosperous white middle class a refuge from the inner-city blacks. Between 1950 and 1960, for example, builders erected one-quarter of all of the residential structures in the nation at that time, and almost all of this growth occurred in the suburbs. Large-scale developments required flexible land use, and zoning decisions ''increasingly [became] the rule of man rather than the rule of law.''[27] Projects such as the massive Levittown, New York development depended on innovations such as the floating-zone concept, in which a local government could craft the ordinance, in the name of the public good, to suit the needs of a particular developer.

Once established, many suburban communities tightened their land-use laws, both to keep others out and to prevent an alteration in the environment that made them appealing in the first place. Snob-zoning ordinances included provisions controlling the size of building lots and floor areas. In the celebrated case of *Lionshead Lake, Inc.* v. *Wayne Tp.* in 1952, the New Jersey Supreme Court sustained such requirements, even though ''[c]ertain well-behaved families will be barred from these communities, not because of any acts they do or conditions they create, but simply because the income of the family will not permit them to build a house at the cost testified to in this case.''[28] The civil rights revolution of the 1960s produced both case and statute law that forbade discrimination in housing based on race, but local governments through their zoning authority continued to set standards that limited the entrance of low-income groups.

Landlord and Tenant

The civil rights movement, public-interest lawyering, and a boom in large-scale luxury apartment buildings contributed to the new landlord–tenant law of the 1960s. Until the 1960s the common law remained favorable to the landlord, and public regulation was the exception. State civil rights legislation included fair housing codes that prohibited discrimination based on race, ethnicity, or religion, and the same principles, under Title VIII of the Civil Rights Act of 1968, applied where federal funds financed apartment construction. The crumbling of traditional deference to the landlord in the case law was also "traceable in no small degree to the fact that, under the Johnson administration's 'Great Society' programs, legal assistance was made much more accessible to indigent persons than it had been in the past."[29] Mundane landlord–tenant cases became vehicles by which activist lawyers engaged in social engineering. The slums, however, were not the only places from which new legal demands flowed. Tenants in large-scale luxury apartment buildings hired legal counsel to press their demands for greater control over their premises from impersonal corporate landlords.

The most far-reaching judicial assault on the common law of landlord and tenant occurred in the District of Columbia. Many states, especially California and New York, passed legislation that restricted the traditional rights of landlords, and some localities even imposed rent controls. Neither Congress nor local government in the District of Columbia had undertaken similar measures; yet the district, with its low-income black population and highly transient white population, was plagued by problems. Furthermore, Judge J. Skelly Wright, a philosophical liberal trained in the civil law system of Louisiana, presided over the District of Columbia Circuit Court of Appeals, which was in the forefront of consumer law reform. Wright's civil law background was important because in that system "the law has always viewed the lease as a contract, and . . . that perspective has proved superior to that of the common law [which viewed it as property]."[30]

The District of Columbia Circuit Court of Appeals between 1960 and 1970 decided three landmark cases that sketched the outlines of what might be called a tenants' bill of rights. In *Whetzel* v. *Jess Fisher Management Co.* (1960), the court permitted a tenant to bring a suit for injuries suffered because the landlord had failed to maintain the building in keeping with the city code. In *Edwards* v. *Habib* (1968), the court overturned the practice of retaliatory eviction. A tenant had rented on a month-to-month basis and, when she complained to the city about sanitary code violations, the landlord ordered her out. The court held that even through the tenant's lease had expired, the landlord was not allowed to evict the tenant because she had blown the whistle. Finally, in *Javins* v. *First National Realty Corp.* (1970), the court eliminated at one stroke several common law rules that had long aided landlords. The court found that landlords had a positive duty with respect to the conditions of the premises, that the tenant was bound to pay rent only when the premises met the conditions agreed to by the landlord, and that a tenant did not have to vacate a residence before asserting the right to refuse to pay rent based on the conditions of the premises. These opinions had their most dramatic effect on the poor, but the revised common and statutory law of landlord and tenant also protected more affluent individuals, who had greater access to counsel and sounder financial resources.

The "new" property, zoning, and the revised law of landlord and tenant manifested the ethos of liberal legalism that pervaded the postwar United States. Zoning and landlord–tenant law fostered some government control over property for the public good, but such activity was clearly within the broad traditions of U.S. legal history and did nothing to redistribute property between haves and have-nots.

Contract Law: Dead or Alive?

As with the law of property, so in the law of contract, what had been largely private matters in the nineteenth century became increasingly public concerns in the era after

World War II. The social welfare state spewed forth a stream of statutes and administrative regulations that removed some contract matters (e.g., insurance and labor employment) from the free market altogether, while antitrust laws limited other traditional commercial activities. Courts increasingly framed public policy, expressed by interpreting statutes and regulation, rather than scrutinizing and enforcing "private agreements under rules and standards formulated in the judicial process."[31] The late-nineteenth-century faith in objectivity and formalism dwindled. For example, the long-standing doctrines of *caveat emptor* and consideration (that which is given or done for the promise or act of another) lost authority to new concerns about fairness and efficiency in the mass-consumption society. Yale Law School Professor Grant Gilmore, after surveying the legal landscape in 1974, proclaimed "The Death of Contract" through "what might be called the process of doctrinal disintegration."[32]

Contract law lost its nineteenth-century position as *the* organizing concept in U.S. law, but reports of its death were greatly exaggerated. The principle of contract (of mutually agreed-to and enforceable private bargains) continued to sustain important social and economic relationships, with lawmakers advancing new doctrines, most notably reliance and unconscionability.

Arthur Corbin, a Harvard Law School professor, more than any other person developed the equitable concept of reliance interest. Corbin authored a major treatise on contract law, but he also served as the assistant to Samuel Williston, another Harvard professor, in preparing the first *Restatement of Contracts*. Corbin successfully argued that judges had historically decided some contract cases based on reliance interest. This concept returned contract to the equitable principles of the colonial era, stressing as it did that once a person relied in good faith on the actions of another a binding agreement had been formed. Section 90 of the *Restatement of Contracts* (second) enshrined the reliance concept, and courts repeatedly invoked it, just as Corbin suspected that they would. For example, the Wisconsin Supreme Court, in *Hoffman* v. *Red Owl Stores* (1965), a milestone in the development of the reliance concept, found that the repeated promises made by the agents of the Red Owl Grocery Company to provide a franchise to Hoffman had established a reliance interest, even though a contract to that effect had never been signed.

Modern courts have also invoked the doctrine of unconscionability. It means that provisions of an agreement that take advantage of another person, even though they had been agreed to as part of the contract, are not to be considered binding. Section 3-302 of the Uniform Commercial Code (UCC) spelled out the doctrine of unconscionability. Karl Llewellyn, a realist, had supervised the preparation of the UCC under the auspices of the American Law Institute during the late 1940s. Because much of the law of contract was also commercial law, the UCC became an important distillation of contract law. Llewellyn completed his work around 1950, and state legislatures gradually adopted the UCC. Today, forty-nine states, plus the District of Columbia and the Virgin Islands, have enacted the UCC, and Louisiana, whose civil law had long ago anticipated many of the practices set out by the UCC, has adopted portions of it.

Public-interest lawyers used the unconscionability provisions in the UCC to frame consumer protection appeals, especially where the poor were involved. The leading case was *Williams* v. *Walker-Thomas Furniture Company* (1965), decided by Judge J. Skelly Wright, the same federal judge who contributed to the reform of landlord–tenant law. A Washington, D.C. furniture store had sold goods, including a stereo, to

Mrs. Walker, a recipient of welfare. She signed a standardized installment sales contract employed by ghetto merchants who serviced what they considered to be poor credit risks. The contract included a "cross-collateral" clause, the effect of which was to "keep a balance due on every item purchased until the balance due on all items, whenever purchased, was liquidated."[33] This provision meant that as long as the purchaser drew on an installment account with Walker-Thomas, the furniture store could repossess *all* the goods purchased.

Judge Wright's opinion left little doubt that he considered the agreement unconscionable. "[T]he primary concern," he found, "must be with the terms of the contract considered in light of the circumstances existing when the contract was made."[34] The case was returned to the lower court, and after a new trial Mrs. Walker was released from the terms of her contract. Subsequent litigation, almost all of it in state courts, refined Judge Wright's somewhat ambiguous phrasing. To prove unconscionability, an aggrieved party had to demonstrate that there was both lack of freedom of choice and unreasonable terms.

Legislatures also passed consumer legislation requiring the full disclosure of credit terms, interest payments, potential safety and health hazards, and limiting the methods by which unpaid goods could be repossessed. These statutes, as in property law, served not just the poor, but middle-class consumers as well.

Nowhere was the problem of adapting contract law to new social circumstances more evident in the 1980s than in human reproduction and family composition. Most states, for example, banned couples from paying for adopted children, but social attitudes outraced the law. In an adoption market that required a waiting period of up to seven years, desperate infertile couples turned to surrogate mothers, hiring women to be impregnated artificially by the sperm of the husband and then to carry the child. The celebrated case of Baby M in 1987, in which a surrogate mother refused to abide by the terms of her contract to surrender the newborn, underscored the complex problems raised by the practice. A New Jersey judge ordered the surrogate mother to surrender the infant to the contracting couple in fulfillment of the contract. This emphasis on traditional contract rules stirred great furor, given the lower socioeconomic status of the surrogate mother in comparison to the parents and the deep emotional bond between the surrogate and the infant. Several state legislators bestirred themselves, proposing intricate rules to govern such contracts, but as of 1987 only Arkansas had passed legislation, providing that the child of an unmarried surrogate mother belonged to the couple who had contracted for it.

Even in the more mundane areas of human activity, the law declared by the courts consisted of only the most visible of disputes involving contracts. The growing intervention of lawmakers into consumer contracts was paralleled by the decreasing use by business interests of courts to settle contract disputes. They turned to commercial arbitration and formalized dispute settlement procedures. This behavior can be attributed, in part, to some of the better-known consequences of the litigation explosion, including a growing lack of confidence in the courts, high litigation costs, and delays in reaching settlements. Equally important, however, were considerations of business morality favoring promise keeping and the need to maintain goodwill among businesses engaged in recurring transactions.

Despite the decline in doctrinal certainty and purity, contract remained an important legal category through which Americans continued to organize themselves. The scope and implementation of contract law changed in response to the demands of a legal culture that placed increasing weight on equitable solutions to disputes rather than strict adherence to the idea that private parties, left to themselves, could best maximize their interests.

Torts and Products Liability

Modern tort law and liability insurance developed hand-in-hand. Through premiums paid by many policyholders, insurance companies spread the costs of accidents while making a profit through the shrewd investment of premiums. Profit was the reward for undertaking the socially useful yet risky task of insuring against accidents and encouraging beneficial technologies.

Late-nineteenth-century employers first used liability insurance, purchasing it to protect themselves against lawsuits brought by employees on the job. When worker's compensation dried up this market in the early twentieth century, the underwriters extended their lines of coverage in many other directions, including to automobile operators. Liability insurance by the 1940s had made tort law "public law in disguise" that provided "a remedy . . . for the everyday hurts inflicted by the multitudinous activities of our society."[35]

After World War II, tort law went through dramatic changes, especially in the areas of comparative negligence, no-fault automobile insurance, strict liability in the manufacture of consumer products, and medical malpractice. In each of these areas the emphasis in tort law shifted from the nineteenth-century concern with fault and blameworthiness to the contemporary stress on compensation of injured persons.

Comparative negligence, which first appeared in the mid-nineteenth century, did not receive widespread attention until the early twentieth century, when it won support in railroad cases as a modification of the harsh doctrine of contributory negligence. Comparative negligence apportioned fault among those persons involved in the accident and provided that recompense would be based on the extent of their responsibility. Between 1908 and 1941 Congress and nine states adopted some form of comparative negligence statutes, but the movement for its adoption slowed thereafter.

During the 1970s it attained new vitality as a way of stabilizing the rising costs of liability insurance. Personal-injury lawyers supported its adoption because it offered, in the face of rising demands by consumer groups for reform, an alternative that retained the negligence system against the even worse fate of no-fault insurance. By 1987 every state, through either legislative or judicial action, had adopted some form of comparative negligence, doing so in response to the growing costs of insurance and the rising demands of consumer groups.

No-fault automobile insurance, however, gained wide acceptance in the 1970s as the social demands placed on the tort system shifted from blameworthiness to compensation. In its pure form, no-fault insurance required that claims for personal injury (and sometimes property damage) were made against the claimant's own insurance company, regardless of who was at fault. With fault abolished, the costs and delays of out-of-court settlements or trials were eliminated. The debate over no-fault insurance extended back to the early twentieth century, but not until the 1960s did it receive sustained attention as a solution to the soaring costs of liability insurance and clogged court dockets. By midcentury, highway wrecks constituted up to 40 percent of the cases docketed in state appellate courts. Consumer activists such as Ralph Nader, and insurance underwriters anxious to better estimate costs, lined up against personal-injury lawyers.

Massachusetts in 1970 became the first state to enact a no-fault statute. Consumer activists in the state, responding to what were then the highest premiums in the nation for automobile insurance, successfully lobbied lawmakers, but the personal-injury bar did win concessions. The modified no-fault law provided that in cases of serious personal injuries and high medical costs, victims could still bring an action for damages against the other party and his insurance company. By 1987 more than one-half of the states had adopted some form of no-fault liability. These statutes reduced the numbers of cases involving automobile accidents, but their effect on the costs of insurance were hotly disputed. Even no-fault programs absorbed vast amounts of resources, primarily in marketing policies and settling claims.

The fault principle also waned in the area of products liability. Judge Benjamin N. Cardozo, of the New York Court of Appeals, in 1916 gave the initial impetus to the field with an innovative opinion in *MacPherson* v. *Buick Motor Co.* The case involved a wheel "made of defective wood," whose spokes "crumbled into fragments" and led to serious injury for MacPherson.[36] Under prevailing doctrine, MacPherson had no basis on which to bring suit against the automobile company because he lacked "privity of contract." This term meant that in order to bring suit a person had to have dealt directly with the manufacturer, and in this instance MacPherson had purchased the car from a dealer. Cardozo, however, relied on nineteenth-century cases involving obviously ultrahazardous activities (such as preparing medicines) to hold that privity of contract did not apply to dangerous manufactured items, a category into which he placed automobiles. Manufacturers, according to Cardozo, had to know that a third-party consumer would use their product and that they therefore had an absolute duty to make it "carefully."[37] Cardozo's opinion, however, stopped short of holding manufacturers strictly liable without fault.

The courts only gradually embraced a strict liability theory in consumer transaction cases. As late as 1955, William Prosser, the twentieth century's most distinguished writer on tort law and a champion of products liability, concluded that "the majority of courts still refuse to find any strict liability without privity of contract."[38] The New Jersey Supreme Court in 1960 decided the first important case, *Henningsen* v. *Bloomfield Motors.* The judges set aside the disclaimers of a warranty to find that a consumer could sue when the steering system went awry resulting in a crash. Four years later, the New York Court of Appeals held in *Goldberg* v. *Kollsman Instrument Corp.* (1963) that the beneficiary of a person killed in an airplane accident could proceed against the manufacturer of the defective altimeter that had caused the accident.

The most far-reaching opinion came in 1963 from the pen of Chief Justice Roger Traynor of the California Supreme Court, perhaps the most important judge and the most important court in the creation of products liability law. In *Greenman* v. *Yuba Power Products* (1963), Traynor found that a person injured by a defective power tool could sue the manufacturer in strict liability. His opinion summed up the circumstances that made this new area of tort law so changeable. The purpose of strict liability in consumer products cases, Traynor concluded, was "to insure that the costs of injuries resulting from defective products are borne by the manufacturers that put such products on the market rather than by injured persons who are powerless to protect themselves.''[39]

Prosser, the author of *Restatement of Torts* (second), enshrined this conception of strict liability in section 402A. "[P]ublic policy demands," this section proclaimed, that "the cost of injuries due to defective products be placed on those who market them; and, such injuries are properly treated as a cost of production and insurable risks by those in the best position to seek such protection.''[40] Not all legal scholars in the 1980s agreed with this view. Richard Posner, for example, complained that products liability law was economically inefficient because it contributed to inflation, and was morally unacceptable because it failed the important social test of impartially fixing blame.

Rights-conscious consumers, a decline of deference to figures of authority, and social interdependency converged during the 1970s and 1980s to subject doctors, nurses, teachers, and lawyers to greater scrutiny. In the nineteenth century and well into the twentieth century, professional malpractice cases were rare. Between 1960 and 1964, for example, there were only 60 malpractice cases brought in Cook County, Illinois, which included Chicago. Between 1975 and 1979, however, there were 142, an increase of 137 percent.

In the mid-1970s and again in the mid-1980s, the profits of the highly cyclical insurance business were buffeted by unfavorable interest rates in the money markets and claims that exceeded premiums. Insurance companies raised premiums, creating a sense of panic and forcing some physicians in especially sensitive areas, such as obstetrics and orthopedic surgery, to hike their fees and even withdraw from practice. Doctors engaged in elaborate and often needless testing to protect themselves from the dreaded day in court, and insurance companies retaliated by requiring that patients secure second and sometimes third opinions before undergoing certain procedures. The American Medical Association and the American Bar Association took sides, and their squabbling further contributed to the decline in public respect accorded the professions. Lawmakers responded with a grab bag of statutes that limited the contingent fees charged by lawyers, placed ceilings on awards and premiums, and established special medical-malpractice insurance pools among the carriers. These measures took the tort system further out of the realm of private control and reemphasized that its principal function was to provide compensation rather than to establish blameworthiness.

No other area of law contributed more to the concept of the law explosion. Before 1900, awards in accident cases were modest, and in the early twentieth century the largest award probably was no more than $750,000 in current dollars.[41] Since then, however, the *average* amount awarded in tort cases has climbed steadily, often with spectacular effect. For example, the Ford Motor Company in 1983, had to pay a judgment of $10 million as a result of an accident in which the brakes on a car it had manufactured failed, resulting in horrible burns to the driver. Such awards were the exception, but they nevertheless grabbed public attention and added to the sense of a legal system out of control.

Domestic Relations: No-Fault Divorce

By the late nineteenth century the private world of the family was increasingly subjected to public scrutiny. This trend continued throughout the twentieth century. Lawmakers, for example, intervened in such matters as child custody, legitimacy of bastard children, abortion, contraception, teenage sexuality, artificial insemination and surrogate motherhood, and the control exercised by parents and educators over children. Social welfare agencies exercised discretion in judging the fitness of parents to retain their children.

An equally important development, however, was the increasing incidence, discussed in the following chapter, of the Supreme Court's involvement with the family. In an age of rights consciousness, people challenged the traditional hegemony exercised by the states over the family, seeking through litigation in the federal courts to privatize matters such as abortion and contraception.

Divorce law, however, was the one area in which the authority of the state and of judges in particular receded and, as in tort law, a no-fault standard gained acceptance. The deregulation of divorce law was a vivid example of the way in which changes in general cultural and social practices forced new lines of development in the legal culture. The modern companionate family had shed many traditional functions, making the family increasingly a source of love and companionship. Divorce became common because, with expectations of marriage so high, "it was inevitable that they [would] not be fully achieved."[42] Furthermore, as women entered the work force in growing numbers, the possibilities of their escaping from an unsatisfactory marriage increased.

Many states during the Progressive era had modified many of the stiff requirements imposed by nineteenth-century law on divorce. But the notion of immorality and the consequent need to establish blame in order to end a marriage died hard. The ship of divorce law, however, foundered under the weight of the world's highest divorce rate; it had become "a fake" that "cheapen[ed] not only the tribunal but the members of the legal profession who [were] involved."[43] The dramatic increase in the divorce rate placed enormous pressures on the legal system and removed the former stigma that had been attached to the practice.

No-fault divorce first appeared in California in 1970. The California statute, which served as a model for the rest of the country, provided that either party in the marriage could assert that the union had broken down and dissolve it without providing an explicit basis (e.g., cruelty, irreconcilable differences) for doing so. No-fault divorce was cheap, easy to obtain, and quick. Only matters of custody and child support remained, and these tasks fell to divorce and family courts. The system quickly swept the country; in 1987 only Illinois and South Dakota did not have some form of no-fault divorce.

Criminal Justice, Crime Control, and the Rehabilitative Ideal

The prevention, detection, and punishment of crime, like developments in the legal profession and substantive law, were influenced by changes in postwar U.S. culture. Two models of criminal justice were in a tense relationship: "crime control" and "due process," both of which Herbert Packer, the period's most important writer on criminal law, described in an influential essay, "Two Models of the Criminal Process," published in 1968.[44] The crime control model emphasized the efficient suppression of crime through a swift and certain criminal process. The due-process model, however, stressed procedural regularity as a limit on the discretionary powers of criminal justice officials, as a protection for individual liberties, and as a guide to social justice. The assumptions behind the crime control model surfaced in the response of police and penal officials to public demands for tougher treatment of criminals.

The Crime Control Model, the Police, and Community Relations

The connection between crime control and police professionalization was typified in the Los Angeles Police Department. Under Chief William Parker during the 1950s and 1960s, it became the paragon of police efficiency, held up to public acclaim in the popular television program, *Dragnet*. Parker was influenced by J. Edgar Hoover, who, by the 1950s, had become the most revered figure in criminal justice. The Los Angeles police force carried the notions of scientific crime detection and a military style of police organization to their limits. Parker was a severe disciplinarian, and corruption in the department was rare. According to Parker, the purpose of the police was to wage a war on crime, and, in the sprawling city of Los Angeles, he developed the most effective motorized patrols and the most sophisticated radio communications network in the nation.

The impersonal and militaristic style adopted by the Los Angeles police met increasing resistance in the urban ghettos, like Watts, especially as the civil rights revolution and Great Society programs raised expectations. Big-city police departments were predominately white, and enforcement efforts in black communities were greeted with charges of police brutality and insensitivity. The problem became shockingly apparent between 1964 and 1968 when a wave of urban violence swept the nation. Both the plight of ghetto dwellers and the role of the police became the focus of national attention. President Johnson appointed the National Advisory Commission on Civil Disorders to investigate the rioting, and it reported, only a month before the assassination of Martin Luther King, Jr., in 1968, that "our nation is moving toward two societies, one black, one white—separate and unequal."[45]

A new police–community relations effort began amid the rubble of the rioting. Denounced by antiwar protesters as "pigs" and condemned as well by many well-intentioned white middle-class liberals, the police bore the brunt of criticism for precipitating the rioting. Major urban departments gradually changed their policies by establishing liaisons with black community leaders, decentralizing police administration into the neighborhoods, and instituting sensitivity training for officers. The hiring of black officers in large numbers was the most enduring of these reforms. By the 1980s, blacks had risen to positions of police leadership in such major cities as Detroit and New York. But efforts to accelerate the promotion of black officers (and later women) over white males with greater seniority, and sometimes higher scores on qualification tests, stirred controversy.

Decline of the Rehabilitative Ideal

Since the early nineteenth century, the purposes of punishment (retribution, deterrence, and rehabilitation) had existed in uneasy cyclical tension. In the 1960s, there was a new burst of enthusiasm in favor of rehabilitation through individualized treatment. The California prison system led the way, along with the U.S. Bureau of

Prisons, but by the 1980s the promise of these years, and of the rehabilitative ideal, had faded.

California developed a model correctional system based on the indeterminate sentence and two new institutions: the Youth Authority (1941) and the Adult Authority (1944). After finding the defendant guilty, a judge could either grant probation or commit the offender to the appropriate authority. The staff of the authority determined the eventual date of release and the particular correctional facility to which the convict would be sent, each of which was designed to deal with a given category of offender. Besides granting parole, the authority supervised the parolees. The prison population exploded and so too did the costs of its administration. In California, it jumped from 5700 prisoners in 1944 to more than 52,000 in 1986. This population was subject to new correctional routines, the most innovative of which was the group therapy session.

As with law enforcement, corrections became mired in racial antagonism. In the South, the rehabilitative ideal made inroads, as major scandals exposed the brutality of a system long run by political hacks. There as elsewhere, however, the rhetoric of reform never quite matched the reality of practice. Prison populations not only grew but they shifted in racial composition, and by the late 1950s a majority of inmates were black or Hispanic. Prison administrators and guards, however, were almost entirely white. Moreover, political and civil rights activism penetrated the prisons, and inmates pressed claims for equal rights that struck a public panicked by crime as ridiculous.

Prison violence became endemic, in part because of racial tension, in part because of the more assertive mood of the prison population, and in part because prison officials lacked funds and personnel to do their jobs. In California, the model of the modern prison system, the number of inmates stabbed by other inmates rose from 56 in 1969 to 168 in 1972. In 1970 alone there were seventy major prison disturbances. A year later Attica prison in New York exploded in the worst prison rioting in U.S. history, leaving forty-three persons dead, including ten hostages.

The debacle at Attica marked the beginning of the decline of the rehabilitative ideal. The Committee for the Study of Incarceration examined events at Attica in the context of the entire penal system, and its report, *Doing Justice* (1976), concluded that the offender should be "treated *as though he deserves* the unpleasantness that is being inflicted on him."[46] The report mirrored public attitudes that wanted the prisoner to pay for what he or she had done rather than for what they might be expected to do. Flat-time or determinate sentencing gained renewed favor, both from proponents of harsher treatment of prisoners who thought it would close the revolving door in prisons created by parole, and by prisoner rights advocates who considered indeterminate sentencing a tool by which prison administrators oppressed the inmate population. In 1987 the U.S. Sentencing Commission, created by Congress, endorsed curbs on judicial discretion through mandatory flat-time sentences and an end to parole of federal prisoners.

The tougher stance toward crime surfaced in other ways. State appellate courts refused to adopt a more liberal interpretation of the insanity test, known as the *Durham* rule, continuing instead to invoke the nineteenth-century *McNaghten* test. The new emphasis on retribution and deterrence also revitalized the death penalty, even though studies showed that it had no deterrent effect and that it was disproportionately applied to blacks who killed whites. Executions declined from a peak of 199 in 1933 to 2 in 1967. The ACLU and NAACP raised through litigation serious constitutional challenges to the death penalty, and the next execution did not take place until after the

Gregg v. *Georgia* (1976) decision, when the Supreme Court reaffirmed its approval of capital punishment. The following year, Gary Gilmore died before a firing squad in Utah. Over the next decade the pace of executions picked up speed, with the Supreme Court in 1987 removing the final hurdle by holding that even though the death penalty was applied unequally to blacks, a condemned person could escape the executioner only by proving direct racial prejudice.

The Federal Government and Crime Control

The federal government expanded its role in crime control, just as it intervened directly in other areas of public life that had historically been the province of state and local officials. The FBI continued as both a model and a scientific, technical, and training resource for local police departments. The Great Society was premised on the belief that social harmony and justice would follow if the conditions fostering the pathology of crime were eliminated. But Johnson in 1965 also persuaded Congress to create the Office of Law Enforcement Assistance (OLEA) to support training, research, and demonstration projects to improve crime control. OLEA was a landmark in that it was the first time that the federal government had provided direct crime-fighting funds to local officials, who snapped up the money.

Urban rioting and soaring crime rates, according to a new generation of conservative criminal justice experts, such as James Q. Wilson of Harvard, and politicians, notably Richard Nixon and George C. Wallace, revealed that the social welfare programs of the Great Society merely abetted criminals and that a due-process revolution carried out by the Supreme Court only encouraged greater lawbreaking. In the midst of a clamor for law and order, Congress passed the Omnibus Crime Control and Safe Streets Act of 1968, which created a new federal agency, the Law Enforcement Assistance Administration (LEAA), to replace OLEA. Congress built LEAA on a scheme of cooperative federalism and block grants. To receive federal funds, the states had to establish a State Planning Agency and develop a comprehensive anticrime strategy. Each state agency then distributed the funds to local criminal justice officials, based on applications they had made. While the federal funds were intended to apply to corrections and courts, most of the money was diverted to the purchase of police equipment as a "war on crime" mentality swept the country in the early 1970s.[47]

Administrative Law and the Regulatory State since World War II

LEAA was only one example of the postwar response of federal agencies in solving the era's complex problems. By the late 1940s, administrative bodies became an accepted feature of the legal system. Many of the New Deal lawyers, once considered radicals for supporting the regulatory state, entered private practice, taking their expertise with them. Over the next four decades, "Washington lawyers" (experts in regulatory matters) rivaled "Wall Street lawyers" for influence.

The ABA leadership, after initial hostility, decided to tame rather than fight the regulatory state. It sponsored the Administrative Procedures Act (APA) of 1946, a federal law that imposed procedural order on often unruly administrative agencies and facilitated the expanded role of lawyers in the regulatory state. The APA, which applied to all federal agencies, rationalized and harmonized the role of administrative bodies. It outlined the way in which agencies should act rather than what the agencies should act upon, dividing the administrative process into two broad categories: rulemaking and adjudication. In the former, the act required agencies to provide preliminary notice, a period for comment, and a statement of basis and purpose. The act also formulated guidelines for the adjudication of disputes about rules. On this count, the act was much more stringent. It created a fairly elaborate scheme for evidentiary requirements and hearing examiners, forcing agencies to proceed about the way courts did in determining the merits of an individual claim.

APA ushered in two decades of consensus about the value of administrative oversight. Matters of regulatory reform and the impulse to redefine the relationship between the public and private sectors were temporarily in abeyance. The federal judiciary, for example, granted broad discretion to regulatory bodies based on their supposed expertise and experience in dealing with the areas they regulated. The growing influence of the agencies further weakened the traditional dichotomy between public and private spheres of responsibility.

Although the Republican party sometimes railed against the newly powerful regulatory state during the 1950s, in practice the administration of Dwight D. Eisenhower supported it. Government by regulation expanded, not contracted, often because business perceived its value. The most notable example was the Atomic Energy Act of 1946, which established the Atomic Energy Commission (AEC). The AEC played a vital role in expanding the nuclear power industry, adapting advances in atomic weaponry to peaceful purposes by encouraging the development of technologies, granting licenses to operators, and overseeing the construction of facilities. Congress complemented this new body with the Price–Anderson Act of 1957, which was "designed, in part, to insulate the nuclear industry from liability suits for damages from serious accidents" by giving "companies the courage to risk massive amounts of money in a complex and potentially very dangerous technology."[48]

The prevailing consensus about the value of regulation did not mean an end to fighting over what the agencies should do. One of the most notable features of the United States after World War II was the way in which contending social and economic groups competed to influence these bodies. In the case of nuclear power, for example, coal operators, fearful that they would lose their virtual monopoly over supplying fuel for electrical generation, lobbied against Price–Anderson in Congress and testified before the AEC about the inadequacies of nuclear power plant safety programs. In another area, labor and business also sharply differed over what powers the NLRB should exercise. Business in 1947 won a major victory in the Taft–Hartley Act, which limited NLRB discretion and made it significantly more sensitive to business interests. The act, for example, banned the closed shop (in which all persons working in the place of employment had to belong to the union) and required certain unions to abide by a sixty-day cooling-off period before striking.

The Public-Interest Era: Consumer Rights and Environmentalism

The consensus that enveloped administrative regulation crumbled in the late 1960s, and a decade later a full-blown movement toward deregulation was under way. The attack on the regulatory state came from many directions. Consumer and environmen-

tal advocates complained that businesses under regulation had captured their regulators, making the agencies into little more than tools of the regulated. Ralph Nader,
the most visible and articulate consumer activist of the era, directed particularly strong
attacks against the Federal Trade Commission (FTC) and the Food and Drug Administration. The business community was equally adamant, charging that the agencies
had driven up costs by imposing unworkable and costly regulations. The federal
judiciary abandoned its deference, questioning the extent to which many federal agencies provided due-process guarantees in both rulemaking and adjudication.

Congress poured forth a stream of consumer and environmental legislation, further
tipping the federal system in favor of the central government and continuing the
tradition of cooperative federalism initiated in the Progressive era. Federal and state
regulatory officials ostensibly shared responsibility for planning and funding, but
federal officials, with superior resources, usually held the whip hand.

The beginning of the era of public-interest law dated from the Auto Safety Act of
1966, which imposed federal safety standards in automobiles, an area traditionally
reserved to the states. The Wholesome Meat Act of 1967, also influenced by Nader,
extended federal standards to meat-processing plants doing *intrastate* business. The
Magnuson–Moss Warranty and FTC Improvements Act of 1972 was designed to
overcome the deficiencies in the handling of consumer matters by the FTC. The
establishment a year later of the Consumer Product Safety Commission gave consumers a separate agency. The Occupational Safety and Health Act of 1970 brought the
federal government into direct regulation of the work place.

Environmentalists won important victories as well. Congress in 1970 passed the
National Environmental Policy Act (NEPA) and the Clean Air Amendments (CAA).
The former directed the Council on Environmental Quality to monitor environmental
trends. What was an otherwise broad statement of national policy did contain one
provision with significant regulatory consequences: the environmental impact statement. It required both developers and regulators, in all agencies, to take into account
the environmental consequences of their actions.

The CAA was equally pathbreaking in restricting administrative discretion and
forcing action on the part of regulators and the regulated. The Environmental Protection Agency (EPA) administered CAA, but EPA relied on the states for implementation, imposing fines and penalties when states failed to cooperate. The act forced both
administrative and state action by specifying rigid time periods during which certain
actions had to take place. The act made the EPA into a policing agency, charging it not
cnly with monitoring state compliance but also with overseeing the directives issued to
auto manufacturers to reduce exhaust emissions dramatically.

Consumer and environmental groups did not want to do away with regulation; they
just wanted to make federal agencies more responsive. During the late 1960s and early
1970s these groups frequently charged that "economic regulation was adrift in a sea of
irresolution."[49] They complained that regulatory bodies failed to delineate long-term
policies and that they had inappropriately mixed promotional and regulatory objectives.

The AEC was a notable example. Congress established it to promote and regulate
nuclear energy in the United States. In 1974, however, as the complexities of building
nuclear power stations became evident, and as a small but active grassroots antinuclear
movement pressed for greater controls on nuclear plants, Congress abolished the AEC,

replacing it with two new bodies: the Nuclear Regulatory Commission (NRC) and the Energy Research and Development Administration (ERDA). The NRC was later merged into the Department of Energy.

Other critics complained that the regulatory state, intended to serve the public, had become oppressive. Yale Law Professor Charles Reich in 1964 complained that the largess doled out by government agencies constituted a "new property," the control of which properly belonged to elected officials and judges rather than bureaucrats.[50] Reich also accused regulators of failing to abide by their own rules and, even when they did, with adjudicating cases in ways that violated traditional due-process guarantees.

The federal courts obliged the demands by consumer and environmental groups that regulatory bodies consistently follow their procedures and respect due process. Two cases during the mid-1960s challenged the self-proclaimed wisdom of regulatory agencies as the exclusive guardians of the public interest. The first was *Office of Communication of the United Church of Christ* v. *FCC,* decided by the Circuit Court for the District of Columbia in 1966, and the other was *Scenic Hudson Preservation Conference* v. *FPC,* decided by the U.S. Second Circuit Court of Appeals in 1965.

The former involved an application by a Jackson, Mississippi television station to have its license renewed after repeated instances of denying civil rights advocates access to the public. For example, the station cut off transmission just as an NAACP representative was about to speak. The Federal Communications Commission (FCC) granted the station a new license without allowing blacks who were opposed to renewal an opportunity to testify. The federal circuit court reversed the decision, finding that the FCC had failed to abide by its own rules requiring that the listening public have an opportunity to comment.

Scenic Hudson was an even more important case, marking the beginning of the environmental movement's use of the federal courts. In this instance, the Federal Power Commission (FPC) issued a license to construct a hydroelectric power plant at Storm King Mountain, a scenic area on the Hudson River. The FPC refused to hear testimony about the impact of the plant on fisheries, and it rejected the application of expert witnesses on the environment to add their testimony to the record. The second circuit court rebuked the actions of the FPC and directed it and the project developers to prepare a statement weighing the intangible concerns about the environment with economic considerations.

These decisions were important precedents in the growth of judicial oversight of administrative and regulatory agencies. The New Deal had placed great weight on the idea that expertise could override the consequences of political decision making; but in the 1970s, many former prophets of regulation claimed that technical expertise had to be balanced by respect for procedure, and the federal courts emerged as watchdogs by imposing a stringent level of judicial review on administrative decision making.

Courts and regulators plunged into areas that presented often intractable controversies over the need for a clean environment and the requirement for economic growth. Quantifying aesthetic and environmental values was troubling enough, but matters became even more complicated when hazardous materials, often essential to industrial production, were involved. The EPA, for example, was often placed in the difficult position of having to devise regulations about the use of these materials based on uncertain evidence about their safety and health effects.

A classic example was the struggle over the Reserve Mining Company's operations in Minnesota on the shore of Lake Superior between 1969 and 1975. The EPA ordered the company to cease dumping of taconite tailings into the lake, charging that they contained asbestos fibers widely believed to cause cancer. The company claimed that the EPA had failed "to establish, under traditional standards of proof, that the tailings" were harmful to human health.[51] In 1975, the U.S. Eighth Circuit Court of Appeals, in *Reserve Mining Co.* v. *EPA,* found that the burden of proof lay with the Reserve Mining Company to show that the tailings were not dangerous rather than on the injured parties. The plant closed. By the mid-1980s, the problem of latent-toxic torts (ones whose effects did not become noticeable until years and in some cases decades later) was burgeoning.

In the late 1970s, the attack on the regulatory state took a new turn as a bipartisan consensus emerged in favor of deregulation. The dramatic rise in inflation, sagging industrial productivity, and the loss of market share by U.S. producers to foreign companies encouraged this reassessment. Consumer activists deplored the new reform effort, but, after years of criticizing federal agencies, their arguments rang hollow. Congress responded to the demands for deregulation by enacting statutes aimed at transportation, the oldest of the regulated industries. The Airline Deregulation Act of 1978 provided for a phased ending to fare setting and to entry restrictions on air travel. The Motor Carrier Reform Act of 1980 and the Staggers Rail Act of the same year relaxed rate and entry regulations on motor carrier and rail traffic, respectively. The Depository Institutions Deregulation and Monetary Control Act of 1980 eliminated interest rate ceilings on time and savings deposits.

Republican President Ronald Reagan, elected to office in 1980, while trumpeting the personal virtues of Franklin Roosevelt, engaged the powers of the presidential office to subvert rather than support the regulatory state. Reagan pledged to get the federal government "off the peoples' backs" by ending the welfare state. He appointed agency heads sympathetic to his views. For example, the National Highway Traffic Safety Administration (NHTSA) in 1977 adopted during the administration of President Jimmy Carter a regulation mandating by 1984 the use of passive restraints in automobiles either by the use of airbags or seat belts. When Reagan came into office, he appointed a new head of NHTSA who proceeded to revoke the mandatory restraint requirement, arguing that the costs of compliance outweighed the effects to be achieved. The Supreme Court, in *Motor Vehicle Manufacturers Association* v. *State Farm Mutual Auto Insurance Co.* (1983), found the agency's reasoning inadequate, and it overturned the new regulation and remanded it to the agency for further consideration.[52] In response, the president directed that all of his appointees to the federal bench embrace his own skeptical attitude toward the regulatory state.

Reagan's efforts produced more show than substance. The administrative state, which had begun in the nineteenth century as a modest enterprise, had grown by the 1980s into a distinct branch of government that was essential to the functioning of a complex and interdependent society. Moreover, the regulatory state after the New Deal was compatible with the ideology of liberal legalism. The administrative law and regulatory agencies did not force a redistribution of wealth; there was no requirement that the polluters give money to those who were injured. That goal was only available through lawsuit. As Richard Posner argued, regulation did have costs, but the prevailing view, as in tort law, was that business should internalize and pass them on to consumers in the form of higher prices. The regulatory system was a means by which to restrict unacceptable activities rather than a program of planned social activity.

The Law Explosion and Contemporary Legal Culture

Chief Justice Warren Burger, appointed by President Nixon in 1969, complained bitterly in 1982 that the nation's legal system had become burdened by a law "explosion during this generation." Burger claimed that "[r]emedies for personal wrongs that once were considered the responsibility of institutions other than the courts are now boldly asserted as legal 'entitlements'." "The courts," he concluded, "have been expected to fill the void created by the decline of church, family, and neighborhood unit."[53] Burger was correct: there were more lawyers, more lawsuits, a vastly expanding regulatory and welfare state, and a pattern of much private law taking on a public character. But did these events amount to a profound disruption that unsettled social relations, added to the costs of doing business, and promoted social contentiousness? Moreover, proponents of the law explosion theory usually failed to include the dramatic upsurge in police and corrections as being in some way bad. When they did take notice, they invariably suggested that the criminal justice system was too lax and too sympathetic to criminals. They complained that there was not enough law. To some extent, the law explosion was a lament by a generation unsettled by the events of the 1960s for a quieter and less perplexing time.

When placed in historical perspective, the major features of the legal system seemed remarkably unchanged and wholly connected to trends extending back at least to the Progressive era. The system remained genuinely federal, characterized by diversity in the substantive law among different jurisdictions and, even though cooperative federalism tilted toward greater national control, state and local lawmakers and regulators retained significant autonomy. Legislation and regulation diminished the breadth of the common law, but it remained, as it had for centuries, a vital component of the legal system.

The quantitative and qualitative changes that swept through the legal system after World War II are best understood as evidence of legal culture resonating, as it had for the previous two centuries, to changes in the underlying general culture. Under the influence of the dominant ideology of liberal legalism, Americans expected more and came to rely more on their legal system. As Lawrence M. Friedman had argued, there emerged in the mid-1960s a general "expectation of justice" and an accompanying "general expectation of recompense" for wrongs.[54] Americans got more law because they wanted more, and the Supreme Court promoted this heightened sense of rights consciousness through a revolution in public law, a revolution in which, ironically, Chief Justice Burger participated.

16

The Imperial Judiciary and Contemporary Social Change

The Changing Public Law Agenda and the Imperial Judiciary

The Supreme Court and Its Business

The transformation of the general culture produced new demands on public as well as private law. The Supreme Court, which had long since established its position as the final arbiter of the Constitution, both reflected and contributed to the heightened sense of rights consciousness that pervaded the contemporary United States. After the constitutional revolution of 1937, the justices turned their attention from matters of economic regulation to issues of civil liberties and civil rights. The civil liberties portion of this new agenda included freedom of speech, press, and religion, and the rights of the accused; the civil rights side dealt with blacks and women. In both of these areas, special-interest groups, like the NAACP, the Sierra Club, the ACLU, and the National Organization for Women, were the agents of social change, pushing back the frontiers of constitutional law.

The composition of the Court revealed the rapidity with which changes in the general culture penetrated the legal culture. President Lyndon Johnson in 1967 appointed the first black, Thurgood Marshall (1967–   ), and Ronald Reagan in 1981 selected the first woman, Sandra Day O'Connor (1981–   ). In 1945 the appointment of either a black or a woman would have been inconceivable.

The Court has been a dynamic institution; in no similar period have the justices issued more concurring and dissenting opinions. Their ranks also changed over these four decades. Twenty-seven justices served on the high bench, and four of these were chief justices: Fred M. Vinson (1946–1954), Earl Warren (1954–1969), Warren Burger (1969–1987), and William H. Rehnquist (1987–   ). Of these, Warren was the dominant force because he was a leader who left a lasting stamp on the Court and the nation.

Analyzing the Court based on the tenures of chief justices is misleading. The history of the Court after World War II can be better understood as two long cycles that overlapped in the early 1970s. The first of these ran from 1946 to 1969, an era in which the appointees of Franklin D. Roosevelt, especially Hugo Black (1937–1971), Felix Frankfurter (1939–1962), and William O. Douglas (1939–1975), combined with three Eisenhower appointees, Chief Justice Earl Warren, John Marshall Harlan (1955–1971), and William J. Brennan (1956–   ) to form the Court's intellectual core. The careers of Warren and Brennan revealed the difficulty that presidents often have in attempting to give the Court a particular ideological cast. They were the most forceful advocates of liberal legalism, so much so, in the case of Warren, that the conservative Eisenhower observed that his selection was "the biggest damnfool mistake I ever made."[1] Warren presided over a far-ranging reinterpretation of black civil rights, church–state relations, voting rights, and the rights of the accused.

The second era began about the time of President Richard M. Nixon's appointment of Chief Justice Burger. Nixon campaigned against many of the Warren Court's decisions, promising to forge a conservative majority on the bench that would support law and order and "strictly construct" the Constitution. By strict construction, the president meant that the justices would read it literally and, when it was unclear, defer to the legislative branch. The Senate's Democratic majority, however, frustrated these plans, rejecting two of Nixon's nominees, G. Harold Carswell and Clement Haynesworth, because of the inadequate qualifications of the former and the membership of both in all-white private clubs. Nixon then turned to able lawyers and judges who were, with the exception of conservative William H. Rehnquist, political moderates.

The Court consolidated the work of the first era and, in some instances, such as civil rights for women and the law of libel, expanded on it. In the area of the rights of the accused, it granted police officials somewhat greater discretion and sustained the death penalty.

The Court was the featured but not the sole actor in the theater of public law. The same interest groups that litigated before it also turned to Congress for legislation and even constitutional amendments. In the 1980s, they also successfully urged many state supreme courts to supplement federal constitutional rights with an expanded interpretation of state constitutional guarantees of liberty. Throughout the postwar era, however, the Supreme Court was at the hub of controversy, with legal scholars, politicians, and even the justices clashing over its role in modern society.

Process Jurisprudence, Neutral Principles, and the Imperial Judiciary

The sociological jurisprudence of Roscoe Pound and Louis D. Brandeis gave way in the 1930s to the legal realism of Karl Llewellyn and Jerome Frank. In the 1940s, legal realism was squeezed on the private law side by the "policy science" approach of Myers McDougal and Harold Laswell and, on the public law side, by process jurisprudence. The last of these began with the critique of legal realism made by Lon Fuller, a Harvard Law School professor, in the 1930s and 1940s, and it blossomed into "a full-blown political science theory in the 19[50]s, prescribing carefully defined roles for courts, legislatures, and administrative agencies."[2]

Process jurisprudence, like "policy science," emerged from the consensual intellectual atmosphere of the Cold War era, and it was an effort to establish guidelines by which appellate judges could operate in a democratic polity. Where realists had taken an essentially fatalistic approach to unchecked judicial power and to judicial whim, exponents of process jurisprudence aimed to rein in judicial authority. Process jurisprudence stressed that there were limits to judicial power and that judges had to defer to the legislative branches. Those limits involved the ways (i.e., the processes) by which judges reached their opinions. According to this theory, judges were to follow a course of "reasoned elaboration" rooted in the best skills of being a lawyer rather than to follow the more open-ended, political compromising that characterized legislative decision making. Substance was subordinated to process, and nothing was as important as "thinking like a lawyer."[3] Process jurisprudence was not antagonistic to judicial creativity and to substantive change in the law; rather, it insisted that such activity be set in a way that would make it legitimate for judges (as judges and not legislators) to undertake to bring about meaningful change, by ensuring that they decided cases based on "impersonal and durable principles."[4]

Professors Herbert Wechsler of Columbia University Law School and Alexander Bickel of the Yale Law School in the 1960s and 1970s carried the idea of process jurisprudence a step further, in reaction to the Warren Court's role in formulating public policy. Wechsler in 1959 published a highly influential essay, "Toward Neutral Principles of Constitutional Law," which stressed that judicial review could only contribute to the growth of democracy when it was "genuinely principled" and based "on analysis and reasons quite transcending the immediate result that it achieved."[5] The most significant limit, according to Wechsler, was "professional constraint"; that is, the craft techniques of the legal profession justified the substitution of the judiciary's judgment for that of electorally accountable representatives. Bickel also worked within the concept of process jurisprudence, but he concluded in *The Morality of Consent* (1975) that even neutral principles and correct processes could not ensure that the decisions of unelected justices would be legitimate. The Supreme Court could be a great moral teacher, but it could not pretend to be able to do what the popular branches of government were unwilling to do.

In the 1950s and 1960s a second line of scholarly debate emerged about the role of the judiciary in American democracy. It was also liberal, but it stressed the importance of the justices in achieving substantive results, and it might be termed substantive liberal jurisprudence. Former liberal critics of judicial power, which the regulatory and social welfare state secured from judicial scrutiny by the constitutional revolution of 1937, became proponents of judicial review as a tool to force social change. "The power of judicial review," Yale Law Professor Eugene Rostow wrote in 1953, "stands . . . as an integral feature of the living constitution, long since established as a working part of the democratic political life of the nation."[6] Proponents of substantive liberalism argued that judicial review, while in the formal sense undemocratic, was actually a necessary instrument of democracy because it permitted justices to break down practices like racial segregation that prevented the United States from becoming a genuinely open society. Substantive liberalism meant that the justices had a responsibility to overturn practices that were clearly antithetical to the broad purposes of American life: open discourse and social egalitarianism. The process used to end racial discrimination, for example, was less important than that it be ended. In public law, substantive liberalism was the fullest expression of liberal legalism.

The debate over process and substance also occurred within the Court. Felix Frankfurter and John Marshall Harlan were the strongest proponents of process jurisprudence. Frankfurter was a longtime adherent of liberal causes, notably Sacco and Vanzetti, but his reaction to their fate was typical of his beliefs. He supported them less from the belief that they were innocent or that they had been singled out because of their ethnic backgrounds and political ideas, and more because he believed that they had not had a fair trial and that the process had failed. As a justice, Frankfurter went out of his way to appear disinterested in liberal causes and to stress repeatedly the theme of judicial restraint. Reason and the professional skills of a lawyer should guide the outcome of the case not the wishes of the judge. Justice Harlan agreed with Frankfurter, arguing that the Court should not attempt to do what legislatures were unwilling to do.

Earl Warren, however, had a substantially different conception of the judicial role. He believed that the Court had a positive responsibility to intervene where social injustice was evident. Warren was much more skeptical than Frankfurter about the efficacy of the political process, believing that it too often was insensitive to the values for which the United States should stand. Moreover, Warren found that the construction of legislative authority was such that it would block meaningful change. Without the prodding of the Court, why then would an all-white legislature ever adopt a position to do away with racial segregation? Why would malapportioned state legislatures, with rural areas far outweighing much more heavily populated urban areas, ever agree to change the existing system upon which rural domination rested? When asked to name the most important decision of his tenure, Warren chose *Baker* v. *Carr* (1962), a case in which the Court mandated the apportionment of legislative districts based on the principle of "one man, one vote."[7] Warren and Black, in short, believed that the Court should promote humanitarian values.

The concept of substantive liberalism evoked a growing chorus of complaints that the justices were substituting their values for those of the framers. In the 1970s and 1980s, the debate about judicial review and judicial power shifted increasingly toward the issue of original intent—that is, the role that the intentions of the framers of the Constitution (and the various amendments) should have in judicial interpretation. Conservative legal scholars, judges, and politicians argued that the Court had become a lawmaking body. Raoul Berger of Harvard University Law School condemned the substantive liberalism of the Warren Court and concluded that the justices had formed themselves into an "imperial judiciary," substituting their vision of the good society for that of the framers.[8] President Ronald Reagan and Attorney General Edwin Meese echoed this theme in the 1980s. Meese urged that the Court return to a jurisprudence of "original intention" and that the justices refuse to decide matters that properly belonged to the states and the legislative branches.[9] Ronald Reagan underscored the depth of his commitment in 1987 by appointing William Rehnquist (the most outspoken proponent of the idea of original intent) as chief justice and Antonio Scalia (a federal appeals court judge, also noted for his strict constructionist views) as an associate justice. After a fierce battle in the judiciary committee, the full Senate rejected the nomination of Robert Bork, a federal appeals court judge and former Yale Law School professor, to the high court. Liberal and moderate senators concluded, somewhat incorrectly, that Bork mouthed the doctrine of original intent as a means of legitimating his conservative goals.

Civil Liberties

Ordered Liberty and Preferred Positions

The modern reconsideration of civil liberties and civil rights began in the 1930s. At the same time that the Court was jettisoning its concern with economic rights and government regulation, it announced clearly its intentions to take on new issues involving matters of human freedom.

The Court moved cautiously to "nationalize" the Bill of Rights through its selective incorporation into the Fourteenth Amendment. In *Palko* v. *Connecticut* (1937), the justices considered a claim that the Fourteenth Amendment's due-process clause incorporated the Fifth Amendment's protection against double jeopardy. Justice Benjamin N. Cardozo rejected the argument in this instance, but he did find that there were some rights that were so "fundamental" that liberty and justice could not exist if they were sacrificed. Cardozo made clear that First Amendment rights were "the indispensable condition" of nearly every other form of freedom, and that they had been fully incorporated. But other rights, notably jury trials, indictments, immunity against compulsory self-incrimination, and double jeopardy "might be lost, and justice still be done." Incorporation of the different parts of the Bill of Rights, therefore, depended on how fundamental they were to a "scheme of ordered liberty."[10] Selective incorporation meant that the justices would have broad authority to pick and choose in the future, but that in doing so they would not interfere with the state systems of criminal justice. The Court reiterated this position in a five-to-four decision in *Adamson* v. *California* (1948), another criminal justice case involving the Fifth Amendment, leaving the process of incorporation to go on selectively.

The justices also signaled their intention to switch the agenda to matters of civil liberties and civil rights in *United States* v. *Carolene Products Co.*, a case decided a year after *Palko*. Justice Harlan Fiske Stone initiated the famous preferred-positions doctrine in a footnote to an otherwise unremarkable case. Stone indicated that in the future the Court was going to give special attention to noneconomic freedom, so much so that it was willing to impose a double standard of review. On the matter of state economic policy, the Court would defer to the legislature; but on issues involving civil liberties and civil rights, Stone announced that the justices would apply special scrutiny to legislative actions and give a preferred position to liberties and rights. Legislative efforts to curb liberties and rights would have to be more securely founded than would measures involving the economy. The preferred-positions doctrine, even buried as it was in a footnote, was an invitation to litigants to bring civil liberties and civil rights appeals to the Court. Judicial review, Stone concluded, was necessary because of "prejudice against discrete and insular minorities, which tends seriously to curtail the operation of those political processes ordinarily to be relied on to protect minorities, and which may call for a correspondingly more searing judicial inquiry."[11] The Court was setting itself up as a guardian of social minorities.

Armed with the concepts of "ordered liberty," selective incorporation, and preferred positions, the postwar Court expanded the sphere of civil liberties, although its actions were not without contradictions. When national-security issues were involved, as in the Japanese relocation cases, the Court was far more willing to defer to Congress than when security issues were not present.

The Cold War and the New Red Scare

Anticommunism was a persistent theme in twentieth-century political life, one that became all the more pronounced as the nation moved to a position of world power. For example, John Bricker, the Republican vice-presidential candidate in 1944, charged that "Communist forces have taken over the New Deal and will destroy the very foundations of the Republic."[12] Red hysteria gripped the nation during the Cold War. The House Committee on Un-American Activities invoked the Smith Act to investigate anyone even suspected of being a Communist. President Harry S. Truman, who replaced Roosevelt in 1945 and won election on his own three years later, undertook on political grounds to purge the government of Communists, and in 1946 he issued Executive Order 9835 creating a Federal Employee Loyalty Program that permitted government officials to screen more than 2 million federal employees for political deviance.

The Red Scare and Senator Joseph McCarthy of Wisconsin became synonymous during the early 1950s. In 1950 McCarthy initiated a four-year reign of terror, when he proclaimed in a speech in Wheeling, West Virginia that he had a list of 205 card-carrying Communists who "are still working and shaping policy in the State Department."[13] McCarthy then hauled a long list of prominent and not-so-prominent Americans before his Senate investigating committee, charging them with being Communists or communist sympathizers. With Americans dying on a distant battlefield against the communist armies of North Korea and China, McCarthy ran roughshod. His campaign finally collapsed in the mid-1950s under the weight of unfounded accusations and peace on the Korean peninsula.

The hysteria of the Red Scare posed questions about the balance to be struck between the government's authority to protect itself and the individual's freedom of association and expression. In 1948, under the authority of the Smith Act, the Truman administration won the indictment and conviction of twelve national leaders of the Communist party of the United States, including its General Secretary, Eugene Dennis. A lengthy and bombastic trial followed in New York City, with all twelve convicted of conspiring to advocate the overthrow of the government by force and violence. The defendants subsequently appealed to the Supreme Court in *Dennis* v. *United States* (1951), but without success. The justices affirmed the conviction and the constitutionality of the Smith Act, relying on a transformed version of Holmes's once-libertarian doctrine of clear and present danger. Chief Justice Vinson, writing for a six-to-two majority, made it into a clear and *probable* danger test, observing along the way that "[t]he government had to protect itself against communism."[14] The First Amendment, Vinson concluded, certainly did not mean that "before Government may act, it must wait until the *putsch* is about to be executed, the plans have been laid and the signal awaited."[15] Justices Black and Douglas dissented, correctly claiming that Vinson's opinion repudiated the true meaning of the clear and present danger test, a position that they also unsuccessfully pressed in cases involving state loyalty programs.

Congress strengthened the anticommunist attack with the McCarran Act of 1950. This measure required Communists to register with the government, revoked passports of those suspected of being Communists, and established provisions for setting up concentration camps for subversives in the event of a national emergency. The law also created the Subversive Activities Control Board (SACB) and gave it extensive powers to administer the loyalty program.

The Supreme Court gradually whittled down the board's authority, although as late at the mid-1960s it was still an effective force. As the Cold War menace receded, the Court became increasingly bold. In *Albertson* v. *SACB* (1965), the justices ruled that the board could not force individuals to register under the McCarran Act without engaging in an unconstitutional violation of the Fifth Amendment right against self-incrimination. Two years later, the Court threw out another provision that made it a crime for any member of a communist-action organization "to engage in any employment in any defense facility."[16] "The statute quite literally establishes guilt by association alone," the Court observed, "without any need to establish that an individual's association poses the threat feared by the Government in proscribing it."[17]

The Court also broadened the base of First Amendment rights outside of the area of national security. Following the *Dennis* decision, the Court consistently avoided the precise language of the clear and present danger test, with some justices believing that the test protected speech too little and others that it protected it too much. In its place, they substituted the concept of overbreadth as a restraint on government. In *Brandenburg* v. *Ohio* (1969), for example, the Court considered the constitutionality of an Ohio state criminal syndicalism statute that was used to prosecute a leader of the Ku Klux Klan for advocating terrorism. The Court struck the Ohio law down as too vague in its definition of what constituted criminal activity. The breadth of the statute was overly restrictive, because it limited advocacy as well as the right of assembly.

The Broadening of Civil Liberties

The overbreadth doctrine was an important advance in the area of First Amendment liberties because it was oriented to the current political reality. Judges had to make a determination about what was happening, not about what would happen in some remote future. The doctrine also gave the Court significant room to maneuver in resolving First Amendment disputes, and increasingly the justices took an expansive view, so much so that critics of the Court claimed that they were assigning protection of the First Amendment to activities that the framers of the Constitution would not have countenanced. The Court's decisions in matters of libel, the press, obscenity, the rights of the accused, and privacy all became highly controversial.

Libel, Commercial Speech, and the Press

Under the common law of libel in most U.S. states after World War II, there was no necessity for a defamed person to prove that he or she had actually been harmed. If a statement reflected badly on an individual, it was "libelous per se," and the question of whether a statement had been made against an individual was exclusively for determination by a jury. It was unreviewable by an appellate court. The theory behind the common law was that "indiscriminate political defamation should not be allowed to wound the reputations of important public figures."[18] The law, in effect, protected the "best men," who, if not able to defend themselves easily from defamatory statements, would withdraw from public life and deny society a valuable resource. The

Supreme Court had consistently refused to intervene in what was widely understood to be exclusively a state matter.

Amidst the uproar over the civil rights movement of the 1960s, however, the Court changed direction in momentous fashion, with implications for public figures and the press. *New York Times* v. *Sullivan* (1964) grew out of a full-page advertisement published in the *New York Times* by civil rights activists appealing for funds to secure the defense of Martin Luther King, Jr., in Alabama against charges of perjury. The advertisement charged that the police and city officials of Montgomery, Alabama had unleashed "an unprecedented wave of terror" against blacks engaged in nonviolent demonstrations.[19] L. B. Sullivan, a city commissioner, claimed that this and other statements, some of which were not true, had defamed him, even though he had not been mentioned by name. A jury agreed with Sullivan, ordering the *Times* to pay him $500,000. Such suits had become common tactics by white opponents of civil rights in the South, and by 1964 the newspaper had a total of $5 million in libel claims pending against it.

The case was reminiscent of the late 1790s, when the Federalists had invoked the idea of seditious libel in the Sedition Act of 1798. Simply accusing a public figure of wrongdoing was itself libelous under this old theory, which the common law had enshrined. The Court, however, overturned the old rule, bringing libel under the umbrella of the First Amendment. The Court held that public officials could recover for defamatory falsehoods about their official conduct or fitness for office only if they could prove that the defendant (in this case the *New York Times*) had published with "actual malice."[20] This term was defined as "knowledge that [the statement] was false or with reckless disregard of whether it was false or not."[21] The Court proceeded not only to overturn the judgment against the *Times,* but also to find that based on the facts there could be no subsequent suit. In essence, the Court had put itself into the highly unusual position of passing on the facts and not just the law in the case. Even false statements, the Court found, could be socially useful. The decision effectively immunized the press from libel suits, and it may well have reflected an erosion of faith in public leaders.

The decision in *New York Times* v. *Sullivan* had another effect. It opened up the concept of commercial free speech. The Supreme Court had long held that commercial advertising was a matter of commerce and not speech. But in *Sullivan* the matter in question was advertising, and the Court had earlier brought movies and books, which were commercial ventures, under the protection of the First Amendment. The justices, as their decision in *Sullivan* indicated, were aware that the goals they were pursuing in matters of civil rights could be restrained by permitting the continued exclusion of commercial speech from First Amendment protection. The justices of the Burger Court, moreover, extended the doctrine. For example, in *Bigelow* v. *Virginia* (1974), the Court overturned a statute that regulated the advertising of abortion services. The justices did not give an absolutely free rein to any kind of commercial speech, but instead demanded that state governments prove that the need to regulate commercial speech was more important than the First Amendment right to speak. For example, the justices agreed in *Metromedia Inc.* v. *San Diego* (1981) that communities could restrict billboards for both aesthetic and traffic safety reasons.

The Court also reaffirmed that the First Amendment granted extensive protection to the press. The most important case of the postwar era was *New York Times* v. *United States* (1971), more commonly known as the Pentagon Papers case. It involved the publication by the *New York Times* and the *Washington Post* of illegal copies of a top-secret Pentagon report about the conduct of the war in Vietnam. President Nixon gained from a lower federal court an order directing the newspapers to halt publication. The Supreme Court, however, vacated the injunctions as a prior restraint on the press, something that the Court had declared impermissible four decades earlier in *Near* v. *Minnesota*. Chief Justice Burger and Justices John Marshall Harlan and Harry Blackmun (1970–   ) dissented, claiming that the government had a legitimate right to suppress the publication of material harmful to the nation and that the executive authorities ought to be given latitude to determine such matters. The dissenters reiterated what the Court had repeatedly held with regard to the press: the First Amendment did not provide publishers an absolute right to publish anything they wanted. But the case, especially in the superheated atmosphere of the period, reaffirmed that government carried a very heavy burden of proof when it attempted to exercise prior restraint over the press. The Court, in the end, believed that it was better able to determine the national-security risks posed by publication of the materials than was the executive branch.

Obscenity, Church–State Relations, and Privacy

The nation had a long history of attempting to legislate moral behavior. For example, by the mid-twentieth century state and local government had sought under their police powers to proscribe obscene books and movies, to require that children pray in public schools, and to prohibit adults from using contraceptive materials. Each of these matters, however, came under increasing scrutiny, with the ACLU seeking to have these laws struck down and to have the First Amendment interpreted to give the fullest scope to individual expression. The nation's ethnic and racial heterogeneity and an increasingly open attitude toward sexual matters raised these issues to questions of important constitutional debate. Yet, no other area of postwar constitutional law was as fraught with controversy, in large measure because Americans were deeply divided. The Court's obscenity, church–state relations, and privacy decisions were at once products of and contributions to a growing sense of rights consciousness. They also fueled the attack on the Court as an imperial judiciary.

The Court struggled fitfully and ultimately unsuccessfully with the problem of whether to protect obscene material under the First Amendment. In 1957 the Court decided *Roth* v. *United States* and *Alberts* v. *California*. The first case involved a federal statute prohibiting the mailing of obscene materials; the second entailed a state obscenity statute. The Court in these cases was acutely aware that, while the states might prohibit obscene material, it did not follow that they should be left to define what was obscene, because that power would give lawmakers far too much discretion. But the Court did not define the term; rather, it said what was protected, and that was any idea having "the slightest redeeming social importance."[22] Operators of erotic book-shops and movie theaters then dressed up their offerings, claiming that they constituted high art or that they were really lessons in anatomy. The *Roth* test proved so elusive that Justice Potter Stewart (1959–1981) observed that, while he could not define obscenity, "I know it when I see it."[23] As another commentator observed, however, "[w]hen sex is a public spectacle, a human relationship has been debased into a mere animal connection."[24]

The pornography industry grew apace during the 1960s, fueled by an atmosphere of open sexuality. The consideration of the interest of the state in the morality of its citizens took on new emphasis, as both local public officials, concerned about the urban blight that inevitably accompanied "sleaze shops," and religious groups designed ordinances intended to curb pornography mills. In *Miller* v. *California* (1973) the Court began to respond to these demands, giving local authorities somewhat greater control. The justices affirmed that obscene material was not constitutionally protected, but they modified the *Roth* test. They substituted in its place the idea that obscene material was "lacking serious literary, artistic, political or scientific value."[25] The determination of obscenity, however, was left to a local jury in which "the average person, applying contemporary community standards," decided whether the material in question "taken as a whole appeals to the prurient interest" as defined by state law.[26] Three justices dissented in the case, and their disagreements reflected that the United States was still divided on the relationship of law to morality and on the meaning of free speech. Nor has the community-based standard of *Miller* stemmed the tide of commercial pornography. Moreover, the women's rights movement in the 1980s attacked pornography on new grounds, seeking to discourage men from viewing "females as anonymous, panting playthings, adult toys, dehumanized objects to be used, abused, broken and discarded."[27]

The connection between morality and the law also figured in the divisive reaction created by the Court's decisions in matters of church–state relations, especially prayer in the public schools. The most important case was *Engle* v. *Vitale* (1962), which involved a prayer composed by the Board of Regents of the State of New York. The prayer was a bland invocation; a product of a committee. "Almighty God, we acknowledge our dependence upon Thee," and it continued, "we beg Thy blessings upon us, our teacher, and our country."[28] The prayer was strictly voluntary, for both school districts in the state and children in schools that did adopt it. Furthermore, religion was a regular feature of public life, even to the phrase "In God We Trust" printed on pennies. Yet well-meaning (and not so well-meaning) teachers brought subtle pressures to bear on young students, especially of non-Christian denominations.

The Court, with only Justice Potter Stewart dissenting, struck the New York prayer down as a violation of the establishment clause of the First Amendment. Justice Hugo Black held that the clause had erected a high wall of separation between church and state, and the prayer was a state-ordained religious practice.

The decision sparked great controversy. Some politicians seized on it to attack the Court generally, not just in its civil liberties decisions but in those cases involving civil rights as well. Thus, Congressman George W. Andrews of Alabama, an opponent of racial integration, proclaimed that the justices had "put the Negroes in the schools" and "now they have driven God out."[29] By the late 1970s, as Christian fundamentalism gathered strength, efforts were undertaken to secure an amendment to the Constitution permitting school prayer, a measure that President Reagan approved but with little success. The Court's ruling, moreover, was widely circumvented.

The justices also became embroiled in moral controversies involving state regulation of birth control devices. The case of *Griswold* v. *Connecticut* (1965) involved an 1879 statute that prohibited the use of any drug or device to prevent conception, and also penalized persons who advised on or provided contraceptive devices. Griswold was the director of the Planned Parenthood League and one of the doctors in the league's clinic who prescribed contraceptives to a married person.

The Supreme Court, with Justice Douglas writing the opinion, held the law unconstitutional by a vote of seven to two. The decision was one of the most important of the twentieth century, and in its argument and effect it revealed much about the way in which the Court was attempting to adapt the Constitution to new realities, one of which was a revolution in birth control and the increasing incidence of women working and seeking to protect themselves from pregnancy. Douglas recognized that the law did not violate any specific guarantee of the Bill of Rights. However, he discovered a new right—that of privacy—to fill in the vacant space. Legal scholars and the Court had previously hinted at such a right. Louis D. Brandeis and Samuel Warren, Jr., had published in 1890 a pioneering essay in the *Harvard Law Review* on the subject. Later Brandeis, while on the bench, had written in *Olmstead* v. *United States* (1925) (a case involving wiretapping) that the framers of the Constitution had "conferred, as against the government, the right to be let alone—the most comprehensive of rights and the right most valued by civilized men."[30]

Douglas located this right of privacy in a "penumbra" of the Constitution, which were the emanations of rights that came from the document without being specifically stated. Other members of the Court agreed with Douglas without taking such an advanced and controversial position. They concluded that the Ninth Amendment, which recognized the existence of rights outside those specifically mentioned in the Constitution, was applicable. Marital privacy was one of those rights; the Connecticut law was an intolerable intrusion by the state into the bedroom. Still other members of the Court found that such a right was based on the idea of substantive due process of law, and they relied on the old economic-regulation decisions to affirm this new civil liberty. Justice Hugo Black dissented because he thought that the Court—having rejected his view of total incorporation in *Adamson* (1948)—was simply invoking principles "to keep the Constitution in tune with the times," a task that lay beyond its power or duty.[31]

It was this reasoning that paved the way for the Court's decision in an even more controversial case eight years later, *Roe* v. *Wade*. In this case, the justices struck down a state abortion statute as a denial of due process of law and held that the interests of the state and the rights of women had to be balanced. Thus, Justice Harry Blackmun, speaking for the majority, concluded that the state could only intervene in restricting abortions after the first six months of pregnancy, when the fetus had become viable. Abortions had always been available to women who had the money to pay for them, and the state laws had not so much discouraged abortions (although they certainly did that) as they drove women who were desperate to terminate a pregnancy into frequently dangerous treatment by unqualified abortionists.

The *Roe* opinion generated powerful protests that went beyond even the reactions registered in the school prayer decisions, although fundamentalist Christians and the Catholic Church played an important role in opposing the decision. The pro-life movement argued that the fetus had rights as well, and that there were better solutions to unwanted pregnancies. Informational picketing aimed directly at women using abortion clinics was combined with a political effort to persuade lawmakers to undertake a constitutional amendment to outlaw abortion. Once again, President Reagan threw his support behind the proposed amendment, but, as with school prayer, with little effect. The nation was as divided over abortion as it was with school prayer, placing the amending process, with its requirement of a two-thirds vote in Congress to propose and a three-quarters vote by the states to ratify, beyond the political grasp of the pro-life forces.

There were limits to the Court's willingness to fine-tune the Constitution to the exigencies of the sexual revolution. Homosexuality, while still a highly controversial practice, had lost some of its social stigma. Gays came out in the open, and they pooled their resources to promote their interests through politics and litigation. For example, they succeeded in winning passage of "gay bills of rights" in several cities, most of which were based on the model fashioned by the powerful homosexual community in San Francisco. The effect has been to decriminalize homosexual conduct and to permit homosexuals some limited rights with regard to parenting and public employment. Significant barriers remain, and the Court has demonstrated that it is unwilling to subject statutes dealing with homosexuals to the same level of scrutiny that it had previously applied to blacks. The Court, in *Bowers* v. *Hardwick* (1986), ruled that state sodomy laws, which banned private relationships between consenting homosexual adults, were fully within the police power of the states.

The Bill of Rights and the Accused

State and local authorities had historically controlled the criminal justice system, and the Bill of Rights protections (e.g., the Fourth, Fifth, and Sixth amendments) that embodied the rights of the accused had historically applied only against the national government. These amendments outlined basic criminal procedures: the Fourth involved search and seizure, the Fifth provided that individuals could not be compelled to testify against themselves, and the Sixth granted right to counsel in a criminal proceeding. After World War II the Supreme Court nationalized each of these amendments, bringing their protection to bear against state action by incorporating them under the due-process clause of the Fourteenth Amendment. The Court's actions, as in other areas of incorporation, spawned a great public and political outcry, which had special poignancy given the sharp rise in criminal activity that was going on at the same time the decisions were rendered.

The most controversial aspect of the Fourth Amendment was the extension of the so-called exclusionary rule to the states. This judge-made rule provided that evidence that was illegally seized through an improper search could not be introduced as evidence in a trial. The Court formulated the doctrine in *Weeks* v. *United States* in 1912, but it had consistently refused to apply it to the states. The Court in *Wolf* v. *Colorado* (1949) did hold that the Fourth Amendment applied to the states, but the badly divided justices refused to extend the exclusionary rule. The justices worried that by applying the rule against the states they would be placed in the position of second-guessing local officials.

The Court finally nationalized the exclusionary rule in *Mapp* v. *Ohio* (1961), one of the most controversial and important cases of the modern era. As was typical in the area of criminal procedure, the Warren Court in many ways was merely ratifying what the states had already undertaken. By the time that the Court decided *Mapp* (a case involving a wreckless search of the home of a suspected drug dealer in Cleveland, Ohio), more than half of the states had adopted the exclusionary rule. Furthermore, the majority of the justices recognized that incorporation of the Fourth Amendment meant little if there was no means of enforcing its provisions against the states. Justice Tom

Clark wrote that to deny enforcement through the exclusionary rule was tantamount to granting "the right but in reality [withholding] its privilege and enjoyment."[32] The Court in the 1980s, however, backed partially away from its strong support of the exclusionary rule, holding in *United States* v. *Leon* (1984) that the rule would not apply where the police had acted in "good faith."

The justices also nationalized the provision against self-incrimination in the Fifth Amendment. By the early 1950s, especially with the second Red Scare, taking the Fifth Amendment was viewed as evidence of guilt. Historically, however, the amendment was rooted in the idea of preventing government from coercing individuals into confessing to crimes that they had not committed. In *Brown* v. *Mississippi* (1936), for example, the Court had thrown out, based on the due-process clause of the Fourteenth Amendment, confessions gained as a result of whipping. But it was not until 1964, in *Malloy* v. *Hogan,* that the justices incorporated the Fifth Amendment protection against self-incrimination through the Fourteenth Amendment, and three years later it provided in *In Re Gault* that these same protections applied to juvenile delinquents. The *Gault* decision thus stripped local juvenile courts of a great deal of the discretion that they had enjoyed since the early twentieth century. Juveniles, at least for purposes of the criminal justice system, were brought under the Constitution's protection for the first time.

Even more controversial was the Court's decision in the landmark case of *Miranda* v. *Arizona* (1966). Miranda was a small-time thug who had kidnapped and raped a woman. He was subsequently arrested and taken to the stationhouse where, after a few hours of questioning, he confessed to the crimes. The police, however, had not informed Miranda of his right to remain silent, and after his conviction he appealed. A sharply divided Court decided in favor of Miranda, and Chief Justice Warren made clear that suspected criminals had to be read their rights to remain silent, to know that anything they said could be used against them, and that if they had no money the state was obliged to provide them with counsel. This "Miranda warning" became a standard feature of police practice, but it was also highly controversial, because it appeared that the justices were coddling criminals. Yet the changes wrought by *Miranda* have been better police practices and, according to some studies, a higher incidence of convictions. Despite much outcry against the rule, moreover, the Supreme Court has carved out only limited exceptions.

The right to counsel was also nationalized. In *Gideon* v. *Wainwright* (1963), the justices considered a handwritten plea brought by Clarence Earl Gideon from his Florida prison cell. Gideon was a small-time thief who had been found guilty of breaking into a pool hall in Panama City, Florida. Gideon had represented himself at his trial because he had no money to pay for counsel. Florida, unlike more than half of the states, had no law requiring that indigents be provided counsel in felony trials. The Supreme Court had first dealt with the issue of incorporating the Sixth into the Fourteenth Amendment in *Powell* v. *Alabama* (1932), the great Scottsboro rape case, but they had not followed a consistent course, proceeding rather on a case-by-case basis, sometimes finding that the protection applied and other times that it did not. The importance of the *Gideon* decision, which the Court decided unanimously, was that it totally applied the incorporation doctrine, meaning that nationally every defendant in a felony trial had a right to counsel and that, if a person was indigent, then the state had to provide counsel. What made the *Gideon* ruling controversial was that the justices applied it retroactively, meaning that the states had to retry convicts properly, by giving them counsel, or let them go, which was usually what happened. Moreover, the Court has consistently expanded the right to counsel, applying it to misdemeanors and requiring that counsel be made available in the early phases of processing a criminal suspect in the stationhouse.

The Supreme Court has dramatically enhanced the scope of civil liberties since World War II. Judicial review has been an instrument by which the justices have restrained majority will in order to preserve individual liberty. The continuing respect for the Court has been underscored by the repeated failure of efforts to trim its appellate jurisdiction or to overturn its decisions through constitutional amendments. The federal judiciary has become in this century a policy-making institution, but Americans seem to approve its actions on the whole.

Civil Rights

The Brown *Decision and the Legal End of Separate but Equal*

Along with the ACLU, the NAACP pioneered special-interest litigation as a means of realizing goals that it could not attain through the regular political process. This strategy became a model for women's, environmental, consumer, and other groups beginning during the 1960s. Organized litigation in the federal courts was not new, but the NAACP developed it to a high art, deploying the lawyers of the Legal Defense Fund to argue the most promising cases. The entire point of the strategy was to bring cases before the Supreme Court that would create a beachhead from which the NAACP could expand its attack on legal segregation and overturn its lynchpin, the doctrine of separate but equal announced in *Plessy* v. *Ferguson* (1986).

During the 1940s, the NAACP scored significant victories. In the area of voting discrimination, for example, it won a particularly important decision from the high court in *Smith* v. *Allright* (1944), which outlawed the all-white party primary. Local southern officials quickly devised registration techniques that reduced black voter turnout. The NAACP lawyers also successfully hacked away at separate but equal, winning two important cases in higher education, *Sweatt* v. *Painter* (1950) and *McLaurin* v. *Oklahoma State Regents* (1950). The strategy of the Legal Defense Fund lawyers in these cases was to stay within the confines of separate but equal, but to expand the doctrine so fully that it would cease to have meaning. The counsel of the NAACP argued that separate but equal should take into account the reputation of the faculty that served blacks, the companionship of one's peers, the quality of the library, and the access of students to the best minds in the class. The Court found that practices such as requiring black students to eat in a roped-off area and to study in a separate part of the library violated separate but equal. The Court added in *Sweatt* that inadequate facilities for blacks were unacceptable. These decisions left segregation intact, but they eroded the legal position of segregationists.

The NAACP leadership changed in 1950. Following the death of Charles Houston, Thurgood Marshall took charge of directing the campaign against segregation. Marshall made the momentous decision to abandon the strategy of gradually expanding separate but equal into irrelevance in favor of a direct assault. Such a strategy seems, in retrospect, to have been clear enough and not particularly dangerous. At the time, however, there was profound disagreement within the NAACP ranks as well as among the justices about whether the Court would abandon a precedent that had such great social importance and, in any case, whether it was the institution to tackle the job.

The NAACP took the risk and won. Marshall started litigation in four states and the District of Columbia that culminated in *Brown* v. *Board of Education of Topeka, Kansas* (1954), which consolidated the state cases along with *Bolling* v. *Sharpe* (1954), which applied to the District of Columbia. The cases had originally been argued in 1953, but they were held over for reargument because the justices could not agree about how to proceed. In one of those curious turns of historical fate, Chief Justice Fred Vinson, who resisted the NAACP's strategy, died and was replaced by Earl Warren. The new chief justice's leadership, combined with the legal arguments of Thurgood Marshall, proved decisive.

Marshall confronted John W. Davis at the bar of the Supreme Court. Davis was a West Virginian, distinguished corporate lawyer, and a former ABA president who had steadfastly opposed racial integration of the association. Marshall addressed his brief in *Brown* to more than just the inequities fostered in black schools, arguing that as a matter of history and sociology the Court should decide against separate but equal. Marshall asserted that the framers of the Fourteenth Amendment had not intended to permit segregation and he produced evidence gathered by social psychologist Kenneth Clark that showed that black children educated in segregated schools had low self-esteem. Davis countered by asserting that the history of the Fourteenth Amendment revealed that its framers were supportive of segregation and that Marshall's social scientific arguments were irrelevant, because the Court was bound to consider only the law. The appropriate standard by which to judge separate but equal, Davis concluded, was whether the states were providing equal funding and physical facilities for blacks, something that he argued (incorrectly) was true. The arguments produced among the lawyers were a microcosm of the clash between a realist and strictly doctrinal approach to constitutional law.

Chief Justice Warren wanted to end segregation, but he had two concerns. First, he knew that the fullest possible public support for the decision depended on fostering the fullest possible agreement among the justices. Second, Warren concluded that the historical and sociological arguments were not dispositive and that resting the decision on them would only invite controversy. These two matters converged into one, because if the Court could broaden the ground upon which it could stand, the possibilities of public acceptance would increase. What Warren hoped to avoid was any nitpicking legal exchanges that would simply give ammunition to the supporters of separate but equal.

"Does segregation of children in public schools solely on the basis of race . . . deprive the children of the minority groups of equal education opportunities?" Warren asked. He concluded that it did, but he rejected both sociology and history as authoritative. Warren's substantive liberalism showed through. The unanimous opinion found that the doctrine of "separate but equal had no place. Separate educational facilities are inherently unequal. . . . Any language in *Plessy* v. *Ferguson* contrary to these findings is rejected."[33] The justices did not overturn *Plessy,* however; instead they left the decision in place, sweeping it into irrelevance while avoiding further annoyance to southern sentiment. Nor did the justices provide a remedy; they merely announced their findings and directed the NAACP to present them with separate briefs about the remedy to be ordered.

The following year the justices heard *Brown* II. The Court remanded the cases back to the federal district courts, directing that the principles enunciated in *Brown* I were to be implemented with "all deliberate speed."[34] This ambiguous phrase reflected concern on the part of the Court that too rapid change in the South would prove disruptive and damage the credibility of the original *Brown* ruling. The strategy was to grant federal district court judges discretion in finding the most appropriate ways within each community to bring an end to segregation with the least social upheaval. The unhappy phrase, however, made it easier for opponents of the decision to obstruct its implementation.

The *Brown* decisions were milestones in the legal history of American race relations, the use of judicial power by the Supreme Court, and in the possibilities of effecting social change through a well-conceived litigation strategy. All of these lessons became a part of the contemporary legal culture, contributing to a growing sense of rights consciousness. But the law in action and the law on the books proved difficult to reconcile. Southerners committed to legal segregation did not change their ideas or their habits once the Supreme Court declared the practice unconstitutional. Moreover, President Dwight D. Eisenhower made the transition to a new era of race relations all the more difficult by his halting national leadership.

Reaction and Counterreaction: The Post-Brown Movement for Black Civil Rights

White southern political leaders displayed some ambivalence about how to react. Big Jim Folsom, the governor of Alabama, observed that "[w]hen the Supreme Court speaks, that's the law."[35] Many more white politicians denounced the decision and began a campaign of "massive resistance" that fused traditional states' rights arguments with blatant racism. Southerners spoke of interposition, that is, of blocking the enforcement of the federal Constitution through state action.

White opposition reached a crescendo in September 1957 amid efforts to integrate Central High School in Little Rock, Arkansas. Governor Orval Faubus, caught in a tight election campaign, made integration of the Little Rock schools a political football and, in his words, adopted the strategy of "outniggering" his opponents.[36] Faubus claimed that the schools could not be integrated because of danger to the students. After considerable delay President Eisenhower, embarrassed by Faubus's practice of breaking promises, federalized the Arkansas National Guard, taking them away from the governor's control, and sent in regular Army troops to restore order. The television pictures of whites taunting black children provided the first image in the North of the depth of race bitterness in the South. Eight black children were enrolled for the full academic year.

Governor Faubus, however, in early 1958 ordered the schools closed for the next academic year and, along with the state legislature, proclaimed that Arkansas would not abide by the *Brown* decision. Faubus insisted that *Brown* was an unconstitutional usurpation of power by the Supreme Court. The justices in *Cooper* v. *Aaron* (1958) not only ordered that a more aggressive integration program be implemented forthwith but held as well, in an opinion signed by all nine of them, that they still fully supported *Brown* and that they alone could interpret the Constitution conclusively.

White intransigence sparked renewed efforts by blacks to claim the full measure of their rights. Beginning in 1955, with the Montgomery, Alabama bus boycott and continuing into the mid-1960s, black civil rights leaders adopted more aggressive tactics. The Montgomery boycott lasted more than one year, and about 90 percent of the blacks refused to ride the city-owned buses until they were integrated. Events in Montgomery made Martin Luther King, Jr., into a national civil rights leader, and under his direction blacks adopted an increasingly militant strategy of nonviolent civil disobedience. In 1960 in Greensboro, North Carolina the sit-in protests began, and they quickly spread throughout the South. White southerners threw the criminal justice system against the protesters, just as the civil rights leaders hoped that they would. Pictures of white police officers turning dogs and fire hoses against blacks filled the nightly newspapers and the television.

The Federal Legislative Response

The federal response to the growing crisis of racial injustice and law and order in the South emerged gradually in the 1960s and followed three lines of development: police, legislative, and judicial. The first was through the use of federal troops and law enforcement officials. The administration of John F. Kennedy, while giving rhetorical support to the civil rights movement, dragged its feet when it came to using federal power, concerned in part about the political consequences of alienating white southerners from the Democratic party. Events overwhelmed the administration, and when Governors Ross Barnett of Mississippi in 1962 and George C. Wallace of Alabama in 1963 attempted physically to block the admission of blacks to the major universities of those states, Kennedy dispatched federal marshalls and troops.

The second phase in the federal response was legislative. Following the assassination of Kennedy in late 1963, Lyndon Johnson, a Texan, undertook a more vigorous stance on civil rights. Congress in the space of four years passed two Civil Rights Acts, the first major enactments since Reconstruction, as well as the Voting Rights Act of 1965. Taken together, these measures composed the modern legislative program against racial discrimination.

The Civil Rights Act of 1964 was the most far-reaching civil rights measure in U.S. history. It ranged, in eleven separate titles, over a wide variety of civil rights problems, including voting rights (Titles I and VIII), court actions to challenge segregated public facilities (Titles III and IV), the power of the attorney general to intervene in civil rights disputes (Title IX), the establishment of a Community Relations' Service to assist communities in resolving discrimination disputes (Title X), and a reinvigorated Civil Rights Commission (Title V), which had been established in the weakly worded Civil Rights Act of 1957.

The most important provisions of the Act were Titles II, VI, and VII. Title II prohibited discrimination in public accommodations based on "race, color, religion or national origin" in any establishment if it "affects commerce or if discrimination is supported by state action."[37] Title VI prohibited discrimination in federally assisted programs, and Title VII prohibited employment discrimination. The act produced through federal enforcement a powerful set of changes in the public life of southern communities and more generally in the American work place.

The Voting Rights Act of the following year was equally significant. Previous measures, including the Civil Rights Act of 1964, had made some provision for dealing with the problem of effectively guaranteeing the right to vote. In 1964, for example, only 6.4 percent of the eligible black population had registered to vote; even in Louisiana, where the percentage was 31.8, white voter registration was above 80 percent. The Voting Rights Act of 1965 and its amendments in 1970, 1975, and 1982 fundamentally changed the face of political power in the South and in big cities with substantial populations of non-English-speaking immigrants. The most important provision of the act was a preclearance requirement that applied to states or political subdivisions with low voter registration or participation. In such jurisdictions, the act suspended literacy, educational, and character tests of voter qualifications that had historically been the primary devices by which to exclude black enfranchisement. The result was that the gap between white and black voting registration dropped significantly; the number of elected black officials tripled between 1970 and 1986, and white politicians like George C. Wallace dropped their segregationist diatribe in order to appeal to the heavy black voting populations of the states of the Deep South.

The Civil Rights Act of 1968 was the final element in the legislative program. Its most important feature was contained in Title VIII, which was the nation's first comprehensive open-housing law. It prohibited discrimination in the sale, rental, financing, and advertising of housing, and in membership in real estate brokerage organizations. The measure also included provisions dealing with the rights of native Americans. Yet the 1968 act was also a product of its times, because it included, in the wake of antiwar and civil rights protests, antiriot provisions. So controversial was the measure that it passed, in large measure, because southerners had delayed consideration of the bill until after the assassination of Martin Luther King, Jr. Even then it barely passed the House of Representatives.

The Federal Judicial Response

The courts composed the third element of the federal response, and because its members were unelected the federal judiciary came in for increasing criticism as it attempted to work out the implications of the *Brown* decision. In effect, the justices and the lower federal courts upon whom they placed the burden of implementing *Brown* recognized that in practice ''all deliberate speed'' had turned into indefinite delay. The Court attempted to correct this matter by taking on an increasing number of segregation cases, hoping that on a case-by-case basis it could prod the South into action. For example, the justices in *Green* v. *County School Board* (1968) declared that they would no longer use a good-faith standard to measure compliance by local districts, but would instead look at effective change in terms of the numbers of students placed in integrated schools. So-called freedom-of-choice plans that let pupils go wherever they wanted were declared discriminatory and unacceptable.

Perhaps the simplest fact about the role of the Court in the implementation of the *Brown* decision was that it lost control over the process. Federal district judges had that task thrust upon them, and many of them acted with courage in the face of substantial personal danger. The most controversial of the remedies developed involved the busing of children among different schools to achieve integration. Busing had long been employed to move public schoolchildren about, making possible the elimination of the one-room schoolhouse and, some believed, making the movement back and forth to school safer for students than walking. As late as 1970 about 40 percent of all students were bused. Furthermore, at the heart of the problem of integrating neighborhood schools was the practice of de facto residential segregation, coupled with school boundary policies that sent blacks to one school and whites to another. The school bus offered one means of overcoming that problem, and it was with precisely that objective in mind that a federal district judge in Charlotte, North Carolina ordered it. The Supreme Court, in *Swann* v. *Charlotte-Mecklenburg Board of Education* (1971) supported the measure and in two subsequent cases in 1973 and 1979 approved the extension of it to western and northern communities.

These decisions stirred profound controversy and were widely (and somewhat incorrectly) believed to have stimulated white flight from the urban areas to the suburbs. The Court, moreover, indicated that it would not accept (except in the most unusual circumstances) busing on a metropolitan scale that combined big-city and suburban school systems.

The justices extended the logic of the *Brown* decision to other areas of public activity, and they also gave strong endorsement to the civil and voting rights legislation. The commerce power had provided much of the authority for the Civil Rights Act of 1964, and the justices, who had historically given Congress great latitude in employing that power, held that it could be extended to "public" facilities such as hotels and restaurants. The justices refused, however, to stretch this logic to small associational groups such as fraternal groups, and the Civil Rights Act had left mom-and-pop facilities free of its provisions.

A fundamental legal revolution involving the rights of blacks took place in the forty years after World War II. Much of the success of that effort stemmed from the courage and skill of black civil rights organizers and lawyers, who made effective use of the legal system, both to work within it and, when appropriate, to hold it up to public ridicule. Constitutional law in 1987 was substantially different on matters of race relations than it had been in 1945 and radically different from what it had been in 1896. De jure segregation was at an end, but de facto segregation persisted.

Women and the Law in the Post–World War II Era

Background to the Issue of Gender Discrimination

Through its tactics, its message, and its moral tone, the civil rights movement provided a model of mobilization for women. Betty Friedan, for example, published *The Feminine Mystique,* the early gospel of the women's movement, in 1963, the same year as the great civil rights march on Washington, D.C. Young women were also active in many civil rights and antiwar groups, including the Student Nonviolent Coordinating Committee (SNCC), the Congress of Racial Equality (CORE), and Students for a Democratic Society (SDS), although they usually held subordinate positions outside the main avenues of policy making. As one observer noted in somewhat exaggerated fashion about the 1965 SDS convention, "women made peanut butter, waited on tables, cleaned up, got laid. That was their role."[38] Women learned that the kind of race-based discrimination suffered by blacks was similar to the subordinate social position in which their gender placed them.

The framers of the Constitution composed a gender-neutral document, relying on words such as persons, people, and electors and avoiding any explicit discrimination based on sex. Until the Civil War amendments, the states had dealt exclusively with matters of gender, most notably through the married women's property acts. Women had no formal political rights, either to vote or to hold office.

This period of federal neglect ended in the early 1870s. A few women tested the meaning of the due-process and equal-protection provisions of the Fourteenth Amendment as they applied to matters of gender. The response was overwhelmingly negative, with the justices refusing to extend to women even the protection that they accorded to blacks. In *Bradwell* v. *Illinois* (1873) the Court rejected the claim of a Chicago woman that the right to practice law was an attribute of citizenship protected by the privileges and immunities clause of that amendment. Two years later, in *Minor* v. *Happersett,* the justices found that the states could restrict the suffrage to men, because the Fourteenth Amendment did not confer the right to vote on women. In 1894 the Court went a step further and held in *In Re Lockwood* that states could confine the word "person" in the Fourteenth Amendment to men alone. Even when the justices did find in favor of state legislation designed to protect female workers (e.g., *Muller* v. *Oregon* [1908]), they endorsed long-standing paternalistic attitudes toward women by all-male lawmakers. Equitable treatment for women did not mean equality before the law.

The women's movement in the early twentieth century sought to secure both suffrage protection and constitutional equality. It gained the former but not the latter. The states in 1920 ratified the Nineteenth Amendment, which gave half of the U.S. population the right to vote. Alice Paul, a leader of the National Woman's party, tried during the 1920s to have Congress pass another constitutional amendment that would have prohibited discrimination based on gender. This Equal Rights Amendment (ERA), however, never received sufficient votes in Congress to send it to the states for ratification. The Supreme Court, moreover, repulsed every effort to expand the legal basis of protection for women under the Constitution. In *Fay* v. *New York* (1947), for example, the justices held that the Nineteenth Amendment did nothing more than give women the right to vote and that it did not extend to women the right to serve on juries. In 1961, while the Supreme Court was busy dismantling race-based discrimination, it held in *Hoyt* v. *Florida* that a state could rationally find that it was a necessity to spare women from the obligation of jury service because of their place at "the center of home and family life."[39]

In the 1960s, however, women's roles changed dramatically. Employment of middle-class white and married women became the norm rather than the exception; birthrates plunged and so did family size. The consumer culture made two incomes necessary, and by 1970, 60 percent of all familes with an income over $10,000 had working wives. By 1987 it was almost 80 percent. Yet through much of the 1960s and 1970s, the larger culture considered working women as less than full-fledged members of the work force; rather, they were "helping out" with the family income while men engaged in more substantial pursuits.

Change indeed began in the 1960s, but it was legislative rather than judicial. In 1963 Congress amended the Fair Labor Standards Act to require equal pay for equal work without regard to sex. The Civil Rights Act of 1964 included in Title VII a ban on discrimination in employment on the basis of sex. Southerners had originally introduced the amendment in the hope that it would kill the entire measure, but Representative Martha Griffin of Michigan succeeded in keeping it, although the federal government was slow to enforce it.[40] Founded in 1966, the National Organization of Women (NOW) had as one of its principal goals to build a legislative foundation for women's rights, while pursuing a litigation strategy in the federal courts that would make gender-based discrimination as subject to searching judicial inquiry as was racial discrimination.

Women and the Supreme Court in the 1970s and 1980s

The Republicans appointed to the Supreme Court beginning in 1969 were supposedly chosen for their devotion to judicial restraint and strict construction. Yet in the area of women's rights, they broke new ground as the earlier Court before World War II had done for blacks. In *Reed* v. *Reed* (1971), a unanimous Court, speaking through new Chief Justice Burger, invalidated an Idaho estate law that gave men preference over similarly situated women as administrators of estates. The Court found that such legislation effectively denied women the equal protection of the law. In *Phillips* v. *Martin Marietta Corporation* (1971), the justices decided that a company's refusal to hire women with preschool-aged children violated the Civil Rights Act of 1964, because the company policy did not apply equally to men. The justices in 1977 also relied on the Civil Rights Act to overturn an Alabama law that used height and weight requirements for prison guards to block women from such employment.

The justices have yet to extend the same standards of scrutiny to gender discrimination as they have to racial discrimination. They have refused, in short, to make gender a suspect classification, as is the case with race. Such status would mean that any time a legislature based its actions on gender it would automatically become suspect and subject to the most searching review by the Court. But the Court has rigorously applied the concept of equal protection of the laws. In *Frontiero* v. *Richardson* (1973), for example, the justices declared invalid provisions of the Fair Labor Standards Act and the Civil Rights Act of 1964 that exempted the military from granting to women the same health and housing benefits that went automatically to men. The justices came within one vote in this case of declaring that gender would be treated as a suspect classification.

The Court has taken the position that the state and federal governments may have some reasonable basis on which to invoke gender. The Court in *Kahn* v. *Shevin* (1974) upheld a state law exempting widows from a special property tax and in *Schlesinger* v. *Ballard* (1975) it gave women naval officers a longer period in which to win promotion than was given to male officers. Finally, in *Rostker* v. *Goldberg* (1981) it held, by a vote of six to three, that Congress could exclude women from the military draft.

The Court's decisions involving women were important in another way. They coincided with the effort to pass the ERA, and to some extent they may have contributed to its failure. Congress in 1972 sent the proposed amendment to the states for ratification within seven years. Within months about half of the states necessary for ratification had agreed, but enthusiasm waned, as was typically the case with amendments. Supporters of the ERA won an extension of the ratification deadline to June 1982, but by then only thirty-five states, three short of the required number, had ratified the amendment and it failed. Had the ERA passed, federal courts would have undoubtedly treated sex as a suspect classification.

Opposition to the ERA reflected substantial disagreement in the ranks of women about the quest for equality. The most effective proponent of the campaign against it was Phyllis Schafly, an articulate and traditional woman who organized STOP ERA, a coalition of conservative groups anxious to retain the existing status of women. These same women were also vocal in their objections to *Roe* v. *Wade,* and they expected that the Reagan administration would help to pass an antiabortion amendment.

Affirmative Action

The most controversial contemporary aspect of civil rights law has been affirmative action programs aimed at overcoming past discrimination based on race and sex. "Our Constitution is color-blind," John Marshall Harlan had written in *Plessy* v. *Ferguson* (1896), "and neither knows nor tolerates classes among citizens."[41] By the 1960s, these ringing words had taken on new meaning with legally imposed racial segregation overturned. Yet past discrimination had created injuries to generations of Americans, or so President Johnson had argued. In a sense, the generation of the era after World War II had been the victim of previous discrimination, and that new generation had, according to Johnson, some basis to demand compensation for the injuries done to their mothers and fathers. Affirmative action meant that mere equality of opportunity was no longer sufficient; that is, it was not enough to do away with prior racial barriers. Under affirmative action programs, the purpose was not to strike neutrality but to use racial and sexual classifications as a basis on which to secure increased employment opportunities, job promotions, and admissions to colleges and universities for racial minorities and women.

Affirmative action policies took two forms beginning in the 1970s. The first involved efforts to accelerate aggressive recruiting and remedial training. The idea behind such programs was to bring people into a position where they could compete equally for positions. These programs drew little resistance, and they seemed wholly justified as means of compensating for wrongs done in the past without disturbing the rights of nonminorities.

Much more controversial, however, were affirmative action programs involving quotas that set aside certain benefits to be given to identifiable racial groups and women. These programs became controversial because they took opportunities away from one group of people and gave them to another, and they did so on the basis of race and gender. The equal-protection clause of the Fourteenth Amendment had held that all people were to be treated equally before the law, but affirmative action, which came to be derisively termed "reverse discrimination," took race and sex into consideration. One person's affirmative action was another's reverse discrimination. The matter was especially troubling for the Supreme Court, which had essayed the revolution in civil rights, because it had to pass on rulings by lower-court judges, legislators, and private employers seeking to apply remedies that would promote social equality. Furthermore, in deciding cases involving affirmative action, the Court has been placed in the ironic position of interpreting the Civil Rights Act of 1964 in light of suits brought by white males charging racial or gender discrimination. The rights consciousness of the era cut in several directions.

The Court has accepted affirmative action programs, but it has struggled in doing so. The justices first decided the merits of an affirmative action program in *Regents of the University of California* v. *Bakke* (1978). The medical school of the University of California at Davis had set aside sixteen of its one hundred openings each year for minority students, who could be admitted even if they had grades and test scores lower than rejected white applicants. Allan Bakke, a white male, had a score just below the cutoff point for majority applicants and higher than the scores of several of the minority admittees. If he had been black, he would have had a place in the class. Bakke sued, claiming that the quota system denied him the equal protection of the law.

The Supreme Court found for Bakke. Though sharply divided, the justices concluded that the use of a rigid quota based on race violated the equal-protection clause of the Fourteenth Amendment and the Civil Rights Act of 1964. The justice also held, however, that race could be used as one of many factors (the Court called it a "plus" factor) in making decisions about admissions. For example, a university could reasonably want a diverse student body as one of its goals, and it was free to pursue that goal so long as it did not establish quotas.

Since then the Court has taken a somewhat tortured path forward. It has approved private affirmative action programs, as in *United Steelworkers* v. *Weber* (1979), even though they appear to violate the Civil Rights Act of 1964. The justices have also given approval to set-aside programs created in the Public Works Employment Act of 1977, which required at least 10 percent of federal funds for public-works projects to be spent on services or supplies from minority business enterprises. In *Fullilove* v. *Klutznick* (1980), the Court sustained the law by a vote of six to three. Justice John Paul Stevens (1975–   ) entered a powerful dissent, suggesting sarcastically that the government would soon be in the position of having to devise a version of the Nazi laws that defined who was a Jew, musing that "our statute books will once again have to contain laws that reflect the odious practice of delineating the qualities that make one person a Negro and make another white."[42]

Affirmative action has become the law of the land. The justices, most recently, have upheld affirmative action programs for both blacks and women. They found in *United States* v. *Paradise* (1987) that a program of promoting one black for every white officer promoted in the Alabama Department of Highway Safety did not violate the Civil Rights Act of 1964 or the equal-protection clause of the Fourteenth Amendment. The justices have also held in *Johnson* v. *Santa Clara County* (1987) that in making promotions within job categories in which women have been historically underrepresented, a public employer may give a preference to women over better-qualified men.

These decisions reveal once again that recompense for past harms, rights consciousness, substantive liberalism, and judicial power have converged to reshape American legal culture. These decisions were among the most controversial aspects of the qualitative side of the contemporary law explosion, and they underscore in dramatic terms the breadth of federal judicial authority in the era after World War II.

The Imperial Judiciary and Social Change

The idea of the imperial judiciary was a variation on the theme of the law explosion. The proof of the greater role of law in American life was the intervention by the high-court justices into areas that were historically the sole province of the state legislatures and Congress. Moreover, the justices, in sketching out a revolution in due process and equal protection under the laws contributed directly to increased litigation. That the Court's power has expanded dramatically and that its role in the American legal system is far more crucial than two centuries ago, seems beyond dispute. What is unclear and subject to constant reevaluation, is whether the justices' actions have moved U.S. law toward ideals for which the nation stood in 1787 and for which its citizens would want to stand today. The answer to that question is perhaps unknowable, but that Americans keep asking it is itself a sign of the health of the constitutional order and of the continuing connection between social and legal change.

Epilogue:
More Like a River than a Rock

Unity within diversity, constancy within change: those have been dominant themes in American legal history. In scope and complexity, the legal system has grown enormously, as has the penetration of government into the daily lives of Americans. While lawmakers have always played a role in the distribution of economic costs, benefits, and rewards, that role, and the judicial, administrative, and regulatory apparatus that supports it, is far greater than anything within the imaginations of the generation that created the nation, let alone the first white colonists. The substance and structure of the legal system have changed accordingly, reflecting the values and assumptions of past generations. The legal culture has historically been the product of changes in the general culture, and legal adaptation in both private and public law have been essential to the legitimacy of the legal system.

We should exercise great caution in thinking about *the* legal history of *the* American law. Our legal system had its origins in the ambiguities of a colonial experience in which white settlers had to adapt their carried legal tradition to a new environment. Even with nationhood, Americans did not create a national law; rather, they settled on a constitutional system that, while giving important powers to the national government, purchased unity by leaving the police powers to the states and granting them significant autonomy over the conduct of their political, social, and economic affairs. Variations among the legal systems of the states, the regions, and between the states and the national government have been one of the principal features of American legal history. The federal system has made the law important at both the core and the periphery, or at both the local and the national level. Even today, when Congress and the Supreme Court exercise authority on an unprecedented scale, state lawmakers, state constitutions, state judges, and state common law remain vital, even essential, elements in the legal system. As was the case two centuries ago, so it is today, there are many common law systems (and even a strong civil law system in Louisiana).

The institutions of the legal system have changed yet remained the same. Administrative and regulatory bodies today constitute a fourth branch of government, but legislative regulation dates to the colonial era. The rise of a separate structure (the independent regulatory agency) was wholly compatible with the principle forged early in the history of the republic that law and politics should be separated in the interests of moral authority and efficiency. The authority of appellate courts has expanded dramatically, and the practice of judicial review, a dimly understood and little-used power in the eighteenth century, has become an essential ingredient of the legal system. Through it, the Supreme Court has established a virtual monopoly over the interpretation of the Constitution. The entire nature of the judicial role has changed as well, with judges ceasing to apply precedent mechanically and instead turning to an expansive, legislative-like role in which they draw on extralegal as well as legal sources in applying the common law, balancing competing constitutional claims, and interpreting statutes. Yet courts remain reactive institutions, far more so than the notion of an imperial judiciary would suggest. Today, as was true centuries ago, courts must wait for cases and controversies before they can act and they remain, even in an age in which legal realism has become a commonplace idea, bound by the necessity of explaining what they do in terms of the law.

State and congressional legislation has grown prodigiously, especially since the late nineteenth century, and it has seemed that in this age of statutes the common law would be submerged. In this sense, the law explosion has been a long time in coming. Yet, even as the statute books explode in girth, the common law continues, as it has historically, to be an important means through which the legal system adapts to social change.

The adaptive process appears in the changing nature of substantive private and public law rules and in the goals of the criminal justice system. Contract, property, and tort law, for example, which were privatized in the early nineteenth century, are today becoming increasingly public. The concept of substantive due process of law, which secured certain economic rights from government interference in the late nineteenth century, has since 1937 been transformed by the Supreme Court into a doctrine to sustain such noneconomic rights as abortion and access to birth control materials. Behind the increasing convergence of public and private law is a sense of rights consciousness, one that has been supported since the New Deal by the Supreme Court's far-reaching reconceptualization of civil liberties and civil rights. Fairness, just compensation, and equality before the law have emerged as persistent themes in modern legal culture. They have also found expression in the criminal justice system, although its tradition of popular control has created a tension among the goals of rehabilitation, deterrence, and retribution.

The ideological basis of American legal culture has also displayed consistency within change. American law in the early twentieth century, and certainly by the New Deal, shifted from its eighteenth- and nineteenth-century republican origins, which had stressed the commonwealth idea, to liberal legalism, with its interest-group orientation and its emphasis on individual rights. Lawmakers have historically invoked the concept of the rights of the public to intervene legitimately against private rights, although they have never done so in order to redistribute wealth on a broad scale. The incessant rhetoric of laissez-faire and individualism in American legal thinking should not detract from the simple truth that, from the beginning of the nation, the law has fostered a mixed economy. The central tendency of lawmakers has been to involve themselves in matters of private economic decision making, not to leave those decisions to exclusively private interests. Indeed, much of the political history of the nation has involved the continuing efforts of different economic interests to secure public power, hence lawmaking authority to serve their own ends.

The American legal system has taken private rights seriously, although not all rights have been protected equally at all times. Until the early twentieth century, public and private law threw up sort of a shield around economic rights and property. That protection was never complete and, in any case, the changing nature of property made inevitable the reformulation of legal doctrines to shield it. Legal formalism, substantive due process of law, and freedom to contract were important but not conclusive barriers to government intervention in the economy. They were indicative of sensitivity to rights under the rule of law. Since the constitutional revolution of 1937, federal courts have deferred to legislatures on matters of economic regulation, but they have recalibrated the yardstick of judicial oversight to take greater account of civil liberties and civil rights. Only in the past two decades, amid the heated controversy over affirmative action and the public-interest law explosion, have judges and lawmakers come to reexamine the balance between individual liberty and economic well-being.

The legal culture has reflected the general culture's commitment to the idea of equality, though equality of a particular, and to the minds of some, limited sort. Americans have clung to the idea that the rule of law implies only that the playing field be level, not that every player on it be similarly endowed. Equality of status (the idea that all persons should be similarly situated as a result of the law) has been alien to most Americans and, hence, to the legal culture. American culture, even in this age of liberal legalism, has rejected the idea that government should redistribute wealth and social power in the name of the collective good. At the same time, it has also proved resistant, even in the nineteenth century, to an opposite vision of radical individualism, of strict laissez-faire policy, and of the nightwatchman state.

Our legal history reflects back to us generations of pragmatic decision making rather than a quest for ideological purity and consistency. Personal and group interests have always ordered the course of legal development; instrumentalism has been the way of the law.

Who have been the winners and losers? The answer is hardly clear-cut. The rule of law in American history has made possible widespread economic and political power, and the long-term trend has been toward the greater dissemination of both, as the evolving legal history of blacks and women suggests. The legal culture has supported the creation of a significant middle class, enhanced the development of new technologies in the service of the public, and maintained social control sufficiently for the realization of individual ambition.

Yet our legal past is studded with injustice. Neither wealth, political power, social standing, nor civil liberties and civil rights have ever been equally distributed. Often the legal system has abetted racial and gender discrimination, maldistribution of wealth, exploitation and political powerlessness. Through a tradition of popular justice, Americans have frequently and savagely stepped outside the rule of law to administer criminal justice. The juggernaut of economic growth has spread considerable havoc; its costs can be tolled in pollution to the environment and in personal injury (and even death) to those whose labors made growth possible. Lawmakers have frequently, as with slavery, pulled on the masks of the law, permitting rather than alleviating injustice. Our legal past has had a persistently dark side; the history of American law has not been the history of uninterrupted human progress.

Its history has been one of systematic change, of law and society reacting to and reinforcing one another. If we know something of the story of law, we can then appreciate more fully the history of the society of which it is a part. Habit and culture incline us to think of the legal system as stable, certain, orderly, and fair. Yet our legal history suggests that it has been more a river than a rock, more the product of social change than the molder of social development. As Oliver Wendell Holmes, Jr. observed almost a century ago, through our legal history we discover that we are what we have been.

Notes

Introduction

1. Oliver Wendell Holmes, Jr., *The Speeches of Oliver Wendell Holmes* (1891), p. 17.
2. *The American Heritage Dictionary of the English Language* (1976), p. 741.
3. Donald Black, *The Behavior of Law* (1976), p. 1.
4. Lawrence M. Friedman, *American Law* (1984), pp. 138–53. I am indebted here and elsewhere in this book to Professor Friedman.
5. Robert Paul Wolf, ed., *The Rule of Law* (1971), pp. 243–52. See also Howard Zinn's discussion of "The Conspiracy of Law," from which I have drawn.
6. John Henry Schlegel, "Notes toward an Intimate, Opinionated, and Affectionate History of the Conference on Critical Legal Studies," *Stanford Law Review* 36(January 1984):411.
7. James Willard Hurst, *Law and the Conditions of Freedom in the Nineteenth-Century United States* (1956).
8. Harry N. Scheiber, "American Constitutional History and the New Legal History: Complementary Themes in Two Modes," *Journal of American History* 68(September 1981):337–50.

Chapter 1

1. Quoted in C. H. Lincoln, *Revolutionary Movement in Pennsylvania* (1901), pp. 17–18.
2. As quoted in Richard Hofstadter, *America at 1750: A Social Portrait* (1973), p. 5.
3. As quoted in Richard B. Morris, *Studies in the History of American Law, with Special Reference to the Seventeenth and Eighteenth Centuries* (1930), p. 25.
4. As quoted in David Burner et al., *An American Portrait: A History of the United States*, 2nd Ed., 2 vols. (1985), vol. 2, p. 22.
5. As quoted in Stephen Botein, *Early American Law and Society* (1983), p. 33.
6. Ibid., p. 26.
7. As quoted in Samuel Walker, *Popular Justice: A History of American Criminal Justice* (1980), p. 26.
8. Bradley Chapin, *Criminal Justice in Colonial America, 1606–1660* (1983), p. 36.
9. Botein, *Early American Law*, p. 18.

10. L. Alston, introduction to Thomas Smith, *De Republica Anglorum* (reprinted 1970), p. xxxiv.

11. Julius Goebel, Jr., "King's Law and Local Custom in Seventeenth-Century New England," *Columbia Law Review* 31(1931):416.

12. Julius Goebel, Jr., and T. Raymond Naughton, *Law Enforcement in Colonial New York: A Study in Criminal Procedure, 1664–1776* (1970), pp. 497–507.

13. David T. Konig, *Law and Society in Puritan Massachusetts, Essex County, 1629–1692* (1979), pp. 89–116. See also Bruce H. Mann, *Neighbors & Strangers: Law and Community in Early Connecticut* (1987), pp. 162–70.

14. D. Hening, *Statutes of Virginia,* vol. 1, p. 486.

15. Robert Summers, "Law in Colonial New York: The Legal System of 1691," *Harvard Law Review* 80(1967):1762.

16. Joseph H. Smith, *Appeals to the Privy Council from the American Plantations* (1950), p. 660.

17. Stanley N. Katz, "The Politics of Law in Colonial America: Controversies over Chancery Courts and Equity Law in the Eighteenth Century," in Donald Fleming and Bernard Bailyn, eds., *Law in American History* (1971), p. 283.

18. Daniel J. Boorstin, *The Americans: The Colonial Experience* (1958), p. 197.

19. As quoted in Anton-Herman Chroust, *The Rise of the Legal Profession in America* (1965), vol. 1, p. 297.

20. As quoted in Botein, *Early American Law,* p. 35.

21. Ibid.

22. Ibid., p. 56.

23. Ibid.

24. Peter Hoffer and N. E. H. Hull, *Impeachments in America, 1635–1805* (1984), p. 42.

25. As quoted in Clarence Ver Steeg, *The Formative Years 1607–1763* (1964), p. 253.

26. Ibid.

27. As quoted in David Grayson Allen, *In English Ways: The Movement of Societies and the Transferral of English Local Law and Custom to Massachusetts Bay in the Seventeenth Century* (1981), p. 39.

28. Jon C. Teaford, *The Municipal Revolution: Origins of Modern Urban Government* 1650–1825 (1975), p. 16.

29. Allen, *In English Ways,* p. 57.

30. Mann, *Neighbors & Strangers,* p. 168.

Chapter 2

1. M. Eugene Sirmans, *Cultural South Carolina* (1966), p. 228.

2. As quoted in Jackson Turner Main, *The Social Structure of Revolutionary America* (1965), p. 227.

3. Douglas L. Jones, "The Strolling Poor: Transiency in Eighteenth Century Massachusetts," *Journal of Social History* 9(1975):45.

4. Pennsylvania, Guardians of the Poor, *A Compilation of the Poor Laws of the State of Pennsylvania from the Year 1700 to 1788, Inclusive* (reprinted 1971), pp. 12–13.

5. Bradley Chapin, *Criminal Justice in Colonial America, 1606–1660* (1983), p. 114.

6. David T. Konig, *Law and Society in Puritan Massachusetts, Essex County, 1629–1692* (1979), p. 174.

7. Douglas Greenberg, *Crime and Law Enforcement in the Colony of New York 1691–1776* (1976), p. 27.

8. As quoted in Stephen Botein, *Early American Law and Society* (1983), p. 26.

9. Lawrence M. Friedman, *A History of American Law,* 2nd ed. (1985), p. 72.

10. As quoted in Chapin, *Criminal Justice in Colonial America*, p. 128.

11. William H. Seiler, "The Anglican Parish in Virginia," in James Morton Smith, ed., *Seventeenth-Century America* (1969), p. 134.

12. *Colonial Records of Rhode Island* (reprinted 1971), p. 113.

13. Ibid.

14. As quoted in Chapin, *Criminal Justice in Colonial America*, p. 55.

15. Richard B. Morris, *Studies in the History of American Law, with Special Reference to the Seventeenth and Eighteenth Centuries* (1930), p. 16.

16. Marylynn Salmon, *Women and the Law of Property in Early America* (1986), p. 185.

17. As quoted in Linda Grant De Pauw, "Women and the Law: The Colonial Period," *Human Rights* 6(1977):112.

18. Ibid.

19. Mary Ryan, *Womanhood in America: From Colonial Times to the Present* (1975), p. 22.

20. As quoted in Botein, *Early American Law and Society*, p. 12.

21. William W. Hening, ed., *The Statutes at Large: Being a Collection of All the Lawes of Virginia etc. (1819–1823)*, vol. 2, p. 43.

22. William W. Wiecek, "The Statutory Law of Slavery and Race in the Thirteen Mainland Colonies of British America," *William and Mary Quarterly* 34(1977):276.

23. Ibid., p. 270.

24. Friedman, *History of American Law*, p. 79.

25. Hening, ed., *Statutes*, vol. 2, p. 268.

26. Ibid., p. 394.

27. As quoted in Paton Yoder, "Tavern Regulation in Virginia: Rationale and Reality," *The Virginia Magazine* 87(1979):262.

28. Carl Bridenbaugh, *Cities in Revolt* (1952), p. 148.

29. Richard Hofstadter, *America in 1750: A Social Portrait* (1973), p. 10.

30. John T. Farrell, ed., *The Superior Court Diary of William Samuel Johnson, 1772–1773* (1942), p. xxxv.

31. Hening, ed., *Statutes*, vol. 9, p. 226.

32. As quoted in C. Ray Keim, "Primogeniture and Entail in Colonial Virginia," *William and Mary Quarterly* 25(October 1968):549.

33. Morton J. Horwitz, *The Transformation of American Law, 1780–1860* (1977), p. 32.

34. A. W. Brian Simpson, "The Horwitz Thesis and the History of Contracts," *The University of Chicago Law Review* 46(1979):557.

Chapter 3

1. "The Declaration of Independence," in Henry Steele Commager, ed., *Documents of American History*, 7th Ed. (1963), p. 100.

2. Ibid.

3. As quoted in Gordon Wood. *The Creation of the American Republic, 1776–1787* (1969), p. 259.

4. William E. Nelson, *The Americanization of the Common Law: The Impact of Legal Change on Massachusetts Society, 1760–1830* (1975), p. 67.

5. Bernard Bailyn, *The Ideological Origins of the American Revolution* (1967), p. 200.

6. Ibid.

7. As quoted in Wood, *Creation of the American Republic*, p. 17.

8. Ibid., p. 264.

9. John M. Murrin, "The Legal Transformation: The Bench and Bar of Eighteenth Century Massachusetts," in Stanley N. Katz and John M. Murrin, eds., *Colonial America: Essays in Politics and Social Development* (1983), pp. 540–72.

10. Ibid., pp. 568–71.

11. As quoted in Charles Adams, ed., *The Works of John Adams, Second President of the United States* (1850), vol. 10, p. 248.

12. M. H. Smith, *The Writs of Assistance Case* (1978), p. 101.

13. Bernard Bailyn, *The Ordeal of Thomas Hutchinson* (1974), p. 24.

14. Smith, *Writs of Assistance,* p. 101.

15. Peter Oliver, *Peter Oliver's Origin and Progress of the American Revolution,* edited by Douglas Adair and J. Schutz (1961), p. 35.

16. As quoted in Stephen B. Presser and Jamil S. Zainaldin, eds., *Law and American History* (1980), p. 73.

17. Bernard Bailyn, ed., *Pamphlets of the American Revolution* (1965), p. 413.

18. As quoted in Wood, *Creation of the American Republic,* pp. 292–93.

19. As quoted in John P. Reid, *In Defiance of the Law: The Standing Army Controversy, the Two Constitutions, and the Coming of the American Revolution* (1981), p. 5. Emphasis added.

20. Ibid., p. 215.

21. Richard Maxwell Brown, *Strain of Violence: Historical Studies of American Violence and Vigilantism* (1975), p. 45.

22. Ibid., pp. 95–133.

23. As quoted in Pauline Maier, "Popular Uprisings and Civil Authority in Eighteenth-Century America," in Roger Lane and John J. Turner, Jr., eds., *Riot, Rout, and Tumult: Readings in American Social and Political Violence* (1978), p. 43.

24. Ibid.

25. Brown, *Strain of Violence,* pp. 41–66.

26. Maier, "Popular Uprisings," p. 45.

27. Hiller B. Zobel, *The Boston Massacre* (1970), p. 182.

28. Ibid., p. 116.

29. Wood, *Creation of the American Republic,* p. 265.

30. Ibid., p. 264.

31. Willi Paul Adams, *The First American Constitutions: Republican Ideology and the Making of the State Constitutions in the Revolutionary Era* (1980), p. 104.

32. As quoted in Peter S. Onuf, "A New Constitutional Order," in Herman Belz, ed., *This Constitution: A History* (1987), p. 29.

33. Ibid., p. 8.

34. W. P. Adams, *First American Constitutions,* p. 63.

35. Peter S. Onuf, *The Origins of the Federal Republic: Jurisdictional Controversies in the United States, 1775–1787* (1983).

36. W. P. Adams, *First American Constitutions,* p. 64.

37. Ibid.

38. Thomas Jefferson, *Notes on the State of Virginia,* edited by William Peden (1955), p. 121.

39. As quoted in Onuf, "New Constitutional Order," p. 18.

40. R. R. Palmer, *The Age of Democratic Revolutions* (1959), vol. 1, p. 214.

41. As quoted in Onuf, "New Constitutional Order," p. 21.

42. Wood, *Creation of the American Republic,* p. 383.

43. Ibid., p. 388.

44. Bayard v. Singleton, 1 Martin 42 (N.C. 1787), p. 90.

45. George Washington to Henry Knox, December [4], 1786, George Washington Papers, Library of Congress.

46. Jack N. Rakove, *The Beginnings of National Politics: An Interpretive History of the Continental Congress* (1979), p. 371–75.

Chapter 4

1. As quoted in Jamil S. Zainaldin, *Law in Antebellum Society: Legal Change and Economic Expansion* (1983), p. 13.

2. As quoted in Richard E. Ellis, *The Jeffersonian Crisis: Courts and Politics in the Young Republic* (1971), p. 268.

3. Forrest McDonald, *Novus Ordo Seclorum: The Intellectual Origins of the Constitution* (1985), p. 287.

4. As quoted in ibid., p. 202.

5. Cecilia M. Kenyon, "Men of Little Faith: The Anti-Federalists on the Nature of Representative Government," *William and Mary Quarterly* 15(1955):3–43.

6. As quoted in Gordon Wood, *The Creation of the American Republic, 1776–1787* (1969), p. 527.

7. Ibid., p. 532.

8. Ibid.

9. McDonald, *Novus Ordo Seclorum*, p. 259.

10. *The Federalist Papers* (1961), p. 83. (Referred to in text as *Federalist.*)

11. As quoted in McDonald, *Novus Ordo Seclorum*, p. 277.

12. Harry N. Scheiber, "Federalism and the Constitution: The Original Understanding," in Lawrence M. Friedman and Harry N. Scheiber, eds., *American Law and the Constitutional Order: Historical Perspectives* (1978), p. 88.

13. Ibid.

14. U.S., *Constitution*, Art. I, sec. 18.

15. McDonald, *Novus Ordo Seclorum*, p. 270.

16. Ibid., p. 269.

17. As quoted in Scheiber, "Federalism and the Constitution," p. 89.

18. *Federalist Papers*, p. 469.

19. Ibid.

20. U.S., *Constitution*, Art. III, sec. 1.

21. Max Farrand, ed., *The Records of the Federal Constitutional Convention* (1966), vol. 2, p. 76.

22. Ibid., p. 299.

23. U.S., *Constitution*, Art. IV, sec. 2.

24. Edward S. Corwin, "The Constitution as Instrument and Symbol," *American Political Science Review* 30(1936):1071, 1078.

25. James Sterling Young, *The Washington Community 1800–1828* (1966), p. 13.

26. "Jefferson's First Inaugural Address," in Henry Steele Commager, ed., *Documents of American History*, 7th Ed. (1963), p. 187.

27. Julius Goebel, Jr., *Antecedents and Beginnings to 1801* (1971), p. 458.

28. Ibid., p. 553.

29. As quoted in Robert G. McCloskey, *The American Supreme Court* (1960), p. 31.

30. Mary K. B. Tachau, *Federal Courts in the Early Republic: Kentucky, 1789–1816* (1978).

31. As quoted in McCloskey, *The American Supreme Court*, p. 35.

32. United States v. Mitchell, 26 Federal Cases 1277 (C.C.D. Penn., 1795).

33. Stephen B. Presser, "A Tale of Two Judges: Richard Peters, Samuel Chase, and the Broken Promise of Federalist Jurisprudence," *Northwestern University Law Review* 73(1978):92.

34. As quoted in ibid., p. 93.

35. Ibid., p. 92.

36. Ibid., p. 93.

37. Ibid., p. 97.

38. As quoted in Ellis, *Jeffersonian Crisis*, p. 15.

39. Ibid., p. 20.

40. As quoted in Zainaldin, *Law in Antebellum Society*, p. 10.

41. Leonard W. Levy, *Thomas Jefferson and Civil Liberties: The Darker Side* (1963).

42. As quoted in Ellis, *Jeffersonian Crisis*, p. 113.

43. Ibid., p. 113.

44. Ibid., p. 51.

45. Ibid., p. 52.

46. U.S., *Constitution*, Art. II, sec. 4.

47. Peter C. Hoffer and N. E. H. Hull, *Impeachment in America, 1635–1805* (1984), p. 209.

48. As quoted in Ellis, *Jeffersonian Crisis*, p. 80.

49. Charles Warren, *The Supreme Court in United States History* (1947), vol. 1, p. 70.

50. G. Edward White, *The American Judicial Tradition: Profiles of Leading American Judges* (1976), p. 11.

51. As quoted in Albert J. Beveridge, *The Life of John Marshall (1916–1919)*, vol. 3, p. 144.

52. Marbury v. Madison, 1 Cranch 177–78 (1803).

53. "Judiciary Act of 1789," in Commager, ed., *Documents*, p. 154.

54. As quoted in Dwight F. Henderson, *Congress, Courts, and Criminals: The Development of Federal Criminal Law, 1801–1829* (1985), p. 28.

55. As quoted in Presser, "Tale of Two Judges," p. 59.

56. United States v. Hudson and Goodwin, 11 Cranch 32 (1812).

57. Alexis de Tocqueville, *Democracy in America*, vol. 1, edited by Phillips Bradley (1945 Ed.), p. 290.

58. Ellis, *Jeffersonain Crisis*, p. 283.

Chapter 5

1. Hector St. John de Crevecouer, *Letters from an American Farmer* (1904), pp. 52–56.

2. Alexis de Tocqueville, *Democaracy in America*, vol. 2, edited by Phillips Bradley (1945 Ed.), pp. 247–48.

3. Thomas Jefferson, "Inaugural Address," *Journal of the Executive Proceedings of the U.S. Senate* 1(1828):393.

4. James Willard Hurst, *Law and Markets in United States History: Different Modes of Bargaining among Interests* (1982), p. 22.

5. James Willard Hurst, *The Growth of American Law: The Law Makers* (1951), p. 82.

6. Harry N. Scheiber, "Property Rights and Public Purpose in American Law," *Proceedings of the International Economic History Association, 7th Congress* 1(1978):234.

7. As quoted in Stuart Bruchey, *The Roots of American Economic Growth 1607–1861* (1968), p. 125.

8. As quoted in Jamil S. Zainaldin, *Law in Antebellum Society: Legal Change and Economic Expansion* (1983), p. 20.

9. As quoted in David Burner et al., *An American Portrait: A History of the United States*, 2nd Ed., 2 vols. (1985), vol. 2, p. 214.

10. Ibid., p. 245.

11. "Jackson's Veto of the Bank Bill," in Henry Steele Commager, ed., *Documents of American History*, 7th Ed. (1963), p. 274.

12. U.S., *Constitution*, Art. I, sec. 8.

13. Earle v. Sawyer, 8 Fed. Cas. 254 (C.C.D. Mass. 1825).

14. 5 Statutes at Large 117, 119, 120 (Act of July 4, 1836).

15. Lawrence M. Friedman, *A History of American Law,* 2nd Ed. (1985), p. 256.

16. Bruchey, *Roots of American Economic Growth,* p. 125.

17. William E. Nelson, *The Roots of American Bureaucracy 1830–1900* (1982), p. 11.

18. George Rogers Taylor, *The Transportation Revolution, 1815–1860* (1951).

19. As quoted in John G. Burke, "Bursting Boilers and Federal Power," *Technology and Culture* 71(1966):21.

20. Ibid., p. 21.

21. Leonard W. Levy, *Chief Justice Lemuel Shaw and the Law of the Commonwealth* (1957), p. 305.

22. *Massachusetts Laws,* 1833, chap. 215.

23. James Willard Hurst, *Law and Social Order in the United States* (1977), p. 70.

24. Harry N. Scheiber, "Federalism and Legal Process: Historical and Contemporary Analysis of the American System," *Law and Society Review* 14(1980):705.

25. Ronald E. Seavoy, *The Origins of the American Business Corporation, 1784–1855* (1985), p. 6.

26. Hurst, *Law and Markets,* p. 48.

27. As quoted in Harold M. Hyman and William M. Wiecek, *Equal Justice under Law: Constitutional Development 1835–1875* (1982), p. 29.

28. Seavoy, *Origins of the Business Corporation,* p. 6.

29. *Register of Debates,* 19th Congress, 1st Sess., May 1, 1826, p. 647.

30. Peter J. Coleman, *Debtors and Creditors in America: Insolvency, Imprisonment for Debt, and Bankruptcy, 1607–1900* (1974), p. 16.

31. As quoted in ibid., p. 5.

32. As quoted in Charles Warren, *Bankruptcy in United States History* (1935), p. 21.

33. Harry N. Scheiber, *Ohio Canal Era* (1968), p. 297.

34. David M. Gold, "Public Aid to Private Enterprise under the Ohio Constitution: Sections 4, 6, and 13 of Article VIII in Historical Perspective," *University of Toledo Law Review* 16(1985):410.

35. Morton Keller, "The Politics of State Constitutional Revision, 1820–1930," in Kermit L. Hall, Harold M. Hyman, and Leon V. Sigal, eds., *The Constitutional Convention as an Amending Device* (1981), pp. 70–71.

36. *Report of the Debates and Proceedings of the Convention for the Revision of the Constitution of the State of Ohio, 1850–51,* vol. 1 (1851), p. 523.

37. Ibid., p. 632.

38. As quoted in Kermit L. Hall, "The Judiciary on Trial: State Constitutional Reform and the Rise of an Elected judiciary, 1846–1860," *The Historian* 44(1983):350–51.

Chapter 6

1. Alexis de Tocqueville, *Democracy in America,* edited by J. P. Mayer, translated by George Lawrence (1969), p. 102.

2. William E. Nelson, *The Roots of American Bureaucracy 1830–1900* (1982), p. 31.

3. Harry N. Scheiber, "Property Rights and Public Purpose in American Law," *Proceedings of the International Economic History Association, 7th Congress* 1(1978):233–40.

4. Morton J. Horwitz, *The Transformation of American Law, 1780–1860* (1977), p. 28.

5. As quoted in ibid., p. 142.

6. As quoted in Lawrence M. Friedman, *A History of American Law,* 2nd Ed. (1985), p. 155.

7. State of New Jersey, *Constitution* (1844), Art. 1, sec. 5.

8. Julius Goebel, Jr., ed., *The Law Practice of Alexander Hamilton,* vol. 2 (1969), p. 20.

9. Horwitz, *Transformation of American Law,* p. 143.

10. *American Jurist* 5(1831):29.

11. Francis Hilliard, *The Elements of Law* (1835), p. vi; William Duane, *The Law of Nations Investigated in a Popular Manner* (1809), p. 3.

12. Commonwealth v. M'Closeky, 2 Rawle 374 (Pa., 1830).

13. Tocqueville, *Democracy in America*, p. 100.

14. R. Kent Newmyer, *Supreme Court Justice Joseph Story: Statesman of the Old Republic* (1985), p. 138.

15. 14 Virginia 315 (1809).

16. "Corporations," in *American Jurist*, reprinted in Charles Haar, ed., *The Golden Age of American Law* (1965), p. 336.

17. Spear v. Grant, 16 Mass. 14 (1819).

18. William E. Nelson, *The Americanization of the Common Law: The Impact of Legal Change on Massachusetts, 1760–1830* (1975), p. 135.

19. Dartmouth College v. Woodward, 4 Wheaton 518 (1819).

20. Ibid.

21. University v. Foy, 1 Murphey 88–89 (N.C., 1805).

22. Newmyer, *Supreme Court Justice Joseph Story*, p. 133.

23. As quoted in George Dargo, *Law in the New Republic: Private Law and the Public Estate* (1983), p. 101.

24. As quoted in Harold M. Hyman and William M. Wiecek, *Equal Justice under Law: Constitutional Development 1835–1875* (1982), p. 48.

25. As quoted in Leonard W. Levy, *Chief Justice Shaw and the Law of the Commonwealth* (1957), p. 184.

26. Ibid., p. 187.

27. Ibid.

28. James Willard Hurst, *Law and the Conditions of Freedom in the Nineteenth-Century United States* (1956), p. 28.

29. William Blackstone, *Commentaries on the Law of England*, vol. 3 (1768), p. 218.

30. Hurst, *Law and the Conditions of Freedom*, p. 28.

31. Harry N. Scheiber, "The Road to MUNN: Eminent Domain and the Concept of Public Purpose in the State Courts," in Donald Fleming and Bernard Bailyn, eds., *Law in American History* (1971), p. 332.

32. As quoted in Horwitz, *Transformation of American Law*, p. 37.

33. Joseph Angell, *Watercourses* (1824), p. 37.

34. Cary v. Daniels, 48 Mass. 476–77 (1844).

35. Irwin v. Phillips, 5 Cal. 146 (1855).

36. Gordon M. Bakken, *The Development of Law on the Rocky Mountain Frontier: Civil Law and Society, 1850–1912* (1983), p. 71.

37. U.S., *Constitution*, Fifth Amendment.

38. Scheiber, "Road to MUNN," pp. 360–76.

39. Ibid., p. 365.

40. Newmyer, *Supreme Court Justice Joseph Story*, p. 225.

41. 11 Peters 544–53.

42. Ibid. *Charles River Bridge* did *not* involve eminent domain issues.

43. 6 Howard 531–32.

44. Dana v. Valentine, 46 Mass. 8 (1842).

45. 1 Grant Cas. 413 (Pa., 1856).

46. As quoted in Levy, *Chief Justice Lemuel Shaw*, p. 121.

47. Horwitz, *Transformation of American Law*, p. 161.

48. William Wetmore Story, *A Treatise on the Law of Contracts*, vol. 1, 5th Ed. (1874), p. 4.

49. Friedman, *History of American Law*, p. 263.

50. McFarland v. Newman, 9 Watts 55 (Pa., 1839).

51. Tony A. Freyer, "Negotiable Instruments and the Federal Courts in Antebellum American Business," *Business History Review* 50(1976):436.

52. Act of September 24, 1789, ch. 20, sec. 34, 1 Stat. 73.

53. Swift v. Tyson, 16 Peters 18–19 (1842).

54. 6 Cush. 296–97 (Mass., 1850).

55. 4 Metcalf 49 (Mass., 1842).

56. Gary T. Schwartz, "Tort Law and the Economy in Nineteenth-Century America: A Reinterpretation," *The Yale Law Journal* 90(1981):1743.

57. Thomas v. Winchester, 6 N.Y. 399 (1852).

58. Robert Rantoul, Jr., *Memoirs, Speeches and Writings,* edited by Luther Hamilton (1854), p. 279.

59. Charles M. Cook, *The American Codification Movement: A Study of Antebellum Legal Reform* (1981), p. 201.

60. Lexington & Ohio Railroad Co. v. Applegate et al., 38 Ky. 310 (1839).

61. Steele v. Curle, 34 Ky. 390 (1836).

62. John Phillip Reid, *Law for the Elephant: Property and Social Behavior on the Overland Trail* (1980), p. 364.

Chapter 7

1. Thomas Jefferson, *Notes on the State of Virginia,* edited by William Peden (1955), p. 138.

2. John T. Noonan, Jr., *Persons and Masks of the Law* (1976), p. 60. On slavery and the Constitution, see Paul Finkelman, "Slavery and the Constitutional Convention: Making a Covenant with Death," in Richard Beeman, Stephen Botein, and Edward C. Carter, II, eds., *Beyond Confederation: Origins of the Constitution and American National Identity* (1987), pp. 188–225.

3. Somerset v. Stewart, Lofft 1, 98 Eng. Rep. 499 (K.B. 1772).

4. Jefferson, *Notes on the State of Virginia,* p. 143.

5. As quoted in Kenneth M. Stampp, *The Peculiar Institution: Slavery in the Ante-bellum South* (1956), p. 207.

6. State v. Mann, 13 N.C. 263 (1829).

7. Ibid.

8. Stampp, *Peculiar Institution,* p. 211.

9. Ibid.

10. As quoted in Stanley Elkins, *Slavery: A Problem in American Institutional and Intellectual Life* (1976), p. 56.

11. Daniel Boorstin, "The Perils of Indwelling Law," in Robert P. Wolff, ed., *The Rule of Law* (1971), p. 85.

12. Philip J. Schwarz, "Forging the Shackles: The Development of Virginia's Criminal Code for Slaves," in David J. Bodenhamer and James W. Ely, Jr., eds., *Ambivalent Legacy: A Legal History of the South* (1984), p. 128.

13. Souther v. Commonwealth, 7 Grattan 673 (Va., 1851).

14. Thomas R. R. Cobb, *An Inquiry into the Law of Slavery in the United States of America* (1858), p. 98.

15. Daniel J. Flannigan, "Criminal Procedure in Slave Trials in the Antebellum South," *Journal of Southern History* 40(November 1974):538.

16. Cato v. State, 9 Fla. 173–74 (1860).

17. Stephen v. State, 11 Ga. 230 (1852).

18. Ford v. Ford, 7 Humphreys 95–96 (Tenn., 1846).

19. State v. Nathan, Slave of Gabriel South, 5 Richardson 219 (S.C. 1851).

20. Stampp, *Peculiar Institution*, p. 446.

21. Thomas D. Morris, " 'As If the Injury Was Effected by the Natural Elements of Air, or Fire,': Slave Wrongs and the Liability of Masters," *Law and Society Review* 16(1981–1982):578.

22. Gallardet v. Demaries, 18 La. 491 (1841).

23. Wright v. Weatherly, 7 Yeager 367 (Tenn., 1835).

24. As quoted in Morris, "Slave Wrongs," p. 588. On the business law of slavery generally, see the symposium articles by Paul Finkelman, Judith Schaffer, and Andrew Fede in *The American Journal of Legal History* 31(1987):269–358.

25. As quoted in Tony Freyer, "Law and the Antebellum Economy: An Interpretation," in Bodenhamer and Ely, eds., *Ambivalent Legacy*, p. 62.

26. Ibid.

27. As quoted in Richard H. Sewell, *Ballots for Freedom: Antislavery Politics in the United States, 1836–1860* (1976), pp. 172–73.

28. William E. Nelson, *The Roots of American Bureaucracy 1830–1900* (1982), p. 58.

29. William M. Wiecek, *The Sources of Antislavery Constitutionalism in America, 1760–1848* (1977).

30. As quoted in Russel B. Nye, *William Lloyd Garrison and the Humanitarian Reformers* (1955), p. 143.

31. As quoted in Don E. Fehrenbacher, *The Dred Scott Case in American Law and Politics* (1978), p. 56.

32. Paul Finkelman, *An Imperfect Union: Slavery, Federalism, and Comity* (1981).

33. Ibid., p. 113.

34. Harold M. Hyman and William M. Wiecek, *Equal Justice under Law: Constitutional Development 1835–1875* (1982), p. 154.

35. As quoted in ibid., p. 155.

36. Ibid.

37. Jones v. Van Zandt, 13 Fed. Cas. 1048 (C.C.D. Ohio, 1843).

38. William E. Barker, ed., *The Works of William H. Seward*, vol. 1 (1884), p. 74.

39. Dred Scott v. Sandford, 19 Howard 407 (1857).

40. Fehrenbacher, *Dred Scott Case*, p. 439.

41. As quoted in Hyman and Wiecek, *Equal Justice under Law*, p. 96.

42. As quoted in ibid., p. 315.

43. Donald G. Nieman, *To Set the Law in Motion: The Freedmen's Bureau and the Legal Rights of Blacks, 1865–1868* (1976).

44. Hyman and Wiecek, *Equal Justice under Law*, p. 234.

45. U.S., *Constitution*, Art. XIII.

46. U.S., *Constitution*, Article XV.

47. As quoted in Harold U. Faulkner, *Politics, Reform and Expansion, 1890–1900* (1959), p. 7.

48. As quoted in Jonathan Lurie, *Law and the New Nation, 1865–1912* (1983), p. 16.

49. *The Civil Rights Cases*, 109 U.S. 3 (1883).

50. William Cohen, "Negro Involuntary Servitude in the South, 1865–1940: A Preliminary Analysis," *The Journal of Southern History* 42(February 1976):32.

51. Howard Rabinowitz, *Race Relations in the Urban South, 1865–1890* (1978), pp. 196–97.

52. Plessy v. Ferguson, 163 U.S. 537 (1896).

53. Cherokee Nation v. Georgia, 5 Peters 1 (1831).

54. As quoted in Morton Keller, *Affairs of State: Public Life in Late Nineteenth Century America* (1977), p. 459.

55. James B. Thayer, "A People without a Law," *Atlantic Monthly* 68(1891):540–51, 676–87.

56. Yik Wo v. Hopkins, 118 U.S. 356 (1886).

57. As quoted in Keller, *Affairs of State,* pp. 443–44.

58. Chae Chan Ping v. U.S. (Chinese Exclusion Case), 130 U.S. 594 (1889).

59. John Wunder, "The Chinese and the Courts in the Pacific Northwest: Justice Denied," *Pacific Historical Review* 52(May 1983):208.

60. Sir Henry Maine, *Ancient Law* (1861, reprinted 1917), p. 100.

Chapter 8

1. John Demos, *A Little Commonwealth: Family Life in Plymouth Colony* (1970), p. x.

2. Ibid., p. 82.

3. Throughout this chapter I have drawn extensively from Michael Grossberg, *Governing the Hearth: Law and the Family in Nineteenth-Century America* (1985), p. 7.

4. Robert L. Griswold, *Family and Divorce in California, 1850–1890: Victorian Illusions and Everyday Realities* (1982), p. 13.

5. Joel P. Bishop, *First Book of Law* (1868), p. 216.

6. Wightman v. Coates, 15 Mass. 4 (1818).

7. Weaver v. Bachert, 2 Pa. 81–82 (1843).

8. McPherson v. Ryan, 59 Mich. 39 (1886).

9. Grossberg, *Governing the Hearth,* p. 65.

10. James Kent, *Commentaries on American Law* (1826–1830), vol. 2, p. 75.

11. Rodenbaugh v. Sanks, 2 Watts 9–10 (Pa., 1833).

12. Grossberg, *Governing the Hearth,* p. 78.

13. Joseph Chamberlain, "Eugenics and the Limitation of Marriage," *American Bar Association Journal* 9(1923):429.

14. As quoted in Grossberg, *Governing the Hearth,* p. 98.

15. Devanbaugh v. Devanbaugh, 5 Paige 557 (N.Y., 1836).

16. True v. Raney, 21 N.H. 54–55 (1850).

17. Reynolds v. U.S., 98 U.S. 162, 167 (1878).

18. State v. Hairston and Williams, 63 N.C. 452, 453 (1877).

19. Frasher v. State, 3 Tex. Ct. of App., 276 (1877).

20. As quoted in Grossberg, *Governing the Hearth,* p. 139.

21. Buck v. Bell, 274 U.S. 200 (1927).

22. Suzanne Lebsock, *The Free Women of Petersburg: Status and Culture in a Southern Town, 1784–1860* (1984), p. 61.

23. Norma Basch, "Equity vs. Equality: Emerging Concepts of Women's Political Status in the Age of Jackson," *Journal of the Early Republic* 3(1983):318.

24. Act of Apr. 7, 1848, ch. 200, 1848 N.Y. Laws 307.

25. As quoted in Grossberg, *Governing the Hearth,* p. 176.

26. Dio Lewis, *Chastity, or Our Secret Sins* (1874), p. 183.

27. Queen v. Hicklin, 3 Q.B. 371 (1868).

28. Ex Parte Jackson, 96 U.S. 736 (1877).

29. As quoted in Grossberg, *Governing the Hearth,* p. 190.

30. People v. Sanger, 22 N.Y. 192 (1918).

31. As quoted in Grossberg, *Governing the Hearth,* p. 162.

32. As quoted in James Mohr, *Abortion in America. The Origins and Evolution of National Policy* (1978), p. 187.

33. Viviana A. Zelizer, *Pricing the Priceless Child: The Changing Social Value of Children* (1985), p. 5.

34. As quoted in Griswold, *Family and Divorce in California,* p. 20.

35. Lawrence M. Friedman, "Rights of Passage: Divorce Law in Historical Perspective," *Oregon Law Review* 63(1984):862.

36. Anonymous, 55 Ala. 433 (1876).

37. Joel P. Bishop, *Commentaries on the Law of Married Women*, vol. 2 (1871), p. 74.

38. Grossberg, *Governing the Hearth*, pp. xi–xii.

Chapter 9

1. Charles Loring Brace, *The Dangerous Classes of New York, and Twenty Years' Work among Them* (1872), pp. 28–29.

2. David J. Rothman, *The Discovery of the Asylum: Social Order and Disorder in the New Republic* (1971), p. 15.

3. William E. Nelson, "Emerging Notions of Modern Criminal Law in the Revolutionary Era: An Historical Perspective," in Lawrence M. Friedman and Harry N. Scheiber, eds., *American Law and the Constitutional Order: Historical Perspectives* (1978), pp. 167–68.

4. Lawrence M. Friedman, *A History of American Law*, 2nd Ed. (1985), p. 294.

5. Cited in Samuel Walker, *Popular Justice: A History of American Criminal Justice* (1980), p. 37. I have relied extensively on Walker's work in this chapter and elsewhere.

6. Ibid., p. 38.

7. As quoted in Adam Hirsch, "From Pillory to Penitentiary: The Rise of Criminal Incarceration in Early Massachusetts," *Michigan Law Review* 80(1982):1235.

8. Kathryn Preyer, "Crime, the Criminal Law, and Reform in Post-Revolutionary Virginia," *Law and History Review* 1(1985):53–85.

9. As quoted in Walker, *Popular Justice*, p. 47.

10. Act of Pennsylvania, April 22, 1784, 3 Sm. L. 186.

11. Benjamin Rush, *Considerations on the Injustice and Impolicy of Punishing Murder by Death* (1792), p. 18.

12. George Keith Taylor, *Substance of a Speech Delivered in the House of Delegates in Virginia, on the Bill to Amend the Penal Laws of this Commonwealth* (1796), p. 31.

13. Tunis Wortman, *An Oration on the Influence of Social Institutions upon Human Morals and Happiness* (1796), pp. 4–5.

14. As quoted in Walker, *Popular Justice*, p. 49.

15. William V. Wells, *The Life and Public Services of Samuel Adams*, vol. 3 (1866), p. 246.

16. *Memoirs of Stephen Burroughs* (1798), p. 126.

17. David J. Bodenhamer, *The Pursuit of Justice: Crime and Law in Antebellum Indiana* (1986), p. 73.

18. As quoted in ibid., p. 56.

19. As quoted in Walker, *Popular Justice*, p. 111.

20. "Diary Notes on the Rights of Juries," in L. Kinvin Wroth and Hiller Zobel, eds., *The Adams Papers: Legal Papers of John Adams*, vol. 1 (1968), p. 230.

21. As quoted in Bodenhamer, *Pursuit of Justice*, p. 84.

22. Rothman, *Discovery of the Asylum*, p. 62.

23. As quoted in ibid., p. 97.

24. Ibid., p. 88.

25. Walker, *Popular Justice*, p. 79.

26. Eric H. Monkkonen, *Police in Urban America, 1860–1920* (1981), p. 31.

27. As quoted in ibid., p. 41.

28. As quoted in ibid., p. 35.

29. Harold M. Hyman and William M. Wiecek, *Equal Justice under Law: Constitutional Development 1835–1875* (1982), p. 509.

30. Lawrence M. Friedman and Robert V. Percival, *The Roots of Justice: Crime and Punishment in Alameda County, California, 1870–1910* (1981), p. 32. There is considerable disagreement about these matters as well as about how to measure, label, and interpret criminal

activity. See Eugene Watts, "Police Response to Crime and Disorder in Twentieth-Century St. Louis," *Journal of American History* 70(1983):340–58.

31. As quoted in Walker, *Popular Justice,* p. 84.

32. Walker, *Popular Justice,* p. 91.

33. Anthony Platt, *The Child Savers: The Invention of Delinquency* (1969).

34. Wilbur R. Miller, *Cops and Bobbies: Police Authority in New York and London, 1830–1870* (1977), p. 80.

35. Edward L. Ayers, *Vengeance and Justice: Crime and Punishment in the Nineteenth-Century American South* (1984), p. 176.

36. 8 Eng. Rep. 718 (1843).

37. John S. Hughes, *In the Law's Darkness: Isaac Ray and the Medical Jurisprudence of Insanity in Nineteenth-Century America* (1986), p. 60.

38. David A. Jones, *History of Criminology: A Philosophical Perspective* (1986), p. 142.

39. Isaac Ray, *A Treatise on the Medical Jurisprudence of Insanity,* 3rd Ed. (1855), p. 263.

40. Walker, *Popular Justice,* p. 123.

Chapter 10

1. Richard L. McCormick, "The Party Period and Public Policy: An Exploratory Hypothesis," *Journal of American History* 66(September 1979):279–98.

2. As quoted in David Burner et al., *An American Portrait: A History of the United States,* 2nd Ed., 2 vols., vol. 2 (1985), p. 425.

3. As quoted in James A. Henretta et al., *America's History* (1987), p. 623.

4. Ibid.

5. Ibid., p. 624.

6. Lawrence M. Friedman, *A History of American Law,* 2nd Ed. (1985), p. 166.

7. Morton Keller, *Affairs of State: Public Life in Late Nineteenth Century America* (1977), p. 165.

8. Harry N. Scheiber, "Property Law, Expropriation, and Resource Allocation by Government, 1789–1910," in Lawrence M. Friedman and Harry N. Scheiber, eds., *American Law and the Constitutional Order: Historical Perspectives* (1978), p. 139.

9. Gordon M. Bakken, *Rocky Mountain Constitution Making, 1850–1912* (1987), pp. 29–34.

10. Scheiber, "Property Law, Expropriation, and Resource Allocation," p. 139.

11. As quoted in Keller, *Affairs of State,* p. 431.

12. Ibid.

13. Charles W. McCurdy, "The *Knight* Sugar Decision of 1895 and the Modernization of American Corporation Law, 1869–1903," *Business History Review* 53(Autumn 1979):304–42.

14. James Willard Hurst, *Law and the Conditions of Freedom in the Nineteenth-Century United States* (1956), p. 73.

15. Richard Hofstadter, *The Age of Reform: From Bryan to FDR* (1955), p. 248.

16. As quoted in Friedman, *History of American Law,* p. 446.

17. Ibid., p. 450.

18. Charles W. McCurdy, "American Law and the Marketing Structure of the Large Corporation," *The Journal of Economic History* 38(September 1978):643.

19. Lawrence M. Friedman, "Freedom of Contract and Occupational Licensing 1890–1910: A Legal and Social Study," *California Law Review* 53(May 1965):487–534.

20. As quoted in Keller, *Affairs of State,* p. 404.

21. Viviana A. Zelizer, *Pricing the Priceless Child: The Changing Social Value of Children* (1985), p. 5.

22. Friedman, *History of American Law,* p. 562.

23. State of Utah, *Constitution* (1895), Art. XVI, sec. 6.

24. Lawrence A. Friedman and Jack Ladinsky, "Social Change and the Law of Industrial Accidents," in Friedman and Scheiber, eds., *American Law and the Constitutional Order*, p. 275.

25. Stephen Skowronek, *Building a New American State: The Expansion of National Administrative Capacities, 1877–1920* (1982), p. 139.

26. William E. Nelson, *The Roots of American Bureaucracy 1830–1900* (1982), p. 81.

27. As quoted in ibid., p. 82.

28. Skowronek, *Building a New American State*, p. 123.

29. As quoted in Henry Steele Commager, ed., *Documents of American History*, 5th Ed. (1949), p. 129.

30. Jonathan Lurie, *Law and the Nation 1865–1912* (1983), p. 35.

31. Commager, ed., *Documents of American History*, p. 136.

32. Lurie, *Law and the Nation*, p. 36.

33. Commager, ed., *Documents of American History*, p. 280.

34. Friedman, *History of American Law*, p. 480.

35. As quoted in ibid., p. 551.

36. Ibid.

Chapter 11

1. Burton J. Bledstein, *The Culture of Professionalism: The Middle Class and the Development of Higher Education in America* (1976), pp. 86–87.

2. *American Lawyer* 1(1893):5.

3. Wayne K. Hobson, "Symbol of the New Profession: Emergence of the Large Law Firm," in Gerard W. Gawalt, ed., *The New High Priests: Lawyers in Post-Civil War America* (1984), p. 6.

4. Ibid., p. 20.

5. Jerold S. Auerbach, *Unequal Justice: Lawyers and Social Change in Modern America* (1976), p. 25.

6. Gawalt, ed., *New High Priests*, p. xii.

7. Ibid., p. xiii. But on the important role of attorneys in "New South" economic development see Gail Williams O'Brien, *The Legal Fraternity and the Making of a New South Community* (1986).

8. Lawrence M. Friedman. *A History of American Law*, 2nd Ed. (1985), p. 166.

9. As quoted in Morton Keller, *Affairs of State: Public Life in Late Nineteenth Century America* (1977), p. 351.

10. Ibid., p. 352.

11. Ibid.

12. Michael de L. Landon, "Another False Start: Mississippi's Second State Bar Association, 1886–1892," in Gawalt, ed., *New High Priests*, p. 198.

13. As quoted in Friedman, *History of American Law*, p. 651.

14. Gawalt, ed., *New High Priests*, p. x.

15. Gary B. Nash, "The Philadelphia Bench and Bar, 1800–1861," *Comparative Studies in Society and History* 7(1965):203.

16. As quoted in Friedman, *History of American Law*, pp. 238–39.

17. As quoted in W. Hamilton Bryson and E. Lee Shepard, "The Virginia Bar, 1870–1900," in Gawalt, ed., *New High Priests*, p. 174.

18. Friedman, *History of American Law*, p. 639.

19. Maxwell Bloomfield, "From Deference to Confrontation: The Early Black Lawyers of Galveston, Texas, 1895–1920," in Gawalt, ed., *New High Priests*, p. 152.

20. Maxwell Bloomfield, *American Lawyers in a Changing Society, 1776–1876* (1976), pp. 338–39.

21. As quoted in Robert Stevens, *Law School: Legal Education in America from the 1850s to the 1980s* (1983), p. 98.

22. Gerard W. Gawalt, "The Impact of Industrialization on the Legal Profession in Massachusetts, 1870–1900," in Gawalt, ed., *New High Priests*, p. 108.

23. Friedman, *History of American Law*, p. 616.

24. Harold M. Hyman and William M. Wiecek, *Equal Justice under Law: Constitutional Development 1835–1875* (1982), p. 347.

25. As quoted in John W. Johnson, "Retreat from the Common Law? The Grudging Reception of Legislative History by American Appellate Courts in the Early Twentieth Century," *Detroit College of Law Review* (1978):416.

26. Christopher G. Tiedeman, *A Treatise on the Limitations of Police Power in the United States* (1886), p. 150.

27. Budd v. New York, 143 U.S. 517 (1892).

28. As quoted in William E. Nelson, *The Roots of American Bureaucracy 1830–1900* (1982), p. 147.

29. As quoted in Keller. *Affairs of State*, p. 346.

30. Thomas K. McGraw, *Prophets of Regulation: Charles Francis Adams, Louis D. Brandeis, James M. Landis, and Alfred E. Kahn* (1984).

31. John W. Johnson, *American Legal Culture, 1908–1940* (1981), p. 30.

Chapter 12

1. Michael Les Benedict, "Laissez-Faire and Liberty: A Re-Evaluation of the Meaning and Origins of Laissez-Faire Constitutionalism," *Law and History Review* 3(Fall 1985):311.

2. Melvin Urofsky, "State Courts and Protective Legislation during the Progressive Era: A Reevaluation," *The Journal of American History* 72(June 1985):64. I have relied extensively on Urofsky's work here and elsewhere in this chapter.

3. John W. Johnson, "Retreat from the Common Law? The Grudging Reception of Legislative History by American Appellate Courts in the Early Twentieth Century," *Detroit College of Law Review* (1978):413–414.

4. Robert Silverman, *Law and Urban Growth: Civil Litigation in the Boston Trial Courts, 1880–1900* (1981).

5. Robert A. Kagan et al., "The Business of State Supreme Courts, 1870–1970," *Stanford Law Review* 30(November 1977):133.

6. Richard A. Posner, *The Federal Courts: Crisis and Reform* (1985), p. 59.

7. Tony A. Freyer, *Forums of Order: The Federal Courts and Business in American History* (1979).

8. The statistics are from American Law Institute, *A Study of the Business of the Federal Courts*, 2 vols. (1934), vol. 1 (p. 107); vol. 2, p. 111; and Gerhard Casper and Richard A. Posner, *The Workload of the Supreme Court* (1976), p. 12.

9. James Willard Hurst, *The Growth of American Law: The Law Makers* (1950), p. 119.

10. William M. Wiecek, "The Reconstruction of Federal Judicial Power, 1863–1876," *American Journal of Legal History* 13(1969):333–59.

11. Freyer, *Forums of Order*, p. 130.

12. Lawrence M. Friedman, *A History of American Law*, 2nd Ed. (1985), p. 355.

13. Margaret V. Nelson, *A Study of Judicial Review in Virginia, 1789–1928* (1947), p. 54.

14. Morton Keller, *Affairs of State: Public Life in Late Nineteenth Century America* (1977), p. 362.

15. Kermit L. Hall, *The Supreme Court and Judicial Review in American History* (1985), p. 27.

16. As quoted in Keller, *Affairs of State,* p. 366.

17. William E. Nelson, *The Roots of American Bureaucracy 1830–1900* (1982), p. 150.

18. Wynehamer v. People, 13 N.Y. 378 (1856).

19. People v. Gillson, 109 N.Y. 390 (1888).

20. State v. Santee, 111 Iowa 1, 4–7 (1900).

21. As quoted in Lawrence M. Friedman, "Freedom of Contract and Occupational Licensing 1890–1910: A Legal and Social Study," *California Law Review* 53(May 1965):513.

22. Slaughterhouse Cases, 16 Wallace 36 (1873).

23. Keller, *Affairs of State,* p. 176.

24. Munn v. Illinois, 94 U.S. 113, 126, 130 (1877).

25. ICC v. Alabama Midland Railway Co., 168 U.S. 144 (1897).

26. Chicago, Milwaukee and St. Paul Railway Co. v. Minnesota, 134 U.S. 458 (1890).

27. James Willard Hurst, *Law and the Conditions of Freedom in the Nineteenth-Century United States* (1956), p. 44.

28. Charles W. McCurdy, "The *Knight* Sugar Decision of 1895 and the Modernization of American Corporation Law, 1869–1903," *Business History Review* 53(Autumn 1979):314.

29. U.S. v. E.C. Knight, 156 U.S. 12 (1895).

30. Christopher G. Tiedeman, *A Treatise on State and Federal Control of Persons and Property of the United States, Considered from Both a Civil and Criminal Standpoint,* 2 vols. (1900), vol. 1, p. 13.

31. In Re Jacobs, 98 N.Y. 98 (1885), as quoted in Urofsky, "State Courts and Protective Legislation," p. 68.

32. Urofsky, "State Courts and Protective Legislation," pp. 70–71.

33. State v. Shorey, 48 Or. 398 (1906).

34. Urofsky, "State Courts and Protective Legislation," p. 71.

35. As quoted in Urofsky, "State Courts and Protective Legislation," p. 71.

36. Ritchie v. People, 155 Ill. 111 (1893).

37. People v. Williams, 189 N.Y. 134 (1907).

38. Burcher v. People, 41 Colo. 495 (1907).

39. Commonwealth v. Beatty, 15 Pa. 8 (1900).

40. Urofsky, "State Courts and Protective Legislation," p. 74.

41. People v. Orange County Road Construction Co., 175 N.Y. 84 (1903).

42. Atkins v. Kansas, 191 U.S. 222–223 (1903).

43. State of Utah, *Constitution,* as amended, originals, and amendments, comp. Utah State Archives (1959), p. 106.

44. Urofsky, "State Courts and Protective Legislation," p. 78.

45. As quoted in ibid., p. 79.

46. Lochner v. New York, 198 U.S. 56 (1905).

47. Ibid., p. 75.

48. As quoted in Urofsky, "State Courts and Protective Legislation," p. 80.

49. Godcharles & Co. v. Wigeman, 113 Pa. 437 (1886).

50. State v. Fire Creek Coal & Coke Co., 33 W.V. 189 (1889).

51. Urofsky, "State Courts and Protective Legislation," p. 83.

52. Coppage v. Kansas, 236 U.S. 15 (1915).

53. Felix Frankfurter and Nathan Green, *The Labor Injuction* (1930), p. 21.

54. As quoted in Urofsky, "State Courts and Protection Legislation," p. 90.

55. Bogni v. Perotti, 224 Mass. 156 (1916).

Chapter 13

1. As quoted in James A. Henretta et al., *America's History* (1987), p. 730.

2. See Alfred H. Kelly, Winfred A. Harbison, and Herman J. Belz, *The American Constitution: Its Origins and Development,* 6th Ed. (1983), p. 523 n.

3. 13 Stat. 370.

4. 22 Stat. 58.

5. 32 Stat. 1213.

6. As quoted in David Burner et al., *An American Portrait: A History of the United States,* 2nd Ed., 2 vols, vol. 2 (1985), p. 534.

7. As quoted in Kelly et al., *American Constitution,* p. 528.

8. Carol S. Gruber, *Mars and Minerva: World War I and the Uses of Higher Learning* (1975), pp. 157–58.

9. Paul L. Murphy, *World War I and the Origin of Civil Liberties in the United States* (1979), pp. 102, 132.

10. Joseph Gusfield, *Symbolic Crusade: Status Politics and the American Temperance Movement* (1963).

11. Paul L. Murphy, *The Constitution in Crisis Times 1918–1969* (1972), p. 217.

12. As quoted in Peter Irons, *Justice at War: The Story of the Japanese American Internment Cases* (1983), p. 19.

13. Ibid.

14. Murphy, *Constitution in Crisis Times,* p. 233.

15. Edward S. Corwin, *Total War and the Constitution* (1947), p. 91.

16. Samuel Walker, *Popular Justice: A History of American Criminal Justice* (1980), pp. 161–83.

17. Ibid., p. 165.

18. Mark H. Haller, "Urban Crime and Criminal Justice: The Chicago Case," in Lawrence M. Friedman and Harry N. Scheiber, eds., *American Law and the Constitutional Order: Historical Perspectives* (1978), p. 305.

19. Walker, *Popular Justice,* p. 181.

20. Haller, "Urban Crime and Criminal Justice," p. 313.

21. Walker, *Popular Justice,* p. 173.

22. Sanford Ungar, *FBI* (1971), ch. 16.

23. Walker, *Popular Justice,* p. 186.

24. Ibid., p. 188.

25. Ibid., p. 193.

26. Jerold S. Auerbach, "Book Review," *Harvard Law Review* 87(1974):1100.

27. Robert Stevens, *Law School: Legal Education in America from the 1850s to the 1980s* (1983), p. 280.

28. James Willard Hurst. *The Growth of American Law: The Law Makers* (1950), p. 280.

29. Stevens, *Law School,* p. 113.

30. As quoted in William H. Harbaugh, *Lawyer's Lawyer: The Life of John W. Davis* (1973), p. 118.

31. Stevens, *Law School,* p. 101.

32. Jerold S. Auerbach, *Unequal Justice: Lawyers and Social Change in Modern America* (1976), pp. 121–22.

33. Ibid., p. 66.

34. Murphy, *World War I and the Origin of Civil Liberties,* p. 246.

35. Auerbach, *Unequal Justice,* p. 139.

36. As quoted in ibid., p. 140.

37. Ibid., p. 198.

38. Ibid, p. 215.

39. Charles H. Martin, *The Angelo Herndon Case and Southern Justice* (1976), p. 12.

40. Murphy, *World War I and the Origin of Civil Liberties,* p. 40.

41. Schenck v. United States, 249 U.S. 47 (1919).

42. Ibid., p. 52.

43. Abrams v. United States, 250 U.S. 616 (1919).

44. Ibid.

45. U.S., *Constitution,* First Amendment.

46. Gitlow v. New York, 268 U.S. 562 (1925).

47. Stromberg v. California, 283 U.S. 359 (1931).

48. Norman L. Rosenberg, *Protecting the Best Men: An Interpretive History of the Law of Libel* (1986), p. 216.

49. William B. Hixson, Jr., "Moorfield Storey and the Struggle for Equality," in Friedman and Scheiber, eds., *American Law and the Constitutional Order,* p. 337.

50. As quoted in Irons, *Justice at War,* p. 366.

51. Ibid.

Chapter 14

1. John W. Johnson, *American Legal Culture, 1908–1940* (1981), p. 59.

2. As quoted in N. E. H. Hull, "The New Jurisconsults: The Intellectual and Social Origins of the American Law Institute," unpublished paper presented at the Annual Meeting of the American Society for Legal History (1985), p. 3.

3. *Proceedings of the American Law Institute,* I (1923), pp. 49–50.

4. Laura Kalman, *Legal Realism at Yale 1927–1960* (1986), p. 14.

5. Wilfred E. Rumble, Jr., *American Legal Realism: Skepticism, Reform, and the Judicial Process* (1968), p. 156.

6. Kalman, *Legal Realism at Yale,* p. 17.

7. G. Edward White, *Patterns of American Legal Thought* (1978), p. 117.

8. As quoted in Grant Gilmore, *The Ages of American Law* (1977), p. 77.

9. As quoted in White, *Patterns of American Legal Thought,* p. 123.

10. As quoted in ibid., p. 128.

11. As quoted in Kalman, *Legal Realism at Yale,* p. 56.

12. Edward A. Purcell, Jr., "American Jurisprudence between the Wars: Legal Realism and the Crisis of Democratic Theory," in Lawrence M. Friedman and Harry N. Scheiber, eds., *American Law and the Constitutional Order: Historical Perspectives* (1978), p. 374.

13. Gerald L. Fetner, *Ordered Liberty: Legal Reform in the Twentieth Century* (1983), p. 40.

14. As quoted in James A. Henretta et al., *America's History* (1987), p. 746.

15. 48 Stat. 195 (1933).

16. Ibid., p. 198.

17. As quoted in Peter H. Irons, *The New Deal Lawyers* (1982), p. 10.

18. Ibid.

19. Donald Richberg, *The Rainbow* (1936), p. 177.

20. Christopher Tomlins, *The State and the Unions: Labor Relations, Law, and the Organized Labor Movement, 1880–1960* (1985), p. 147.

21. Irons, *New Deal Lawyers,* p. 3.

22. Felix Frankfurter and James M. Landis, *The Business of the Supreme Court* (1927), p. 283.

23. Nebbia v. New York, 291 U.S. 556 (1934).

24. Irons, *New Deal Lawyers,* pp. 55–56.

25. Ibid., p. 56.

26. As quoted in ibid., p. 87.

27. 295 U.S. 553 (1935).

28. 297 U.S. 68 (1936).

29. As quoted in Irons, *New Deal Lawyers,* p. 275.

30. *Congressional Record,* vol. 81, pt. 1 (75th Cong., 1st Sess.), pp. 877–78.

31. As quoted in Alpheus T. Mason, *Harland Fiske Stone: Pillar of the Law* (1956), p. 444.

32. 301 U.S. 41–42 (1937).

33. Alfred H. Kelly, Winfred A. Harbison, and Herman J. Belz, *The American Constitution: Its Origins and Development,* 6th Ed. (1983), p. 519.

34. Irons, *New Deal Lawyers,* p. 295.

35. Ibid.

Chapter 15

1. As quoted in James A. Henretta et al., *America's History* (1987), p. 84.

2. Allen J. Matusow, *The Unraveling of America: A History of Liberalism in the 1960s* (1984).

3. Lawrence M. Friedman, *Total Justice* (1985), p. 42.

4. *U.S. News & World Report,* December 4, 1978, p. 50.

5. Marc Galanter, "Reading the Landscape of Disputes: What We Know and Don't Know (and Think We Know) about Our Allegedly Contentious and Litigious Society," *UCLA Law Review* 31(1983):38.

6. A lawyer is defined as any person licensed to practice law. See Barbara A. Curran, *The Lawyer Statistical Report: A Statistical Profile of the U.S. Legal Profession in the 1980s* (1985), p. 9.

7. *Statistical Abstract of the United States,* 10th Ed. (1986), p. 402. The Census classifies a lawyer as any person saying that they are one even if not licensed to practice.

8. Marion S. Goldman, *A Portrait of the Black Attorney in Chicago* (1972), p. 49.

9. Robert Stevens, *Law School: Legal Education in America from the 1850s to the 1980s* (1983), p. 246.

10. 421 U.S. 773 (1975).

11. Jerold S. Auerbach, *Unequal Justice: Lawyers and Social Change in Modern America* (1976).

12. 433 U.S. 350 (1977).

13. Gerald L. Fetner, *Ordered Liberty: Legal Reform in the Twentieth Century* (1983), p. 95.

14. John P. Heinz and Edward O. Laumann, *Chicago Lawyers: The Professions of the Bar* (1982), p. 111.

15. Stevens, *Law School,* p. 207.

16. Ibid., p. 210.

17. Ibid., p. 277.

18. G. Edward White, *Tort Law in America* (1980), p. 140.

19. Laura Kalman, *Legal Realism at Yale 1927–1960* (1986), p. 179.

20. Stevens, *Law School,* p. 266.

21. Ibid., p. 275.

22. G. Edward White, "From Realism to Critical Legal Studies: A Truncated Intellectual History," *Southwestern Law Journal* 40(June 1986):843.

23. Charles A. Reich, "The New Property," *Yale Law Journal* 73(1964):733–87.

24. Seymour I. Toll, *Zoned America* (1969), p. 184.

25. Ibid., p. 186.

26. 272 U.S. 388 (1926).

27. As quoted in Richard F. Babcock, *The Zoning Game: Municipal Practices and Policies* (1966), p. 8.

28. 10 N.J. 182 (1952).

29. Mary Ann Glendon, "The Transformation of American Landlord–Tenant Law," *Boston College Law Review* 23(May 1982):521.

30. Javins v. First National Realty Corp., 428 F. 2d 1075 n. 13. Judge Wright and the court did *not* conclude, however, that leases were to be treated as contracts for all purposes.

31. Edward J. Murphy and Richard E. Speidel, eds., *Studies in Contract Law,* 3rd Ed. (1984), p. 12.

32. Grant Gilmore, *The Death of Contract* (1974), p. 101.

33. 350 F. 2d 445, (D.C. Cir. 1965).

34. Ibid.

35. White, *Tort Law in America,* p. 150.

36. As quoted in Lawrence M. Friedman, *A History of American Law,* 2nd Ed. (1985), p. 684.

37. Ibid.

38. As quoted in White, *Tort Law in America,* p. 168.

39. Ibid., p. 202.

40. *Restatement (Second) of Torts,* sec. 402A(c) (1965).

41. Friedman, *Total Justice,* p. 61.

42. Carl N. Degler, *At Odds: Women and the Family in America from the Revolution to the Present* (1980), p. 454.

43. Lawrence M. Friedman, "Rights of Passage: Divorce Law in Historical Perspective," *Oregon Law Review* 63(1984):666.

44. As quoted in Samuel Walker, *Popular Justice: A History of American Criminal Justice* (1980), p. 128.

45. Ibid., p. 224.

46. Ibid., p. 248.

47. Ibid., p. 237.

48. John W. Johnson, *Insuring against Diseaster: The Nuclear Industry on Trial* (1986), p. viii.

49. Robert L. Rabin, "Federal Regulation in Historical Perspective," *Stanford Law Review* 38(May 1986):1286.

50. Reich, "The New Property," p. 783.

51. Rabin, "Federal Regulation in Historical Perspective," p. 1305.

52. 463 U.S. 29 (1983).

53. Warren Burger, "Isn't There a Better Way," *American Bar Association Journal* 68(1982):275.

54. Friedman, *Total Justice,* p. 43.

Chapter 16

1. As quoted in Paul L. Murphy, *The Constitution in Crisis Times, 1918–1969* (1972), p. 476n.

2. G. Edward White, "From Realism to Critical Legal Studies: A Truncated Intellectual History," *Southwestern Law Journal* 40(June 1986):827.

3. Laura Kalman, *Legal Realism at Yale 1927–1960* (1986), p. 222.

4. Ibid., p. 223.

5. Herbert Wechsler, "Toward Neutral Principles of Constitutional Law," *Harvard Law Review* 73(1959):12.

6. Eugene V. Rostow, "The Democratic Character of Judicial Review," *Harvard Law Review* 66(1952):193.

7. Baker v. Carr, 369 U.S. 186 (1962).

8. Raoul Berger, "Paul Brest's Brief for an Imperial Judiciary," *Maryland Law Review* 40(1981):38.

9. "Speech of Attorney General Edwin Meese, III," July 9, 1985, Washington, D.C.

10. Palko v. Connecticut, 302 U.S. 325 (1937).

11. United States v. Carolene Products Co., 304 U.S. 153 n. 4 (1938).

12. William Chafee, *The Unfinished Journey: America since World War II* (1987), p. 97.

13. As quoted in ibid., p. 105.

14. As quoted in Michal Belknap, *Cold War Political Justice: The Smith Act, the Communist Party, and American Civil Liberties* (1977), p. 137.

15. Dennis v. United States, 339 U.S. 509 (1950).

16. As quoted in Murphy, *Constitution in Crisis Times,* p. 448.

17. United States v. Robel, 389 U.S. 258 (1967).

18. Norman L. Rosenberg, *Protecting the Best Men: An Interpretive History of the Law of Libel* (1986), p. 11.

19. New York Times v. Sullivan, 376 U.S. 256 (1964).

20. Ibid.

21. Ibid.

22. Roth v. United States, 354 U.S. 476 (1957).

23. As quoted in Murphy, *Constitution in Crisis Times,* p. 396.

24. As quoted in Steven Shiffrin, "Obscenity," in Leonard W. Levy and Kenneth L. Karst, eds., *Encyclopedia of the American Constitution* (1987), p. 1336.

25. Miller v. California, 413 U.S. 24 (1973).

26. Ibid.

27. Shiffrin, "Obscenity," p. 1336.

28. Engle v. Vitale, 370 U.S. 421 (1962).

29. As quoted in Murphy, *Constitution in Crisis Times,* p. 392.

30. Olmstead v. United States, 279 U.S. 849 (1925).

31. Griswold v. Connecticut, 381 U.S. 479 (1965). See also Adamson v. California, 322 U.S. 46 (1948).

32. Mapp v. Ohio, 367 U.S. 643 (1961).

33. Brown v. Board of Education, 347 U.S. 493, 495 (1954).

34. Brown v. Board of Education 349 U.S. 301 (1955).

35. As quoted in Chafee, *Unfinished Journey,* p. 153.

36. Ibid., p. 161.

37. Civil Rights Act of 1964, Title II.

38. Chafee, *Unfinished Journey,* p. 334.

39. Hoyt v. Florida, 368 U.S. 62 (1961).

40. Chafee, *Unfinished Journey,* p. 330.

41. Plessy v. Ferguson, 163 U.S. 559 (1896).

42. Fullilove v. Klutznick, 448 U.S. 448 (1980).

Glossary

The law is a technical subject and has its own professional language. I have attempted to keep the use of legal terms and phrases to a minimum, and when I have used them I have tried to explain briefly their meaning. This glossary provides some definitions that could not be readily fitted into the text. It is not intended to be comprehensive. A fuller explanation of the technical words, concepts, and phrases associated with the law can be found in Henry Campbell Black, *Black's Law Dictionary,* 5th Ed. (1979).

Actus reus (Latin, "wrongful deed"). One of the essential elements of a completed crime (the other being ***mens rea***), namely the human conduct which if done with *mens rea* is contrary to law. Commonly, *actus reus* is the commission of some act, e.g., assault, but it may also be an omission, e.g., failing to turn off a car's lights.

Absolute liability. A concept in tort law that establishes liability without regard to fault or negligence. Also known as strict liability in products liability cases.

Admiralty. The law of the sea, historically covering both civilian subjects (e.g., marine insurance, salvage, torts at sea) and military subjects (prize and capture). Juries are not used in admiralty courts.

Amicus curiae (Latin, "friend of the court"). Courts sometimes permit parties not directly involved in the litigation but affected by it to participate in the argument. Typically, such parties have some special expertise that would be useful to the court.

Assumption of risk. The doctrine which holds that plaintiffs cannot collect damages for injuries to which they voluntarily expose themselves.

Bankruptcy. The condition in which persons are placed when they are unable to pay their debts when they become due.

Bill of exchange. A form of commercial paper widely used by merchants in the eighteenth and nineteenth centuries. A orders B to pay a sum of money to C at a fixed future time. The bills circulated as a kind of paper money.

Certiorari (Latin, "to be made more certain"). A discretionary writ that a superior court can choose to issue in order to examine the records of a lower court. Following the Judiciary Act of 1925 it became the principal means by which the Supreme Court of the United States structures its docket.

Clear and present danger test. Doctrine first formulated in *Schenck* v. *U.S.* (1919), providing that governmental restrictions on freedom of speech and press will be upheld if necessary to prevent grave and immediate danger to interests which government may lawfully protect.

Commercial paper. Various forms of legally enforceable orders between private parties, such as promissory notes, checks, or bank accounts, and other kinds of negotiable instruments.

Common law. The system of law developed by judges and based on precedents. In theory, common law grows out of usage and custom. It contrasts with the civil law systems of Europe and Latin America, which are based on codes and derived from Roman law. America, like Great Britain, is a common-law jurisdiction. Common law is also contrasted with statutory (or positive) law, which is made by legislatures.

Comparative negligence. Under this doctrine, negligence is apportioned on a percentage basis among those involved in an accident, and damages are diminished accordingly. It has replaced **contributory negligence** in many states.

Consideration. The inducement (the impelling influence) offered to make a contract.

Contributory negligence. Conduct by a plaintiff that contributes, along with that of the defendant, to an accident. In many states the defense of contributory negligence has been replaced by **comparative negligence.**

Coverture. The condition or state into which a woman passes when she marries. Under coverture, wife and husband are united, but the husband is the dominant legal presence.

Deed. A document used to convey real property from one person to another.

Diversity jurisdiction. Jurisdiction conferred by Article III, section 2 of the Constitution on the federal courts. It covers suits between citizens of two different states, who are said to be in diversity to one another.

Dower. The provision made through law for a widow, out of the husband's lands, for her support and that of her children. If the husband dies intestate (without a will), the widow can claim one third of the estate. Dower has been abolished in a majority of states and materially altered in most others.

Durham Rule. A liberalization of the traditional insanity defense (the so-called right-wrong or McNaghten Rule) developed by Judge David J. Bazelon in *Durham* v. *United States* (1954). Also known as the irresistible impulse test of criminal responsibility. When there is some evidence that the accused suffered from a diseased or defective mental condition at the time of the unlawful act, he or she cannot be held responsible. Most jurisdictions have widely ignored the rule.

Ejectment. The name of an action in common law used to recover the possession of lands and to claim damages for its wrongful holding by another.

Entail. A means of limiting the succession of real property to certain heirs.

Equity. A body of Anglo-American law that developed parallel to the common law. Its purpose is to provide equitable rather than legal solutions to conflicts, and it developed historically as a means of providing discretion in the application of common-law rules. In England a chancellor administers equity in separate courts, but in America, although the title ''chancellor'' is still used, most equity jurisdiction (since the nineteenth century) has been merged with common-law courts, meaning that often the same judges that administer equity also administer common law.

Establishment clause. That provision of the First Amendment to the U.S. Constitution which provides that Congress shall make no law respecting an establishment of religion (or prohibiting the free exercise thereof). Because of this clause the state and federal governments are prohibited from setting up state religions or passing laws which aid religion or force belief in a religion.

Ex parte (Latin, ''on the side of''). A judicial proceeding or order that is undertaken on behalf of one party only, with the opposing party either absent or nonexistent. Under this action, opposing parties have notice or opportunity to be heard.

Federal questions. Cases within the jurisdiction of the federal courts and based upon interpretation of the Constitution, laws, or treaties of the United States.

Fellow servant rule. A common-law doctrine that holds that an employee cannot recover damages against an employer as a result of an action taken by another worker (a "fellow servant"). The doctrine has been largely abrogated by workers' compensation acts and the Federal Employers' Liability Act.

Grand jury. A jury of inquiry charged with receiving and hearing complaints and, if they are satisfied of possible wrongdoing, returning indictments.

Habeas corpus (Latin, "you should have the body"). A group of writs that command someone restraining an individual to produce that person before a judge for the purpose of reviewing the legality of the detention.

Information. An accusation leveled by a prosecutor against a person for some criminal offense, without an indictment, although the information has the effect of an indictment. An indictment is issued by a grand jury. Indictments and informations are the way a criminal proceeding is begun under the common law.

Injunction. A judicial order, originating in equity rather than in common law, that commands an individual to perform an act, or prohibits him or her from performing some act. An injunction acts on persons and not on things, and it is commonly used where there is no adequate remedy in the law.

Judicial review. The power of courts to hold a statute or an act of the executive in violation of a constitution, and therefore to refuse to enforce it. Both state and federal judges exercise judicial review, but state judges cannot declare federal laws unconstitutional.

Loan of credit. A practice by which nineteenth-century state legislatures "loaned" their credit to counties, cities, and towns. Unlike a direct loan, which involved a lender and a borrower, a loan of credit also involved an underwriter, who actually put up the money. The purpose of the loan of credit was to help a corporation raise money for an enterprise that the voters or local legislative authorities deemed desirable.

Mandamus (Latin, "we command"). A writ that commands an officer of government to perform some act required by law. Under common law it was also termed an extraordinary writ.

Mens Rea (Latin, "guilty mind"). A knowledge by a person that an act is wrong; the guilty mind or mental state required for the commission of a particular crime. One of the elements necessary (the other being **actus reus**) to establish criminal liability.

Negotiability. The legal characteristic of an instrument, such as a check or bank note, that makes it possible to transfer it from one party to the next and, in so doing, to provide the second or subsequent party with all or most of the rights that went to the original holder.

Peine forte et dure (French, "severe and hard punishment"). A special form of punishment in old English law (also used in the Salem witch trials) for those persons who refused to plead or put themselves on trial. The individuals were placed under increasingly heavy weights of stone until they relented or died.

Peonage. A condition of servitude compelling persons to perform labor to pay off a debt. It is prohibited by the Thirteenth Amendment, but forms of it appeared in the post-Civil War South.

Petit jury. The ordinary trial jury of a civil or criminal action. It is so called to distinguish it from the **grand jury.**

Prerogative courts. Certain non-common-law English courts, such as the Star Chamber, which were instruments of royal power. The Whiggish opposition to the Crown viewed them as a threat to liberty.

Primogeniture. The right of the eldest son to succeed to the estate of his father. The condition gives primacy to the most senior male heir in a family to the exclusion of younger sons.

Quit rent. A rent paid by the tenant of a freehold, by which he is discharged from any other rent.

Retaliatory eviction. An act taken by a landlord to evict a tenant because he or she entered a complaint or engaged in a tenant's union or some similar behavior with which the landlord does not agree.

Riparian rights. The rights of the owners of lands on the banks of rivers and streams (so-called watercourses), relating to the water, its use, and that of lands contiguous thereto. The doctrine had different implications in arid and humid climates, as its development in the eastern and western United States makes clear.

Seditious libel. A communication written with the intent of inciting the people to change the government by other than legal means, or advocating the overthrow of the government by force and violence.

Separate equitable estate. The individual property of a woman held apart from that of her husband. The doctrine arose as a means of providing women control over property that would have otherwise been lost to the control of her husband through **coverture.**

Substantive due process. A concept closely connected to the idea of vested rights and which grew in significance in American constitutional law after the Civil War. It meant not only that due process required procedural fairness when life, liberty, or property were governmentally regulated, but that there were certain aspects of life, liberty, and property that government could not be permitted to regulate at all. Thus there were certain *substantive* rights (embraced particularly by the words ''liberty'' and ''property'') that were beyond the legitimate reach of governmental power. Under this concept persons (including corporations) could not be deprived of substantive rights by any procedure regardless of how fair.

Ultra vires (Latin, ''beyond the power [of]''). A doctrine of corporate law by which a court determines that some corporate act was taken beyond the authority of the corporation as defined by its charter. Much more important in the nineteenth than in the twentieth centuries.

Vested rights. Rights that have so completely settled in an individual that they are not subject to defeat by an act of another person, and which government is bound to protect. Such rights became a source of conflict in American constitutional history as they clashed with demands for technological progress.

Bibliographical Essay

The bibliographical essay that follows recognizes those scholars in history, law, political science, and criminal justice studies on whose work I have relied heavily. However, this essay is not comprehensive, in that it covers neither all of the literature from which this book is drawn nor all of the literature bearing on particular subjects. Readers seeking a broad bibliography can turn to several guides. The most extensive is Kermit L. Hall (compiler), *A Comprehensive Bibliography of American Constitutional and Legal History*, 5 volumes (1984). Also useful are the bibliographies that accompany the major historical texts in public and private law. The former is covered in Alfred H. Kelly, Winfred A. Harbison, and Herman J. Belz, *The American Constitution: Its Origins and Development*, 6th Ed. (1983) and Melvin I. Urofsky, *A March of Liberty: A Constitutional History of the United States* (1988). The latter is the subject of Lawrence M. Friedman, *A History of American Law*, 2nd Ed. (1985).

The American Constitution and *A History of American Law* have significance much beyond their fine bibliographies. Both have shaped the course of teaching and writing about the history of public and private law, and both (less Friedman than Belz, et al.) have perpetuated the traditional division between public and private law themes. In the past decade or so, however, scholars working on the history of American legal culture have sought to merge the two fields. The reasons behind this development are complex, but in the simplest terms they reflect the tremendous impact of social history on the writing of all American history. The main lines of development are addressed in Kermit L. Hall, "The Magic Mirror: American Constitutional and Legal History," *International Journal of Social Education* 1 (1987). The most cogent argument for the reciprocal and reinforcing nature of constitutional and legal history can be found in Harry N. Scheiber, "American Constitutional History and the New Legal History: Complementary Themes in Two Modes," *The Journal of American History* 68 (1981). On the enduring ties between constitutional and social history, see James G. Randall, "The Interrelation of Social and Constitutional History," *The American Historical Review* 35 (1929). A similar call for a balancing of the traditional case law approach with an external history of constitutional development has been made by Paul L. Murphy in "Time to Reclaim: The Current Challenge of American Constitutional History," *The American Historical Review* 69 (1963). William E. Nelson, in an equally cogent treatment, concludes that efforts at integration are likely to fail and questions whether legal history—under ideological pressure from the right and left—can ever mature into a distinct field: "Standards of Criticism," in *The Literature of American Legal History,* edited by Nelson and John P. Reid (1985). Most of this volume is devoted to review essays that examine major developments in writing about legal history since the early 1960s. This volume is an ideal starting point for anyone interested in understanding the torrent of writing in legal history during the past two decades. An even more extensive collection, discussing almost every major area of the history of American legal culture, can be found in Kermit L. Hall, ed., *United States Constitutional and Legal History: Major Historical Essays,* 20 volumes (1987). The first volume, *Main Themes in United States Constitutional and Legal History,* covers all of the major historiographical and interpretive views about the history of American legal culture, including the radical attack of the critical legal studies (CLS) movement on American legal institutions and practices. Wythe Holt, ed., *Essays in Nineteenth-Century American Legal History* (1976), is also useful, as is Lawrence M. Friedman and Harry N. Scheiber, eds., *American Law and the Constitutional Order: Historical Perspectives* (1978). Another particularly good collection of essays dealing with American legal history was published as a symposium issue in *William & Mary Law Review* 23 (1982). Wythe Holt's essay on the contributions of Morton J. Horwitz and his influence on CLS is particularly instructive.

During the bicentennial of the federal Constitution, several journals produced special issues devoted to the document's history. See, for example, "The Constitution in American Life: A Special Issue," *Journal of American History* 74 (1987) and "The Constitution of the United States," *The William and Mary Quarterly* 44 (1987). Most bicentennial efforts, including those listed above, concentrated on the federal document, much to the neglect of state constitutions, constitution making, and constitutionalism. The best introduction to state developments can be found in a symposium issue, "State Constitutional Design in the Federal System," *Publius: The Journal of Federalism* 12 (1982).

Just as the scholarly literature has grown, so too has the availability of teaching materials. The texts of Belz et al. and Friedman have educated the modern generation of Americans about its legal heritage. Both books offer an external rather than a technical view (Friedman more than Belz, et al.) of American legal development, and Friedman has pioneered the concept of legal culture, a theme he addresses in both *American Law* (1984) and in *Total Justice* (1985) and one I have drawn on heavily. Friedman's *A History of American Law* was a pathbreaking study that helped to set the agenda for further study of legal history. As Friedman's impressive list of publications makes clear, he, along with James Willard Hurst and Harry N. Scheiber, are the dominant figures in the history of American legal culture. Another important scholar is Melvin I. Urofsky, whose *The March of Liberty: A Constitutional History of the United States* (1988) offers a liberal analysis of major public-law themes with some passing attention to the development of private law and legal institutions. Also, Borzoi Books/Knopf has brought out a series of short paperbacks, which together cover the main periods of American legal development by combining brief interpretive essays of a period with representative documents. See Stephen Botein, *Early American Law and Society* (1983); George Dargo, *Law in the New Republic: Private Law and the Public Estate* (1983); Jamil S. Zainaldin, *Law in Antebellum Society: Legal Change and Economic Expansion* (1983); Jonathan Lurie, *Law and the Nation, 1865–1912* (1983); and Gerald L. Fetner, *Ordered Liberty: Legal Reform in the Twentieth Century* (1983). The casebook method has also found its way into the teaching of American legal culture. *Law and American History: Cases and Materials* (1980), edited by Stephen B. Presser and Jamil S. Zainaldin, treats both private and public law developments, although it does so with disappointingly little attention to such matters as the sociolegal history of women, free blacks, children, and criminals. Other works that broadly conceptualize the nation's legal history are Grant Gilmore, *The Ages of American Law* (1977), which needlessly dismisses the first three hundred years of the nation's history as irrelevant to the study of its legal past, and Samuel Walker, *Popular Justice: A History of American Criminal Justice* (1980), which is a valuable survey of the evolution of the American criminal justice system. Also useful is Herbert A. Johnson, *History of Criminal Justice* (1988). John T. Noonan, Jr., *Persons and Masks of the Law: Cardozo, Holmes, Jefferson, and Wythe as Makers of the Masks* (1976), while far from a comprehensive history of American legal culture, does offer an essentially legal realist vision cloaked in Platonic moral imperatives, arguing that too often American lawmakers have chosen to cling to neutral rules—the "masks of the law"—rather than forging a "person-centered" legal culture. G. Edward White, *The American Judicial Tradition: Profiles of Leading American Judges* (1976), surveys the individual performances of notable judges to show how economic, social, political, and especially intellectual trends have shaped great judicial decisions and to reveal the ways in which the awesome mantle of judicial power often transformed political partisans into judicial statesmen and middle-of-the-road politicians into ideologues.

No other scholar has had greater influence on the field of legal history than James Willard Hurst. His *The Growth of American Law: The Law Makers* (1950) marked the beginning of the contemporary surge in writing about legal history. Not only was this book the most accessible of Hurst's works, but it also demonstrated the ways in which private and public law themes could be integrated. Hurst also argued persuasively that legal history encompassed what he called the "agencies of law": constitutional conventions, legislatures, administrative bodies, and the bar. Hurst certainly took the work of judges and courts seriously, but he made the basic point, often forgotten by scholars who worship his name but show signs of not having read his work, that the variety and diversity of lawmaking bodies has been an important feature of the nation's legal history. Hurst's other work was significant for the stress that it placed on the interaction of legal and economic development. In works such as *Law and the Conditions of Freedom in the Nineteenth-Century United States* (1956), *Law and Economic Growth: The Legal History of the Lumber Industry in Wisconsin, 1836–1915* (1964), and *Law and Markets in United States History: Different Modes of Bargaining among Interests* (1982), Hurst portrayed an essentially pluralist-consensus view of the relationship of law and economic growth, with the law distributing broadly the fruits of economic development. Hurst pursued this theme of consensus in another important book, *Law and Social Order in the United States* (1977).

Hurst's conclusions have come under increasing attack from scholars who believe that the evidence reveals a legal past in which the law encouraged a maldistribution of wealth: the rich got richer. Several CLS historians have taken direct aim at Hurst's arguments. Morton J. Horwitz, Mark V. Tushnet, and Robert Gordon, for example, have authored important criticisms of Hurst's findings (but not about his scholarship). Their attack, which centers on Hurst's assessment of the distributive consequences of American law, is summarized and analyzed in Kermit L. Hall, "The Magic Mirror: American Constitutional and Legal History," *International Journal of Social Education* 1 (1987). An cogent critique of Hurst's work and of his contributions to the field, is presented in Harry N. Scheiber, "At the Borderland of Law and Economic History: The Contributions of James Willard Hurst," *The American Historical Review* 75 (1970) and Scheiber, "Constitutional History and the New Legal History."

Hurst also stressed the sectional and regional differences in American legal culture, and historians have recently moved beyond the restricted confines of New England and the Middle Atlantic states. While legal historians accept that a degree of diversity has characterized legal developments in the states and regions, they are hardly of one mind about the extent of these differences. For a discussion of the issue of intersectional variety in legal culture, see, for example, the essays in David J. Bodenhamer and James W. Ely, Jr., eds., *Ambivalent Legacy: A Legal History of the South* (1984); Kermit L. Hall and James W. Ely, Jr., *An Uncertain Tradition: Constitutionalism and the History of the South* (1988); and Kermit L. Hall, "The 'Magic Mirror' and The Promise of Western Legal History," *The Western Historical Quarterly* 18 (1987). On the persistent provincialism behind much American law, whether positive or common law, see Harry N. Scheiber, "Xenophobia and Parochialism in the Early History of American Legal Process: From the Jacksonian Revolution to the Sagebrush Rebellion," *William*

& *Mary Law Review* 23 (1982). An excellent collection of essays on the Louisiana civil law system is Edward F. Haas, ed., *Louisiana's Legal Heritage* (1983).

The Colonial Era

The history of colonial America rests on a rich historiographical tradition, but historians of American legal culture have often treated it as merely a prelude to the *national* history of American law. Stanley N. Katz, "The Problem of Colonial Legal History," in *Colonial British America. Essays in the New History of the Early Modern Era*, edited by Jack P. Greene and J. R. Pole (1984), vigorously challenges this practice and urges legal historians to take the colonial era seriously. For an excellent example of what can be done, see David T. Konig, *Law and Society in Puritan Massachusetts, Essex County, 1629–1692* (1979). Although the disregard of colonial legal history was never as great as Katz argued, it has only recently begun to receive its scholarly due. George L. Haskins and Julius Goebel, Jr., were pioneers in the field. Haskins's *Law and Authority in Early Massachusetts: A Study in Tradition and Design* (1960) connected social, political, and legal developments and, as such, offered a model of sorts for what came to be called the "new" legal history, which sought an external perspective on the internal developments of the law. Goebel pursued a similar tact in "King's Law and Local Custom in Seventeenth-Century New England," *Columbia Law Review* 31 (1931). Along with T. Raymond Naughton, Goebel also opened up the study of the colonial criminal justice system, and *Law Enforcement in Colonial New York: A Study in Criminal Procedure, 1664–1776* (1970) has been particularly influential. There is no general history of colonial legal development, although Botein's *Early American Law and Society*, on which I have drawn heavily, offers a fine survey full of imaginative insights. Also useful is David H. Flaherty, ed., *Essays in the History of Early American Law* (1969), although subsequent scholarship in the fast-developing field has dated some of the essays. One example of the way in which new writing has reshaped understanding of basic themes, such as the reception of the common law, is David Grayson Allen, *In English Ways: The Movement of Societies and the Transferral of English Local Law and Custom to Massachusetts Bay in the Seventeenth Century* (1981). The actual work of the county courts, which were the backbone of the legal system in many of the colonies, is ably treated in Hendrick Hartog, "The Public Law of a County Court: Judicial Government in Eighteenth-Century Massachusetts," *The American Journal of Legal History* 20 (1976). Richard B. Morris, *Studies in the History of American Law, with Special Reference to the Seventeenth and Eighteenth Centuries*, 2nd Ed. (1959), remains valuable, although his judgment about the place of colonial women before the law has come under withering attack. Indeed, writing about the legal history of colonial women has attracted considerable attention, especially as it relates to property rights and inheritance. On these matters, see, for example, Marylynn Salmon, *Women and the Law of Property in Early America* (1986), and Linda Grant De Pauw, "Women and the Law: The Colonial Period," *Human Rights* 6 (1977). On the legal development of inheritance (for both women and men), see Carole Shammas, Marylynn Salmon, and Michel Dahlin, *Inheritance in America from Colonial Times to the Present* (1987).

Other aspects of colonial law and society have also received treatment. The literature on the law of slavery is quite dense, but William W. Wiecek, "The Statutory Law of Slavery and Race in the Thirteen Mainland Colonies of British America," *The William and Mary Quarterly* 34 (1977), is particularly valuable. The collision between white settlers and native Americans is analyzed in Yasuhide Kawashima, *Puritan Justice and the Indian: White Man's Law in Massachusetts, 1630–1763* (1986).

Colonial criminals, the social bases of crime, and dispute resolution in general have received attention, although much more work, especially on the southern colonies, remains to be done.

Particularly valuable are Bradley Chapin, *Criminal Justice in Colonial America, 1606–1660* (1983); Douglas Greenberg, *Crime and Law Enforcement in the Colony of New York 1691–1776* (1976); and Joseph H. Smith, ed., *Colonial Justice in Western Massachusetts (1639–1702), The Pynchon Court Record, an Original Judges' Diary of the Administration of Justice in the Springfield Courts of Massachusetts Bay Colony* (1961), the last of which contains an informative introduction. Also valuable, on the civil side, is William E. Nelson, *Dispute and Conflict Resolution in Plymouth County, Massachusetts, 1725–1825* (1981). Nelson's *The Americanization of the Common Law: The Impact of Legal Change on Massachusetts Society, 1760–1830* (1975), while covering the era of the Revolution and the early nation, nonetheless offers valuable insights into the operation of late colonial law and society. Bruce Mann's *Neighbors and Strangers: Law and Community in Early Connecticut* (1987) is particularly good at showing the way in which once-neighborly modes of dispute settlement yielded, by the American Revolution, to a legal system that treated neighbors and strangers alike.

The development of substantive private law and the legal profession in the colonial era both require much more attention than historians have given them. Paton Yoder, "Tavern Regulation in Virginia: Rationale and Reality," *The Virginia Magazine* 87 (1979), suggests what can be done to link the former with economic developments. John M. Murrin, "The Legal Transformation: The Bench and Bar of Eighteenth-Century Massachusetts," in *Colonial America: Essays in Politics and Social Development*, edited by Stanley N. Katz and John Murrin (1983), provides considerable insight into the evolution of colonial legal institutions and lawyers.

The Revolution, the Constitution, and Law in the New Nation

The literature on the American Revolution and the Constitution is enormous, although little of it assesses the ways in which the Revolution transformed American legal culture. Hendrick Hartog, ed., *Law in the American Revolution and the Revolution in the Law* (1981), offers a good starting point. So, too, does the work of John Phillip Reid, who has written extensively on the legal background of the Revolution and who has integrated these concerns into a general history of early American constitutional development. See, for example, Reid's *In Defiance of the Law: The Standing Army Controversy, the Two Constitutions, and the Coming of the American Revolution* (1981), and *Constitutional History of the American Revolution: The Authority of Rights* (1986). In this book, I have given substantial emphasis to the Writs of Assistance Cases as examples of the way in which legal quarrels were escalated into constitutional conflicts over basic rights. M. H. Smith, *The Writs of Assistance Case* (1978), is the authoritative study. Equally valuable is Hiller B. Zobel, *The Boston Massacre* (1970). On the emergence of constitutional values before the Constitution, see George Dargo, *Roots of the Republic: A New Perspective on Early American Constitutionalism* (1974).

The rise of revolutionary ardor, the emergence of republican constitutional theory, and the relationship of both to the rule of law are examined in several important works. Gordon Wood's *The Creation of the American Republic, 1776–1787* (1969) is seminal, but it should also be read along with Reid's works cited above and Forrest McDonald's brilliant *Novus Ordo Seclorum: The Intellectual Origins of the Constitution* (1985). The role of the states in the development of constitutional norms, and the importance of the states as laboratories in constitution making, are explored in Willi Paul Adams, *The First American Constitutions: Republican Ideology and the Making of the State Constitutions in the Revolutionary Era* (1980). The problem of the place of the states in the new federal system is the subject of Peter S. Onuf, *The Origins of the Federal Republic: Jurisdictional Controversies in the United States, 1775–1787* (1983), a book that delivers far more than its title promises. Perhaps the most important essay about the origins of American federalism, a concept that figured prominently in the history of the nation's legal culture, is Harry N. Scheiber, "Federalism and the Constitution: The Original Understanding," in *American Law and the Constitutional Order: Historical Perspectives,* edited by Friedman and Scheiber (1978). The argument that slavery was crucial to the formation of the Constitution is ably made by Paul Finkelman, "Slavery and the Constitutional Convention: Making A Covenant with Death," in *Beyond Confederation: Origins of the Constitution and American National Identity,* edited by Richard Beeman, Stephen Botein, and Edward C. Carter, II (1987). The emergence of American citizenship in the Revolution and the subsequent impact of the Civil War amendments on it is ably analyzed in James H. Kettner, *The Development of American Citizenship, 1608–1870* (1978).

The emergence of a distinctive legal culture in the new nation is examined in several works. On the practice of judicial review, see Kermit L. Hall, *Judicial Review in American History* (1985), and, for its political implications in early state and national politics, see Richard E. Ellis, *The Jeffersonian Crisis: Courts and Politics in the Young Republic* (1971). The beginnings of the federal judicial system are analyzed in Julius Goebel, Jr., *Antecedents and Beginnings to 1801* in *The Oliver Wendell Holmes Devise History of the Supreme Court,* vol. 1 (1971), and, for the lower federal courts, Mary K. B. Tachau, *Federal Courts in the Early Republic: Kentucky, 1789–1816* (1978). The use of impeachment as a means of separating law from politics, a concern of many public figures in the new nation, is explored by Peter C. Hoffer and N. E. H. Hull, *Impeachment in America, 1635–1805* (1984). Leonard W. Levy, *Thomas Jefferson and Civil Liberties: The Darker Side* (1963), asserts that the Federalists were not the only partisans in the new nation willing to merge their political ambitions with legal authority.

Much of the early debate about the breadth of the national government's legal authority centered on the question of whether there was a federal common law of crimes. Dwight F. Henderson, *Congress, Courts, and Criminals: The Development of Federal Criminal Law, 1801–1829* (1985) not only assesses this issue but shows as well the limited instruments of early federal law enforcement. Stephen B. Presser, "A Tale of Two Judges: Richard Peters, Samuel Chase, and the Broken Promise of Federalist Jurisprudence," *Northwestern University Law Review* 73 (1978), is also a good source on these matters, as is George Dargo, *Law in the New Republic: Private Law and the Public Estate* (1983).

The development of the bar and of the culture of the nation's first lawyers is explored in several works. Particularly valuable is Maxwell Bloomfield, *American Lawyers in a Changing Society, 1776–1876* (1976). Also useful are the collections of edited legal papers of such notable figures as Daniel Webster, Alexander Hamilton, Andrew Jackson, and John Marshall. See, for example, *The Law Practice of Alexander Hamilton: Documents and Commentary,* 5 volumes (1964–1980). R. Kent Newmyer, *Supreme Court Justice Joseph Story: Statesman of the Old Republic* (1985), masterfully reveals the value of biography for legal history.

The Nineteenth Century

By far the richest writing in the history of American legal culture has dealt with the nineteenth century, stressing the interaction of law, politics, economics, and social change. Recently, much of the best work has concentrated on particular aspects of the law of personal status and domestic relations (especially slavery, the family, women, and children), although much remains to be done. Historians tend to view the Civil War as a major breaking point, and this approach makes some sense given the enormous implications of the war for public law. Yet considerable thematic and interpretive unity bind the eras before and after the Civil War. Harold M. Hyman and William M. Wiecek, *Equal Justice under Law: Constitutional Development 1835–1875* (1982), provides, despite its subtitle, the best introduction to both public and private law developments during most of the century.

Law and the Economy

Historians have devoted considerable attention to the distributive economic consequences of American law. The general issues of law and economic development are ably presented in Zainaldin, *Law in Antebellum Society* (1983), which draws heavily on the work of Hurst, whose books and essays provide the starting point for any assessment. Hurst made the important point that legislators as well as judges played vital roles in structuring market relations and allocating scarce resources. Not all scholars, however, have embraced Hurst's description of the broadly distributional consequences of lawmaking. For example, Morton J. Horwitz, in *The Transformation of American Law, 1780–1860* (1977), brilliantly argued the position that judges crafted a body of common law that benefited a relatively few well-heeled entrepreneurs at the expense of workers and farmers. Horwitz's work is one of the best, and most controversial, examinations of the development of nineteenth-century substantive law, notably torts, contracts, and real property. During the course of the century, Horwitz argues, judges became increasingly formal in their opinion writing as they consolidated the gains won by the capitalist class in alliance with the rising legal profession. Historians agree that antebellum judges grew increasingly attentive to policy making, but, as the reaction to Horwitz's book makes clear, they disagree sharply about the breadth and purposes of such policy making, let alone its distributive economic consequences. On these matters, see A. W. Brian Simpson, "The Horwitz Thesis and the History of Contracts," *The University of Chicago Law Review* 48 (1979); and Gary T. Schwartz, "Tort Law and the Economy in Nineteenth-Century America: A Reinterpretation," *The Yale Law Journal* 90 (1981).

Perhaps the most original challenge to the Horwitz thesis comes from John P. Reid, an expert in the history of the legal culture of the American West. The notion that an underlying behavioralism of law guided nineteenth-century Americans in their economic relations is imaginatively argued by Reid in *Law for the Elephant: Property and Social Behavior on the Overland Trail* (1980). Other studies of western legal history have raised still more questions about the Horwitz thesis, which drew most of its examples from New England and the Middle Atlantic states. Gordon Bakken, for example, paints a complex picture of public and private law developments in the Rocky Mountain West that tends to support many features of the Hurst thesis. See, for example, *The Development of Law on the Rocky Mountain Frontier: Civil Law and Society, 1850–1912* (1983), and Bakken, *Rocky Mountain Constitution Making, 1850–1912* (1987). On developments in western water law that run counter to the stark outlines of the Horwitz thesis, see Donald J. Pisani, "Enterprise and Equity: A Critique of Western Water Law in the Nineteenth Century," *The Western Historical Quarterly* 18 (1987). Pisani makes the important point, echoed in the work of Scheiber and others, that courts often took a broader view of economic development than state legislatures, which were much more susceptible to political and economic pressures. The problem of western legal history, of course, is one of assessing properly the relationship between economic, ecological, and legal change. Indicative of what can be done is Arthur F. McEvoy, *The Fisherman's Problem: Ecology and Law in the California Fisheries 1850–1980* (1986).

The Horwitz thesis has encountered difficulties in other areas. Horwitz refused to take public-law developments seriously, and he badly neglected statutory developments. As Kent Newmyer shows in his splendid biography of Joseph Story, *Supreme Court Justice Joseph Story: Statesman of the Old Republic* (1985), private and public law themes in this important nineteenth-century jurist responded to the republican values of the Revolution rather than to any crass materialism. Moreover, Harry N. Scheiber argues that judicial policy making was also compatible with the idea that the public had certain rights that judges were bound to uphold through the law. The influence of this so-called public-interest or public-purpose doctrine is treated in Scheiber, "The Road to MUNN: Eminent Domain and the Concept of Public Purpose in the State Courts," in *Law in American History,* edited by Donald Fleming and Bernard Bailyn

(1971). Scheiber has elaborated other parts of this important argument in several articles, including "Property Rights and Public Purpose in American Law," *Proceedings of the International Economic History Association, 7th Congress* 1 (1978). Tony A. Freyer has worked on many of the same themes, and his "Negotiable Instruments and the Federal Courts in Antebellum American Business," *Business History Review* 50 (1976) challenges parts of the Horwitz thesis. Moreover, Freyer has raised significant questions about the applicability of the Horwitz thesis to the nineteenth-century South as a whole. See "Law and the Antebellum Southern Economy: An Interpretation," in *Ambivalent Legacy*, edited by Bodenhamer and Ely (1984).

Important aspects of American economic growth occurred beyond the immediate reach of the courts. Legislators, for example, engaged in various schemes of economic development, responding as they did to the variety of political pressures that played on them. A particularly good study of the interaction of government and the economy during the period is Harry N. Scheiber, *Ohio Canal Era: A Case Study of Government and the Economy, 1820–1861* (1969), which fits legislative activity to the concept of distributive economic justice. These issues of state intervention in support of internal improvements often sparked heated constitutional debate in the states. The broad outlines of these developments are sketched in Morton Keller, "The Politics of State Constitutional Revision, 1820–1930," in *The Constitutional Convention as an Amending Device*, edited by Kermit L. Hall, Harold M. Hyman, and Leon V. Sigal (1981).

Legislative authority shaped other areas of economic activity. On corporation law, see Ronald E. Seavoy, *The Origins of the American Business Corporation, 1784–1855* (1985); on debtor–creditor relations, see Peter J. Coleman, *Debtors and Creditors in America: Insolvency, Imprisonment for Debt, and Bankruptcy, 1607–1900* (1974); and on bankruptcy Charles Warren, *Bankruptcy in United States History* (1935).

The relationship among technological, economic, and legal changes has received only cursory attention, but it deserves much more. For good examples of what can and should be done, see Stanley I. Kutler, *Privilege and Creative Destruction: The Charles River Bridge Case* (1971); John G. Burke, "Bursting Boilers and Federal Power," *Technology and Culture* 71 (1966); and Elizabeth B. Monroe, "Spanning the Commerce Clause," *The American Journal of Legal History* 32 (1988).

All of this vigorous involvement by the state (whether through judges, through legislators, or later in the century, through regulators) calls into question the traditional notion of laissez-faire. The responsiveness of lawmakers to constituent economic interests, the rise of protective legislation for women and children in the industrial work place, and the emergence of economic regulation in the name of the public interest are skillfully analyzed in William E. Nelson, *The Roots of American Bureaucracy 1830–1900* (1982). Nelson's book is an excellent example of the connections between themes of legal, intellectual, and social development before and after the Civil War. Nelson stresses the way in which the social scientific revolution, the quest for legal science, and the moral energies of reform combined during the Industrial Revolution to produce new regulatory schemes that limited traditional distributive politics.

A similar reevaluation of the relationship of the late-nineteenth-century judiciary to corporate interests is also under way. Michael Les Benedict, "Laissez-Faire and Liberty: A Re-Evaluation of the Meaning and Origins of Laissez-Faire Constitutionalism," *Law and History Review* 3 (1985), stresses that conservative law scholars and judges during the era denounced protective legislation in part because it offended their social and political sensibilities, but Benedict also shows that they had a sincere interest in liberty as a matter of constitutional right. Melvin Urofsky, "State Courts and Protective Legislation during the Progressive Era: A Reevaluation," *The Journal of American History* 72 (1985), argues that both state and federal appellate court judges sometimes delayed the acceptance of protective legislation, but that they ultimately blocked very little of it.

The relationship of industrialization to legal change (of the relative places of capital, labor, and the legal profession) is an important yet unresolved issue in the literature of American legal history. Morton Keller, *Affairs of State: Public Life in Late Nineteenth Century America* (1977), is particularly good at connecting constitutional, legal, and political change. Keller makes an important case for the promotional role played by legislators at the state and federal level during these years, and he gives serious attention to tax policy. Keller also shows the ways in which the regulatory state emerged to deal with the complex of problems created by industrialization. Harry N. Scheiber, in "Property Law, Expropriation, and Resource Allocation by Government, 1789–1910," in *American Law and the Constitutional Order,* edited by Friedman and Scheiber (1978), also stresses the interventional and developmental role of government. Other scholars, however, believe that efforts to control the consequences of industrialization through regulation proved fitful and ineffective. Stephen Skowronek, *Building A New American State: The Expansion of National Administrative Capacities, 1877–1920* (1982), deemphasizes the importance of national administrative bodies, arguing that the traditional politics of patronage and distribution of economic goods severely limited national regulatory initiatives. Skowronek, unlike Keller, fails to give sufficient attention to developments in the states, where regulation made its most important strides. Both Skowronek and Keller can be usefully complemented by reading Thomas K. McGraw, *Prophets of Regulation: Charles Francis Adams, Louis D. Brandeis, James M. Landis, and Alfred E. Kahn* (1984).

Other aspects of business activity have received serious consideration. Charles W. McCurdy, "The *Knight* Sugar Decision of 1895 and the Modernization of American Corporation Law, 1869–1903," *Business History Review* 53 (1979), argues that corporation law became increasingly national in scope as federal judges resisted the continuing efforts by the states to carve out special preserves for local businesses. McCurdy has also shown, in "American Law and the Marketing Structure of the Large Corporation," *The Journal of Economic History* 38 (September 1978), how technological advances in the late nineteenth and early twentieth centuries reformulated traditional business relationships and corporate structures. The tension between localism and nationalism is also assessed by Tony A. Freyer, *Forums of Order: The Federal Courts and Business in American History* (1979).

Race and the Law of Personal Status

Some of the best writing in the history of nineteenth-century legal culture has involved race relations. Thomas Jefferson's *Notes on the State of Virginia,* edited by William Peden (1955), remains a valuable source. *Persons and Masks of the Law* (1976), by John T. Noonan, Jr., assesses the moral conflicts generated by a commitment to the rule of law in the name of racially based slavery. A similar tack was taken by Robert M. Cover, *Justice Accused: Antislavery and the Judicial Process* (1975). Cover emphasized that the peculiar institution was permitted to continue because the best judicial minds of the nineteenth century simply refused to acknowledge in action that it was a moral evil. A good general study of slavery with close attention to its "legal" character is Kenneth M. Stampp, *The Peculiar Institution: Slavery in the Ante-bellum South* (1956). It can be usefully supplemented by Mark V. Tushnet, *The American Law of Slavery* (1981). Tushnet's Marxist interpretation of the legal framework of slavery, while intriguing, is also insensitive to the historian's most important concern: change over time.

The study of the American law of slavery has become increasingly rich, both in its treatment of slaves and fugitives. Some of the most provocative work has been undertaken by Thomas D. Morris, who has published a series of articles that extend our understanding of slave law into matters of tort, contract, and credit. See, for example, " 'As If the Injury Was Effected by the Natural Elements of Air, or Fire,': Slave Wrongs and the Liability of Masters," *Law and Society Review* 16 (1981–1982). Paul Finkelman, Judith Schaffer, and Andrew Fede have also done much to expose the ways in which the business law of slavery became a distinctive feature of the

South's legal culture. Their efforts are contained in a special issue of *The American Journal of Legal History* 31 (1987). Fugitive slaves have also received increasing attention, so much so that the historian John Reid has concluded that one of the few areas of American legal history where we have a comprehensive body of understanding has to do with fugitive slavery. See, in particular, his essay, "The Lessons of Lumpkin," *The William & Mary Law Review* 23 (1982). Paul Finkelman has contributed significantly to this important new body of scholarship, and his *An Imperfect Union: Slavery, Federalism, and Comity* (1981) is especially valuable, although his counterfactual arguments remain controversial. The great work on the law of fugitive slavery and its relationship to the politically destructive tensions that divided North and South is Don E. Fehrenbacher, *The Dred Scott Case in American Law and Politics* (1978). Fehrenbacher blends themes of public and private law while displaying great sensitivity to the personal and political dynamics on the Supreme Court.

The antislavery and proslavery positions, both of which figured in the legal definition of slavery, and hence, the personal status of slaves, have been the subject of intense scrutiny. The varied constitutional assumptions and political goals underlying the efforts of the abolitionists have been cogently dissected by William M. Wiecek, *The Sources of Antislavery Constitutionalism in America, 1760–1848* (1977). Wiecek has also shown that the American law of slavery and the legal debate about abolitionism were different from their English counterparts. See Wiecek, "Slavery and Abolition before the United States Supreme Court, 1820–1860," *The Journal of American History* 65 (1978). The entire debate about the legal character of slavery (was it harsh? mild? in between?) is covered in A. E. Keir Nash, "Reason of Slavery: Understanding the Judicial Role in the Peculiar Institution," *Vanderbilt Law Review* 32 (1979). A particularly valuable case study of the abolitionists' response to the law and slavery is Howard Jones, *Mutiny on the Amistad: The Saga of a Slave Revolt and Its Impact on American Abolition, Law, and Diplomacy* (1987).

Less attention has been devoted to the legal status of the free black and other racial minorities, notably native Americans and Chinese. Leon Litwack's *North of Slavery: The Negro in the Free States, 1790–1860* (1961) remains an invaluable source for legal historians. Hyman and Wiecek, *Equal Justice under Law*, contains a useful discussion of the status of native Americans, free blacks, and the Chinese, and it provides an especially good discussion of the way in which changes wrought by the Fourteenth Amendment had potentially enormous consequences (most of which were not realized until the twentieth century) for all three groups. Donald G. Nieman's *To Set the Law in Motion: The Freedmen's Bureau and the Legal Rights of Blacks, 1865–1868* (1976) is valuable for the treatment accorded newly freed blacks in the South. Robert J. Kaczorowski, *The Politics of Judicial Interpretation: The Federal Courts, Department of Justice and Civil Rights 1866–1876* (1985), explains the important role of the federal bench and the Department of Justice in the collapse of black rights in the postbellum South. C. Van Woodward's classic, *The Strange Career of Jim Crow,* 2nd Rev. Ed. (1966), remains useful for its analysis of the origins of legal segregation in the South, but it should be supplemented by J. Morgan Kousser, *The Shaping of Southern Politics: Suffrage Restriction and the Establishment of the One Party South* (1974). Also valuable as a case study is Charles Lofgren, *The Plessy Case: A Legal-Historical Interpretation* (1987). William Cohen, "Negro Involuntary Servitude in the South, 1865–1940: A Preliminary Analysis," *The Journal of Southern History* 42 (1976), provides an excellent account of the legal measures that kept most Southern freedmen in a status of quasi peonage.

The legal history of the Chinese in America is only now being written, but John Wunder has made an important start. See, for example, "The Chinese and the Courts in the Pacific Northwest: Justice Denied," *Pacific Historical Review* 52 (1983); and "Chinese in Trouble: Criminal Law and Race on the Trans-Mississippi West Frontier," *The Western Historical Quarterly* 17 (1986).

Domestic Relations: The Family, Children, and Women

One of the fasting growing areas of writing in American legal (and social) history involves gender and family issues. The discovery of the family as an integral part of American social history surfaced in the several town and community studies of the 1960s and 1970s. See, for example, John Demos, *A Little Commonwealth: Family Life in Plymouth Colony* (1970). Since then, study of the family has taken an even more explicitly legal turn. Particularly valuable is Michael Grossberg, *Governing the Hearth: Law and the Family in Nineteenth-Century America* (1985), which traces the evolving legal status of parents and children within the family and on which I have relied heavily. According to Grossberg, children had by 1900 achieved a new legal status in which they enjoyed the right not to be abused, mistreated, neglected, or exploited. Grossberg also insists that patriarchal control of the family declined, to be replaced by greater and greater judicial administration of family affairs. Viviana A. Zelizer, *Pricing the Priceless Child: The Changing Social Value of Children* (1985), argues that one of the consequences of the Industrial Revolution was to increase the emotional value of the child to the family at the same time that its economic worth declined.

The evolving legal status of women has also come in for increased attention. Carl Degler's *At Odds: Women and the Family in America from the Revolution to the Present* (1980) is especially useful in fitting women into a general social history context, although many scholars of women's history reject his argument that the position of women has gradually improved. Robert L. Griswold's *Family and Divorce in California, 1850–1890: Victorian Illusions and Everyday Realities* (1982) is not just good on legal developments; it also does away with many of the traditional assumptions about why marriages ended in divorce. Nelson M. Blake, *The Road to Reno: A History of Divorce in the United States* (1962), is still valuable on the legal evolution of the practice of divorce. Paula Petrik argues convincingly that the frontier environment of the West helps to explain why women there were the first to secure the electoral franchise. See Petrik, *No Step Backward: Women and the Family on the Rocky Mountain Mining Frontier, Helena, Montana, 1865–1900* (1988).

Although scholarly concern about the legal status of women has mushroomed, much remains to be done. A good idea of the present state of research in women's history can be found in D. Kelly Weisberg, ed., *Women and the Law: The Social Historical Perspective*, 2 volumes (1982), but there is no "general" legal history of women. The tension inherent in the legal treatment of women between granting them equity or equality is nicely summarized in Norma Basch, "Equity v. Equality: Emerging Concepts of Women's Political Status in the Age of Jackson," *Journal of the Early Republic* 3 (1983). Basch has also contributed an important volume, *In the Eyes of the Law: Women, Marriage, and Property in Nineteenth-Century New York* (1982), to the growing literature on the married-women's property acts. The best treatment of the implications of the law of property for the conduct of female behavior is provided in Suzanne Lebsock, *The Free Women of Petersburg: Status and Culture in a Southern Town, 1784–1860* (1984). Abortion, one of the central concerns of the modern women's movement, continues to draw historical attention. James Mohr, *Abortion in America. The Origins and Evolution of National Policy* (1978), is a valuable introduction to the complex of legal, class, and economic issues behind this practice.

The Nineteenth Century Criminal Justice System

Social and legal historians have stimulated each others' interest in deviancy and dependency. Much of their research, however, has stressed the external and social implications of crime rather than examining substantive criminal law developments. One of the ironies of contemporary American life is that for a nation so consumed with a fear of crime, its historians know next to nothing about the evolution of substantive criminal law. A good deal more effort has gone into the social determinants of crime and the crime rate. There is a growing consensus that indus-trialization and urbanization did not bring about more crime, but scholars are at a loss to explain why the per capita crime rates dropped through most of the nineteenth and well into the twentieth centuries. On these developments, see Eric H. Monkkonen, "A Disorderly People? Urban Order in the Nineteenth and Twentieth Centuries," *The Journal of American History* 68 (1981). Monkkonen's position has been hotly disputed. Much of the debate about crime rates turns on the issue of what crime was. The evidence does suggest that, on the whole, concern with crimes of morality gave way at the end of the eighteenth century to a new awareness of crimes against person and property. The intellectual background of this change is sketched in William E. Nelson, "Emerging Notions of Modern Criminal Law in the Revolutionary Era: An Historical Perspective," *New York University Law Review* 42 (1967). Friedman's *A History of American Law*, 2nd Ed. (1985) also contains useful details about the social, intellectual, and economic foundations of changes in criminal law and the criminal justice system. Samuel Walker's *Popular Justice* (1980) devotes less attention to law and more time to the criminal justice system. Much the same can be said for David J. Bodenhamer, *The Pursuit of Justice: Crime and Law in Antebellum Indiana* (1986), which is valuable for its treatment of grand and petit juries, a subject almost ignored in the literature. The connections between social change and penology are ably examined in Francis A. Allen, *The Decline of the Rehabilitative Ideal: Penal Policy and Social Purpose* (1981).

Other parts of the criminal justice system have received attention. Eric H. Monkkonen, *Police in Urban America, 1860–1920* (1981), distinguishes the changing roles played by the police as urban America developed. Wilbur R. Miller, *Cops and Bobbies: Police Authority in New York and London, 1830–1870* (1977), shows the importance of cultural differences in expectations about policing. These and other studies of the police have complemented an equally imaginative literature on the prison and jails. David J. Rothman's *The Discovery of the Asylum: Social Order and Disorder in the New Republic* (1971) gave far too little emphasis to develop-ments outside the North, but he brilliantly connected social change and the role of the asylum where he did look. Edward L. Ayers, *Vengeance & Justice: Crime and Punishment in the Nineteenth-Century American South* (1984), suggests that Southerners believed in jails but that the region's peculiar race relations created its own special problems of providing criminal justice. A similar theme can be found in Michael Hindus, *Prison and Plantation: Crime, Justice, and Authority in Massachusetts and South Carolina, 1767–1878* (1980). Children's crime (juvenile delinquency) is discussed in Anthony Platt, *The Child Savers: The Invention of Delin-quency* (1969). Lawrence M. Friedman and Robert V. Percival, *The Roots of Justice: Crime and Punishment in Alameda County, California 1870–1910* (1981), is a remarkable study of the operation of an entire criminal justice system in one place over a period of time. Friedman and Percival, like other recent students of criminal justice, stress that urbanization and industrializa-tion seem to have fostered a social discipline and rhythm that lowered rather than raised the crime rate.

The connection between criminality, insanity, and eugenics has received attention. David A. Jones, *History of Criminology: A Philosophical Perspective* (1986), is a good general introduc-tion to these matters. John S. Hughes, *In the Law's Darkness: Isaac Ray and the Medical Jurisprudence of Insanity in Nineteenth-Century America* (1986), is a valuable treatment of one of the nation's great teachers on medical jurisprudence.

Professionalization of the Bench and Bar

Growing professionalization of the bench and bar accompanied the social and economic transfor-mation of the nineteenth century. The professionalization of law and other occupations is discussed in Burton J. Bledstein, *The Culture of Professionalization: The Middle Class and the*

Development of Higher Education in America (1976). Professional and political pressures, which have always been in tension, were not entirely resolved, themes analyzed by Maxwell Bloomfield in *American Lawyers in a Changing Society, 1776–1876* (1976). Bloomfield not only discusses the various themes of law versus politics, but includes a valuable discussion of the rise in the era after the Civil War of a small corps of black lawyers. The subsequent impact of industrialization on the profession is treated in Gerard W. Gawalt, ed., *The New High Priests: Lawyers in Post–Civil War America* (1984). These essays cover the emergence of the American Bar Association, the development of the large corporate law firm, and the social backgrounds and training of lawyers and judges. The role of attorneys in shaping economic development and race relations in one local community in the South is skillfully examined in Gail Williams O'Brien, *The Legal Fraternity and the Making of a New South Community, 1848–1882* (1986). The development of legal education during these years is the subject of Robert Stevens, *Law School: Legal Education in America from the 1850s to the 1980s* (1983). The codification movement is ably treated in Charles M. Cook, *The American Codification Movement: A Study of Antebellum Legal Reform* (1981).

The evolution of the bench and judicial behavior is the subject of G. Edward White, *The American Judicial Tradition: Profiles of Leading American Judges* (1976), which devotes considerable attention to distinguishing nineteenth- and twentieth-century styles of judging. One area where law and politics did meet was through the practice of electing state appellate judges, although professional goals and political accountability were far more compatible than was once presumed. See Kermit L. Hall, "The Judiciary on Trial: State Constitutional Reform and the Rise of an Elected Judiciary, 1846–1860," *The Historian* 44 (1983). On the middle-class backgrounds of nineteenth-century federal judges (both in the states and the territories), see Hall, " 'The Children of the Cabins': The Lower Federal Judiciary, Modernization, and the Political Culture, 1789–1899," *Northwestern University Law Review,* 32 (1980). On the territorial judiciary of the post-Civil War West, see John D. W. Guice's fine study, *The Rocky Mountain Bench* (1972).

The nation's expanding economy created more work for courts and judges, both in the form of more common law actions and in the need to review more statutes and administrative findings. On the connections between economic change and judicial behavior in the state appellate courts, see Robert A. Kagan et al., "The Business of State Supreme Courts, 1870–1970," *Stanford Law Review* 30 (1977). A similar pattern of development is traced in Richard A. Posner, *The Federal Courts: Crisis and Reform* (1985). The jurisdiction of the federal courts expanded in response to the dynamic national economy, although, as William M. Wiecek explains in "The Reconstruction of Federal Judicial Power, 1863 1876," *The American Journal of Legal History* 13 (1969), much of the growth in federal judicial power that served the interests of business was at its inception in Reconstruction designed to aid the enforcement of black civil rights. Greater legislative activism, by both Congress and state legislatures, meant that appellate judges, practiced in common law interpretation, had increasingly to take account of the legislative history of major acts. As John W. Johnson has shown in "Retreat from the Common Law? The Grudging Reception of Legislative History by American Appellate Courts in the Early Twentieth Century," *Detroit College of Law Review* (1978), this development forced judges (and the lawyers who argued before them) to search for new kinds of materials, such as statistics, to bring to bear in the courtroom.

Did the legal profession react uniformly to social and economic change? Of course not. Yet the most visible and professional part of the bar, with its ties to emerging corporate capitalism growing ever closer, protected its interests rather than the public good, at least according to Jerold S. Auerbach, *Unequal Justice: Lawyers and Social Change in Modern America* (1976). Auerbach shows that racial, ethnic, and gender prejudice impeded access to the legal profession by minority groups and hampered the delivery of legal services to a society ever more in need of them.

The Twentieth Century

The history of American legal culture in the twentieth century is only beginning to be written. Even the second edition of Lawrence M. Friedman's *A History of American Law* (1985) gives only passing attention to the period. There is no single legal history of the century, although students of American public law have lavished great attention on the Supreme Court and developments surrounding it. Paul L. Murphy, *The Constitution in Crisis Times 1918–1969* (1972), offers a good introduction to basic developments in constitutional law set against Murphy's fine understanding of the social and cultural context of the period. Murphy's *World War I and the Origin of Civil Liberties in the United States* (1979) is particularly good at connecting the experiences of the war with the development of interest in the preservation of civil liberties. In a somewhat related vein, Norman Rosenberg, *Protecting the Best Men: An Interpretive History of the Law of Libel* (1986), brings shape to twentieth-century developments in another important area of First Amendment law.

Scholars have only begun to explore the history of contemporary criminal justice, but Mark H. Haller, "Urban Crime and Criminal Justice: The Chicago Case," *Journal of American History* 57 (1960), provides an excellent example of the ways in which professional policing, crime control, and social upheaval in the cities shaped the behavior of the criminal justice system. On the growth of the federal criminal enforcement machinery, see Richard G. Powers, *Secrecy and Power: The Life of J. Edgar Hoover* (1987), and Kenneth O'Reilly, *Hoover and the Un-Americans: The FBI, HUAC, and the Red Menace* (1983).

Civil rights have been an important theme during the century, one that grew in significance after the Supreme Court began in the early 1940s to give greater attention to it and the NAACP developed a coherent litigation strategy. For a critical assessment of the relationship of the bar to these developments, see Jerold S. Auerbach, *Unequal Justice: Lawyers and Social Change in Modern America* (1976). On the early development of the NAACP's litigation strategy, see William B. Hixson, Jr., "Moorfield Storey and the Struggle for Equality," *Journal of American History* 60 (1968). The role of the black bar and the Communist party is discussed in Charles H. Martin, *The Angelo Herndon Case and Southern Justice* (1976). Yet another vantage point on these matters is William H. Harbaugh, *Lawyer's Lawyer: The Life of John W. Davis* (1973), a fine biography of the man who represented segregationist interests in *Brown v. Board of Education* (1954). The most authoritative (and critical) treatment of the NAACP's Legal Defense Fund lawyers is Mark V. Tushnet, *The NAACP's Legal Strategy against Segregated Education, 1925–1950* (1987). On the difficulties of implementing the *Brown* decision, see Tony A. Freyer, *The Little Rock Crisis: A Constitutional Interpretation* (1984).

Twentieth-century legal thought is another area that has received considerable attention, especially the rise of the legal realist movement. Interpretations vary considerably, however. Wilfred E. Rumble, Jr., *American Legal Realism: Skepticism, Reform, and the Judicial Process* (1968), is good at connecting the movement in law schools to larger philosophical developments. G. Edward White, *Patterns of American Legal Thought* (1978), is also valuable, as are John W. Johnson, *American Legal Culture, 1908–1940* (1981) and Laura Kalman, *Legal Realism at Yale 1927–1960* (1986). Edward A. Purcell, Jr., "American Jurisprudence between the Wars: Legal Realism and the Crisis of Democratic Theory," *The American Historical Review* 75 (1969), does a good job of showing how legal realism crumbled before the twin challenges of nazism and Catholic natural law theology. The connections between legal realism and critical legal studies (with some attention to the policy science and law and economic approaches) is examined in G. Edward White, "From Realism to Critical Legal Studies: A Truncated Intellectual History," *Southwestern Law Journal* 40 (1986).

The extent to which legal realism penetrated the New Deal remains in dispute. Christopher Tomlins, *The State and the Unions: Labor Relations, Law, and the Organized Labor Movement, 1880–1960* (1985), argues that the labor reforms wrought by the New Deal had little real consequence for workers and that, on balance, they were probably of greater value to corporate managers. Peter H. Irons, *The New Deal Lawyers* (1982), has fashioned an insightful study of lawyers as litigators and administrators in the New Deal. It is in this group of lawyers that Irons locates the beginnings of contemporary legal liberalism.

There has been considerable debate about the extent to which legal culture after World War II differed from earlier generations. The "law explosion" is addressed in Marc Galanter, "Reading the Landscape of Disputes: What We Know and Don't Know (and Think We Know) about Our Allegedly Contentious and Litigious Society," *UCLA Law Review* 31 (1983). Substantive legal developments have attracted some attention, although much remains to be done. The concept of the "new property" (e.g., entitlements) is examined in Charles A. Reich, "The New Property," *Yale Law Journal* 73 (1964). The evolution of landlord–tenant relations is the subject of Mary Ann Glendon's "The Transformation of American Landlord–Tenant Law," *Boston College Law Review* 23 (1982). The increasing importance of zoning law is discussed in Seymour I. Toll, *Zoned America* (1969). Contract law has received serious attention, especially when taken in comparison with the spread of tort and tortlike concepts. Grant Gilmore, *The Death of Contract* (1974), argues that classical contract law had given way before increasingly powerful tort concepts. Edward J. Murphy and Richard E. Speidel, eds., *Studies in Contract Law*, 3rd Ed. (1984), insist that contract law retained considerable vitality. G. Edward White, *Tort Law in America* (1980), places the debate in its intellectual context and shows why tort has captured this century's legal imagination, just as contract did in the nineteenth.

These and other areas require more scholarly attention. Historians know more about the origins of the regulatory state than they do about its operation in this century, especially in the era after World War II. The best (and only) general survey is Robert L. Rabin, "Federal Regulation in Historical Perspective," *Stanford Law Review* 38 (1986). One part of the regulatory apparatus, that involving nuclear power, is treated in John W. Johnson, *Insuring against Disaster: The Nuclear Industry on Trial* (1986), although most of Johnson's attention is devoted to litigation surrounding the Price–Anderson Act rather than day-to-day regulation.

Scholars of every ideological stripe and in numerous scholarly disciplines have lavished attention on the Supreme Court and contemporary American constitutional development. Often what scholars believe the justices should do in the future has informed their analyses of what they did in the past. Some conservatives have argued that the federal courts generally, and the Supreme Court specifically, have composed an "imperial" force that has overridden the wishes of the popularly elected branches. Raoul Berger, for example, has argued that federal judges should be bound by the concept of original intent (what the framers said goes, and if they were silent then the matter belongs to the legislature and not the courts), while liberals believe that judges ought to measure the framers' intentions against present realities and that judges have the duty to protect minority rights from majority encroachment. The debate is nicely summarized in Raoul Berger, "Paul Brest's Brief for an Imperial Judiciary," *Maryland Law Review* 40 (1981). Berger's historical reasoning, however, is effectively challenged in H. Jefferson Powell, "The Original Understanding of Original Intent," *Harvard Law Review* 98 (1985). That the Supreme Court has been far from accepting of all minorities, however, is ably demonstrated in Michal Belknap, *Cold War Political Justice: The Smith Act, the Communist Party, and American Civil Liberties* (1977). The propensities of the federal legal system to mete out harsh penalties to dissenters and oddballs is discussed in Stanley I. Kutler, *The American Inquisition: Justice and Injustice in the Cold War* (1982). Finally, for an able study of the Court's history in brief compass, see William M. Wiecek, *Liberty and the Law: The Supreme Court in American Life* (1988).

Table of Cases

Index